The Hamlyn
WORLD ATLAS

Published by The Hamlyn Publishing Group Limited
London · New York · Sydney · Toronto
Astronaut House, Feltham, Middlesex, England.

Designed and produced for The Hamlyn Publishing Group Limited
by Intercontinental Book Productions.
Copyright © 1980 Intercontinental Book Productions.
Map pages, Political Information Tables and Index pages © Rand
McNally & Company from *The International Atlas* © 1969 Rand
McNally & Company, re-edited for *The Earth and Man* © 1972, Thematic
Maps from *Goode's World Atlas* © 1978 Rand McNally & Company.

ISBN 0 600 30490 6

Printed in Italy

Editorial acknowledgements
Geographical consultant: David E. Elcome M.Sc.
Contributing editor: Emma Wood B.A.

Photographs
All photographs were supplied by Colour Library International
Limited except for those listed below.

Picture credits are by page number/picture number.
Australian News and Information Service: 109/1, 109/2, 109/3
British Antarctic Survey: 165/1, 165/2, 165/3
British Petroleum Company: 17/1
Camera Press: 41/2, 41/3, 41/4, 53/1, 79/1, 154/1
Bruce Coleman Limited: 164/1
Rosemary Hartill: 138/1, 141/2
Italian State Tourist Office: 19/2
Novosti Press Agency: 58/3, 59/1, 59/2, 59/3, 60/1, 60/2, 61/2, 170/1
Volkswagen UK Limited: 17/3

Front end paper: Kleine Scheidegg Junfrau, Switzerland
Back end paper: Tahiti

The Hamlyn
WORLD ATLAS

Brian P. Price B.Sc., F.R.G.S.

Hamlyn
London · New York · Sydney · Toronto

CONTENTS

13 EUROPE

57 USSR

67 ASIA

87 AFRICA

107 OCEANIA

121 MIDDLE AMERICA

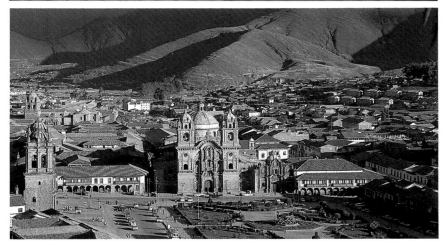

FOREWORD

Atlases have held me in thrall since my childhood. I used to gaze in juvenile wonder, and with a pride induced by my teachers, at the vast areas coloured red on the world map which marked the bounds of the Empire's dominions beyond the seas. Later, I found a fascination in the physical aspects of geography, trying to conjure up in my mind's eye the mountainous regions of the globe from the shades of brown, with exciting areas of white to show those challenging heights above the snow-line; in contrast with the greens of the plains and valleys, and the blues of the oceans. Now, in later age, maps bring back memories of journeys to distant places, of people who accompanied me, and of the experiences we shared together; they beckon me still with the same persuasion as ever in the past, to set forth again.

As one whose allegiance to geography is more romantic than academic, I was surprised to discover, on becoming President of the Royal Geographical Society, how widely drawn are its boundaries; how diverse the disciplines with which it is allied. Some aspects of science which fall properly within one ambit of geography have become more important than they were in my youth. There are, for instance, large question marks over our food resources in a world whose population has increased by leaps and bounds in the past fifty years, and which is still growing. The problems of feeding the world's masses become more acute as the expectations of the developing countries rise, and as the industrialized nations look to them as sources from which, with their technology, more food can be extracted in the humid and arid soils of the tropics. New sources of energy to supplement and replace the diminishing supplies of oil; the problems of urban population: not least, the need for people living in cities to have outlets into unspoilt countryside; these are but a few examples of the challenges which confront us as we approach the turn of this century, and are challenges for which solutions must be sought within the bounds of human and physical geography.

'The Hamlyn World Atlas' is an atlas with a difference. The author has contrived to combine the maps with photographs which bring into the sight of the reader those physical features which so intrigued my childish mind some sixty years ago; which bring to life the peoples who inhabit every part of the earth's surface and whose way of life, conditioned by differences in climate and natural environment, is changing under the impact of new technologies. The maps and photographs are interpreted by a text which, with statistical diagrams, speaks eloquently of the human impact on geography in changing the nature of the land under man's insatiable urge to improve his material circumstances and, in pursuit of that quest, to exploit the resources available to him.

For all who love the natural landscape and who feel concern about the impact of progress on people in undeveloped areas, the quickening changes to our planet may be a source of some regret. But change is inevitable and, provided that it is managed and controlled with good sense and sensitivity, some things of lasting value can be conserved or adapted for the benefit of future mankind.

This atlas, whose publication falls fortuitously in the 150th year of the Royal Geographical Society, will perform a valuable service in making us more aware of the dangers, no less than the opportunities, in our quickening world.

The Lord Hunt of Llanfair Waterdine KG CBE DSO

Lord Hunt is President of the Royal Geographical Society and was leader of the Everest expedition which first conquered the mountain on May 29th 1953.

INTRODUCTION

At any given moment the minds of most people are concerned primarily with their own immediate world: the farmer with his land, animals and crops, the office worker with his piles of paper, the housewife with her home and family. Think, though, of man in relation to the earth, with its surface area of 500 million km² (nearly 200 million sq ml), which is seemingly large enough to accommodate and provide for all of mankind. The contribution, then, of any one person to world achievement is minute.

Population has accelerated alarmingly in the last 130 years. From 1,200 million in 1850, world population rose to 2,485 million in 1950, 2,982 million in 1960 and 3,635 million in 1970. By 1978, the figure was 4,119 million. The world's population will almost certainly have doubled again in the half century 1930–'80. And by the year 2000, at the present rates of growth, it could be over 6,500 million.

At the same time as man's numbers have increased, so too have his overall demands on the earth. Granted there are great differences between the demands of the developed world and those of the developing world. Yet the living standards of a large proportion of the world's population are now far higher than those of their ancestors. There has been more than a proportionate increase in the demands for food, raw materials and material possessions. Such trends cannot go on for ever. Men must become aware of the consequences of their own actions, be it building up population pressure, abusing nature or wasting limited resources.

Water has long been taken from the rivers and seas, but what do we put back? Sewage, poison wastes from industries, fertilizers and pesticides washed from the land, radioactive waste in 'safe' containers – all these are mixed up in the seas. If unchecked, such noxious substances could one day make the water which is essential to life a danger to that life.

Until comparatively recently people have also taken the earth's resources for granted, without much thought for the coming generations. Fossil fuels are the classic case, and it is now likely that the world's oil riches will have been largely squandered during the twentieth century. Where will man turn next for a new source of energy?

Careless use of the land must not go unremarked. In the long history of developing new lands, man has sometimes made his own catastrophes by stripping the natural vegetation. On a large scale, the dust bowl of the southern interior of the USA created in the late 1920s and early '30s was a classic case. But, on many smaller scales, the use of shifting agriculture in many areas of the Third World also leads to a waste of the land.

In the past then, we have tended to be rather rash and careless in our use of the environment. Fortunately, the inventive and enquiring minds of modern scientists have been ever busy. In the field of agriculture, new strains of seeds, new breeds of animals and new techniques of farming have led to increases in the amount of food which can be grown on a given area. In industry, new inventions and techniques have greatly increased the speed of producing many materials and goods and decreased the production costs. In science and technology, the opening up of new areas of knowledge, such as electronics and computing, enable more tasks to be done for more people by fewer.

Thus, more and more should we regard this as the quickening world, thankful for the inventiveness of men's minds, thankful for the apparent riches of the earth yet ever conscious of the fact that man treads a tightrope from which he could so easily fall through his own thoughtlessness and stupidity.

How to Use this Atlas

The conventional continental division of the world is no longer ideal for modern purposes. The USSR, for instance, which straddles two continents, is important and large enough to be given separate treatment. Further, the Americas are increasingly divided into three: the largely English-speaking North, the Spanish/Portuguese heritage of the South, and the patchwork of predominantly Latin mainland states together with the Caribbean and other islands of Middle America. In this atlas, therefore, the world has been divided into nine major areas: Europe and Asia, with the USSR as a separate entity; Africa; Oceania; the three Americas as described and, in addition, the Polar Regions.

Each continental section within the atlas is self-contained, and each section, with the exception of the Polar Regions, contains the following features:

Political maps
Mainly on two scales, the smaller (1:13,200,000) presenting the continents as a whole on one or more maps, the larger (1:3,300,000) showing countries or areas in greater detail. The maps emphasize political features and show the main physical features.

Text
Each continental section begins with a Physical Profile, giving details of world location, size, landscape and climate. Further information covers the continent's history, culture, population, politics, industry, commerce, communications, agriculture, forestry, fishing, natural resources and economy. Rounding off each continent, under the heading '. . . . . . . Countries', is information on the individual countries. There are entries for every country, arranged in alphabetical order.

Travelogues
Interspersed with the 1:3,300,000 maps of Europe, expanded text and picture coverage give lighter, general summaries of selected European countries.

Opposite: Golden Pavilion of the Kinkaku-Ji Temple, Kyoto, Japan

Illustrations
Throughout the book 300 colour illustrations (numbered for ease of reference) reveal the great variety of natural environments, and also show aspects of industry, agriculture, architecture, or everyday life. Extended captions complement the pictures.

Diagrams
In measures of world activity, growth and standards, three main criteria have been used. National trade figures (imports and exports) give an impression of the extent to which a country has developed and is involved in the world scene. The average earnings of the population indicate the living standards of the people. Finally, the average amounts of energy used per capita relate to one of the key issues in the world and are also a barometer of levels of development. Using common scales throughout the book for ease of cross reference, three diagrams within each continental section show the ranges within these sets of figures for selected countries. The diagrams are based on the most recent available statistics.

Mineral production tables
Within the main continental sections, under the heading 'Natural Resources', each table gives world production of ores, the continental share per ore and the principal producing countries.

Country reference tables
This table, which is found at the end of the country entries, covers every country within the continent, giving details of political status on the following classification:

A Independent countries.
B Countries with internal independence, yet under the control of another country at least for foreign and defence matters.
C Colonies which are completely dependent on another country. Also component units within certain countries.
D Component states or provinces within selected federal countries.

State capitals are listed, followed by data on national area, population, birth rates, death rates and, finally, the average annual percentage increase in the national populations in recent years. Comparisons of these figures reveal clearly the centres of the world population explosion. When compared with the existing populations and densities of populations, they give an added indication of the parts of the world where sheer population pressure, regardless of the local ability to cater for its needs, is greatest.

Following the continental sections other features are as follows:

Polar Regions
Due to their similarities of climate the Arctic and the Antarctic have been treated as a unit. A general introduction is followed by maps of the Arctic and the Antarctic and detailed information.

Thematic maps
In the 'World to View' section are world maps on the subjects of languages, literacy, predominant economies, population density and climatic regions. Each is accompanied by explanatory text.

Index
Found at the end of the book this is an alphabetical list of the names appearing on the maps, giving a page reference, coordinates and, where applicable, a symbol indicating the nature of the feature.

The above breakdown is a guide to the scope of the atlas's component units. Used in conjunction with the Contents, Index and Major Data page references (opposite) it will provide an invaluable key to the information you need.

For example, you may want to find out about Poland's economy and how this rates in world terms. Turn firstly to the individual entry for Poland (p. 24) under the heading 'European Countries'; this gives general details of the Polish economy. Within the main European section are the diagrams showing imports/exports, per capita income, and energy usage (pp. 17, 18, 19): these provide specific data on key areas of the economy. Polish figures can be readily compared with those for other European countries. Reference to diagrams in other continental sections give worldwide comparisons.

Also within the main European section, under the headings 'Industry, Commerce and Communications', 'Agriculture, Forestry and Fishing', 'Natural Resources', and 'European Economy' (pp. 15–19), is information on aspects of the European economy as a whole, with specific references to Poland. The table of mineral production (p. 16), under 'Natural Resources', shows the principal minerals Poland produces.

The map of Central Europe (pp. 36–37), at a scale of 1:3,300,000, includes Poland, showing something of her physical relief and indicating her position in relation to her neighbours. Following this there is a brief reference to the Polish economy under the travelogue heading 'Eastern Europe' (p. 41).

Finally, in the 'World to View' section, the world map of 'Predominant Economies' (pp. 170–171) indicates Poland's principal economic activities.

Important data appears in the diagrams and tables in each continental section. Page references are listed below, continent by continent.

MAJOR DATA: page references

	DIAGRAMS			TABLES	
	Imports/ Exports	Income	Energy	Mineral Production	Country Reference
Europe	17	18	19	16	24
USSR	59	60	60	60	61
Asia	71	72	73	71	78
Africa	89	90	91	90	98
Oceania	109	110	110	110	114
Middle America	123	124	125	123	128
South America	135	136	137	137	142
North America	152	153	154	153	159

Key to Maps

Inhabited Localities

The symbol represents the number of inhabitants within the locality

1:3,300,000	• 0—10,000	1:13,200,000	• 0—50,000
1:6,600,000	○ 10,000—25,000		⊕ 50,000—100,000
	⊙ 25,000—100,000		⊡ 100,000—250,000
	⊡ 100,000—250,000		⊠ 250,000—1,000,000
	▣ 250,000—1,000,000		■ >1,000,000
	■ >1,000,000		

▭ Urban Area (area of continuous industrial, commercial, and residential development)

The size of type indicates the relative economic and political importance of the locality

Écommoy	Lisieux	**Rouen**
Trouville	**Orléans**	**PARIS**

Hollywood □ Section of a City, Neighborhood
Westminster

Bi'r Safājah ° Inhabited Oasis   Kumdah   Uninhabited Oasis

Capitals of Political Units

BUDAPEST   Independent Nation

Cayenne   Dependency (Colony, protectorate, etc.)

GALAPAGOS (Ecuador)   Administering Country

Villarica   State, Province, etc.

White Plains   County, Oblast, etc.

Alternate Names

Basel	**MOSKVA**	English or second official language names are shown
Bâle	**MOSCOW**	in reduced size lettering

Ventura	Volgograd	Historical or other alternates in the local language
(San Buenaventura)	(Stalingrad)	are shown in parentheses

Political Boundaries

International (First-order political unit)

1:3,300,000
1:6,600,000
1:13,200,000

———·———·——— Demarcated, Undemarcated, and Administrative

——·——·——— Disputed de jure

———————— Indefinite or Undefined

———————— Demarcation Line

Internal

———————— State, Province, etc. (Second-order political unit)
GUAIRA

·················· County, Oblast, etc. (Third-order political unit)
WESTCHESTER

ANDALUCIA   Historical Region (No boundaries indicated)

Miscellaneous Cultural Features

PARQUE NACIONAL CANAIMA   National or State Park or Monument

FORT CLATSOP NAT. MEM.   National or State Historic(al) Site, Memorial

BLACKFOOT IND. RES.   Indian Reservation

FORT DIX   Military Installation

TANGLEWOOD   Point of Interest (Battlefield, cave, historical site, etc.)

STEINHAUSEN   Church, Monastery

UXMAL   Ruins

WINDSOR CASTLE   Castle

AMISTAD DAM   Dam

World Index Map

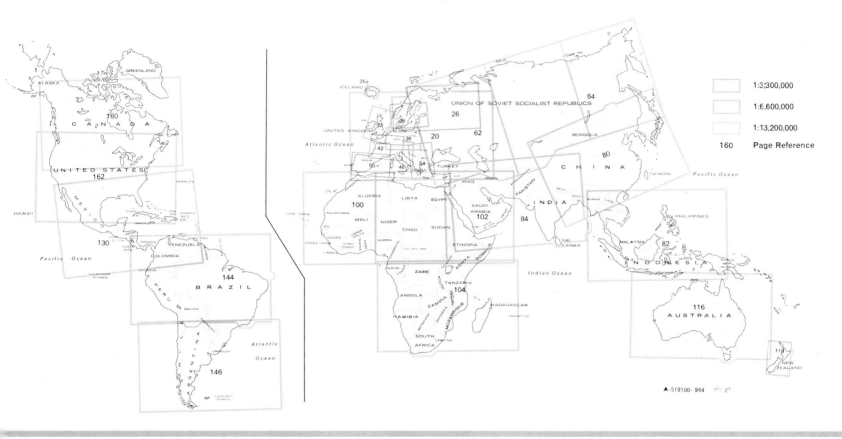

1:3,300,000
1:6,600,000
1:13,200,000
160   Page Reference

A-519100-964

Transportation

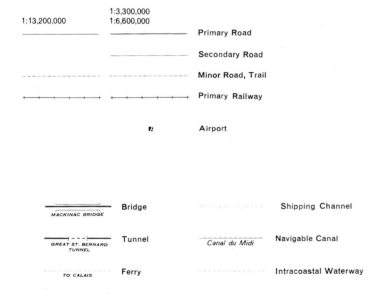

1:13,200,000	1:3,300,000 1:6,600,000	
		Primary Road
		Secondary Road
		Minor Road, Trail
		Primary Railway
		Airport

Bridge
MACKINAC BRIDGE

Tunnel
GREAT ST. BERNARD TUNNEL

Ferry
TO CALAIS

Shipping Channel

Navigable Canal
Canal du Midi

Intracoastal Waterway

Metric-English Equivalents

Areas represented by one square centimetre at various map scales

1:3,300,000
1,089 km²
421 square miles

1:6,600,000
4,356 km²
1,682 square miles

1:13,200,000
17,424 km²
6,725 square miles

Metre=3.28 feet
Kilometre=0.62 mile

Metre² (m²)=10.76 square feet
Kilometre² (km²)=0.39 square mile

Hydrographic Features

	Shoreline	
	Undefined or Fluctuating Shoreline	
Amur	River, Stream	
	Intermittent Stream	
	Rapids, Falls	
	Irrigation or Drainage Canal	
	Reef	
764	Depth of Water	

The Everglades — Swamp

SEWARD GLACIER — Glacier

L. Victoria — Lake, Reservoir

Tuz Golu — Salt Lake

Intermittent Lake, Reservoir

Dry Lake Bed

(395) — Lake Surface Elevation

Topographic Features

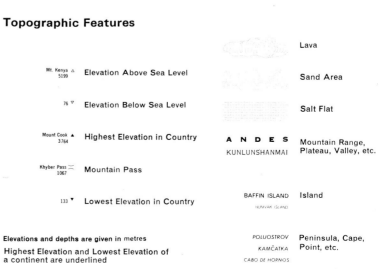

Mt. Kenya △
5199   Elevation Above Sea Level

76 ▽   Elevation Below Sea Level

Mount Cook ▲
3764   Highest Elevation in Country

Khyber Pass ═
1067   Mountain Pass

133 ▼   Lowest Elevation in Country

Elevations and depths are given in metres
Highest Elevation and Lowest Elevation of a continent are underlined

Lava

Sand Area

Salt Flat

A N D E S
KUNLUNSHANMAI   Mountain Range, Plateau, Valley, etc.

BAFFIN ISLAND   Island
NUNIVAK ISLAND

POLUOSTROV   Peninsula, Cape,
KAMČATKA   Point, etc.
CABO DE HORNOS

9

ARCTIC OCEAN

Beaufort Sea

GREENLAND
(Den.)

Baffin Bay

Thule

Godhavn

UNITED STATES
Arctic Circle

Nome

Inuvik

Mackenzie

VICTORIA ISLAND

BAFFIN ISLAND

Angmagssalik

Godthåb

ICELAND

Reykjavik

FAEROE ISLANDS
(Den.)

Mount

Anchorage

Fairbanks

Yellowknife

Hudson Bay

Churchill

Goose Bay

U.S.S.R.

Bering Sea

Gulf of Alaska

ROCKY

C A N A D A

Edmonton

Calgary

Winnipeg

Lake Superior

Lake Huron

St. Lawrence

Québec

Montréal

NEWFOUNDLAND

St. John's

Glasgow

Dublin

IRELAND

KING

ALEUTIAN ISLANDS

Portland

Seattle

NORTH AMERICA

Salt Lake City

Denver

Minneapolis

Lake Michigan

CHICAGO

L. Erie

DETROIT

Ottawa

Toronto

L. Ontario

Boston

NEW YORK

PHILADELPHIA

Washington

Halifax

ATLANTIC OCEAN

Porto

PORTUGAL

Lisboa

SPA

P A C I F I C

SAN FRANCISCO

UNITED STATES

St. Louis

APPALACHIAN MOUNTAINS

AÇORES AZORES
(Port.)

GIBRALTAR

LOS ANGELES

Phoenix

Mississippi

Atlanta

Rabat

Casablanca

MOROCCO

O C E A N

San Diego

El Paso

Dallas

Rio Grande

Houston

New Orleans

BERMUDA
(U.K.)

ARQUIPÉLAGO DA MADEIRA
(Port.)

MIDWAY ISLANDS
(U.S.)

Tropic of Cancer

CABO SAN LUCAS

Gulf of Mexico

Miami

BAHAMAS

ISLAS CANARIAS
CANARY ISLANDS
(Sp.)

WESTERN SAHARA

HAWAIIAN ISLANDS
(U.S.)

Honolulu

MEXICO

CIUDAD DE MÉXICO

La Habana

CUBA

DOMINICAN REPUBLIC

MAURI-TANIA

JOHNSTON ISLAND
(U.S.)

Guadalajara

HAITI

PUERTO RICO (U.S.)

San Juan

Santo Domingo

GUADELOUPE (Fr.)

Nouakchott

CAPE VERDE

Tombouctou

P

GUATEMALA

BELIZE
(U.K.)

JAMAICA

Kingston

Port-au-Prince

MARTINIQUE (Fr.)

SENEGAL

Dakar

O

San Salvador

HONDURAS

Tegucigalpa

Caribbean Sea

BARBADOS

TRINIDAD AND TOBAGO

GAMBIA

Banjul

Bamako

L

EL SALVADOR

Managua

NICARAGUA

Port of Spain

GUINEA-BISSAU

GUINEA

CLIPPERTON
(Fr. Poly.)

COSTA RICA

San José

Panamá

PANAMA

Caracas

VENEZUELA

GUYANA

Georgetown

Paramaribo

FRENCH GUIANA

SIERRA LEONE

Conakry

IVORY COAST

Y

LINE ISLANDS

Equator

Bogotá

COLOMBIA

Monrovia

LIBERIA

Abidjan

Equator

N

CANTON AND ENDERBURY (U.K.–U.S.)

ARCHIPIÉLAGO DE COLÓN
GALAPAGOS ISLANDS
(Ec.)

ECUADOR

Quito

Manaus

Amazon

Belém

E

PHOENIX ISLANDS

Guayaquil

Iquitos

Fortaleza

CABO DE SÃO ROQUE

S

TOKELAU ISLANDS
(N.Z.)

ÎLES MARQUISES

Trujillo

Juruá

B R A Z I L

Natal

Recife

I

WALLIS AND FUTUNA SAMOA
(Fr.)

W. SAMOA

AM. SAMOA

ÎLES TUAMOTU

Lima

SOUTH AMERICA

Salvador

ATLANTIC OCEAN

Apia

ÎLES

A

FIJI

NIUE
(N.Z.)

ÎLES DE LA SOCIÉTÉ
SOCIETY ISLANDS

Arequipa

La Paz

BOLIVIA

Goiânia

Brasília

Belo Horizonte

TONGA

COOK ISLANDS
(N.Z.)

FRENCH POLYNESIA

Sucre

PARAGUAY

Paraná

SÃO PAULO

RIO DE JANEIRO

Tropic of Capricorn

PITCAIRN
(U.K.)

ISLA DE PASCUA
EASTER ISLAND
(Chile)

Antofagasta

ISLA SAN AMBROSIO
(Chile)

Asunción

Santos

Curitiba

International Date Line

CHILE

Pôrto Alegre

P A C I F I C

Valparaíso

Santiago

Córdoba

Rosario

URUGUAY

Montevideo

CHATHAM ISLAND
(N.Z.)

ISLAS JUAN FERNÁNDEZ
(Chile)

Co. Aconcagua
6959

Concepción

BUENOS AIRES

ARGENTINA

Mar del Plata

O C E A N

Bahía Blanca

FALKLAND ISLANDS
ISLAS MALVINAS
(U.K.)

SOUTH GEORGIA
(Falk. Is.)

Punta Arenas

CABO DE HORNOS
CAPE HORN

SOUTH ORKNEY ISLANDS
(B.A.T.)

Antarctic Circle

LARSEN ICE SHELF

Ross Sea

Bellingshausen Sea

Weddell Sea

Vinson Massif
5140

A N T A R

ARCTIC OCEAN

Barents Sea
ZEML'A FRANCA-IOSIFA
NOVAJA ZEML'A
Karskoje More
More Laptevych
NOVOSIBIRSKIJE OSTROVA

Hammerfest
Murmansk
Narjan-Mar
Vorkuta
Dikson
Nordvik
Chatanga
Tiksi
Arctic Circle

SWEDEN
FINLAND
Helsinki
Archangel'sk
Salechard
Noril'sk
Jenisej
Igarka
Lena
Verchojansk
Jakutsk
Anadyr

Stockholm
Leningrad
Vologda
Perm
Čel'abinsk
Omsk
Irtyš
Novosibirsk
Krasnojarsk
Bratsk
Čita
Magadan

København
POLAND
Warszawa
MOSKVA
Gor'kij
Sverdlovsk
UNION OF SOVIET SOCIALIST REPUBLICS
Sea of Okhotsk
Bering Sea
Petropavlovsk-Kamčatskij
ALEUTIAN (U.S.)

BERLIN
G.D.R.
Bonn
Kijev
Volgograd
Ural
Karaganda
Ozero Balchaš
OSTROV SACHALIN
Južno-Sachalinsk
KURIL'SKIJE OSTROVA

Milano
Budapest
ROM.
Astrachan'
Aral'skoje More
Alma-Ata
Taškent
TIEN SHAN
ALTAJ
Ulaanbaatar
MONGOLIA
Chabarovsk
Vladivostok
Sapporo
Sea of Japan
JAPAN

Roma
Beograd
Bucureşti
Black Sea
Istanbul
Ankara
Baku
Wulumuqi
GOBI
Haerbin
N. KOREA
Pyongyang
S. KOREA
Pusan
HOKKAIDO
TŌKYŌ
OSAKA
HONSHU

Napoli
BUL.
Sofija
Athinai
TURKEY
SYRIA
Tehrān
Kabul
AFGHANISTAN
HIMALAYAS
Lasa
Chengdu
BEIJING PEKING
Tianjin
Lüda
Qingdao
Yellow Sea
SHANGHAI
Nanjing
Wuhan
Fukuoka
Kyūshū

CYPRUS
LEB.
Baghdad
IRAN
IRAQ
Eşfahān
CHINA
Chongqing
Changsha
Fuzhou
T'aipei
TAIWAN
PACIFIC OCEAN

Mediterranean Sea
MALTA
Tarabulus
Tripoli
ISRAEL
JORDAN
KUWAIT
Ābādān
PAKISTAN
DELHI
New Delhi
Kunming
Guangzhou
HONG KONG (U.K.)
Ha-noi
HAINANDAO
OGASAWARA-GUNTŌ (Jap.)
NANSEI-SHOTŌ
WAKE ISLAND (U.S.)

Banghāzī
Al-Iskandarīyah
CAIRO
QATAR
UNITED ARAB EMIRATES
Karāchi
Ahmadābād
Tropic of Cancer
BANGL.
BURMA
Rangoon
THAILAND
VIETNAM
South China Sea
MANILA
Philippine Sea
MARIANA ISLANDS
GUAM (U.S.)
PACIFIC ISLANDS TRUST TERRITORY (U.S.)

LIBYA
EGYPT
Aswān
Ar-Riyād
SAUDI ARABIA
Masqat
OMAN
INDIA
BOMBAY
Hyderābād
CALCUTTA
Krung Thep
Bangkok
KAM.
Phnum Pénh
Ho Chi Minh
Thanh-pho
PHILIPPINES
MICRONESIA
MARSHALL ISLANDS

Red Sea
NIGER
CHAD
Al-Khurtūm
SUDAN
YEMEN
P.D.R. OF YEMEN (P.D.R. of Yem.)
SUQUTRĀ (S. Yem.)
RAS ASIR
Arabian Sea
Bangalore
Madras
ANDAMAN ISLANDS (India)
BRUNEI (U.K.)
Medan
CAROLINE ISLANDS

NIGERIA
Kano
Ndjamena
CEN. AFR. EMP.
DJIBOUTI
Djibouti
Adis Abeba
ETHIOPIA
Cochin
SRI LANKA
Colombo
NICOBAR ISLANDS (India)
MALDIVES
MALAYSIA
Kuala Lumpur
Singapore
SUMATRA
BORNEO
SULAWESI
Equator
NAURU
GILBERT ISLANDS (U.K.)

CAMEROON
Douala
Yaoundé
EQUATORIAL GUINEA
Libreville
GABON
CONGO
ZAIRE
RWANDA
BURUNDI
Bujumbura
UGANDA
Kampala
KENYA
Nairobi
Kilimanjaro 5895
TANZANIA
SEYCHELLES
CHAGOS ARCHIPELAGO (B.I.O.T.)
INDONESIA
JAKARTA
JAWA
Palembang
Banjarmasin
Ujung Pandang
Surabaya
TIMOR
PAPUA NEW GUINEA
Mount Wilhelm 4509
GUINEA
Port Moresby
SOLOMON ISLANDS
MELANESIA

Brazzaville
Kinshasa
Luanda
Lobito
ANGOLA
Lubumbashi
ZAMBIA
Lusaka
Lake Victoria
Mombasa
Zanzibar
Dar-es-Salaam
INDIAN OCEAN
CHRISTMAS ISLAND (Austl.)
Darwin
CAPE YORK
Gulf of Carpentaria
Cairns
NEW HEBRIDES (Fr.-U.K.)
Suva
FIJI

NAMIBIA (S. Afr. Admin.)
Windhoek
Walvisbaai (S. Afr.)
BOTSWANA
Gaborone
ZIMBABWE RHODESIA
Salisbury
Mozambique Channel
MADAGASCAR
Antananarivo
MAURITIUS
RÉUNION (Fr.)
Tropic of Capricorn
AUSTRALIA
Alice Springs
Coral Sea
NEW CALEDONIA (Fr.)
Nouméa

SOUTH AFRICA
Johannesburg
Pretoria
Maputo
SWAZILAND
LESOTHO
Durban
Cape Town
CAPE OF GOOD HOPE
Port Elizabeth
ÎLES KERGUELEN (F.S.A.T.)
Perth
Adelaide
Melbourne
Mount Kosciusko 2228
Canberra
Sydney
Darling
NORTH ISLAND
Auckland
NEW ZEALAND
Wellington

TASMANIA
Hobart
Tasman Sea
SOUTH ISLAND
Christchurch

International Date Line

Antarctic Circle
ENDERBY LAND
AMERY ICE SHELF
WILKES LAND

ANTARCTICA

Copyright © by Rand McNally & Co.
Map prepared by Rand McNally & Co.
A-510000-264   -6   12"

Kilometres   0   1000   2000   3000   Km.
Statute Miles   0   1000   2000   3000   Mi.

One centimetre represents 825 kilometres.
One inch represents approximately 1320 miles.
Robinson Projection
Scale 1:82,500,000

11

EUROPE
Physical Profile

World Location and Size

Europe is joined to the continent of Asia. Its eastern limits can be regarded as the Ural Mountains which run north to south across the Soviet Union at about 60°E. Although the huge country of the USSR is thus divided between Europe and Asia, for the purposes of this atlas the USSR is being treated as a separate geographical unit.

Europe is situated in the Northern Hemisphere. Its north to south extent is some 4,000 km (2,500 ml) from North Cape in Norway within the Arctic Circle at 71°N to the island of Crete in the Mediterranean Sea at 35°N. From west to east, mainland Europe extends from the Portuguese coast immediately west of Lisbon at nearly 10°W to the margins of the Black Sea in Romania at 29°E, a distance of approximately 3,400 km (2,100 ml). Beyond the mainland, Iceland, the Azores and parts of the Irish Republic lie even farther west.

Within the whole bounds of 35° to 71°N and 10°W to 29°E there is also a large area of ocean and sea. The precise outline of Europe is as intricate as that of any continent, and for a land area of its total size it has a long coastline. The Baltic, Adriatic and Aegean Sea coasts, as well as the fjord coastline of Norway, the margins of all the islands and the more regular-shaped coasts of France and Iberia, together make over 48,000 km (30,000 ml) of coast.

Landscape

The three main physical regions of Europe are two areas dominated by uplands, one in the north-west and the other in the south, and one lowland area fanning out from a narrower north-south extent in the west to a wider one in the east. This pattern persists even where the continental area is interrupted by expanses of sea. There are no great open expanses of relatively monotonous landscape such as are found in some other continents. Not even the lowlands surrounding the Baltic Sea are as expansive as, say, the interior lowlands of North America, the Great Siberian Plain or Amazonia.

The uplands of the north and west are mostly of Caledonian age and are the remains of a chain of mountains formed about 350 million years ago. Today these reach heights of 2,472 m (8,104 ft) in Norway and 1,343 m (4,406 ft) in Scotland. Not all parts of the continent which were formed in Caledonian times are similarly mountainous. Parts of Sweden and all Finland, for example, have been

Opposite: The Colosseum, Rome, Italy

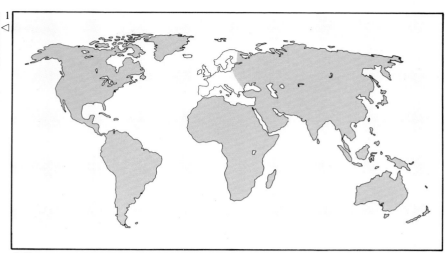

Europe's contrasting physical scope: 1 Mojacar, Almeria – Spanish hilltop town; 2 Hammerfest, Norway – the world's northernmost town. The sun never sets from May to August and never rises from November to February

reduced over the ages by erosion to their present lower physique. The mountains of Iceland were mainly produced by more recent volcanic activity, Iceland being one of the few places in Europe which is volcanically active today.

The lowlands which lie east-west across Europe occupy the largest area of the three major regions. Geologically they are younger than the northern uplands, but older than much of the area to the south. The landscape often has a gently rolling appearance, being a succession of low hills, referred to as scarps, with vales between. Such landscapes dominate much of lowland Britain and northern France. For the most part these lowland areas are less than 150 m (500 ft) above sea level.

Geologically, the mountains of the south are among the youngest parts of the continent, being of Alpine age, less than 100 million years old. They are part of the great system of mountains which lies west-east from northern Spain, through Italy, Switzerland, Austria and the Balkan countries and then on into the USSR and Asia. These are the highest mountains within Europe, rising to 4,807 m (15,771 ft) in Mont Blanc.

As well as the high mountains of the Alpine system, other older upland areas are found in southern Europe. The south central parts of France, parts of central and southern Germany and of western Czechoslovakia are eroded mountain systems which were formed about 200 million years ago in the Hercynian age. In the Massif Central of France these rise to 1,885 m (6,188 ft).

In very recent geological times, northern Europe and the higher parts of the southern mountain areas have been covered with ice. Much smaller areas of northern and mountain Europe are glaciated today. At its maximum advance, the ice covered most of the continent north of about 52°N. It eroded the landscape in many places, and today such features

as the Norwegian fjords and the Scottish lochs are evidence of this glaciation. In other places, the ice carried and then deposited much fertile soil which is today the basis of some of the rich farmlands of the central lowlands.

Europe is a continent of comparatively short rivers. No location in the whole continent is more than about 650 km (400 ml) from the sea. The longest river and largest river system is the Danube, rising in southern Germany and flowing eastward to the Black Sea.

Climatic Background

Europe lies on the west side of the world's largest single land mass, Eurasia, almost entirely north of 40°N and south of the Arctic Circle. Since there are no mountain barriers running parallel to the Atlantic coast except in Norway, the warming influences of the west-east moving maritime airs are felt well into the central parts of the continent. Thus most of Europe experiences temperate climates either of the cool or the warm varieties.

Most of western Europe has no month of the year in which the average temperature is less than 0°C (32°F) or above 22°C (72°F). Rainfall is spread fairly evenly throughout the year with no marked 'wet'

and 'dry' seasons. Rainfall totals are almost all above 550 mm (22 in) and in upland areas of the west coast far higher.

Southern Europe also experiences average monthly temperatures always above 0°C (32°F) and in many places always above 6°C (43°F). In some places, particularly in the eastern Mediterranean area, the average monthly temperature in the summer can easily reach as high as 27°C (80°F).

In Eastern Europe and much of Scandinavia, from Bulgaria northward to Finland and much of Sweden, the winters are colder, with the average monthly temperature falling below 0°C (32°F) in mid winter. In the north of this region, the average monthly temperature in the summer months may rise to only 17°C (62°F), while in the south, in Romania and Bulgaria, it rises to above 24°C (75°F), giving the highest temperature range in all of Europe. This pattern is typical, since temperature ranges increase in places which are farther from the moderating effects of an ocean. Northern Europe extends sufficiently far to contain a small area of Polar climates in which no month has an average temperature higher than 10°C (50°F), such conditions being found in the extreme north of Scandinavia and much of Iceland.

EUROPE

Throughout history Europe has been the birthplace of most major developments in Western Civilization, from the democratic principle as originated in Greece, through parliamentary government as developed in the United Kingdom and the evolution of colonial systems as operated by a number of West European countries, to the growth of the industrial and now the technological age. Many of these fundamentals have been adopted by countries in other parts of the world.

Thus, despite being the second smallest of the eight sectors under review, with only Middle America having a smaller total area, there is little doubt that Europe's influence on the whole world has been collectively greater than that of any other

continental area. In more recent times, however, other continents have become increasingly important, both politically and economically, due largely to the influence of individual countries, particularly the United States of America and the Soviet Union.

Recent Historical and Political Background

Twice within twenty-five years Europe has been torn apart by wars which subsequently embroiled much of the rest of the world. In the aftermath of both wars, her statesmen struggled to forge a lasting peace – first, in the international arena, through the ill-fated League of Nations. Now Europe is shaping her own destiny with trading links and economic agreements which have joined one-time enemies together as peacetime partners.

Today's unity between British and German politicians, or between governments in Paris and Bonn would have been unthinkable in the high summer of 1914. Then a more powerful Austria and Germany fought Russia, France, Italy, the United Kingdom and the British Empire and, later the USA. The inevitable cost in millions of lives and in the economic impoverishment of virtually the whole continent, left Europe and the rest of the world seeking a way to prevent any similar future catastrophe. Many of the former European kingdoms had been replaced by republics, often controlled by dictators at the head of one-party government systems. Pre-World War I prosperity was not easy to restore, and the world of the 1920s and early '30s was a breeding ground for tension and international anxiety.

The League of Nations was bedevilled by dissent between the

major power blocs and its influence was reduced, partly by the severe attitude taken towards their 1914–18 enemies by the western allies, and partly because the USA, for all her help, was not a member, and the Soviet Union did not join until 1934. At the same time, a succession of trade cycles resulted in economic uncertainty and social unrest in many parts of Europe. Germany's share of these problems produced Adolf Hitler and the Nazi party whose nationalist, expansionist policies led the world into a second global war only twenty-one years after the first had ended.

This time, after an initial period in which Germany, Italy and Japan (the Axis powers) together expanded their territory to almost the whole of continental Europe, parts of North Africa, the USSR, the Middle East and much of SE Asia, the Allies (The United Kingdom and the British Commonwealth, the USA, the USSR, China, France and some other European countries) stemmed the Axis tide and, in 1945, were victorious. But again, the resultant economic and social damage was enormous.

Since 1945, Europe has been divided into two broad groups of countries: in the West, those which are essentially democratic and pursue the principles of freely-elected government; in the East, those which are Socialist (Communist) states, with a one-party system of government. Within both groups, the existence of a large number of small political units, compared with the geographically and demographically large units of the new powers in the world, such as the USA, the USSR, and now China, led Europeans to think of various kinds of unification and co-operation. Thus, in Western Europe in the last thirty years a number of supra-national organizations with defence, economic and general political links have been established, forming what we know today as the European Community.

In 1948, Belgium, the Netherlands and Luxembourg established an economic union called Benelux. The aims of this union were to establish economic and social uniformity in such matters as prices, wages, taxation and social security, and to remove trade restriction between the three member countries. Then, following a lead given in 1945 by the French politician Jean Monet, the European Coal and Steel Community (ECSC) was set up in 1951. In 1958 the European Economic Community (EEC) and the European Atomic Energy Commission (Euratom) were set up. Initially, six countries (Belgium, France, West Germany, Italy, Luxembourg and the Netherlands) were members of these groups.

1 Forth Bridges, Scotland; 2 Life Guards in the Mall, London, England; 3 Greek windmill; 4 Grand Canal, Venice, Italy; 5 Memorial to the Discoveries, Lisbon, Portugal; 6 Eiffel Tower, Paris, France; 7 Cheese Market, Gouda, the Netherlands

Switzerland and Sweden, traditionally neutral countries, were not prepared to compromise such a position, and the United Kingdom was understandably concerned about the impact of membership of the European Community on the Commonwealth. These three joined with Austria, Denmark, Norway and Portugal in 1959 to establish what was termed 'little Europe', EFTA (The European Free Trade Association), and later extended it to include Iceland and links with Finland. The objectives of EFTA were purely economic, with the eventual establishment of free trade between all members.

In 1973, the United Kingdom and Denmark transferred to the European Community which, with the admission of Eire, expanded its membership to nine, and began to pursue common aims over wider economic, industrial and agricultural policies. Also, since that time, EFTA and the EEC countries have developed closer economic links.

Since World War II, Western Europe has seen the establishment of other international groups, giving evidence of the new spirit of co-operation in place of the earlier dominance of nationalism. Western Europe also has mutual defence links with the USA and Canada through the North Atlantic Treaty Organization (NATO).

At the same time, the countries of Communist eastern Europe have been establishing their own international organizations, with the USSR playing a dominant role. The Warsaw Pact (the equivalent of NATO) provides for the maintenance of peace through the mutual defence of Albania, Bulgaria, Czechoslovakia, East Germany, Hungary, Poland, Romania and the USSR. The Council for Mutual Economic Assistance (COMECON) is the East European equivalent of the European Community. All Warsaw Pact countries except Albania are members, together with Cuba and Mongolia, two non-European members, and some associate members.

Industry, Commerce and Communications

European industry has developed over the last 250 years so that today the great industrial complexes of West Germany, France, the United Kingdom, the Benelux countries, northern Italy, East Germany, Poland and Czechoslovakia, as well as many other smaller areas within Spain, southern Sweden, Denmark, Austria and Switzerland add up to the largest single industrial concentration in the world. Within this area, the all-important iron and steel industry provides a base for the production of a wide range of metal goods, from heavy engineering and shipbuilding, through vehicle and aircraft construction to a whole range of consumer goods and, at the other end of the scale, intricate precision engineering. Other major European manufacturing industries are textiles, electrical engineering and food processing.

Many Europeans work in what are broadly termed the service industries, some 28 percent of the working population being employed in offices, another 15 percent in the retail and wholesale trades and a further 6 percent in transport and distribution services. Overall then, two out of every five working Europeans are engaged in non-manufacturing activities, but still play an essential part in both the European and world economy. For example, London, Zurich and other smaller financial centres within Europe conduct a large part of all the world's banking and insurance services.

Europe is made up of many great trading nations. As most countries have a coastline, a series of major sea ports have developed. Rotterdam, London, Antwerp and Marseilles, for example, handle large quantities of imports and exports every year. Within continental Europe large rivers and canal systems also handle much cargo.

Similarly, European road, rail and air networks are as densely developed as anywhere in the world. Today's railways tend to concentrate on two types of passenger transport, carrying workers (commuters) from their homes to their work, usually within or around the large towns and cities, and inter-city travel, rather than rural as in the past. Freight transport by rail, albeit diminishing, has been modernized and remains viable.

Major road-building schemes in the last half-century mean that Europe now has a complex network of high speed roads, known variously as autobahnen in Germany, autostrada in Italy, motorways in the United Kingdom, and so on.

Air travel within Europe increases annually. Although still comparatively expensive for distances over 400 km (250 ml) it is quicker, centre to centre, than either rail or road. Today, European air services are used by a wide range of passengers, from businessmen to tourists.

Europe's complex coastline and many offshore islands necessitate frequent ferry services. Ferries are numerous in Scandinavia and the Mediterranean Sea, as well as being available to reach many continental countries from the UK.

Agriculture, Forestry and Fishing

Before man developed the European landscape, forests dominated the natural scene. In the western parts throughout the British Isles, Denmark, France, the low countries and West Germany, as well as in parts of Scandinavia and the Danube Basin, these forests were largely deciduous. In parts of northern Sweden and the lower mountain areas of south and south-eastern Europe, coniferous trees were dominant. Mixed forests covered much of eastern Europe, while in the south there was predominantly Mediterranean vegetation. Upland Norway, Iceland and the highest parts of the Alps were clothed in short Alpine vegetation.

Today, much of this natural cover has been removed in the lowland areas and the land developed, mainly for commercial agriculture. Many of the soils of lowland Europe are either rich loess and limon deposited by the wind in recent glacial times or fertile clays and loams. On the areas of poorer soils of lowland Europe, and many parts of upland Europe, the original forest has often been developed commercially and programmes of forest management introduced.

Around the land mass the width of the continental shelf varies greatly. The shallow waters of the shelf provide rich fishing grounds, especially within the North Sea, around Iceland, to the west of the British Isles and in the Mediterranean.

Of all the large temperate regions of the world, Europe has had the longest period of development, and many of the world's great strides forward in terms of agricultural development have been made in the continent. Commercial farming, for the most part highly efficient, has been established and developed in recent times. Broadly, dairying plays a major role throughout much of the British Isles and in a belt through northern France, the low countries, Denmark, northern Germany and Poland as well as southern Sweden and Finland. Crop farming and livestock raising are more important in the areas south of the main dairying belt. In the extreme south, crops suited to the warmer Mediterranean type climate dominate the agricultural scene.

The temperate European lowlands provide some of the richest farmlands in the world. Even so, Europe as a whole needs to import much of its foodstuffs, and within the continent there is much trading of specific crops which are produced abundantly in one area but less so in others.

Remember that the land area of

European retailing has many faces: 1 Sponge seller, Athens, Greece – divers take living sponges from the seas; 2 Basket shop, Dinan, France – a typical French provincial scene; 3 Oxford Street, London, England – the world-famous shopping street is lined with large department stores

EUROPE

Europe is only 3.5 percent of the world total but its population nearly 12 percent of the world total. Thus, in proportional terms, where Europe's share of world production of a given crop or raw material exceeds both these figures she must rate as a significant producer in those fields. The following figures give examples of her role in world production.

The Mediterranean lands of the south, grow about 15 percent of the world's citrus fruits. About 75 percent of world olive oil also comes from these areas. Together with parts of south-east and middle Europe, these lands also produce 30 percent of the world's hemp fibre, 13 percent of its annual maize production of over 330 million tonnes and 12 percent of its tobacco.

Wheat is by far the most important European cereal, being grown in nearly every country, with France, Italy and West Germany as the leading individual producers. Yet, despite producing over 22 percent of the world total of over 400 million tonnes per year, the continent still has to import large quantities. Barley is also grown widely in Europe, about 36 percent of the world total of 180 million tonnes per year being produced here, particularly in France, the United Kingdom, West Germany and Denmark. Of all other crops, Europe is a major producer of oats (33 percent of the world's output of 51 million tonnes), sugar beet (50 percent of the world's total of 46 million tonnes), vines which yield over 70 percent of the world's wine, and apples (49 percent of the world's annual production of over 22 million tonnes).

Much European farming may be classified as mixed in that crop growing and animal husbandry exist side by side. Cattle farming is most concentrated in the lowlands, for both beef and dairy production. Some 11 percent of all the world's cattle are found in a broad belt from Eire to Poland and the Balkans. Sheep farming, particularly in the upland areas, concentrated in Spain, parts of France, the United Kingdom, Italy and the countries of south-east Europe, accounts for 12 percent of the world's total. As well as lamb and mutton production, these countries supply nearly 10 percent of the world's wool. Pig farming is also concentrated in certain regions, often in association with dairy farming because pigs can be fed on skimmed milk. South-east England, northern France, the Netherlands, Denmark, both East and West Germany and Poland are the most significant areas.

Much of the continent is still forested, especially in Scandinavia, and middle and eastern Europe. Both softwoods (conifers) and temperate hardwoods are grown and felled. In a typical year Sweden, Finland and Norway provide most of Europe's 41 percent share of the world's total wood pulp and pulp products. Likewise, Sweden, Finland, Austria and Romania lead in sawn timber production; Europe accounts for 20 percent of the world's total.

Many European countries have large fishing fleets and her fishermen account for about 18 percent of the world's total annual catch. In recent years, however, it has become necessary to control fishing and prevent the depletion of stocks.

Natural Resources

For such a relatively small continent, Europe has a wide range of mineral resources and large deposits of some of them. Modern industrial economies are based largely upon supplies of fuel and power. Europe has a number of important coal fields which were among the first ever to be developed. Today, the major coal fields of Silesia, the Ruhr, the United Kingdom and some smaller European fields, account for about 20 percent of the world's hard coal production (bituminous coal and anthracite) which is currently about 2,300 million tonnes per year. In addition, East Germany is the world's leading producer of soft coal (lignite), and there are other important fields of lignite in West Germany, Czechoslovakia, Poland and south-east Europe.

Until recently, western Europe produced very little fuel oil and natural gas, although eastern Europe fared better with major oil fields in Romania. However, the last twenty years have seen much oil and natural gas exploration under the western parts of the European lowlands. So far the richest fields have been found beneath the North Sea, the lowlands of the Netherlands and North Germany. New fields may soon be found in these and other parts of lowland western Europe.

Only about one-tenth of the world potential for hydro-electric power (HEP) has yet been developed. Europe, a continent of comparatively short rivers, many of which have small discharges when compared with the rivers of the other continents, may only possess about 5 percent of the world's total potential of 3,000 million kilowatts installed capacity. However, some European countries have made great strides to develop HEP, particularly those without large deposits of coal and/or oil. Norway and Sweden lead in this respect and still have more rivers to harness. France and Italy have both developed over 75 percent of their potential, while other alpine countries with a smaller potential have steadily developed this valuable resource.

The second raw material upon which modern industrial economies are based is iron ore. In this, Europe is also reasonably well endowed for a continent of its size, producing about 9 percent of the world's total of approximately 540 million tonnes (iron content) per year. France accounts for about 35 percent of Europe's output, mainly from the extensive, rich deposits of Lorraine. Sweden has two large deposits, one just north of the Arctic Circle and the other in the Bergslagen district farther south. Between them, these two account for almost 50 percent of Europe's output. Spain, Norway and the United Kingdom are Europe's other leading iron ore producers. That Europe's share of world iron ore production has fallen from over 18 percent to its present figure in the post World War II era is more a reflection of increasing production elsewhere than of the continent's declining output. It is currently estimated that Europe still possesses 9 percent of the world's proven reserves of over 260,000 million tonnes (iron content).

Other valuable ores are found in Europe in varying quantities, summarized in the table above.

Ore	Average Annual World Production (million tonnes)	Europe's Share (percent)	Principal European Producing Countries
bauxite	80.3	15	Hungary, Greece, France
chrome	7.2	12	Albania
cobalt	0.03	11	Norway, France, Finland
copper	7.4	10	Poland, Yugoslavia
lead	3.2	20	Yugoslavia, Bulgaria, Sweden, Poland
nickel	0.733	3	Greece
silver	0.01	9	Poland, Sweden, Yugoslavia
tungsten	0.036	5	Portugal, France
vanadium	0.02	12	Finland, Norway
zinc	5.4	18	Poland, West Germany, Sweden

1 Olive groves, Alcaudete, Spain – half a million tonnes of olive oil are produced yearly by the Spaniards; 2 Burgundy Château and vineyard, France – one of the great wine regions; 3 Commercial harbour, Rhodes – fishing by traditional methods continues in the Greek Islands

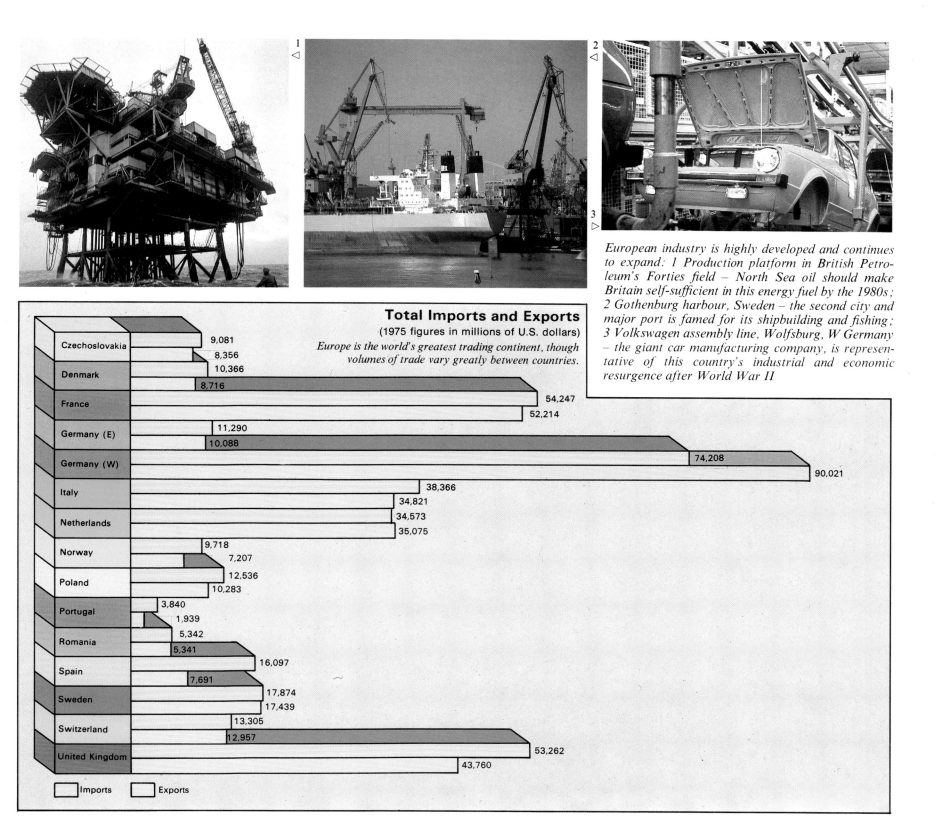

European industry is highly developed and continues to expand: 1 Production platform in British Petroleum's Forties field – North Sea oil should make Britain self-sufficient in this energy fuel by the 1980s; 2 Gothenburg harbour, Sweden – the second city and major port is famed for its shipbuilding and fishing; 3 Volkswagen assembly line, Wolfsburg, W Germany – the giant car manufacturing company, is representative of this country's industrial and economic resurgence after World War II

Total Imports and Exports
(1975 figures in millions of U.S. dollars)
Europe is the world's greatest trading continent, though volumes of trade vary greatly between countries.

Country	Imports	Exports
Czechoslovakia	9,081	8,356
Denmark	10,366	8,716
France	54,247	52,214
Germany (E)	11,290	10,088
Germany (W)	74,208	90,021
Italy	38,366	34,821
Netherlands	34,573	35,075
Norway	9,718	7,207
Poland	12,536	10,283
Portugal	3,840	1,939
Romania	5,342	5,341
Spain	16,097	7,691
Sweden	17,874	17,439
Switzerland	13,305	12,957
United Kingdom	53,262	43,760

☐ Imports   ☐ Exports

European Economy

The population map of Europe shows the greatest concentration of people in a broad belt extending from Wales, England and northern France in the west, across the low countries and Germany to southern Poland in the east. Elsewhere, much of Italy, western France and the Rhône-Saône Valleys, and parts of southeast Europe also have an overall density exceeding 150 persons to the square kilometre (390 persons to the square mile). The least heavily peopled parts of the continent are the cooler upland areas of the north and the upland areas of Mediterranean and south-east Europe.

Europe is, of course, highly urbanized in many parts, more than 20 millionaire cities having grown up in recent times. Of these, Paris, London, Madrid, Rome, Athens, West Berlin and Budapest are the largest, each having more than 2 million inhabitants. In some areas,

groups of towns and cities close together make up large conurbations or concentrations of many millions of people. The largest conurbations are in midland and northern England, north-east France, Belgium and the Netherlands, northern Germany and the industrial cities of southern Poland.

By world standards the population of Europe is currently fairly static. Birth rates in excess of 40 per 1,000 are found in Africa and Asia and, when coupled with lower death rates, combine to make annual increases in population in excess of 4 percent. European birth rates rarely exceed 20 per 1,000 and are often as low as 11 or 12, so that overall the normal increase in European population is less than 1 percent per annum.

Most of the European countries are among the world's leading developed economies either in the free market (democratic) or planned (socialist) world, and many European countries have been and still are

great trading nations. How then does Europe as a whole and its individual member countries stand in comparison to other continental areas today?

Between 1939 and 1958 the worldwide values of both imports and exports rose by 4.5 times; between 1958 and 1975, by nearly 8 times. Such figures demonstrate the considerable growth in world trade during these periods and, despite the confusing effects of inflation on the units of measurement, act as a relevant yardstick against which to measure the trade of a continental area or even an individual country.

European imports in the same two periods rose by only 3.9 times and just over 8.5 times. Her exports rose by 4.7 times and just over 8.5 times. Collectively then, the countries of Europe have performed better than average in the league tables of world trade.

The performance of individual European countries and groups of trading countries during the periods

1938–'58 and 1958–'75 reveal considerable differences, as shown in the following examples. Compare the figures with those quoted above for the whole continent.

As a group, the nine countries now in the EEC reduced their share of European imports during these periods from 75.8 to 64.9 percent, but their share of exports remained comparatively steady, at 72.0 and 72.5 percent. The EFTA group of countries has fared less well: their share of imports has fallen overall (14.3 to 14.1 percent) but so has their share of exports (15.8 to 13.0 percent). Where figures for individual countries are concerned, those for the UK show the most marked decline both for imports (35.0 to 12.1 percent) and exports (27.3 to 10.8 percent). Other countries which have lost ground, for both imports and exports, include Austria, Denmark, the Irish Republic and Norway.

Some countries, however, have increased their share of both imports

Comprising many great trading nations, Europe has excellent communication links, with its many islands relying heavily on sea transport: 1 Hydrofoil at St Helier, Jersey, Channel Islands; 2 Tower Bridge, London, England – up river, the Thames sees few merchant ships; 3 Europe's longest road bridge links the Swedish mainland with Öland island

EUROPE

and exports. The 1945 partition of Germany makes it impossible to compare her performance since 1938, but certainly West Germany has improved her position considerably since 1958; imports have risen from 15.0 to 16.8 percent of the European total, but exports from 19.3 to 22.1 percent. Three others, France, the Netherlands and Switzerland, have fared similarly, increasing their share of exports more than imports.

The trading position of other countries has no single pattern. For some, such as Bulgaria, Poland and Spain, the increasing share of imports has outstripped that of exports. For others, like Belgium, Czechoslovakia, Finland, Hungary, Greece and Sweden, the share of imports has risen but that of exports has declined.

It is also possible to compare the change in the incomes of countries and groups of countries in percentage terms. For example, the overall rise in per capita incomes in the non-Communist world between 1960 and 1974 was 186 percent, as compared to a rise of 290 percent in all Europe.

The rise in European per capita incomes thus outstripped that of all other *continental* areas; only Oceania with a rise of 279 percent came anywhere near it, though the countries of the Middle East, a subregion of Asia, surpassed it with 445 percent.

Marked differences can be seen between individual European countries. For example, Austrian per capita incomes rose by 386 percent, French by 275 percent, Portuguese by 404 percent, Swedish by 267 percent and British by 147 percent. The absolute dollar values must also be taken into account. The Portuguese

for example, have obviously improved their incomes over five times, but are still relatively poor. Within the five selected countries, the United Kingdom, in comparison, has fared badly in both absolute and relative terms, slipping from second to fourth place.

Energy production and consumption figures and, perhaps more significantly, the figures for per capita consumption of energy, are further ways in which the state of the European economy can be compared with other parts of the world. For all its reserves of coal, Europe is well

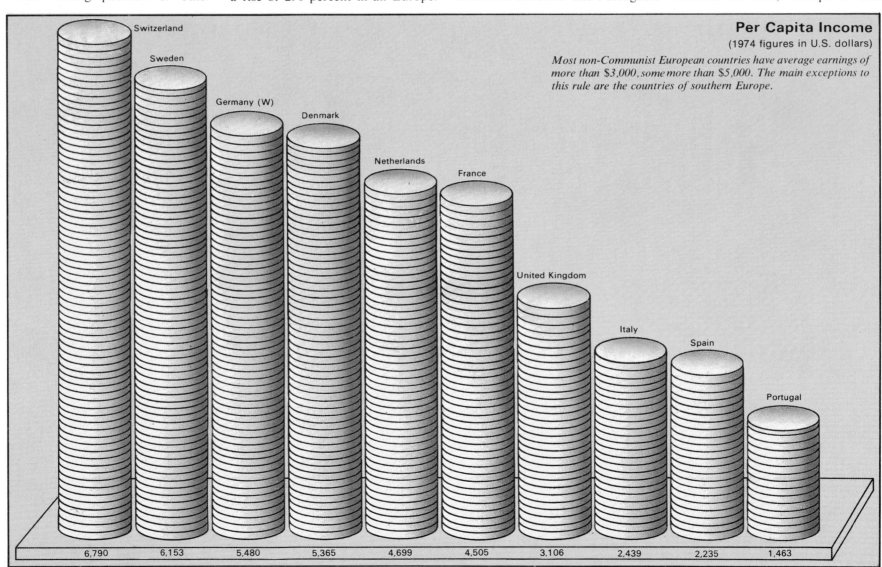

Per Capita Income
(1974 figures in U.S. dollars)

Most non-Communist European countries have average earnings of more than $3,000, some more than $5,000. The main exceptions to this rule are the countries of southern Europe.

Switzerland	Sweden	Germany (W)	Denmark	Netherlands	France	United Kingdom	Italy	Spain	Portugal
6,790	6,153	5,480	5,365	4,699	4,505	3,106	2,439	2,235	1,463

known to be a great energy-deficient area. It has yet to prove and develop its own oil reserves fully, and is still heavily dependent upon the world's oil rich areas.

Overall, when energy figures are reduced to a common unit of million tonnes coal equivalent, Europe produced 1131.74 mtce in 1975 yet consumed 2021.75 mtce. She thus produced 13.2 percent of the world's energy but consumed 25.3 percent. Among the large energy-consuming countries, Czechoslovakia imported 23 percent, France 77 percent, East Germany 30 percent, West Germany 50 percent, Italy 84 percent and the United Kingdom 38 percent each of their needs. In all Europe, Romania

is just self-sufficient while only the Netherlands and Poland are significant exporters of energy.

A final index of Europe's position in a quickening world is the amount of energy consumed per head of population. In the continent as a whole in 1975 the figure was 4,227 kilograms per head (kg/ca), very high by overall world standards, reflecting the area's great industrial activities. Yet there are great differences from country to country. Luxembourg, with its small population and substantial iron and steel industry used the phenomenal amount of 15,504 kg/ca, while at the other end of the scale, Albania used only 741 kg/ca and Portugal 983. In general, south-

ern European countries have a lower energy consumption than northern ones, reflecting both the climate and the lower industrial development.

Many European countries developed their economies early and reached a mature stage by or before the mid-twentieth century. At present, with new political and economic incentives, the continent as a whole is just managing to hold its relative position in the trading world, with an overall slight improvement in the last two decades.

Over the last five years, however, her overall relative position has worsened. Such fluctuations in fortune over a brief time span can also be seen in variations from

country to country for the same period, as revealed most significantly in the individual trade and per capita incomes figures.

We have now moved from an era in which energy self-sufficient Europe was the great industrial heart of the world to one in which European industry is heavily dependent upon imported energy. In the short term, as Europe develops her own oil resources this situation may improve. By the end of this century, as global oil resources run down, world technology will need to harness new energy sources. It must be hoped that a significant contribution, as yet an unknown quantity, will be made by Europe.

Many traditional cottage industries are still preserved throughout Europe: 1 Thatcher, Bideford-on-Avon, Warwickshire, England – cottages roofed with varieties of reed are found mainly in the southern parts, but this is one of many country crafts experiencing a modern nationwide revival; 2 Cheese making in the Emilia-Romagna region of Italy – food processing, in particular cheeses for which the country is renowned, is the main occupation of this fertile area which stretches across northern Italy; 3 Lace maker in national dress, Bruges, Belgium – hand-made lace, especially from this medieval town, is much prized and a great tourist attraction

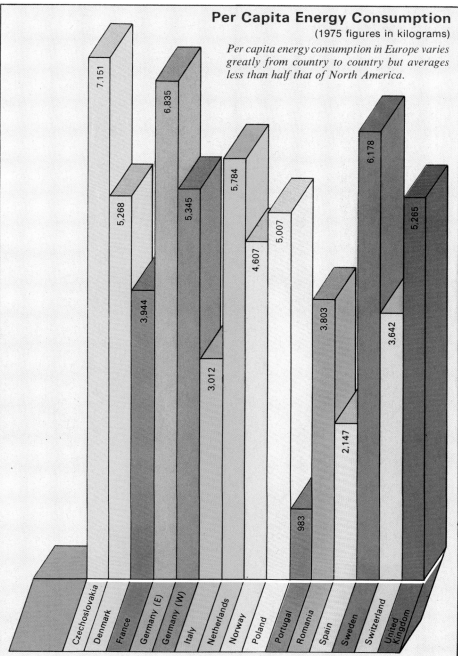

Per Capita Energy Consumption
(1975 figures in kilograms)

Per capita energy consumption in Europe varies greatly from country to country but averages less than half that of North America.

Czechoslovakia	7,151
Denmark	5,268
France	3,944
Germany (E)	6,835
Germany (W)	5,345
Italy	3,012
Netherlands	5,784
Norway	4,607
Poland	5,007
Portugal	983
Romania	3,803
Spain	2,147
Sweden	6,178
Switzerland	3,642
United Kingdom	5,265

Kilometres 0 200 400 Km.

Statute Miles 0 200 400 600 Mi.

Scale 1:13,200,000

One centimetre represents 132 kilometres.
One inch represents approximately 210 miles.
Miller Oblated Stereographic Projection

European Countries

Albania

A mountainous country, bordering the Adriatic Sea, Albania boasts a language unlike any other, based on ancient Illyrian. Previously predominantly Moslem, the country has been officially atheist since 1967 when all places of worship were closed. This Socialist peoples' republic and member of the Warsaw Pact is unique in the Eastern bloc in that it is not a member of COMECON, but has strong political and economic links with China, 70 percent of all trade being with that country. In recent years, minerals such as chrome ore, copper, lignite and crude oil have been steadily developed. Farming is restricted to the coastal lowlands and the Korçë Basin, with maize, wheat and sugar beet as the main crops grown there.

Andorra

Situated high in the Pyrenees Mountains, Andorra is curiously semi-independent politically, paying taxes to neighbours France and Spain and using the currency of both countries. In recent years tourism has outpaced agriculture as a source of revenue, although many Andorrans still grow a variety of crops and keep sheep and goats.

Austria

Prior to 1914 the Austro-Hungarian state dominated Central Europe. Austria was established as a separate, smaller country between the two world wars, and after World War II its independence was re-established in 1955. It is now a member of EFTA. Austria today is perhaps best known for its tourist attractions – cities like Vienna and Salzburg and the mountain ski resorts. Many are employed in dairying and cereal farming. Minerals extracted include iron ore, lignite and graphite from one of the world's major deposits.

Belgium

A founder member of the EEC, Belgium now plays host to the Community in its capital, Brussels. Belgians are predominantly Roman Catholic, but are divided culturally between the northern areas where Flemish, a language similar to Dutch, is spoken, and French-speaking Walloonia in the south. The north and west of this small, densely populated kingdom bordering the North Sea, comprises low-lying rich agricultural land, while to the south and south-east are the forest uplands of the Ardennes. Farming in the north is very intensive, with dairying and pig production following close on the heels of major crops such as sugar beet, potatoes and cereals. Although coal and iron ore mining have both declined recently, a wide range of heavy and manufacturing industries still flourishes.

Bulgaria

The Peoples' Republic (Socialist) of Bulgaria is a member of both the Warsaw Pact and COMECON, 80 percent of all her trade being with the European Communist countries. A limited mineral production is on the increase, especially lignite, iron ore and copper outputs. Both arable and dairy farming play a major part in the lives of many Bulgarians, whose language is one of the simplest in the Slavonic group. Most people follow the Eastern Orthodox faith.

Channel Islands

Some 140 km (90 ml) south of the British mainland, the nine inhabited Channel Islands are a British crown possession with internal self-government. English is the main language, though a form of Norman-French is also spoken. Jersey, the largest island, relies heavily on tourism and agriculture. Guernsey, next in size, with seven smaller dependencies, is famed for its cows, greenhouses, tomatoes and flowers.

Czechoslovakia

A landlocked Central European federal Socialist republic, Czechoslovakia is a member of both the Warsaw Pact and COMECON, 67 percent of all her trade being with the European Communist countries. After a period of unrest in 1968, more liberal leaders took control of the country. They were soon deposed, following the occupation of the land by armed forces from other Warsaw Pact countries. Czechoslovakia was established in 1918 following the break up of Austria-Hungary, and both Czech and Slovak languages are spoken today. Czechoslovak agriculture is highly efficient, dairying and pig farming playing a major part, with sugar beet, wheat, potatoes and barley the principal crops. Forestry also contributes greatly to the national economy. Coal and iron ore are the most important of the country's limited mineral resources. In recent years a range of basic manufacturing industries has been successfully established.

Denmark

The kingdom of Denmark comprises a low-lying peninsula and groups of islands separating the North and Baltic Seas. The Danish farming system is highly organized and very efficient. Dairy cattle dominate the green pastures, although some root crops and barley are grown, mainly for animal feeding. Food processing, especially bacon and dairy products, is of prime importance to the economy. In recent years, however, a wide range of manufacturing industries has been established, and today nearly three times as many people work in such industries as on the land. Denmark joined the EEC in 1973.

Faeroe Islands

A group of 21 islands 500 km (310 ml) south-east of Iceland, the Faeroes belong to Denmark but have had internal self-government since 1948. The name Faeroes is taken from the Danish for 'sheep islands' and sheep farming, along with fishing, is the most important occupation. Fish, fresh and processed, and craft products are exported mainly to Scandinavia and the United Kingdom.

Finland

The most northerly country of mainland Europe, Finland has a low-lying, forested and lake-strewn landscape. Such severe winters grip the land that even the capital, Helsinki, in the south of the country, is ice-bound. Generally, farming, forestry, mining, especially for copper and iron, and manufacturing industries all play their part in the economy. A democratic republic which steers a careful political course between the Soviet Union and Western Europe, Finland has a treaty of friendship and co-operation with the USSR and is also an associate member of EFTA. Like the other Scandinavian peoples, most Finns are members of the Lutheran National Church.

France

The largest country in Western Europe, France is a democratic republic. It has coastlines facing in three directions (north, west and south), a variety of rich agricultural lowlands and less prosperous upland areas, including parts of the Alps which rise to a maximum height of 4,807 m (15,771 ft) and a wide range of climates. A major tourist country,

1 Schröcken, Vorarlberg, Austria – dairying is a major occupation in this picturesque mountain region; 2 East Berlin, E Germany – the modern TV Tower rises alongside the ancient cathedral in this physically divided city; 3 Market day, Split, Yugoslavia – spectacular Roman ruins and the fine harbour attract tourists and commerce to this Dalmatian port

rightly famed for its capital, Paris, France remains predominantly rural. It is the world's largest producer of wines, mainly from the Rhône and Saône river valleys, the Loire valley, Bordeaux and Champagne. In addition to large outputs of cereals and vegetables, cattle and sheep farming both play a major part in French agriculture. Industrially, iron ore production is most important, while coal production is declining; there is a large iron and steel industry. The automobile, aircraft, textile, chemical and food processing industries are all large. France is a founder member of the EEC and most of her trade is with other members of this group.

Germany (Democratic Republic of East)

About a third of the geographical area of the united Germany of the inter-war years now forms the Socialist Democratic Republic of East Germany. A member of both the Warsaw Pact and COMECON, some 75 percent of all its trade is with the European Communist countries. East Germany's lignite (soft coal) output is the largest for any single country in the world. Mineral production and a range of industries generate about 70 percent of the national income, although forestry, and crop and animal farming are also important.

Germany (Federal Republic of West)

Occupying over half of the area of the old united Germany, the Federal Republic of West Germany comprises ten main states (Länder) and the western parts of Berlin. West Berlin, with a population of about 2 million, remains the largest city in the Federal Republic. Bonn, in North Rhine–Westphalia, with a mere 300,000 population, has been the capital since 1949. Since World War II, West Germany has developed as a leading member of the Western European group of countries, being a founder member of the EEC and trading mainly with fellow members. It is the biggest hard coal producer of West Europe, and has the largest iron and steel industry within the EEC. A range of major manufacturing industries are concentrated in the northern Ruhr area, the port cities of the North Sea coast and the large cities of the south. The northern lowlands form the major agricultural area, followed by the areas of rolling landscapes in the south. Sugar beet, potatoes, barley and wheat are the main crops, pigs and cattle the most numerous farm animals. German wines from the Rhine and Mosel valleys play a valuable part in the economy, as does forestry.

1 △   2 ▽   3 ▽

Gibraltar

Guarding the western entrance to the Mediterranean, Gibraltar rises steeply from its base on the south Spanish coast to a height of 429 m (1,408 ft). The Rock of Gibraltar thrives on air and naval activities – its artificial harbour and airfield are of great strategic importance – tourism and commercial ship repairing. Although the Spaniards claim that it is part of their country, Gibraltar has been a British crown colony since 1704. The small, rocky promontory has apparently little wish to become entirely independent, although it has a large degree of self-government, and in 1967 it voted by over 12,000 to 44 to retain British links.

Greece

A mountainous peninsula and island country in the extreme south-east of Europe, Greece relies heavily on the many tourists who annually sample its ancient treasures and modern amenities. Although much of the land is unsuitable for agriculture, cereals, cotton, tobacco, olives, grapes and citrus fruit are grown.

Major industries are food processing, textile and chemical production. A few minerals are produced in modest quantities and some are exported. Greece is currently negotiating to become a member of the EEC.

Hungary

Over 60 percent of all Hungary's trade is with the European Communist countries, as this peoples' republic (Socialist) is a member of both the Warsaw Pact and COMECON. The leading industries are food processing, metal, textile and chemical production. Coal – both hard and soft – and bauxite are the major minerals. Arable farming, especially maize, wheat, sugar beet and potatoes, as well as raising pigs, sheep and cattle, is of prime importance to the economy. Free to follow any religion, the Hungarians speak a language, Magyar, which is most akin to Finnish.

Iceland

A volcanic island in the North Atlantic Ocean just south of the Arctic Circle, Iceland was formerly part of the Danish realm; its language is

related to both Danish and Norwegian. It achieved independence in 1918 and declared itself a democratic republic in 1944. Iceland, whose economy is based on fishing, is a member of EFTA.

Irish Republic

Comprising 26 counties in the southern part of Ireland, the modern independent republic (Eire) was formerly united with Great Britain and Northern Ireland, but finally severed all links with the Commonwealth in 1949. Both English and Gaelic are spoken. Most of the Irish are Roman Catholics. Known as 'the Emerald Isle', from the rich, green landscape, southern Ireland is predominantly agricultural. Food processing and brewing are the leading industries. The Irish Republic has been a member of the EEC since 1973.

Isle of Man

Lying in the middle of the Irish Sea, this attractive island relies heavily on tourists, although sheep and cattle are raised, as are some crops. A member of the Commonwealth, the Isle

23

European Countries

of Man has internal government by the Court of Tynwald but United Kingdom control of external affairs.

Italy

A democratic republic of Mediterranean Europe, Italy freely elects the members of both houses of parliament. The state religion is Roman Catholicism to which almost everyone adheres. As fountainhead of the ancient Roman Empire, Italy has a great range of cultural and religious treasures which attract many tourists every year to the centres of Rome, Venice and Florence. Other popular holiday areas are the Riviera coast, the isle of Capri and the Italian lakes on the border with Switzerland. The 'boot' of Italy is a long peninsula whose backbone is the Apennine Mountains which extend to the very 'toe' in the south; the southern ranges of the Alps dominate the extreme north. Still primarily agricultural, the richest and most extensive farmlands are within the basin of the River Po. In addition to temperate crops like wheat, sugar beet and potatoes, Italy grows rice, tobacco, olives and citrus fruit. Crude oil production has expanded rapidly in recent years, especially in Sicily, and modest quantities of a range of minerals are also produced. Italian textiles, particularly silk, are world famous. Most industry is concentrated in the north, especially in the large cities. Southern Italy is less developed. Italy was a founder member of the EEC.

Liechtenstein

This small, independent alpine principality is united with Switzerland for diplomatic and customs purposes. Dairying is the most important agricultural activity of this picturesque mountainous area, and in recent years industries such as precision engineering, food processing and ceramics have developed.

Luxembourg

The Grand Duchy of Luxembourg is a small but rich independent state situated between Belgium, France and West Germany. Both at the end of the Franco-Prussian War and World War I its people decided to remain independent of the surrounding larger powers. Since 1948, however, Luxembourg has abandoned its neutral status and has been a member of NATO. French and German are spoken, but most of the people use the Letzeburgesch dialect. A founder member of the EEC, Luxembourg's greatest strengths economically are its iron ore deposits and the iron and steel industry based on them.

Malta

Greeks, Romans, Carthaginians, Phoenicians and Arabs all used Malta at some time. For 268 years it was the base of the Knights of St John, but became a British colony following the Napoleonic Wars. Today it is a small, independent Mediterranean island republic within the Commonwealth. It was of enormous strategic importance during World War II, when the valour of its people in withstanding attacks from the Axis powers led in 1942 to the award of the George Cross, the highest British award for civilian bravery. The subsequent decline of its role as an important air and naval base has led to the development of a number of new industries such as textiles and rubber and food processing to replace the decreasing dock activities.

Monaco

Enclosed on the land side by France, the small, independent Mediterranean principality of Monaco enjoys a special administrative relationship with its powerful neighbour. Next to the Vatican it is the world's smallest sovereign state. Most of the revenue comes from tourism.

Netherlands

Often mistakenly referred to as Holland, the Netherlands is a low-lying kingdom bordering the North Sea. It has one of the highest population densities in Europe. Much of the Netherlands lies below sea level, behind protecting dykes and sea-walls, and some of its richest farmlands have been reclaimed from the sea in recent times. Dutch agriculture is highly organized and efficient, as is a wide range of industries near to the great ports of Rotterdam and Amsterdam. The Netherlands was a founder member of the EEC.

Norway

An independent kingdom since 1905, Norway has been closely linked with its neighbours Sweden and Denmark throughout its history. Famed for its mountains and fjords, most Norwegian land is unproductive, only 3 percent being farmed and some 23 percent forested. The economy rests largely on forestry, fishing and mining (especially of high grade iron ore and copper) and their associated processing industries. A member of EFTA, Norway earns much foreign currency from its large ocean-going merchant navy, and from tourism. Its government successfully negotiated entry to the EEC, but the Norwegian people voted against the move in a referendum late in 1972.

Poland

Now over 1,000 years old, the country of Poland has not always enjoyed independence and its precise geographical boundaries have changed frequently. It is today a people's republic (Socialist) which is a member of both the Warsaw Pact and COMECON, although its foreign trade is almost as great with the western world as with the Soviet bloc. Poland possesses the second largest coal field in Europe, upon which the many industries of Silesia are based. Principal farm products are cereals, root crops and dairy products.

Portugal

Together with Spain and Gibraltar, Portugal is situated in the Iberian peninsula. The Atlantic islands of Madeira and the Azores are parts of metropolitan Portugal. Less than half the land is farmed, a quarter forested and the remainder is unproductive. Famed for its vines and the production of port wine, Portugal also produces more than half of the world's cork. Other leading exports are wood pulp, resins and sardines. Portugal is a member of EFTA.

COUNTRY REFERENCE: EUROPE

European Countries	Political Status	State Capital	Area km²	Area sq ml	Population	Population Density per km²	Population Density per sq ml	Births per Thousand Persons	Deaths per Thousand Persons	Mean Annual Percentage Increase in Population
Albania	A	Tirane	28,748	11,100	2,655,000	92	239	33.3	8.1	3.1
Andorra	A	Andorra	453	175	28,000	62	160	20.1	4.6	3.7
Austria	A	Vienna	83,849	32,374	7,500,000	89	232	12.3	12.7	0.5
Belgium	A	Brussels	30,513	11,781	10,005,000	328	849	12.3	12.0	0.4
Bulgaria	A	Sofia	110,912	42,823	8,820,000	80	206	16.6	10.3	0.6
Channel Islands	C	St Peter Port (Guernsey)	78	30	54,000	692	1,800	11.5	13.1	1.1
	C	St Helier (Jersey)	116	45	75,000	647	1,667			
Czechoslovakia	A	Prague	127,876	49,373	15,095,000	118	306	19.5	11.5	0.6
Denmark	A	Copenhagen	43,069	16,629	5,090,000	118	306	14.1	10.2	0.6
Faeroe Islands	C	Torshavn	1,399	540	40,000	29	74	19.9	7.3	1.0
Finland	A	Helsinki	337,032	130,129	4,770,000	14	37	14.2	9.4	0.4
France	A	Paris	543,998	210,039	53,208,000	98	253	15.2	10.4	0.8
Germany (E)	A	East Berlin	108,178	41,768	16,695,000	154	400	10.8	14.3	0.2
Germany (W)	A	Bonn	248,533	95,959	61,070,000	246	636	9.7	12.1	0.6
Gibraltar	C	Gibraltar	6	2	30,000	5,000	15,000	19.8	7.0	0.5
Greece	A	Athens	131,944	50,944	9,340,000	71	183	15.6	8.9	0.5
Hungary	A	Budapest	93,032	35,920	10,690,000	115	298	18.4	12.4	0.3
Iceland	A	Reykjavik	103,000	39,800	225,000	2.2	5.7	20.6	6.9	1.3
Irish Republic	A	Dublin	70,285	27,137	3,210,000	46	118	21.6	10.	1.1
Isle of Man	C	Douglas	588	227	64,000	109	282	11.7	16.7	2.9
Italy	A	Rome	301,250	116,313	56,710,000	188	488	14.8	9.9	0.8
Liechtenstein	A	Vaduz	160	62	25,000	156	403	12.6	7.3	0.8
Luxembourg	A	Luxembourg	2,586	998	365,000	141	366	11.2	12.2	0.2
Malta	A	Valletta	316	122	275,000	870	2,254	18.7	9.7	-0.2
Monaco	A	Monaco	1.5	0.6	26,000	17,333	43,333	8.2	12.3	0.9
Netherlands	A	Amsterdam and The Hague	40,844	15,770	13,945,000	341	884	13.0	8.3	1.0
Norway	A	Oslo	323,878	125,050	4,060,000	13	32	14.0	9.9	0.7
Poland	A	Warsaw	312,677	120,725	34,865,000	112	289	19.0	8.7	0.9
Portugal	A	Lisbon	92,082	35,553	9,660,000	105	272	19.6	11.0	0.2
Romania	A	Bucharest	237,500	91,699	21,760,000	92	237	19.7	9.1	0.9
San Marino	A	San Marino	61	24	21,000	344	875	17.4	7.7	0.6
Spain	A	Madrid	504,750	194,885	36,530,000	72	187	18.2	8.1	1.1
Sweden	A	Stockholm	449,750	173,649	8,265,000	18	48	12.6	10.8	0.4
Switzerland	A	Bern	41,288	15,941	6,270,000	152	393	12.4	8.8	1.2
UK	A	London	244,013	94,214	55,890,000	229	593	12.4	11.8	0.3
Vatican	A	Vatican City	0.4	0.2	1,000	2,500	5,000	—	—	—
Yugoslavia	A	Belgrade	255,804	98,766	21,875,000	86	221	18.1	8.6	0.9
EUROPEAN TOTAL (exc. USSR)			4,870,569.9	1,880,566.8	479,207,000	98	255	—	—	—

1 Monte Carlo, Monaco – the yacht harbour and casino of this Riviera capital attract an internationally famous clientele; 2 Iceland – hot springs are found all over this volcanic island; 3 Amsterdam, the Netherlands – the capital's famous canals, running through the city, are home for a floating population of houseboat dwellers, including lots of cats!

Romania

A member of both the Warsaw Pact and COMECON, Romania is a mountainous Socialist republic bordering on the Black Sea. Oil and natural gas are produced in substantial quantities. Coal, iron ore and other minerals are extracted, and a wide range of manufacturing industries has been developed. Tourism is a modern growth industry. Principal exports, mainly to other East European countries, are oil products, cereals, chemicals and machinery. The Danube lowlands of the south and east and other western lowlands are the most important agricultural areas.

San Marino

Founded in the fourth century, San Marino claims to be the world's oldest republic. Tourism and the sale of postage stamps bring in much foreign currency to this small state. It is surrounded entirely by Italy with whom it has a long standing treaty of friendship. Wines, textiles and ceramics are the major exports.

Spain

One of the largest yet least developed countries of Western Europe, Spain, together with Portugal and Gibraltar, occupies the whole of the Iberian peninsula. Following an economically disastrous Civil War in the late 1930s, Spain was ruled as a dictatorship by General Franco until 1975 when it returned to being a monarchy with an elected parliament. With over 30 million visitors each year, the Spanish economy depends a great deal on tourism. Spain is still largely an agricultural country, roots and cereals being the major temperate crops, with vines, olives and citrus fruit grown widely. A range of mineral deposits is currently being developed, but only iron ore is mined on a large scale. Textiles are the major manufacturing industry.

Sweden

The Scandinavian kingdom of Sweden is one of the most prosperous countries of Western Europe. With a long tradition of neutrality, Sweden is today a member of EFTA, but not of any European political union. Only a small part of the land is farmed, but over half is forested, forming the basis of the country's all-important timber industries. Swedish high quality iron ore deposits are large and provide another major export item, along with smaller amounts of copper, zinc and lead.

1 △

2 ▽

3 ▽

Switzerland

Neutral Switzerland is a member of EFTA and provides the headquarters for many international organizations. Tourists are attracted throughout the year to this landlocked alpine federal republic, especially for the scenery and traditional winter sports. Switzerland's agriculture is highly organized, dairying being the main activity. The most successful industries are precision and electrical engineering and toy making.

The United Kingdom

England, Scotland, Wales and Northern Ireland comprise the United Kingdom which occupies most of the British Isles, a group of islands separated from mainland Europe by the North Sea and the English Channel. It is a constitutional monarchy with a two chamber parliament, the House of Commons being freely elected and the House of Lords composed of hereditary and nominated peers. Britain was the mother country of an extensive Empire until the twentieth century. In recent years most of the former dependent countries and dominions have achieved independence. Today, many are members of the Commonwealth of Nations which has no constitution yet exists for mutual co-operation and assistance. The English language is today the most widely spoken in the world and the established Anglican Church is the second largest in the Christian world. Geographically, the southern and eastern parts of the country are lower-lying and agriculturally more productive than the more rugged northern and western areas. Farming is well developed and efficient, but 40 percent of the nation's food still has to be imported. Previously a member of EFTA, the United Kingdom did not join the EEC until 1973.

Vatican City

A tiny sovereign state within the city of Rome, the Vatican provides an independent base for the headquarters of the Roman Catholic Church. Governed by the Pope, it has its own coins and stamps, and a radio station which broadcasts in 31 different languages.

Yugoslavia

Created in 1918 by the union of the south Slavic peoples, Yugoslavia is a Balkan country bordering on the Adriatic Sea. A number of Slavonic languages are spoken, the most widespread being Serbo-Croat. Yugoslavs have religious freedom; the Eastern Orthodox, Roman Catholic and Islamic faiths are the strongest. Although a Socialist federal republic, among the European Communist countries Yugoslavia has always maintained most independence from the Soviet bloc, being neither a member of the Warsaw Pact nor of COMECON. Leading agricultural crops are maize, wheat, potatoes and tobacco. A range of valuable ores are mined in addition to coal and iron. The main industries are metals, chemicals and textiles.

Kilometres
Statute Miles

One centimetre represents 66 kilometres.
One inch represents approximately 105 miles.

Scale 1:6,600,000

Lambert Conformal Conic Projection

27

NORWEGIAN SEA

NORTH SEA

Skagerrak

Kattegat

NORWAY NORGE
SWEDEN SVERIGE
DENMARK DANMARK
FED. REP. OF GER. B.R.D.

Bergen
Stavanger
Haugesund
Kristiansand
Oslo
Drammen
Tønsberg
Skien
Porsgrunn
Moss
Fredrikstad
Halden
Sarpsborg
Ålesund
Trondheim

Göteborg
Gothenburg
Uddevalla
Trollhättan
Borås
Jönköping
Halmstad
Helsingborg
Landskrona
Malmö
Trelleborg
Kristianstad
Karlskrona
Kalmar
Växjö
Karlstad
Karlskoga
Örebro
Västerås
Uppsala
STOCKHOLM
Eskilstuna
Södertälje
Norrköping
Nyköping
Linköping
Motala
Skövde
Visby
GOTLAND
ÖLAND
BORNHOLM

København
COPENHAGEN
Roskilde
Odense
Svendborg
Næstved
Helsingør
Ålborg
Århus
Randers
Silkeborg
Herning
Viborg
Horsens
Vejle
Kolding
Fredericia
Esbjerg
Flensburg
Schleswig
Rendsburg
Kiel
Neumünster

The annexation of Latvia and Est in 1940 by the Soviet Union has r been officially recognized by the United States Government.

Copyright © by Rand McNally & Co.
Map compiled by Esselte Map Service AB, Stockholm.
Map produced by Rand McNally & Co.
A-554400 264

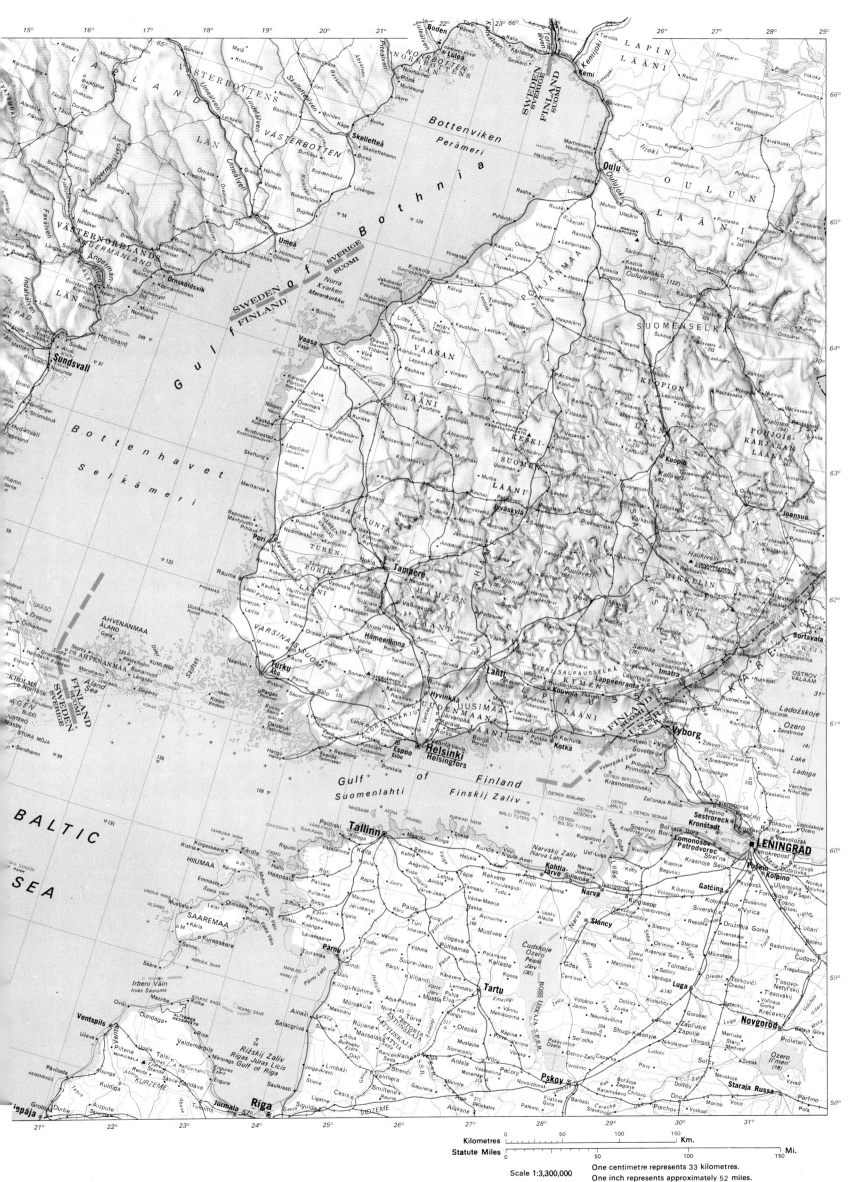

Kilometres

Statute Miles

Scale 1:3,300,000

One centimetre represents 33 kilometres.
One inch represents approximately 52 miles.

Conic Projection, Two Standard Parallels

29

Scandinavia

Alike, yet different; sophisticated but simple; vast open spaces and intimate cities; an advanced economic society, yet one that includes a race of nomadic herdsmen. All these contradictions are to be found in the four countries which make up Europe's northern attic, Scandinavia, a land of wild beauty, friendly peoples and room to move.

Think of Scandinavia and you think of the great outdoors, where mountains, lakes and forests combine in one marvellous year-round winter sports centre. Water is ever-present, from Sweden's thousands of lakes, to Norway's spectacular fjords and glaciers, Finland's sailing waters and the sea around Denmark. Trees too stretch away as far as the eye can see, especially in Sweden, the largest country. Here, log cabins are scattered across remote landscapes and many different types of wood products are manufactured, all with the clear-cut lines that are the trademark of Scandinavian design. In northern Norway, 'land of the midnight sun', there are prolonged hours of summer daylight. And farther north, the reindeer herding Lapps cope happily with the extremes of almost continual summer light and winter darkness.

By contrast, the Scandinavian capitals are places of warmth and sophistication. Few can resist the charm of little Denmark's 'wonderful Copenhagen', a cosmopolitan city where, contrary to popular myth, sexual licence is not all-pervasive. Here, visitors can relax in the famous Tivoli gardens funfair or eat hearty Smørrebrød – Danish open sandwiches. Stockholm, the 'Venice of the north', epitomizes Swedish style and cleanliness, the old town with its narrow streets and cluttered shops contrasting with the modern business centre and spacious lakeside suburbs. Today a major port, Oslo, the Norwegian capital, is as fair as its Viking forefathers while Helsinki, in Scandinavia's most unspoiled country, Finland, mixes modern amenities with a picturesque setting.

1 Romsdal area, Norway; 2 Sergels Torg, Stockholm, Sweden; 3 Olavinlinna Castle, Savonlinna, Finland; 4 Engelsholm Castle, Jutland, Denmark; 5 Log cabins at lakeside, Hjarpesto, Sweden; 6 Norwegian fjord; 7 Little Mermaid, Copenhagen, Denmark; 8 Kornhamnstorg to the south of the Royal Palace, Stockholm, Sweden

6 △

7 ◁

8 ▷

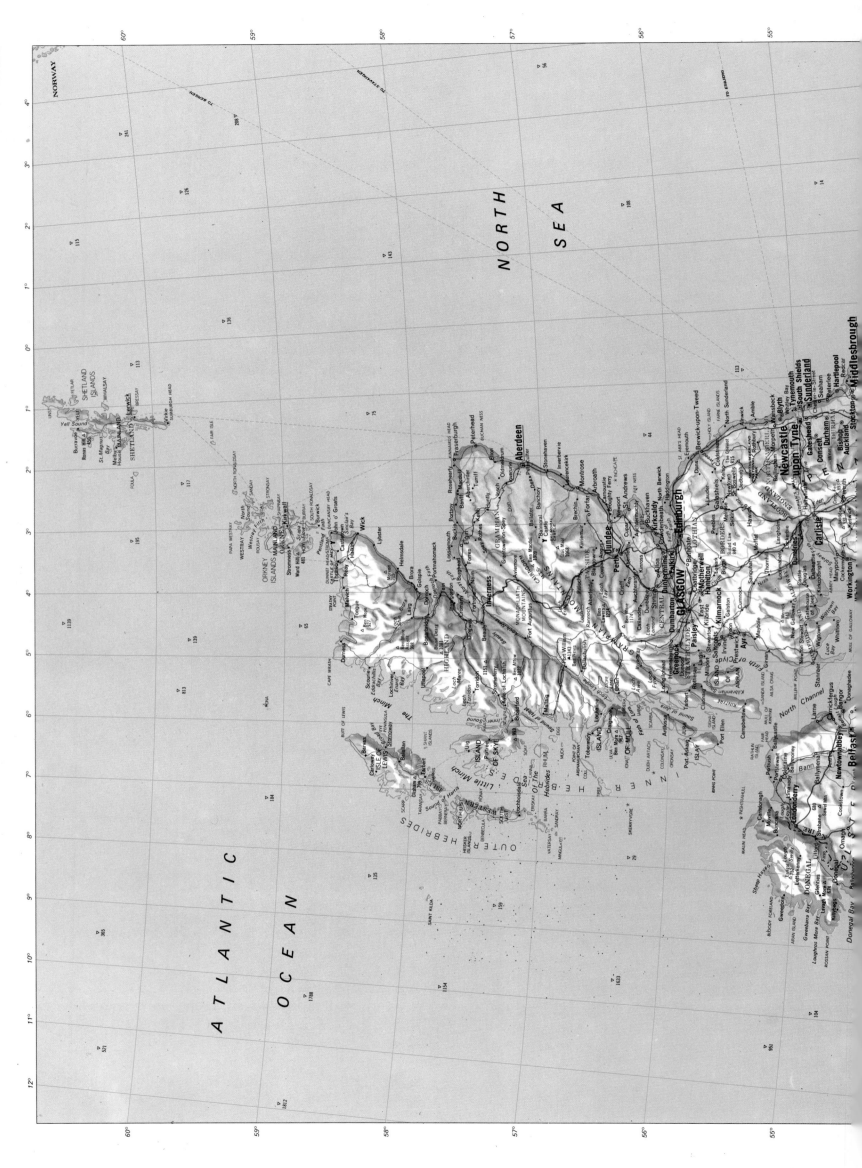

NORWAY

N O R T H   S E A

A T L A N T I C   O C E A N

SHETLAND
ISLANDS

ORKNEY
ISLANDS

OUTER   HEBRIDES

The Minch

Little Minch

HIGHLAND

GRAMPIAN
MOUNTAINS

MONADHLIATH
MOUNTAINS

Aberdeen

Peterhead
Fraserburgh

Inverness

Dundee
Perth

GLASGOW
Paisley
Motherwell
Hamilton
Kilmarnock
Ayr

Edinburgh
Kirkcaldy

BORDERS

SCOTLAND

Newcastle
upon Tyne

Sunderland

Carlisle

Middlesbrough
Hartlepool
Stockton
Durham
Bishop
Auckland
Workington

Belfast
Londonderry
DONEGAL
Newtownabbey

British Isles

In a changing world, Shakespeare's 'sceptred isle' still retains much of its individuality and tradition. The sunset of Empire, an increased European awareness, dissent in Northern Ireland and demands for a national voice from the Scots and Welsh, have not lessened overall pride in the British heritage. The monarchy is still respected by the mass of the people as representing the values of patriotism and family life. Small wonder then that immigrants, exiles and visitors alike are won over by this liberal society surrounded by a wealth of history.

London still represents England to those who have ventured no farther than Piccadilly Circus and the Tower, Buckingham Palace and Westminster Abbey. Visitors to the ancient university cities of Oxford and Cambridge, or the architectural splendours of Regency Bath, may feel they know more of the country. But England stretches from the glorious West Country coast through soft Cotswold villages and the sweeping landscapes of Constable's Suffolk to the remote splendour of the Northumberland moors. Football may be the national craze, but the English sporting occasion still reigns supreme: Wimbledon tennis, rowing at Henley, racing at Ascot and cricket at Lords.

In the north, Scotland also combines a fierce love of tradition with the modern pace of industrial life as the country benefits from the discovery of offshore oil. The golfer's paradise, the naturalist's delight, this land of lochs and mountains offers the cosmopolitan delights of the capital, Edinburgh, the wild beauty of the highlands and islands as typified by remote crofts and grey fishing villages.

Ireland, too, is a place of beauty and contrasts, made all the more apparent and heartbreaking by the present internal conflict. But everywhere, from the northern loughs to the southern mountains, from urbane Dublin to the comparative poverty of the west, this land of Yeats and Shaw exudes a sense of hospitality and pride. And in Wales, where music and rugby football are equal gods, that same warmth is extended in the Celtic tongue, through Cardiff and the industrial valleys of the south to Snowdonia.

1 Tower of London, England; 2 Canterbury Cathedral, Kent, England; 3 Scarborough harbour, Yorkshire, England; 4 Derwent Water, Cumberland, England; 5 Ruins of Melrose Abbey, Roxburghshire, Scotland; 6 The docks at sunset, River Clyde, Glasgow, Scotland; 7 Menai Suspension Bridge, linking Anglesey, Gwynedd, to mainland Wales; 8 Vale of Clara, County Wicklow, Irish Republic; 9 Thirteenth century Caerphilly Castle, Glamorgan, Wales

NORTH SEA

Kilometres
Statute Miles

Scale 1:3,300,000

One centimetre represents 33 kilometres.
One inch represents approximately 52 miles.
Conic Projection, Two Standard Parallels.

1 △

2 ▽

3 ▽

West Germany, Austria and Switzerland

West Germany dominates this part of the map as it does the European economy. Yet the industrial landscapes of the Ruhr and Saarland are only as representative of this multi-faceted country as the vine-clad slopes of the Rhine and Mosel rivers, the nightlife of Hamburg's famous Reeperbahn, the romance of Heidelberg and the fairytale scenic splendours of Bavaria. A cultural giant too, this country can claim to have produced such great writers as Goethe and Schiller, and to have an especially powerful musical inheritance in the works of Beethoven and Brahms. By contrast, East Germany, while containing the manufacturing centres of Leipzig, Magdeburg and Dresden, has not enjoyed a similar economic recovery since World War II. The united Germany's traditional capital, Berlin, since 1961 divided by the concrete wall built by the East, retains a particular significance for both countries.

What they lack in size and economic power, the neighbouring countries of Austria and Switzerland make up for in outstanding scenery and solid worth. Austria's renowned cultural centres of Vienna, Innsbruck and Salzburg are equalled in appeal by the mountainous Tirol region, winter sports centres and health spas. In Switzerland, home of financial wizards, precision watch making and dairying, the scenery is no less spectacular with beautiful lakes and splendid peaks such as the Matterhorn, and the ski resorts of St Moritz and Davos are world-famous.

1 Neuschwanstein Castle, Bavaria, W Germany; 2 The port, Hamburg, W Germany; 3 Heidelberg, W Germany; 4 Belvedere Palace, Vienna, Austria; 5 Castle near Salzburg, Austria; 6 Herd of dairy cows, near Interlaken, Switzerland; 7 Skiing, Switzerland

4 △

5 △   6 ▽

7
▷

The Netherlands, Luxembourg and Belgium

No longer banded together as an economic threesome, the 'Benelux' countries of Belgium, Luxembourg and the Netherlands still remain a delightful entity while retaining their individual charm. Situated at the mouth of the Rhine, the Netherlands is rightly called the 'gateway to Europe'. Known the world over as a land of cheese, canals and bulbs, more importantly it houses the world's largest seaport in Europoort, Rotterdam, and Amsterdam, the friendly capital, is the world centre for diamond cutting. Belgium, now destined to be home to EEC bureaucrats, is undervalued as a tourist country, except for the capital, Brussels, with its magnificent market place, and the medieval pearl of Bruges. The wooded heights of the Ardennes region, in particular, are a walker's and a gastronome's delight. These roll on into little Luxembourg, itself a land of magic castles, rivers, forests and enchanting towns.

1 Vianden, Luxembourg; 2 Bruges, Belgium; 3 National Monument in Dam Square, Amsterdam, the Netherlands; 4 Drainage mills, the Netherlands

Eastern Europe

The political map of Central Europe has been changed twice in this century, once in 1919 and again in 1945. In the modern Soviet satellite countries the vast rolling estates and artistic splendours which characterized Central Europe before World War I have disappeared. But the spirit of the peoples remains unquenched. The Hungarian Magyars, once part of two great empires, still mainly work the land, retaining their old traditions and culture.

A land of great scenic attractions, with its extensive Bohemian forests and magnificent Carpathian Mountains, Czechoslovakia too is in many ways outwardly unchanged. Many beautiful buildings, such as the medieval Charles Bridge, are now being restored in the capital, Prague, one of Europe's most charming, relatively 'undiscovered' cities.

Poland, a once-proud nation which then lost its identity for over 100 years is, of course, etched in the annals of the twentieth century as the country which sparked the fires of World War II. Since then, aided by the valuable mining areas of Silesia, and by other industries around the capital, Warsaw, it has re-asserted itself to secure a tolerable amount of freedom from its Soviet masters.

1 Ols Village, East Hungary; 2 Old town square, Prague, Czechoslovakia; 3 Town Hall, Poznan, Poland; 4 Svetla glassworks, Bohemia, Czechoslovakia

1 △

2 ◁

3 ▷

4 ◁

Kilometres

Statute Miles

Scale 1:3,300,000

One centimetre represents 33 kilometres.
One inch represents approximately 52 miles.

Lambert Conformal Conic Projection

43

1 △

2 ▽

France

France has so much in its favour that less well-endowed countries might be forgiven a passing resentment at such good fortune. Rich in natural resources, with a pleasing position and climate, there is small wonder that the inhabitants of this large and lovely country often seem to have little time for the world outside. For, despite its size and wealth, France is predominantly a nation of small towns and villages, where home and family, the church and trade rule supreme.

Is it not strange then, that a land so indisputably rural, with a still large and vociferous peasantry, should be renowned the world over for its enviable chic and its undoubted naughtiness? Thus the influence of the capital, Paris, is asserted far beyond its own region. Indeed, its dictates in the world of fashion and the arts are followed more slavishly in London and New York than in its own country. France has been in the forefront of true western culture for centuries, and Paris itself has been the cradle of writers and artists too numerous to mention. Look around at the museums, galleries, artistic treasures and monuments, and you can see the past glory of the mighty French Empire, the golden Bourbons and the military might of Napoleon, all part of an historic heritage which continues unbroken to the present day, despite the major upheaval of Revolution in 1789.

France in the 1980s is strongly placed on the economic front with its major manufacturing centres at Lille, Lyons and Paris and the port of Marseille in the south. But it is for its splendid beaches that the Riviera coast is best known; the elegant resorts of Nice and Cannes vying with St Tropez and its starlet strip. Farther west the wild, swampy Camargue region with its roaming horses and wealth of wildlife is a great attraction for naturalists. Inland, the ancient towns of Arles, Avignon and Nîmes are much visited. The south-west also has fine beaches, the forests of the Landes area and, above all, Bordeaux, the greatest wine area in the world. Others may prefer the wilder Brittany coastline, the quiet charm of the Loire region with its magnificent chateaux or the gently pastoral area of the Dordogne. All this, and much, much more, is France.

1 Arc de Triomphe, seen from the Champs Elysées, Paris; 2 Château de Chenonceaux, Loire; 3 Seafood market in Quimper, Brittany; 4 Grape harvest, Bordeaux area; 5 Le Grande Motte, near Montpellier

3 △

4 ◁

5 ▷

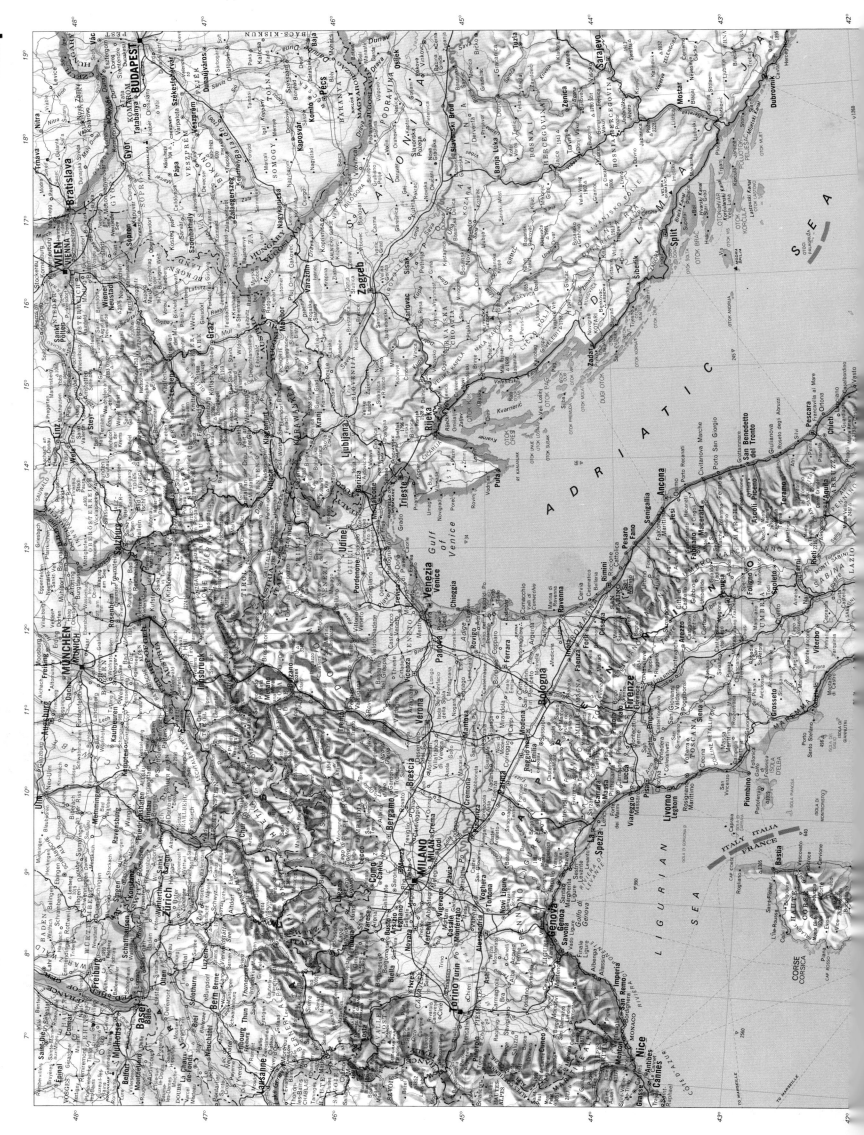

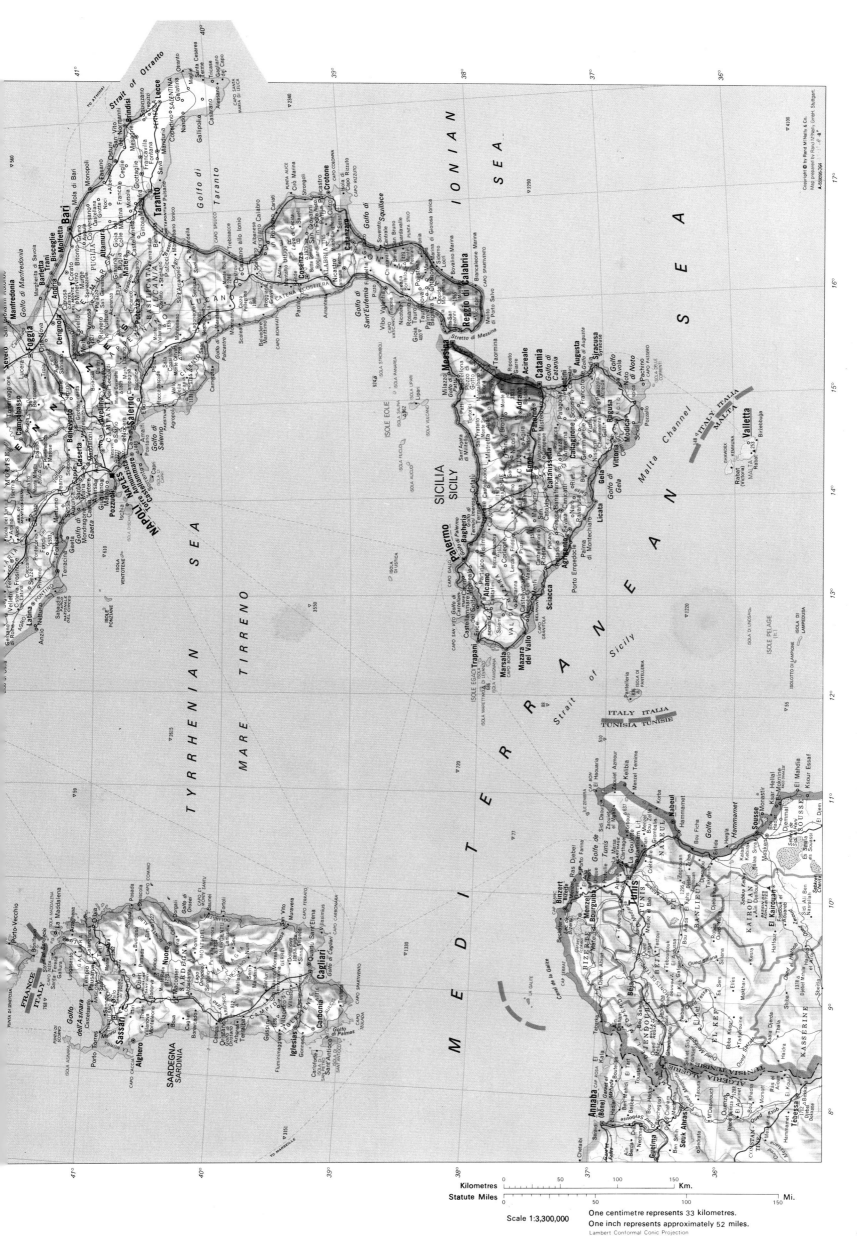

Kilometres
Statute Miles

One centimetre represents 33 kilometres.
One inch represents approximately 52 miles.

Scale 1:3,300,000

Lambert Conformal Conic Projection

47

Italy

Like its people, Italy can be by turns volatile and subdued, extremely wealthy or gratingly poor, spontaneous and welcoming or cunningly calculating. It is, above all, a cultural colossus where the influence of the Roman Catholic Church is all-pervasive. Sadly, as in the case of Venice, where little is being done to prevent this unique island city of gondolas, canals, St Mark's Square and the Rialto, from slipping back into the sea, this pre-eminence is in danger of disappearing under the ravaging hordes of over-enthusiastic sightseers and under-energetic city fathers.

At its peak during the Roman Empire which spread its influence throughout the world, Rome itself, the Eternal City, contains more architectural and artistic masterpieces than any other place in the world. Among these are the Colosseum, first used in AD 80, a year after Pompeii was destroyed by the eruption of Vesuvius, and the Forum, built in the fifth century AD. At Rome's heart is the Basilica of St Peter and the Vatican, home of the Roman Catholic Church. Rome also has such favourite haunts as the Trevi Fountain and the Spanish Steps.

Golden Florence, in Tuscany, birthplace of the Renaissance, combines a wealth of priceless treasures in its buildings and museums with the prosperity of a modern city. Classic monuments, like Michelangelo's David, and historic architecture, such as the sixteenth-century Ponte Vecchio, rub shoulders with students and tourists alike. Then there is Milan, Italy's economic pulse, with its truly awe-inspiring cathedral.

And there is more to this country of hot summers and superb scenery. Positano on the fashionable Costa Amalfitina, the artistic haven of Portofino and the Italian coast resorts all have much to offer. Inland, the Italian Lakes lie serenely at the foot of the Alps, while to the north-east are the dramatic Dolomites with their famous skiing resorts.

1 Cathedral, Baptistry and Leaning Tower, Pisa, Tuscany; 2 Gondolier, Venice, Veneto; 3 Portofino, Liguria; 4 Milan Cathedral, Lombardy; 5 Positano, Campania; 6 Cortina d'Ampezzo, Dolomites; 7 Spanish Steps, Rome, Latium

4 △

5 ◁

6 ▷

7 ◁

MEDITERRANEAN SEA

Scale 1:3,300,000

One centimetre represents 33 kilometres.
One inch represents approximately 52 miles.
Conic Projection, Two Standard Parallels

51

Spain and Portugal

Despite their physical togetherness, Spain and Portugal are two very different countries. The traveller may come to appreciate both, but his heart will always belong to the one first visited. Enter Iberia across the hot, arid countryside of Don Quixote's Spain, and you will remain forever in the thrall of this land of fiesta and flamenco, where Moslem palaces vie with endless olive groves, sun-bathed beaches and snow-clad mountains. But Portugal, with its softer landscape, gentle people, white-walled villages and haunting fado music, has a special appeal. Undisturbed by the last two great wars, Lisbon, the capital, retains much of its past glory, the elegant nineteenth-century buildings and boulevards contrasting sharply with the winding alleyways of the old Arab quarter, the Alfama. Close by, the dignified resorts of Estoril and Cascais provided a pleasant exile for many of Europe's deposed ruling families, suitably near to the old royal palaces at Byron's beloved Sintra, and Quelez. Along the coasts, brightly-painted small boats, often crewed by men in traditional garments, still go out to fish in the time-honoured way.

If previously best known throughout the world for their fortified wines – Spanish sherry from Jerez and port from Portuguese Oporto – both countries now rely heavily on the benefits of tourism. While Portugal's Algarve area, still comparatively unspoiled, is becoming increasingly popular, Spain, in particular, is recognized as Europe's holiday playground. Here, the vast hotel blocks on the highly commercialized Costas Brava and del Sol contrast starkly with the unchanged lifestyle of the interior where hilltop villages and vast plains give way to thriving, historic cities.

At its heart, Spain remains the land of Hemingway, where bulls still run in the streets of Pamplona, and the land of El Greco, whose magnificent paintings in Toledo are matched by the town's spectacular location. Home to the plundering conquistadors, the civilizing Moors and the feared Spanish Inquisition, Spain continues to be, above all, the land of the *feria* where holy processions and modern celebrations combine in annual outbursts of gaiety and reverence throughout the country.

1 Benidorm, Costa Blanca, Spain; 2 Barcelona Cathedral, Catalonia, Spain; 3 Matador at a Spanish bull fight; 4 Portuguese vineyard; 5 Seville horse fair, Andalusia, Spain; 6 Fishermen, Sesimbra, Portugal

1 △

2 ◁

3 ▷

4 ▷

5 ◁

6 ▷

1 Erechtheion, Acropolis, Athens, Greece; 2 Lake Bled, Yugoslavia; 3 Corinth Canal, Greece; 4 Farm houses, Yugoslavia; 5 Monastery at Meteora, Greece; 6 Greek Orthodox priests; 7 Island of Mykonos, Greece

Greece and Yugoslavia

In many ways remarkably different, historically, politically and ethnically, Greece and Yugoslavia jointly epitomize life in south-eastern Europe. Greece, home of some of Europe's earliest civilizations, now relies heavily on tourism which is also increasing in the less commercially-developed yet spiritually resilient Socialist Yugoslavia.

Today, 'the glory that was Greece' is still seen in breathtaking ancient ruins. Placed atop the rock of the Acropolis, the classical architectural simplicity of the Parthenon (fifth century BC), represents the high point of the great age of Athens, the modern capital.

The largest of the Balkan countries, Yugoslavia remains primarily agricultural, although its Serbian capital, Belgrade, and Zagreb in Croatia, are growing industrial centres. The country is perhaps best known for its beautiful Adriatic coastline.

USSR Physical Profile

World Location and Size

The world's largest country, the USSR straddles the conventional boundaries of two continents, Europe and Asia. Mainland USSR extends from nearly 78°N in the Taymyr Peninsula to almost 35°N on the Afghanistan border, a distance of about 4,800 km (3,000 ml). Beyond the mainland, Soviet islands in the Arctic extend beyond 81°N. From west to east the USSR stretches from the Czechoslovak border at 22°E to the Bering Strait at 170°W, thus extending nearly half way round the globe in the Northern Hemisphere. In time terms, when it is 8 a.m. in Moscow it is 6 p.m. in the Cukotskij Peninsula.

Of a total area of nearly 22,275,000 km² (8,600,350 sq ml), 25 percent is in Europe and 75 percent in Asia. For such a land mass, the USSR has only limited stretches of effective coastline which are ice-free throughout the year. In the north-west only a small part of the Arctic coast is ice-free all year and in the west, parts of the Baltic freeze in winter, but most of the Black Sea coast and its ports remain open all the time. The north-flowing rivers are blocked for up to seven months each year.

Landscape

Most USSR land borders are in mountainous parts of the country. The south and east are the highest areas while the northern, central and western parts are dominated by plains.

European USSR is dominated by the eastern parts of the North European Plain. Only the Central Russian Uplands, the Valdai Hills, rising to 346 m (1,125 ft) north-west of Moscow, and the uplands of the Kola Peninsula rising to 1,191 m (3,907 ft) stand above this. The lower plains continue eastward through the basins of the Rivers Don, Volga and North Dvina to the Ural Mountains which form the only major north-south divide in western USSR.

To the south of this lowland region lies the Black Sea with its outlet to the Mediterranean Sea and the Caspian Sea which is a focus of inland drainage. The Carpathian Mountains on the border with Romania rise to 2,061 m (6,762 ft) and the Caucasus Mountains between the Black and Caspian Seas rise to 5,633 m (18,481 ft).

East of the Caspian Sea lies the Turanian Plain and an area of inland drainage focusing on the Aral Sea. Uplands surround this whole region, particularly to the south and east where the boundaries with Afghani-

Opposite: St Isaac's Cathedral in the centre of Leningrad, Russia

stan and China lie within the Pamir and the Tien Shan ranges. Here is the highest land in the USSR rising in Communism Peak to 7,495 m (24,590 ft). East and north-east of the Turanian Plain are the Lake Balkash Basin and the Kazakh Uplands.

West of the River Yenisey and east of the Urals is the extensive West Siberian Plain. This has a total area of over 2.5 million km² (1 million sq ml) and constitutes the largest single area of plain land in the world.

The landscape east of the Yenisey is more varied and elevated. The Central Siberian Plateau between the Yenisey and the Lena Rivers is

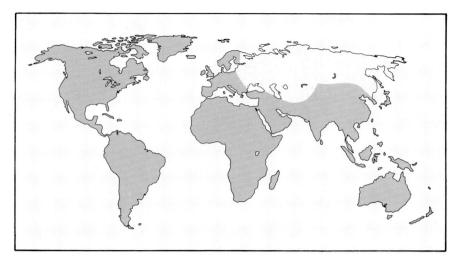

generally above 300 m (1,000 ft) and in the south reaches to above 3,000 m (10,000 ft) in the Sayan and Yablonovy Mountains. The Putoran Mountains of the north rise to a maximum height of 1,701 m (5,581 ft). The remote region east of the Lena River is dominated by a series of mountain ranges, Verkhoyansk, Cherskiy, Chukot and Sredinny which reach a maximum of 4,750 m (15,584 ft) in the Kamchatka Peninsula.

The USSR is a land of great rivers draining in four directions. In the west are comparatively short rivers, like the Don, the Dnepr and the Dvina flowing to the Black or Baltic Seas. In the east, the Amur and many smaller rivers flow eastward to the Pacific. About half the country is drained northward by the Ob, Yenisey and Lena River systems. Finally, the Volga and Ural flow to the Caspian Sea and the Amu-Darya and Syr Darya to the Aral Sea, in the largest inland drainage basin of the world.

Climatic Background

The Soviet Union is the most extensive west-east land mass in the world. It is almost entirely north of the 40°N parallel, is flanked on its southern borders by highland areas and is climatically little influenced by either the Atlantic or Pacific Oceans. Seen overall, the country's climates are characterized by large temperature ranges and low precipitation.

The southern parts of Soviet Central Asia experience a mid-latitude desert climate. Over a large area, the average monthly temperature in January falls to −10°C (14°F) but in July rises to 30°C (86°F). Nowhere does annual precipitation rise above 200 mm (8 in) and it is often far less.

In a broad belt from the southern Ukraine to the Mongolian and Chinese borders lies the area of the dry mid-latitude steppe climate. The temperature range here is higher in the east than in the west, say −30°C (−22°F) to 16°C (61°F) compared

Spassity Tower, Kremlin, Moscow − one of the 18 towers in the wall circling the citadel at the heart of the capital

with −4°C (25°F) to 22°C (72°F). Low annual rainfall, less than 400 mm (16 in), comes mainly in the summer.

In the extreme north of the country, polar climates extend from west to east. Most places in this area have at least one month when the average temperature is above freezing, but no month's average rises above 10°C (50°F).

Between these southern desert/steppe and the northern polar climates, most of the USSR has a more humid climate with a wide annual temperature range. In the west, the July average temperature may approach 22°C (72°F) with the winter average going as low as −10°C (14°F). Precipitation, with a summer maximum, comes throughout the year and may total 700 mm (28 in). This decreases farther east and the temperature range increases.

USSR

The Union of Soviet Socialist Republics did not exist when the twentieth century began. Now it rivals the USA in military might and its potential and economic sphere of influence is larger than that of the British Empire at its zenith. At its heart, Russia – still ruled by the feudal Tsars at the start of World War I – mastered modern technology to put the first man in space. The birthplace of Communism, a major battleground of World War II, Russia created the modern USSR amid the smoke of the uneasy peace of the mid-1940s and '50s.

A decade later, the world held its breath when the Cuban missile crisis brought the USA and the USSR, by now the world's two most powerful nations, to the threshold of nuclear war. But later, when Warsaw Pact forces put down the Czech revolt in 1968, the West did not intervene and subsequent confrontations have been confined to the United Nations, strategic arms limitation talks or to the set-piece Helsinki conference which served as the trigger for another flashpoint, human rights.

Population Growth

Although dominated by Russia, the Soviet Union comprises more than 100 national groups of which perhaps two dozen each have a population of over one million. Many of these groups are concentrated in particular geographical areas which are thus accorded appropriate administrative status.

Russians (137.1 million), Ukrainians (49.9 million) and White Russians (9.5 million) make up over 75 percent of the population. These peoples are all slav-speaking.

The major Altayan peoples of Soviet Central Asia (the Central Asian Republics) are Uzbeks (9.2 million), Tatars (5.3 million) and Kazakhs (4.4 million). Other peoples with populations in excess of one million include, among the Uralian group, Mordovians, Karelians and Estonians.

Throughout recent times, the peopling of the Soviet Union has taken place in a number of distinct phases. Between 1600 and 1850, within European Russia, the main movements were from the forested northern lands into the more open steppe lands of the south and southeast. From 1800 onward, and particularly after the abolition of serfdom in 1860, the Russians moved eastward to the steppe lands beyond the Urals. In the first decade of the twentieth century Russians were migrating eastward at a rate of 600 per day. Throughout this time there had been a steady trickle of migrants from the west into the Russian Empire. Thus, the imperial population grew by natural increase and immigration to 171 million by 1913.

Then, from 1914 to 1926, years of world war, revolution, civil war and emigration, on average the national population fell by 2 million per year.

The next thirteen years saw a complete reversal of this trend and by 1940 the population of the USSR had risen to its highest ever. During World War II, 20 million Soviet lives were lost, a large proportion being young males. Thus, by the war's end, the total population was still only 173 million and the sex and age structure within that total had suffered a major imbalancing blow. Still, during the next thirty years or so the numbers rose to 260.1 million.

Political Development

The Russian Empire prior to 1917 expanded over a thousand year period. It grew from a relatively small area between the Gulf of Finland in the north and a line well north of the Black Sea in the south, to include most of the present territories of the USSR and also modern Finland, parts of Poland and parts of Turkey. The USSR as we know it today is administratively and politically the product of little over 60 years.

Russia's long history up to 1917 is dominated by certain individuals and families. In the mid-sixteenth century, the first Tsar of all the Russias, Ivan the Terrible, established autocratic control over a much enlarged territory. The Romanov Dynasty was established in the mid-seventeenth century. Peter the Great (1689–1725) introduced new social and industrial ideas from the then advanced countries of Western Europe. Later, in the 1780s under Catherine the Great, Russia's extent was pushed as far west as it was ever to be. During the nineteenth century, the country expanded eastward into Moslem Central Asia and on to the Pacific.

By the beginning of the present century, the empire was not only having difficulties with some neighbouring countries, but internally revolutionary pressures were growing against the oppressive regime of the Romanovs. War with Japan led to territorial losses in the east; fighting against Germany in World War I, the Imperial Russian Armies suffered heavy losses. In 1917, the Communist revolution broke out.

From 1918 to 1922 the country was gripped by civil war. Eventually the Bolsheviks defeated the non-Communist White Russians supported by the western allies. They had lost some lands in the west where Finland, Estonia, Latvia, Lithuania and Poland had been re-established as separate countries.

During World War II, Germany attacked the USSR in June 1941 and the western allies joined forces with the Soviets. After making immense territorial gains, the Germans were eventually forced back, and by 1945 the Soviet armies had overrun Eastern Europe. Since the end of the war, the Soviet Union has had a dominant interest in the maintenance of Communist governments in the eastern bloc of European countries.

Since the creation of the Soviet Union, a system of internal political control has evolved which provides varying degrees of self-government for particular areas. Soviet Socialist Republics (SSRs) are the highest administrative unit, within which smaller units may exist.

Industry, Commerce and Communications

Before the revolution, Russia was predominantly agricultural. Since 1928, a series of five-year plans have been implemented. The early plans sought to establish heavy industries and the rational development of mineral resources. When World War II caused much damage to the industries of the western areas, newer, strategically safer locations farther east were developed. Since then, more emphasis has been placed on manufactured, consumer goods than on heavy industry.

One of the largest concentrations of the iron and steel industry is in the southern Ukraine; iron ore comes from Krivoy Rog and coking coal from the Donbas area. The largest production centres are Donetsk and Zaporozhye. The Urals contain the next most significant places, with Magnitogorsk and Chelyabinsk being the largest individual centres. Farther east, Temirtau and Novokuznetsk were established in the 1930s and smaller plants have been set up more recently in the far east.

1 Summer Palace, Leningrad, Russia;
2 Interior of GUM, the largest store in the world, Moscow, Russia;
3 Harvesting wheat, Dmitrovski state farm, Yakut Autonomous Republic

Large concentrations of the petro-chemical industries, especially in the southern Ukraine, the Greater Moscow Region, the Urals area and the Kuzbas region farther east have developed since the 1930s.

Leningrad, Moscow, Gorki, the Urals and Ukraine towns are variously the main centres of heavy industrial equipment, vehicles, railway and farming equipment manufacture. Lighter engineering is more widely scattered. Textiles and clothing have long been concentrated in the European areas but have more recently been established in Soviet Central Asia and Transcaucasia. Food processing is usually market orientated and is thus predominantly in the west, but is tending to spread eastward.

The USSR is an advanced industrial society, yet 22 percent of the working population, about 25 million workers, are still employed in farming. Some 26 percent are employed in manufacturing industries, 10 percent in transport and communications and 6 percent in trade and commerce.

Communications in the USSR are all state controlled. Railways provide some 60 percent of the freight mileage and 50 percent of the passenger mileage. The rail network is densest in the west. Beyond the Urals are a number of routes to Soviet Central Asia, two to the Lake Baykal region and one to the Pacific.

By Western standards the Soviet road network is ill-developed. Car ownership and long-distance road haulage are limited. Only in the west is the system truly efficient and well maintained. For long distance passengers and mail, as well as for wider purposes in the remote areas, planes are increasingly used. Today, some 100 million air passengers are carried internally each year. Despite the problems of the winter freeze, many rivers of the west are used for barge and larger ship movements. Links exist between the Baltic, Black, White and Caspian Seas.

Agriculture, Forestry and Fishing

Perhaps 30 percent of the USSR could be used for crop farming, but only about one-third of that is currently so utilized. Twice as much land is given over to pasture and grazing. About half of the national area is forested and the remainder is either tundra of the north, deserts of the south or mountains.

During the 1920s and '30s and following World War II, agriculture took a back seat in the total national economic scene, while industrial development was given higher priority. Since 1953, following the death of Stalin, farming has been made modern and more efficient. All land is nationalized and organized in state farms (Sovzhoz) and collectives (Kolkhoz).

The forest zone extends from the Finnish and Baltic margins in a broad belt to the Pacific. There are over 7.5 million km² (3 million sq ml) of forests, two-thirds in the Asiatic

parts of the country. These, and the European forests are being systematically exploited from the southern margins. In European Russia, sawmills, pulp and paper making plants and wood chemical works are widely scattered. Farther east, so much of the forests are as yet untouched. Currently, timber production stands at about 390 million cubic metres and paper at 4 million tonnes per year. Nearly 85 percent of the wood produced is soft and only 15 percent hard. In total, the Soviet Union accounts for 16 percent of the world's timber production.

The USSR is the world leader in wheat production, growing as much as 24 percent of the 400 million tonnes produced each year. It is also the leading producer of barley – 37 percent of the world's 190 million tonnes, oats – 34 percent of the world's 50 million tonnes, and rye – 43 percent of the world's 28 million tonnes. By contrast, only 3 percent of the world's maize comes from the USSR.

Nearly 30 percent of the world's potatoes are grown in the USSR and it is again the world leader. It comes second only to the USA in growing tomatoes, producing 9 percent of the world's total. The USSR also produces a phenomenal major share of the world's sugar beet: 34 percent, nearly four times as much as the second largest producer, the USA. In contrast the USSR figures poorly in world fruit growing, though it does account for 9.5 percent of the world's grapes. Of the beverage crops, the USSR accounts for about 5.5 per-

cent of the global tea production.

The USSR figures prominently in the production of industrial, vegetable fibres, being the leader in cotton lint production, the producer of nearly three-quarters of the world's flax and only marginally second to India in accounting for 25 percent of the world's hemp.

The Soviet Union is also well placed in the world's livestock and animal products league tables having 9 percent of the 1,214 million cattle, 9 percent of the 645 million pigs and 14 percent of the 1,038 million sheep. Nearly one-quarter of the world's cows' milk, one-eighth of its hens' eggs, one-sixth of its greasy wool and one-twelfth of its raw silk also originate here.

Finally, the Soviet Union is currently second only to Japan as a world fishing nation. Its large long-range fleet catches some 14 percent of the world's fish total. In addition, Soviet whalers also gather half of all the world's catch of the diminishing stocks of whales.

Natural Resources

The Soviet economy is based very heavily upon home production of fuel and power. The country has major coal fields in both the developed west and in the developing central and eastern areas. In total, the USSR accounts for about 25 percent of the world's hard coal production (bituminous and anthracite) which is currently about 2,300 million tonnes per year. The Soviet Union is also the world's second most important

producer of soft coal (lignite). About 175 million tonnes per year, 20 percent of the world total, comes from the Moscow Basin and recently developed fields farther east.

By 1976 the USSR had become the world's largest single producer of crude oil with 520 million tonnes, 18 percent of the world total. The Baku oil fields, formerly the major source, have now been overtaken by the Ural-Volga fields. The USSR is thought to have the largest natural gas reserves in the world, producing over 300 million cubic metres per year. This represents some 24 percent of world output, and puts the USSR second in the world production tables. The fields of Soviet Central Asia and the area north of Tyumen are most important.

It is estimated that the Soviet Union's hydro-electric potential is the highest of any single country in the world, over 400 million kilowatts installed capacity. Much of this lies in the valleys of the great north-flowing rivers of the Soviet heartland. Around 10 percent has been installed and the annual HEP production is third in the world, behind the USA and Canada. One-eighth of the Soviet's consumed electricity is derived from hydro sources.

The Soviet Union is by far the world's leading producer of iron ore, contributing about 140 million out of the world's total of about 540 million tonnes (iron content) per year, 26 percent of the total. The iron ore fields of Krivoy Rog in the Ukraine are the largest, the long-developed fields of the Ural region

Soviet agriculture is generally highly mechanized and is organized on collective lines: 1 Festival of reindeer tenders, Moma state farm, Yakut Autonomous Republic – fishing, trapping and cattle raising are also carried out in this Siberian republic of very cold winters; 2 Piling up cotton at Tedjen state farm, Turkmen – this is the most valuable crop of this primarily desert region; 3 Caviar weigher at the Ust-Kamchatka fish factory, Russia – the part-nomadic people of this remote eastern territory hunt and fish for a livelihood

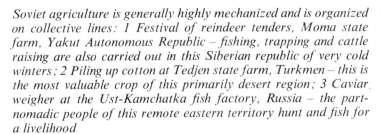

USSR Imports		36,969
USSR Exports		33,310

☐ Imports ◼ Exports

Total Imports and Exports
(1975 figures in millions of U.S. dollars)

The modern trade figures for the USSR are similar to those of Canada, and show remarkable recent growth.

USSR

are the second largest. Ore deposits farther east, particularly those of the Kuznets area, are now being developed systematically. The USSR's estimated iron ore reserves are over 260,000 million tonnes, 44 percent of the world total.

The USSR contains a wide range of other mineral ores, some of them in significant quantities, as the table right shows.

Soviet Economy

The distribution of population in the USSR is very uneven. The greatest concentrations are in the west, south of the 60th parallel. Here are the richest and most advanced agricultural lands and most of the large urban developments. Other centres of high average population density are found in Soviet Central Asia. In both, densities in excess of 100 per sq km (250 per sq ml) are found over large areas. About two-thirds of the population are living on the plain lands of European USSR, that is on about one-sixth of the national area.

Elsewhere, the line of the Trans-Siberian Railway and the river valleys are at the centres of the belt of higher population density. In all other places, population is thinly scattered.

Compared with the USA and the countries of Western Europe, a lower proportion of the population is concentrated in large urban areas, 100.2

Ore	Average Annual World Production (million tonnes)	USSR Share (percent)	Principal USSR Locations
bauxite	80.3	8	Urals
chrome	7.2	27	Urals
cobalt	0.03	5	Urals
copper	7.4	16	Kazakh, Urals, Central Asian Republics and Transcaucasia
gold	1 million kg	31	East Siberia and the Far East
lead	3.2	16	Central Asian Republics
manganese	22.8	39	Nikopol and Chiatura
molybdenum	0.084	11	The Far East
nickel	0.733	17	Urals and Yenisey Basin
silver	0.01	17	Karelia and the Far East
tungsten	0.036	20	East Siberia
vanadium	0.02	23	Central Asian Republics
zinc	5.4	13	Central Asian Republics, Urals and Salair region

million being classified as rural and 159.9 million as urban. There are 13 millionaire cities in the USSR of which only Moscow, Leningrad and Kiev have populations in excess of 2 million. Of the others, only Tashkent, Novosibirsk and Sverdlovsk are east of the Urals. This location pattern of the largest cities is a further indication of the economic dominance of the west in the country as a whole.

Yet, population changes and increases during recent years show how the areas east of the Urals are growing in importance. For example, between 1961 and 1976 percentage increases were 74.1 in Uzbek, 37.6 in Kazakh and only 16.1 in Byelorussia. The overall growth rate is 0.9 percent per annum, though in Asiatic USSR it is more than double that figure. Two distinctive features of the population of the USSR are the imbalance between the sexes and the gap in the age pyramid caused by the large losses of World War II.

Soviet emphasis has been on industrial growth: 1 Bratsk Power Station, Irkutsk, Russia; 2 Temirtau iron and steel plant, Kazakh SSR

When analysing the USSR's economic progress we must remember that some data may not always be directly comparable with that for non-Communist countries. For instance, where finance figures are concerned, there is the problem of using a meaningful exchange rate.

Available trade figures over the years 1938, '58 and '75 show remarkable growth when compared, for example, with those of the USA or a number of European countries. Imports rose from $273 million to $4,350m (1,493 percent increase) and then to $36,969 million (750 percent increase). The comparable export figures were $255 million to $4,298 million (1,585 percent increase) and then to $33,310 million (675 percent increase). In essence these reflect the lack of trade between the USSR and the outside world before World War II, its rapid growth thereafter, especially through trade with other Communist countries and, in the later period, an increasing volume of trade with non-Communist world.

The Soviet Union makes no regular return on per capita incomes, and comparisons over a period are thus not possible. However, occasional figures are available for particular years, of which a figure of $2,790 for 1976 can be usefully compared with certain other countries: USA $5,923,

West Germany $5,480, France $4,505 and UK $3,106.

In the mid 1970s the USSR had an energy surplus, 1,650 million tonnes coal equivalent (mtce) being produced and 1,410 mtce consumed. Coal output stood at 712 million tonnes, 43 percent of the national energy production, being a higher proportion of the national total than for any other large energy-producing country except China. Oil and oil products are the major energy export, and have increased their share of total national energy production from around 14 percent in 1945 to 45 percent in 1976.

The per capita consumption of energy in 1975 was 5,546 kg, a fraction over half that of the USA. Much of this figure is expended in industrial production and services rather than in direct personal use.

The modern economy of the USSR has shown remarkable growth; in little over half a century it has mushroomed from a revolutionary catastrophe, has been seriously curtailed by world wars and has been centrally planned by governments which have on occasion, brought large changes of emphasis in the development of the country. Since World War II, the Soviet Union has been the dominant power in the Communist world and has, in many respects, narrowed the gap, if not closed it, between itself and the other great world power, the USA.

How will the Soviet Union develop internally and act in the international scene in the coming years? As the present leadership of the USSR will change fairly soon, forecasting is especially difficult. However, some significant points can be noted. Economic growth has been slowing down slightly in recent years, which must cause concern in a country with so many agricultural workers and so much extractive and heavy industry. It is becoming increasingly necessary to exploit the comparatively expensive resources of the eastern frontiers. Although industrial productivity now grows at a little over 3 percent per annum, the maintenance of even this figure seems unlikely. Oil exports, a valuable source of overseas currency, seem bound to decline in the 1980s.

At the same time, the Soviet Union is increasing its defence expenditure by 4.5 percent per annum. If it continues to do this while the national growth rate stagnates, it may be able to hold its present military position vis-a-vis the West only at the expense of a fall in the home living standard. Then, unless trends in productivity take an upturn, the country may lose ground in the constant struggle to maintain military parity with the non-Communist world.

Yet such matters cannot be looked at in isolation. Other considerations, such as the growth rates of the Western economies and the role of Communist China in the next decade or so must also be taken into account. The potential of the USSR is enormous; the way in which it will be harnessed must depend on a balance of internal decisions and the general consensus of other leading world powers.

Per Capita Energy Consumption

(1975 figures in kilograms)

Energy consumption in the USSR is little more than half that of North America.

5,546

USSR

Per Capita Income

(1976 figures in U.S. dollars)

Average earnings in the USSR work out at about half those of the USA.

USSR

2,790

USSR Republics

Russia

More than 75 percent of the whole USSR lies in this uniquely constituted federal republic. Stretching from the Baltic to the Pacific, it has a huge range of landscapes and climates. In value terms it accounts for over two-thirds of the country's agricultural output and about 60 percent of its industrial output. Extensive croplands stretch across the south; here, and to the north, pastoral farming is also extensive. The great forest lands lie even farther north. In the Urals area and elsewhere, coal, iron ore and crude oil are all extracted in large quantities. The population is most densely settled in the west, with Moscow (7.6 million) and Leningrad (4.3 million), but a string of millionaire and other cities has developed in the 'new lands' east of the Urals and to the Pacific. These collectively contain virtually every industrial activity found in the country.

More than any other republic, Russia is sub-divided into smaller political units. There are 16 Autonomous Soviet Socialist Republics (ASSRs), the largest of which is the Yakut ASSR covering over 3 million km² (nearly 1.2 million sq ml). Each ASSR is largely settled by one racial group and now enjoys a great deal of local political control. There are also 5 Autonomous Regions (ARs) in Russia, each of which has less local political control.

The Baltic Republics – Estonia, Latvia and Lithuania

Once part of the Russian Empire, these achieved independence in 1919 but were subsequently admitted to the USSR in 1940. Formerly their economies were firmly based on agriculture, but in recent years a range of industries has become increasingly important. All three, but particularly Estonia, have valuable timber and pulp industries. In Estonia shale is used for gas making and peat for firing electricity stations. In Latvia and Lithuania, textiles, food processing and engineering are other major industries. Agriculturally, rye, oats and vegetable growing as well as some pastoral farming are the main activities.

Three European Republics – Byelorussia, Moldavia and the Ukraine

Some of the richest agricultural and industrial landscapes of the whole USSR are found in Europe. The Ukraine in particular, produces over one-quarter of all the Soviet's grains and three-fifths of its sugar beet. Maize, potatoes, flax, sunflower seeds and fruits are produced widely in the southern parts. Peat cutting and timber production are more signifi-

cant farther north. Industrially, 60 percent of the USSR coal reserves lie beneath Ukrainian soil; today 30 percent of the annual output comes from here, 50 percent of the iron ore and 60 percent of the manganese. Nearly half the Soviet iron and steel production also comes from the Ukraine. Other major industries include food processing, petrochemicals, engineering including vehicle and farm equipment manufacturing, textiles and leather. Besides individual large cities in each republic, the cluster of major cities in south-east Ukraine is the largest in the whole union.

Soviet Central Asia – Kazakh, Kirghiz, Tadzhik, Turkmen and Uzbek

Kazakh is by far the largest of these republics. Kirghiz and Tadzhik are mountainous, the others mainly dry plain lands. Irrigation plays a large part in agriculture. Nomadic herding

of cattle and sheep is traditional and valuable. Apart from wheat, sugar beet and vegetables, tobacco, cotton, citrus fruit and rice are also grown here. Raw materials extracted include coal, iron ore, crude oil, natural gas, tungsten, copper and lead. The range of industries in the largest cluster of Soviet large towns east of the Urals includes food processing, iron and steel, petrochemicals, engineering, textiles and leather working. Tashkent (1.5 million), capital of Uzbek, is the fourth largest city in the USSR.

Transcaucasia – Armenia, Azerbaidzhan and Georgia

Created out of the former Transcaucasian SSR in 1936, these three SSRs are situated between the Black and Caspian Seas, bordering Iran, Turkey and Russia. Mountains and large river basins dominate the landscapes. Irrigation is employed in some areas to grow a wide range of

1 Eleventh century church, Novgorod, Russia – one of the oldest towns in the Republic; 2 Bridge over the Dnieper, Kiev, Ukraine – the USSR's third largest city is a major communications centre; 3 Domes of the Kremlin; 4 Changing guard, Lenin's Tomb, Red Square, Moscow

subtropical and temperate crops, of which wheat, cotton, subtropical fruits, grapes, maize and potatoes are the most valuable. Sheep are more numerous than cattle and goats. A wide range of industries have been established on a modest scale; these include food processing, textiles and leather goods, metal working, light engineering, vehicle and railway construction. The extraction and processing of oil in the Caspian lowlands is of great national importance.

The Transcaucasian republics also contain a number of smaller political divisions: Azerbaidzhan has 1 ASSR and 1 AR; Georgia has 2 ASSRs and 1 AR.

REFERENCE TABLE: USSR

USSR Republics	Political Status	State Capital	Area km²	Area sq ml	Population	Population Density per km²	Population Density per sq ml
Armenia	D	Jerevan	29,800	11,500	2,887,000	97	251
Azerbaidzhan	D	Baku	86,600	33,450	5,801,000	67	173
Byelorussia	D	Minsk	207,600	80,150	9,520,000	46	119
Estonia	D	Tallinn	45,100	17,400	1,456,000	32	84
Georgia	D	Tbilisi	69,700	26,900	5,046,000	72	188
Kazakh	D	Alma-ata	2,715,000	1,048,300	14,592,000	5.4	14
Kirghiz	D	Frunze	198,500	76,650	3,433,000	17	45
Latvia	D	Riga	63,700	24,600	2,601,000	40	106
Lithuania	D	Vilnius	65,200	25,150	3,381,000	52	134
Moldavia	D	Kisinov	33,700	13,000	3,902,000	116	300
Russian SFSR	D	Moscow	17,075,400	6,592,850	137,053,000	8.0	21
Tadzhik	D	Dusanbe	143,100	55,250	3,538,000	25	64
Turkmen	D	Aschabad	488,100	188,450	2,627,000	5.4	14
Ukraine	D	Kiev	603,700	233,100	49,941,000	83	214
Uzbek	D	Tashkent	449,600	173,600	14,332,000	32	83
USSR TOTAL	A	Moscow	22,274,900	8,600,350	260,110,000	12	30

Note: For the whole USSR, Birth rate per thousand persons 18.2
Death rate per thousand persons 9.3
Mean annual percentage increase in population 0.9

BARENTS SEA

NOVAJA ZEML'A

KARSKOJE MORE
KARA SEA

MORE LAPTEVYCH

LAPTEV SEA

OSTROVA KOMSOMOLEC
SEVERNAJA ZEML'A

Pečorskoje More

Arctic Circle

SEVERO SIBIRSKAJA NIZMENNOST

POLUOSTROV TAJMYR
GORY BYRRANGA

ZAPADNO-

ROSSIJSKAJA

Noril'sk

PLATO PUTORANA

SREDNE-

SIBIRSKAJA

Tomsk

SOVETSKAJA

FEDERATIVNAJA SOCIALISTIČESKAJA

SIBIRSKOJE

Novosibirsk

SOVIET

RUSSIAN SOVIET FEDERATED SOCIALIST REPUBLIC

PLOSKOGORJE

RESPUBLIKA

Krasnojarsk

SOCIALIST

REPUBLICS

Barnaul

Novokuzneck

Bratsk

Jenisej

Lena

STANOVOJE NAGORJE

STANOVOY MOUNTAINS

Semipalatinsk

ZAPADNYJ SAYAN

VOSTOČNYJ SAJAN

Čeremchovo

Irkutsk

Ozero Bajkal
Lake Baykal

JABLONOVYJ CHREBET

Ust'-Kamenogorsk

SAJANY
SAYAN MOUNTAINS

Ulan-Ude

Čita

CHINA

MONGOLIA

CHINA

Ulaanbaatar

Kilometres 0   200   400   600 Km.

Statute Miles 0   200   400   600 Mi.

Scale 1:13,200,000

One centimetre represents 132 kilometres.
One inch represents approximately 210 miles.
Lambert Conformal Conic Projection

Copyright © by Rand McNally & Co.
Map prepared by Esselte Map Service AB, Stockholm.

63

BARENTS SEA

KARSKOJE MORE
KARA SEA

MORE LAPTEVYC
LAPTEV SEA

NOVAJA ZEMLA

OSTROV
KOMSOMOLEC
SEVERNAJA ZEML'A

ARCTIC CIRCLE

Vorkuta

GYDANSKIJ POLUOSTROV

SEVERO - SIBIRSKAJA NIZMENNOST

TAJMYR
GORY BYRRANGA

Noril'sk

PLATO
PUTORANA

SREDNE-
SIBIRSKOJE

ZAPADNO
SIBIRSKAJA
NIZMENNOST'

SOVIET
UNION

SOVETSKAJA
FEDERATIVNAJA
SOCIALISTIČESKAJA
RESPUBLIKA

RUSSIAN SOVIET FEDERATED SOCIALIST REPUBLIC

PLOSKOGORJE

SOVIET OF SOCIA

Omsk
Tomsk
Novosibirsk
Kemerovo
Anzero-Sudzensk
Krasnojarsk
Leninsk-Kuzneckij
Prokopjevsk
Novokuzneck
Abakan
Barnaul
Belovo
Kiselovsk

Bratsk

STANOVOJE NAGORJE

Pavlodar

STANOVOY MOUNTAINS

Semipalatinsk
Rubcovsk

Ust'-Kamenogorsk

ZAPADNYJ SAJAN
VOSTOČNYJ SAJAN
SAJANY

Čeremchovo
Usolie-Sibirskoje
Angarsk
Irkutsk

Ozero Bajkal
Lake Baykal

Ulan-Ude

JABLONOVYJ CHREBET

KAZACHSKAJA
S.S.R.

CHINA
SINKIANG
XINJIANG WEIWUER ZIZHIQU

MONGOLIA

Ulaanbaatar

Yining
Kuldja

Scale 1:13,200,000

Kilometres
Statute Miles

One centimetre represents 132 kilometres.
One inch represents approximately 210 miles.
Lambert Conformal Conic Projection

Copyright © by Rand McNally & Co.
Map prepared by Esselte Map Service AB, Stockholm
▲-579395-264   -3°

SIBIRSKOJE
OSTROVA

VOSTOČNO- SIBIRSKOJE MORE

EAST SIBERIAN SEA

Chukchi

Sea

OSTROV
VRANGELA

Proliv Longa

Arctic Circle

SAINT LAWRENCE ISLAND

NUNIVAK ISLAND

EKATAPSKIJ CHREBET

ANADYRSKOJE

ANADYRSKIJ
Zaliv

PLOSKOGORJE

KOLYMSKAJA NIZMENNOST

Bering Sea

JUKAGIRSKOJE

ANJUSKIJ CHREBET

SAINT MATTHEW ISLAND

KORJAKSKOJE NAGORJE

PLOSKOGORJE

MOMSKIJ CHREBET

CHREBET ČERSKOGO

KOMANDORSKIJE
OSTROVA

Zaliv
Šelichova

SREDINNYJ CHREBET

CHREBET

CHREBET SUNTAR- CHAJAT

Jakutsk

Magadan

POLUOSTROV
KAMČATKA

Petropavlovsk-
Kamčatskij

REPUBLICS

CHREBET DŽUGDŽUR

SEA OF OKHOTSK

OCHOTSKOJE MORE

Pervyj Kuril'skij
Proliv

STANOVOJ CHREBET

ŠANTARSKIJE
OSTROVA

Sachalinskij
Zaliv

OSTROV
SACHALIN
SAKHALIN

KURIL'SKIJE OSTROVA

KURIL ISLANDS

Proliv Kruzenšterna

Komsomol'sk-
na-Amure

BUREINSKIJ CHREBET

Zaliv
Terpenija

MYS TERPENIJA

Amur

SICHOTE ALIN

OSTROV TURUP
Habomai, Shikotan, Kunashiri, and
Etorofu, occupied by the U.S.S.R.
since 1945, are claimed by Japan
pending a final peace treaty.

Blagoveščensk

Južno-Sachalinsk

Chabarovsk

Zaliv
Aniva

Proliv
Jekateriny

CHINA

MANCHURIA

La Perouse Strait

HEILONGJIANG

Yichun

Hegang

Asahikawa

Kushiro

Haerbin

HOKKAIDO

Sapporo

PACIFIC

JILIN

Muroran

Hakodate

JAPAN

Mudanjiang

Hachinohe

Ussurijsk

Aomori

Vladivostok

SEA OF JAPAN

HONSHU

Akita

Morioka

OCEAN

65

ASIA
Physical Profile

World Location and Size

Asia is joined to both Europe and Africa. Its western limits are the Ural Mountains, lying north to south in the USSR at about 60°E, the Caspian Sea, Asia Minor, the eastern Mediterranean coast and the Red Sea. The main land mass is clearly defined to south, east and north by the Indian, Pacific and Arctic Oceans, but Asia also includes a large number of islands, especially off its south-east and east coasts. As we are treating the USSR as a separate geographical unit, the area here under review as Asia is but the southern portion of the whole continent.

Asia is predominantly in the Northern Hemisphere. The continent's west-east extent is from the Aegean Sea at 26°E to the Japanese island of Hokkaido at 146°E, a third of the way around the world at about 40°N latitude. Although the USSR extends north of the Arctic Circle, for our purposes Asia extends from the northernmost part of China, in Manchuria at 53°N to the Indonesian Islands at 10°S; even that is one-third of the distance between the North and South Poles.

Landscape

Asia may be divided into five distinct physical units, each separated from its neighbour by a line of mountains. South-west Asia includes all countries south of the border with the Soviet Union, from the Mediterranean and Red Seas east to Afghanistan and western Pakistan. Its northern area is rugged and mountainous, reaching 5,604 m (18,387 ft) in the Elburz Mountains of northern Iran. Within the broad mountain region lie some extensive plateaus such as the Plateau of Iran. Turkey and northern Iran are both prone to earthquakes.

South of this general area it is geologically more complex. Its western region is part of the great Rift Valley which extends from East Africa to Syria. The mountains of the Arabian peninsula rise to 3,760 m (12,336 ft). East of these, the land level falls across the great desert expanse of the Arabian Peninsula to the lowland belt occupied by the Persian Gulf and the south-east flowing Tigris and Euphrates rivers.

Central Asia, farther east, is the most remote and physically extreme area of the whole world. Bounded in the north by the Tien Shan and the Sayan Mountains, it extends southward across western China, Mongolia and Tibet to the Himalayas. Within Sinkiang Province, China, the

Opposite: Twelfth century Jagannath temple, Puri, eastern India

Turfan Depression descends to a level of 154 m (505 ft) below sea level. In contrast, Mount Everest in the Himalayas is the world's highest point, some 8,848 m (29,028 ft) above sea level. Though encircled by mountains, the area's heartland is a series of plains, predominantly uninviting dry lands including the Takla Makan and Gobi Deserts, and the Tibetan Plateau.

Still farther east lie the large river valleys of Eastern Asia, flanked by the hills and low tablelands of eastern China. Also within this region lie Korea, the Japanese islands and Taiwan. The islands are essentially the tops of a great mountain ridge rising steeply from the floor of the Pacific Ocean. They are part of the 'Pacific Ring of Fire', a zone of modern active volcanoes and frequent earthquake activity. This is much the smallest of the areas covered so far, yet the most important in population and broad development terms.

South of the mountains of Central Asia lies the Indian subcontinent which is composed of two distinctly different areas. Much of the Deccan, a triangular-shaped tableland which occupies the southern parts of the peninsula, lies at 500 m (1,650 ft) to 700 m (2,300 ft). Its margins rise in the Western and Eastern Ghats to greater heights, 2,695 m (8,842 ft) and 1,680 m (5,512 ft) respectively. Then, between the Deccan and the Himalayas are the great valleys of the Indus, Ganges and Brahmaputra Rivers.

South of China and east of India/Bangladesh lie the intricately shaped peninsulas of South-east Asia, and the islands beyond. The northern flanks are mountainous, the principal mountain axis being north to south. Lower mountain chains then extend into peninsulas, particularly into Burma, Malaysia, Laos and Vietnam. A number of large rivers flow southward across broad plains in Burma, Thailand and Kampuchea. In the islands farther south, the mountain axis changes to north-west/south-east (Sumatra) and then west/east (Java). The easternmost islands lie in the 'Pacific Ring of Fire'.

Climatic Background

Situated on the east and south-east side of the world's largest single land mass, Asia extends from the equatorial region to temperate mid-latitudes and contains several very high mountain ranges. Consequently, it exhibits a wide range of climatic types, including the unique three season pattern of the monsoon lands. The extreme west, on the littoral of Turkey, in Cyprus, the Levant coast and into parts of lowland Iraq, has a Mediterranean type of climate. The summer is very dry, and total precipitation may be only 500 mm (20 in). Average temperatures in the hottest month may be well into the low

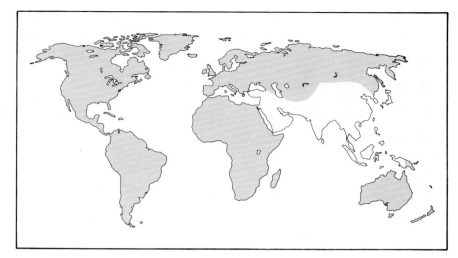

Japan's advanced bullet train passes through snow near Maibara: a mountainous country with active volcanoes and prone to earthquakes, Japan has a monsoonal climate with heavy summer rains and cold winters in parts

20°sC (mid 70°sF) on the fringe of the Mediterranean. Farther east, annual temperature ranges increase, summer monthly averages rise higher and total precipitation decreases.

The transition zone between a humid subtropical climate and the dry climates of desert and steppe lands is thus quickly crossed. So much of Asia falls within these two climatic categories. The Arabian Peninsula, the Plateau of Iran, the Makran coast, much of Pakistan and parts of north-west India experience a true hot desert climate. Average annual precipitation nowhere exceeds 250 mm (10 in) and is often less than half that. Monthly average temperatures are never below freezing and in the high sun season exceed 32°C (90°F).

North of this region, throughout much of interior Iraq, Iran, Afghanistan and, in India, south of the Great Desert and east of the Western Ghats, extends a belt of steppeland climates. Annual rainfall is slightly higher and the range of temperatures lower. Then, within the Anatolian Plateau, in Mongolia and parts of north-east China, lower precipitation with lower temperatures produce the mid-latitude steppe climates. In these the lowest winter average monthly temperature falls below 0°C (32°F), and the summer temperature rises into the low 20°sC (mid 70°sF).

The great upland heart of Asia experiences mountain climates in which altitude is the predominant factor. Precipitation is very variable, but is often low. Average temperatures are surprisingly low for the latitude, with readings below freezing for as many as six months.

In Eastern Asia, most of lowland China, Korea and Japan the annual precipitation is much higher and the

average temperatures lower. To the north, the rains fall throughout the year or, on the mainland, largely in summer. Farther south, in southern Honshu and Kyushu as well as in much of southern China and northern Laos, Vietnam and Thailand, summer average temperatures exceed 27°C (80°F) and annual precipitation exceeds 1,250 mm (50 in).

Much of peninsula India, Burma, Malaysia, southern Thailand, Laos, Vietnam, Kampuchea and the islands of SE Asia experience tropical rainy climates. The average temperature of even the coolest month exceeds 18°C (64°F) and the high summer average temperatures reach the high 20°sC (low 80°sF). Near the equator the average monthly temperatures stay near 27°C (80°F) all year.

Precipitation is constant throughout the year in many of the islands, but India, Bangladesh and Sri Lanka are subject to the unique monsoons. From mid-December to early March dry, comparatively cool air from central Asia crosses the Himalayas and then blows out into the Indian Ocean. From then to the end of May the heat builds up. In June, when low pressure develops over central Asia, hot wet winds blow onshore bringing with them very heavy rains. The exact amount of rainfall varies but, at its most extreme, the world's highest average annual precipitation of 11,610 mm (457 in) is experienced 1,311 m (4,300 ft) up in the Assam hills, at Cherrapunji.

ASIA

Asia is something of an enigma in the modern world. The contrasting economies found there today, in large measure conceal the great ages in the continent's past. Herein lies the scene of many early civilizations – the Sumerians in Mesopotamia over 5,000 years ago, the great Indus Valley cultural centre over 4,000 years ago, the Chinese dynastic developments culminating in the artistic excellence of the Chou some 1,000 years BC, the empire of Alexander the Great 700 years later.

Asia has also been the birthplace of most of the world's great religions – Buddhism founded in India and Confucianism in China in the sixth century BC, Christianity in Palestine, and Mohammedanism in Arabia in the sixth century AD.

More recently, before European intervention, great empires have come and gone and centuries of wars have swept the area – the Byzantine Empire from the fourth century onward, the Mongols led by Genghis and Kubla Khan in the thirteenth century, the sixteenth century Ottomans. Then the British, French and Dutch, in particular, moved into parts of Asia to establish outposts of their recent empires. Today even these connections have mainly crumbled and the continent is made up of independent countries.

Asia's sheer size underlines its conflicting characteristics. It includes the new, rising economic generation of the Middle East and Japan. China and India in particular embrace rich histories yet have unrealized potential in the modern world. Its differences in life styles, languages, religions and politics are greater than those found in any other single continent – from the Tibetans who never leave their mountain aeries to the Arab teenagers who commute by jet to shop in Europe's capital cities. Here lies the quickening world in perhaps its most dramatic form.

The Peoples and Their Life-Styles

Asia is the most heavily peopled continent. It is also the one whose population is growing most rapidly. Indeed, total population has increased at alarming rates this century. Living standards for so many people are extremely low; life expectancy is also low by modern standards. Birth rates in Asia are high and death rates lower.

In recent times parts of Asia have developed economically along Western lines, especially Japan and Israel. The oil-rich Arab countries are also developing fast, though not for the benefit of all their peoples. Generally, despite some large urban centres and growing industries, the rest of Asia is still dominated by subsistence farming. In a continent of territorial and climatic extremes, millions of Asians thus face the almost annual consequences of crop failure and famine, as well as disastrous floods and tropical storms.

Among the great number of racial groups to be found in Asia, the main ones are the Mongoloids, the Caucasoids, and the Negroids. And just as there are many races, so there are many religions, with different areas being dominated by different faiths. India is predominantly Hindu, the Arab world is largely Moslem, China presents a mixture of Buddhism and Confucianism, and Japan a mixture of Buddhism and Shintoism.

Industry, Commerce and Communications

Compared with the leading areas of the developed world, particularly Europe and North America, Asia is, as a whole, industrially ill-developed. Whereas Western Europe accounted for nearly 31 percent of the world's value added in manufacturing industries in 1975, the USA 29 percent and the USSR nearly 16 percent, Asia accounted for only 10.6 percent. Certain individual countries such as Japan, China, and India are, however, comparatively well developed as are Hong Kong, Singapore, Java, Israel and Turkey.

Japan, for instance, is now one of the world's leading industrial nations, noted for such products as shipbuilding (first in the world), cars (world second) and precision engineering, such as optics, electrical and electronics (world first for both radio and TV manufacture). In all Asia, Japan's trade with the outside world is greater than any other. She also currently rates third in world steel production, third also in the production of aluminium and second in pig iron. Such placings all show remarkable progress during the post World War II era.

China too has made great strides forward since the Communist revolution and the establishment of the People's Government in 1949. While agriculture has been given priority over industry in many respects, China is now the world's fourth largest pig iron producer, fifth largest steel producer and fourth tin producer. By contrast, in the same field, India, with its longer history of development, rates consistently lower: tenth for pig iron, fifteenth

1 △ 2 ▽

3 ▽

1 China – the Great Wall, 2,400 km (1,500 ml) long, at Zhang Jia Khou;
2 Hong Kong – Typhoon Shelter;
3 Japan – Tokyo's lively Ginza area

for steel and fourteenth for aluminium. In comparison with Japan, however, both China and India, with their far larger populations, are still striving to satisfy home demands and are not major world traders.

Taking these same two countries, 74 percent of their combined working population is engaged on the land, about 10 percent in manufacturing, 2 percent in extractive industry and 2 percent in building. Only 4 percent are engaged in trade and commerce, 2 percent in transport and communications and 6 percent in the other service industries. Such figures show the extent to which Asian economies are still agriculturally-based, apart from Japan, Hong Kong and Israel, and the very small part of the economies which are within the service industries. Overall, it is doubtful if more than one in twenty of the whole Asiatic population are thus employed.

Asia plays a fragmented role in world trade. As already indicated, Japan is unique. Some South-east Asian countries trade in specialist products like rubber, tea, hardwoods, rice, jute and cotton textiles. The Arab states of South-west Asia make a major contribution to world trade in that some 45 percent of all crude oil originates there and the great bulk of this is exported.

Apart from the specialist oil terminals, Asia has few major sea and air ports. Karachi, Bombay, Calcutta, Bangkok, Singapore, Hong Kong, Canton, Shanghai, Tokyo/Yokohama and Osaka/Kobe are the most important coastal cities with large airports. Inland waterways also play a substantial role in China, and to a lesser extent in India.

Considering the nature of the terrain, the population distributions and the average per capita incomes in many countries, it is hardly surprising that much of Asia is ill-provided with road and rail facilities. India, the Malay peninsula, Asia Minor and Japan have the most effective transport networks, unlike China, South-west and South-east Asia. On the railways, steam haulage is still important in India, though improved diesel services are now being introduced. By contrast, Japan has modern rail facilities with heavily congested urban networks within and around the large cities as well as some rapid inter-city travel.

Agriculture, Forestry and Fishing

In its natural state the vegetative cover of Asia was very varied. In the south-west the landscape was dominated by desert. Farther north, along the Levant coast and in Asia Minor, a more luxuriant broadleaf and mixed shrub vegetation was found. To the east of this, in a broad belt extending to the lowlands of eastern China, in an area bounded to the south by the Persian Gulf and the Himalayas, was desert or grassland. Broadleaf deciduous woodland occupied much of central India, eastern China, Korea and inland Burma and Thailand. The hotter,

1 △

2 ◁

3 ▷

4 ▽

The rich tapestry of Asia is shown in contrasts – rich memorials to the dead and squalid living conditions, luxuriant islands and arid deserts, modern industry and folk art: 1 Masad, Iran – dominated by the golden domed tomb of the Imam Riza, the sacred city is also a commercial centre; 2 Rice paddy workers, Bali – coffee and copra are also grown in this fertile Indonesian island; 3 Tibetan refugees weaving rugs, Nepal – many Tibetans followed their leader, the Dalai Lama, to India in 1959 when the revolt against the occupying Chinese was put down; 4 Rubber tapping, Malaysia – this quite wealthy country owes its prosperity mainly to rubber

ASIA

wetter environments of South-east Asia were covered with broadleaf evergreen forests or mixed forest of broadleaf evergreen and deciduous trees.

The economic potential of those areas with a rainfall deficiency is very limited, and the high mountain areas and desert regions are largely void of population and agricultural activity. By contrast, in the great northern areas where grassland takes over from true desert, extensive animal herding dominates the landscape.

Throughout much of the heavily forested areas of the south-east, including most of the islands, primitive agriculture prevails. Much of India and Bangladesh, the Indus valley, parts of Burma, Thailand and the Mekong river system, parts of Malaysia and Indonesia, eastern and southern China, Korea and Japan contain the most attractive farming lands. Here, well over 60 percent of the large population depend upon small holdings, or on state farms in the Communist countries.

The dominant cereal crops are rice and wheat. Rice is particularly demanding where rainfall and temperature are concerned; wheat is less restricted by these particular factors. Rice is grown primarily in the areas influenced by the monsoon winds and rains, but wheat can be grown in the drier places. World rice production now averages some 350 million tonnes per year, of which China accounts for 33 percent, India 20 percent, Indonesia 6 percent and Bangladesh and Japan 4 percent each. In total, Asia grows over 85 percent of the world's rice. Over 95 percent of this is for home consumption, although over 60 percent of world trade in rice, amounting to about 10 million tonnes, originates in Asia. In all, Asia produces about 29 percent of the world's wheat. World production now exceeds 400 million tonnes in an average year. China accounts for about 10 percent of this and India 7 percent, with only the Soviet Union and the USA producing more.

Asia accounts for nearly one-fifth of the world's maize, which comes mainly from China, India, Java, Pakistan and Turkey, and a slightly larger proportion of its barley with some two-thirds of this being grown in China, followed by Turkey, India and Japan. Oats and rye are comparatively unimportant being grown only in the cooler parts of China, Japan and Turkey. By comparison, millet and grain sorghum production in Asia dominate the world output,
China growing nearly a half of the world's millet and India over one-sixth of the world's total sorghum production.

Asia is the world leader in tea. Overall some 83 percent of the world's total comes from this continent, and over 70 percent of world tea trade originates here. Individually, India grows 31 percent, China 20 percent, Sri Lanka 12 percent, Japan 6 per cent and Indonesia 4 percent.

More than two-fifths of world sugar cane output also comes from Asia, mainly in the tropical and equatorial parts, with India producing 21 percent of the world total, China, 6.5 percent, Pakistan, 4 percent, the Philippines, 4 percent and Thailand, 2.5 percent. Smaller quantities of sugar beet are grown farther north and west in China, Turkey, Iran and Japan.

Asia dominates world natural rubber production, some 92 percent of the annual 3.4 million tonnes total coming from South-east Asia, in particular Malaysia (44 percent of the world total), Indonesia (24 percent) and Thailand (11.5 percent).

Except for flax, vegetable fibres grow readily in the humid parts of Asia. China is second only to the USSR in world cotton production with 19 percent. India is the leading world producer of hemp fibre with 29 percent of the total. Finally, over 95 percent of the world's jute is grown in Asia, especially in China, India and Bangladesh.

Asiatic production contributes greatly to world totals of a number of other tropical and subtropical crops: over four-fifths of the coconuts come from the Philippines, Indonesia and the Indian subcontinent; three-fifths of the peanuts come, especially, from India and China, and nearly a half of the world's tobacco comes from China, India and Turkey.

Asia has more cattle than any other continent, but the sacred significance of the animal in many parts makes this fact somewhat meaningless where food value is concerned. India has more cows than any other country, China is fifth in the world tables and Bangladesh ninth. India, China, Turkey, Iran, Pakistan, Bangladesh, Indonesia and Yemen account for about half the world's goats. China alone has nearly two-fifths of the world's pigs. What is most remarkable is the fact that no other single country in the world has a quarter of this massive total. Pigs are of little significance elsewhere in the continent. China, Turkey, India, Iran, Pakistan, Afghanistan and Mongolia together account for about 28 percent of the world's sheep population.

Asia is rich in a variety of woods. South-east Asia and the Islands, as well as parts of the Indian subcontinent, have tropical hardwoods, while farther north in China and Japan temperate hardwoods and some softwoods are found. In total, over a quarter of the world's sawn timber comes from these areas, with China, Indonesia, India, Japan and the smaller islands leading. Japan

1 △

2 ▽

3 ▽

Asia is home for the world's great religions: 1 Marble Temple, Bangkok, Thailand – Buddhist monks also act as village school teachers; 2 Bar Mitzvah, western Wailing Wall, Jerusalem, Israel/Jordan – in the old part of this divided city stands one of the Jews' most sacred places; 3 Manikanika Ghat, Varanasi, India – from these steps, thousands of Hindu pilgrims bathe in the Ganges

and China are the major Asiatic exporters.

The seas off eastern and southern Asia are rich in a range of fish. Of an average world catch of about 70 million tonnes, Japan and China alone account for about one quarter. India, South Korea, Indonesia, Thailand, the Philippines and Vietnam contribute a further sixth of the world total. Japan also accounts for one-third of the world's whale catch.

Natural Resources

Asia's natural resource base is not yet fully appreciated as large parts of the interior have not been comprehensively surveyed. Thus, modern developments of fossil fuels and minerals are currently somewhat regionalized, with only vague indications of riches elsewhere.

Major bituminous coal and anthracite fields are found in eastern and southern Asia. In total, Asia produces over a quarter of the world's average annual output of hard coal. China alone accounts for some 450 million tonnes per year, then India produces about 100 million tonnes annually, followed by Japan and North Korea. Lignite output in Asia is small, coming mainly from China.

Over 45 percent of the world's annual oil output originates in Asia, particularly the south-western countries. Saudi Arabia is now second only to the USSR, producing over 420 million tonnes per year (15 percent of the world total). Iran, Iraq, Kuwait and other small Persian Gulf States account for a further 22 percent of world production, giving the Arab states a very strong position in today's crude oil markets. The remainder of Asia is of minor importance in oil production. Natural gas is also of little significance in Asia, either for local use or export, only Iran and China producing significant amounts.

Although the dry lands of Asia have little HEP potential, the countries of the east and south-east have far more. With the exception of Japan, however, little of this potential has yet been developed. Japan now rates as the world's fourth largest HEP producer, with a total of 86,000 million kwh per year. India, with greater potential, has only installed about 10 percent of it, producing 31,000 million kwh per year. Countries with less development thus far are China, which is estimated to have over 8 percent of the world's potential, Burma, Indonesia and Vietnam.

Asia is somewhat scantily provided with the iron ore upon which modern industry relies heavily. Her proven reserves are more limited than those of any other continent except Africa, standing at little over 6 percent of the world 260,000 million tonnes (iron content). Chinese reserves are considerable, however, and current annual production, mainly from the fields of Shansi, Hopei, Shantung and Tayeh is about 40 million tonnes iron content. This is over twice that of India, the second largest Asiatic producer.

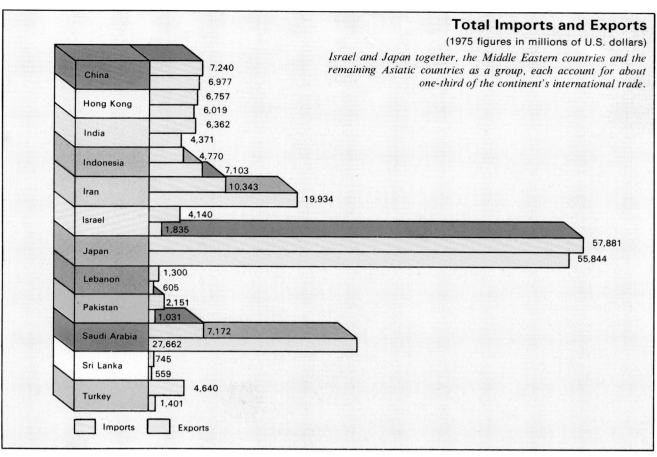

Total Imports and Exports
(1975 figures in millions of U.S. dollars)

Israel and Japan together, the Middle Eastern countries and the remaining Asiatic countries as a group, each account for about one-third of the continent's international trade.

Country	Imports	Exports
China	7,240	6,977
Hong Kong	6,757	6,019
India	6,362	4,371
Indonesia	4,770	7,103
Iran	10,343	19,934
Israel	4,140	1,835
Japan	57,881	55,844
Lebanon	1,300	605
Pakistan	2,151	1,031
Saudi Arabia	7,172	27,662
Sri Lanka	745	559
Turkey	4,640	1,401

☐ Imports ☐ Exports

The Middle East oil bonanza has brought new wealth, amenities and western life styles: 1 Desalination plant, Abu Dhabi, UAE – in a land where water is at a premium, new agricultural systems use treated sea water; 2 Oil rig, Qatar – crude oil production may be all-important to this barren land, but many tribesmen prefer to rear camels; 3 TV recording session for a 'pop' show, Jedda, Saudi Arabia – oil revenues have introduced some dubious western culture to a primarily desert country

Other mineral ores and precious metals are found in Asia, but apart from tin and tungsten current production of many is very limited, as the table below shows.

Asian Economy

Apart from Europe, including the European parts of the Soviet Union, no other contiguous part of the world is anywhere near as consistently densely peopled as either the Indian subcontinent or the eastern and southern parts of China. Japan too is similar to the British Isles both in size and population. And, beyond these major areas, other smaller regions such as Asia Minor, the Levant coast, the lower river valleys of South-east Asia and parts of Indonesia and the Philippines are also highly peopled. By contrast, most of the continent is sparsely populated. South-west and south-central Asia as well as western China have less than 5 persons per km² (12 per sq ml).

A predominantly agricultural and developing continent, Asia surprisingly contains some 62 millionaire cities. There are 21 in China, of which 7 have populations in excess of 2 million, and 10 in Japan, where Tokyo, with 11.6 million, ranks first, about equal in the world league with

Ore	Average Annual World Production (million tonnes)	Asia's Share (percent)	Principal Asiatic Producing Countries
bauxite	80.3	5	Indonesia, India
chrome	7.2	22	Turkey, India, Philippines, Iran
copper	7.4	8	Philippines, China, Japan
gold	1 million kg	4	Japan, Philippines
lead	3.2	8	China, N Korea, Japan
manganese	22.8	8	India, China
molybdenum	0.084	2	China, Japan, S Korea
nickel	0.733	4	Philippines, Indonesia
silver	0.01	3	Japan
tin	0.2	58	Malaysia, Thailand, Indonesia, China
tungsten	0.036	50	China, N & S Korea, Thailand, Japan, Burma
zinc	5.4	11	Japan, N Korea, China, Iran

ASIA

New York. India has 8, four of which have populations between 2 and 7 million. Thereafter, Indonesia and South Korea each have 3, Pakistan, Turkey and Vietnam 2 each, and Bangladesh, Burma, Kampuchea, Hong Kong, Iran, Iraq, North Korea, the Philippines, Singapore, Taiwan and Thailand 1 each.

Asia's population changes are volatile, in some countries increasing at rates as high as anywhere in the world. Many Asian countries have birth rates in excess of 40 per 1,000, and some of these, like Bangladesh, Indonesia, Thailand and Vietnam, already have large populations. India, the second most populated country, has a birth rate of nearly 35 per 1,000 and China, with over 850 million population, has a birth rate of 27 per 1,000. Death rates, though high by the standards of more advanced countries, are far lower than birth rates, the average is in the high teens and a few countries have developed medical services to a point where death rates have fallen below 8 per 1,000. The combination of these two sets of figures leads to an overall annual population increase of over 2.5 percent. Herein lies the greatest focus of the population explosion which has carried the world total to

over 4,000 million in the recent years.

Even by the kindest definitions, few Asian countries can be classified as developed market economies. Most are developing, China as the second largest centrally planned economy, and the oil producing states have uniquely lopsided economies. Compare the performance of Asia in general and some individual countries in world trade during the periods 1938–'58 and 1958–'75 with overall world performances. In imports, Asian totals rose by 2.6 and 8.9 times (compared with world figures of 4.5 and 8.0); in exports Asian totals rose by 2.3 and 11.3 times (compared with world figures of 4.5 and 8.0). Taking into account the impact of inflation, these figures are remarkable in revealing how the continent lagged behind world trends until way into the 1950s but has performed so much better since then.

This is in large measure due to economic growth in particular areas. Japan alone, Asia's largest trading nation by far, increased its imports by 1.8 and then 18 times in the two periods of time, and its exports by 1.6 and then 18.5 times. The oil-producing states increased imports by 5.8 and 13.7 times, and exports by 8.7 and 18.7 times. But the figures for the remainder of free Asia were 2.5 and only 5.7 times for imports, 1.4 and only 6.1 times for exports.

1 △   2 ▽

Asian industry and commerce remain comparatively under-developed in contrast with the west, apart from one or two notable exceptions: 1 Hong Kong and Shanghai Bank, Hong Kong – – banking revenue helps offset an adverse trade balance in this place of thousands of small factories; 2 Industrial pollution, Japan – Asia's major producing and trading country pays the penalty for its industrial success with an unclean atmosphere

Per Capita Income
(1974 figures in U.S. dollars)

The average earnings of most east and south-east Asians are less than $500. Yet the figures for citizens of some oil-producing states, Japan and Israel, are very much higher.

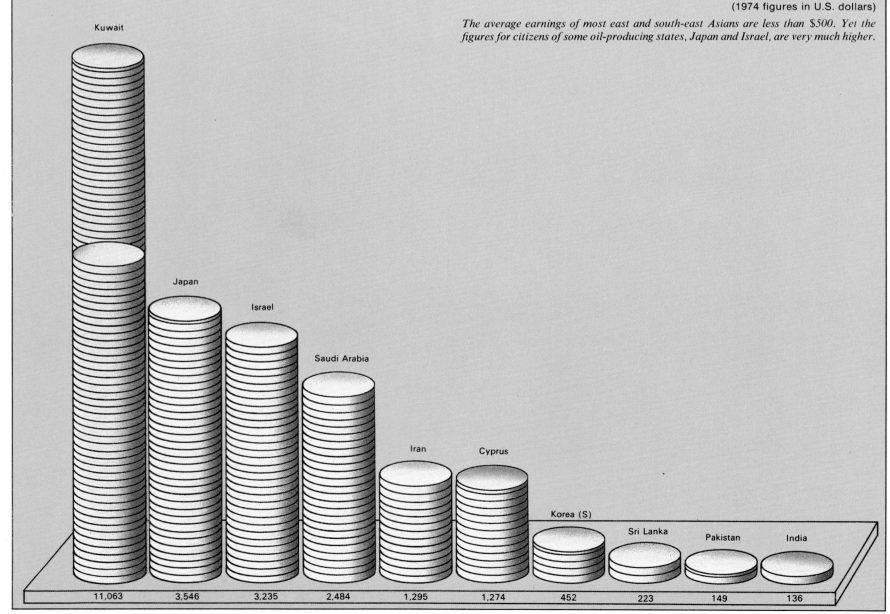

Kuwait	Japan	Israel	Saudi Arabia	Iran	Cyprus	Korea (S)	Sri Lanka	Pakistan	India
11,063	3,546	3,235	2,484	1,295	1,274	452	223	149	136

Available per capita income figures for Asia are not as revealing as in many other continents, since the distribution of wealth is more uneven than in many parts of the world. This is particularly true in the oil-producing states. Worldwide, averages rose by 186 percent between 1960 and 1974; in the oil states they rose by 445 percent, in free southern and eastern Asia by 330 percent, in Japan by 750 percent.

However, such percentage figures must be viewed cautiously and absolutes stressed to illustrate the poverty of much of Asia compared with, say, European and North American countries. In 1974, the per capita income of the USA was $5,923, of West Germany $5,480 and of the UK $3,106. In Asia, Kuwait topped the table with $11,063 (an exceptional case), while Japan was top of the large countries with $3,546, Israel next with $3,235, then Saudi Arabia with $2,484. Among the lowest average incomes recorded were Sri Lanka $223, Pakistan $149 and India $136.

Overall, Asia is a marked energy surplus continent, entirely due to the oil riches of the Middle East. In 1975, 2,470 million tonnes coal equivalent (mtce) were produced and 1,410 mtce consumed. The Middle East countries accounted for 1,508 mtce of the product but only used 127 mtce, thus providing a phenomenal surplus. The remainder of free Asia had to import large quantities since production was only 317 mtce and consumption 658 mtce. China, North Korea, Vietnam and Mongolia, the planned economies, together had a small surplus. Individually, India needs to import a mere 14 percent of her total needs of 132 mtce, while Japan has to import 90 percent of her total needs of about 400 mtce. Other noteworthy examples of importing and exporting are Indonesia and Brunei with their large oil surpluses, and South Korea which imports about half of its needs of 36 mtce.

Asia's range of energy consumptions (expressed in kilograms per head per year) is as large as any in a single continent. Though total consumption is small, some of the oil-producing states are world leaders in per capita terms. Even the 11,000 kg/ca of the USA looks small compared with the 35,300 kg/ca used by the 280,000 people living in Qatar. But figures of less than 100 kg/ca are often recorded – Bangladesh 28, Burma 51, Kampuchea 16, Laos 63, Nepal 10 – in the least developed countries.

Overall it is difficult to generalize about Asia's economic position in the modern world. However, individual parts and separate countries can be commented on. Japan is the continent's one great example of a developed economy, its phenomenal recovery after the devastation of World War II providing one of the economic miracles of the last quarter century. The oil-producing countries, especially those of the Middle East, currently have the energy-deficient countries of the developed world at

Everyday life in Asia: 1 Supermarket, Abu Dhabi, UAE – new prosperity, new products; 2 Fish shop near the Galata Bridge, Istanbul, Turkey – ancient Byzantium now relies mainly on trade and tourism; 3 Children welcome guests to a Chinese commune – nearly 75,000 People's Communes now work the land

their mercy. Their potential power has yet to be finally assessed. Nevertheless, at this time, these countries have immense riches and will continue to accumulate foreign currency and overseas investments as long as their liquid gold lasts and they remain politically stable.

China and, to a lesser extent the other Communist states of Southeast Asia, are currently developing in diverse and often unknown ways. The economic potential of these countries which contain nearly a quarter of the world's population is enormous, but it will be some years before the state plans for industry and agriculture achieve their possible greatness. By contrast, India is something of an enigma. Another heavily peopled land with a lengthy history and connection with Britain, its progress is far more lumbering. Finally, growth and progress in the rest of South-east Asia appears varied.

Wherein lies the economic future for this continent? How will the oil-rich states utilize the economic strength which their limited resources give them? Can Japan maintain its present remarkable position in world industry and trade? How rapidly can China emerge from its largely isolated position of the last quarter of a century, develop internally and become a leading world trader? These are some of the questions to which the coming decades may provide surprising answers.

Per Capita Energy Consumption
(1975 figures in kilograms)

Apart from high amounts in the oil-producing countries, Asiatic energy consumption per head ranges from Japan's modest figure to the minute ones of many third world countries.

China	693
Hong Kong	1,119
India	221
Indonesia	178
Iran	1,353
Israel	2,806
Japan	3,622
Lebanon	928
Pakistan	183
Saudi Arabia	1,398
Sri Lanka	127
Turkey	630

Asian Countries

Afghanistan

Formerly a kingdom, Afghanistan has been a republic since 1973. Its economy is based largely on the agriculture of the valleys and plains areas, which occupy less than one-tenth of the country, the rest being mountain or desert. Raising Persian lambs, wheat, fruit and cotton farming are important activities, with lamb skins, raw cotton and fruit being the main exports. Less than one-twentieth of the population live in large towns; three times as many are nomadic. The USSR, India and the USA are her main trading partners.

Bahrain

Composed of a number of low-lying islets near Qatar, off the east coast of Saudi Arabia, Bahrain has a fierce, desert climate. Completely independent since 1971, for the previous 90 years the country was an independent sheikdom enjoying British protection. The ruling family, the Al Khalifa dynasty, have been in control for 200 years. Home-produced crude oil and oil piped from Saudi Arabia is refined locally before being exported. Aluminium smelting, engineering and ship repairing are growing rapidly. Her main trading partners are the USA, the UK, West Germany and other West European countries.

Bangladesh

Formerly the eastern province of Pakistan, since 1971 Bangladesh has been a separate independent republic within the Commonwealth. It is a densely-peopled, lowland country which centres on the deltas of the Ganges and Brahmaputra. Disastrous floods have impeded her economic progress. Agriculture is the base of the economy, with rice, jute, tea and sugar cane the main crops. Textiles, paper making and sugar refining are valuable industries.

Bhutan

This small landlocked Himalayan state is independent, but neighbouring India officially guides her foreign affairs. Traditionally, crop and animal farming as well as forestry have provided the economic base. Now mining, hydro-electric power production and tourism are being developed steadily.

British Indian Ocean Territories

Formed in 1965 from a number of scattered islands in the western Indian Ocean, this British colony today comprises the Chagos Archipelago, some 1,700 km (1,000 ml) south-west of Sri Lanka. The small population mainly fish and grow food crops.

Brunei

A member of the Commonwealth, this self-governing sultanate in North Borneo enjoys British protection. Most of the land is untouched forest and the cleared areas are now mainly planted with rubber trees. The oil and natural gas fields of Seria and those offshore provide about 90 percent of the country's exports. Rubber and native crafts account for much of the other foreign earnings, mainly from the UK, her main trading partner, followed by Australia and New Zealand.

Burma

A Socialist republic since 1974, Burma left the then British Commonwealth in 1948 to become an independent federal country. All its borders are mountainous. Agriculture is the leading activity, with rice, wheat, maize, millet, tea, sugar cane and rubber as major crops. Hardwoods, especially teak, are an important source of foreign earnings. Crude oil is produced in modest quantities; lead, tungsten and tin to a lesser extent. International trade is still limited, rubber, cotton and crude oil being the leading items. Relies heavily on internal waterways.

China

After the USSR and Canada, the People's Republic of China is the largest country in the world. It contains about 20 percent of the world population. Most Chinese live in small settlements and derive their living from the land, although there are a number of large modern cities in the east. After 3,000 years' rule by a series of powerful dynasties, twentieth-century China has been torn by conflict and revolution culminating in the establishment of the Communist state in 1949. Until about 1970 the country was virtually closed to the outside world. The dominating figure of Chairman Mao-Tse-Tung was responsible for the Great Proletarian Cultural Revolution initiated in 1966. During and after this period China began to develop more contacts with the outside world, a policy continued by Mao's successor, Hua-Kuo-Feng. The ideological conflict between Peking and Moscow also continues.

Agriculture was reorganized after 1949 and today the country is self-sufficient in all needs except cotton. Cereals, root crops, industrial crops and livestock, especially pigs, have priority. The total area of controlled irrigation is the highest for any country in the world. Mineral pro-

1 Phosphate industry, Jordan – this is the chief resource of this desert area; 2 Peking, China – despite slow moves to western ways, bicycles remain the Chinese capital's most common form of transport; 3 Wall of fort, Lahore, Pakistan – the country's second largest city is known mainly for its carpets and textiles

duction is considerable, headed by coal, iron ore, crude oil, tungsten and tin.

Since the Communist state was created, industry has been developed in a series of five-year programmes. While the old cottage industries persist, new textile, heavy metallurgical, chemical, vehicle, engineering, cement and paper industries have been established. Today 80 percent of China's international trade is with the non-Communist world, with Japan, Hong Kong, Australia and Canada being her main partners.

Christmas Island

Lying 350 km (210 ml) south of Java in the eastern Indian Ocean, Christmas Island is now under Australian sovereignty. The extraction of phosphates is the island's major industry. Exports are mainly to Australia, New Zealand, Singapore and Malaysia.

Indonesia

Java, Sumatra, Sulawesi and most of Borneo are the largest islands in this independent republic which was a Dutch colony from 1600 till 1941. Three-quarters of the people live by farming, many growing subsistence crops. Rubber, coffee, tea and sugar cane are the main commercial crops. Indonesia has rich deposits of oil, tin and bauxite. Crude oil, tin, rubber, palm oil and kernels and coffee are the main exports. Rice, chemicals, machinery and consumer goods are the major imports.

Iran

Lying between the Persian Gulf and the Caspian Sea, Iran (formerly Persia) has a history which goes right back to the Persian Empire of 2,500 years ago. Normally, crude oil production is the main base of the economy. Other important products and exports are cotton, carpets, wool and hides. Wheat, sugar beet, oats and rice are the most extensively grown crops. For all that the country earns great revenue from its oil exports, it is a land of stark contrasts in living standards; most of the population is rural and very poor. In recent years, civil unrest has grown so that in 1979 the ruler, the Shah, reputedly one of the world's richest men, was forced to leave the country. An islamic republic has been established, re-introducing all the ancient laws.

Iraq

This former kingdom became a republic in 1958. It is centred on the fertile basin of the Rivers Tigris and Euphrates. Much land is irrigated and part of the large revenues of the national oil companies are used to introduce still more irrigation schemes. Apart from oil, dates, wool and cotton are the major exports. For home consumption, wheat, barley, rice and livestock products are important.

Israel

In 1948 the independent country of Israel was established within much of the former British mandated territory of Palestine, and proclaimed as a homeland for the Jews. Since then, tension has existed between this young home for Zionism and its Arab neighbours. This has resulted in two short wars (in 1967 and 1973) which have threatened to escalate into large-scale international conflict. However, in 1979 a peace treaty between Israel and Egypt was signed, following mediation by the USA. There is a new mood of cautious co-existence between the two nations, though this is not shared by other Arab states. The country is by far the most economically developed and balanced of all in western Asia. Agriculture, mining and industry are highly organized. The main exports are processed diamonds, chemicals, oil products and citrus fruit.

1 Rooftop view of Jerusalem, Israel/Jordan – this 4,000 year old city, sacred to Jews, Moslems and Christians, remains a continuing source of conflict; 2 Nha-Trang, Vietnam – the Communist regime has led to a growing tide of refugees from the old South; 3 Fishing boats and nets, Macau, China – fish is the main export of this Portuguese territory

Cocos Islands

These lie 1,000 km (600 ml) west of Christmas Island. Their control was passed from Singapore to Australia by the British government in 1955. The meteorological station there provides information for eastern Indian Ocean weather forecasting.

Cyprus

The eastern Mediterranean island of Cyprus is an independent republic within the Commonwealth. Agriculture and mining are its main activities. Potatoes, wine and grapes, copper, asbestos and iron pyrites are its major exports. Fuel oils, cereals and textiles are the main imports. The Cypriot population of 80 percent Greek orthodox and 20 percent Turkish Moslem do not coexist happily.

Hong Kong

This British crown colony comprises the main island of Hong Kong, some other islands and a small part of the Chinese mainland near the mouth of the Pearl River. There are estimated to be over 33,000 factories in the colony, many very small. These produce a wide range of consumer goods for the world market, of which textiles, electronic and electrical goods, clocks and watches, toys and plastic goods are major examples. The adverse balance of visible trade is offset by earnings from banking, insurance, tourism and other services.

India

This subcontinental area has a history of civilization which dates back to about 2500 BC. Modern India, the largest part of the former British viceroyalty, is now a republic and has been an independent member of the Commonwealth since 1947. It is a strange mixture of long-standing traditions and attempts to bring the country fully into the late twentieth century. Over 80 percent of the modern population are Hindus, subdivided by the caste system – Priests and Scholars (Brahmins), Warriors (Kshatriyas), Merchants (Vaishyas),

Workers (Sudras). Moslems are the second largest population group. India, though only about one-third the size of China, is today Asia's second largest country, with about 75 percent of the population of that country. The concentrations of people in the plains of the north are some of the densest in the world.

Most Indians live off the land, many deriving a meagre existence from it. Recent attempts have been made to improve agriculture, and progress in the introduction of new strains of seeds, modern equipment and fertilizers is steady. Rice, wheat, millet, tea, sugar cane, cotton and jute are the leading crops. Draught animals are kept, but the Hindu religion regards the cow as sacred so it is not generally eaten. Sheep and goats are raised for slaughter. Indian mineral reserves are great but have yet to be systematically exploited. Iron ore, coal, manganese, bauxite and copper are at present extracted. The leading industries are iron and steel, cotton and silk textiles and carpet making. Jute and cotton manufactures, tea, iron ore and leather goods are the major exports; imports are wheat, oil products, machinery and fertilizers. India's main trading partners are the USA, Japan, Iran, the UK and the USSR.

Asian Countries

Japan

Asia's most advanced country comprises a large series of over 3,000 islands off the east coasts of China, Korea and the USSR. Most of the population live on the four main islands of Honshu, Hokkaido, Kyushu and Shikoku. Japan has been ruled by the same dynasty since being united as one nation nearly 1,800 years ago. During the present century it has been involved in a series of conflicts with Russia, Manchuria and China and then joined forces with Germany and Italy in World War II. Defeat in 1945 came after the only two nuclear bombs ever used in war had destroyed the cities of Hiroshima and Nagasaki. In the last 30 years the Japanese economy has been remarkably re-established, and the country now enjoys one of the highest living standards in all Asia.

Only one-sixth of the whole country is suitable for farming, and now little more than 10 percent of the labour force works on the land. Crop production has been diversified recently. The demand for rice has fallen and though it is still a major crop, wheat, barley, sugar beet and cane and fruits are of increasing significance. The mountains and steeper slopes are mainly forested, yielding valuable timber. While Japan is no longer the world's leading fishing nation, she still accounts for about 17 percent of the world's annual catch.

The country is ill-endowed with minerals. However, Japanese industry is now well established and organized, highly competitive and very diversified: ship building, vehicle making, textiles, optics and electronics are but a few of her major activities. These depend to a large extent on the importing of raw materials. Japan trades with all parts of the world, but especially with the USA, her South-east Asia neighbours, Australia and Canada.

Jordan

The modern Arab kingdom of Jordan was established in 1949. Most of the country is desert land, only 10 percent being cultivated. Irrigation plays a vital part in farming. Wheat, watermelons, citrus fruit and tomatoes are the most important crops. Phosphate rock production and exporting is an important part of the national economy. To date, the search for oil in Jordan has yielded no commercial return.

Kampuchea

Formerly known as Cambodia and then the Khmer Republic, Kampuchea was part of the former country of French Indo-China. Increasing economic problems and the infiltration of Communist guerillas from neighbouring Vietnam led to the removal of the ruler Prince Sihanouk in 1970. Following a short period of civil war, the Communist forces of the Khmer Rouge defeated the republicans in 1974. Farming, fishing and forestry are the main occupations. Rice, rubber, maize and fresh water fish are the most important products. A little phosphate, iron ore, limestone and some precious stones are mined.

Korea (North)

The northern part of the Korean peninsula is a people's democratic (Socialist) republic. Here, mineral production is far more important than agriculture. Coal, iron, lead, zinc and copper are the leading minerals. A wide range of industries employ about 40 percent of the national workforce. Rice, maize and other grains are the leading crops, all farms now being collectivized. Most trade is with Russia.

Korea (South)

The southern part of the Korean peninsula is officially known as the Republic of Korea. Its economy is more evenly based than that of the north. Rice, barley, wheat, beans and tobacco are the leading crops. A large ocean-going fishing fleet is kept. The extraction of coal, iron ore,

1 △

2 △

3 ▽

copper and lead is limited; only tungsten, in which Korea is a world leader, is produced in great quantities. A range of manufacturing industries have been developed. Most trade is with the USA and Japan.

Kuwait

This tiny, independent sheikdom on the Persian Gulf is an almost entirely flat desert land, with very little cultivated area. In the last thirty years, since oil was first extracted, it has developed into one of the world's major oil-producing countries. It is estimated that nearly 14 percent of the world's oil reserves lie beneath such a small land.

Laos

Formerly part of French Indo-China and then a civil-war torn kingdom, this landlocked country is now an independent people's democratic (Socialist) republic. One of the least developed countries of SE Asia, its agriculture is largely subsistent and primitive. Forest products, sawn timber (especially teak), plywood and matches, are the main export items apart from tin, which is the only exploited mineral from the wide range known to exist.

Lebanon

This small republic bordering the eastern Mediterranean is unique among Arab countries in that the majority of the population are Christian. Less than 40 percent of the country can be cultivated. Citrus and other fruit, tobacco, olives and wool are exported in large quantities to pay for imported foodstuffs and manufactured goods. Iron ore and other minerals exist but to date have been little developed.

Macau

Two islands and part of a Chinese peninsula near the mouth of the Canton River have formed the Portuguese territory of Macau since 1557. Its importance as a trading centre is small compared with nearby Hong Kong, but it has a large fishing industry.

Malaysia

An independent federal country within the Commonwealth, Malaysia comprises the Malay Peninsula (West Malaysia) and parts of northern Borneo (East Malaysia). Rubber, tin, timber and palm oil account for about 75 percent of the national exports. Agriculture centres on rice,

1 Looking towards the channel, Penang, Malaysia – the state capital and main port, George Town, like the island, is known simply as Penang; 2 Kyrenia, Cyprus – this attractive Mediterranean island relies mainly on farming and tourism; 3 Isa New Town, Bahrain – much oil revenue is being pumped back into new community projects and developing industry

1 Sampans, Singapore – en route from Europe to the Far East, the island's main port is an excellent trading venue; 2 Rice terraces, Banaue, Philippines – rice, the islands' major food crop, is grown everywhere, but still has to be imported to feed the population of over 44 million; 3 Ploughing with oxen, Afghanistan – farming is difficult in this arid, mountainous land

palms, fruits, sugar and tea. The population is 45 percent Malay, 35 percent Chinese and 20 percent Indian, Pakistani and smaller tribal groups.

Maldive Islands

Now an independent republic, this collection of over 2,000 coral atolls lying south-west of Sri Lanka was a British protectorate until 1965. Fishing, especially for bonito, is the main activity. Tourism has been growing in importance in recent years.

Mongolia

The Mongolian People's (Socialist) Republic is a sparsely populated landlocked country lying between the USSR and China. Most Mongols, modern descendants of Genghis Khan, are herdsmen, and animals and their products provide the great majority of the country's exports. Coal, copper, molybdenum and phosphates are the main minerals found. There is little industry. A member of COMECON, Mongolia trades mainly with its Communist neighbours and currently relies on them to support a substantial trade deficit.

Nepal

Landlocked between Tibet and India, Nepal is a Hindu kingdom situated in the Himalayas. Farming is the most important activity, with rice, maize, wheat, millet and jute the chief crops. What small deposits of coal and iron ore are known are not yet exploited. Textiles, sugar milling, leather and shoe making and native crafts are the major industries. Most international trade is with India.

Neutral Zone

From 1922 to 1966 part of the Arabian Desert was declared a neutral zone to be jointly administered by Saudi Arabia and Kuwait. Since 1966 it has been partitioned, but the natural resources extracted from the area, especially oil, are shared by the two countries.

Oman

This independent sultanate is largely desert in the south-eastern part of the Arabian peninsula. Dates, fruit and sugar cane are grown on parts of the coastal lowlands, the hills and at oases. Since the mid-1960s oil production has grown steadily, and is now the major source of foreign revenue. Most trade is conducted

with the United Kingdom, India, Australia and Japan.

Pakistan

The independent Moslem republic of Pakistan was established in 1947. Its original eastern province has since become the separate country of Bangladesh. The majority of the population lives by farming. Wheat, maize, cotton, millet, barley and fruits are the main products. Small quantities of a range of minerals are extracted. A large programme of water control for irrigation and hydro-electric power production is helping agricultural and industrial development. Food processing and textiles are the main industries.

Philippines

Only one-tenth of the 7,000 islands in the independent republic of the Philippines are inhabited. Most of the population live on 16 of them, about half on Luzon. Crop farming,

forestry and fishing are important activities. The islands have a wide range of mineral resources: gold, silver, iron, copper and chromite are most valuable. Food processing, leather processing and native craft production are the major industries. Most trade, via Manila, is with the USA.

Qatar

This is an independent sheikdom on the Persian Gulf. In the last thirty years oil production has risen steadily. Natural gas is also produced. Some nomadic tribesmen herd livestock and a little fishing is carried out along the coast. Among the uses to which the considerable oil revenues are put is the provision of free social service, education and health.

Saudi Arabia

This largely desert kingdom occupies most of the Arabian peninsula. About half the population are still engaged

in nomadic herding and oasis agriculture. Dates, alfalfa, barley and citrus fruit are the main crops. Since oil was first discovered in the 1930s the country has rapidly become a world leader in crude oil production. Oil refining is now a major industry and other oil is exported unrefined. Her main trading partners are Japan, the USA, West Germany and the United Kingdom.

Singapore

Singapore became an independent republic within the Commonwealth in 1965, having previously been part of the Malaysian federation. This small island country has a mainly Chinese population. Its economic importance derives from commerce, transit trading and processing. Chemicals, timber, rubber, tin and plastic industries are most important. In recent years a major fishing industry has been established. Most trade is with Malaysia, Japan and the USA.

Asian Countries

Sri Lanka

Formerly known as Ceylon, Sri Lanka is an island lying south of the Indian peninsula. It is a democratic republic within the Commonwealth. The majority of the people live by agriculture, mainly producing tea, rice, rubber and coconuts. Tea is the major export. Graphite is the most important mineral extracted and exported; a range of gem stones are also mined. Food processing, chemicals, cement and textile production are the leading industries. Among her trading partners are China, Japan, Australia and United Kingdom.

Syria

This east Mediterranean Arab republic is agriculturally self-sufficient. Wheat, barley, cotton and tobacco are the main crops. Cattle and sheep are also important. Textiles and food processing are the major industries. The mineral wealth of the country is not fully realized, although phosphates are worked, and lead, copper, nickel and chromite have been found. Natural gas has been discovered and the search for oil, present beneath so many parts of the Middle East deserts, continues, though it has so far not met with success.

Taiwan

Formerly called Formosa, Taiwan is a large island 160 km (100 ml) from the Chinese mainland. It became part of China in 1945 but since mainland China became a people's republic, Taiwan has been a separate non-Communist country, receiving support from the USA. About as many people farm as work in industry. Sugar cane, rice, sweet potatoes and tropical fruits are the main crops. Metal manufacture, textiles, chemicals and cement making are the major industries. Coal is the most developed mineral, and reserves of copper, sulphur and oil are also being successfully investigated. Taiwan's main trading partners are Japan, the USA, West Germany and the United Kingdom.

Thailand

This South-east Asian kingdom used to be known as Siam. Farming and forestry are the main activities. Rice is the most valuable product, followed by rubber. Other leading crops are sugar cane, tapioca, maize and coconuts. Teak, yang and other trees are felled. Of a wide range of minerals, fluorite, gypsum, iron and lignite are most important. Fishing is also a significant activity. Food and rubber processing, as well as handicrafts, are the main industries.

Turkey

Since 1923, Turkey has been an independent republic. It occupies the whole of Asia Minor and a small part of south-east Europe on the opposite side of the Turkish Straits. Based largely on its historic and cultural attractions, such as those in Istanbul, tourism is growing steadily. More than 65 percent of the population live by farming. Cereals, cotton, tobacco, fruits, olives and grapes are the main products. Important minerals include hard and soft coal, iron ore, crude oil and chromite; others have yet to be commercially exploited. Raw materials are exported and manufactured goods imported.

United Arab Emirates

This independent country in Southwest Asia was formed in 1971 from seven sheikdoms formerly known as the Trucial Oman or the Trucial States. The whole area is predominantly desert, with the exception of the Buraimi Oasis in Abu Dhabi which provides a significant area of farmed land. The economy otherwise is entirely based on the oil produced and exported, mainly from Dubai and Abu Dhabi. Oil exploration in the other emirates has been intensified in recent years.

Vietnam

Once part of French Indo-China, Vietnam was partitioned into two states in 1954, the North being Communist and the South non-Communist. During the 1960s, Communist infiltration, supported by the USSR, was a growing problem in the South. Increasingly the USA supported the democratic South, eventually deploying a large army in its defence. The Vietnam war officially ended in 1973; two years later, Communist infiltration led to the fall of Saigon, the southern capital, and the creation of a united Socialist republic. The problem of giving sanctuary to boatloads of refugees fleeing from the present regime occupies neighbouring countries.

Most Vietnamese are farmers, producing mainly rice, maize, sugar cane, sweet potatoes and cotton. Rubber is the main export. Coal mining is important. The existence of a range of other minerals including gold, chromite and oil is known, but to date there has been little development of these. Textiles and food processing are the main industries. Since reunification, the USSR and China have been her main trading partners and aid-givers.

Yemen

This Arab republic borders the Red Sea. Where irrigation schemes have been established, agriculture is the main activity. Millet, maize, fruits, dates and coffee are the major crops. Sheep and goats are also kept. Salt extraction and export is important. Other exports include hides, coffee and qat, a narcotic. Japan and China are the main trading partners.

Yemen (People's Democratic Republic)

In 1967 the 17 sultanates of the Federation of South Arabia were overrun by a nationalist organization, and renamed. Today, the country is sometimes distinguished from the neighbouring Arab republic (see above) by being called Southern Yemen. Agriculture is the main activity, with sorghum, sesame and millet as the chief crops. Long-staple cotton is now being grown and is a major export. Fishing exports also provide valuable foreign earnings. Aden, a former British colony, is an important oil-bunkering port.

COUNTRY REFERENCE: ASIA

Asian Countries	Political Status	State Capital	Area km²	Area sq ml	Population	Population Density per km²	Population Density per sq ml	Births per Thousand Persons	Deaths per Thousand Persons	Mean Annual Percentage Increase in Population
Afghanistan	A	Kabul	647,500	250,000	20,565,000	32	82	49.2	23.8	2.4
Bahrain	A	Al-Manamah	598	231	268,000	448	1,160	30.0	—	3.1
Bangladesh	A	Dacca	142,775	55,126	84,605,000	593	1,535	49.5	28.1	2.4
Bhutan	B	Paro & Thimbu	47,000	18,200	1,245,000	26	68	43.6	20.5	2.1
British Indian Ocean Territory	C	Victoria, Seychelles	47	18	1,800	38	100	—	—	—
Brunei	B	Bandar Seri, Begawan	5,765	2,226	190,000	33	85	33.4	4.3	2.5
Burma	A	Rangoon	678,033	261,790	31,815,000	47	122	39.5	15.8	2.4
China	A	Peking	9,561,000	3,691,500	855,546,000	89	232	26.9	10.3	1.7
Christmas Island	C	The Settlement	135	52	3,600	27	69	10.1	—	—
Cocos Islands	C		14	5	700	50	140	—	—	—
Cyprus	A	Nicosia	9,251	3,572	645,000	70	181	22.2	6.8	0.3
Hong Kong	C	Victoria	1,034	399	4,445,000	4,299	11,140	19.7	5.2	1.8
India	A	New Delhi	3,183,643	1,229,210	627,990,000	197	511	34.6	15.5	2.1
Indonesia	A	Jakarta	1,919,270	741,034	138,180,000	72	186	42.9	16.9	—
Iran	A	Tehran	1,648,000	636,300	34,160,000	21	54	45.3	15.6	2.8
Iraq	A	Baghdad	434,924	167,925	12,069,000	28	72	48.1	14.6	3.3
Israel	A	Jerusalem	20,770	8,019	3,610,000	174	450	28.3	7.2	3.2
Japan	A	Tokyo	372,197	143,706	114,650,000	308	798	17.2	6.4	1.3
Jordan	A	Amman	97,740	37,738	2,900,000	30	77	47.8	14.7	3.5
Kampuchea	A	Phnom Pénh	181,035	69,898	8,712,000	48	125	46.7	19.0	2.8
Korea (N)	A	Pyongyang	120,538	46,540	16,855,000	140	362	35.7	9.4	2.7
Korea (S)	A	Seoul	98,477	38,022	36,735,000	373	966	28.8	8.9	1.7
Kuwait	A	Al-Kuwait	16,000	6,200	1,091,000	68	176	47.1	5.3	5.6
Laos	A	Vientiane	236,800	91,400	3,485,000	15	38	44.6	22.8	2.4
Lebanon	A	Beirut	10,230	3,950	3,096,000	303	784	39.8	9.9	3.0
Macau	C	Macau	16	6	284,000	17,750	47,333	—	—	1.8
Malaysia	A	Kuala Lumpur	332,633	128,430	12,845,000	39	100	38.7	9.9	3.0
Maldives	A	Male	298	115	141,000	473	1,226	50.1	22.9	2.0
Mongolia	A	Ulan Bator	1,565,000	604,200	1,552,000	1.0	2.6	38.8	9.3	3.0
Nepal	A	Kathmandu	140,797	54,362	13,280,000	94	244	42.9	20.3	2.3
Neutral Zone			5,700	3,560				—	—	—
Oman	A	Muscat	212,457	82,030	824,000	3.9	10	—	—	3.1
Pakistan	A	Islamabad	895,496	345,753	77,040,000	86	223	36.0	12.0	3.3
Philippines	A	Manila	300,000	115,831	44,505,000	148	384	43.8	10.5	3.0
Qatar	A	Doha	11,000	4,247	100,000	9.1	24	—	—	3.0
Saudi Arabia	A	Riyadh	2,149,690	830,000	9,645,000	4.5	12	49.5	20.2	3.0
Singapore	A	Singapore	581	224	2,320,000	3,993	10,357	17.7	5.1	1.7
Sri Lanka	A	Colombo	65,610	25,332	14,085,000	215	556	29.5	7.7	2.3
Syria	A	Damascus	185,180	71,498	7,968,000	43	111	45.4	15.4	3.3
Taiwan	A	T'Aipei	35,961	13,885	16,770,000	466	1,208	—	—	—
Thailand	A	Bangkok	514,000	198,500	44,600,000	87	225	43.4	10.8	3.2
Turkey	A	Ankara	780,576	301,382	41,605,000	53	138	39.6	14.6	2.4
United Arab Emirates	A	Abu Dhabi	83,600	32,300	239,000	2.9	7.4	—	—	3.1
Vietnam	A	Hanoi	332,559	128,402	48,475,000	146	378	41.9	13.8	2.2
Yemen	A	San'a	195,000	75,300	5,690,000	29	76	49.6	20.6	2.9
Yemen People's Democratic Republic	A	Aden	287,683	111,075	1,825,000	6.3	16	49.6	20.6	3.3
ASIA TOTAL (exc. USSR)			27,526,613	10,629,290	2,346,665,100	85	221	—	—	—

1 Troglodyte dwellings, Cappadocian Province, Urchisar, Turkey; 2 Folk dancers, Tehran, Iran – the traditional arts and crafts of Persia still abound in the modern, oil-producing Moslem nation; 3 Damnoen Saduak, outside Bangkok, Thailand – this rural floating market has more to offer than its counterpart in the capital; 4 Oil derrick, UAE – Abu Dhabi is by far the largest oil-producing emirate, followed by Dubai, though oil exploration continues in the other emirates

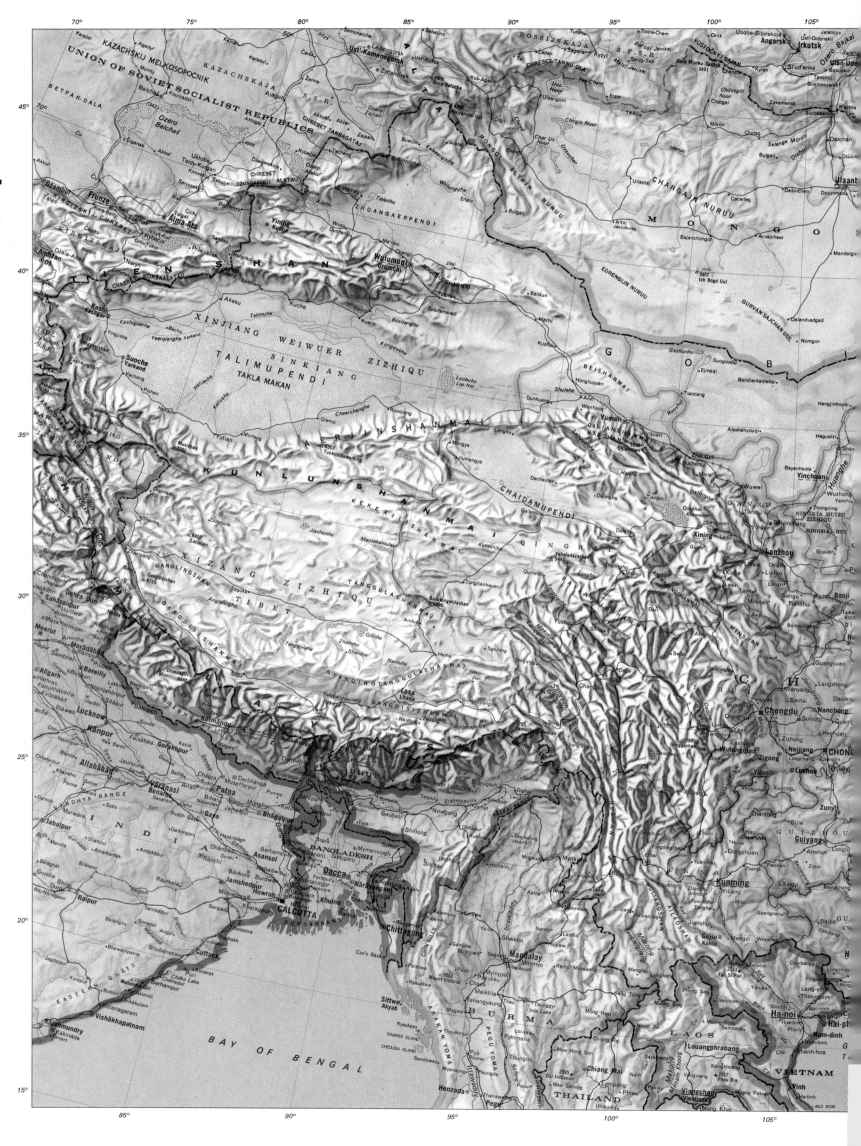

Kilometres
Statute Miles

Scale 1:13,200,000

One centimetre represents 132 kilometres.
One inch represents approximately 210 miles.
Lambert Conformal Conic Projection

81

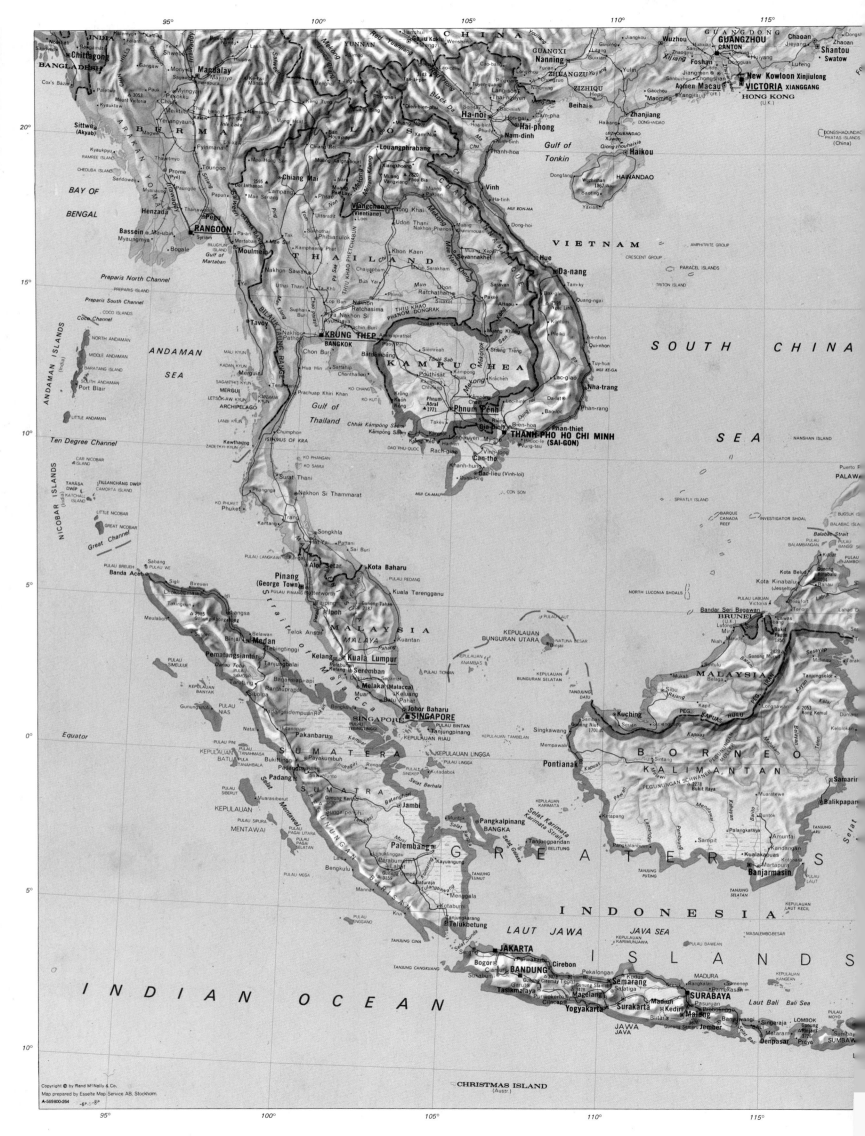

Scale 1:13,200,000

Kilometres

Statute Miles

One centimetre represents 132 kilometres.
One inch represents approximately 210 miles.

Lambert Conformal Conic Projection

83

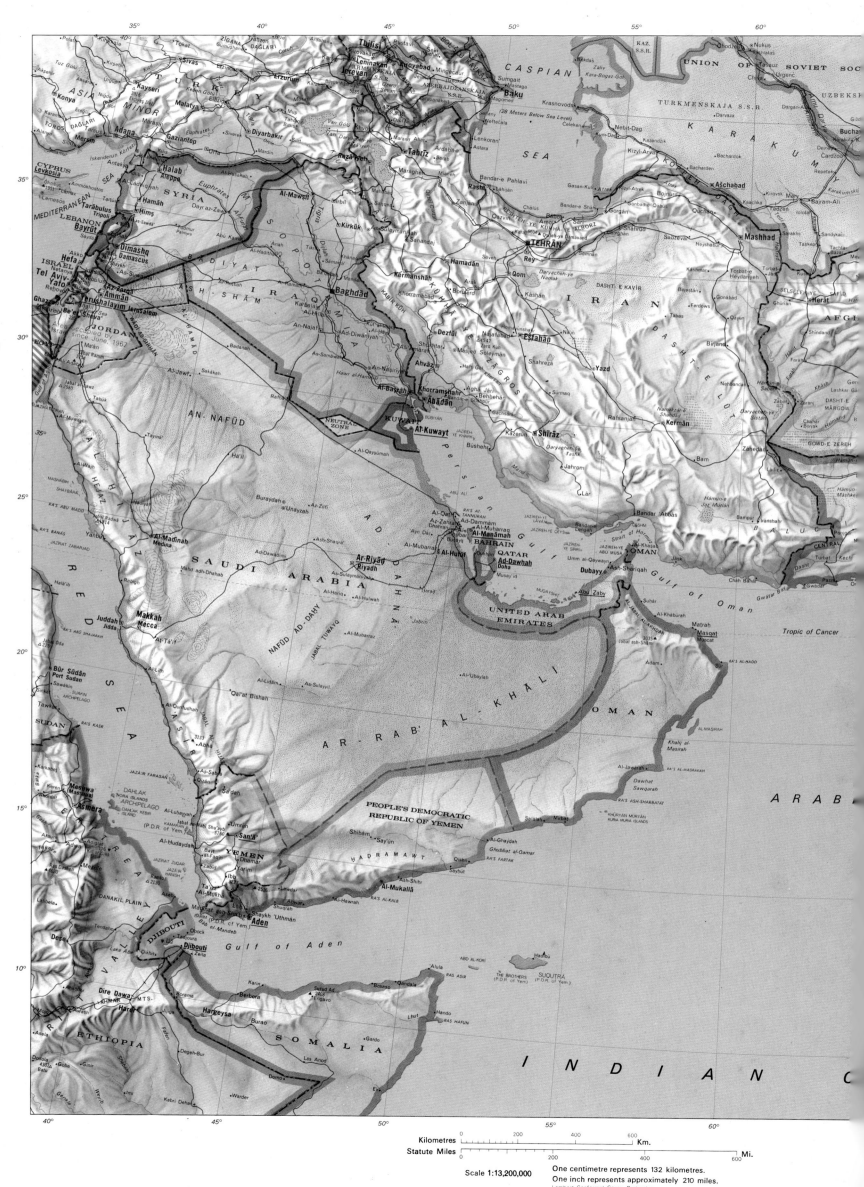

Tropic of Cancer

Scale 1:13,200,000

Kilometres

Statute Miles

One centimetre represents 132 kilometres.
One inch represents approximately 210 miles.
Lambert Conformal Conic Projection

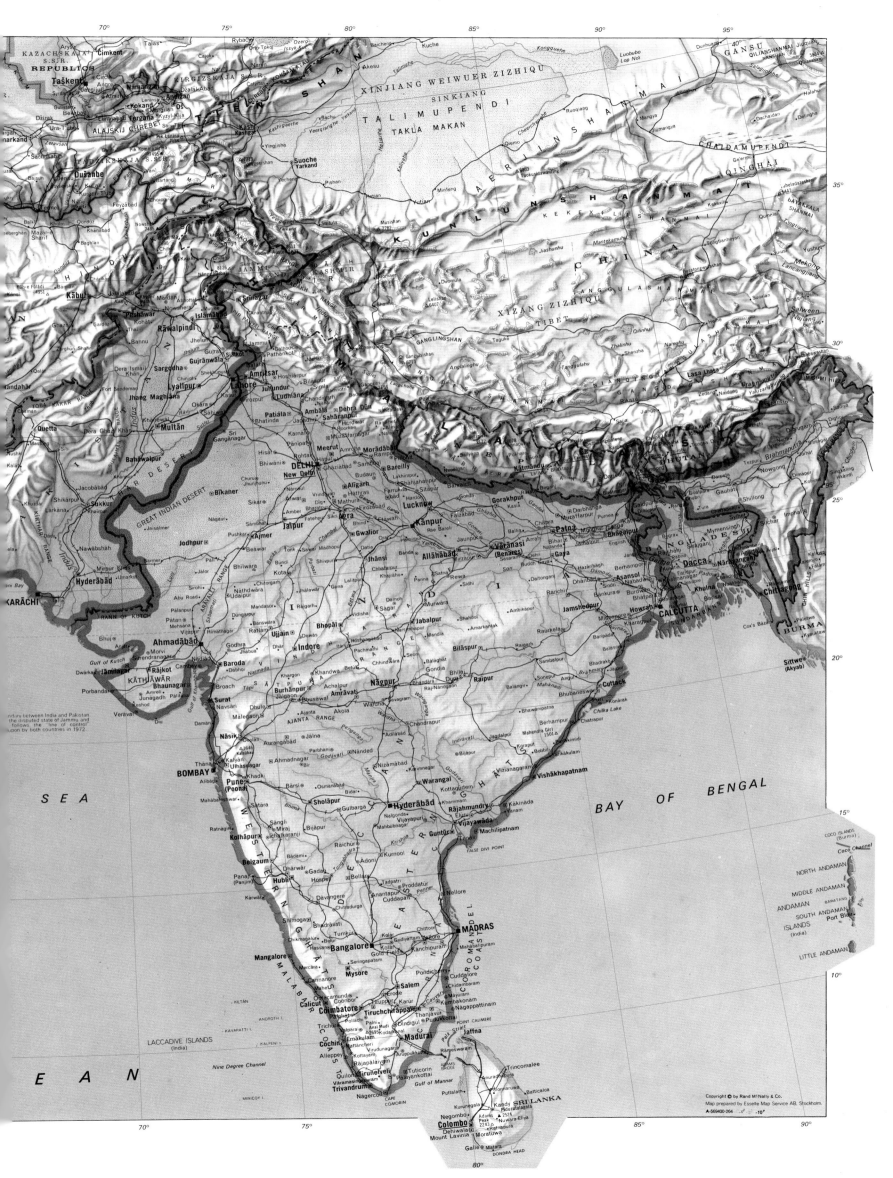

AFRICA
Physical Profile

World Location and Size

Africa is geographically separated from Asia by the Suez Canal and from Europe by the Straits of Gibraltar. It is a compact continent which sits uniquely astride the equator, extending from 37°N in Tunisia to almost 35°S in South Africa, a north-south distance of some 7,900 km (4,900 ml). Its west to east extent is greatest in the Northern Hemisphere where it stretches from Dakar in Senegal at 17°W to the Horn of Africa in Somalia at 51°E, some 7,100 km (4,450 ml). Geographically, it includes the large island of Madagascar and a number of smaller island groups in the Indian and Atlantic Oceans.

Landscape

Plateaus dominate the African landscapes, most of the continent being above 180 m (600 ft). These plateaus are found at different heights, usually with a steep edge between them. This is especially so where the lowest plateau falls to the coastal plains which are very narrow in all parts of the continent except the west and north-east coasts of the Sahara region and in Mozambique and Somalia. In general the level of the highest plains is greater in the south – average height 1,000 m (3,300 ft) – than in the north – average height 300 m (1,000 ft).

The eastern third of Africa contains the greatest relief, provided by the spectacular feature of the Great Rift Valley, an enormous belt of faulting in the earth's crust extending from Lake Nyasa in the south to the Red Sea and onward into Asia in the north. This rift system divides in two across the East African Plateau of Kenya, Tanzania and Uganda, and is up to 160 km (100 ml) wide and 5,100 km (3,200 ml) long in Africa alone. Most of the continent's great natural lakes are found within the system. Lake Victoria lying between the two main valleys, has a surface area of nearly 69,500 km² (26,830 sq ml), being second only to Lake Superior as the world's largest fresh water lake.

Close to the Rift Valley are a number of mountainous areas, some still containing active volcanoes, which rise to Africa's highest point at Mount Kilimanjaro, 5,895 m (19,340 ft). The most extensive mountain range, the Ethiopian Highlands, rises to 4,620 m (15,158 ft).

In the north-west the barrier of the Atlas Mountains of Morocco and Algeria, rising to 4,167 m (13,665 ft), effectively divides the coastal strip from the Sahara. At the other end of

Opposite: Table Mountain from Cape Town, Republic of South Africa

the continent, the Drakensberg Mountains of South Africa reach 3,660 m (12,008 ft). Only two other mountain regions approach a maximum height of 3,000 m (10,000 ft), the Ahaggar Mountains of southern Algeria and the Tibesti Massif.

Some parts of Africa, such as the Lake Chad Basin and the northern Kalahari Desert area focusing on the Okavango Swamp, are internal drainage basins. Elsewhere, there are many comparatively short rivers flowing to the Atlantic and Indian Oceans. The world's longest river, the Nile, flows northward for 6,700 km (4,160 ml) from the East African lakes to the

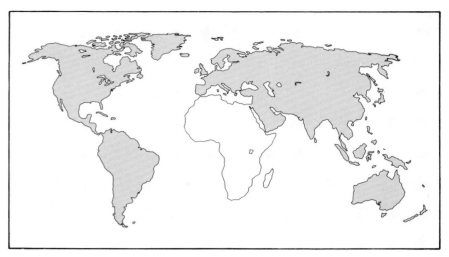

Mediterranean Sea. In West Africa, the Niger follows a circuitous course for 4,190 km (2,595 ml) between the highlands of Sierra Leone and its delta in Nigeria. The Zaire Basin, in equatorial Africa, occupies 12 percent of the continent, with the Zaire River (formerly River Congo) as its main channel. In the south-east, the Zambesi flows for 2,600 km (1,615 ml) from Angola eastward to the Indian Ocean, cascading over the Victoria Falls en route. All African rivers contain similar waterfalls and cataracts, where they drop from one plateau level to a lower one.

Climatic Background

Since the continent sits astride the equator, certain climatic features are mirrored on the opposite sides of the 0° latitude. In the extreme north of Morocco, Algeria and Libya, as well as the southern tip of South Africa, the climate is pleasantly subtropical. Summers here are dry, with the highest monthly average temperature above 22°C (72°F) and no winter average monthly temperature below 10°C (50°F). The South African plateau, farther east, has a cooler subtropical climate with no dry

season and the greater part of its rainfall in summer.

In a belt of central and western Africa within 5° of the equator, and on the east coast of Madagascar, equatorial climates provide rainfall throughout the year with totals in excess of 1,500 mm (60 in) and often more than 2,500 mm (100 in). Monthly average temperatures never fall below 18°C (64°F) and reach 27°C (the low 80°sF) at their maximum.

In a broad area around the equatorial belt shaped like a giant horseshoe lying on its side, precipitation becomes less intense, and, although temperatures never fall below 18°C (64°F) in any month, they show a greater seasonal range. These are the climates of the tropical savanna lands which, due to the effects of altitude in much of east and south central Africa, are markedly cooler than they might be.

North and south of the savanna lands lie the areas of semi-arid and true desert climates. In the north, the Sahara constitutes the world's largest single desert area. Average summer temperatures in the arid regions may reach 37°C (98°F) in one month, the winter monthly average temperature falling back only to 15°C (59°F) and

Mount Kilimanjaro in Tanzania, soars above the giraffes in the Amboseli game reserve, Kenya – Africa's highest mountain, at 5,894 m (19,340 ft), is always covered in snow at its peak

the precipitation, often negligible, rarely exceeding an average of 125 mm (5 in). Rain, when it does fall, is brief but torrential.

Overall, two characteristics dominate African climates. Firstly, 75 percent of the continent has a water supply problem. Average rainfalls may appear to be sufficient but, except in the equatorial areas, the variation in rainfall from one year to the next creates great potential difficulties unless enormous water control schemes are introduced. Secondly, for all its intertropical situation, the fact that so much of Africa is mid and high level tableland modifies the heat, so that consistently high temperatures are the exception to the rule outside the desert areas. Thus, while the temperature on the Kenyan coast may be unpleasantly high, on the East African Plateau, still on the equator but 1,500 m (5,000 ft) above sea level, it is lower; (for every 100 m (330 ft) of altitude, the temperature falls 1°C (0.55°F).

AFRICA

International observers refer to the world in three distinct divisions: the developed free nations, the developed Communist nations and the remaining developing 'Third World'. With the exception of South Africa, all of the African continent lies within this Third World. Here is the largest single group of newly independent countries which provide one of the great international challenges of our time. Within the developed world, the democratic countries of the West are anxious not to seem to be interfering too much in Africa's struggle for identity and economic advance. Yet they are keeping a keen eye on pro-African moves from the Communist bloc. One of the most fascinating international questions for the rest of this century concerns the development of the African continent and the roles which will be played by the free and the Communist world in that process.

The Peoples and Their Cultures

Africa may well have been the birthplace of mankind. Certainly East Africa has provided the oldest known skeleton of a prehistoric man, thought to be nearly 4 million years old. Today the population of this continent includes every major racial group. The Sahara separates the two main native groups, the Caucasian peoples to the north, and the Negroes to the south.

The Caucasians are similar to those peoples found in Europe and the Indian sub-continent. Though the colour of their skin varies they are all swarthy with black hair. The Hamite group includes the nomadic peoples of the Sahara, Tuareg and Fulani, and the Berbers of north-west Africa. Farther east, live the Semite group, thought to have migrated from south-west Asia perhaps as recently as only 1,500 years ago. Together these make up the Arab peoples.

The Sudanese Negroes of West Africa are regarded as the purest of this group. They include the large populations of Yorubas, Ibos, Wolofs and Mandinkas, as well as a number of smaller tribal groups. In southern Africa, the other main group, the Bantu, are not pure blooded Negroes, being of mixed stock.

Intermarriage between peoples has also produced the Nilotes of the Nile Valley and the half-Hamites of East Africa. Diminutive peoples include the Bushmen and Hottentots of the southern desert lands and the Zaire Basin Pygmies. Distinct from both the Arabs and the Negroes are the Madagascar peoples, descended from Polynesians whose forefathers must have arrived here by westward migration across the Indian Ocean.

Within very recent times parts of Africa have been settled by Europeans, some of whom left when their adopted countries became independent. Likewise small populations of South-east Asian settlers in East Africa have recently been reduced, largely through expulsion by the newly-independent African governments. South Africa, however, is still politically controlled by a substantial white minority population, and, until 1979, Zimbabwe-Rhodesia was similarly controlled.

Despite European and eastern influence over two centuries, the new governments of Black Africa are understandably anxious to build their countries in a manner reflecting their ancient cultures. There is much emphasis for instance on the tribe and family where the ties of kinship are preserved through many generations. Individual Africans are conscious of their blood relationships with far more people than are, say, Europeans and Americans. African religion too is still a powerful influence, despite the introduction of Christianity and the Islamic faith.

Prior to the colonial period, little of African development was recorded except in the northern parts. History was largely known through spoken accounts and recall rather than in documentary evidence. Now, the numerous African languages are widely used in both written and spoken form. Swahili and Yoruba dominate literature and writing, though both French and English are widely used, as are other European languages.

Political Development

For a period of over 500 years, from 1415 onward, Africa increasingly attracted the attention of the powerful European nations who were anxious to spread their influence. Portugal, Holland, Britain and France all looked for sources of slave labour for other parts of their expanding empires, and later for raw materials for their own developing industries.

During the nineteenth century, names such as Livingstone, Stanley, Speke, Caillié and Nachtigal became famous for their exploration of the African interior. This led to great rivalry between the European nations in the opening up of this 'dark continent'. By 1900, often regardless of tribal territories, the map had been filled in with claims by the British, French, Portuguese, Germans, Spanish and Italians. Particularly in those colonies with less inviting climates, the imperial powers' objectives were solely exploitation. Where a colony's climate was more suited to the Europeans themselves, they became settlers. For the next half century or so each colony provided materials for the mother country without any real preparation for the ultimate responsibilities of self-government which was to follow.

African nationalism increased greatly after World War II. Whereas in 1951 only three African countries were independent, by now there are few parts of the continent which have not achieved that status. From 1956 to 1968, 38 new independent countries emerged, many changing their colonial names for ones with greater African significance. For example, the Gold Coast became Ghana, the Belgian Congo became the Congo Democratic Republic and later Zaire, Nyasaland became Malawi and Northern Rhodesia became Zambia.

Today, the Arab-dominated north and the white-ruled south apart, the new countries face enormous problems. Since their boundaries are based on fossilized European colonial claims rather than the real African tribal areas, what internal cohesion do some of the countries have? How does each state govern itself; by Western democratic ideas or along one-party lines, by some different tribal system, or does it fall victim to

1 General view of Johannesburg, Republic of South Africa; 2 Tribal dancers in traditional dress, South Africa; 3 Tississat Falls, on the Blue Nile, near Bagar Dar, Ethiopia, north-east Africa

military rule? What form of unity or co-operation should there be between nations whose peoples have much in common? More than any other continent, Africa, in this early phase of independence for such a large proportion of its peoples, faces large political as well as economic problems.

Industry, Commerce and Communications

With a few exceptions, especially South Africa with its extensive range of raw materials and climates which were most appealing to European settlers, the African countries show less development than any other comparable group. If South Africa is excluded, the value of goods manufactured in the whole continent is less than that of such individual countries as the Netherlands, Sweden or Belgium. Raw materials are largely exported to other continents instead of being used for local industry.

On a global map showing the principal locations of manufacturing industries, with its great concentrations in the developed world, only South Africa, Egypt, Ghana and Nigeria show up with marked agglomerations. Elsewhere, in Africa, manufacturing industries, where they exist at all, are comparatively small and scattered.

For most African countries, development at the present time is very difficult. Small-scale local industries, such as food processing, wood, clothing and leather working may be set up with limited capital. But for larger scale developments, it is necessary either to receive financial aid from overseas or to earn large quantities of foreign currency by exporting valuable raw materials. The first alternative is not always easy, as the conditions placed upon international loans are not always attractive to the borrowers. The second is harder for most African countries which lack adequate concentrations of the raw materials. Even when such resources exist, their development also needs overseas investment before they can be exploited on a sufficiently large scale. Herein lies a chicken and egg situation which bedevils so many national aspirations in a continent like Africa. Even the oil- and mineral-rich countries are finding that the road to steady development is not easy.

Communications in Africa are severely hindered by the natural conditions. Dense forests, extensive desert areas, and wide rivers which contain frequent waterfalls, all make travel difficult. Many original roads and railways were developed only to take raw materials from their sources to the coast. Even now, rail networks are only effectively developed in a few countries, mainly South Africa and parts of the Mediterranean countries. Slowly, new railways are being developed but, like industry, these are hampered by lack of capital. Outside many African cities and the better developed areas in the south, roads are largely ill-made, being dusty in the hot season and muddy in the wet one. Rivers and lakes are usable in parts. Travel over long distances, from Kenya to Nigeria or Egypt to South Africa, is only really possible now that air routes have been developed.

Agriculture, Forestry and Fishing

When assessing Africa's contribution to world output of given products, remember that the continent's land area is just over one-fifth, and its population just over one-tenth that of the whole world.

Farming is still the sole occupation of most of the population although much of the land is ill-suited to agriculture. The people live by subsistence farming, trying to make a meagre living by growing enough food for themselves and their families, with perhaps a little extra for use as barter. In many areas shifting cultivation is employed whereby a patch of forest is cleared and worked until the soil is exhausted, then the people move on to clear another area and so on. Simple tools such as hand hoes and machetes are used. The prevalence of the tsetse fly and its accompanying diseases makes large-scale animal raising impossible. The main subsistence crops are yams, maize, cassava and peanuts.

In more developed areas, where the climate will allow, some of these crops and others are grown in a more systematic way. Commercial farming is found in some of the better developed areas. Then it will often be found that one or two crops are most important, and will contribute much to the country's exports. On the savanna lands, maize especially, peanuts, yams, and cassava are the leading crops with cotton, millet and tobacco of lesser importance.

In a west-east belt from Guinea to Nigeria, in the Sudan and Ethiopia, as well as in scattered parts of eastern and southern Africa, millet and sorghum are the major cereal crops. Africa produces 18 percent of the world's combined total of nearly 82 million tonnes, half of Africa's output coming from Nigeria and the Sudan. Mainly from South Africa, Egypt and Zimbabwe-Rhodesia, Africa contributes nearly 10 percent of the world's sugar cane production. World production of cassava is currently over 105 million tonnes, of which Africa accounts for about 37 percent.

In equatorial and tropical areas, harvesting tree crops is a major activity. Over 67 percent of the world's output of about 1.4 million tonnes of cocoa comes from equatorial Africa. 28 percent of the world's coffee production of about 3.6 million tonnes comes from a wider area.

Africa is second to Asia as the most important rubber-producing continent, with Nigeria, Liberia, Zaire, Ivory Coast and the Cameroon accounting for 7 percent of the world total. Dates are the main cash crop at the Sahara oases which produce nearly 40 percent of the world's output, especially in Egypt, Algeria, the Sudan and Morocco. Vegetables, fruit, and some cotton is also grown at the oases. Cotton is grown in far larger quantities in the Nile valley of Egypt and the Sudan.

In the extremes of the continent, in South Africa and the Mediterranean coastlands, grapes, citrus fruit and temperate cereals, especially wheat and barley are all grown. The areas which are suited to such crops are but a tiny part of the whole continent, so African contribution to world output will be relatively small.

Successful livestock raising is carried out in some tropical parts and the two extremes of the continent. 9 percent of the world's sheep are found in South Africa, Ethiopia, Morocco and the Sudan; they are kept both for wool and meat. South Africa is the world's fifth most important producer of wool. Nearly 7 percent of the world's cattle are herded on the plateaus of Ethiopia, the Sudan, Tanzania, South Africa, Nigeria and Kenya. In the desert, camels provide milk as well as being beasts of burden. Goats are also herded in many semi-arid regions.

Fishing is of minor importance in Africa. South Africa alone in the continent is one of the world's 20 most important fishing nations, accounting for 2 percent of the fish

Ways of earning a living in the world's second largest continent are many and varied: 1 Fishing the river Niger, Nigeria – most of the population live by farming but a wide range of industries is developing; 2 Tea picking, Kenya – this is one of the major crops of the cooler highland areas; 3 Picking coconuts, Casamance, Senegal – the main crop here is peanuts which is one of the country's major exports

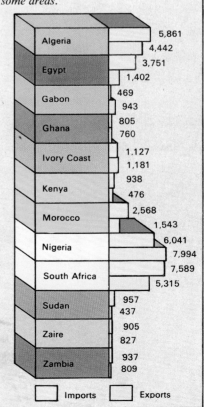

Total Imports and Exports
(1975 figures in millions of U.S. dollars)
Few African countries are large traders despite the recent discovery of oil in some areas.

	Imports	Exports
Algeria	5,861	4,442
Egypt	3,751	1,402
Gabon	469	943
Ghana	805	760
Ivory Coast	1,127	1,181
Kenya	938	476
Morocco	2,568	1,543
Nigeria	6,041	7,994
South Africa	7,589	5,315
Sudan	957	437
Zaire	905	827
Zambia	937	809

AFRICA

catch and 6 percent of whales. Recently however, both in the natural and the man-made lakes of the interior, schemes to introduce commercial fishing systematically have been started.

Much of equatorial and tropical Africa is clothed in extensive and valuable hardwood forests which have been developed to a limited extent. Where world production of hardwood is concerned, Nigeria (5 percent), Tanzania (2.5 percent), the Sudan (1.6 percent) and Ethiopia (1.6 percent) are the leading producers.

Natural Resources

Africa's mineral base differs from that of many other continents in that there are no widespread reserves of coal and iron ore. Likewise the other raw materials found widely in other parts of the world are also ill-distributed here. Colonial exploitation and lack of overseas investment may have hindered previous industrial growth, but this lack of raw materials will inevitably continue to limit traditional industrial development.

South Africa, economically the most advanced country, produces about 75 million tonnes of coal each year (3.8 percent of world output) while the rest of the continent, notably Zimbabwe-Rhodesia and Nigeria, accounts for less than half this figure.

Those few African countries which do have iron ore reserves are largely exploiting it for export. Liberia accounts for some 18 million tonnes iron content per year, South Africa 9 million, Mauritania 5 million and Angola 3 million tonnes. Thus, in total the continent produces less than 8 percent of the world's annual output; and her proven reserves are less than 3 percent of the world total.

Africa's contribution to world production of other minerals and precious stones is very variable, but her proven reserves may be conservatively estimated on account of under-exploration. She does make a leading contribution to world outputs of cobalt, vanadium, manganese and chrome, and very especially of gold and diamonds.

Only in the last two decades have the oil reserves of northern and western Africa begun to be realized. Now, the riches beneath the Sahara and the lowlands bordering the Gulf of Guinea are the subject of much

exploration and exploitation. By 1976 Nigeria had risen to eighth place in the world crude oil production tables, accounting for nearly 103 million tonnes (3.7 percent of world output); Libya 93 million tonnes and Algeria 50 million tonnes are next most important.

In all, just over 10 percent of the world's crude oil comes from Africa, the great bulk of which is exported. For the future, it is estimated that she has about 10.5 percent of known world reserves.

Africa also has about 10 percent of the world's proven natural gas reserves, although currently these are not so well developed, with less than 4 percent of the world's natural gas production coming from Algeria and Libya combined. The continent plays a more significant role in current uranium production and may contribute more in the future as she possesses over a quarter of the world's

Ore	Average Annual World Production (million tonnes)	Africa's Share (percent)	Principal African Producing Countries
bauxite	80.3	11	Guinea
chrome	7.2	37	S Africa, Zimbabwe-Rhodesia
cobalt	0.03	69	Zaire, Zambia, Morocco
copper	7.4	19	Zambia, Zaire, S Africa
diamonds	42.7 million carats	66	Zaire, S Africa, Botswana, Ghana, Namibia, Sierra Leone
gold	1 million kg	57	S Africa, Zimbabwe-Rhodesia, Ghana
lead	3.2	4	Morocco, Namibia
manganese	22.8	33	S Africa, Gabon, Ghana, Morocco
nickel	0.733	5	S Africa, Botswana, Zimbabwe-Rhodesia
silver	0.01	3	S Africa, Morocco, Zaire
tin	0.2	6	Zaire, Nigeria, S Africa
vanadium	0.02	43	S Africa, Namibia
zinc	5.4	5	Zaire, S Africa

reserves. South Africa, Nigeria and Gabon together account for 23 percent of current world production. Algeria and Madagascar have as yet untouched deposits.

Equatorial and tropical Africa have an estimated quarter of the world's HEP potential, mainly in the rivers of the Zaire Basin and East and West Africa, the Nile valley and Madagascar. Yet only a tiny fraction of this has been developed, so that Africa produces less than 3 percent of the world's total. Her main internationally famed HEP installations are at Volta Dam (Ghana), Kariba Dam (Zambia and Zimbabwe-Rhodesia), the Aswan High Dam (Egypt) and Cabora Bassa Dam (Mozambique). Of course, these and other proposed schemes can only be worthwhile when a demand for electricity is there, wherein lies part of the vicious circle ensnaring Africa's development.

African Economy

The population map of Africa shows well over 95 percent of the total area of the continent to have less than 10 persons to the km^2 (25 per sq ml). Only in limited parts – the Nile valley, the north-west coastal strip, parts of West and East Africa, around Lake Nyasa and in South Africa – are there large areas with populations in excess of 100 per km^2 (250 per sq ml).

Within these areas of high concentration, Africa has a few large cities which dominate the individual country's livelihood. The nine millionaire cities within the continent in size order are: Cairo, Alexandria, Kinshasa, Casablanca, Algiers, Lagos, Johannesburg, Addis Ababa and Cape Town.

African population is currently growing at a considerable rate. Most countries have birth rates in excess of 40 per 1,000, many in excess of 45 and some 50 per 1,000. Death rates are mainly in excess of 20 per 1,000 and sometimes higher. Such figures resemble those of parts of Asia, though there the death rates are often lower. The annual increase in each African country's population is often between 2.5 and 3.0 percent, and only rarely in excess of 3.5 percent, high figures by modern world standards.

Overall, African countries are among the world's least developed economies anywhere. Even excluding the islands and smaller mainland countries, the great majority of African countries have annual imports and exports valued at less than $500 million (contrast France and

Apart from South Africa, the continent is industrially under-developed: 1 Gold mine shaft heads, Johannesburg, S Africa – in the middle of the world's richest gold field, the country's largest city is an important manufacturing centre; 2 Ebony carver, Nigeria – local crafts are the main industry of many communities

Per Capita Income
(1974 figures in U.S. dollars)

Overall, the average earnings of Africans are the lowest of all the continental areas, being little over $300. Only South Africans earn more than $1,000.

South Africa	Algeria	Mauritius	Ivory Coast	Tunisia	Zambia	Morocco	Nigeria	Egypt	Kenya
1,146	870	612	600	596	504	370	340	251	197

the United Kingdom with 100 times and the USA with 200 times such a figure). There are however, eight countries whose annual imports and exports are each valued at more than $1,000 million.

The growth of African trade over the years 1938–'58 and 1958–'75 was as follows: imports up by 3.9 and 4.9 times respectively and exports up by 4.6 and 6.0 times respectively. But, the absolute figures show the poor performance as a whole. By 1975 imports were worth only $44,700 million and exports $40,400 million.

The exceptions to the pattern of poor development lie at the north and south extremes of the continent, plus Nigeria and the Ivory Coast. The Mediterranean countries of Africa were more advanced than those of black Africa early in the twentieth century and today some of their trading performances have been enhanced by oil development. Thus, Libya's imports rose from $47 m to $97 m to $3,554 million and her exports from $6 m to $14 m to $6,837 million in the years 1938, '58 and '75. Algeria's advance has been slightly less dramatic. Egypt, Tunisia and Morocco, all in the top eight trading nations of Africa, advanced, but more slowly.

In West Africa, Nigeria ranked as a modest trading nation before World War II, with imports and exports valued at $42 million and $47 million. Now, thanks to comparatively rapid development soon after 1945 and then, in the last decade the development of oil resources, these figures have risen to $5,041 million and $7,994 million respectively. The Ivory Coast has advanced at about the same rate but with consistently lower absolute figures.

South Africa is the trading giant of Africa, but even so is only comparable with, say, Hungary or India. Modern performance is $7,589 million imports and $5,315 million exports.

Where such figures exist, per capita incomes act as a further measure of the lack of development and lower standards of living found in the continent. Remembering that the EEC countries in 1974 had an average per capita figure of $4,000, and that in the USA the figure was $5,923, the overall African figure was $350. Many countries have no accurate measure but may be reckoned to be no higher than $100. In heavily-populated Egypt the 1974 figure was $260, Nigeria with its oil revenues and large population, $320, and Algeria with its growing oil revenues and lower population, $870. Some other countries with different resources have comparatively high average per capita incomes, such as Ivory Coast ($600), Tunisia ($596), Zambia ($504) and Morocco ($370), but this does not necessarily mean a higher overall standard of living. Again, South Africa is the exception to all African patterns. Here over the whole population, average incomes in 1974 were $1,146.

Africa's energy production and consumption figures again demon-

Trading and bartering are an essential part of African life: 1 The Kasbah, Tetúan, Morocco – the souk *is an instant tourist trap in all North African countries; 2 Street market, Ghana – a more western life-style characterizes one of the first African countries to become independent. Ghana is the world's leading cocoa producer; 3 Road-side market, Tanzania – the economy here is based on producing crops for home use*

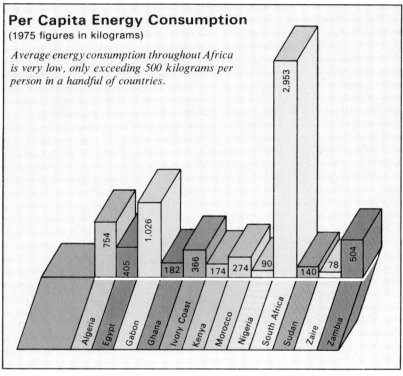

Per Capita Energy Consumption
(1975 figures in kilograms)

Average energy consumption throughout Africa is very low, only exceeding 500 kilograms per person in a handful of countries.

Algeria 754 · 405 · Egypt · Gabon 1,026 · Ghana 182 · Ivory Coast 366 · Kenya 174 · Morocco 274 · Nigeria 90 · South Africa 2,953 · Sudan 140 · Zaire 78 · Zambia 504

strate the lack of development. The following figures need to be viewed remembering the overall lack of coal, the recent discoveries of oil and the largely untapped HEP resources. In 1975 all Africa produced 456 million tonnes coal equivalent (mtce) and used 157 mtce. The continent is thus a net exporter of energy, largely due to Algeria (83 mtce produced, 13 mtce used), Libya (111 mtce produced, 3 mtce used) and Nigeria (131 mtce produced, 6 mtce used). Elsewhere, few countries consume more than 1 mtce or produce that much. South Africa is again the exception with production of 70 mtce and consumption of 84 mtce.

Energy consumption is only 393 kg/ca overall, and in many countries it is below 100. It is rising so that in the northern oil-rich countries, Algeria (754) and Libya (1,299) are among the continent's leaders. South Africa has the highest use with over 2,950 kg/ca, but even this is low by developed world standards.

In making an overall review of Africa's future prospects it is important to remember the exceptions to the rule. For instance, Africa north of the Sahara is very different from black Africa. It is part of the Arab world with its newly found oil riches.

These will bring in quick though only temporary revenues for use in western style projects. The overall standard of living may be greatly improved by new industries, changes in agricultural methods and the further development of tourism.

South Africa, with its advanced economy and white minority control, is a country apart. The national policy of racial segregation, apartheid, is widely abhorred inside Africa and elsewhere. In the coming years, it may well lead to internal problems far greater than those already experienced. Today Zimbabwe-Rhodesia has a similarly mixed population with more acute political problems, and the outside world, which has taken various initiatives to try to help in their solution, awaits the outcome.

Despite the few nations which have developed specific resources and thus gained a comparative lead over the rest, in general, black Africa is seeking advancement but seems not to know how best to go about it. Since 1963 independent countries have formed the Organisation for African Unity, with headquarters in Addis Ababa, to encourage co-operation and unity between nations and to oppose colonialism in general and European rule in South Africa. There

are now 44 member nations. All black Africa's independent countries are members of UNO. Many were former British colonies and are now members of the Commonwealth and some other countries are members of the French Community. A number have set up special trading agreements with the EEC. Still others which prefer the Socialist to the capitalist model have developed links with China, the USSR and Cuba.

Understandably, after the colonial experiences of their forefathers, modern Africans and their leaders may regard their relationships with the former imperial powers circumspectly. They may view their new alliances with non-African nations in the same light, and some even have reservations about the relationships with other African countries. A period of trust and stability is very much needed so that the development of this large continent can be accelerated soon. Whether the great human and economic potential here can be harnessed in the near future, or whether the whole continent will become embroiled in the black/white confrontations of South Africa and Zimbabwe-Rhodesia is a question which greatly occupies the developed world at the present.

African Countries

Algeria

A French possession until 1962, since when it has been an independent republic, Algeria is the second largest country in Africa, but over 90 percent of its area is part of the Sahara desert. Near the Mediterranean coast, cereal, citrus fruit and grape production are important. Forestry and herding dominate the mountains to the immediate south. Iron ore, phosphates, zinc and lead have, for a long time, been valuable minerals. Since 1957, Algeria has developed oil and natural gas fields beneath the Sahara, and these now provide over 90 percent of foreign earnings. France and other EEC countries are her major trading partners.

Angola

A Portuguese overseas territory until 1975, Angola is now an independent peoples' republic in south-west Africa. Much of the land is very dry and infertile. Most of the population live by subsistence farming, growing maize, peanuts or rice. Coffee, cotton and palms are grown commercially in some parts. There is valuable oyster fishing off the south coast. Coffee, maize, oysters and palm oil are all exported. Diamonds and iron ore have been worked and exported for many years: more recently crude oil extraction and exporting has been started. The chief imports are textiles, foodstuffs and machinery.

Benin

Formerly called Dahomey, Benin was part of French West Africa until 1960, since when it has been an independent republic. It is a small country bordering the Gulf of Guinea. Most of the population live off the land, growing maize and cassava. In the south, palms are the main crop, palm products being the country's leading exports, followed by cocoa. Coffee and cotton production have been steadily stepped up in recent years. Small quantities of chromite, gold and iron ore are mined.

Botswana

This independent, landlocked republic in southern Africa was known as the Bechuanaland protectorate until 1966. It is a member of the Commonwealth. Much of the country is an arid tableland. Most of the Bantu population live by herding cattle and dairying. Crop farming is unreliable on account of the variable rainfall, though it is more reliable where boreholes have been drilled. Animal products are the chief exports but diamonds, copper and nickel exports are rapidly rising. Machinery and metal products, foodstuffs and fuel oils are the main imports. Botswana is a member of the South African Customs Union and conducts most of her trade with countries in that group and the United Kingdom.

Burundi

Since 1962, the southern part of the former United Nations Trust Territory of Rwanda-Burundi has been the independent republic of Burundi. It is a small, densely-peopled, landlocked country on the highland margins of the East African Plateau. Subsistence agriculture is most important, with beans, cassava, maize, sweet potatoes and peanuts being among the major crops. Cattle are also kept. Coffee is grown for export, as is cotton, but the latter is being superseded by tea. Minerals are little developed though large reserves of nickel have been proved. Textiles, foodstuffs and vehicles are the major imports. The EEC countries and the USA are her main trading partners.

Cameroon

From 1919 till the early 1960s, France and the United Kingdom controlled two trusteeship territories in western Africa. Since then most of these two areas have been the federal republic of the Cameroon. Most of the people live by subsistence farming. The main cash crops are cocoa, coffee and bananas. Cotton and rubber are of lesser importance. Bauxite is the only exploited mineral and is mainly exported. A range of hardwoods is felled and exported as well. The EEC countries, especially France, and the USA are her main trading partners.

Cape Verde

Formerly a Portuguese overseas territory, these fifteen islands off the west coast of Africa have been independent since 1975. Eventually, union with Guinea-Bissau, another former Portuguese territory on the mainland, is a distinct possibility. The islands are mountainous and volcanic. Coffee, bananas and cassava are grown in the valleys and a range of livestock is kept.

Central African Empire

In 1960 this former part of French Equatorial Africa, known as Ubangi Shari, became the landlocked, independent Central African Republic, and in 1976 it changed its name in part. It is mainly a savanna land with forests in the south. Most of the people live by subsistence farming, with maize, peanuts and sorghum as the main crops. Cotton and coffee are the leading export produce. Diamonds and gold are also mined and exported.

Chad

Part of French Equatorial Africa until 1960, since when it has been an independent, landlocked country, Chad is desert land in the north and savanna land in the south. It has one of the lowest population densities in all Africa. In the north, nomadic herdsmen roam the dry lands with their animals. Farther south, subsistence farming and commercial cotton, peanut and sugar cane growing are the major activities. Cotton and meats are the only exports; fuel oils, fibres and machinery are the main imports.

Comoro Islands

Four islands in the Mozambique Channel formed the French overseas

1 Viergen de las Nieves, Las Palmas, Canary Islands – although belonging to Spain, this group of North Atlantic islands is only 96 km (60 ml) from Africa; 2 Harar, Ethiopia – this ancient walled city is the country's chief Islamic centre; 3 Musicians, Brikama, The Gambia – tourism is being developed to broaden the one-crop economy based on peanuts

1 △

2 △

3 ▽

territory of the Comoro Islands from 1960 to 1976. Then, three became the independent country of the Comoro Islands and the other, Mayotte, became an overseas department of France. A range of commercial crops are planted in small areas: copra, sisal, vanilla, perfume plants and coffee are most important. Subsistence farming centres on cassava, sweet potatoes and other vegetables, but much foodstuff has to be imported. France is her main trading partner.

Congo

Formerly part of French Equatorial Africa, under the name of the Middle Congo, the republic became independent in 1960 and is now a member of the French Community. The country sits astride the equator and is largely clothed in equatorial rain forest. Most of the population live near the River Zaire or the coast. Subsistence farming is the main activity. A little lead, zinc and gold are mined and exported. Timber, palm products and peanuts are also exported. Crude oil was discovered in 1969 and production is now rising.

Djibouti

Until 1977, The Afars and Issas was a French overseas territory. Since then, newly named, it has been an independent republic. Lying on the Gulf of Aden in East Africa, the land is mainly a stony desert. Most of the population are nomadic, herding goats, sheep and camels. Some market gardening is found around the main towns and at the Ambouli Oasis. A few minerals have been proved, but none has been developed. Fishing for pearls, sponges and shellfish is conducted in the coastal waters. Foodstuffs and fuel oils are the main imports, hides and cattle the main exports.

Egypt

The Arab republic of Egypt occupies the extreme north-east corner of Africa, and extends into Asia. It is mainly a desert land, but its present population centres and ancient civilizations which developed over 5,000 years ago and lasted for nearly 2,500 years centred around the Nile and its delta. Today such monuments to this golden age may be seen in the Pyramids, the Sphinx and the Temple of Abu Simbel. In recent years Egypt has been one of the main Arab states in conflict with Israel, which its borders. Territory formally recognized as Egyptian is still occupied by Israelis. Yet a new mood of cautious

1 Fishing boats, Monrovia, Liberia – the 'home' port for the world's biggest merchant navy operating under flags of convenience was opened in 1948; 2 Gebel Togo, Aswan, Egypt – a Nubian village which has remained unchanged for centuries; 3 Flocks at Colomb-Béchar, Algeria – the oasis town of Béchar, in the Atlas foothills, is known for its date palms

coexistence is growing up between the two countries, following the signing of a peace treaty in 1979.

For home consumption wheat, maize and millet are the main crops. Cotton, citrus fruit, potatoes, rice and sugar cane are grown for export. The Aswan High Dam in the south has revolutionized irrigation control and provides hydro-electricity for industry and the urban areas generally. Textiles, chemicals, foodstuffs and cement production are the major industries. Leading minerals are iron ore, phosphates and salt: crude oil production is rising again following the regaining of the Sinai field from Israel. The Suez Canal, a major international waterway for conventional shipping, not supertankers, crosses Egypt from the Red Sea to the Mediterranean. Since reopening in 1975, after eight years of closure, following the Arab/Israeli War, it has provided valuable foreign revenue in dues, and is now being developed as a tax-free industrial zone.

Equatorial Guinea

Since 1968 the mainland area of Rio Muni, the Corisco Islands and Fernando Póo have been independent. Previously a Spanish colony, they now rely economically upon Spain, the USSR and Cuba. Hardwoods from the rain forests together with cocoa and coffee are the main exports, although political uncertainties since independence have led to a lack of confidence in the economy so that production and exports have fluctuated greatly.

Ethiopia

Formerly known as Abyssinia, Ethiopia has a very long and legendary history. Until 1975 it was a kingdom ruled by a house said to be descendants of King Solomon and the Queen of Sheba. Since then it has had a series of military governments. It is an upland country and most people live on the central tableland. Coffee, sugar cane, maize, barley and tobacco are among the main crops. Sheep and cattle are raised. Food processing and the textiles industries are being steadily developed. Coffee is the major export, foodstuffs, machinery and fuel oils the main imports. The USA, Italy, West Germany and Japan are her main trading partners.

Gabon

Now a member of the French Community, the independent republic of Gabon was formerly part of French Equatorial Africa. Lying close to the equator in West Africa the land is mainly clothed in dense rain forest. Subsistence farming and a little coffee, cocoa and peanuts grown for export are important activities. Mahogany and okoumé are valuable woods felled and exported. Iron ore, manganese, uranium and crude oil are all produced, but overall development is slow. Principal trading partners are the USA and members of the EEC.

African Countries

Gambia

Formerly a British colony, since 1970 this narrow strip of land stretching along either bank of the Gambia River in West Africa, has been an independent republic within the Commonwealth. The economy balances on the growing and exporting of peanuts and their products. Rice production for home consumption is increasing. Foodstuffs, textiles, machinery and fuel oils are the main imports. The United Kingdom and USA are her main trading partners.

Ghana

Formerly known as the Gold Coast, a British colony, and the trusteeship territory of Togoland, Ghana was one of the first African countries to achieve independence in 1957. Predominantly agricultural, it is the world's leading producer and exporter of cocoa. Coffee and rubber production are being increased. Maize, rice, cassava and yams are the main foods grown for home consumption. Gold,

1 Camel handler, Nabeul, Tunisia – these long-suffering camels remain the desert lands' most useful animal; 2 Nairobi, Kenya – the administrative capital also attracts many visitors to the nearby National Park; 3 Fishermen's cottages, Camara de Lobos, Madeira – part of Portugal, this volcanic island group lies 640 km (400 ml) west of the coast of Africa

diamonds, manganese and bauxite are the most valuable minerals. Since independence, the world's largest man-made lake, for irrigation control and the production of HEP, has been created behind the Volta dam. Foodstuffs, fuel oils, chemicals, machinery and manufactured goods are the chief imports. Her chief trading partners are the EEC, the USA and other West African countries.

Guinea

Part of French West Africa until 1958, Guinea then became an independent republic outside the French Community. West Africa's most mountainous country, it is an important mining area. Bauxite accounts for 60 percent of exports, and iron ore and diamonds are also important. The main crops are coffee, rice, cassava, palms, bananas, pineapples and peanuts. Large herds of cattle are raised in the uplands.

Guinea-Bissau

Formerly the Portuguese overseas province of Portuguese Guinea, this Atlantic coast country has been independent since 1974. It aims to unite with the Cape Verde Islands. Subsistence farming and some cash cropping are the main activities; rice, cassava, palms and peanuts are the main crops. Inland, cattle raising is carried out on the plateau country. There are large reserves of bauxite but development has hardly begun.

Ivory Coast

Until 1960 the Ivory Coast was a part of French West Africa, but is now an independent republic. It is potentially one of the richest countries of West Africa. Coffee and cocoa are the leading crops both by production and as exports. Cotton production is rising steadily. For home consumption yams, cassava and rice are the main crops. Sheep, cattle and goats are herded in the interior. Diamonds, manganese and iron ore are major minerals. Timber is the most valuable export. Main imports are machinery, cement and fuel oils. Her chief trading partners are the EEC countries, especially France, and the USA.

Kenya

Since 1963, the former British East African colony of Kenya has been an independent republic within the Commonwealth. Sitting astride the equator, the land may be divided into two, the cooler western uplands and the hotter eastern lowlands. In the west, wheat, maize, coffee and tea are the main crops and cattle are raised. Coconuts, cotton, maize and sugar cane are important in the east. In the highest areas, forestry is significant; a range of minerals is extracted but together they add less to the economy than timber production. Tourism is a growing activity, with game parks and the highland areas being the major attractions. The United Kingdom, Japan, West Germany and the USA are her main trading partners.

Lesotho

The former British protectorate of Basutoland, a small, upland, landlocked area of southern Africa, became the independent country of Lesotho within the Commonwealth in 1966. It is primarily agricultural. Maize, wheat and sorghum are the chief crops, and sheep, goats and cattle are raised. There is a small diamond mining industry, but many of the Bantu population now work in the mines of neighbouring South Africa. Cattle, wool and mohair are the main exports; foodstuffs, fuel oils and machinery the main imports. Most trade is with the United Kingdom and other African countries.

Liberia

This is the oldest independent country in West Africa, having been established in 1822 as an American settlement for freed slaves and granted independence 25 years later. Iron ore and rubber are the most important exports, and timber, coffee and cocoa are also exported. Rice, cassava and sugar cane are grown as well. The main imports are foodstuffs, machinery and manufactured goods. Most trade is with the EEC countries and the USA.

Libya

A North African republic, Libya was established in 1951 by the United Nations from three provinces which were then under French and British control, following World War II. The land is largely desert, with a fertile coastal belt and a few oases and irrigated areas. Dates, olives, citrus fruit and cereals are the main products. Sheep and goats are the most valuable animals. Leather and food processing and other small industries have been established. More recently, Libya has become a

1 Desert patrol near Gadames, Libya – at the borders with Tunisia and Algeria, this Saharan town is an important stop-over for the camel caravans; 2 Sugar cane harvest, Mauritius – this crop is the basis of the economy, accounting for nearly all its exports; 3 Harbour, Mozambique – this country with its long coastline handles trade for neighbouring landlocked states

leading world producer of crude oil, and now has a substantial annual trade balance which is being used in part to develop agriculture and industry.

Madagascar (Malagasy)

From 1896 till 1958 this island, lying some 400 km (240 ml) off the southeast African coast, was a French colony. Since independence it has been known variously as the Democratic Republic of Malagasy or Madagascar. Agriculture is the base of the economy. Rice, millet, maize and cassava are the main food crops. Coffee, vanilla and cloves are exported, as are animal products. Chromite is the major mineral, while graphite, phosphates and mica are extracted in smaller amounts. The range of processing industries is being steadily increased. Foodstuffs, metalware and chemicals are the main imports. Most trade is with the EEC.

Malawi

This landlocked independent republic in southern Africa was the British Protectorate of Nyasaland until 1964 and is a member of the Commonwealth. It is predominantly rural and about 80 percent of foreign earnings come from agricultural exports. The most important subsistence crops are maize, millet and cassava. Tobacco, tea, cotton and peanuts are the main cash crops. The few known minerals have yet to be exploited. Major imports are foodstuffs, machinery, vehicles, fuel oils and building materials. Most trade is conducted with the United Kingdom, other EEC countries and the USA.

Mali

Until 1958 this landlocked country of the western Sahara was known as French Sudan. It then federated with Senegal to become the Mali Federation, but less than two years later became a separate republic. In the dry areas, nomadic herding is the main activity. Irrigation schemes elsewhere enable millet, peanuts, rice, maize and cotton to be grown. Iron ore, manganese and phosphates are known but are little exploited. Exports are mainly cotton, rice, peanuts and animal products; foodstuffs, machinery, fuel oil and building materials are the main imports. Most trade is with the EEC, especially France, and the USA.

Mauritania

In 1960 the French protectorate of

Mauritania became an independent republic. Its territory was expanded in 1976 when it took in part of the former Spanish Sahara. It is largely a dry desert tableland facing the Atlantic Ocean in West Africa. In the south, near the Senegal river, maize, millet and peanuts are mainly grown. Elsewhere, the population are mostly nomadic herdsmen. Iron ore and copper are both important minerals, accounting for over 90 percent of foreign earnings and giving the country a substantial balance of payments surplus. Much trade is with the EEC, especially France, and the USA.

Mauritius

This group of islands in the Indian Ocean some 800 km (500 ml) east of the Malagasy Republic, has been an independent republic within the Commonwealth since 1968. Prior to being a British colony, it had belonged to first the Dutch and then the French. The republic's economy depends heavily on the production of sugar cane which is sometimes adversely affected by tropical storms. Other crops being developed for export are tea and tobacco. Forestry is also of increasing importance. While agri-

cultural products account for nearly all exports, the country imports a wide range of foodstuffs, oil and consumer goods. Most trade is with Commonwealth countries, especially the United Kingdom, Australia and Canada as well as South Africa.

Mayotte

From 1960 till 1976 Mayotte was part of the French overseas territory of the Comoro Islands, a group of four islands in the Mozambique Channel. Since then, the others have been independent but Mayotte has become an overseas department of France. In part this separation is religion-based, since Mayotte has a predominantly Catholic population while the other islands are predominantly Moslem.

Morocco

Independent since 1956, this northwest African kingdom was previously partly a French and partly a Spanish protectorate. More recently, in 1976, the country has incorporated part of the former Spanish Sahara into its bounds. Most of the population live on the coastal lowlands, and 70 per-

cent of them live off the land. Wheat, barley, vegetables, olives and citrus fruit are the main crops. Stock raising, wine production, fishing and some forestry are also significant. Phosphates are the most valuable mineral; lead, manganese and iron ore are of lesser importance. Fruit and minerals are the main exports, manufactured goods the main imports. France and West Germany are her main trading partners.

Mozambique

This former Portuguese overseas territory has been independent since 1975. With a long coastline on the Indian Ocean, its ports serve not only its own needs but also those of the three neighbouring landlocked states of Malawi, Zimbabwe-Rhodesia and Zambia, as well as parts of South Africa. Subsistence farming is practised widely, but in the more fertile valleys and along the north coast, sugar cane, cashew nuts, cotton, copra, sisal and tea are produced for export. Africa's largest HEP scheme is located at Cabora Bassa and will provide power when completed for Mozambique and her neighbours.

African Countries

Namibia

Until World War I this dry corner in the south-west of the continent was a German colony. Since then it has been first a mandated territory and then a United Nations trusteeship territory administered by South Africa. It is now the newest independent country in the continent. Diamonds extracted from the coastal alluvial terraces are the main base of the economy. Livestock herding is widespread, crop farming being largely limited to the northern areas.

1 △

2 △

Karakul pelts (from a small sheep) are the major agricultural product. Fishing is an important coastal activity, pilchards and lobsters being valuable catches. International trade, except with South Africa, is conducted through Walvis Bay.

Niger

Since 1960 this former part of French West Africa has been an independent republic within the French Community. Landlocked, it is mainly desert and savanna land. In the driest areas nomadic herding is the main activity. Elsewhere, subsistence farming with millet, rice and maize as the main crops is important. Mineral resources include uranium, which has been developed in the last ten years, salt and tin. Peanuts, gum arabic, salt, uranium and animal products are the main exports. Most trade is with France and other EEC countries. Most trade is conducted through Niamey on the main north-south Saharan road.

Nigeria

A federal republic of West Africa and a member of the Commonwealth, Nigeria achieved independence from Britain in 1960. Its population is by far the greatest in all Africa, and the density of population the highest apart from that of some of the smaller countries and islands. The natural vegetation ranges from semi-desert in the north to mangrove swamp on the Gulf of Guinea coast in the south. While most of the population live by farming, the economy is increasingly dependent on mineral production and exports. Palm kernels, cotton, cocoa and peanuts are the main cash crops. Maize, millet, rice and cassava are of lesser importance. Nigeria is one of the few African countries to produce coal. Tin and columbite have also been mined for many years. Since the 1960s, oil and natural gas have developed to provide well over 90 percent of the country's foreign earnings. Among tropical African countries, Nigeria has the widest range of developing and expanding manufacturing industries.

The country takes its name from the river which flows from its north-west corner to the south coast. Together with its tributaries, the Niger River is the largest system in West Africa. The area to the west and south of the river, the former lands of the Yoruba peoples, is today the economic heart of the country. Here lie the Yoruba Highlands at heights between 300 m (1,000 ft) and 500 m (1,700 ft). Elsewhere heights of up to 1,200 m (4,000 ft) are reached, but the levels of development are lower in these remoter regions.

Reunion

This Indian Ocean, volcanic island, some 900 km (560 ml) east of Madagascar, is a French overseas department, and as such sends representatives to the National Assemblies in Paris. Sugar cane is the main crop and export, and feeds a number of processing factories on the island. Rum, maize, essences and tobacco are also produced. Pigs, sheep and cattle are raised. Rice and cement are the main imports. Most trade is with France and other European countries.

1 Pounding corn, Cap Vert-Tiaroye, Senegal – farming is the major occupation here; 2 Termite hill, Tsavo National Park, Kenya – Africa's famous wildlife is protected from big game hunters in such reserves; 3 Cape Town, South Africa – dominated by the flat-topped Table Mountain, the provincial capital is rightly famed for its beauty and climate

Rwanda

The former United Nations trust territory of Rwanda-Burundi divided into two independent nations in 1962. The republic of Rwanda is landlocked, small and one of the most heavily populated parts of all Africa. Most of the people live by subsistence agriculture; beans, cassava, maize and sorghum being among the leading staple food crops. Coffee, tea, cotton and pyrethrum are produced as cash crops. A little tin ore is mined and exported.

St Helena

This small volcanic island 1,900 km (1,200 ml) west of the African mainland is a British colony. A number of other islands are associated with it, particularly Ascension Island 1,100 km (700 ml) to the north-west and Tristan da Cunha 2,400 km (1,500 ml) to the south-south-west. Only small areas are cultivated, flax being the main product feeding a small lace-making industry. Vegetables and fruit are grown for local consumption. Each island group is very remote. At one time they were important centres for shipping and wireless communications.

Sao Tome and Principe Islands

Lying some 200 km (130 ml) off the coast of West Africa in the Gulf of Guinea, these islands were formerly a Portuguese overseas territory. Since 1975 they have been a democratic republic. The volcanic soils are very fertile and much land is used for producing cocoa, copra, coconuts, coffee, bananas and palm oil. As well as the natural labour force, migrant workers from the mainland come each year to work on the plantations. The considerable farming exports provide the base for a healthy balance of trade. Most trade is conducted with European countries which sell manufactured goods in return.

Senegal

The oldest French colony in Africa until 1958, when it became a partner with French Sudan in the independent federation of Mali, since 1960 Senegal has been a separate republic. Extensive areas are farmed, peanuts and millet being the major crops. Sheep, goats and cattle are kept in large numbers. Rich fishing grounds lie off the coast. Phosphates are currently the most important mineral produced. Recently large iron ore reserves have been discovered which may be the richest in all Africa. Peanuts, phosphates and fish are the main exports, rice, sugar, fuel oils and textiles the main imports. Most trade is conducted with the EEC countries and the USA.

Seychelles

This group of about 90 volcanic islands in the Indian Ocean some 1,600 km (1,000 ml) east of the

Kenyan coast was formerly a British colony, but since 1976 it has been an independent republic within the Commonwealth. At that time, Aldabra, Farquhar and Desroches Islands, which had previously been part of the British Indian Ocean Territories within Asia, joined the new nation. Food crop production is being stepped up, as is fishing for both home consumption and export. Copra and cinnamon bark are the main cash crops and exports. Rice, sugar, fuel oils and manufactured goods are the leading imports. Tourism is becoming increasingly important. Her main trading partners are the United Kingdom, Kenya, Australia and South Africa.

Sierra Leone

In 1961 this former British colony in West Africa became an independent member of the Commonwealth. The coastal lowlands are covered with tropical forest while the interior undulating plateau is a savanna land. Rice is the main staple food crop, cassava, maize and vegetables being of subsidiary importance. Fishing is increasing steadily but still does not provide all the home needs. Cash crops, and the main agricultural exports include cocoa beans, peanuts, coffee, ginger and palm kernels. Diamonds and bauxite are important products, accounting for over 65 percent of the country's foreign earnings. Foodstuffs, manufactured goods and fuel oils are the main imports. The United Kingdom and Japan are her main trading partners.

Somali Republic

Lying in the eastern 'horn' of Africa, this democratic republic was created as an independent country in 1960 from the former British Somaliland protectorate and the Italian trusteeship territory of Somalia. It is essentially a hot, dry country. Most of the population are nomadic herdsmen raising cattle, goats and camels. Near the main rivers of the south, cotton, sugar cane, bananas, other fruit and maize are grown. Tuna and mother of pearl are both taken from the Indian Ocean. The known reserves of iron ore, gypsum, berylium and columbite have yet to be developed. A little uranium is mined. Fruit, livestock and animal products are the main exports.

South Africa

This republic is economically the most advanced country in all Africa. Of the total population of 25.8 million, about 4 million are white. Its internal policy of separate development for the white settlers and the black natives (apartheid) led to its withdrawal from the Commonwealth in 1961. The climate of many parts of the country, both on the coast and the plateau, is particularly attractive to Europeans. Agriculture is well developed commercially, maize and wheat being the leading cereals; deciduous and citrus fruit are also important, as is pastoral farming.

Mineral production is far more significant to the overall economy. South Africa is the world's leading gold producer. Coal production is the highest for any African country; diamonds, copper, manganese, asbestos, iron ore and chrome are all mined in considerable quantities. A wide range of manufacturing industries have been developed, with food processing, heavy industry and engineering, chemicals, textiles and small industries accounting for nearly 23 percent of the national product. Now, more foreign earnings come from manufactured goods than either mineral or agricultural exports. Imports are mainly machinery, vehicles, manufactured goods and fuel oils, plus chemicals. EEC countries, especially the United Kingdom and West Germany, the USA, Japan and other American countries are her main trading partners.

Sudan

The largest single country in Africa was administered jointly by the United Kingdom and Egypt until 1956, since when it has been an independent republic. The Nile and its tributaries provide the main focus of economic activity, much of the rest of the country being desert. The Sennar Dam provides water for the large irrigated area of the Gezira. Here and elsewhere in lowland Sudan, long staple cotton is the major crop. Besides cotton, peanuts, oil seed and gum arabic are the main exports. Fertilizers, machinery, sugar and

fabrics are the main imports. China, Italy and West Germany take 40 percent of Sudanese exports. The United Kingdom and the USA are the leading sources of imports.

Swaziland

Since 1968, this landlocked country of southern Africa has been an independent member of the Commonwealth. While the majority of Swazis live by subsistence agriculture, the national economy is broadly and firmly based on a range of agricultural products and minerals. Sugar, and wood pulp from the forested mountains are the main exports. Other valuable crops are citrus fruit, rice, cotton, maize and sorghum. Cattle and goats are both widely kept. Iron ore and asbestos are the most important minerals. Swaziland is joined in a customs union with South Africa. It currently enjoys an annual balance of payments surplus with the rest of the world.

Tanzania

The East African mainland country of Tanganyika became independent in 1961, as did the nearby islands of Zanzibar and Pemba in 1963. Together they now form the United Republic of Tanzania. The mainland agricultural economy is currently being diversified. Cotton is the major crop, sisal is of declining importance and the production of other crops like citrus fruit, cocoa, maize and

Pyramids, Egypt – one of the ancient world's great civilizations, Egypt under the Pharaohs employed vast manpower and primitive tools to create architectural wonders such as the tomb of Tutankhamen, the huge temples at Luxor and Karnak and, above all, the magnificent pyramids at Gizeh, 2650–2550 BC, one of the wonders of the ancient world

nuts is being increased. Cattle ranching and dairying are also being developed. Hardwoods are of increasing export importance. Zanzibar and Pemba are the major world source of cloves. Mineral production in Tanzania is dominated by diamonds. Foodstuffs and manufactured goods form the bulk of the country's imports. The United Kingdom, other EEC countries, Japan and China are her main trading partners.

Togo

Since 1960, this former West African United Nations trusteeship territory has been an independent republic within the French Community. The shape of the country is long and narrow with its main axis lying north-south. The coastal strip is low and swampy while the interior is an undulating plateau region. Maize, yams and cassava are the main subsistence crops. Coffee, cocoa, palm products, peanuts and cotton are the main cash crops. Since independence, mining activity has increased. Phosphates are the most important product; reserves of bauxite and iron ore

African Countries

have yet to be exploited on a large scale. Phosphates, coffee and cocoa account for nearly 90 percent of the foreign earnings. Most trade is with EEC countries.

Tunisia

Lying between Algeria and Libya on the north coast of Africa, this independent Arab-speaking republic was a French protectorate from 1881 till 1956. A wide range of crops are produced for both home consumption and export, with citrus fruit, olives, cereals, grapes and dates all being important. Sheep, cattle and goats are the most widely kept animals. Phosphates are the leading mineral, with iron ore, lead and zinc of lesser importance. Tourism is growing. France and the USA are her main trading partners.

Uganda

This landlocked East African independent republic is a member of the Commonwealth. It is mainly a savanna land, set high up on the East African Plateau. Cotton and coffee are the leading commercial crops and exports. Tea, tobacco, peanuts and maize are of lesser importance. Copper is the most valu-

able mineral in terms of both output and exports. Most trade is conducted with the United Kingdom, the USA, Japan and West Germany.

Independent Uganda was controlled by a civil government for more than eight years. Then, in 1971, the eight year rule of General Amin began. Only in early 1979 was this ended with the aid of troops from neighbouring Tanzania.

Upper Volta

Formerly part of French West Africa, Upper Volta has been an independent republic since 1960. Subsistence and livestock farming are the main activities of this landlocked country. Cattle, sheep and goats are most numerous animals. Maize, sorghum, millet and peanuts are the main crops. Some cotton is grown for export. Mineral exploitation is limited by remoteness, manganese being the leading product. Her main trading partners lie in the EEC, especially France, and the USA.

Zaire

This central African republic was a large Belgian colony until 1960, called the Belgian Congo. It then became independent as Congo (Kinshasa) and changed its name to Zaire in 1972. The country centres on the extensive equatorial forests of the Congo Basin and has a short Atlantic

coastline. Subsistence and commercial farming have both declined in recent years and are now subject to a 'revival programme'. Palm products, coffee, rubber, tea and timber are the main exports from the land. However, the national economy is based more on mining, mainly in the southern area of Shaba, with copper, zinc, gold and cobalt being the leading products. Copper alone accounts for 65 percent of the foreign earnings.

Zambia

Formerly known as Northern Rhodesia, this independent republic was established in 1964. It is a member of the Commonwealth. The national economy of this landlocked country rests heavily on the production of copper ore and products. Other minerals of lesser importance are zinc, cobalt and lead, as well as coal. The country also rates highly in the African development of HEP. Over 70 percent of the population live off the land, but their contribution to the national product is only 10 percent. Maize, tobacco, cotton and peanuts are the principal products. Cattle, sheep and goats are found over a wide area. Copper, copper products and tobacco are the main exports; machinery, vehicles, fuel oils, chemicals and manufactured goods the main imports. EEC and EFTA countries as well as the USA are her main trading partners.

Zimbabwe–Rhodesia

Formerly known as Southern Rhodesia, this landlocked country of southern Africa was once part of the British Empire and then Commonwealth. Currently about 277,000 of the population are white and 6,220,000 black. In 1965 its white minority government made a unilateral declaration of independence, thus effectively severing relations with the United Kingdom and the Commonwealth. Since that time, there have been various initiatives by the UK, the USA and others trying to restore constitutional government, based on some form of revised system of franchise introducing majority rule. Early in 1979 elections were held to establish the first ever parliament with a majority of black members. It remains to be seen if this settlement will be successful.

Among the leading crops grown are maize, tobacco, sugar, cotton, oranges and coffee, but since 1965 when Rhodesian international trade was made subject to United Nations sanctions, production figures have been unpublished.

1 Looking down into Ngorongoro Crater, Tanzania – one of Africa's most memorable landscapes; 2 Pigmy woman and child, Uganda – most Ugandans are of the Bantu tribe and speak Swahili; 3 Beach scene, Seychelles – a profitable tourist industry

COUNTRY REFERENCE: AFRICA

African Countries	Political Status	State Capital	Area km²	Area sq ml	Population	Population Density per km²	Population Density per sq ml	Births per Thousand Persons	Deaths per Thousand Persons	Mean Annual Percentage Increase in Population
Algeria	A	Alger	2,381,741	919,595	18,073,000	7.6	20	47.8	15.4	3.2
Angola	A	Luanda	1,246,700	481,353	7,214,000	5.8	15	47.2	24.5	1.8
Benin	A	Porto Novo	112,622	43,484	3,405,000	30	78	49.9	23.0	3.1
Botswana	A	Gaborone	600,372	231,805	718,000	1.2	3.1	45.6	23.0	3.4
Burundi	A	Bujumbura	27,834	10,747	4,003,000	144	372	48.0	24.7	2.0
Cameroon	A	Yaoundé	475,442	183,569	6,725,000	14	37	40.4	22.0	1.9
Cape Verde	A	Praia	4,033	1,557	314,000	78	202	29.2	8.8	2.1
Central African Empire	A	Bangui	622,984	240,535	1,923,000	3.1	8.0	43.4	22.5	2.2
Chad	A	Ndjamena	1,284,000	495,800	4,255,000	3.3	9.0	44.0	24.0	2.1
Comoro Islands	A	Moroni	2,079	803	314,000	151	391	46.6	21.7	3.1
Congo	A	Brazzaville	342,000	132,000	1,455,000	4.3	11	45.1	20.8	3.1
Djibouti	A	Djibouti	23,000	8,900	152,000	6.6	17	—	—	—
Egypt	A	Al-Qahirah	1,002,000	386,900	39,320,000	39	102	35.5	12.4	2.2
Equatorial Guinea	A	Malabo	28,051	10,830	325,000	12	30	36.8	19.7	1.7
Ethiopia	A	Addis Ababa	1,221,900	471,778	29,775,000	24	63	49.4	25.8	2.5
Gabon	A	Libreville	267,667	103,347	537,000	2.0	5.2	32.2	22.2	1.0
Gambia	A	Banjul	11,295	4,361	559,000	49	128	43.3	24.1	2.5
Ghana	A	Accra	238,537	92,100	10,905,000	46	118	48.9	21.9	2.7
Guinea	A	Conakry	245,857	94,926	4,695,000	19	49	46.6	22.9	2.4
Guinea-Bissau	A	Bissau	36,125	13,948	539,000	15	39	40.1	25.1	1.5
Ivory Coast	A	Abidjan	322,463	124,504	7,095,000	22	57	45.6	20.6	2.5
Kenya	A	Nairobi	582,644	224,960	14,545,000	25	65	48.7	16.0	3.6
Lesotho	A	Maseru	30,355	11,720	1,622,000	53	138	39.0	19.7	2.2
Liberia	A	Monrovia	111,369	43,000	1,810,000	16	42	49.8	20.9	2.3
Libya	A	Tarabulus	1,759,540	679,362	2,678,000	1.5	4.0	45.0	14.7	4.2
Madagascar	A	Antananarivo	587,041	226,658	8,399,000	14	37	46.0	25.0	1.5
Malawi	A	Lilongwe	118,484	45,747	5,385,000	45	118	50.5	26.5	2.5
Mali	A	Bamako	1,239,710	478,655	6,050,000	4.9	13	50.1	25.9	2.5
Mauritania	A	Nouakchott	1,030,700	397,950	1,484,000	1.4	3.7	44.8	24.9	2.7
Mauritius	A	Port Louis	2,045	789	901,000	441	1,142	25.1	8.1	1.0
Mayotte	C	Dzaoudzi	373	144	43,000	115	299	46.4	21.5	3.0
Morocco	A	Rabat	446,550	172,415	18,595,000	42	108	46.2	15.7	—
Mozambique	A	Maputo	783,763	303,771	9,745,000	12	32	43.1	20.1	2.3
Namibia	C	Windhoek	823,168	317,827	910,000	1.1	3.0	45.0	16.7	2.3
Niger	A	Niamey	1,267,000	489,200	4,925,000	3.9	10	52.2	25.5	2.7
Nigeria	A	Lagos	923,768	356,669	66,190,000	72	186	49.3	22.7	2.7
Reunion	C	Saint-Denis	2,510	969	525,000	209	542	28.1	7.1	2.4
Rwanda	A	Kigali	26,338	10,169	4,421,000	168	435	50.0	23.6	2.9
St Helena	C	Jamestown	419	162	8,000	19	49	24.9	8.1	—
Sao Tome & Principe Islands	A	Sao Tome	964	372	83,000	86	223	45.0	11.2	1.8
Senegal	A	Dakar	196,722	75,955	5,295,000	27	70	55.4	23.9	2.4
Seychelles	A	Victoria	404	156	61,000	136	352	32.8	8.8	2.8
Sierra Leone	A	Freetown	71,740	27,699	3,252,000	45	117	44.7	20.7	1.5
Somali Republic	A	Mogadisho	637,657	246,201	3,391,000	5.3	14	47.2	21.7	2.6
South Africa	A	Pretoria & Cape Town	1,222,161	471,879	27,061,000	22	57	42.9	15.5	2.6
Sudan	A	Al-Khurtum	2,505,813	967,500	16,726,000	6.7	17	47.8	17.5	2.5
Swaziland	A	Mbabane	17,366	6,705	515,000	30	77	49.0	21.8	3.1
Tanzania	A	Dar-es-Salaam	945,087	364,900	16,154,000	17	44	47.0	22.0	2.7
Togo	A	Lome	56,000	21,600	2,366,000	42	110	50.6	23.3	2.6
Tunisia	A	Tunis	164,150	63,379	5,875,000	36	93	33.9	13.8	2.4
Uganda	A	Kampala	256,886	91,076	12,521,000	53	137	45.2	15.9	3.3
Upper Volta	A	Ouagadougou	274,200	105,800	6,376,000	23	60	48.5	25.8	2.3
Zaire	A	Kinshasa	2,345,409	905,567	26,705,000	11	29	45.2	20.5	2.8
Zambia	A	Lusaka	752,614	290,586	5,406,000	7.2	19	51.5	20.3	3.3
Zimbabwe-Rhodesia	A/C	Salisbury	390,580	150,804	6,860,000	18	45	47.9	14.4	3.5
AFRICA TOTALS			30,336,232	11,704,988	429,164,000	14	37	—	—	—

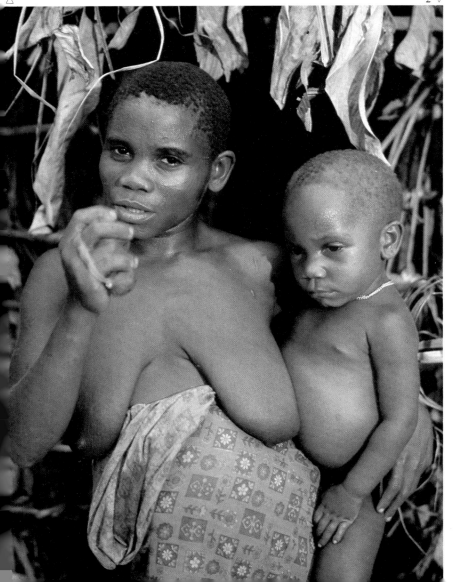

ARQUIPÉLAGO DA MADEIRA
MADEIRA ISLANDS
(Portugal)

Funchal

ISLAS CANARIAS
CANARY ISLANDS
(Spain)

Santa Cruz
de Tenerife

Las Palmas de
Gran Canaria

Western Sahara has been occupied
by Morocco and Mauritania

Tropic of Cancer

WESTERN
SAHARA

ATLANTIC

MAURITANIA

Nouakchott

CAPE VERDE

Saint-Louis

SENEGAL

Dakar

Kaolack

Banjul

GAMBIA

OCEAN

GUINEA-
BISSAU   Bissau

GUINEA

MALI

Bamako

UPPER VOLTA

Ouagadougou

Conakry

SIERRA
LEONE

Bobo Dioulasso

Freetown

IVORY COAST

GHANA

Monrovia

LIBERIA

Kumasi

Abidjan

Accra

Cape Coast
Sekondi-Takoradi

SPAIN   Málaga

Gibraltar

Ceuta (Sp.)

Tétouan

Rabat

Casablanca

Meknès   Fès

Marrakech

MOROCCO

Equator

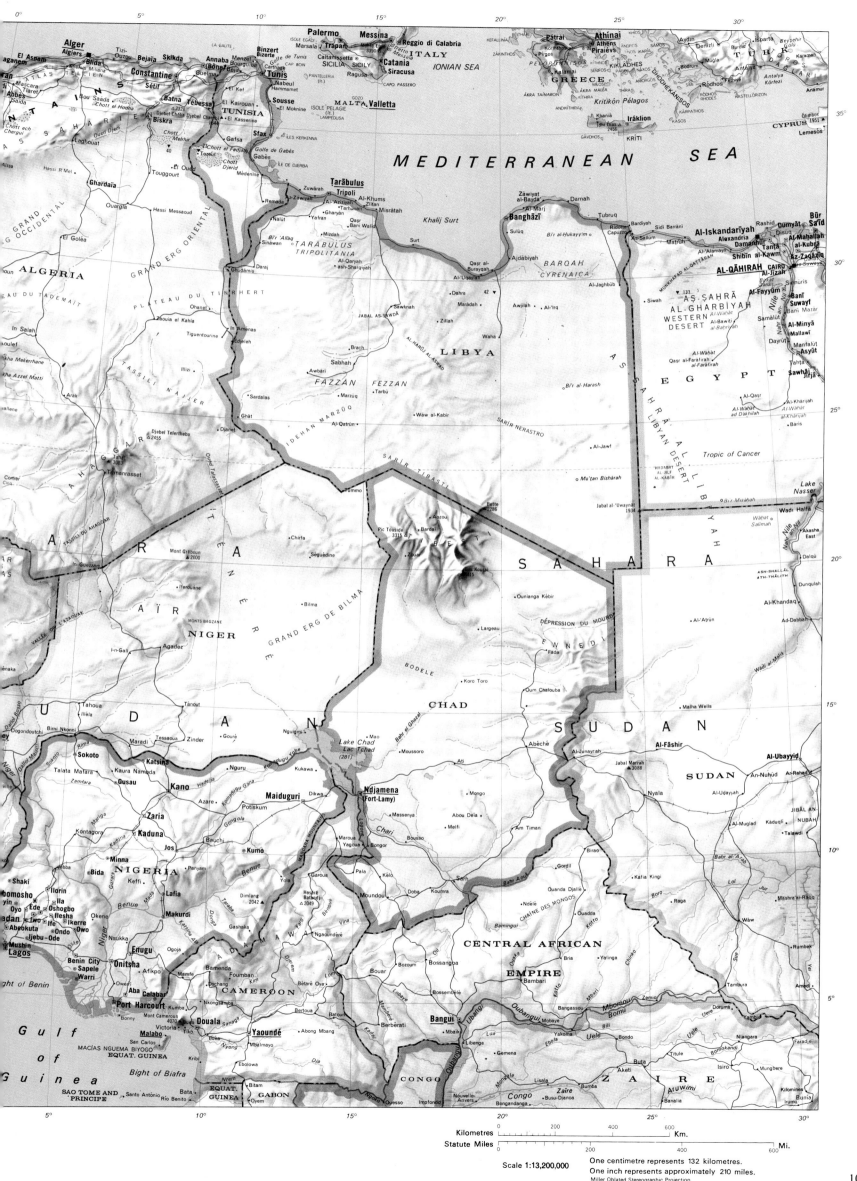

Kilometres
Statute Miles

Scale 1:13,200,000

One centimetre represents 132 kilometres.
One inch represents approximately 210 miles.
Miller Oblated Stereographic Projection

101

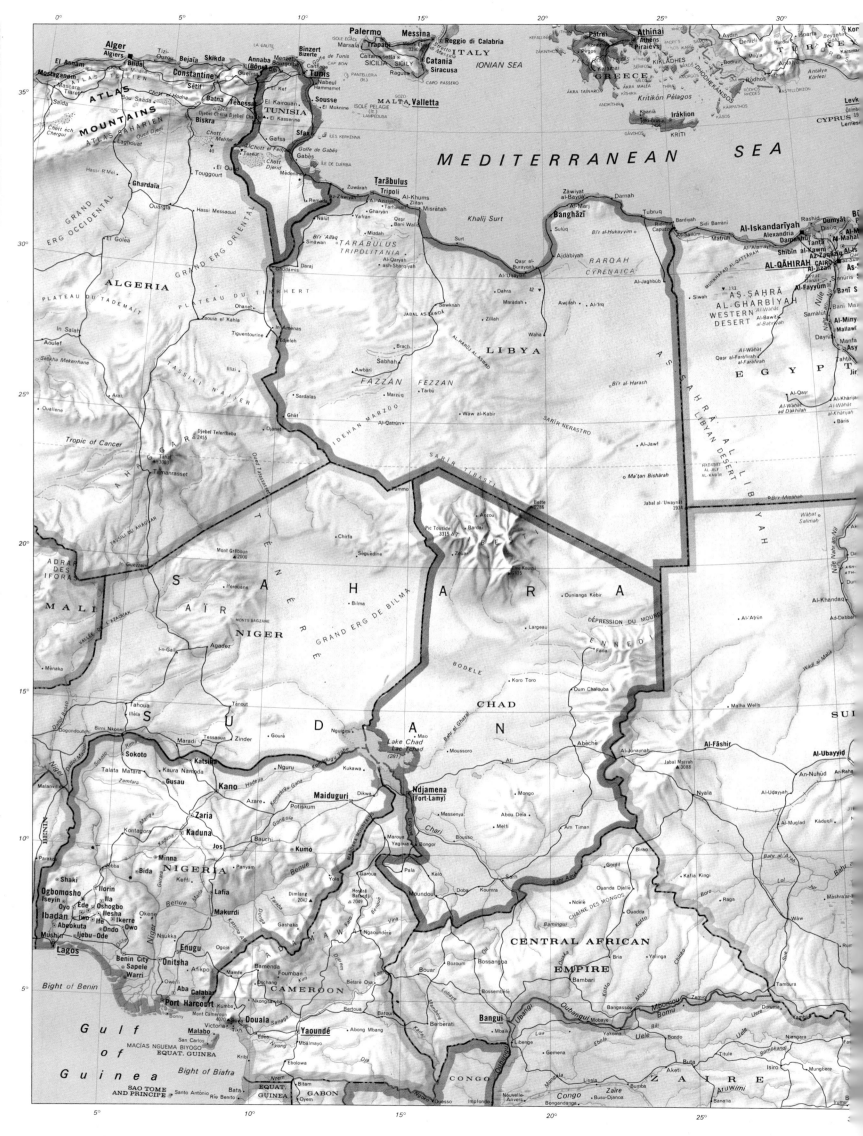

MEDITERRANEAN SEA

IONIAN SEA

ITALY

GREECE

TURKEY

CYPRUS

Palermo
Messina
Reggio di Calabria
Catania
Siracusa
SICILY

Athens
Athínai
Piraiévs

KRITI

Alger
Algiers
Blida
El Asnam
Mostaganem
Mascara
Saïda

ATLAS MOUNTAINS

ATLAS SAHARIEN

Constantine
Batna
Biskra
Sétif
Annaba
(Bône)
Guelma

TUNISIA
Tunis
Bizerte
El Kef
El Kairouan
Sousse
Sfax
Gabès
Médenine

Tarābulus
Tripoli
Al-Khums
Misrātah

MALTA Valletta

GRAND ERG OCCIDENTAL

ALGERIA

PLATEAU DU TADEMAIT

GRAND ERG ORIENTAL

Ghardaïa
El Golea
Ouargla
Hassi Messaoud
In Salah

TARABULUS
TRIPOLITANIA

PLATEAU DU TINRHERT

LIBYA

FAZZAN FEZZAN

Sabhah

BARQAH
CYRENAICA

Banghāzī
Darnah
Tubruq

EGYPT

AS-SAHRĀ
AL-GHARBĪYAH
WESTERN DESERT

Al-Iskandarīyah
Alexandria
AL-QĀHIRAH
CAIRO

Tropic of Cancer

AHAGGAR

TASSILI DU AHAGGAR

Tamanrasset

Djanet
Ghāt

SAHARA

MALI

NIGER

AÏR

Agadez

TÉNÉRÉ

GRAND ERG DE BILMA

Bilma

TIBESTI

Pic Tousside
3315

Emi Koussi
3415

ENNEDI

Fada

CHAD

SUDAN

NIGERIA

Sokoto
Katsina
Kano
Zaria
Kaduna
Jos
Maiduguri
Ndjamena
(Fort-Lamy)

Lake Chad
Lac Tchad

Abéché

Al-Fāshir

Al-Ubayyid

Nyala

BENIN

Lagos
Ibadan
Ogbomosho
Ilorin
Benin City
Onitsha
Enugu
Port Harcourt
Calabar

CAMEROON

Yaoundé
Douala

Bight of Benin

Gulf
of
Guinea

SAO TOME
AND PRINCIPE

EQUAT. GUINEA

GABON

CONGO

CENTRAL AFRICAN
EMPIRE

Bangui

ZAIRE

Congo

102

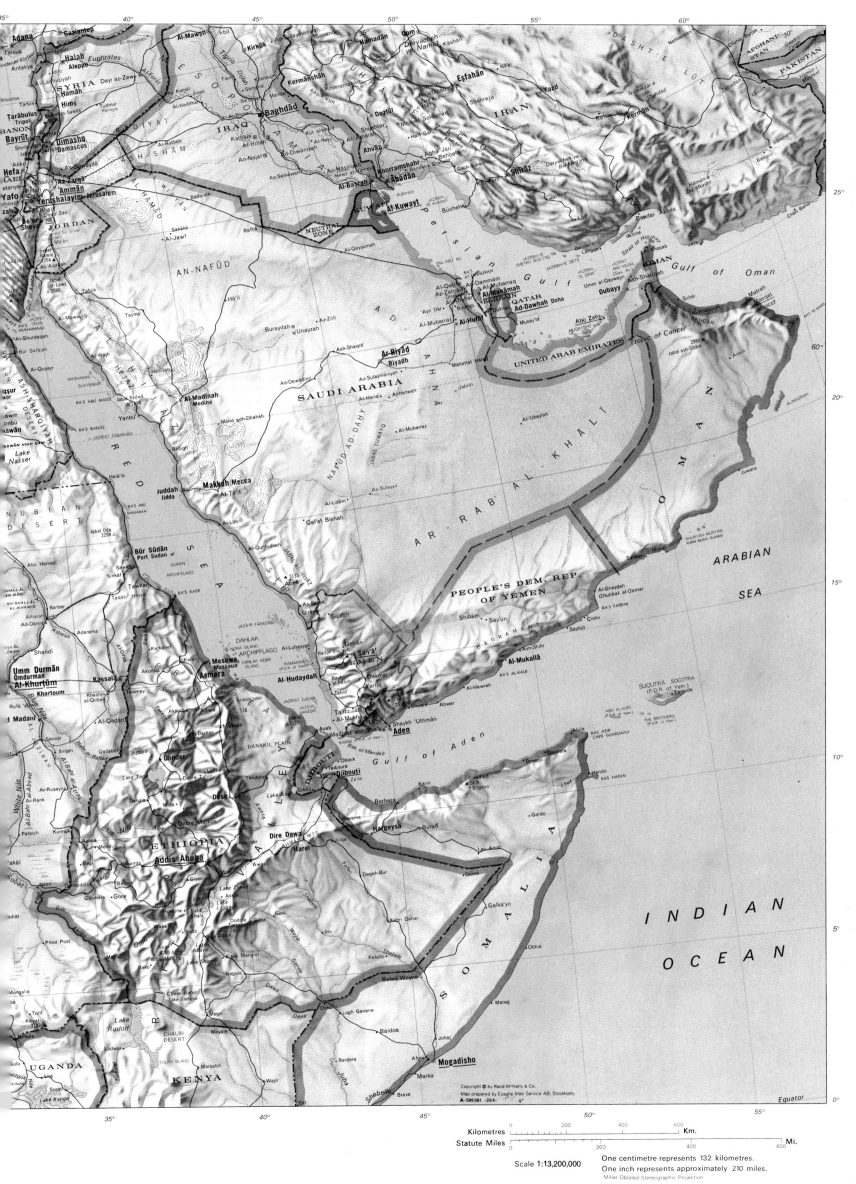

Kilometres |____|____|____|____| Km.
        0   200   400   600
Statute Miles |____|____|____|____| Mi.
        0   200   400   600

Scale 1:13,200,000

Copyright © by Rand McNally & Co.
Map prepared by Esselte Map Service AB, Stockholm.
A-589391 -264- -9"

One centimetre represents 132 kilometres.
One inch represents approximately 210 miles.
Miller Oblated Stereographic Projection

103

SAO TOME AND
PRINCIPE

PRINCIPE Santo Antônio
SÃO TOMÉ • São Tomé

PAGALU
(Equat. Gui.)

CAP LOPEZ

Port-Gentil

GABON

Libreville

EQUATORIAL
GUINEA

CAMEROON

ZAIRE

Kinshasa
(Léopoldville)

Brazzaville

Pointe-Noire

CABINDA
(Angola)

Boma
Matadi

Luanda

ANGOLA

A T L A N T I C

O C E A N

Lobito
Benguela
Huambo
(Nova Lisboa)

Moçâmedes
Porto Alexandre

CAPE FRIA

The United Nations declared an end to the mandate
of South Africa over Namibia in October, 1966.
Administration of the territory by South Africa
is not recognized by the United Nations.

OVAMBOLAND

NAMIBIA

KAOKOVELD

DAMARALAND

Swakopmund
Walvisbaai
Walvis Bay
(S. Afr.)

Windhoek

Tropic of Capricorn

HOLLAM'S BIRD
ISLAND
(S. Afr.)

(S. Afr. Admin.)

GREAT NAMALAND

Lüderitz

KINGDOM OF LESOTHO

Kinshasa

Kikwit

Kananga
(Luluabourg)

Mbuji-Mayi
(Bakwanga)

KATANGA PLATEAU

Kamina

Kolwezi
Likasi
(Jadotville)
Lubumbashi
(Elisabethville)

BAROTSELAND

KALAHARI

DESERT

BOTSWANA

Lake Ngami
Lake Xau

Okavango
Swamp

CAPRIVI STRIP

Livingstone
VICTORIA
FALLS
Wankie

ZAMBIA

Lusaka

Kabwe
(Broken Hill)

Chingola
Kitwe
Luanshya

Mufulira
Ndola

ZIMBABWE
RHODESIA

Bulawayo

Gwelo

Gaborone

Pretoria

JOHANNESBURG
Krugersdorp
Germiston Benoni
Vereeniging
Potchefstroom
Klerksdorp

SWAZILAND
(Lourenço Marques)

Mbabane

Kroonstad

Welkom

Virginia

Kimberley

Bloemfontein

LESOTHO

Maseru

SOUTH
AFRICA

Pietersburg

Pietermaritzb
Durban

GREAT KARROO
LITTLE KARROO

East London
Oos-Londen

Queenstown

Port Elizabeth

Cape Town
Kaapstad
Stellenbosch

CAPE OF GOOD HOPE

CAPE AGULHAS

RWANDA

BURUNDI

Bujumbura

Kigali

Bukavu

Lake
Tanganyika

Kalemi
(Albertville)

Kisangani
(Stanleyville)

Congo

Zaire

ZAIRE

Mbandaka
(Coquilhatville)

Kasai

Lac
Mai-Ndombe

Kasai

Lake
Kariba
KARIBA DAM

Zambezi

104

INDIAN OCEAN

Equator

SOMALIA

KENYA
Nairobi

Mombasa

Tanga
Zanzibar
Dar-es-Salaam

TANZANIA

MOZAMBIQUE

Beira

Blantyre

Lake Nyasa

MALAWI

SEYCHELLES
Victoria

AMIRANTE ISLANDS
(Sey.)

ALDABRA ISLANDS
(Sey.)

COMOROS
Moroni

Diégo-Suarez

MADAGASCAR

Majunga

Antananarivo

Tamatave

Antsirabe

Fianarantsoa

Tuléar

Fort-Dauphin

Port Louis
MAURITIUS
Saint-Denis
RÉUNION

MASCARENE
ISLANDS

Tropic of Capricorn

INDIAN OCEAN

Rhodesia unilaterally
declared its independence
from the United Kingdom
on November 11, 1965.

Copyright © by Rand McNally & Co.
Map prepared by Esselte Map Service AB, Stockholm
A-569200-264

Kilometres
Km.
Statute Miles
Mi.
Scale 1:13,200,000

One centimetre represents 132 kilometres.
One inch represents approximately 210 miles.
Miller Oblated Stereographic Projection

105

OCEANIA

Australia, New Zealand, Papua New Guinea and a number of island countries scattered over the south and central Pacific Ocean comprise Oceania. Together, the three named countries make up nearly 99 percent of the total land area and contain nearly 92 percent of the total population. Australia alone has over 90 percent of the land area and nearly two-thirds of the total population.

The principal Pacific islands and island groups within Oceania may be regarded in three areas, Melanesia, Micronesia and Polynesia. Occupy-ing the smallest area, Melanesia lies closest to Australia. It extends north-west to south-east from New Guinea to the Solomon Islands, New Caledonia, New Hebrides and Fiji. Melanesia means the black isles, and these are inhabited by dark-skinned peoples with short frizzy hair.

Micronesia, meaning the little isles, contains no islands as large as the main ones of Melanesia. Farther to the north, it covers a larger area of ocean. Lying more west-east, it extends from the Caroline Islands and Guam in the west to the Gilbert Islands in the east. Micronesian peoples have a dark brown skin and long straight black hair.

Polynesia covers the largest area of the three, extending from 25°N to 40°S and from 160°E to 100°W. Some of its islands are associated politically with either the USA or Chile and are described in the appropriate continental sections. Polynesians are generally tall with light brown skin and black hair.

Mainly because of Oceania's fragmented nature it is difficult to identify any unifying character. The islands comprise such a small part of the whole and, for all their wide variety of longitudinal and climatic positions, have mainly simple economies. In contrast, the largest land masses had strong ties with the United Kingdom for a long time. Although Australia and New Zealand are still members of the Commonwealth, their geographical remoteness, Britain's reorientated position viz-a-viz Europe and the Common Market, and the development of new resources and markets around the Pacific mean that these two countries are now reducing the proportion of their trade conducted with Europe and increasing that conducted elsewhere.

Australian Physical Profile

World Location and Size

Australia extends through nearly 3,700 km (2,300 ml) north to south, from Cape York in Queensland to South-East Cape in Tasmania. Its west-east distance is similar from the Western Australia coast at 113°E near Carnarvon to the Pacific margins of Queensland and New South Wales at nearly 154°E. Situated entirely in the Southern Hemisphere, it straddles the Tropic of Capricorn.

Landscape

For the most part the country is a vast undulating plateau. The great exceptions are: the eastern mountains extending from Cape York in the north to Victoria in the south, which are rarely more than 160 km (100 ml) inland from the coast and reach 2,230 m (7,316 ft) in Mount Kosciusko, New South Wales; the lowland area of the Central Basin extending from eastern South Australia to the Gulf of Carpentaria; and the plains which are found around most of the coast, wide in some parts like the central southern area and narrow in the extreme south-east.

Water resources are a great problem in much of Australia whose rivers fall into two main types. Many comparatively short rivers flow toward the east coast from the divide of the Eastern Highlands, and a few in the north and the south-west are reliable in their flow. Also, parts of the interior are crossed by major river systems of which the Murray and its tributaries is the largest example. These rivers have a large discharge in their headwaters but lose much of this as they flow westward across the drier interior lands of the Central Basin. Parts of this area are drained by rivers which dry up in the hot season and/or only

Opposite: Expressways near the harbour, Sydney, N S W, Australia

reach lakes whose surface areas vary greatly throughout the year.

A distinctive water feature of Australia is the series of artesian basins. In these, rainfall in the surrounding areas percolates underground and is then brought back to the surface through man-made boreholes. The Great Artesian Basin underlies much of western Queensland, north-east South Australia and north-west New South Wales, extending for 1,554,000 km² (600,000 sq ml). Farther south the Murray River Basin occupies a smaller area. Western Australia also has four smaller basins around its coastal margins.

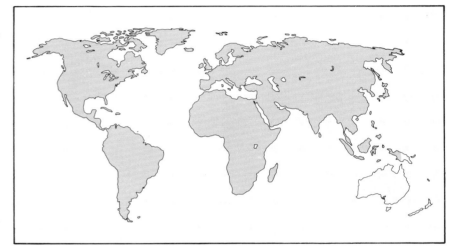

Climatic Background

There are three main groups of climate present in Australia. Only the temperate humid climate is at all attractive to white settlers who are found only in limited parts of the country. Nowhere in the temperate areas does the average temperature of the coldest winter month, July, fall below freezing, and in summer the averages rise above 18°C (64°F), reaching above 22°C (72°F). The extreme south-west of Western Australia has a Mediterranean type of climate with summer temperatures reaching the higher levels and a marked lack of summer rain.

Farther east, in southern South Australia and parts of western Vic-toria, similar summer temperatures are experienced and the rainfall, mainly in the winter, is greater. Still in the temperate group, the east coast climate, from Tasmania to the central Queensland area, shows more even distribution of rainfall in the south to a summer maximum north of the tropic. In the south, the highest monthly average temperatures are below 20°C (68°F) but in the north they are well above 22°C (72°F).

The northern coastal areas of the country experience tropical climates in which even the coolest month has an average temperature above 18°C (64°F) and there is a marked summer maximum in the rainfall, totals exceeding 2,000 mm (80 in) in places.

The great heartland of Australia,

Rain forest village, Malekula, New Hebrides – like many of the Pacific islands, this group is of volcanic origins. Most places have over 2,250 mm (90 in) of rain a year, with high temperatures giving humid conditions

from the Indian Ocean in the west, eastward to the interior slopes of the Highlands of the Pacific bordering states, is an area of marked rainfall deficiency with higher average temperatures than elsewhere in the continent. In the most arid central parts, precipitation rarely exceeds 250 mm (10 in), the summer temperature may reach 27°C (80°F), and in the winter drops only to 12°C (54°F). Around the margins, less extreme climates may be found.

OCEANIA
Historical and Political Background

Situated on the opposite side of the globe from Europe, this part of the world was among the last places to be visited by the 'Old World' explorers. In 1606 Dutch navigators landed on the north coast and the Cape York Peninsula. Little impressed by the hot lands, the Dutch took no further interest in this area which they called New Holland. Some 82 years later, the English explorer William Dampier reached the barren wastes of the north-west coast, and reported unenthusiastically of his finds on his return home.

Only in 1770 were the more inviting parts of south-east Australia discovered by Captain Cook who first sailed to Tahiti and New Zealand before reaching the coasts of what are now New South Wales and Queensland. Cook laid formal claim to this land for the British crown and reported enthusiastically on its potential when he returned home.

However, interest in this distant land did not grow until after Britain had lost her American colonies a few years later. The earliest settlement centred on Port Jackson, which has subsequently developed into the large city of Sydney. For the first thirty years or so the Blue Mountains presented an impenetrable barrier to westward expansion. Then, in 1813, a route was pioneered to the rich plains of the interior, and very soon development of the plain around Bathurst and the Darling Downs country farther north began.

During the first half of the nineteenth century many new settlements were established: Tasmania in 1803, Brisbane in 1824, the Swan River colony in the distant south-west in 1829, Melbourne in 1835 and Adelaide in 1836. At about the same time, despite domination by the original settlement in New South Wales, separate provinces or colonies were being established: Tasmania (1825), Western Australia (1831), South Australia (1834), Victoria (1851), Queensland (1859). By 1850 the population had risen to just over 400,000. But it was not until the early 1860s, when the population had risen to over 1 million, that the first south-north crossing of the country was made.

The initial attraction of the new lands was for farming. Merino sheep from Spain soon flourished there and produced the world's finest wool. Also, in 1851, mineral prospecting received a great lift with the discovery of gold at Bathurst, and nearly ten years later in Western Australia.

By the end of the century, when the separate colonies federated to become the Commonwealth of Australia under the British crown, the population had risen to 3.7 million. From that time it grew steadily by natural increase and further immigration; in 1940 it was 7 million, in 1960 it was 10.2 million and now it is over 13.6 million.

The indigenous population of Australia are the Aborigines, who came originally by sea from south-east Asia. Their forebears probably arrived about 16,000 years ago. They now number about 40,000 and live mainly on special reserves.

Today the six original colonies have been added to by the creation of the Northern Territory and the Australian Capital Territory of Canberra. These eight constitute an independent federal country which is a member of the Commonwealth. As one of the most developed countries in its area it also plays a leading part in a number of organizations for collective development and security, such as the Colombo Plan Countries and SEATO.

Industry, Commerce and Communications

Prior to World War II Australia was essentially a primary producer, exporting agricultural products and some raw materials, largely to countries within the then British Empire and Commonwealth, and importing most of her manufactured needs. Since then a wide range of manufacturing industries have been developed so that today the Australian economy is far more balanced. The main centres of these industries are near to the coasts especially around the major cities and towns of the south-east, from Adelaide to Brisbane, and in the extreme south-west of the country.

The present labour force, excluding those in agriculture, is about 4.75 million. Of these, 1.2 million are employed in manufacturing, 0.95 million in wholesale and retail trade, 1.6 million in public services such as administration, community service, health and education and 0.35 million in transport industries.

Australia's communications networks are best developed in the east and the south-west. Roads have been developed right around the coasts; Victoria, New South Wales and Queensland are well served but south-north routes across the heart of the country are few. Likewise, railways link Western Australia across the Nullarbor Plain with South Australia then on into Victoria, New South Wales and Queensland, but the line from Adelaide to Darwin has never been completed. In recent years isolated lines serving the rich iron ore fields of the north-west have been constructed to the nearest harbours. Aircraft are of considerable use in Australia, both city to city and city to 'the outback' – the remote areas, popularly exemplified by the Flying Doctor Service. Remote parts also find the radio a great boon for communication. For example, Australia

1 Sheep shearing, Australia; 2 The Southern Alps, South Island, New Zealand; 3 Native dancers, Suva, Fiji, south-west Pacific; 4 Herd of cattle crossing the Davidson river, Tully, Queensland, Australia

uses the radio as an educational aid for families in the outback.

Agriculture, Forestry and Fishing

In their natural state the Australian native forests are principally hardwoods. Over 90 percent of those forests are comprised of the distinctive Eucalypts, popularly known as 'gum trees'. These range in form from the 100 m (330 ft) tall giant trees of the dense forests of the south-east to the shrub-like form of the mallee extending across south-central Australia. Broadly, the natural vegetation of the country is densest in the south-west, the east and the north. Farther inland, grass becomes increasingly important as the mulga and other acacias grow ever more thinly over the ground. Ultimately the arid heart of the country is true sand desert.

First and foremost, Australian farming is based on animals. There are nearly 150 million sheep here, more than in any other country, being some 15 percent of the total world population. These produce over 750 thousand tonnes of greasy wool each year, about 30 percent of the world total. This represents the best yield per animal anywhere in the world. Individually, only the USSR and China produce more mutton and lamb. Australia also has over 33 million head of cattle, nearly 3 per-

cent of the world total. Beef rearing is more important than dairying, and the country is the world's seventh largest beef producer.

Today the richest areas for crop farming are in the best watered parts of the interior eastern plains, the lower parts of the great Murray-Darling river basin and the southern parts of South Australia, most of Victoria and parts of south-west Western Australia. Australia ranks highly in the production of cereals. Wheat, grown in the better watered parts of the temperate south, is the foremost example. In all some 12 million tonnes are produced each year, that is about three-quarters of the French output and more than twice that of the United Kingdom. Barley and oats are also grown in the temperate parts. In each of these crops, Australia ranks among the top fifteen world producers.

Tropical Queensland is a major producer of sugar cane, Australia being ninth in this world table. Nearly 24 million tonnes, 3.5 percent of the world's output, is grown here. However, Australia plays a very limited part in the growing of other tropical crops. By contrast, temperate fruits and grape growing have been fairly extensively developed. Australia, especially Tasmania, produces 1.5 percent of the world's apples (324,000 tonnes). Over 2 percent of the world's pears and 1.3 percent of the

world's grapes are grown in the south-east.

Australia does not rank highly in fishing, though it is the world's fifth largest whaling nation. A range of timber is also produced in modest quantities, particularly in the south-east and Tasmania.

Natural Resources

Modern Australian expansion has grown outwards from the temperate lands of the south. Initially, the land resources and farming potential were most valued in the east as well as south-west, but then the gold, coal and iron ore resources were realized. More recently as the land has been more extensively surveyed and explored, far richer reserves of iron ore have been proven in the drier areas and the tropical north, as well as a large range of other minerals.

In world terms, Australia is a comparatively modest bituminous coal producer. From the fields of eastern New South Wales, annual output is now approaching 75 million tonnes per year. Assessing this figure in terms of population rather than area, it places Australia quite high in the world tables. The same applies to lignite production, with Victoria's rich deposits now yielding over 31 million tonnes per year.

Australian crude oil production is now increasing steadily, with the

fields off the south-east coast being most significant. The annual output of 20 million tonnes is less than 0.75 percent of the world total but puts Australia eighteenth in the world table. Natural gas production, currently around 6,000 million cubic metres per year is also increasing. Perhaps more interestingly, uranium production is as yet very small but it is estimated that over one-fifth of the world's reserves lie in the extreme Northern Territory and in the west of Queensland. South-east Australia is also an area of considerable HEP potential, exemplified by the Snowy Mountains scheme. As yet less than a fifth of this has been harnessed, but that alone provides more than one-fifth of the country's total electricity needs.

Within the last two decades Australia's iron ore production has been dramatically increased by opening up the resources of arid Western Australia. The fields of South Australia and southern Western Australia once supplied only Australia's needs, but now the country is the world's second largest producer, mining about 60 million tonnes (iron content) per year, much of which is exported to Japan. Present known reserves are only 6.4 percent of the world total but it is likely that further fields will be discovered in the drier areas.

One of the world's richest deposits

Agriculture, particularly raising sheep, is the prime Australian occupation, but important mineral deposits have created industry and a large urban population: 1 Harvesting sugar cane, Rocky Point, Queensland – this is the main crop of the eastern region of the second largest state; 2 Boning meat, Rockhampton, Queensland – like the state capital, Brisbane, this large port has important meat works and exports meat products; 3 Blast furnaces at the AIS plant, Port Kembla, New South Wales – iron and steel works predominate in this industrial centre; 4 Zinc and phosphate works, Derwent river, Tasmania – the island has large mineral resources, including zinc and copper, and metals are its leading exports, ahead of newsprint and paper products from its forestry industry

Total Imports and Exports
(1975 figures in millions of U.S. dollars)

Australia and New Zealand dominate Oceania's world trade. The islands' figures are all low. Overall there is a visible balance of payments deficit.

	Imports	Exports
Australia	9,811	11,575
Fiji	268	159
New Caledonia	348	289
New Zealand	3,152	2,152
Papua New Guinea	483	475

OCEANIA

of bauxite has been developed in the Cape York Peninsula within the last twenty years. Smaller fields in the Northern Territory and south-west Western Australia have also been opened up. Collectively these make Australia the world's most important producer of this ore with 21 million tonnes, over 29 percent of the world's annual output.

Australia contributes variously to the world production of other mineral ores. She is the third largest producer of lead, mining 391 thousand tonnes (lead content) per year, i.e. 12 percent of the world total, largely from the Broken Hill area of New South Wales and from western Queensland. Largely from the same two areas comes nearly 8 percent of the world's zinc, of which Australia is again the third most important world producer. Nickel production of 75 thousand tonnes nickel content, just under 10 percent of the world total, puts Australia in fourth position in this world table. The country's output of some other resources is summarized in the table below:

The Australian Economy

Taken as a single unit the population density of Australia is extremely low, being only 1.8 per km^2 (4.6 per sq ml). No other large country in the world which includes areas developed along western industrial lines has so low an average figure. Well over 80 percent of the country has fewer than 1 person per km^2 (2.5 per sq ml) while only a few very limited areas around the state capitals have densities in excess of 100 per km^2 (250 per sq ml).

By far the largest state capitals are Sydney (2,874,000) and Melbourne (2,584,000). These are the only two millionaire cities in the country, though Brisbane, Adelaide and Perth now have populations in excess of three-quarters of a million people.

Ore	Average Annual World Production (million tonnes)	Australia's Share (percent)
cobalt	0.03	3
copper	7.4	3
gold	1 million kg	2
manganese	22.8	7
silver	0.01	8
tin	0.2	4
tungsten	0.036	3

Taken as a whole, Australia's population is growing at a rapid rate by most western standards. This is partly due to the continuing policy of attracting new settlers, mainly from Europe. Each year some 120–140,000 new migrants are attracted to the country and perhaps 100–115,000 earlier arrivals and others leave. But Australia also has a higher birth rate than many western countries, 17.2 per 1,000 overall, which is far higher than the typical death rate for a 'developed' country of 8.1 per 1,000. There are some marked regional and state differences lying behind the overall growth rate which currently runs at about 1.6 percent per year; Queensland's and Western Australia's populations are rising at much faster rates than any other parts of Australia.

With the growth of her agricultural, mining and other industrial activities in the last twenty years, Australia has moved from a position of deficit in her visible trade to one of surplus. Whereas in 1938 imports and exports were $517 million and $518 million respectively, by 1958 they were $1,776 million and $1,660 million, and by 1975, $9,811 million and $11,575 million. Imports had risen by 2.43 and 4.52 times and exports by 2.20 and 5.97 times. Clearly the last figure, though not as high as some seen in other parts of the world, is the most remarkable index of the country's growth within the last twenty years.

Over the period 1960–'74 Australia's per capita incomes rose from $1,438 to $5,884, a rise of 309 percent. This very high figure is marginally better than that for Europe as a whole and far better than that for the whole non-Communist world for the same period.

Australia had an agreeable energy surplus in 1975 with 111.05 million tonnes coal equivalent (mtce) produced and only 87.56 mtce consumed. The latter figure indicates a per capita consumption of 6,485 kg/ca, comparable with the highest figure for individual European countries, but far lower than those for the USA and Canada.

Australia, which in certain parts displays many characteristics of a well developed country, has an expanding economy. As a country with net immigration it is attracting young people with growing families, and its age pyramid is thus weighted in the younger age groups. In more than one sense this is a country with plenty of youthful energy.

With its wide natural resource base, its growing contacts with other trans-Pacific countries and its traditional links with the Commonwealth, Australia is well set to play an increasingly important part in the world's market and political meeting places.

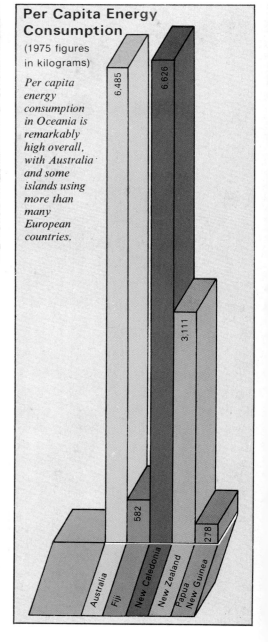

Per Capita Energy Consumption

(1975 figures in kilograms)

Per capita energy consumption in Oceania is remarkably high overall, with Australia and some islands using more than many European countries.

6,485 — Australia
582 — Fiji
6,626 — New Caledonia
3,111 — New Zealand
278 — Papua New Guinea

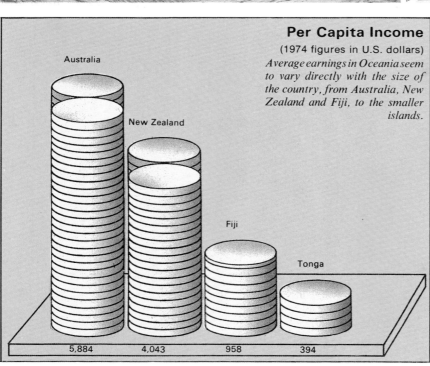

Per Capita Income

(1974 figures in U.S. dollars)

Average earnings in Oceania seem to vary directly with the size of the country, from Australia, New Zealand and Fiji, to the smaller islands.

Australia — 5,884
New Zealand — 4,043
Fiji — 958
Tonga — 394

With such a large land mass, extending through a range of latitudes, Australia is a land of extremes in terrain and climate: 1 Ayers Rock, Northern Territory – part monsoon area with grasslands, forests and swamps, and part desert, these central and northern regions are inhabited by the country's largest number of native aborigines who are mainly nomadic herdsmen, many preferring to resettle their old tribal homelands instead of living in the special reserves set aside for them with health and educational facilities; 2 Bondi Beach, Sydney, New South Wales – perhaps the most famous worldwide, this is just one of the fine beaches and holiday areas to the east of the state capital

Oceanian Countries

Australia

Australian Capital Territory

An area of federal territory within New South Wales was demarcated in 1911 and the federal capital of Canberra established. The city with its provision for central government and administration was developed in the 1920s after World War I. Today the area is almost entirely devoted to government and tertiary services.

New South Wales

Today only the fifth largest Australian state, New South Wales has the highest population of any in the federation. Economically it has a broad base. The most important crops are wheat, barley, hay, rice and oats, while the numbers of sheep, lambs and pigs are the highest, and the cattle population the second highest, for any state. Most of Australia's coal is mined here. Silver, lead and zinc are the other leading minerals. One of Australia's most established centres of iron and steel production is located in New South Wales, and a wide range of manufacturing industries are to be found in the Sydney area. The Blue Mountains have developed as a major tourist area.

Northern Territory

The third largest constituent part of modern Australia is largely desert waste with a northern belt of tropical lands. Overall it is the most inhospitable part of the whole country. Its development is so limited that it still rates only as a territory, not a state. Agricultural research and development is slow. Mineral resources offer a brighter economic prospect, all extracted products being shipped either to other parts of Australia or abroad. Bauxite is currently most valuable, followed by manganese. Iron, lead, zinc and rich deposits of uranium have yet to be effectively developed. This is the area in which most of the Aborigine Reserves have been established.

Queensland

Now the second largest state in the federation, Queensland today has the third largest population, most of which is found on the coastal fringes, especially in the south-east corner. As the northernmost of the tier of states, in the climatically appealing east of the country, Queensland extends to tropical latitudes. It has a distinctive range of crops. Wheat, barley, hay and potatoes are the major temperate crops, and sugar cane, sorghum, pineapples, maize, citrus fruit, peanuts and cotton are important tropical crops. Queensland has more cattle than any other state, and the second highest number of pigs but comparatively few sheep. Bauxite mining in the extreme north is a most valuable part of the economy; coal, copper, silver and lead are also important. Tourism centres on its expansive beaches and the Great Barrier Reef with its attractive coral features and tropical fish.

South Australia

With the bulk of its population clustered in the south-east corner, this is both the fourth largest and the fourth most heavily populated state. Economically it has a broad though somewhat limited base. Farming in the comparatively dry areas depends on careful soil conservation and irrigation. Wheat and barley are the major cereals; temperate and citrus fruit farming is a distinctive activity, as is grape growing and wine making. South Australia's mineral output includes iron ore, lead, copper and gypsum. Metal processing, car manufacturing, ship building and food processing are the most important industries.

Tasmania

This smallest Australian state also has the lowest population total. Its agricultural activities are varied, with hay, potatoes and barley as the major crops. Sheep, cattle and pigs are all found throughout the island. Iron ore, coal, zinc and copper as well as silver and gold are all mined. This state of fast-flowing rivers has large HEP installations, most valuable for the refining of aluminium. Forestry is of especial importance, newsprint and other paper products being second only to metals as exports.

Victoria

This is the second smallest of the six original colonies which federated in 1901, yet it has the second highest population today. Together with parts of New South Wales, South Australia and the island of Tasmania, it is climatically most akin to the home countries of the European settlers. Economically, agriculture is the most important activity. Wheat, hay and barley are the leading crops. Vegetables and fruit farming are also important. The numbers of sheep, cattle and pigs are each third largest for any Australian state and, for the area of this state, very large indeed. Victoria has modest reserves of gold and lignite, and is now the country's leading producer of both crude oil and natural gas. There are also large valuable forests. The Greater Melbourne area is a major focus for industries, especially textiles, petrochemicals, aluminium refining, car manufacturing and food processing.

Western Australia

Australia's largest state comprises so much arid land that the country's fifth highest state population is mainly clustered in the south-west corner, some 2,000 km (1,300 ml) from the nearest large concentration of people around Adelaide in South Australia. Farming is of great importance in the south-west where wheat is the major crop, with hay, barley and oats of lesser significance. Temperate fruit farming and, farther north, orange growing are also important. Only New South Wales has more sheep and lambs. Cattle and pigs play a smaller part. Traditionally, Western Australia mining was dominated by gold but in recent years iron ore, bauxite and now crude oil and natural gas production have assumed far greater significance. New processing plants for these raw materials have developed quickly.

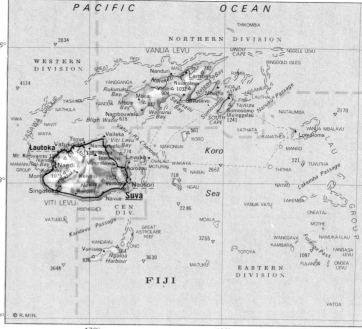

New Zealand: 1 Mt Egmont, 2,518 m (8,260 ft) and farmlands from Tariki, Taranaki, North Island – some 90 percent of the country's all-important dairy cattle graze on the island's lowlands; 2 Aerial view of Queenstown, South Island – on the shores of the beautiful Lake Wakatipu this tourist town is well placed for exploring the area; 3 Bora Bora, Tahiti Viti Levu and Vanua Levu are the two largest islands of Fiji, Oceania's fourth largest country. They lie on the Pacific Ring of Fire

Oceanian Countries

American Samoa

The Samoan Islands are a Polynesian group approximately midway between Australia and Hawaii. The eastern islands have been an unincorporated territory of the USA since 1900. A wide range of tropical crops are grown but little is exported. Fishing, especially for tuna, is more important, providing the major export item. Other exports include pet foods and native crafts. Major imports include building materials, rice, sugar and fuel oils.

Cook Islands

Lying fairly widely scattered some 3,000 km (1,900 ml) north-east of New Zealand in the Polynesian islands of the south-west Pacific, the Cook Islands are mainly of volcanic origin. First discovered in 1773 by

activity and sugar exports produce over 60 percent of foreign earnings. Copra, ginger and gold are the other main exports. Fiji's animal farming is expanding rapidly, and forestry and tourism are being developed systematically.

French Polynesia

Scattered over a wide area in the eastern Pacific, since 1958 the islands of French Polynesia have enjoyed the status of an overseas territory within the French Community. Local

Australia: 1 Aborigine, Wessel Islands – Stone Age arts are practised by the country's oldest inhabitants; 2 Todd River, Alice Springs, Northern Territory, situated in the remote dry heart of Australia

New Caledonia and New Hebrides: both these groups of islands within Melanesia, are of volcanic origins

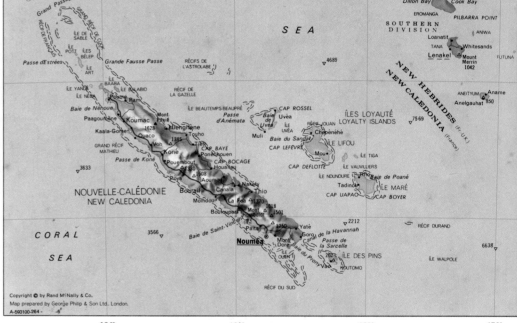

Captain Cook, they were made a British protectorate in 1888 and a New Zealand territory in 1901. Since 1965 they have enjoyed internal self-government. Well over half the population live on the island of Rarotonga (see map p.114); 13 other islands are peopled, the most important being those in the south of the group. Major exports are citrus fruits, bananas, copra and pearl shells.

Fiji

Comprising nearly 850 Melanesian islands in the south-west Pacific, Fiji is the fourth most heavily populated country in Oceania, and the most populated of all the island groups. Today only about 42 percent of the people are of Melanesian descent, with over 50 percent being of Indian origin. A British colony for nearly 100 years, Fiji became independent in 1970, and remains a member of the Commonwealth. Sugar cane growing is the prime

government is thus in the hands of an island-elected assembly under the presidency of an appointed governor. The islands also send representatives to the French Assemblies in Paris. The five groups in the political unit are the Pacific Windward Islands and Leeward Islands (together called the Society Islands), the Tuamotu, the Tubuai Islands and the Marquesas Islands. The economies are essentially agricultural and tourist based. Chief exports are copra, coffee, citrus fruit, vanilla and mother of pearl.

The Gilbert Islands

This larger part of the former British colony of the Gilbert and Ellice Islands also includes Phoenix and Line Islands. They achieved internal self-government in 1976 and full independence nearly three years later, remaining within the Commonwealth. Most of the islands are atolls – Christmas Island is the world's largest atoll – and have very little soil. Only coconuts grow read-

ily; copra and the highly valuable deposits of phosphates form the bases of the national economy.

Guam

This largest and most southerly island in the Marianas Archipelago of Micronesia, is an outlying yet unincorporated territory of the USA, ceded from Spain in 1898. It is the USA's most westerly Pacific outpost and is of major strategic importance both as a naval and air base. About a quarter of the present population are US service personnel and their families. The native population is mainly of Malay origin. Agriculture concentrates on maize, sweet potatoes, cassava, bananas, citrus fruit and vegetable growing, as well as pig and cattle raising and poultry farming.

Nauru

A tiny Micronesian coral island approximately 20 km (12 ml) in cir-

cumference, Nauru's core contains extensive deposits of high grade phosphates, the country's sole export. Foodstuffs and raw materials for the phosphate industry are the main imports. The island was a German colony from 1888–1914, a British colony from 1920–1947, a joint (Australia, New Zealand, United Kingdom) trusteeship territory till 1968, and is now an independent republic which has a special relationship with the Commonwealth.

New Caledonia

The largest volcanic island in Melanesia with a number of small dependencies, New Caledonia is a French overseas territory. Local government is in the hands of an appointed High Commissioner and an island-elected council and territorial assembly. Representatives are also sent to the French Assemblies in Paris. The chief crops produced are coffee, copra, maize and vegetables. The main island is far more important for its mineral production, especially a rich nickel deposit.

New Hebrides

This group of Melanesian islands between New Caledonia and Fiji is politically unique in that, since 1906, it has been an Anglo-French condominium. The islands are a dependent territory whose external administration is shared between London and Paris. Copra, cocoa and coffee are exported. Rich manganese deposits have been developed recently and are now the major export item.

New Zealand

First discovered by Tasman in 1642, New Zealand comprises two main islands plus a number of smaller ones. In 1840, after a period in which Australians had used some of the anchorages for whaling and trading, a treaty was signed with the native Maoris whereby the country became a British colony. The next 30 years were punctuated with misunderstanding and occasional conflict between the British settlers and the Maoris, but peace has reigned for the past 100 years and more. Since 1907 New Zealand has been independent and is a member of the Commonwealth. It is today one of the most successful plural societies in the world.

The two main islands extend from 34°S to 47°S, a distance of nearly 1,500 km (930 ml) and are separated by the Cook Strait. Both islands are mountainous, the South Island having the Southern Alps running northeast to south-west through its whole length, and rising to 3,764 m (12,349 ft) in Mount Cook. The North Island is volcanic, having both active and extinct cones as well as the famous hot springs and geysers. Mount Ruapehu, still active, rises to 2,797 m (9,175 ft). The most extensive lowland area of the country is the Canterbury Plains on the east side of the South Island.

New Zealand's climates are humid temperate and in many respects are similar to those of the British Isles, especially in the South Island. North Island is a fraction warmer with no single monthly average temperature being below 6°C (43°F). Precipitation totals, which are higher in the mountains, reach 625–1,000 mm (25–40 in) in the eastern parts of South Island and up to 1,250 mm (50 in) in the lowlands of North Island.

The New Zealand economy has been dominated by agriculture, especially pastoral farming, throughout this century. Yet, in recent years, the imbalance of the economy has improved as a range of manufacturing industries have been developed. In a country of nearly 10 million cattle and over 56 million sheep, animal farming is still the backbone of the economy. New Zealand is fourth in the world sheep table with 5.4 percent. She produces 12 percent of the world's wool, too.

Food processing is still the most valuable manufacturing industry; for example, 41 percent of the world's butter and 7 percent of its lamb/mutton comes from here. Textiles, metal fabrication, transport equipment, wood and cork processing, paper making, chemical production and boot and shoe making are the leaders in the growing list of other manufacturing industries. New Zealand is ill-endowed with minerals; there is some coal in both islands and natural gas is extracted in North Island. Both islands have developed a considerable capacity for HEP.

Something like 80 percent of all New Zealand exports are related to agriculture with wool, lamb, beef and butter being the four most valuable items. The list of imports is headed by fuel oils, machinery, transport equipment, textiles, chemicals and raw materials. Australia, the UK, the USA and Japan are the main trading partners.

Niue

Geographically within the Cook Islands, Niue's area is more than that of all the other islands in that group together, but its population is far smaller. It achieved separate internal self-government within the New Zealand overseas territories in 1974 but its economy depends heavily upon aid from the mother country. Copra, sweet potatoes and bananas are the main products.

Norfolk Island

An Australian territory 1,400 km (900 ml) east of the New South Wales coast and 700 km (450 ml) northwest of New Zealand, this was originally used as a penal settlement when, in 1856, the 194 *Bounty* descendants moved from Pitcairn at their own request. Today the attractions of the scenery, beaches and climate have led to the development of a large tourist industry. Most foodstuffs have to be imported.

Pacific Island Trust Territory (US)

Following World War II the USA was appointed by the United Nations to act as trustee of all former Japanese mandated islands in the Pacific between 1° and 22°N, and 130° and 172°E. These Micronesian islands, over 2,100 atolls and smaller islands of which only 96 are inhabited, are mainly in the Caroline, Marshall and Marianas Groups. Some 1,857 km² (717 sq ml) of land are scattered over 8 million km² (3 million sq ml) of ocean. Each district has its own elected local government, while an elected Congress of Micronesia exercises 'federal' control.

Papua New Guinea

For nearly a hundred years the territories of Papua and New Guinea (other than the Netherlands western part which is regarded as part of Asia) were administered variously by Australia and the United Kingdom. Since 1975 the combined areas have been a fully independent state within the Commonwealth. A consistent trading deficit has been converted to a large surplus each year since 1970 by the rapid development of rich copper deposits. Copra and coffee are the next most important exports. Foodstuffs, machinery and manufactured goods are the major imports.

Pitcairn Island

Pitcairn lies approximately midway between New Zealand and Panama, in Polynesia. Its original inhabitants in 1767 were 9 mutineers from the *Bounty* and 18 Tahitians. In 1856 the population of 194 moved to Norfolk Island, but 43 returned soon afterwards. Today the population is about 100 and is declining. Since 1898 the island has been an official British dependency; currently the British High Commissioner in New Zealand is the Governor.

Solomon Islands

Comprising one of the largest island groups in Melanesia in the south-west Pacific, to the east of New Guinea, the Solomons became a British Protectorate in the 1890s and achieved independence in 1977. The larger islands are mountainous and heavily forested. Coconuts, copra and rice are the most important crops and forestry is of growing importance.

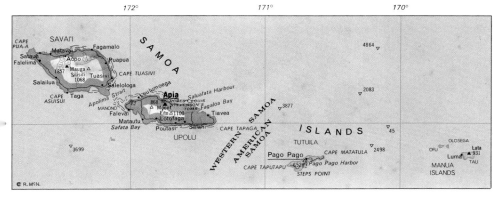

The Samoan Islands of Polynesia, north-east of Fiji, are politically divided – the islands of Western Samoa are members of the Commonwealth and the islands of American Samoa are a territory of the USA; Norfolk Island, between Australia and New Zealand, is a popular vacation spot

1 Growing copra in the Cook Islands – this crop is the coral islands' main export; 2 Ngauruhoe volcano, North Island, New Zealand – one of three active volcanoes in the Tongariro National Park; 3 Band playing during a carnival on the island of Tutuila – the largest island of Pago Pago, American Samoa

Oceanian Countries

Copra, timber, fish products and cocoa are the leading exports. The major imports are machinery, fuels and non-tropical foodstuffs.

Tokelau Islands

These are three Polynesian atolls some 480 km (300 ml) north of Western Samoa. Once part of the Gilbert and Ellice Islands, they have been directly associated with New Zealand since 1926. The economic base of the islands is very insecure and the population rely heavily on that country's aid. Since 1965 there has been a government scheme to resettle many of the population on the New Zealand mainland.

Tonga

About 150 coral and volcanic islands due east of Fiji comprise Tonga. The 'Friendly Islands' are distinctive in that they are a long-standing monarchy, the present monarch being King Taufa'ahau Tupou IV, son of Queen Salote Tupou III. A British protectorate from 1900 to 1970, it has since been an independent member of the Commonwealth. Local agriculture concentrates almost entirely on copra and banana production, two important export items. Pig and cattle farming are also important. In recent years the government has pursued development plans in an attempt to broaden the base of the islands' economy.

Tuvalu

Nine Polynesian islands, south of the Gilbert Islands with whom they were formerly associated as the Ellice Islands, have formed a separate British protectorate since 1975. The colony depends heavily on British aid. There is little cultivable soil. Fishing is the major activity.

Wallis and Futuna

The Wallis Islands with Futuna and Alofi are grouped 600 km (380 ml) north-west of Fiji within Polynesia. From 1842 till 1961 they were a French protectorate associated with New Caledonia. Since then they have been an overseas territory of France enjoying local self government and sending representatives to the French Assemblies in Paris. Farming is important with some fishing as well. Coffee, copra and vegetables are the main crops.

Western Samoa

Four inhabited Polynesian islands and a number of smaller ones northeast of Fiji and west of American Samoa make up Western Samoa. The islands are mountainous, being volcanic with coral fringes. Before World War I they belonged to Germany, were administered by New Zealand from 1920 to 1962 and since that time have been an independent country within the Commonwealth. Tropical crops, mainly bananas, cocoa and copra are grown on the coastal strips.

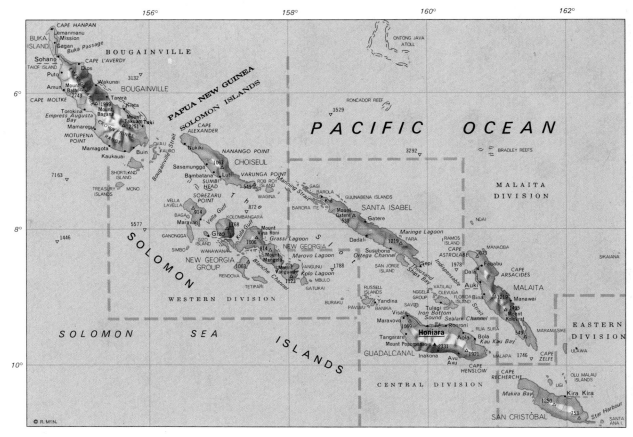

Opposite: 1 Pokutu Geyser, Rotorua, N Island, NZ – hot springs abound here; 2 Village, Western Samoa – food crops are the leading exports; 3 Native musicians, Fiji; 4 Basketmakers, Vavau Islands, Tonga

The Solomon Islands are among the most mountainous of Melanesia; Rarotonga is the most important member of the Cook Islands

COUNTRY REFERENCE: OCEANIA

Oceania Countries	Political Status	State Capital	Area km²	Area sq ml	Population	Population Density per km²	Population Density per sq ml	Births per Thousand Persons	Deaths per Thousand Persons	Mean Annual Percentage Increase in Population
American Samoa	C	Pago Pago	197	76	33,000	168	434	—	—	—
Australia	A	Canberra	7,686,849	2,967,909	13,858,000	1.8	4.7	17.2	8.1	1.6
NSW	D	Sydney	801,428	309,433	4,886,000	6.1	16	18.5	8.7	1.5
Victoria	D	Melbourne	227,618	87,884	3,730,000	16	42	18.7	8.5	1.6
Queensland	D	Brisbane	1,727,522	667,000	2,084,000	1.2	3.1	19.8	8.7	2.7
S. Australia	D	Adelaide	984,377	380,070	1,273,000	1.3	3.3	17.0	8.2	1.5
W. Australia	D	Perth	2,527,621	975,920	1,171,000	0.5	1.2	19.1	7.3	2.9
N. Territory	D	Darwin	1,347,519	520,280	100,000	0.07	0.2	29.3	6.1	7.3
Tasmania	D	Hobart	68,332	26,383	412,000	6	16	18.5	8.4	0.9
ACT	D	Canberra	2,432	939	202,000	83	215	24.2	3.9	10.0
Cook Islands	C	Avarua	241	93	18,000	75	194	32.8	5.7	-2.6
Fiji	A	Suva	18,272	7,055	595,000	33	84	28.8	4.3	1.9
French Polynesia	C	Papeete	4,000	1,550	138,000	35	89	33.7	7.2	3.5
Gilbert Islands	C	Bairiki	857	331	58,000	68	175	22.3	6.5	3.5
Guam	C	Agana	549	212	96,000	175	453	30.4	4.2	2.1
Nauru	A	—	21	8	7,300	348	913	32.2	8.3	—
New Caledonia	C	Noumea	19,058	7,358	141,000	7.4	19	32.2	7.9	3.6
New Hebrides	C	Vila	14,760	5,700	100,000	6.8	18	—	—	2.9
New Zealand	A	Wellington	268,675	103,736	3,245,000	12	31	18.4	8.1	1.9
Niue	C	Alofi	259	100	3,000	12	30	19.0	4.8	-3.2
Norfolk Island	C	Kingston	36	14	2,000	56	143	9.5	5.3	8.2
Pacific Islands (US Trust Territory)	C	Saipan	1,857	717	129,000	69	180	40.0	4.5	2.8
Papua New Guinea	A	Port Moresby	461,691	178,260	2,950,000	6.4	17	40.6	17.1	1.6
Pitcairn Island	C	Adamstown	5	2	70	14	35	—	—	—
Solomon Islands	A	Honiara	29,785	11,500	215,000	7.2	19	36.1	13.0	3.1
Tokelau Islands	C	—	10	4	1,600	160	400	24.5	—	—
Tonga	A	Nukualofa	699	270	92,000	132	341	28.3	3.2	2.9
Tuvalu	C	Funafuti	23	9	7,000	304	769	—	—	—
Wallis & Futuna	C	Matu-utu	255	98	9,500	37	97	43.3	10.6	2.5
Western Samoa	A	Apia	2,842	1,097	170,000	60	155	34.9	7.0	2.1
OCEANIA TOTALS			8,510,941	3,286,099	21,868,470	2.6	6.7	—	—	—

N.B. There are a number of other small islands, island groups and reefs in the Pacific Ocean which are associated with the USA, the UK and New Zealand but are not separately listed here.

1 △

2 ◁

3 ▷

4 ◁

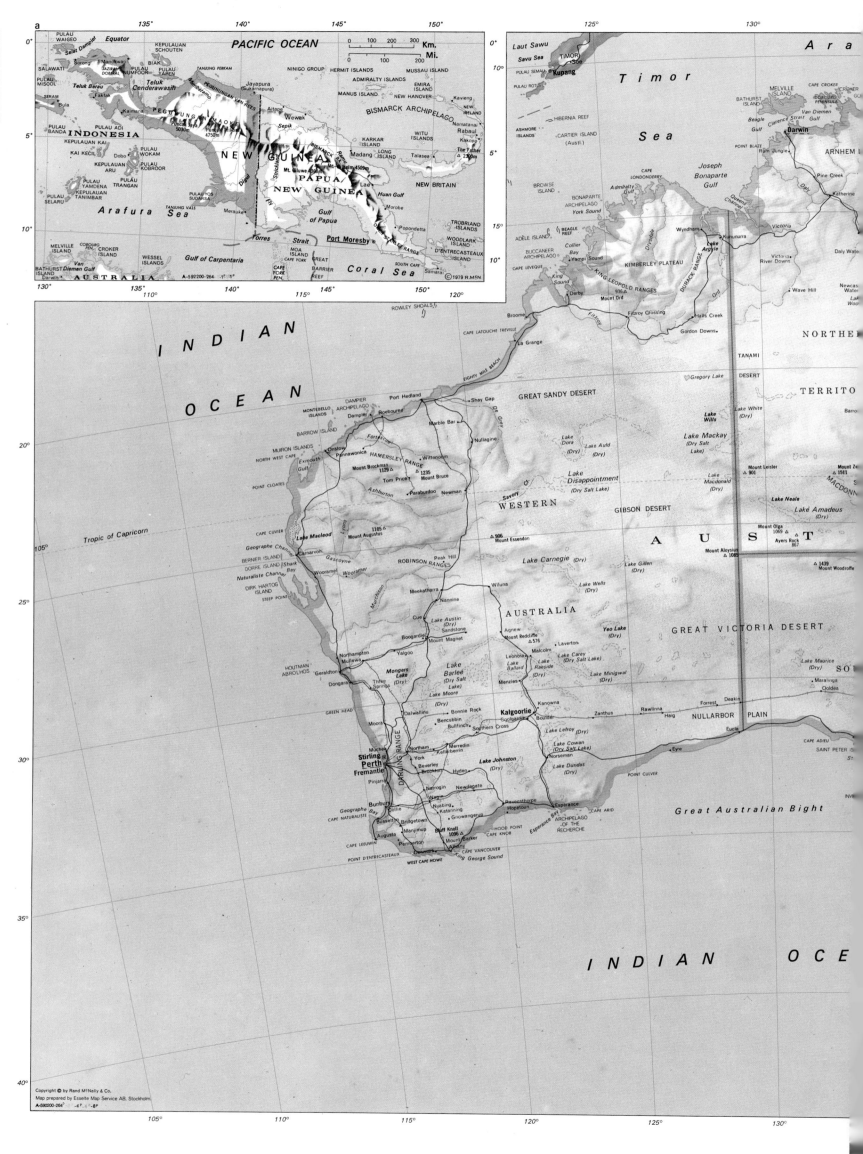

ra Sea

Gulf of
Papua

**PAPUA
NEW GUINEA**
NEW GUINEA

SOLOMON ISLANDS

Solomon Sea

Port Moresby

Torres Strait

Gulf

of

Carpentaria

CAPE
YORK

PENINSULA

C o r a l   S e a

GREAT   BARRIER   REEF

BARKLY TABLELAND

Cairns

Townsville

GREAT   DIVIDING   RANGE

QUEENSLAND

SIMPSON
DESERT

GREAT   ARTESIAN

BASIN

Rockhampton

Tropic of Capricorn

P A C I F I C

O C E A N

AUSTRALIA

Lake Eyre
North

Lake Eyre
South

GREY   RANGE

BARRIER   RANGE

FLINDERS   RANGES

Broken Hill

NEW   SOUTH   WALES

GREAT   DIVIDING   RANGE

Darling

Newcastle

Elizabeth
Adelaide

Parramatta
SYDNEY
Wollongong

Canberra
A.C.T.

RIVERINA

Albury

Murray

VICTORIA

Bendigo
Ballarat
Geelong
MELBOURNE

GREAT

Mount Gambier

T a s m a n

S e a

Bass Strait

King Island

TASMANIA

Burnie Devonport
Launceston

TASMANIA

Hobart

Kilometres   200   400   600 Km.

Statute Miles   200   400   600 Mi.

Scale 1:13,200,000

One centimetre represents 132 kilometres.
One inch represents approximately 210 miles.

Lambert Conformal Conic Projection

117

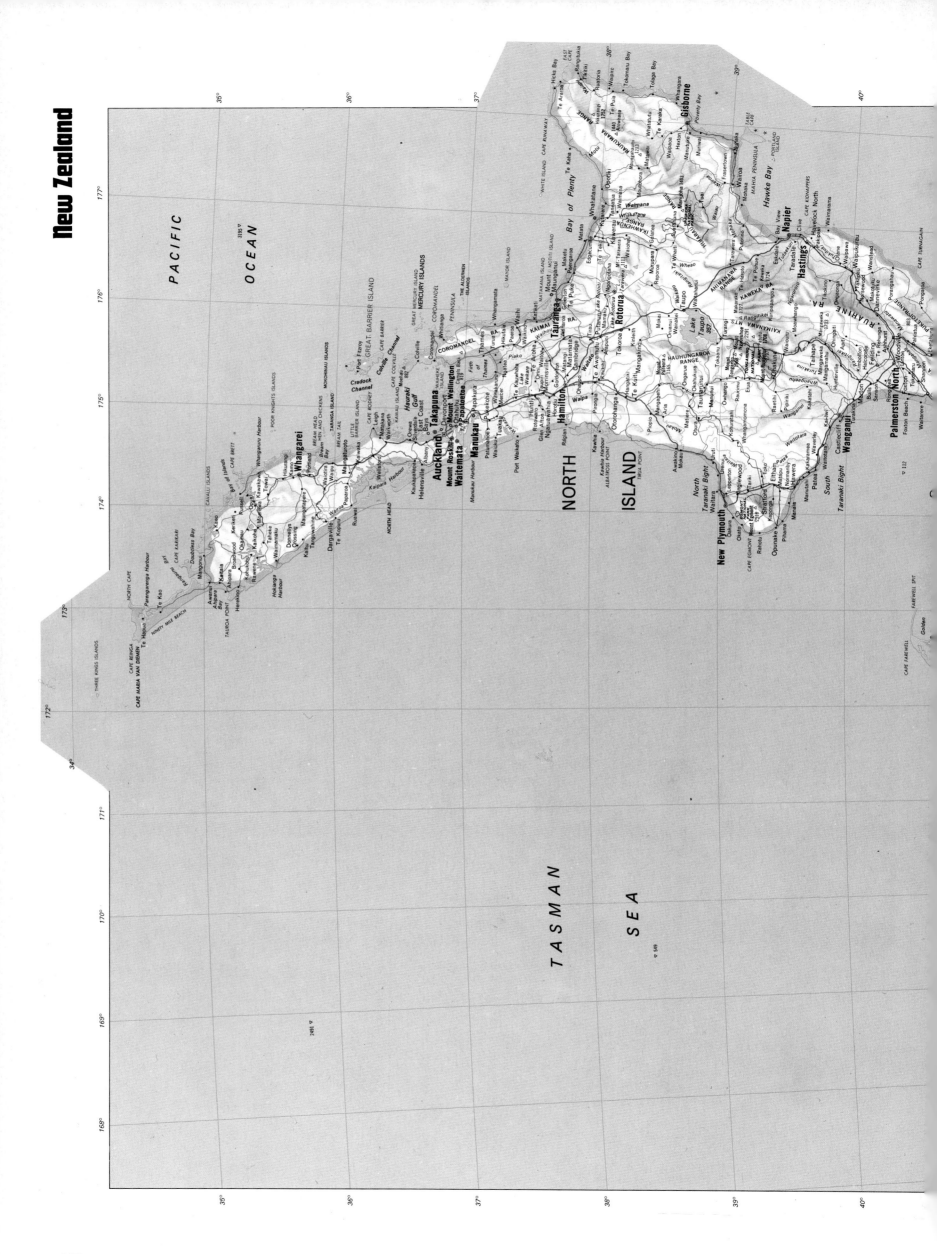

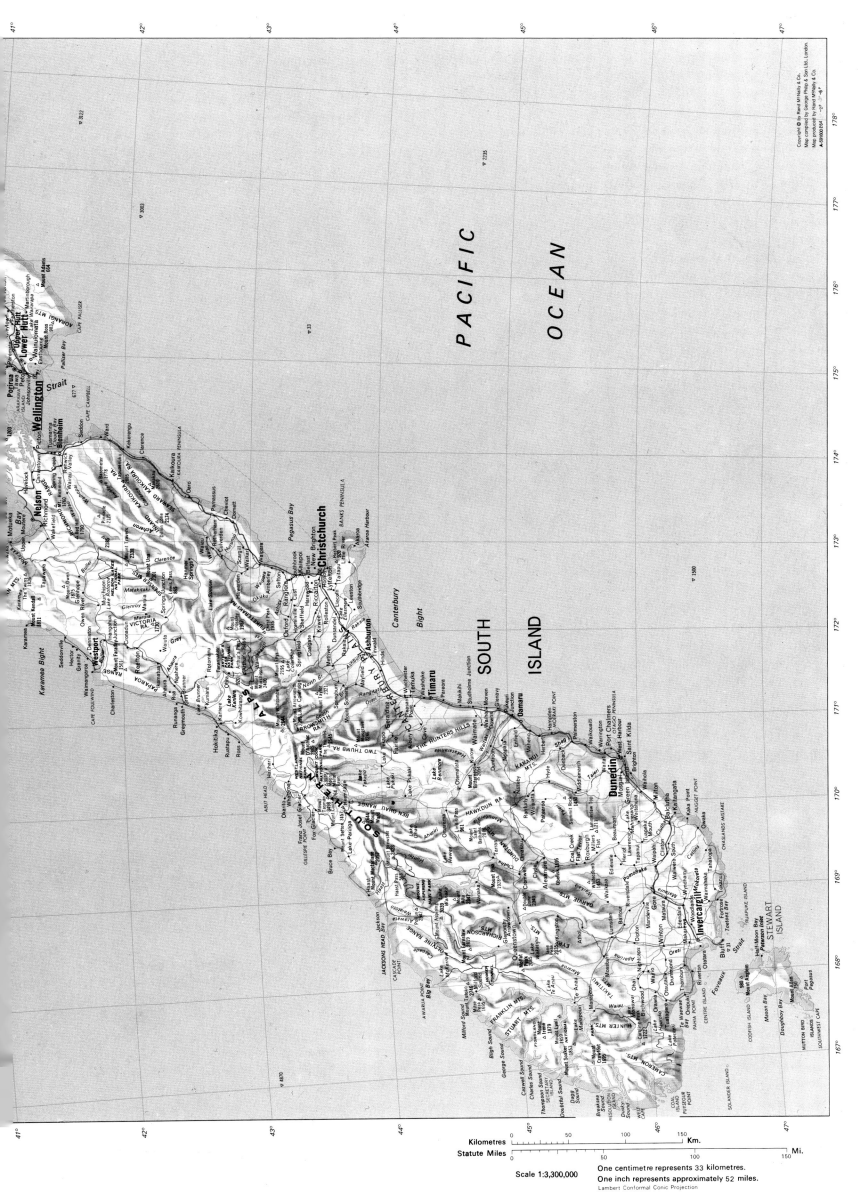

PACIFIC

OCEAN

SOUTH

ISLAND

STEWART
ISLAND

Kilometres

Statute Miles

Scale 1:3,300,000

One centimetre represents 33 kilometres.
One inch represents approximately 52 miles.

Lambert Conformal Conic Projection

119

MIDDLE AMERICA

Physical Profile

World Location and Size

Although it is the smallest of our nine 'continental' areas, Middle America is scattered over a wide area. On the mainland, the Mexico/USA boundary lies at about 33°N, while the Panama/Colombian boundary is at nearly 7°N. The north-west to south-east extent of the mainland is thus some 4,800 km (3,000 ml). Yet this part of the continent is never more than 1,200 km (750 ml) in west-east extent in Mexico and is often far narrower.

Middle America also includes the islands of the Greater and Lesser Antilles and others lying in the seas between the mainland of the three Americas. Many of these are collectively called the West Indies, lying principally within a belt bounded by 17°N and 22°N, and extending as far into the Atlantic as 59°W.

Landscape

Middle America may be divided into three main physical areas. In the north, in much of Mexico as far south as the Isthmus of Tehuantepec, the great mountain system of North America's Western Cordillera continues. The Sierra Madre Occidental runs parallel to the Pacific coast and rises to a maximum of 4,265 m (13,994 ft). The Sierra Madre Oriental runs parallel to the Gulf of Mexico coast and rises to greater heights in some of the volcanic peaks, such as Popocatepetl, 5,452 m (17,887 ft). Between these two ranges, a complex plateau lies at heights of between 1,200 m (4,000 ft) and 2,400 m (8,000 ft). To the west of all these three lies the great depression occupied by the Gulf of California and the elongated Baja California Peninsula, an extension of the Coast Ranges of the USA.

The southern mainland section of Middle America is physically far more complex. In its northern province, between Tehuantepec and Nicaragua, a series of mainly west-east mountain ridges lie across the isthmus from a high volcanic plateau on the Pacific fringe. Each line of mountains is highest in the west. There are limited coastal lowlands in this area, except in the great Yucatan Peninsula which is an extensive low limestone plain. The mountains of southern Nicaragua, Costa Rica and Panama are separated from the others by the depression containing Lakes Nicaragua and Managua. These mountains present a formidable barrier to movement across the isthmus, running north-west to south-east, then west to east. Through the whole of the second area, there are

Opposite: Market fruit stalls, San Miguel de Allende, Mexico

only four clear routes from Pacific to Caribbean: Tehuantepec, the Motagua River, Lake Nicaragua and the vital line of the Panama Canal.

The third physical province is that of the islands, which is itself in need of subdivision. To the north lies the line of coral reefs making up the Bahamas. Then the islands, often large, of the Greater Antilles are an eastern continuation of the mountains of southern Mexico, Guatemala and Honduras. Finally the Lesser Antilles are mainly a volcanic arc. They are a north-eastern extension of the South American Andes. There are also a number of coral islands in

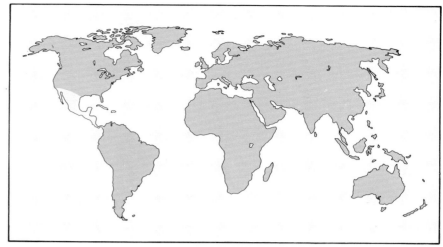

this last area. Thus, the West Indian islands show a great variety of physical features – active volcanoes, extinct volcanoes, coral islands, mountainous islands.

Climatic Background

Virtually all Middle America lies within the tropics. The close proximity to the seas, and the fact that it contains a range of altitudes, accounts for the variety of climates.

Mexico, north of the Tropic of Cancer, experiences dry climates. In the north-west and north-central

parts lies a subtropical desert area where the monthly average temperature never drops below 0°C (32°F) but rainfall is below 250 mm (10 in). More extensively, central and north-eastern Mexico has a subtropical steppe climate in which similar temperatures are accompanied by higher rainfalls, up to 600 mm (24 in).

Except in the high mountain areas, the remainder of the mainland experiences tropical rainy climates, being wetter on the east coast, except in the Yucatan Peninsula, than on the west. Here is the rain forest area where average monthly temperatures

The Pitons, St Lucia, West Indies – the mountainous, wooded Windward Island of volcanic origins

may be around 25°C (77°F) for much of the year and rainfall exceeds 2,500 mm (100 in). In the drier savanna areas of the west, rainfall is only around one-third of this amount.

Many of the islands experience a similar tropical savanna type of climate, though parts, such as the northern coastal strip of Hispaniola and Puerto Rico, have far higher rainfalls. In much of the Caribbean, hurricanes are an occasional menace.

MIDDLE AMERICA

The known history of Middle America dates back to the early settlements of 'Indians' who penetrated from north to south through the Americas about 10,000 BC. Their descendants, the Maya, developed their own civilization to

Population Growth and Political Development

When European settlers first moved to Middle America towards the end of the fifteenth century, there were probably no more than 2 million

American Indians. During the early period of European penetration, the American Indian population of the islands was largely wiped out by disease and the effects of enslavement. Far more survived on the mainland, so that today there are very few pure bred Amerinds on the islands, and they are now most strongly represented in the mainland countries. Nearly half the population of Guatemala, for instance, is of pure Amerind stock.

In contrast, the population of European descent in most Middle American countries is today low. African Negroes, originally introduced as slaves to the plantations, now form a substantial part of the Caribbean population. It is estimated that over four-fifths of the population of Haiti is of Negro stock, for example. Only in Puerto Rico, the Dominican Republic and Cuba, among the islands, are Negroes in a minority. The present total population of the continent is over 112 million, three-fifths of whom live in Mexico.

European influence in Middle America from 1500 onwards was essentially by two groups. The mainland was part of the area allocated to Spain under the 1493 agreements between Spain, Portugal and the Pope; the Caribbean islands were part of the area largely left to the Dutch, French and British. Independence movements developed early in the nineteenth century. Mexico was the first country to experience revolution, leading to independence in 1821. Soon, all Spanish territories had established their independence, though the initial Federation of Central American States lasted for only 14 years until it broke up in 1838. Since then there have been few major political changes. The three largest modern developments have been US interest in the control of Cuba, Puerto Rico and Panama, the granting of independence to most of her West Indian colonies by the United Kingdom since World War II, and the development of a Communist regime in Cuba.

Industry, Commerce and Communications

Industrialization in Middle America is a comparatively recent development. Even today on a world scale, it must rank with all Africa as being one of the two least industrially developed continents. However, individual Middle American countries have seen the advantages of broadening their economies, being less dependent upon the production and exporting of primary products and the importing of others, including manufactured needs. Industrialization also provides one alternative activity for the rapidly expanding population who cannot be absorbed on the land. Not surprisingly, Mexico has led the way: El Salvador, Costa Rica and now Cuba have followed.

Consumer goods are the first group of industries to have been developed. The home market for textiles and footwear, household goods and food-stuffs is large. While all these consumer industries are found in the leading countries, only some of them exist in the smaller countries. They have been followed by the setting up of heavy industry, iron and steel, petrochemicals and cement production in Mexico, refining Venezuelan

1 △

2 ▽

3 ▽

1 Maya ruins, Uxmal, Yucatan, Mexico; 2 Sugar plantation workers, Cuba; 3 Market square, St George's, capital of Grenada, West Indies

oil and fertilizer production in El Salvador, and light engineering in Costa Rica.

Transport networks in mainland Middle America are rather fragmentary. In Mexico, the road and rail networks both focus on Mexico City and have been developed outward to all corners of the country. The road link to the countries of the south-east is complete to Panama, though the Pan American Highway has yet to be completed from here into Colombia. In the other mainland countries rail development has been difficult and costly. Isolated lines serve the more populated parts of most countries. On the islands, rail and road networks are best developed in Cuba and Hispaniola. Throughout the whole of Middle America, air and sea links are also important.

Agriculture, Forestry and Fishing

Farming throughout Middle America was, for a long time, characterized by large estates with much wealth being in the hands of a small fraction of the total population, while the majority of the people were poor, landless peasants, mainly African Negroes. Changes slowly started to take place in the early twentieth century. The Mexican revolution in 1910 brought about a move to introduce communal ownership and working of the land, but so far this has been applied to less than half the land. More recently in Cuba, the Communist regime has tried to make farming more efficient by establishing state farms. However, overall, land reform has proved difficult to implement speedily.

Within Middle America, pastoral, subsistence and commercial farming are all found where the environmental hazards of too much or too little rainfall and/or altitude and steep slopes do not rule them out. So much of the dense forests remain untouched, except at their margins. Similarly, the arid areas of the north are hardly touched except where irrigation schemes have been introduced, as in north-eastern Mexico.

As in the natural grasslands of South America, settlers here soon introduced cattle and sheep, the Mexican plateau being the most inviting environment. Today, Mexico ranks seventh in the world for pigs, with 12 million, eighth for cattle, with nearly 29 million and eleventh for goats with 9,000. Smaller numbers of cattle and pigs are found in many of the other mainland countries and the larger Caribbean islands. Sheep too are found in smaller numbers in some of the mainland countries.

The continent's commercial crop growing is also concentrated in Mexico. It ranks in the world's top ten producers for twelve important crops and has greatest importance for oranges and lemons, third in each; coffee and sorghum, fourth in each; sugar, fifth; pineapples, coconuts and copra, sixth in each. Other Middle American countries mainly appear in

Much of the Caribbean islands' revenue comes from tourism, although some tropical crop production is also important: 1 Cutting bananas in the Bahamas, WI – the poor soil of these coral islands is not generally suited to agriculture; 2 Bridgetown, Barbados, WI – the capital is also the island's only harbour, from which rum is a major export; 3 Going through the Panama Canal – the passage from the Atlantic to the Pacific takes about 8 hours

Total Imports and Exports
(1975 figures in millions of U.S. dollars)

Few Middle American countries rank at all highly as trading nations and most import more than they export.

	Imports	Exports
Bahama Islands	1,565	3,416
Costa Rica	643	454
Cuba	4,001	3,680
Dominican Republic	773	894
El Salvador	601	515
Guatemala	733	624
Jamaica	1,113	732
Mexico	6,580	2,859
Netherlands Antilles	2,790	2,393
Nicaragua	517	375
Panama	870	272
Virgin Islands	2,198	1,933

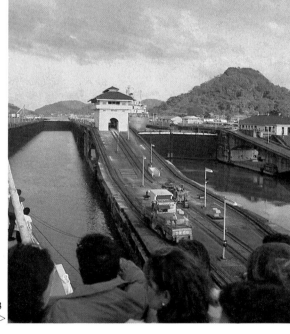

the world tables only for one or two crops, showing an economically dangerous dependence upon them. For example, Cuba is the world's third largest sugar cane producer, yet its second largest product, tobacco, ranks only twenty-fourth; Honduras, Costa Rica and Panama are major banana producers; Guatemala is heavily dependent upon coffee production.

Natural Resources

Middle America is very poorly endowed with mineral resources, having few significant deposits of specific minerals. It lacks coal, even more than South America. Mexico has reserves of over 10,000 million tonnes of coal but produces only about 5

million tonnes each year. Yet, Mexican oil reserves and production are such that she now ranks fifteenth in the world, producing over 40 million tonnes per year, and is of increasing importance to the western world. This may be less than a tenth of the

output of the world leaders, but is a third of that of Venezuela, Latin America's leading oil producer. Oil is also produced in Costa Rica and Cuba, and the Caribbean is regarded as one of the world's greatest prospects for future oil exploration. For

Ore	Average Annual World Production (million tonnes)	Middle America's Share (percent)	Principal Middle American Producing Countries
bauxite	80.3	19	Jamaica
cobalt	0.03	6	Cuba, Honduras
copper	7.4	1	Mexico
lead	3.2	5	Mexico
manganese	22.8	2	Mexico
nickel	0.733	11	Cuba, Dominican Rep.
silver	0.01	16	Mexico, Honduras
tin	0.2	2	Mexico
zinc	5.4	5	Mexico

MIDDLE AMERICA

all its selected areas of high rainfall, Middle America is neither potentially nor actually a great continent for the production of hydro-electric power.

Iron ore is found only in limited quantities in Middle America. Once again Mexico is the leading producer with about 3.6 million tonnes each year, which places it eighteenth in the world tables.

Middle America's contribution to world output of other minerals is very limited as the table on page 123 demonstrates. Mexico's position as the second largest silver producer and the sixth largest lead producer,

Jamaica's as the third largest bauxite producer, Cuba's and the Dominican Republic's as fifth and sixth largest producers of nickel are by far the most significant features.

Middle American Economy

The most extensive area of high average population density in Middle America is the plateau area of southern central Mexico where over 50 per km² (125 per sq ml) are found. Over a wider area in Mexico there are more than 25 persons per km² (60 per sq ml). Elsewhere on the mainland, such figures are only reached in limited areas of the Pacific coast lands of Guatemala, El Salvador and Costa Rica, and in parts of north-east Mexico.

Some Caribbean islands, however, show densities equal to and well above these figures, as can be seen in the table on page 128. In particular, Puerto Rico, Jamaica and the western parts of Cuba among the large islands all have average densities above 150 per km² (375 per sq ml). At the other end of the scale, the least densely-populated parts of the continent are the east side of the Yucatan Peninsula, east Honduras and Nicaragua, the Baja California Peninsula and parts of northern central Mexico.

Parts of Middle America are urbanized, though there are only four millionaire cities. Three of these are in Mexico, where Mexico City with 11.3 million inhabitants, is only marginally smaller than either New York or Tokyo. Guadalajara (2.0

million, Monterrey (1.6 million) and Havana, Cuba (1.0 million), are the other three millionaire cities. The capital cities of the Dominican Republic, Guatemala, Haiti, Jamaica, Nicaragua and Puerto Rico have populations of between half and one million, as do four more Mexican cities.

Birth rates in Middle America vary from over 45 per 1,000, as in the mainland countries of Honduras and Nicaragua, as well as the Dominican Republic, to below 20 per 1,000, as in some of the smaller, more advanced islands. Death rates are far lower, most being below 12 per 1,000 and many being single figures. Such figures in combination indicate age pyramids with a wide base in a situation where improving health facilities have increased life expectancy. The overall increase in population in some countries is now over 3 percent. Mexico, the country which so dominates the continent, has a birth rate of over 40 per 1,000, a death rate of only 7.2 per 1,000 – a figure which is lower than those of both the USA and the UK – and a population growth rate of 3.5 percent per annum.

Compared with the major trading areas, like Europe and North America, this continent plays a minor role in world trade. The value of its imports and exports are about one-twentieth those of all Europe and one-sixth those of North America.

Overall the value of Middle American imports rose by 569 percent and 496 percent, and exports rose by 391 percent and 486 percent between 1938–'58 and 1958–'75 respectively. Together these figures show an unhealthy trend during the first period but improvement in the latter. Although the continent still has a marked balance of payments deficit on visible trade, the position seems to be improving. Some individual countries show a divergence from this norm. For example, Mexico, the largest trader in the continent has a large deficit, and Cuba, Netherlands Antilles and Virgin Islands (US), the next largest traders, smaller deficits each. The Bahama Islands with a substantial trading surplus are unique. Most other Middle American countries are comparatively small traders with deficits on their visible trading.

During the period 1960–'74, per

1 △

2 ▽

Mexico, Middle America's largest country, is industrially the most highly developed, with vast oil reserves, but there is still much poverty outside the modern major city centres. As a result, regular streams of illegal immigrants to the neighbouring United States are frequently apprehended. 1 Cathedral and National Palace, Mexico City – the capital boasts the continent's oldest Christian building as well as fine colonial and modern architecture; 2 Acapulco beach – the world-famous Pacific coast resort, with its warm seas and sandy beaches, is especially popular with US visitors

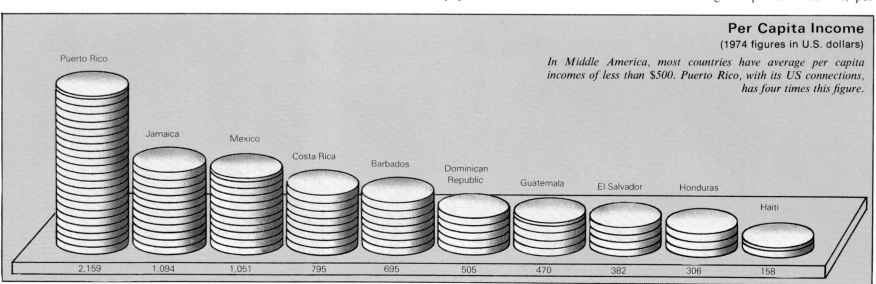

Per Capita Income
(1974 figures in U.S. dollars)

In Middle America, most countries have average per capita incomes of less than $500. Puerto Rico, with its US connections, has four times this figure.

Puerto Rico	Jamaica	Mexico	Costa Rica	Barbados	Dominican Republic	Guatemala	El Salvador	Honduras	Haiti
2,159	1,094	1,051	795	695	505	470	382	306	158

capita income in Middle and South America rose by 220 percent, from $300 to $960. This was slightly better than the overall percentage performance for the non-Communist world. Individually, Middle American countries showed considerable differences. Mexico, on 236 percent, fared better than the average and with its large population dominated the whole scene. Most other countries did worse or far worse. Puerto Rico's per capita income rose by 201 percent, Nicaragua's by 187 percent, Costa Rica's by 123 percent, Guatemala's by 82 percent and El Salvador's by only 71 percent. Absolute values for 1974 make poor comparison with the rest of the world; Puerto Rico had the highest value of $2,159, Mexico had $1,094 but smaller countries had incomes less than $500 per capita.

Middle America is overall a small energy producer and consumer. In 1975, 85.22 million tonnes coal equivalent (mtce) were produced and 115.60 mtce consumed. Mexico's share of these figures was high, 84.44 and 73.43 mtce respectively, showing this to be the only energy surplus country in the continent. All other countries are net importers of energy, Cuba and Puerto Rico each importing about 10 mtce per year. The remaining countries import small amounts, usually far less than one million tonnes, except the Dominican Republic, Jamaica, Netherlands Antilles and the Virgin Islands (US).

When energy consumption per capita is considered, three countries which are either connected with the USA or have oil processing industries have high energy uses: Virgin Islands (US) 50,157, Panama Canal Zone 14,150 and Netherlands Antilles 12,231 kg/ca. Some of the small developed islands have comparatively high consumptions per capita, such as Bahama Islands 6,279 and Bermuda 3,090. Many of the islands have figures between 1,500 and 3,000, while most of the mainland countries consume less than 500kg/ca per year.

There are such large differences in the sizes of individual Middle American countries. Some areas still await effective development, while others have been selectively exploited for specific products over the years. A possible way to more effective and concerted development in the future may be shown by two recent instances of international co-operation. In 1960 El Salvador, Guatemala, Honduras and Nicaragua created the Central American Common Market (ODECA), which was joined in 1962 by Costa Rica. These five have now established free trade in most commodities between themselves and have increased their trade with each other five-fold since the market was created. More recently, between 1973 and 1974, the Caribbean Common Market was established. This now has thirteen member states and aims at economic co-operation and growth. Mexico is outside both groups though it is associated with South American countries through its membership of Latin American Free Trade Association.

1 △

2 △   3 ▽

1 Aruba, Netherlands Antilles – despite idyllic scenes like this, the island's economy, like the other two in the southern part of this Dutch group, depends largely on refining oil imported from nearby Venezuela, South America; 2 Bermuda – the near-perfect subtropical climate with warm winters and trade winds cooling the hot summers, makes the Bermudas fine holiday islands and tourism is the main source of revenue; 3 St Vincent, Windward Islands – the delights of the carnival are enjoyed by the inhabitants as much as the visitors. The 1979 eruption of the volcano, Soufrière, has greatly harmed the island's crop-growing and tourism economy

Per Capita Energy Consumption

(1975 figures in kilograms)

Average energy consumption in Middle America ranges from the extraordinary for the Panama Canal Zone, through comparatively high figures for some developed islands, to the more normal levels of most mainland countries and less advanced islands.

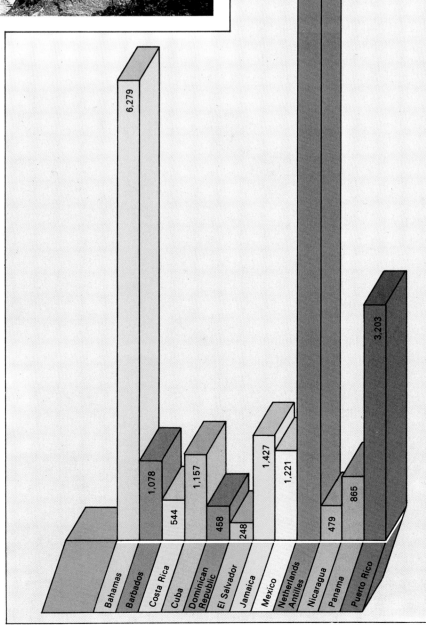

12,231

6,279

3,203

1,078

544

1,157

458

248

1,427

1,221

479

865

Bahamas
Barbados
Costa Rica
Cuba
Dominican Republic
El Salvador
Jamaica
Mexico
Netherlands Antilles
Nicaragua
Panama
Puerto Rico

Middle American Countries

Anguilla

A member of the West Indies Associated States (WIAS), Anguilla was associated with St Kitts-Nevis until 1976. The smallest of the Leeward Islands, it is a member of the Commonwealth with internal self-government, while the UK is responsible for defence and foreign affairs. It is a low coral island with poor soils. Sea salt and fruits are the main products.

Antigua

Together with its dependent islands of Barbuda and Redonda, Antigua is a member of the WIAS. The largest of the Leeward Islands, it has internal self-government. It is a member of the Commonwealth and the UK is responsible for defence and foreign affairs. Mainly a coral island, the remains of an extinct volcano rise to 402 m (1,319 ft) in the south. Sugar and cotton are the main products and exports. The tourist industry is being developed.

Bahama Islands

The Bahamas comprise some 1,700 coral islands and cays north of Cuba and east of Florida. Watling's Island, the first land sighted by Columbus in 1492, is among them. Most are uninhabited. Only New Providence has more than 100,000, and Grand Bahama more than 10,000 inhabitants. Now a member of the Commonwealth, the former British colony achieved complete independence in 1973. The islands' major products and exports are cement, petroleum products, rum, chemicals and fish. A range of small light industries is being developed on the two islands with the largest populations. Tourism is a most important industry.

Barbados

Lying about 170 km (105 ml) east of the Windward Islands, the island of Barbados became an independent country within the Commonwealth in 1966. A British possession for over 350 years, its character earned it the title 'Little England'. Barbados is largely a coral island with a very high population density. Sugar is the dominant crop and the economy is largely dependent upon this, molasses, rum and tourism. Other subsistence crops like yams and cassava are grown.

Belize

Formerly known as British Honduras, this is the only Commonwealth country on the mainland of Middle America. A self-governing colony since 1964, the UK is responsible for its defence, foreign affairs and internal security. It is subject to earthquakes and hurricanes, and in 1961, much of the old capital of Belize City was severely damaged. The building of the new capital city of Belmopan was started in 1967 and the government moved there in 1970. About half the country is forested. Citrus fruit, fruit products, sugar and fish are important to the national economy.

Bermuda

A British island colony within the Commonwealth, some 920 km (570 ml) east of the United States mainland, Bermuda has internal self-government. Of the 150 islands in the group only 20 are inhabited. The attractive climate has led to a great tourist industry, and today one and a half million people visit the islands each year. In 1975 visible exports, of which pharmaceutical products were the major item, brought in about 55 percent of the country's foreign earnings. Tourism and financial services were responsible for the other 45 percent.

British Virgin Islands

East of Puerto Rico and west of the Leeward Islands lies a group known collectively as the Virgin Islands. Those to the west are an unincorporated territory of the USA; the 36 to the east are a British colony which has some measure of internal self-government. The two groups have close social and economic links. Tortola, with a population of just over 8,000, is the largest British island. Farming and fishing are important activities but the developing tourist industry is the biggest source of foreign earnings.

Cayman Islands

Grand Cayman is the most important of the three coral islands which comprise this British colony some 320 km (200 ml) north-west of Jamaica. The main productive activities are fishing, particularly for turtles, boat building and rope-making. However, the country earns far more foreign currency by its flourishing tourist industry and through its international financial services.

Costa Rica

Except for Panama, this independent republic occupies the narrowest parts of the isthmus joining North and South America. Geographically it is divisible into three broad regions; the comparatively wide Caribbean coastal lowlands, the narrower Pacific coast lowlands and the north-west to south-east chain of volcanic mountains rising to heights of up to 3,819 m (12,530 ft). The main centres of population are in the valleys of the central mountain chain and on the Pacific side of them. Farming dominates the Costa Rican economy. Bananas, maize, sugar, coffee, rice and tobacco are all widely grown. Dairying and stock raising are also important, with marked increases in cattle and pig numbers in recent years.

Costa Rica's mineral reserves are limited. Currently a little gold is produced each year. Deposits of iron ore and sulphur have recently been discovered but have yet to be developed. Bananas, coffee and sugar are her main exports. Manufactured goods, transport equipment, chemicals and petroleum products are the main imports.

Cuba

The republic of Cuba comprises the largest Caribbean island, the smaller Isle of Pines and many smaller islets. It is comparatively flat, apart from the east-west mountain ridge of the extreme east which rises to a maximum height of 1,994 m (6,542 ft), and some hills in the central province of Las Villas and in the extreme west. Formerly a Spanish possession, Cuba became independent in 1898, but was economically tied to the USA until 1959. Since then it has severed relationships with the West and established links with the Soviet bloc. The great bulk of Cuba's international trade is with the USSR and other countries of eastern Europe. The economy is centrally planned. It is the world's third largest producer of sugar. Rice, tobacco, coffee

1 Martinique – devastated by a volcanic eruption at the start of the century, this French island is also hurricane-prone; 2 St Thomas, US Virgin Islands – the main island of this group which attracts more holiday visitors yearly; 3 Grand Cayman – the largest of three coral islands in this British colony where fishing, tourism and banking are the main activities

1 △

2 △

3 ▽

holdings. Production of sugar, cocoa, coffee, tobacco and rice is, however, concentrated on large estates. Bauxite and iron ore are the most important minerals. Industries have developed a great deal in recent years, particularly sugar processing and textile production. The chief exports are sugar, minerals, cocoa and coffee. Manufactured goods, fuel oil, vehicles and raw materials are the major imports.

El Salvador

The smallest and the most densely populated of the Middle American republics, El Salvador has been independent since 1841. Physically, the lie of the land is from east to west with a main volcanic mountain ridge near to the south coast, limited tropical lowlands to the south of this and a wider belt of undulating terrain to the north. The largest centres of population are in the valleys of the central upland area and the south. The country's economy is based mainly on crop and livestock farming. Coffee, rice, maize and sugar growing, and sheep and cattle rearing are most important. The forests of El Salvador produce the world's largest quantity of the medicinal gum, balsam. Food processing, textile and footwear production are the leading industries. Over half the country's foreign earnings come from coffee exports. The chief imports are temperate foodstuffs, fuel oil, machinery and manufactured goods.

Grenada

The smallest of the Windward Islands, Grenada was the first to be granted full independence in 1974. A number of tiny islands, the Grenadines, are dependent on her; others are dependent upon St Vincent. Grenada is of volcanic origins and rises to a maximum height of 840 m (2,756 ft) above sea level. On the extensive lower areas a wide range of crops, such as cocoa, nutmegs, bananas, coconuts and citrus fruit are grown.

Guadeloupe

One of the four overseas departments of France, Guadeloupe is a group of two main and five smaller islands. The main western island is dominated by the active volcano, Soufrière; the eastern island is much flatter. They are all situated between the British Leeward Islands and Dominica. Bananas, sugar, rum and pineapples are the principal products and export items. Trade is mainly with France.

Guatemala

This independent mainland republic is physically divided by the mountainous areas of the south and west rising to a height of 4,220 m (13,846 ft) above sea level. Agriculture is vital to the national economy. The Pacific facing coastlands are most important in this respect; the broader lowlands of the north and northeast are less fertile. About two-thirds of the working population are in farming, either subsistence or on the commercial plantations. Coffee, cotton, sugar and beef are the main export items. Large areas of the north and extreme south have valuable hardwood forests which have yet to be developed commercially. Rubber production is being encouraged. Mineral production is very limited. Most industries are connected with food processing, cotton textiles and clothing. Chemicals and foodstuffs are the major imports.

Haiti

The only French-speaking republic in Middle America, Haiti comprises the western third of the island of Hispaniola. It has a large population for its size, over 90 percent of the inhabitants being classified as rural. The standard of living of most Haitians is low when compared with other countries of Middle America. The main commercial crops are coffee, sugar and sisal. Bauxite and copper are both mined by North American companies. Light industries are being developed, and now contribute as much to the country's export earnings as any other single item except coffee. Foodstuffs and fuels oils are the most costly imports.

Honduras

One of the larger Middle American republics, Honduras has an extensive upland interior, a long Caribbean-facing coastal zone and a shorter Pacific coastline. Less than 25 percent of the country is cultivated, though two-thirds of the work force is employed in agriculture. Bananas, coffee, beef cattle and cotton are the principal products and agricultural exports. Some 45 percent of the country is forested with both hard- and softwoods. Forest exports are almost as valuable as coffee. A number of industries have been developed but these employ less than 10 percent of the work force.

Jamaica

The largest and most important Commonwealth country in Middle America, Jamaica became fully independent in 1962 after a period of eighteen years with internal self-government. It is an attractive, mountainous island rising to a maximum height of 2,256 m (7,402 ft). For a long time agriculture was the mainstay of the economy, particularly sugar cane, coconuts, bananas, coffee and citrus fruit production. However, Jamaica has now developed a

and maize are the next most widely produced crops. The forests contain a wide variety of hardwoods which are, as yet, little utilized. Cuban mineral reserves are considerable, with large deposits of nickel, production of which is being rapidly expanded. Iron ore and chromite are also important. A range of industries has been developed, such as textile, cigar and cigarette making and food processing.

Dominica

The largest of the Windward Islands, Dominica is a member of the WIAS. It is of volcanic origins and is by far the highest of the Windward group, rising to 1,447 m (4,748 ft) above sea level. A member of the Commonwealth, it is internally self-governing, but the UK is responsible for defence and foreign affairs. Tropical fruits are most important, especially bananas, limes and cocoa.

Dominican Republic

The independent Dominican Republic forms the eastern two-thirds of the island of Hispaniola. Physically the grain of the country is from east to west, with a central highland ridge rising to 3,175 m (10,417 ft), lowland belts on either side of this followed by coastal ranges and coastal lowlands. Economically, the island is heavily dependent upon agriculture. Half the cultivated area is in small

Middle American Countries

range of industries other than agricultural processing. Textiles, engineering, pharmaceuticals and building construction are all important. The country is also the world's second largest source of bauxite. This and processed alumina now account for two-thirds of Jamaica's foreign earnings. Sugar is the next most valuable export. Raw materials are the main imports. Tourism is of growing importance.

Martinique

Situated between Dominica and the British Windward Islands, this island is one of the four overseas departments of France. The north is dominated by Mount Pelée rising to 1,340 m (4,397 ft), the volcano responsible for one of the worst natural disasters of modern times; on 8 May 1902 its eruption killed 40,000 people. Today, bananas, sugar and rum are the main products and exports of the island. Foodstuffs and manufactured goods are the main imports.

Mexico

By far the largest Middle American country, Mexico is the most northerly. Physically dominated by the Sierra Madre mountains, it has far less forest and far more grassland and desert areas than the others, and ranks among the most developed overall. The population is concentrated in the high plains of the south, the eastern foothills and in the lower valley of the Rio Grande. Mexican agriculture produces a wide range of crops, the major ones by output being sugar cane, maize, coffee, sorghum, wheat, oranges and bananas. Of these, only sugar and coffee are exported in large quantities. Mexican forests, some of which were felled indiscriminately earlier in this century, are now exploited more systematically. Production of a wide range of woods and wood products is now rising steadily. A variety of fish is landed from both the Pacific and the Caribbean.

Mexican mineral reserves are large in a wide range of ores. Crude oil is most valuable to the national economy. One-fifth of the world's silver is mined in Mexico; large uranium deposits are being developed steadily. Manufactured goods, petroleum, coffee, sugar and cotton are the leading exports. Cereals, metal products, electrical goods and vehicles are the main imports. Mexico's chief trading partners are the USA, the EEC countries and Japan.

Montserrat

This scenically attractive island is a British colony situated south-west of Antigua and north-west of Guadeloupe within the Leeward Islands. The economy is heavily dependent on British aid. Sea island cotton, limes, tomatoes and other vegetables are the main products.

Netherlands Antilles

Collectively an internally self-governing Dutch overseas possession, the Netherlands Antilles are found in two groups: the three islands of Aruba, Curaçao and Bonaire lie close to the Venezuelan coast; St Martin, St Eustatius and Saba lie within the Leeward Islands. Over 92 percent of the population live on Aruba and Curaçao. Oil refining is the main activity, with crude oil being imported from Venezuela and refined products being exported to North America and Europe. Phosphates are mined in Curaçao and exported. In the Leeward Islands, fishing, sugar and rum production are the main activities, though they are of far lower value than those of the other islands.

Nicaragua

Middle America's second largest country, this independent republic is quite sparsely populated. Physically it extends from the Pacific to the Caribbean coast where the mountainous backbone of the Middle American isthmus is at its lowest (max height 2,107 m, 6,913 ft). It is also distinctive, physically, for the presence of two large lakes, Nicaragua and Managua. Agriculture is the main occupation with much scope for improved production using irrigation. Cotton, tropical fruits, rice and sweet potatoes are the leading crops grown in the east. Sugar cane, cotton and maize are grown in the west where beef cattle are also raised. Cotton, coffee and meat products are the main exports; manufactured goods, chemicals and fuel oils are the major imports.

Panama

Part of Colombia until 1903, this is the youngest independent republic on the Middle American mainland. Divided in two by the Panama Canal Zone, it occupies the narrowest parts of the Middle American mainland. The land nearest to the canal zone is most heavily populated. Agriculture is not well developed, though it is the mainstay of the national economy. Over 60 percent of the country's foodstuffs is imported. The most important crops grown for local consumption are rice and maize, with only bananas and sugar as significant exports. Mineral developments are just beginning, with the emphasis on three large copper deposits. The economy is, however, largely dependent upon the Panama Canal. The country has a large registered merchant fleet, many of its inhabitants work on the canal, and foreign personnel passing through spend money in the main country.

Panama Canal Zone

Between 1904 and 1914 the USA constructed a most important 58 km (36 ml) long canal across the isthmus of Panama, connecting the Caribbean Sea to the Pacific Ocean. By a treaty with the country of Panama at that time, the USA leased in perpetuity a strip of land about 16 km (10 ml) wide in which they possess full sovereignty rights. In 1978, new treaties were signed to give the zone back to Panama by the year 2000 and to maintain its neutrality. The canal is open to shipping of all nations on payment of tolls. In an average year 13,000 ocean-going vessels pass through, carrying about 150 million tonnes of cargo. Since the canal's opening the amount of ocean-going traffic in the Caribbean area has grown enormously, and Europe's trading relations with the Pacific coasts of all the Americas, Australia and New Zealand have changed radically.

Puerto Rico

Save two smaller islands, Puerto Rico is the most densely populated country in Middle America. An island outlying territory of the USA, it is internally self-governing but dependent upon the US in international affairs. Sugar cane, which is refined into sugar and distilled into rum, is the leading crop but tobacco, cotton,

COUNTRY REFERENCE: MIDDLE AMERICA

Middle American Countries	Political Status	State Capital	Area km²	Area sq ml	Population	Population Density per km²	Population Density per sq ml	Births per Thousand Persons	Deaths per Thousand Persons	Mean Annual Percentage Increase in Population
Anguilla	C	The Valley	91	35	6,000	66	171	—	—	—
Antigua	B	Saint Johns	442	171	75,000	170	439	18.3	7.1	1.4
Bahama Islands	A	Nassau	13,935	5,380	222,000	16	41	18.1	3.9	3.9
Barbados	C	Bridgetown	430	166	250,000	581	1,506	19.5	8.4	0.7
Belize	C	Belmopan	22,965	8,867	150,000	7.0	17	38.7	5.3	3.2
Bermuda	C	Hamilton	54	21	59,000	1,093	2,810	16.3	6.4	1.6
British Virgin Islands	C	Road Town	153	59	10,000	65	170	24.5	7.5	2.4
Cayman Islands	C	Georgetown	260	100	12,000	46	120	24.7	6.0	—
Costa Rica	A	San José	50,900	19,650	2,079,000	41	106	29.5	5.0	2.7
Cuba	A	La Habana	114,524	44,218	9,678,000	85	219	22.3	5.7	1.8
Dominica	B	Roseau	751	290	77,000	103	266	36.4	10.1	1.0
Dominican Republic	A	Santo Domingo	48,734	18,816	5,041,000	103	268	45.8	11.0	2.9
El Salvador	A	San Salvador	21,393	8,260	4,290,000	201	519	40.1	8.0	3.0
Grenada	A	Saint George's	344	133	114,000	331	857	26.2	7.5	0.5
Guadeloupe	C	Basse-Terre	1,780	687	371,000	208	540	28.0	7.3	1.7
Guatemala	A	Guatemala	108,889	42,042	6,525,000	60	155	43.1	12.5	2.5
Haiti	A	Port-au-Prince	27,750	10,714	4,800,000	173	448	35.8	16.3	1.6
Honduras	A	Tegucigalpa	112,088	43,277	2,946,000	26	68	49.3	14.6	4.0
Jamaica	A	Kingston	10,962	4,232	2,080,000	190	491	30.8	7.2	1.7
Martinique	C	Fort-de-France	1,100	425	378,000	344	889	22.4	6.8	1.6
Mexico	A	Ciudad-de-Mexico	1,972,546	761,604	65,555,000	33	86	43.4	7.2	3.5
Montserrat	C	Plymouth	101	39	14,000	139	359	24.3	10.5	—
Netherlands Antilles	C	Willemstad	961	371	242,000	252	652	—	—	1.8
Nicaragua	A	Managua	130,000	50,200	2,347,000	18	47	48.3	13.9	3.3
Panama	A	Panama	75,651	29,230	1,795,000	24	61	31.7	7.1	3.3
Panama Canal Zone	C	Balboa Heights	1,445	558	40,000	28	72	13.2	—	—
Puerto Rico	C	San Juan	8,897	3,435	3,345,000	376	974	23.3	6.5	2.8
St Kitts-Nevis	B	Basseterre	267	103	48,000	178	466	24.1	10.8	0.4
St Lucia	A	Castries	616	238	117,000	190	492	40.9	9.3	1.5
St Vincent	B	Kingstown	388	150	117,000	302	780	34.4	10.0	0.7
Turks and Caicos Islands	C	Grand Turk	430	166	5,000	12	30	34.3	10.4	2.7
Virgin Islands (US)	C	Charlotte Amalie	344	133	102,000	297	766	27.7	5.2	0.5
MIDDLE AMERICA TOTALS			2,729,191	1,053,749	112,890,000	39	101	—	—	—

coffee and tropical fruits are also grown. Dairying is more valuable and provides the leading export products. Since World War II, a large number of industries have been established, particularly the manufacture of metal goods, cement, glass and wood products.

St Kitts-Nevis

These two Leeward Islands are members of the WIAS. Until 1976 they were associated with Anguilla. Members of the Commonwealth, they are internally self-governing though the UK is responsible for their defence and foreign affairs. Both are mountainous islands of volcanic origins. St Kitts is the larger and more densely populated. Its most important products are sugar, molasses and salt, while those of Nevis are sugar and cotton.

St Lucia

Fully independent only since February 1979, St Lucia is a member of the Commonwealth and the WIAS. It is the second largest and scenically the most attractive of the Windward Islands, rising to 950 m (3,117 ft). There is still much evidence of its former state as a French possession. Today bananas, cocoa, copra and coconuts are the main exports. Tourism is growing.

St Vincent

The second smallest of the Windward Islands, a member of the Commonwealth and the WIAS, St Vincent is internally self-governing but has its defence and foreign affairs controlled by the UK. It is the most British of the Windward Islands. Physically it is a volcanic island which rises to

1,074 m (3,524 ft) above sea level. A group of tiny islands, some of the Grenadines, are dependent upon it; others are dependent upon Grenada. Arrowroot is the main product; tropical fruits, vegetables and spices are the other main crops.

Turks and Caicos Islands

These two groups of islands are a British colony lying south-east of the Bahamas. Only six are inhabited. Until 1976 they were associated with the Cayman Islands. Fishing is the most important activity, accounting for over 95 percent of the islands' exports. Imports are mainly foodstuffs and manufactured goods.

Virgin Islands (US)

In 1917 the United States purchased the western group of the Virgin

1 Dominican Republic – US aid has helped develop this troubled state which suffered over 50 revolutions; 2 Looking south from Tortola, British Virgin Islands – sailing and fishing can be enjoyed in these mild, sheltered waters; 3 Antigua, Leeward Islands – this attractive island relies increasingly on tourism

Islands from Denmark, the others being a British colony. They are constitutionally an unincorporated territory of the USA. The islanders elect their own governor and legislative representatives, do not vote in the US presidential elections, but send one non-voting member to the US congress. Tourism is now the base of the islands' economy, with about 1.5 million visitors each year. Manufacturing industries, fruit and vegetable production and building are also important.

Kilometres
Statute Miles

Scale 1:13,200,000

One centimetre represents 132 kilometres.
One inch represents approximately 210 miles.
Oblique Conic Conformal Projection

131

SOUTH AMERICA
Physical Profile

World Location and Size

The dividing line between Middle and South America lies at the Colombian/Panamanian border, the narrowest land bridge dividing the Pacific Ocean from the Caribbean Sea. The northern coast of the continent extends to 12°N. The southernmost point, Cape Horn, lies at 56°S. Thus, the north-south extent of the continent is 7,450 km (4,600 ml). The west to east extent varies greatly, but in the central equatorial parts it extends from 82°W in northern Peru to 35°W in eastern Brazil, an overall distance of some 5,150 km (3,200 ml).

South America is essentially triangular in shape; the north and east coasts are comparatively straight, but the west coast has a straight southern part and then a convex northern part. The continent also includes a number of offshore islands, including Trinidad and Tobago to the north, the Falkland Islands to the south-east, the Galapagos Islands to the west, the Chonos Archipelago to the south-west and Tierra del Fuego to the south. Apart from the latter two islands, the coastline of the continent is largely physically uncomplicated.

Landscape

The continent may be divided into eight distinct physical areas, four of which are essentially lowlands and the rest uplands. Within each of these two groups is a dominant member: the Amazon Basin is by far the most extensive lowland area and the Andes Mountains the most extensive upland area.

The Amazon Basin is an extremely low-lying area dominated by dense tropical rain forest. It covers a part of central and eastern South America which is almost as large as the whole USA. The main rivers discharge more water than any other single system in the world. The Amazon itself is some 6,275 km (3,900 ml) long.

The continent's second largest river system is dominated by the Parana, Paraguay and Uruguay Rivers. These reach the sea in the Rio de la Plata, an inlet of the Atlantic which extends some 330 km (205 ml) inland. The dominant lie of the land here is gently sloping from north to south.

The third, but far smaller river basin is that of the Orinoco in the north which drains a smaller area than the Amazon, from which it is divided by an extremely low water-

Opposite: Forming part of the border between Brazil and Argentina, the spectacular Iguassu Falls would provide great power if harnessed

shed. These rivers drain the eastern and northern flanks of the Andes as well as the Guiana Highlands. Most of the area is known as the *Llanos*, and is dominated by swamplands.

The last area of lowland, along the Pacific coastal fringes, is the most fragmented. The coastal plains are widest in the extreme north and parts of Chile, where they may reach 80 km (50 ml) at their maximum, but elsewhere the mountains are as little as one-tenth that distance from the ocean. The lowlands are crossed in their humid parts by a number of short rivers which plunge steeply westward from the Andes.

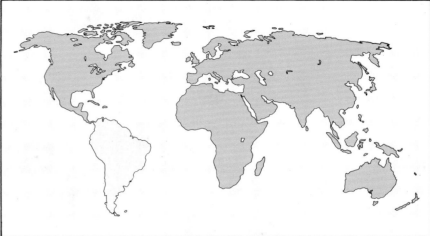

The Andes mountains run parallel to the Pacific coast. In the south there is one main ridge but there are two or three ridges in the north with large valleys between. At its widest, the whole range stretches for about 500 km (310 ml) from west to east. The western slopes are more precipitous than those of the east. The Andes contains a number of active and extinct volcanoes and is still a belt of earthquake activity. It is part of the 'Pacific ring of fire'. Mount Aconcagua in Argentina rises to 6,958 m (22,831 ft), the highest point in the Western Hemisphere.

South and east of the Amazon lies the second largest upland area, the triangular-shaped Brazilian Highlands. These rise quite steeply from the Atlantic fringe and then slope gently into the interior. Their general levels in the south-east average 1,400 m (4,600 ft), and the highest point is 2,890 m (9,482 ft). Geologically, these are far older than the Andes.

The smaller Guiana Highlands of the north, between the Amazon and Orinoco Basins, rise steeply from the former to their highest parts which are over 2,600 m (8,600 ft) up, and then slope gently towards the north.

In the extreme south, the Patagonian Plateau is a lower, irregular, wind-swept tableland rising to a little over 760 m (2,500 ft).

Climatic Background

Extending from the world's largest equatorial basin to the most southerly point in the Southern Hemisphere outside the Antarctic, South America exhibits a wide range of climates. East of the Andes and north of 20°S, is a large area which experiences equatorial and tropical climates which provide for the dense rain forests within 5° to 8° of the equator and the savanna landscapes of parts of the Guianas, Venezuela and much of the Brazilian interior. Average monthly temperatures never fall below 18°C (64°F). Rainfall at its maximum exceeds 2,500 mm (100 in). Similar humid tropical climates are also found on some Brazilian coastal fringes between 12°S and 28°S and on the Colombian coastlands between 9°W and 8°S.

Hot or warm climates are found along the Pacific coastal lowlands from 4°S to 32°S and in a small area east of the Andes around 30°S. Here,

View of the Andes from near Cuzco, Peru; the Inca civilization was centred on this region in an area of magnificent scenery provided by the extensive mountain chain

rainfall is mainly below 125 mm (5 in) per year, and average monthly temperatures reach the high 20°sC (low 80°sF) in the north and the mid 20°sC (mid 70°sF) in the south. The Patagonian Plateau area is one of mid-latitude desert, where rainfall rarely reaches 250 mm (10 in) and average temperatures range between 19°C (66°F) and 0°C (32°F). Steppeland climates are found in a north-south belt east of the Andes and south of 22°S, in north-east Brazil and in a small coastal area of Venezuela.

Warm and cool temperate climates dominate the Pacific coastlines south of 32°S and a triangular area south of 20°S and east of 65°W. In the Pacific strip the north experiences a Mediterranean climate while farther south it becomes cooler and far wetter. The climate in the larger Atlantic-facing area has higher temperatures, with a greater temperature range, and rainfall totals of between 550 mm (22 in) and 1,000 mm (40 in).

SOUTH AMERICA

This, the fifth largest continent, has a well documented history dating back to before the days of the Inca Empire which was at its peak in the second half of the fifteenth century. From about 1500, it attracted European explorers, prospectors and settlers at much the same time as North America, but thereafter the two sister continents developed in entirely different ways. Unlike the North, South America did not unite into large independent countries, but instead a number of separate countries, some of them comparatively small, emerged by the early nineteenth century. Most of these had no ties with European mother countries. In any case, by that time, Spain and Portugal were far from powerful. So, the continent has tended to stagnate during the last 170 years. There is a great potential but it needs harnessing. Well may South America be called 'The Sleeping Giant'.

Population Growth

When Spanish explorers first reached South America in the late fifteenth century, it is estimated that there were some 10–12 million people in the continent. These were all American Indians (Amerinds) whose forefathers had crossed from Asia into North America before those two land masses were divided by the creation of the Bering Strait at the end of the ice age. They then penetrated into the South American continent. It is likely that these people arrived 12,000–15,000 years ago.

From the sixteenth century onwards, European settlers mainly from Spain and Portugal, but also a few from France, the Netherlands and the United Kingdom arrived in this new continent. Eastern South America was settled mainly by the Portuguese and elsewhere by the Spanish migrants. By the early years of the nineteenth century when the Spanish Empire disintegrated, it is estimated that there were nearly 10 million European settlers here.

During the second half of the nineteenth century and the first three decades of this, South America saw a steady stream of arrivals from a number of European countries. Italians, British and Germans emigrated there, as well as more from Iberia, especially into the southern temperate parts. By 1900, nearly 40 million of the continent's inhabitants were either European migrants or their descendants.

The third group of people to arrive in South America were the African Negroes who were initially introduced by the Europeans as slaves. They came mainly to the hotter parts and are most numerous in northern Brazil and Colombia.

Today the Europeans dominate with far smaller numbers of Negroes and Amerinds. Yet, all told these three 'pure' groups make up less than half the total population. In addition, there are large numbers of people descended from mixed marriages, an arrangement never resisted by the Roman Catholic Church, and indeed established from the early settlement days when Spanish and Portuguese men took Amerind wives. Today, the offspring of a European and Amerind marriage are known as mestizos; the children of Europeans and Negroes are mulattos; where Amerind and Negro marry the offspring are called zambos. Intermarriage between these three has led to a further blurring of the racial groups which, in time, will become even harder to distinguish.

The present population of the continent is about 227 million which, as we shall see, is very unevenly distributed. Even the proportions of the different racial groups found in individual countries vary greatly. Brazil has about 75 percent of its 113 million directly descended from European stock, 5 percent from Amerind or Negro stock and the remaining 20 percent from mixed marriages, predominantly mestizo. By contrast, only 20 percent of Venezuelans are of European extraction, 10 percent are of Negro stock and the remaining 70 percent are of mixed marriages, again mainly mestizo.

Political Development

The Inca civilization was centred on the Andes mountains. One of its interests then, and for us today, lies in the great technical skills of these peoples, who yet remained completely ignorant of some things which we would regard as vital. They had built huge palaces and temples and evolved a technique of suspension bridge engineering which amazed the European. An elaborate system of roads stretched from one end of the empire to the other. The Incas were also highly skilled craftsmen working in precious metals. Yet, they knew nothing of iron and had not stumbled upon the wheel, a technical wonder known in Europe for over 1,500 years. Further, they had no written language but depended upon quipu, an intricate system of knotted cords, for keeping records.

In 1531 the Inca Empire was effectively overthrown by Pizarro and the Spanish conquistadors. Today a number of its great landmarks, such as the Machu Picchu ruins high in the mountains of Peru, remain as a symbol of this once grand and powerful system, and are a modern tourist attraction.

The sixteenth to the early nineteenth centuries were characterized by the arrival of Spaniards in the west and south and Portuguese in the east, attracted by the precious metals, especially gold, as described in the legend of El Dorado, and the development of new farming lands. Such crops as tobacco and sugar cane, neither of which could be cultivated in Europe, were important initially. The mineral wealth of the interior was slowly realized in the nineteenth century. Then, at a later stage than in North America, a series of wars of independence was waged, out of which emerged nine separate Spanish-speaking countries and one Portuguese-speaking country. This internal division has subsequently been a great hindrance to the continent's development.

Within the present century some countries have been able to establish reasonably sound economies based on locally strong activities and resources: Argentina is the greatest temperate farming land in the continent, Brazil has developed tropical farming plus a range of mining and industrial ventures, and Venezuela is the greatest oil and mineral producing country. But, many of the rest are still comparatively poor. Today, South American politics tend to be predominantly volatile. The overthrowing of presidents and governments by civil revolution or military uprising is a common, almost everyday, feature.

Both the Communist and the democratic world try to influence the directions in which South American countries develop. For example, the present Brazilian constitution set up in 1967 is essentially democratic, with a two-chamber elected congress, president and vice-president. There is a ban on political parties which work against democratic ideals and fundamental human rights. Likewise, Chile adopted a democratic constitution in 1925. In the presidential elections in 1970 the incoming president, on a minority vote, took the country along completely new lines with a Marxist coalition government. This became unpopular both inside Chile and in the outside world. In 1973 the government was overthrown by the military, who have since established a military government, dissolved the National Congress and banned all Communist parties and all other political activities.

Industry, Commerce and Communications

Prior to World War I, most South American countries exported their agricultural and mined raw materials, mainly to the Northern Hemisphere, and there was very little industrial development. In the sixty-plus years since then, some countries have attempted to broaden their economies, establish a range of industries and thus be less dependent on imports of manufactured goods from North America, Europe and elsewhere. During the two periods of world war and throughout the great inter-war economic slump, those countries dependent upon one or two staple exports suffered severe econ-

1 Incas going to church, Pisco, Peru;
2 Bogota, capital of Colombia

Brazil and Argentina tower above other S American countries as developed economies: 1 Caracas, Venezuela – as with the country, oil is the mainspring of this capital's prosperity; 2 Modern road network, Rio de Janeiro, Brazil – this city and nearby Sao Paulo are the largest urban developments in the whole of the continent; 3 Buenos Aires harbour, Argentina – large meat processing plants surround the capital's busy port, preparing meat for worldwide export

1 △   2 ▽   3 ▽

Total Imports and Exports

(1975 figures in millions of U.S. dollars)

Brazil and Venezuela account for something like two-thirds of all South American trade. Venezuela has a trade surplus, most other countries have a deficit.

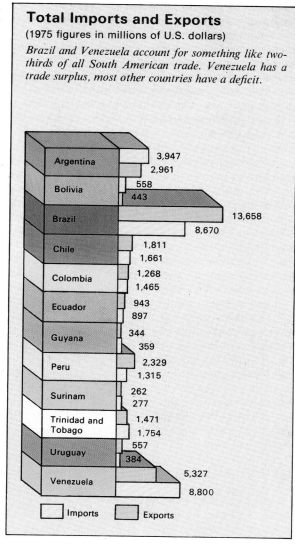

Country	Imports	Exports
Argentina	3,947	2,961
Bolivia	558	443
Brazil	13,658	8,670
Chile	1,811	1,661
Colombia	1,268	1,465
Ecuador	943	897
Guyana	344	359
Peru	2,329	1,315
Surinam	262	277
Trinidad and Tobago	1,471	1,754
Uruguay	557	384
Venezuela	5,327	8,800

☐ Imports   ▨ Exports

omic difficulties, so that diversification in their internal economies became essential.

South American industry is based on a wide range of raw materials, both farm products and mineral resources. Yet the minimal coal deposits hampered development for a long time, and today other energy sources, such as oil, natural gas and HEP have been developed to varying degrees. A second great problem for South American industrialization lies in the limited local markets; if the great majority of the population are poor, demand is limited, industrialization is thus unwarranted so there is little opportunity for the local population to become richer. Yet there is internal pressure to become more independent economically; thus far Brazil, Argentina, Chile and Uruguay have demonstrated most effectively how this can be done. Venezuela, Peru and Colombia are following behind.

The employment structure of Brazil, which has the largest population and probably the most advanced economy in the continent, provides an interesting contrast with those of developing countries in other continents. More than 2 out of every 5 working persons are employed in farming, about 1 in 6 in manufacturing industries, 1 in 10 in trade and commerce, 1 in 20 in transport and communications and the rest in a range of service industries and other activities.

The physical character of the continent and the way in which population has tended to cluster along the Atlantic seaboard and, to a lesser extent, in the Andean valleys and some Pacific fringe locations, have markedly affected the development of the transport networks. The great river systems are beset by rapids, silting and seasonal flow and, for the most part, traverse the least settled parts of the continent. Yet one day they could play a major part in the development of the interior.

Except in the Pampas area of Argentina and in parts of Brazil's Atlantic fringe, the railways are ill-developed. They consist largely of isolated lines for specific purposes or radial routes feeding into a single large city. A problem which has only recently been faced is that presented by the existence of so many different gauges. Air transport, both international and movements between the core region of a country and its remoter areas, was developed initially between the two world wars. It has expanded since World War II and is without doubt the most successful mode of transport for the terrain.

Road networks, like rail networks, are inconsistently developed. In their first phase of development, the inter-war era, the Pampas and south-east Brazil were the most rapidly developed areas, with a few main routes penetrating into the interior of the temperate southern parts and across the Andes to Chile. Since World War II, the often dreamed of Pan American Highway has been developed from Alaska to Argentina, though it is not yet complete. However, within South America it does provide through communications from Colombia southward to Chile, then eastward to Buenos Aires and north-eastward to Rio and Brasilia. Further developments, like the Amazonian Highway, are envisaged, which will aid in the development of the interior.

Agriculture, Forestry and Fishing

Equatorial South America contains the world's largest expanse of broad-leaf forest. While some of this has been cleared, the greater part of the Amazon Basin remains agriculturally unproductive. Much of the Pacific coastal strip from 5°S southward and the Andes Mountains are also unsuitable for farming, as is the Gran Chaco area of the interior.

Beyond these negative areas, grazing lands cover the next largest parts of the continent, dominating the farming landscapes south of about 15°S to southern Argentina. However, more intensive and often far more mixed farming is found on the Atlantic coastal fringes of Brazil, Uruguay and Argentina. Grazing and stock raising are also found in the valleys of the Andes, the Llanos and coastal Venezuela.

Livestock was introduced into South America during the sixteenth century. It was not until nearly 300 years later, however, that technological advances, such as refrigeration, made it possible to develop the great grasslands of the south and east, raising stock to be shipped back to the large markets of the Northern Hemisphere. The tropical grasslands and areas as far as 35°S are mainly cattle territory while sheep dominate the cooler areas from there to Cape Horn and also the Andean valleys.

South American grasslands are more reliable than those of South Africa and Australia, and are as yet nowhere near fully exploited. There is much scope for further development here. In all, the continent has nearly 18 percent of the world's 1,210 million cattle. Brazil, with 95 million, Argentina with 60 million, Colombia with 24 million and Uruguay with 11 million, have the largest numbers. Some 12 percent of the world's 1,040 million sheep can be found in South America. Argentina with 25 million, Peru with 17 million and Uruguay with 16 million have the largest numbers. The Argentine is the world's fourth largest wool producer; 167 thousand tonnes or 7 percent of the world total. Brazil alone has significant numbers of other farm animals, with 36 million pigs and 16,000 goats; 6 and 4 percent of the world totals respectively.

Arable farming in South America is markedly concentrated, crop by crop, in particular areas, with the subtropical and temperate regions of the south again being more important than the hotter parts of the north. Around 3 percent of the world's wheat production comes from this continent, almost entirely from extensive areas of Argentina, where 11 million tonnes are grown each year. Chile, Uruguay and southern Brazil produce far smaller quantities. Some 9 percent of the world's maize is grown in southern Brazil. Brazil, with 18 million tonnes, is the world's third largest producer. The only other cereal to be grown in quantity

SOUTH AMERICA

is sorghum. The Argentine contributes 10 percent of the world output, being second only to India in sorghum production.

Within the tropical areas, a few distinctive products loom large. In a typical year, 45 percent of the world's coffee is grown in Brazil, Colombia, Venezuela, Peru and Bolivia, with Brazil alone accounting for nearly 30 percent of the world total. Brazil again, with Ecuador and to a lesser extent Colombia and Venezuela, also produce a quarter of the world's cocoa. Nearly a quarter of the world's sugar cane comes from Brazil, Colombia, Argentina and Peru.

Brazil is also the world's second largest orange producer. Other citrus fruits are grown there in substantial quantities and in Argentina. Finally, Brazil produces more than twice as many bananas as any other single country in the world. Ecuador, Colombia and Venezuela also contribute to South America's share of just over one-third of the global total, making it the undoubted leader in this field.

The continent's vast forest reserves are little developed. Less than 9 percent of the world's sawn timber comes from here. More than two-thirds of that is produced by Brazil, the world leader for sawn broadleaf timber. Colombia is a poor second in the continent.

The Pacific Ocean is rich in fish and comparatively under-exploited. Peru, once the world's most important fishing nation, is now fourth in the world with 3.5 million tonnes (5 percent world total), and Chile fifteenth with 1.1 million tonnes. Peru is also a leading whaling nation.

Over and above commercial pastoral and arable farming, large areas are still farmed by Amerinds and mixed racial groups on a subsistence basis. Land is held communally or individually, or as a small-holding granted by the plantation owners. Here families grow such crops as maize, manioc, yucca and vegetables for their personal needs. Some of this farming is of a shifting kind, a wasteful practice which it may take a long time to eliminate.

Natural Resources

The power base of this continent goes part way to explain the lack of industrial development. Only Middle America has smaller reserves of coal. Modern outputs are derisory, standing at less than 10 million tonnes per year, of which Colombia and Brazil each contribute around 3 million tonnes. Indeed, South America's coal resources are considerably less than Africa's.

Since 1917, South America has become increasingly important as a crude oil producer. Venezuela, in particular, has rich resources, and is today one of the leading producers of the western world. This country is thought to possess 3 percent of the world's crude oil total. Smaller sources of crude oil are found along the Pacific fringes of Ecuador and Peru and in the extreme south of Chile. Some other small fields have been found and exploited east of the Andes, where further exploration is likely to reveal other reserves. Venezuela and Argentina are the only two significant producers of natural gas.

It is estimated that South America has about 12 percent of the world's HEP potential but only a very small part of this has been harnessed. Many of the finest locations are remote, development and transmission costs would be high and, in many cases, the countries with their comparatively backward economies simply do not have the demand for the electricity. Much of the potential is thus unexploited. As in so many fields, Brazil leads in HEP development, with a number of schemes in the highlands providing the great bulk of the nation's electricity needs.

Both in terms of reserves and modern outputs, the continent is well endowed with iron ore. As an individual country, Brazil has the third richest reserves in the world, and is the fourth largest producer with over 7.5 percent of the world's annual output. Venezuela, Chile and Peru are also in the top 15 producers, placing South America overall as the world's third most important continent in this respect.

The table opposite summarizes South America's production of other ores and precious resources.

South American Economy

More than any other continent, the population map of South America shows the main concentrations to be on the coasts and in the lower river valleys. There are also mountain valley concentrations in the tropical north-west. Around the main towns and cities are limited areas in which over 100 people per km² (250 per sq ml) live, but, outside these, population densities fall off rapidly. In lowland Argentina, Uruguay and Brazil large areas with more than 25 per km² (60 per sq ml) are found. But so much of Amazonia, Patagonia and the mountain areas have less than 1 per km² (2 per sq ml).

South American capitals dominate their countries, along with a few other major cities. Known as primate cities, they present a considerable problem to effective, widespread development. Thus, in Argentina, Buenos Aires has a population of 8.4 million, with no other city having a population one-tenth of that. In Brazil, Sao Paulo has 8 million and Rio de Janeiro 7 million, with the next largest city, Belo Horizonte, having only 1.5 million. Santiago in Chile has 3.2 million, the next largest being one-twelfth that size. Other millionaire cities of the continent

Many S American Indians live only at subsistence level: 1 Peasants at the market, La Paz, Bolivia – the world's highest sizeable city is at 3,600 m (11,800 ft); 2 Amazonian hunters, Brazil – tribes have been wiped out as areas of rain forest have been cleared; 3 Llama flock, Sacsahuamán, Peru – the ancient Inca rock fortress is a good shelter.

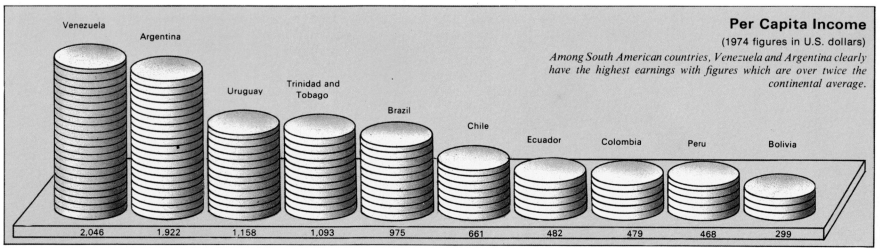

Per Capita Income
(1974 figures in U.S. dollars)
Among South American countries, Venezuela and Argentina clearly have the highest earnings with figures which are over twice the continental average.

Venezuela	Argentina	Uruguay	Trinidad and Tobago	Brazil	Chile	Ecuador	Colombia	Peru	Bolivia
2,046	1,922	1,158	1,093	975	661	482	479	468	299

are Lima (Peru) (3.3 million), Montevideo (Uruguay) (1.2 million), Caracas (Venezuela) (2.2 million), Bogota (Colombia) (2.9 million) and Medellin (Colombia) (1.1 million).

South American birth rates are mainly far higher than world averages. In some countries they exceed 40 per 1,000 though 25–39 per 1,000 is the norm. Uruguay, with 20.9 per 1,000 has the lowest birth rate. Death rates are mainly below 10 per 1,000. Thus, in the majority of South American countries, population grows by more than 2.5 percent each year, and in six by more than 3 percent annually.

Overall the growth of international trade conducted by South American countries in the past forty years has not kept up with world trends. Although world imports and exports grew by 4.5 and 8 times between 1938–'58 and 1958–'75. South America's import figures grew by only 3.2 and 4.5 times, and exports 3.7 and 3.7 times respectively. Obviously some countries are trading giants compared with others and individual performances have varied greatly. In 1938, Argentina, Brazil and Chile were the three leading countries. By 1975 the order had changed and Brazil, Venezuela and Argentina were the leaders. Between them, these three accounted for over two-thirds of the total international trade of the continent.

South American changes in per capita incomes in the period 1960 to 1974 have outstripped the non-Communist world growth of 186 percent; they have grown by 210 percent, though inflation has been more marked here than in other parts of the world. Some countries have growth figures above, others below this average. The largest growth has been in Brazil, with 390 percent. Other growth figures are Argentina 227 percent, Chile 190 percent and Venezuela 138 percent.

South America's energy production and consumption strikingly demonstrate the continent's deficiency in this field. As a whole, in 1975 the continent produced 334 million tonnes coal equivalent (mtce) and used 195 mtce. The export surplus of 139 mtce is due entirely to oil from Venezuela which produced 201 mtce and used only 32 mtce, exporting 169 mtce. Seen another way, the rest of the continent produced 133 mtce and used 168 mtce, showing that they had to import over one-fifth of their meagre energy needs. In this, Brazil played a major part, its production

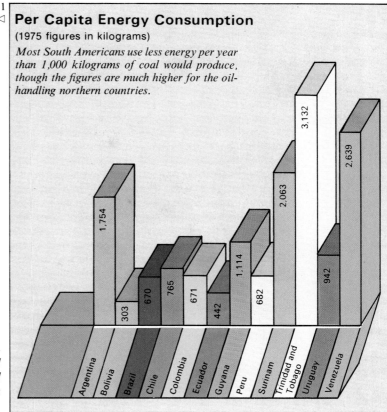

Per Capita Energy Consumption
(1975 figures in kilograms)

Most South Americans use less energy per year than 1,000 kilograms of coal would produce, though the figures are much higher for the oil-handling northern countries.

Argentina 1,754; Bolivia 303; Brazil 670; Chile 765; Colombia 671; Ecuador 442; Guyana 1,114; Peru 682; Surinam 2,063; Trinidad and Tobago 3,132; Uruguay 942; Venezuela 2,639

1 La Compañia Jesuit church, Quito, Ecuador – one of many architectural gems in this old capital; 2 Rio de Janeiro, Brazil – the splendid bay with its famous Sugar Loaf mountain is a fitting setting for this lively capital

being nearly 26 mtce but its consumption almost 72 mtce. Argentina has a fine balance of energy production and consumption of just over 42 mtce. In the rest of the continent, only Colombia produces and consumes more than 10 mtce.

Per capita energy consumption figures range from over 3,000 kg/ca in Trinidad and Tobago, 2,640 in Venezuela, to 303 in Bolivia and 153 in Paraguay. The overall continental average in 1975 was 813 kg/ca. Only Africa, with its average of a little less than 400, and Asia with just over 600 kg/ca, have lower figures.

The expression 'The Sleeping Giant' was used earlier to characterize South America. Experts have suggested that, given an appropriate stimulus or lead, the continent would stir. We have seen some of the problems which it faces, both economic and political. Yet there are signs that it is rousing itself, and will continue to do so in coming decades. South America's natural resources are becoming increasingly attractive as alternative supplies in the developed world are being rapidly used up. Some countries which were heavily dependent upon one or two staple exports, realize how dangerous this

is and are making attempts to diversify their economies. Most South American countries have been politically independent for a long time but have made little economic progress. There is now a growing impatience for economic growth and more economic independence.

Internally the problems of inflation are greater here than in other parts of the world, though these should be checked soon. More hopefully, in the last few years some countries, especially Brazil, have shown growths in their national products which have been well placed in the world tables. Things could go wrong, but given effective government of any sort and a little economic good fortune, the remainder of this century could be the time for comparatively rapid development of many parts of this hitherto backward American continent.

Ore	Average Annual World Production (million tonnes)	South America's Share (percent)	Principal South American Producing Countries
bauxite	80.3	10	Surinam, Guyana
chrome	7.2	2	Brazil
copper	7.4	13	Chile, Peru
lead	3.2	7	Peru, Argentina
manganese	22.8	10	Brazil
molybdenum	0.084	12	Chile, Peru
silver	0.01	18	Peru, Chile, Bolivia
tin	0.2	15	Bolivia, Brazil
tungsten	0.036	9	Bolivia, Brazil, Peru
vanadium	0.02	3	Chile
zinc	5.4	8	Peru

South American Countries

Argentina

The lands around the River Plate were first discovered by Spanish explorers in 1515. They remained under Spanish control until 1816 when Argentina broke away from European rule and became independent. Since 1976 it has been under a military government.

Much of the western part is taken up by the Andes Mountains, rising to 6,959 m (22,831 ft) in Mount Aconcagua. The east of the country is largely plain land. Here, the lush Pampas, one of the world's richest farming regions for both beef and wheat production, is most important to the economy. The Argentinian population is most heavily concentrated in the Plate valley. In the southern area of Patagonia and in the Gran Chaco of the north, as well as in the mountainous west, the population is far smaller.

Argentina is a major trading nation. Her meat exports are the second largest in the world. Wheat, wool, vegetable oils, hides and skins are other leading exports. Among the most valuable imports are chemicals, machinery and electrical equipment and mineral oil. Her main trading partners are the USA, Brazil and West Germany.

Bolivia

Up to one hundred years ago Bolivia extended to the Pacific coast but at that time Chile defeated Bolivia in one of a series of South American wars, and extended her territory northward to the present border with Peru. The area of Bolivia is now little more than one-third of the independent republic of Bolivia which was originally created in 1826. Parts of the original area which extended to the Pacific coast were lost to Chile, Peru, Brazil, Paraguay and Argentina, throughout the nineteenth and early in the twentieth centuries. One of South America's two landlocked countries, Bolivia today largely depends on special arrangements with Peru and Chile for trading through their Pacific coast ports.

Bolivia may be divided into three broad geographical regions: the eastern and northern plains (the *Oriente*), occupying nearly 75 percent of the country; the main eastern ranges of the Andes Mountains running northwest to south-east; the high plains within the Andes (the *Altiplano*), in the west and south-west.

For such a large country, Bolivia is comparatively thinly populated. The greatest centres of population are in the cities and towns in the valleys of the central mountain region and the surrounding farming areas.

Overall, it is a poor agricultural country, though in recent years schemes have been set up to develop the *Oriente* for sugar cane, rice and cotton growing as well as for cattle raising.

Economically, Bolivia depends very largely on the extraction and export of minerals. Some 60 percent of her total foreign earnings come from the sale of tin, zinc, silver, antimony and other minerals. These are mined in difficult conditions high up in the mountains, mainly by Amerinds. Recently, oil and natural gas have been discovered in the south and east of the country; Bolivia is now self-sufficient in both. The chief imports are foodstuffs, machinery, vehicles and other metal manufactures. Most trade is conducted with the USA, Argentina, Japan and West Germany.

Brazil

First discovered in 1500 by the Portuguese, Brazil remained under European influence until it was declared an independent kingdom in 1822. After 67 years and two kings, a republic was established in 1889. Today it is by far the largest single country in South America, occupies nearly 50 percent of the continental area and has just over half of the total population. Unique among the South American republics, the official language of Brazil is Portuguese.

The northern, widest parts contain most of the Amazon Basin. The southern parts are dominated by the Brazilian Highlands. Most of the population is found in the coastal regions and the neighbouring highland fringes, especially around the Tropic of Capricorn. Sao Paulo and Rio de Janeiro between them have a population of over 15 million. In an attempt to open up the heart of the

South American landscape is varied and its features frequently breathtaking: 1 Fernando de Noronha, off Brazil – this wild island, with its dramatic coastline, is part of Brazil's smallest state; 2 Machu Picchu, Peru – the ruins of this Inca city, near Cuzco, on a mountainous terraced site, are a major tourist attraction since their discovery in 1911

1 △

2 ▽

country, a new capital, Brasilia, was created some 1,000 km (620 ml) north-west of Rio in 1960. It grew to a city of over 600,000 within fifteen years.

Over 40 percent of the population is classified as rural. Agricultural and forestry exports are three times as valuable as other commodities: sugar, coffee, cotton and pinewood are the most important exports. Other major crops are maize, bananas, oranges and rice.

Much of the potential of Brazil's wide range of minerals has yet to be developed. So many of the riches lie inland where there are no real communications networks. This country has some of the richest iron ore deposits in the whole world, and also large deposits of rarer minerals such as chrome, mica, graphite, manganese and tungsten.

Brazil's most important industries are textiles, HEP, wood processing and paper manufacture. Her main imports are fuels, wheat and a wide range of mechanical goods including vehicles and chemicals. Principal trading partners are the USA, the Netherlands, West Germany, Japan and the United Kingdom.

Chile

When South America's west coast was discovered by Spanish explorers in the early sixteenth century, the narrow strip of land west of the Andes was established as a single colony and Santiago was settled in 1541. Chile freed itself from Spanish rule in 1818, becoming an independent republic. Since 1973 the country has been run by a military government.

Chile extends through nearly 50° of latitude and has a coastline some 4,120 km (2,560 ml) long; yet its east-west extent is rarely more than 200 km (125 ml). From north to south it may be divided into four areas – the inhospitable arid zone of the Atacama Desert, a Mediterranean region, a wetter, windswept forested region and finally a small grassland area.

The natural difficulties in north Chile have been overcome to develop the rich mineral deposits of the arid region. Copper is the most important single mineral and brings in 80 percent of Chile's foreign earnings. About 14 percent of the world's copper is mined in Chile. Iron ore production is increasing and has now overtaken nitrates to become the second most valuable mineral produced by weight.

Well over 60 percent of Chileans are classified as rural, but farm and forest products account for less than 10 percent of the national wealth. Recent efforts have been made to increase agricultural output and reduce the need to import foodstuffs. Wheat, maize and potatoes are the leading crops. Olives, grapes and citrus fruit are also important. Forestry is valuable both for sawn timber and paper products.

Chilean industry has developed steadily in recent years. Iron and steel production is growing at a new plant near Concepcion. The output

of cellulose and wood pulp now increases each year as does textile production. Chile's principal imports are industrial equipment, foodstuffs, fuels, vehicles and chemicals. West Germany, the USA and Japan are her main trading partners.

Colombia

As seen on the modern map, Colombia has only been in existence since 1886. When the north-western parts of Spanish America, then known as New Granada gained independence in 1819, the state of Greater Colombia included those areas now comprising Panama, Venezuela and Ecuador. Colombia was created from within those areas 67 years later. It is a democratic republic.

The country has both an Atlantic and a Pacific coastline. It may be divided into three broad geographical regions; the south-eastern interior lowlands which are scantily populated and under-developed; the central mountain region where the main concentrations of population are found, and the coastal lowlands which are more extensive and more developed in the northern, Atlantic-facing parts.

With most of the population living at heights of between 1,200–3,000 m (4,000–10,000 ft) above sea level, where the range of climates varies greatly with altitude, it is not surprising that Colombian agriculture produces a wide range of crops. Tropical crops include coffee, cotton, rice and sugar cane. Temperate crops

1 Quito, Ecuador – the picturesque capital is situated below the Pichincha volcano in a basin of the Andes; 2 Panteon National, Plaza de los Heroes, Asuncion, Paraguay – the capital has strong links with near neighbours Brazil and Argentina; 3 Carnival, Trinidad, W Indies – this Caribbean island relies on tourism and refining oil from nearby Venezuela

include barley, potatoes and wheat. Cattle are the most numerous farm animals. Much agricultural potential has yet to be developed.

Colombia is rich in minerals. Her output of gold is the highest in South America, and her deposits of platinum are thought to be the largest in the world. Emeralds, silver, copper, lead and crude oil play a leading part

South American Countries

in the economy. Colombian exports are dominated by coffee, followed by cotton, emeralds and animal products. Machinery and manufactured goods, rubber, chemicals and fertilizers head the list of imports.

Ecuador

The Spanish colony of Ecuador was established in 1532. Following unrest early in the nineteenth century it threw off European rule in 1819 and joined in a federation with Colombia. It became an independent republic in 1830. Since 1972 it has had a military government.

Ecuador may be divided into three distinct geographical regions. In the east lies the tropical jungle of the Upper Amazon Basin (the *Oriente*).

The Andes, rising in Mount Chimborazo to 6,267 m (20,561 ft) dominate central Ecuador. Here are many valleys which are heavily populated, and which produce temperate crops and animal products. Western Ecuador (the *Costa*), has some of South America's widest coastal plains. Tropical crops are grown here, especially bananas, coffee and cocoa. Much of Ecuador is covered by untouched, inaccessible forest lands. The only wood which is sawn and exported in quantity is balsa.

Ecuador is not well endowed with minerals. There is a little working of copper, gold, silver, lead and zinc. In the last few years, oil exploration has been stepped-up and production is rising steadily. Some of this is now exported, but food exports are more important, most trade being conducted with the USA and Europe.

Falkland Islands

A British crown colony whose connection with the United Kingdom is the subject of a dispute with Argentina, the Falkland Islands comprise two large islands, East Falkland with the capital of Stanley, West Falkland, and a number of smaller islands. The whole group lies some 770 km (480 ml) north-east of Cape Horn. Half the population live in Stanley, the rest being scattered over both the main islands. Almost all of the population is descended from British settlers. There are some 650,000 sheep on the islands, providing wool as the main export item. Communication with the outside world is maintained by a weekly air service to Argentina and by an occasional vessel direct to and from the United Kingdom.

A number of other nearby islands in the South Atlantic form the Falkland Island dependencies. South Georgia was once an important whaling and sealing base but is now inhabited only by a small party of scientists of the British Antarctic Survey. No one lives on the South Sandwich Islands.

French Guiana

The Guiana coastlands were originally settled by the Dutch. Following a number of changes involving the French, Portuguese and British, in 1815 the Congress of Vienna created separate colonies, including French Guiana. The smallest of the mainland countries of South America, this is the only one which is not now independent, being one of France's four overseas departments. It has its own local government but also sends representatives to the French National Assemblies in Paris.

The southern boundary of French

1 Montevideo, Uruguay – set in a bay on the shore of the Rio de la Plata, the capital is the main port and industrial city; 2 Shanty town, Buenos Aires, Argentina – much poverty remains away from the heart of the spacious modern city; 3 Indians farming the Altiplano, Bolivia – all agricultural pursuits are difficult on this barren tableland high up in the Andes

1 △

2 ▽

3 ▽

Guiana is the low watershed between the short rivers flowing northwards to the Atlantic and the lower left-bank tributaries of the Amazon. Most of the interior is undeveloped forest land. Small areas of the coastal strip have been developed for agriculture, with manioc, sugar cane, bananas and maize being most widely grown. Little livestock is kept.

Guyana

In 1796 the British seized control of the Guiana coast from the original Dutch settlers, and in 1815 the separate colony of British Guiana was established. This became an independent country with the name Guyana in 1966. It is a member of the Commonwealth.

The main centres of population are along the coast and in the lower valleys of the rivers Demerara, Essequibo and Berbice. The country may be divided into three main geographical regions. The low coastal strip contains the main agricultural areas producing sugar cane, rice, coconuts and citrus fruit. The slightly higher, forested, undulating country contains proven mineral reserves of bauxite, gold, manganese and diamonds. The interior, forested parts of the Guiana Highlands and the tall grasslands extend into Northern Brazil and Venezuela.

For its size, Guyana is an important trading nation, mainly selling to and buying from the USA, the United Kingdom and other countries in the Caribbean area. Sugar, alumina, bauxite, rice, rum and timber products are most important. Imports are headed by vehicles and machinery for the mines and factories, fuels, especially petroleum products, and fertilizers.

There is much scope for expansion and development in Guyana. The forests of the interior are still largely untouched and production could be increased greatly if a road network were developed. In the lower coastal regions, large areas of unimproved land could be settled and developed for tropical crops and grazing land.

Paraguay

The Spanish colony of Paraguay was established in 1535. It became independent in 1811, then suffered heavily in wars against Brazil, Argentina and Uruguay between 1865 and 1870, and against Bolivia between 1932 and 1935. Like Bolivia, it is a landlocked country, depending largely on special arrangements with Argentina to trade with the outside world, using the Rivers Paraguay and Parana and the port of Buenos Aires.

Paraguay is far more thinly populated than the other South American republics, the main centres of population being in the south and southeast. It is also probably the least developed. Much of western and central Paraguay comprises the economically unproductive Gran Chaco.

1 Santiago, Chile – this Andean capital is responsible for the major share of the country's industrial output of such goods as textiles and footwear; 2 Marine iguanas, Galapagos Islands, Ecuador – now a nature reserve, these islands are home for several wildlife species which cannot be found elsewhere, including the large tortoises after which the Galapagos were named. Darwin obtained crucial material here when forming his ideas on evolution in the 1830s; 3 A colourful shopping street scene in La Paz, which is the capital city of Bolivia. La Paz is set high up in the magnificent Andes mountains

South American Countries

In the east and south, soya beans, cotton and wheat are produced. Here, also, some 6 million head of cattle and smaller numbers of pigs and sheep are raised. Large areas of hardwood forest are found in the extreme east, but these have so far been little developed. Paraguay has virtually no commercially exploitable minerals.

By South American standards, Paraguay's foreign trade is very limited. Her main exports are meat products, timber, vegetable oils, tobacco and cotton. Foodstuffs, vehicles, machinery, chemicals and fertilizers are the main imports. The USA, Argentina, Brazil, West Germany and the UK are the main trading partners.

Peru

In pre-colonial days, Peru was the centre of the Inca civilization. It became the most important Spanish colony, achieving independence in 1824. Since 1968 it has been controlled by a military government.

Peru may be divided into four broad geographical regions. From south-west to north-east they are: the Pacific coastal strip averaging about 80 km (50 ml) in width, the coast ranges and the Andes rising to 6,768 m (22,205 ft) with valleys between the main ranges, the high wooded region of the *Montana*, and finally the dense jungle of the Upper Amazon Basin. The main concentrations of population are on the coast and in the Andean valleys.

About 50 percent of the population is classified as rural, but farm products account for only about 16 percent of the value of the national production. Sugar cane, cotton, coffee and wool are the principal items. Sheep, llamas and alpacas are all kept for their wool. Peru is a major world fishing nation in terms of its catch. Anchovies are the most important single fish and are processed into fish meal and exported as an animal feedstuff. Other important fish are tuna and bonito. Peru's fishing industry is now turning to supply the domestic market.

Peru is also an important mineral producer and exporter, especially of lead, copper, iron, silver, zinc and crude oil. Minerals, metals and fish products account for 80 percent of the exports, and agricultural products only 15 percent. Imports are mainly machinery, foodstuffs, chemicals and vehicles. The USA, Japan, West Germany, the Netherlands and the United Kingdom are Peru's main trading partners.

Surinam

Geographically the central country of the three Guiana coast ones, Surinam has always had close ties with the Netherlands, and was a Dutch colony from 1815–1957 known first as Dutch Guiana. In 1975 it gained full independence. Like French Guiana and Guyana, Surinam comprises a settled coastal strip and central valley, beyond which lie expansive forested areas. The latter cover rising ground which reaches the highest parts of the Guiana/Brazil watershed.

Commercial agriculture is limited to the coastal zone and the lower parts of the main valleys. Rice, sugar cane and tropical fruits are the main crops. Livestock numbers are small. The forest reserves are being developed steadily both for sawn timber and wood products like plywood and wood-particle board. Far more important are the rich deposits of bauxite and the alumina and aluminium plants which are fed by these, to account for about two-thirds of Surinam's foreign earnings. Foodstuffs and forest products account for most of the rest. Raw materials and machinery are the main imports.

Trinidad and Tobago

The island of Trinidad, just north of the Venezuelan coast, was discovered by Columbus in 1498 and became a Spanish colony in 1532. In 1802 it became a British colony. Tobago, 30 km (19 ml) to the north-east, became a British colony in 1814. The two islands were united administratively in 1889 and became an independent member of the Commonwealth in 1962.

Trinidad's northern margin comprises a highland ridge rising to 940 m (3,084 ft). The central and southern parts present a lower undulating landscape. Tobago is about one-twentieth the size, and is made of a broad south-west to north-east hilly ridge. The population, mainly of African and true Asiatic Indian descent, is just over 1 million in Trinidad and about 50,000 in Tobago.

Both islands are covered with dense natural forest, large parts of which have now been cleared. The most important planted crops are now sugar cane, cocoa, coconuts and citrus fruit. Trinidad also has considerable oil reserves and the natural 'Pitch Lake', covering nearly half a square kilometre, from which asphalt is recovered. There are metal processing plants and three oil refineries which process both local and imported crude oil.

Crude oil imports and refined product exports are the main items of international trade. Besides refined oil products, sugar, cocoa and tropical fruits are the main exports. Many non-tropical foodstuffs, particularly flour, dairy products, meat and rice, chemicals and a range of manufactured goods have to be imported.

Uruguay

South America's second smallest republic, Uruguay was part of the Spanish territory around the River Plate, and then a province of Brazil. It became an independent country, a buffer state between Argentina and Brazil, in 1828.

Uruguay is low-lying, the highest ground rising to no more than 500 m (1,600 ft) above sea level. The population is fairly evenly spread with the main centres being along the southern coastlands. Agriculture is the base of the national economy with 16.5 million hectares of land farmed. Over 20 million sheep and 8 million cattle are kept on 90 percent of this land and, on the rest, wheat, maize and rice are the three major crops grown. Many factories process agricultural products; meat packing and processing and textiles are most important.

For a country of its size and population, Uruguay has a large foreign trade. Meat products, wool and textiles account for nearly two-thirds of her foreign earnings. Raw materials, fuel oils, chemicals and machinery are the largest imports. Trade is mainly with Brazil and the EEC.

Venezuela

Following the South American Wars of Independence, Venezuela became part of Simon Bolivar's Greater Columbia in 1819. It has been an independent republic since 1830. One of the middle-sized South American republics, it is today the richest of them, largely because of its oil reserves.

First discovered in Venezuela in 1917, oil production rose steadily to just over 2 million barrels per day by the early 1970s. Three-quarters of this output comes from the Maracaibo area. The reserves of the Orinoco region where production has been increasing recently are not yet fully realized.

South of the Orinoco, rich deposits of iron ore are found. These are currently mined and either used in Venezuela or exported, mainly to the USA. Other mined products include gold and diamonds. Rich reserves of manganese, phosphates, nickel and sulphur are also known. With such a broad base of raw materials, Venezuela is in a strong position to establish a wide range of industries. So far, oil refineries, an iron and steel plant and a range of smaller manufacturing industries have already been established.

Venezuela's main farming products are maize, rice, sugar cane, coffee and cocoa. Beef cattle and pigs are the most numerous livestock. Over 40 percent of the population are classified as rural, and a large proportion of them enjoy a low standard of living in a country which is, by South American standards, rich.

Venezuela has a large surplus in her balance of payments. Oil, iron ore and coffee are the three leading exports; imports of raw materials, machinery, foodstuffs and chemicals come mainly from the USA, Japan and the EEC countries.

1 Caracas, Venezuela – the modern Centro Simon Bolivar presents a sharp contrast to some of the capital's suburbs; 2 Carnival dancer, Rio de Janeiro, Brazil – in a superb setting, with the famous Copacabana beach, Rio attracts the international 'jet set'; 3 Cuzco, Peru – the attractive Inca capital contains many splendid relics of the ancient civilization

COUNTRY REFERENCE: SOUTH AMERICA

South American Countries	Political Status	State Capital	Area km²	Area sq ml	Population	Population Density per km²	Population Density per sq ml	Births per Thousand Persons	Deaths per Thousand Persons	Mean Annual Percentage Increase in Population
Argentina	A	Buenos Aires	2,776,889	1,072,162	26,075,000	9.4	24	22.7	9.4	1.3
Bolivia	A	Sucre and La Paz	1,098,581	424,164	4,887,000	4.4	12	43.7	18.0	2.6
Brazil	A	Brasilia	8,511,965	3,286,487	113,815,000	13	35	37.1	8.8	2.8
Chile	A	Santiago	756,945	292,258	10,740,000	14	37	26.3	9.0	1.7
Colombia	A	Bogota	1,138,914	439,737	25,460,000	22	58	40.6	8.8	3.2
Ecuador	A	Quito	283,561	109,483	8,180,000	29	75	41.8	9.5	3.4
Falkland Islands	C	Stanley	11,961	4,618	1,900	0.2	0.4	21.5	13.8	0.8
French Guiana	C	Cayenne	91,000	35,100	66,000	0.7	1.9	28.3	7.8	3.5
Guyana	A	Georgetown	214,969	83,000	781,000	3.6	9.4	31.6	7.2	2.2
Paraguay	A	Asuncion	406,752	157,048	2,839,000	7.0	18	39.8	8.9	3.0
Peru	A	Lima	1,285,216	496,224	16,795,000	13	34	41.0	11.9	3.2
Surinam	A	Paramaribo	163,265	63,037	454,000	2.8	7.2	36.9	7.2	2.6
Trinidad & Tobago	A	Port of Spain	5,128	1,980	1,118,000	218	565	24.0	6.5	1.2
Uruguay	A	Montevideo	177,508	68,536	2,826,000	16	41	20.9	9.5	1.2
Venezuela	A	Caracas	912,050	352,144	13,047,000	14	37	36.1	7.0	3.1
SOUTH AMERICA TOTALS			17,834,704	6,885,978	227,084,900	13	33	—	—	—

1 △

2 △

3 ▽

143

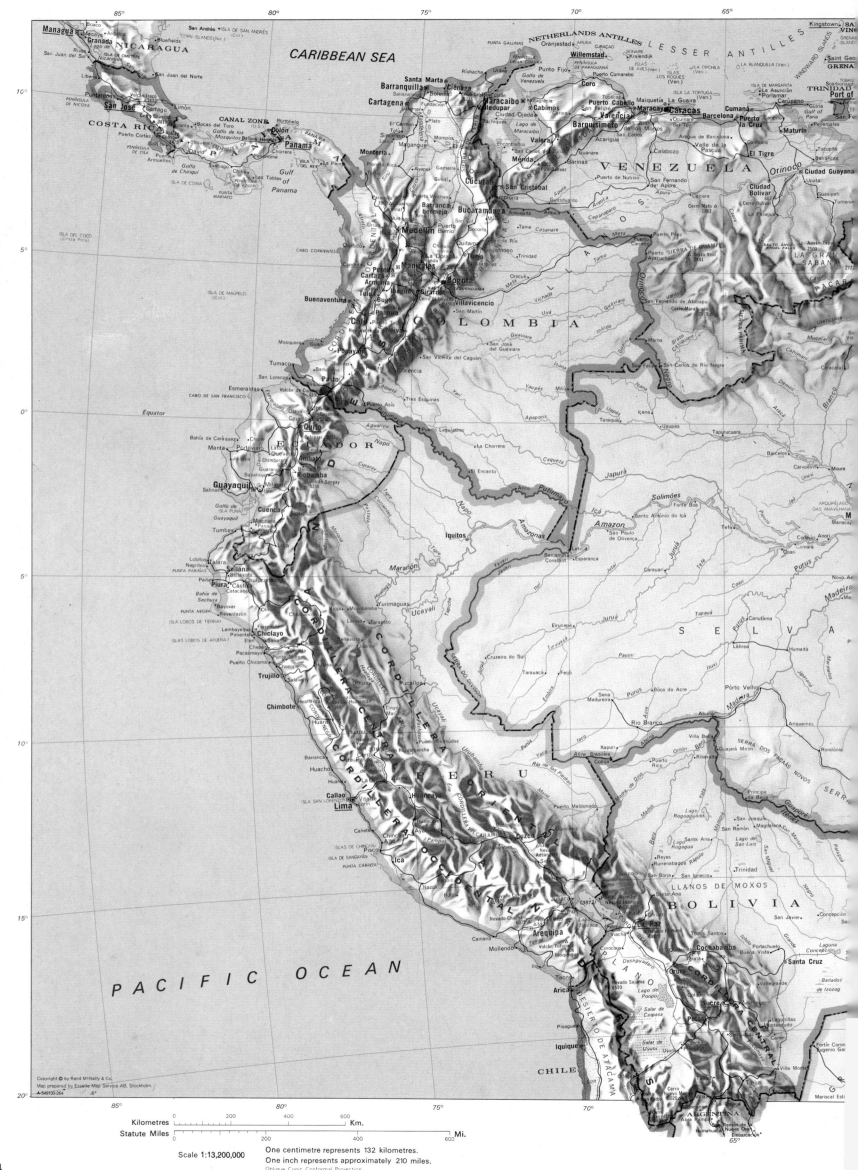

CARIBBEAN SEA

PACIFIC OCEAN

VENEZUELA

COLOMBIA

ECUADOR

PERU

BOLIVIA

CHILE

S E L V A

NICARAGUA

COSTA RICA

PANAMA

NETHERLANDS ANTILLES   LESSER ANTILLES

TRINIDAD

Equator

Kilometres
Statute Miles

Scale 1:13,200,000

One centimetre represents 132 kilometres.
One inch represents approximately 210 miles.
Oblique Conic Conformal Projection

ATLANTIC OCEAN

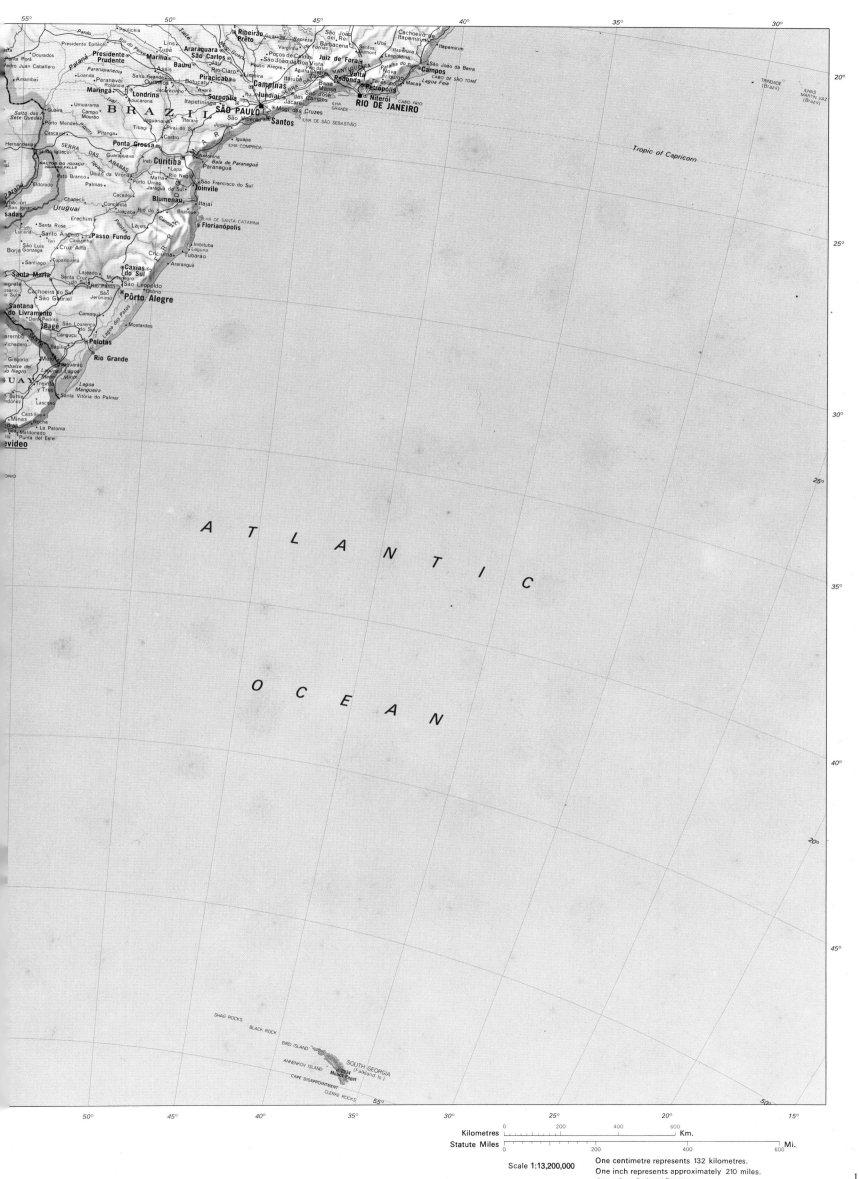

ATLANTIC

OCEAN

Tropic of Capricorn

BRAZIL

São Paulo
RIO DE JANEIRO
Santos
Niterói
Petrópolis
Campos
Curitiba
Florianópolis
Pôrto Alegre
Pelotas
Rio Grande

Montevideo

55° 50° 45° 40° 35° 30°
20°
25°
30°
25°
35°
20°
40°
45°
15°

SHAG ROCKS
BLACK ROCK
BIRD ISLAND
SOUTH GEORGIA
(Falkland Is.)
Mount Paget
ANNENKOV ISLAND
CAPE DISAPPOINTMENT
CLERKE ROCKS

50° 45° 40° 35° 30° 25° 20° 15°
55° 50°

Kilometres   0   200   400   600   Km.
Statute Miles   0   200   400   600   Mi.

Scale 1:13,200,000   One centimetre represents 132 kilometres.
One inch represents approximately 210 miles.
Oblique Conic Conformal Projection

147

NORTH AMERICA
Physical Profile

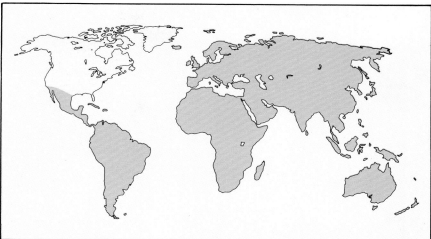

World Location and Size

The Americas stretch from well north of 80°N in the islands of Canada and Greenland to 56°S at Cape Horn. The extent of North America itself is from the northern tips of the Canadian Islands to those of Florida Keys at 24°N, a distance of some 6,250 km (3,900 ml). The most westerly point on the mainland of the continent is at 167°W in Alaska. On the Atlantic coast, Labrador lies at 56°W, but Newfoundland and Greenland extend even farther to the east.

Mainland North America is remarkably compact, being essentially rectangular with appendages in the north-west and south-east. Beyond the mainland lie many islands, especially in the north. Within the main rectangle are hundreds of lakes, with the open sea of Hudson Bay in the north.

The North American coastline shows a number of contrasting features. Parts, such as British Columbia and Maine, have a complex, fretted outline with a number of offshore islands. Elsewhere, the outline is far more simple, as in Oregon and California. In places like Texas and Louisiana the coast is one of bars and lagoons.

Landscape

North America can be broadly divided into four major physical regions. In the north, surrounding Hudson Bay in a great crescent-shaped area, lies the Canadian or Laurentian Shield. It has been stripped of most of its soil during recent glaciations, has hundreds of lakes dotted on its surface and has little agricultural potential. The main interest lies in the mineral resources of the old rocks, and in forestry.

Along the east side of the continent lie ranges of mountains with a maximum height of 2,037 m (6,684 ft) in the Blue Ridge area of the Appalachians. Extending from Alabama in the south to the Canadian border in the north, the Appalachians continue into the mainland Maritime Provinces and Newfoundland.

In the west, the Western Cordillera are far more complex and extensive. The Rocky Mountains are in the east of this belt while farther west lie the Sierra Nevada, the Cascades, the Coast Ranges and the Alaska Range. Between and within these lie a number of plateaus, desert basins, including the notorious Death Valley, and such fertile areas as the Central Valley of California and the Willamette Valley/Puget Sound lowlands

Opposite: Dramatic landscape of the Grand Canyon, Arizona, USA

farther north. These mountains today form the highest areas of the continent, rising to 6,194 m (20,320 ft) in Mount McKinley, Alaska. In this most unstable region of the continent lie the famous geysers of Yellowstone National Park, and the much feared San Andreas Fault which threatens many of the urban areas of California.

A wide lowland area stretches from the Arctic Ocean in the north to the Gulf of Mexico in the south. Part of this is very low, as in the floor of the Mississippi and Mackenzie valleys, but the high plains reach to some 1,600 m (5,000 ft) above sea level at the front ranges of the Rocky Mountains.

North America is a land of great rivers and river basins, most of which drain toward the Atlantic and Arctic Oceans, Hudson Bay and the Caribbean Sea. The central lowlands are drained southward by the 'big-muddy' Mississippi/Missouri Rivers system, and northward by the Mackenzie River and the Saskatchewan/Nelson system. Rivers flowing to the Pacific are mainly shorter, though a few, especially the Colorado, the Columbia/Snake system and the Frazer have developed impressive scenic courses through the mountains to the coast. Another distinctive water feature of the North American landscape is the lakes.

Climatic Background

Climatically, the North American continent extends from the tropics to the polar wastes, and has a full west-east range from one ocean to the other. Parts of mainland Canada, Greenland and other islands lie well inside the Arctic Circle. In the west of the continent lies the great mountain region which acts as a major barrier to the movement of air from west to east. In the east, the Appalachians have a similar barrier effect to air movements. Thus the interior of

the continent is effectively sealed from oceanic influences, though the unimpeded passage for air moving northward and southward from the Gulf or the Arctic does mean that, at times, warm air may penetrate well north or cold air well south.

In the extreme west, limited areas experience warm and cool temperate climates of an oceanic type. In parts, California enjoys a climate akin to that of some Mediterranean areas, but the coast ranges ensure that the Central Valley, for example, has great temperature extremes and, in the south, an acute water shortage. Farther north, in the coastal strip of Oregon, Washington and British Columbia, the average temperature of the coldest month stays above freezing level, but the summer average monthly temperatures never exceed 22°C (72°F).

East of this coastal area, and south of approximately 55°N, the climates of the mountain ranges are largely inhospitable. Then, those of the basins and ranges and the area as far east as about 102°W can be classified as dry, in that annual precipitation is below 250 mm (10 in) and, with the heat of most areas, this moisture has little useful effect. Temperatures are more extreme here than on the coast, the monthly average being below freezing for parts of the year.

Palos Verdes headland – breathtaking coastline lying south of Los Angeles, near Hermosa and Redondo beaches

Such semi-arid areas can be referred to as Steppe lands. In the extreme south-west, in Arizona, Utah and New Mexico, the more extreme conditions of hot deserts prevail, with July temperatures of 33°C (91°F), and 13°C (55°F) in January.

East of 102°W in south-east North America and across the whole continent north of 55°N, the climates may be broadly classified in west-east belts. Except for the tropical tip of Florida, the US south of Kansas, Kentucky and the Virginias enjoys a subtropical climate with rainfall throughout the year and distinctly warm summers. North of this area are progressively cooler and mainly drier zones. Thus the southern parts of the prairie provinces and much of the Great Lakes region enjoy a cool temperature climate, with rainfall increasing to the east.

Still farther north the climates become less and less inviting. Moving through a broad belt of subarctic climates, in the Tundra margins of northern Canada no month has an average temperature in excess of 10°C (50°F). Ultimately, there is Greenland, an area mostly covered by permanent ice.

NORTH AMERICA

European consciousness of the 'New World' dates from only about 1,000 years ago, and it was not until the 'discovery' voyages of Christopher Columbus (1492) and others that any real interest was focused on the vast North American continent.

The early seventeenth century saw small settlements of pioneers from France, Spain, the Netherlands and, above all, Britain, whose Pilgrim Fathers from that historic *Mayflower* voyage of 1620 laid the foundations for early British dominance. Despite an eighteenth-century influx of immigrants from Ireland and Germany, in 1776 when the colonies established an independent Union of the 13 existing states, four out of five of the new Americans still had English or Scots ancestry. The USA is now one of the two great political and economic world powers, a position it has achieved following a relatively short period of development.

The huge and somewhat remote land of Canada was first settled permanently by the French but always with a strong British presence. Ceded to the English by the Treaty of Paris in 1763, Canada remained loyal during the War of Independence and was established as a dominion in 1867.

Population Growth

The North American population has grown continuously over the past two centuries, increasing more rapidly in the climatically more attractive USA than in Canada. Throughout this time, natural increase has been boosted by periods of mass migration, particularly from Europe. From the end of the Napoleonic Wars to the outbreak of World War I, about 30 million people crossed the Atlantic to start a new life in this inviting continent. At the peak, nearly 1,300,000 settlers entered the USA alone in 1907, and 400,000 entered Canada in 1913. In the 1920s, restrictions on new immigrants were imposed, and since that time far smaller numbers of new settlers have been able to enter the continent.

Today, when most modern 'Americans' come from European stock, it is necessary to remember that they are not the descendants of the original settlers of this large land mass, nor the only modern group of any significance. The American Indians are thought to have crossed from Siberia to North America some 20,000 years ago, at a time when the Bering Strait had not been established. Their modern descendants are thus recognized as Mongoloid stock, being related to the Japanese and Chinese. When first encountered by Europeans, in a land originally thought to be India, these people with reddish-brown skins came to be known as 'Red Indians'.

At that time, there may have been about a million Indians in North America, with more in Mexico and the lands farther south. During the great European drive westward, the US Indians suffered greatly, being driven from their lands, but they fared better in Canada, due to a peaceful proclamation in 1763. By the end of the nineteenth century, the total population of North American Indians was very low but has now recovered to over 1 million. Almost half live on Indian Reservations covering nearly 25 million hectares (over 61 million acres) across the continent, and many traditional tribal customs are retained. Overall the modern Indians' standard of living is still below that of the white population.

Other Mongoloid groups whose settlement of the cold, northern margins of North America dates back thousands of years are the Eskimos of Alaska, Northern Canada and Greenland and the people of the Aleutian Islands. While retaining their traditional forms of life based on hunting, fishing and some primitive cultivation, both groups have adopted western habits as settlers have penetrated into the sub-polar areas. The trading post and the mail order catalogue have aided this integration into the main streams of modern American life.

European settlers remained with their fellow countrymen, concentrating on specific parts of the continent. The Spaniards, for instance, who settled mainly in the south, in Mexico and the West Indies, then moved northward into what is now the south-west USA. The English and smaller groups of Germans, Dutch and Scandinavians settled the main Atlantic coastal strip from Georgia to the Atlantic provinces, while the French penetrated the St Lawrence lowlands and later the Mississippi Valley to the Gulf coast.

1 and 2 Calgary Stampede and Ponoka grain stores, Alberta, Canada; 3 White House, Washington DC, USA; 4 Statue of Liberty, New York, USA

Finally, North America today has a substantial black population descended from West African slaves transported in vast numbers in the period 1619 to 1865. These were originally brought over to work on the plantations of the south-eastern states where the climate was far hotter and wetter than the European settlers were accustomed to. With the abolition of slavery at the end of the Civil War between the Federal north and the Confederate south in 1865, some 4.5 million blacks became free yet remained tied to the plantation area. Since then they have spread out over the rest of America, particularly to northern cities, but more than half of the modern total of over 22 million still live in the south-eastern states.

Today, then, no one national group has dominance in the USA. Canada, by contrast has a far higher proportion of its population descended from the English and French, probably over 80 percent. Thus, what may be termed the two 'melting pots' of North American population have produced two very different amalgams: the Canadians have preserved many English and French associations; the US citizens have a strong affection for, and some affinities with, many European countries, but their nation now has a great, newly-created identity.

Political Development

In 1776 the US consisted of that tier of states stretching from New England in the north to Georgia in the south. When peace was established, following the War of Independence, the border was moved westward to the line of the Mississippi River. Twenty years later, the extent of the country was almost doubled by the Louisiana Purchase, whereby the area extending into modern Montana, Wyoming, Kansas, Oklahoma and Louisiana was bought from the French. By 1819, Florida and a small strip of land which now constitutes southern Alabama and Mississippi had been gained from the Spanish.

Next, Texas, then larger than the modern state, seceded from Mexico and joined the USA in 1845. A year later, the Pacific north-west Oregon Territory between 42°N and 49°N entered the union. California and the south-west were added in 1848. In 1853, the Gadsden Purchase added the Gila Valley, thus effectively completing mainland USA excluding Alaska. Since then, Alaska has been purchased from Russia in 1867 and sovereignty was assumed over Hawaii in 1898.

Within each of these broad geographical areas individual states were only declared when a specified population level had been reached. Thus, within the Louisiana Purchase area, Louisiana itself became a state in 1812 and Arkansas in 1836, but Wyoming was only recognized in 1890 and, finally, Oklahoma in 1907. The last of the conterminous states to be declared were Arizona and New Mexico in 1912.

The eastern US/Canadian border was fixed by treaty after the War of Independence, and thereafter by agreement as the frontier of settlement moved west. North of the 49th parallel, agreed from Lake of the Woods to the Pacific in 1818, Canada grew more slowly. After the dominion was established in 1867 new provinces were added in succession: Manitoba in 1870, British Columbia in '71, Prince Edward Island in '73, Alberta and Saskatchewan in 1905.

Canada became an independent country within the then British Empire and Commonwealth in 1931, and was united with Newfoundland in 1949.

Thus, the internal political organization of most of North America can be seen to be one of rapid change over a period of little more than a century and a half. During that time, the continent developed rapidly in economic terms, so that by the inter-war period of the 1920s-'30s, the

whole fortune of the western world was very closely allied to that of the United States.

Since World War II the USA has been the most powerful country within the western world. At a time when the capitalist/Communist rivalry is foremost in all world affairs, the USA has endeavoured to contain the area of the world dominated by the eastern bloc. The Charter of the Organization of American States, designed to establish peace and

USA: Home for many diverse peoples, the United States is a young nation of energy and exuberance: 1 Chinatown, Manhattan, New York City – reflecting just one aspect of this cosmopolitan city which contains more large communities of ethnic minorities than any other world city; 2 San Francisco, California – the unique cable cars which serve this hilly and lovely city are a great tourist attraction; 3 Football game – the American version bears little resemblance to the sport played the world over, but ranks second only to baseball as the national game

NORTH AMERICA

justice, solidarity and collaboration, territorial integrity and independence for its members, was drawn up in 1948. A year later both the USA and Canada were original signatories to NATO, the military treaty to provide a collective shield for Western Europe against the eastern Communist bloc. The USA has also established military links and alliances westward across the Pacific.

Industry, Commerce and Communications

The North American Manufacturing Belt, the main area of industry and commerce, has no rigid boundaries but, in broad terms, extends from southern New England to somewhere west of Chicago. It encompasses many large towns and cities of the north-eastern US, the St Lawrence lowlands and lake shores of Canada. Within this area lie the coalfields of Pennsylvania, Ohio, Indiana and Illinois as well as the iron and steel industry of Pennsylvania, the lakeside towns and the Atlantic seaboard. Many manufacturing industries are closely associated with these extractive and basic industries.

This great complex had a virtual stranglehold on North American industry until World War I, but the last half century has seen other centres of manufacturing established within the continent. New industrial foci have developed along the western seaboard, in and around Los Angeles, San Francisco, Seattle and Vancouver. Other centres have developed in the interior, e.g. Dallas, Denver, St Louis, Kansas City and Minneapolis-St Paul.

Despite North America's importance as a major agricultural area, only 4 percent of the work force is engaged in farming. By contrast, 23 percent are employed in manufacturing industry, 36 percent in trade and commerce, 25 percent in services and 6 percent in transport and communications. Only a very advanced economy can sustain so many of the working population engaged in non-manufacturing work.

Both the USA and Canada are great trading nations. While the St Lawrence and the Great Lakes freeze in winter, their ports nevertheless handle much internal and international traffic in summer. The Atlantic seaboard from Halifax southward contains a series of large sea ports now well geared to handle the world's largest container ships and bulk carriers. On the west coast newer ports have developed primarily to handle trade with Japan, Australia and other trans-Pacific destinations.

Road, rail and air networks are all densely developed in the most settled parts of the continent, east of the Rockies and south of the climatic hazards of mid and northern Canada. North America is the archetypal home of the automobile. Personalized transport is more developed here than anywhere else in the world. Interstate highways, other state and national routes, and transcontinental roads like the Trans-Canada Highway, provide for rapid travel over long distances. At the same time, city centres handle large volumes of daily traffic, suffer from crippling jams and are dotted with parking lots.

The American rail network has been severely pruned in recent years as distance travellers have taken to the air. Intercity air travel is as highly developed here as anywhere in the world, and distances between major cities in excess of 450 km (300 ml) almost invariably have rapid jet links. Smaller centres, particularly in the less populated parts, are usually linked by regular air services using slower aircraft.

Agriculture, Forestry and Fishing

With the exception of the true tropical and equatorial, nearly all the world's natural environments existed within the North American continent. Today, many of these have been modified by man, but much of the natural cover remains.

Forests are thought to have covered about half of North America prior to European settlement. Virtually the whole of the Atlantic fringe was clothed in woodland, from coniferous in the north, through mixed areas of deciduous to subtropical in the extreme south. Such forests also existed well to the west. In the western parts of the interior plains, however, first tall grass prairie and, in the drier west, the short grass prairie replaced trees. Together these two areas of valuable rich soil extended from the Texas coast northward to the southern parts of the Canadian prairie provinces, and as far west as the Western Cordillera.

Today, about two-thirds of the area of the old forests still remain. Three important areas of forest are found in the mountains of the west: on the middle slopes of the Rockies, on the lower 2,500 m (8,000 ft) of the British Columbian and Pacific northwest states and on the lower sections of the coast ranges. Especially in the west, these provide some of the most valuable stands of hardwood in the whole world.

North America's forest industries play a major part in modern world supplies. An average of 350 million cubic metres of coniferous wood is felled each year, about twice as much in the US as in Canada. In total, this amounts to about 32 percent of the world total. In the hardwood league table, the contribution is less significant, the US providing less than 6 percent. However, Canada ranks first in the world and the USA second in both wood pulp and newsprint production.

Except in the mountains and desert areas, all of the US has now been adapted to some form of commercial farming. In comparison, so much of Canada remains non-agricultural.

Overall, North America is a land of great agricultural surplus. The continent covers some 14.5 percent of the world's surface, and its population is only about 5.9 percent of the world total. Compared with these figures, North America's share of

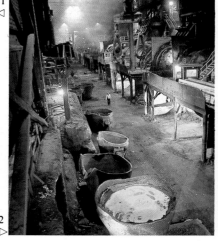

Canada: 1 Mount Royal, Montreal – 213 km (700 ft) above sea level, this park on volcanic soil overlooks the world's second largest French speaking metropolis; 2 International Nickel's copper cliff plant Sudbury, Ontario – the town is a major world nickel producing centre; 3 Alaska Highway – a primarily tourist road from British Columbia to the Yukon

Total Imports and Exports
(1975 figures in millions of U.S. dollars)

The USA is the world's largest trading nation. Remembering that Canada has about one-tenth the population, its trading performance is impressive.

	Imports	Exports
Canada	34,306	31,881
USA	102,984	106,157

world farming production is remarkably high.

Where cereal production is concerned, North America is among the world leaders for most temperate varieties. Currently, each year's world output of wheat exceeds 400 million tonnes. The US accounts for some 15 percent of this and Canada for a further 5 percent. Of maize, the world's second cereal, the USA alone accounts for nearly 48 percent of total production. North America features less significantly in barley production, 5 percent coming from Canada and a fraction less from the USA. World production of oats is only about one-eighth that of wheat and of this 22 percent is grown in North America.

North America is also a major area for the production of many fruits and vegetables. The US alone is the world leader for apples (13 percent), oranges (28 percent), grapefruit (65 percent) and tomatoes (17 percent). It is also a world leader in growing soya beans, sugar beet, potatoes, a range of other fruits, tobacco, cotton and peanuts.

Where livestock are concerned, the USA ranks second to India, with 11 percent of the total population of cattle, and third to China and the USSR with 8 percent of the pigs.

North America as a whole accounts for 15 percent of the world's milk production, 16 percent of its hen eggs and 5 percent of its fish.

Natural Resources

North America is well endowed with the supplies of fuel and power upon which modern industrial economies depend. The continent has, in addition, rich reserves of a wide range of minerals.

After a period in which coal production declined, North American output has again risen in the last decade. Now, only the USSR individually produces more than the USA, and Canada rates twelfth in world production. Over one-third of the world's hard coal is mined in the continent, but lignite (soft coal) is of little importance. On current estimates, over 26 percent of the world's coal reserves lie within North America.

North America again ranks second to the USSR in the production of crude oil, accounting for about one-sixth of world production. Proven reserves are less impressive, however, only 8 percent lying beneath the continent. Reserves of natural gas are also less impressive, standing at only 14 percent, although North

Ore	Average Annual World Production (million tonnes)	North America's Share (percent)	Principal North American Locations
bauxite	80.3	3	Arkansas
cobalt	0.03	6	Margins of the Shield
copper	7.4	27	W Cordillera and Canadian Shield (USA world leader)
gold	1 million kg	6	W Cordillera in both Canada and USA
lead	3.2	28	W Cordillera in both Canada and USA
molybdenum	0.084	75	Colorado
nickel	0.733	34	Canadian Shield (Canada world leader)
silver	0.01	26	W Cordillera
tungsten	0.036	13	USA W Cordillera
vanadium	0.02	19	USA W Cordillera
zinc	5.4	32	W Cordillera, Appalachia and Canadian Shield (Canada world leader)

America accounts for about half of the world's production of natural gas each year. With an eye to the possible future potential of nuclear energy, it should be noted that currently the USA produces 44 percent and Canada 25 percent of the world output of uranium, and their proven respective reserves are 30 and 13 percent of the world total.

As with crude oil, so with iron ore. The US has proven reserves of 7,500 million tonnes, but these represent only 3 percent of world reserves. Canada has far greater reserves, 33,700 million tonnes. Currently the two countries produce 46 million and 34 million tonnes respectively each year, representing together about 15 percent of the world total. Much of the Canadian ore is exported to the USA and Europe. The US also imports from Venezuela.

North America's share of world outputs of other minerals is, in many cases, considerable, as the table shows.

Electricity production and consumption play a relatively minor part in total energy figures, but the absolute totals for North America are at the head of the world league tables. As an industrial country, the US consumes twice as much electricity as any other world power, over 2 billion kilowatt-hours per year. Of this, 15 percent is hydro, 9 percent nuclear and 76 percent thermal. Canada consumes about one-tenth that total, indicating a similar per capita consumption, but no less than 74 percent of this is hydro-electric-power (HEP), 4 percent nuclear and only 22 percent thermal. Of all the continental areas, North America has made the greatest progress in harnessing water power, over half the potential capacity having been installed.

North American Economy

Within the continent, population is most concentrated in the great belt which encompasses Megalopolis from Boston, through New York and Philadelphia to Baltimore and Washington, in the industrial cities of the Great Lakes area and St Lawrence lowlands and in the three large urban concentrations of the Pacific fringes. In all these areas, the average density of population exceeds 200 persons per km^2 (500 per sq ml).

These concentrations apart, the population east of about 98°W is greater than 20 per km^2 (50 per sq ml) in all but the less hospitable areas. West of that line, it is mainly less than 10 per km^2 (25 per sq ml). In Canada, outside the main cities of the east, the prairie provinces and the Vancouver area, it is very thinly spread. There are within the USA 29

1 △

2 ▽

Canada: 1 Sawmill, shore of Lake Slocan, British Columbia – lumbering is a major industry in this westerly mountainous province; 2 Horses grazing on the Great Plains, South Saskatchewan – nearly 70 percent of Canada's wheat output comes from the rolling 'big sky' country of the prairie provinces, much of it going for export

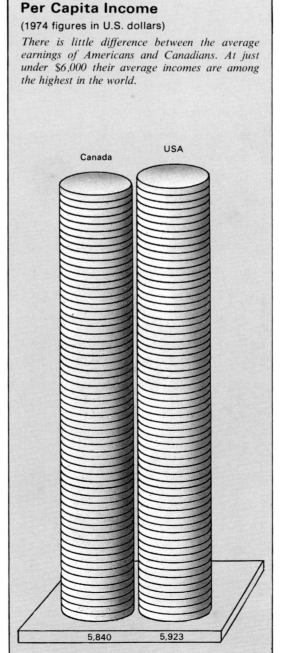

Per Capita Income

(1974 figures in U.S. dollars)

There is little difference between the average earnings of Americans and Canadians. At just under $6,000 their average incomes are among the highest in the world.

Canada   USA

5,840   5,923

NORTH AMERICA

millionaire cities, of which 14 contain more than 2 million people. New York with 17 million people, Los Angeles with 9 million and Chicago with 7.6 million are the three largest. Canada has three cities whose metropolitan areas contain more than a million inhabitants: Toronto and Montreal each with 2.8 million and Vancouver with 1.2 million.

Although world population is currently rising at a little over 4 percent per annum, this figure is nowhere near reached in North America. In the continent as a whole, the birth rate is running at 14.8 per thousand while the death rate is 8.9 per thousand. Thus, the net increase is some 0.8 percent per annum.

Remembering that inflation distorts figures which are compared over the years, there is no denying that the value of all North American imports rose 6.3 times from 1938 to 1958 and 7 times between 1958 and 1975. The corresponding figures for all North American exports were 5.8 and 6.1 times. All four figures are well above the corresponding world averages, giving a clear indication of both the major part played by the US and Canada in world trade and the growth of their contribution during the last 40 years.

The trading performance of the North American countries over the period 1938–'58 and 1958–'75 has advanced as much as that of almost any country in the developed world. Canadian imports rose from $691 million to $5,205 million and then to $34,306 million. As such figures reflect not only genuine growth but also inflation, they represent actual percentage increases of 653 and 559 respectively. Exports rose from $865 million to $5,045 million (483 percent increase) and then to $31,881 million (532 percent increase). The comparable figures for the US were, imports, $2,180 million, $13,298 million and $102,984 million (510 and 675 percent increases) and exports, $3,064 million, $17,775 million and $106,157 million (479 and 498 percent increases).

Thus, over the selected periods, Canada's imports have risen more rapidly than exports, but the recent trends are hopeful for a return to a balance of visible trade. Yet, in the USA where there has always been a surplus on visible trade, growth rates overall are a fraction lower and a little worrying in that imports are growing more rapidly than exports.

As for incomes, in the period 1960 –'74 these rose by 186 percent in the non-Communist world and by 290 percent in Europe. In Canada the rise has been 206 percent and in the USA 137 percent. Clearly, with the population of the USA approximately ten times that of Canada, the average figure for the continent is not surprisingly only 142 percent.

North America ranks as the world's greatest energy consuming continent on a per capita basis and the absolute figures for consumption are also very high. Canada is a net exporter of energy; 268.42 million tonnes coal equivalent (mtce) were produced in 1975 and 225.57 mtce consumed. In the US, the corresponding figures were 2,036 mtce and 2,349 mtce. For a continent which contains less than 6 percent of the world's total population, that North America produces nearly 27 percent of the world's energy in an average year yet consumes about 32 percent of it, is indeed remarkable. In large measure this reflects the high degree of development in both Canada and the US. But, as was clearly recognizable in the attempt of the US federal government to reduce energy consumption during and after the 'oil crisis' of 1973, these figures also reflect a somewhat extravagant attitude to energy consumption in the area. Indeed, in 1975 the USA was still consuming energy at the rate of 11,000 kg/ca and Canada 9,880 kg/ca. Compare this with elsewhere in the world – except for a few very small Middle Eastern countries where per capita figures do not add up to large *total* amounts – where the highest figures are 7,151 in Czechoslovakia, 6,485 in Australia and 6,178 in Sweden.

Although North America is still looked upon as the 'New World', it should be noted that its countries developed their economies only a short time behind those of Europe, the world leaders in industrial and commercial growth. While the US and Canada participated in both twentieth-century world wars which rocked Europe, the North American continent was not physically involved in either. The North American economies continue to grow, though they now face new challenges. There is the rivalry between the USA and the USSR as the leaders of the western and eastern blocs. There is the resurgence of such countries as Japan and the European recovery, including the remarkable economic growth of West Germany. There is the as yet unmeasured growth of China.

The US has been a world leader for more than half a century, at times with hardly a competitor in sight in economic fields. But the age of that unchallenged supremacy is past. As new technologies develop, the economically most advanced countries will be in intense competition. American attitudes to world competition and world change may themselves be subject to considerable adjustment. Remember that the USSR put the first artificial satellite into orbit around the earth but that the US put the first man on the moon. International brinkmanship reached its zenith at the time of the Cuban crisis when America forced the Soviet Union to retract. Later, however, in Vietnam the US had to concede that there could be no 'victory'.

In the Third World where neo-colonialism is replacing the old colonial systems after a short period of independence for the 'new nations', the US pursues policies apparently designed not to upset the global objectives of detente. Problems at home like the political shock of Watergate, a less stable economy and a weakened dollar, and the growth of the environmental and other lobbies must have their effect.

Doubtless North America will continue to contribute much to the advancement of our society, but there can be no denying that the US no longer in the unchallenged position it held previously.

1 △   2 ▽

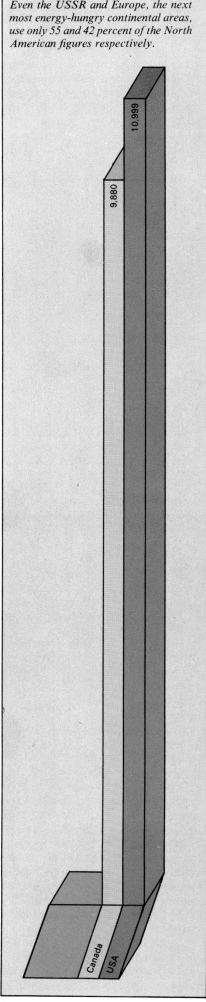

USA: Industrial and agricultural development throughout the country is as varied as the landscape of the 50 states: 1 Ford Rouge Plant, Detroit, Michigan – part of the world's biggest automobile manufacturing complex; 2 Sugar refinery, Hawaii – the last state to join the union has fertile farmland for production of the island's main crops, which are pineapples and sugar cane

Per Capita Energy Consumption
(1975 figures in kilograms)

In North America, energy used per head of population is higher than for almost anywhere else in the world. Even the USSR and Europe, the next most energy-hungry continental areas, use only 55 and 42 percent of the North American figures respectively.

10.999 — USA
9.880 — Canada

North American Countries

Canada

The second largest country in the world, Canada is by far the least populated of all the world's giant states in total and density terms. This is a measure of both its youthful development and its northerly latitude. It is a federal state with ten constituent provinces and two territories, and it is a member of the Commonwealth. The population is now predominantly of English descent but that of Quebec province is predominantly French. In recent times particularly, a separatist movement has received considerable support in French Canada, and eventually Quebec might well secede from the union, which was first created from the four provinces of Ontario, Quebec, New Brunswick and Nova Scotia in 1867. This would leave Anglo-Canada in two parts, the Atlantic provinces in the east, and the larger and economically far more significant portion, in the centre and west.

A land of great potential, Canada is also a land of contrasts. Its range of raw materials is vast; extensive softwood forests and smaller but considerable hardwood forests; a wide range of minerals; rich fishing grounds off both east and west coasts; areas of great agricultural potential. Yet much of it is physically remote and climatically uninviting.

The Atlantic Provinces

New Brunswick, Newfoundland/Labrador, Nova Scotia and Prince Edward Island in the extreme east of Canada are remote from the main population centres. Newfoundland may have been the first part of North America ever discovered by European adventurers as early as AD 1000. All four provinces have important lumbering and fishing industries. Specialist farming is important in some areas, such as the major potato growing provinces of Prince Edward Island and New Brunswick, and fruit production, especially apples, in Nova Scotia. Labrador has an important range of minerals; about half of Canada's iron ore is extracted from a belt which straddles the border with Quebec, and uranium has been discovered. The ports of the Atlantic provinces play a major role in Canadian and US Atlantic trade, especially in winter when the St Lawrence freezes.

Quebec

As with all Canadian provinces, most of the developed and populous parts are found in the south, here straddling the St Lawrence River. Quebec farming, with its distinctive French origins and layout, is dominated by

pasture, hay growing and dairy cattle. About 25 percent of Canada's butter and cheese come from this area. Mineral production, from the same belt as that found across the border in Labrador, is very important; iron, copper and zinc being the major ores extracted. Elsewhere, asbestos production is particularly significant, some 70 percent of Canada's total output coming from the Eastern Townships. Quebec also accounts for about 40 percent of Canada's HEP production. Forestry products – pulp, paper and cardboard – are another major industrial group, the extensive forests of the north accounting for half of Canada's pulp production in a typical year. Montreal, one of Canada's largest and most cosmopolitan cities, has a metropolitan area population equal to that of Toronto, and has a wide range of industries – clothing and textiles, shoe making, food processing, transport equipment and other manufactured goods.

Ontario

Most of the population is clustered along the northern shores of Lakes Ontario and Erie and, to a lesser extent, in an east-west belt along the Ottawa River. This is Canada's leading industrial province, with major centres of iron and steel making, oil refining and chemical industries, automobile assembly, pulp and paper production and food processing being found here. Prior to the opening of the St Lawrence Seaway in 1959, ocean-going vessels could navigate the great river only as far as Montreal, Quebec, which thus developed as the major manufacturing centre. Ports and cities farther west were served only by smaller lake vessels. Now that Toronto and other cities are equally accessible to the ocean, when the St Lawrence is not frozen over, their importance has increased. Ontario's agricultural heart is in the south-west peninsula, between Lakes Erie and Huron. Here, soils, climate and markets combine to create a prosperous arable and dairying area. In addition, large amounts of fruit are grown in the Niagara peninsula. Farther north within the Shield area, Ontario too has rich mineral resources, nickel, copper, iron and gold being the leaders in value terms.

The Prairie Provinces

West from Ontario, the three provinces of Manitoba, Saskatchewan and Alberta present an expansive landscape which rises in a series of steps towards the Western Cordillera. The archetypal prairie farm scene, however, exists only in a semi-elliptical area in the south. Here, wheat farming dominates – though it is often mixed with stock rearing – with Saskatchewan accounting for 65 percent of Canada's sown area and 60 percent of her annual output. Most wheat is marketed via the great cities of the prairies, and much is exported, mainly to Europe. Farther north and west, livestock rearing,

1 △   2 ▽   3 ▽

dairying and mixed farming become increasingly important, especially with the modern rapid growth of the large prairie towns, like Edmonton and Calgary. The prairie provinces also account for the bulk of Canada's fossil fuel production. Coal reserves have long been exploited, and today Alberta's annual output is approximately 10 million tonnes. However, crude oil, oil sands and natural gas discoveries and development during the last 30 years have been rapid. Alberta produces 85 percent of Canada's crude oil and 90 percent of her natural gas. Saskatchewan also possesses the world's largest potash deposits.

British Columbia

The great mountain province of Canada is, in some ways, remote from the rest of the federation. Little of its land is suited to farming, although there are important specialist activities like apple growing in Okanagan Valley and dairying in the lower Frazer Valley. Fishing, though significant, plays a smaller part in the economy of the province than is sometimes thought. Forestry is far more vital. Copper, zinc, lead and to a lesser extent coal, crude oil and natural gas are the leading mineral products.

The population of the metropolitan area of Vancouver is the third highest in all Canada, and is now twice as large as either Edmonton or

1 Las Vegas, Nevada, USA – a name synonymous with gambling and lavish entertainment; 2 Pacific Rim National Park, Vancouver Island, British Columbia; 3 Oil well, Condor, Alberta, Canada – 85 percent of the country's crude oil comes from this mineral-rich prairie province

Winnipeg. It is the largest urban area west of Toronto and is Canada's major outlet to the Pacific.

The Northern Tier

North of the 60th parallel, except for the area east of Hudson Bay, lie the mountain Territory of the Yukon and the more extensive mainland and island parts of the Northwest Territories. Best known to the public from the pioneer days of the Klondike Gold rush, the Yukon is still most important for its mineral wealth. However, the scope of its mineral base is now recognized, with zinc, lead, silver, copper and gold rating most highly in value terms. Forestry has great potential, but has yet to be systematically developed. The Northwest Territories are far more extensive. Here, zinc, lead, gold, silver and copper are the main products. Yellowknife is the largest town and centre of gold production. Furs yield almost as much revenue as gold. A modest production of crude oil from the Mackenzie Basin has been maintained for nearly 60 years. Today

155

North American Countries

larger areas are being searched for further fields. Facing directly across the Polar ice to the north coast of the USSR, this attic of North America has increasing strategic importance for the whole continent.

Greenland

Popularly regarded as the world's largest island, 85 percent of this land is covered by a permanent ice cap. The western coastal strip contains 90 percent of the population who are mainly Eskimo. As Greenland is still part of the Danish realm, the small amount of European inhabitants are mostly from that country and most trade is with Denmark, although Greenland's defence is controlled by a Danish/American agreement. The USA maintain air bases here. Fishing and processing are the most significant activities, though mineral prospecting and extraction is of growing importance. Coal mining ceased recently; cryolite, a rare mineral important in the production of aluminium, has been mined for some time; lead and zinc mining started in 1973; the search for oil is intensifying off the west coast.

St Pierre and Miquelon

This group of eight islands to the immediate south of Newfoundland is an overseas territory of France. As the name suggests, they lie in two distinct sections. Oddly, the far smaller St Pierre group contains 90 percent of the total population. Largely bare rock, the islands are useless for farming. Cod fishing on the Grand Banks is the main occupation; fish processing industries are obviously important.

The United States of America

Created in 1776 when the 3 million inhabitants of the 13 original states on the Atlantic seaboard declared their independence from Britain, the present area of the USA makes it the fourth largest country in the world. In those 200 years the federation of states has grown to a modern total of 50; the country extends from Atlantic to Pacific coasts of the North American continent and has two non-contiguous states, Alaska and Hawaii, as well as a number of outlying territories (classified separately within this atlas). At the last full census in 1970 the country contained over 203 million, and it is now estimated to be approximately 220 million.

In the late nineteenth and twentieth centuries, the USA developed economically into the free world's most powerful country. It is a land of great physical contrasts. Agriculturally it produces a wide range of crops: citrus fruit, sugar cane and cotton from the subtropical south and south-west; great quantities of cereals, especially maize and wheat, as well as tobacco and soya beans, from the mid-latitude continental interior, and market garden crops from the densely populated areas of the north-east. Stock raising, pig rearing, dairying and, to a lesser extent sheep farming, are also important.

The US economy is also based on a wide range of minerals. Coal, natural gas and crude oil are all produced in large quantities, although the latter is now imported from Venezuela and the Middle East. Precious minerals and metal ores are extracted over a wide area. But ultimately the great economic strength of the USA lies in its manufacturing industries. Based on its rich agricultural and mineral resources, the range of industries is such that it would almost be possible for the USA to isolate itself economically from the outside world.

The very size of the USA makes it unrealistic to attempt overall descriptions of its modern geography and economy. Although parts of the country which have a popular image go under such titles as the 'Great Plains', the 'Mid-West' and the 'Manufacturing Belt', such areas do not account for the whole nation, sometimes overlap and are inevitably subject to rather vague notions about their precise extent. We are therefore using the officially-accepted nine standard geographical divisions based on state boundaries.

New England

Comprising six comparatively small states in the extreme north-east of the country, in overall terms this is the smallest division, yet it is the second most densely populated. Maine covers nearly half of the area yet has less than ten percent of the inhabitants, and Vermont too is thinly populated. The great economic heart then is in Massachusetts, Connecticut, Rhode Island and the southern part of New Hampshire.

Much of New England lies within the original area of colonial America and thus has a long history of development. Agriculture today is very specialized, and large areas which were once cleared and farmed have now reverted to forest. Market gardening and dairying are the leading activities. Timber production and fishing, two long-standing occupations, are still significant.

Overall, the division is singularly deficient in minerals. Most important is the manufacturing industry of the many towns lying in a broad belt from Boston in the east toward New York in the south-west. The traditional market leaders of textiles and leather manufacturing have now been surpassed by electrical and electronics industries, instrument making and other metal industries.

One of the increasingly appreciated resources of New England is its tourist potential. In the summer its southern shores provide readily accessible inlets and beaches for the nearby urban population. The coast of Long Island Sound is now dotted with marinas at which many of the population of Megalopolis moor their craft. Farther east, Cape Cod is a retreat from the nearby cities. Farther north, the beaches of Massachusetts and Maine provide a cooler attractive environment, not only for US citizens but also for Canadians from Quebec and Ontario.

The mountains, rivers and lakes of Vermont, New Hampshire and Maine attract both summer and winter tourists. State Parks on the coast and inland at places like Mount Monadnock provide camping, picnicking and walking facilities. The dramatic colours of the forest in 'the fall' attract many visitors. Winter sports are also popular in the region.

Middle Atlantic

To the immediate west and south-west of New England lies the slightly larger but equally compact division of the Middle Atlantic. This comprises only three states (New Jersey, New York and Pennsylvania) and extends across the northern Appalachians from the Atlantic seaboard to the two easternmost Great Lakes. The mountains extending north-east to south-west through the region constitute something of a divide and an agricultural dead heart. It was across this area that so many of the stream of migrants who have entered the USA in the last 200 years and more have passed. Today, the Middle Atlantic as a whole is of enormous importance in the US economy. Herein lies one of the world's largest conurbations and other large centres of population.

Early colonial settlement developed a more broadly based agriculture than that of neighbouring divisions. Today, the demands of the large urban areas have led the farmers to concentrate on two main activities: dairying, largely for milk, not butter and cheese, extending throughout the division, and market gardening on the Atlantic seaboard and the southern shores of Lakes Ontario and Erie. Specialist farming still continues; for example, poultry, tobacco, apples and mushrooms are

1 Greenland – Eskimo hunting walrus, an occupation which, like sealing and whaling, has been replaced by fishing for the majority of the population of these ice-covered parts; 2 Houston, Texas USA – the largest town in the state is at the centre of a wealthy industrial area, as well as being the headquarters of NASA, which is the United States National Aeronautics and Space Administration

1 △

2 ▽

all of great significance in Lancaster County, Pennsylvania, where dairying is the staple activity.

America's earliest iron and steel industry was based here, using the iron of eastern Pennsylvania, charcoal from the Appalachian forests and later coal from the same state. Today, Pennsylvania is the main American focus for both iron and steel production. It also accounts for about 15 percent of the US coal output as well as being the original and a continuing producer of crude oil and natural gas.

New Jersey and New York States have a broader manufacturing base. Food processing, clothing and some textiles, chemical and metal manufacturing are most valuable. Commerce and service industries also dominate many of the cities.

Perhaps, above all, the Middle Atlantic is known for its large urban areas focusing on some of the original colonial settlement ports, New York and Philadelphia, the original capital city of the independent USA of 1776, being the most famous. New York has the advantages of both easy access to the Atlantic and routes to the interior. These are somewhat offset by the disadvantage of its physical site, centring on Manhattan Island between two large rivers, which today manifests itself in the chronic congestion of the central areas of the city. The New York metropolitan area now has more people in it than any other single world city, and as a trading, commercial and manufacturing centre it dominates the whole North American continent.

East North Central

North of the Ohio River, east of the Mississippi and primarily south of the westernmost Great Lakes lies a group of five states, Ohio, Indiana, Illinois, Michigan and Wisconsin. Collectively these contain some of the richest US farmland, parts of two of her most important coal fields and three major industrial centres, Chicago, Detroit and Cleveland.

From east to west the land slopes gently, somewhat monotonously, toward the upper valley of the Mississippi. Much of the area is clothed with rich glacial deposits and the climate is moist enough to maintain the extensive areas of maize in Illinois, Iowa and Indiana at the centre of the 'Corn Belt'. This is largely used as animal fodder, feeding locally reared pigs and cattle brought in from the plains. Farther west and north, wheat growing, hay and dairying are more common. To the east, the poorer soils on the margins of the Appalachians and the demands of the urban dwellers have resulted in an emphasis on dairying and market gardening.

The division comprises the western parts of the US 'Manufacturing Belt'. Heavy industry – iron and steel production, chemicals, glass, rubber etc – is found in Ohio, and particularly in the towns close to Lake Erie, such as Cleveland, Toledo and Youngstown. To the north, the

Detroit area of Michigan contains the world's largest concentration of automobile making, an assembly industry ·which is dependent upon the sheet steel, rubber and other components provided largely from the nearby cities.

Farther west, on the shore of Lake Michigan is Chicago, the second largest single city of the US, after New York. It is at the main head of navigation on the Great Lakes, and is but a short canal journey from a major tributary of the Mississippi system, the Illinois river. It is a great industrial centre, known particularly for its heavy industry, steel production and as the effective 'capital' of the 'Middle West'. It is the largest railroad focus in the whole of the US. The vast metropolitan area sprawls over the flat Illinois landscape. By contrast, Chicago's central business district is, for modern purposes, very crowded, being chiefly centred in the downtown area.

The towns and cities of the south and west of this division are mainly geared to the needs of the surrounding agricultural areas. Food processing, particularly flour milling and meat packing, are the main activities, though some cities have developed agricultural industries.

West North Central

West of the Mississippi, south of the Canadian border and east of the Western Cordillera lie two tiers of states. The seven most northern states, Minnesota, Iowa, Missouri, North and South Dakota, Nebraska and Kansas – constitute this division. In the east, the extensive landscape of the 'Middle West' continues into Missouri, Iowa and Minnesota. Then the landscape rises up to the different levels of the Great Plains, so that

when the foothills of the Rocky Mountains are reached the level of the plains is about 1,600 m (5,000 ft).

Farming in this area responds very critically to the total rainfall. The farther west, the lower the rainfall, so that maize growing diminishes and wheat and sorghum increase in importance. In Missouri, Iowa and Minnesota, these alternative grains are grown mainly for fodder, but in the west of the division cashcrop wheat growing is most important. This, and the modern equivalent of traditional ranching, provide a far more extensive agricultural pattern than that seen farther east. Farm units become larger and the farming activities are such that a smaller population is needed. Much of this area centres on the Missouri River valley; for more than 30 years this has been the subject of federal aid development, though not with the same enthusiasm as is seen in the Tennessee Valley (page 158).

The settlement and industrial development of this area has been understandably less dynamic than that of the Manufacturing Belt to the east. Today the two large urban centres of the southern part, St Louis and Kansas City, have developed from their former roles of agricultural market and transportation centres into more broadly based industrial centres. Farther north, Omaha on the Missouri, as well as Minneapolis/St Paul on the Mississippi, are the only other cities with over 300,000 population. These, and the smaller towns and cities, each act as a local service centre and manufacturing focus. Overall, the area is not well endowed with minerals, though in the extreme north, the Mesabi, Vermilion and Cuyuna Ranges in Minnesota are the major US source of iron ore.

1 Toronto, Ontario, Canada – the CN Tower, the world's tallest free-standing structure, dominates the capital of the province as seen from Ontario Place; 2 Indian, New Mexico, USA – many of North America's original inhabitants still live in this southern state, bordering Mexico, Middle America; 3 Livermore Falls, Maine, USA – the largest of the New England states is, like its north-eastern neighbours, especially beautiful in the 'fall'

South Atlantic

Between Pennsylvania in the north and Florida in the south lies a line of Atlantic seaboard states which are nearly all sandwiched between the ocean and the Appalachian watershed: Maryland, Delaware, the District of Columbia, West Virginia, Virginia, North and South Carolina, Georgia and Florida. The northern tier were part of the original group of 13 which declared their independence from Britain in 1776; five of the states in the division were on the side of the South in the Civil War. Along with the states of the lower Mississippi Valley these comprise the area known as the 'South', with its popular image of cotton and tobacco plantations, the land of the American Negro slaves in the pre-Civil War days and, in some ways, the poor relation states. Today, such outmoded, if historically accurate concepts, should be replaced by a more realistic factual assessment.

Physically the South Atlantic states contain a largely infertile coastal belt of sands, swamps and forests, and a western mountain belt. Between these lie the main agricultural areas where the principal crops vary with the latitude. In Georgia, cotton still dominates. Farther north, tobacco is the most important crop. Timber is

North American Countries

also valuable, North Carolina being the fifth most important state of the union for forestry products.

The Virginias are also important for tobacco production, but derive far more of their economic prosperity from their fossil fuel reserves. West Virginia produces more coal than any other single state, while Virginia is seventh in this category.

Food processing apart, textiles is the area's most important manufacturing industry. The southern states gained steadily on the previous major producer, New England, in the first half of this century and now have the lead.

Near to the extremes of this division are two areas of different distinction. In the north, Washington, the nation's capital, lies within the District of Columbia. Formerly part of Maryland and Virginia, this small area has been the seat of the national government and administration since 1790. Spaciously laid out on the banks of the Potomac River, the capital now attracts many home and overseas visitors, not only to the government buildings and national monuments but also to the cultural centres such as the National Gallery and the Smithsonian Institution.

In the south, Florida extends farther south than any other continental part of the union. This subtropical state has developed rapidly in the last 30 years. It is now most significant as a major US source of citrus fruit, as well as producing sugar cane, tobacco and vegetables for the early markets.

East South Central

Traditionally regarded as part of the 'South', Kentucky, Tennessee, Alabama and Mississippi lie between the Appalachians and the Mississippi south of the Ohio River. Within these lies the Tennessee River, the subject of a federal development scheme which has been a major boost to the economy and morale of the area – the creation of the Tennessee Valley Authority (TVA).

Prior to 1933, the Tennessee River was a menace; its flow fluctuated from season to season, it was of little navigational value, and it was a flood hazard. Agriculture in its whole basin was at a low ebb. By constructing a series of dams, many with by-passing canals, the river is now controlled, navigable and is the source of much HEP. Within the river basin, schemes to prevent soil erosion have been pursued and the quality of farming has thus improved. Long and bitter political arguments through the years concerning the TVA have tended to breathe caution on similar programmes elsewhere, such as the Missouri Valley and the Columbia River Scheme.

The Gulf states of Mississippi and

Alabama lie largely south of the TVA area. Save in the extreme northeast where the Appalachians extend into Alabama, both are largely flat with subtropical agriculture dominating their economies. Soya beans are the most valuable field crop and cotton second. Poultry, pigs and cattle account for slightly more farm income than do crops. In Alabama, the coal and iron deposits associated with the Appalachians farther north are once again found. These were a major factor in the growth of Birmingham as a major iron and steel centre.

West South Central

Between the Mississippi and the Western Cordillera south of about 37°N lie Arkansas, Louisiana, Oklahoma and Texas. Texas alone amounts to over 7 percent of the total area of the US. In the west is the archetypal Great Plains landscape with its cattle ranges; in the east, Arkansas and Louisiana are the western extremities of the old 'Deep South'; in the south lies the modern, prosperous Gulf coastal strip.

Arkansas and Louisiana are still major cotton producing states today, with a yield per hectare (acre) among the highest for any state. In Texas, where modern irrigation

schemes have greatly enlarged the crop area, the area of cotton growing is very large but yields are lower. Among a wide range of other crops grown throughout the area, subtropical citrus fruit, rice and peanuts are most noteworthy. Texas is a major beef stock state but also contains the greatest single concentration of sheep in the whole of the US.

The farther west, the lower the rainfall. In this area of the division, where parts of the great dust bowl of the 1920s and '30s can still be seen, the threat of soil erosion persists and conservation measures are applied rigorously. In Oklahoma, the greatest farming trend of the last forty years has been the conversion of arable land to grazing.

In the extreme east, New Orleans on the Mississippi delta is an old-established port at the focus of the river, rail and road network, with sea-going traffic for Middle and South America as well as Africa and Europe. Its French character, revealed in streets, squares, buildings and names, and its connections with the origin of jazz music, make it a most distinctive city. Other ports on the Gulf coastlands have now overtaken it in terms of the volume of traffic handled each year.

Farther west on the Gulf coast and

inland, modern prosperity rests predominantly on mineral wealth and the associated industrial development; in particular, the production of crude oil and natural gas. Here is the largest concentration of these resources in the US. Oil refining and the petrochemical industries have developed rapidly.

Mountain

The physical problems present in the inland states west of about 105°W, Montana, Idaho, Wyoming, Utah, Nevada, Colorado, Arizona and New Mexico, are enormous. Here lies the great complex of mountains stretching north-south from the Canadian to the Mexican borders; to the east, the various local ranges which collectively make up the Rocky Mountains; then such ranges as the Bitterroots and the Wasatch and, still farther west, on the Californian border, the Sierra Nevada. Between many of the ranges lie the great plateaus and desert basins. The finest index to the inhospitable nature of the area lies in the average population density of the eight states, 4.3 per km² (11.0 per sq ml). Without such large cities as Denver, Phoenix and Salt Lake City, these figures would be even lower.

1 △

2 ▽

1 Dallas, Texas, USA – a centre of the oil industry – with other industries such as aircraft, machinery and cotton textiles – this second biggest town in the 'lone star' state, Dallas, an important industrial and commercial city, is also known for the Texas State Fair, held yearly; 2 Niagara Falls, USA/Canada – about half way down the river which forms part of the North American frontier, the Falls attract thousands of tourists who don waterproofs to view the torrent up close. The Canadian Horseshoe Falls shown here – at over 670 m (2,210 ft) wide and 54 m (178 ft) high – are bigger than the American Rainbow Falls.

Lack of water is the farmers' greatest problem. In the Great Salt Lake depression, the Snake River area of south Idaho and the Gila Basin in Arizona, however, such aridity has been countered by irrigation and a wide range of crops is now grown. Ranching and lumbering are still the main activities, on a far more extensive scale than anywhere else in the continental part of the union.

The mountain states also contain a wide range of minerals, many discovered by the early pioneers as they moved west along the trails. These 'strikes' gave rise to the mining settlements which enjoyed a limited period of intense activity before becoming ghost towns. Today, copper is the most valuable single ore, a number of mines in Arizona, the open pit mine at Bingham, Utah and the deeper deposits of Butte, Montana, being the largest sources. Southwest Montana and north Idaho have valuable deposits of zinc. Silver is still a major resource of Idaho.

In the summer, the scenic variety of all but the hottest desert areas attract many visitors from both east and west. Winter tourism is based on sports areas like Sun Valley, Idaho and Aspen, Colorado; this is the time of the year to visit the Arizona desert and Death Valley.

Pacific

Of all the US Divisions, only the Pacific is non-contiguous. Three of its states in main, continental USA, Washington, Oregon and California, are bounded by the Pacific coast; Alaska, the largest state in the union, is detached from the rest by Canada, and Hawaii is set in mid-ocean. As the US has developed from east to west, these westernmost outposts of the union have shown their most dramatic developments recently.

Much of Washington state, Oregon and California are mountain and plateau country, but the lowland areas and parts of the coastal belt have given rise to great centres of population where large industrial complexes have developed. In Washington state, where the economy was previously based on farming, forestry, fishing and mining, each of which still has its part to play, aircraft and aerospace industries now dominate the manufacturing sector which has become the most valuable activity. Oregon's economy is, however, still based on primary products like timber from the extensive forests.

Today, California, with the highest state population in the union, has a popular image of being the great boom state of the post World War II era. It certainly has a range of activities and products greater than that of any other single state. Crude oil and natural gas production and the petrochemical industries are second only in value to those of the western Gulf states. A range of minerals is extracted from the mountains, in particular around 4 million troy ounces of gold per year. A wide range of modern manufacturing industries has developed.

The value of fish landed is the highest for any US state; farming products range from cotton, sugar beet and rice through all the temperate cereals, temperate and subtropical fruits, including grapes which generate the largest US production of wine. Irrigation is vital for many of the farming activities. Cattle, sheep and pigs are all raised.

The Los Angeles urban area, a group of individual cities which have been dubbed as being centreless, is arguably the largest in the world and certainly the most famous complex of highways in the world, generating, in the still atmosphere of this southwest corner of the country, the equally famous smog. By comparison, San Francisco with only 4.5 million inhabitants, is small indeed.

Alaska, at the opposite end of the US climatic spectrum, only joined the union in January 1959. By far the largest state, it is the least densely populated. Originally prized for its strategic importance, and its forestry and fishing resources, it is now most valued for the proven and further suspected oil reserves.

Hawaii, whose economy is based mainly on tourism, is the most recent state to join the union in March 1959.

COUNTRY REFERENCE: NORTH AMERICA

North American Countries	Political Status	State Capital	Area km²	Area sq ml	Population	Population Density per km²	per sq ml
CANADA	A	Ottawa	9,976,139	3,851,809	23,625,000	2.4	6.0
Alberta	D	Edmonton	661,185	255,285	1,889,000	2.9	7.4
British Columbia	D	Victoria	948,596	366,255	2,534,000	2.7	6.9
Manitoba	D	Winnipeg	650,087	251,000	1,050,000	1.6	4.2
New Brunswick	D	Fredericton	73,437	28,354	696,000	9.5	25
Newfoundland	D	St John's	404,517	156,185	573,000	1.4	3.7
NW Territories	D	Yellowknife	3,379,683	1,304,903	44,000	0.01	0.03
Nova Scotia	D	Halifax	55,491	21,425	851,000	15	40
Ontario	D	Toronto	1,068,582	412,582	8,492,000	7.9	21
PEI	D	Charlottetown	5,657	2,184	121,000	21	55
Quebec	D	Quebec	1,540,680	594,860	6,406,000	4.2	11
Saskatchewan	D	Regina	651,900	251,700	947,000	1.5	3.8
Yukon	D	Whitehorse	536,324	207,076	22,000	0.04	0.1
GREENLAND	C	Godthåb	2,175,600	840,000	50,000	0.02	0.06
ST PIERRE AND MIQUELON	C	Saint Pierre	242	93	6,000	25	65
USA	A	Washington DC	9,363,125	3,615,123	217,264,300	23	60
New England							
Connecticut	D	Hartford	12,973	5,009	3,142,500	242	627
Maine	D	Augusta	86,026	33,215	1,086,800	13	33
Massachusetts	D	Boston	21,386	8,257	5,832,600	273	705
New Hampshire	D	Concord	24,097	9,304	838,000	35	90
Rhode Island	D	Providence	3,144	1,214	922,400	293	760
Vermont	D	Montpelier	24,887	9,609	483,300	19	50
NE TOTAL			172,513	66,608	12,305,600	71	185
Middle Atlantic							
New Jersey	D	Trenton	20,295	7,836	7,358,700	363	939
New York	D	Albany	128,401	49,576	18,102,300	141	365
Pennsylvania	D	Harrisburg	117,412	45,333	11,896,700	101	262
MA TOTAL			266,108	102,745	37,357,700	140	364
East North Central							
Illinois	D	Springfield	146,075	56,400	11,277,200	77	200
Indiana	D	Indianapolis	93,993	36,291	5,306,000	56	146
Michigan	D	Lansing	150,779	58,216	9,121,800	60	157
Ohio	D	Columbus	106,764	41,222	10,669,100	100	259
Wisconsin	D	Madison	145,438	56,154	4,616,500	32	82
ENC TOTAL			643,049	248,283	40,990,600	64	165
West North Central							
Iowa	D	Des Moines	145,790	56,290	2,880,900	20	51
Kansas	D	Topeka	213,063	82,264	2,337,200	11	28
Minnesota	D	St Paul	217,735	84,068	4,026,900	18	48
Missouri	D	Jefferson City	180,486	69,686	4,800,800	27	69
Nebraska	D	Lincoln	200,017	77,227	1,564,900	7.8	20
North Dakota	D	Bismark	183,022	70,665	650,500	3.6	9.2
South Dakota	D	Pierre	199,551	77,047	688,400	3.4	8.9
WNC TOTAL			1,339,664	517,247	16,949,600	13	33
South Atlantic							
Delaware	D	Dover	5,328	2,057	587,600	110	286
District of Columbia	D	Washington	174	67	689,000	3,960	10,284
Florida	D	Tallahassee	151,670	58,560	8,651,000	57	148
Georgia	D	Atlanta	152,488	58,876	5,032,400	33	85
Maryland	D	Annapolis	27,394	10,577	4,190,000	153	396
North Carolina	D	Raleigh	136,197	52,586	5,538,600	41	105
South Carolina	D	Columbia	80,432	31,055	2,900,500	36	93
Virginia	D	Richmond	105,716	40,817	5,114,200	48	125
West Virginia	D	Charleston	62,628	24,181	1,846,100	29	76
SA TOTAL			722,027	278,776	34,549,400	48	124
East South Central							
Alabama	D	Montgomery	133,667	51,609	3,725,300	28	72
Kentucky	D	Frankfort	104,623	40,395	3,482,400	33	86
Mississippi	D	Jackson	123,584	47,716	2,379,200	19	50
Tennessee	D	Nashville	109,411	42,244	4,276,400	39	101
ESC TOTAL			471,285	181,964	13,863,300	29	76
West South Central							
Arkansas	D	Little Rock	137,539	53,104	2,143,700	16	40
Louisiana	D	Baton Rouge	125,674	48,523	3,905,500	31	80
Oklahoma	D	Oklahoma City	181,089	69,919	2,823,100	16	40
Texas	D	Austin	692,405	267,339	12,834,700	19	48
WSC TOTAL			1,136,707	438,885	21,707,000	19	49
Mountain							
Arizona	D	Phoenix	295,023	113,909	2,359,600	8.0	21
Colorado	D	Denver	269,998	104,247	2,644,400	9.8	25
Idaho	D	Boise	216,412	83,557	854,900	4.0	10
Montana	D	Helena	381,086	147,138	763,800	2.0	5.2
Nevada	D	Carson City	286,297	110,540	637,000	2.2	5.8
New Mexico	D	Santa Fe	315,113	121,666	1,201,600	3.8	9.9
Utah	D	Salt Lake City	219,931	84,916	1,263,800	5.7	15
Wyoming	D	Cheyenne	253,596	97,914	406,900	1.6	4.2
M TOTAL			2,237,456	863,887	10,132,000	4.5	12
Pacific							
Alaska	D	Juneau	1,518,800	586,412	407,500	0.3	0.7
California	D	Sacramento	411,013	158,693	22,017,500	54	139
Hawaii	D	Honolulu	16,705	6,450	914,200	55	142
Oregon	D	Salem	251,180	96,981	2,372,700	9.4	24
Washington	D	Olympia	176,616	68,192	3,697,200	21	54
P TOTAL			2,374,314	916,728	29,409,100	12	32
NORTH AMERICA TOTALS			21,515,106	8,307,025	240,945,300	11.2	29.0

NOTE:	Canada	Greenland	St Pierre & Miquelon	USA
Birth rate per thousand persons	15.4	19.2	16.6	14.8
Death rate per thousand persons	7.4	6.9	9.1	9.0
Mean annual percentage increase in population	1.3	1.6	0.9	0.8

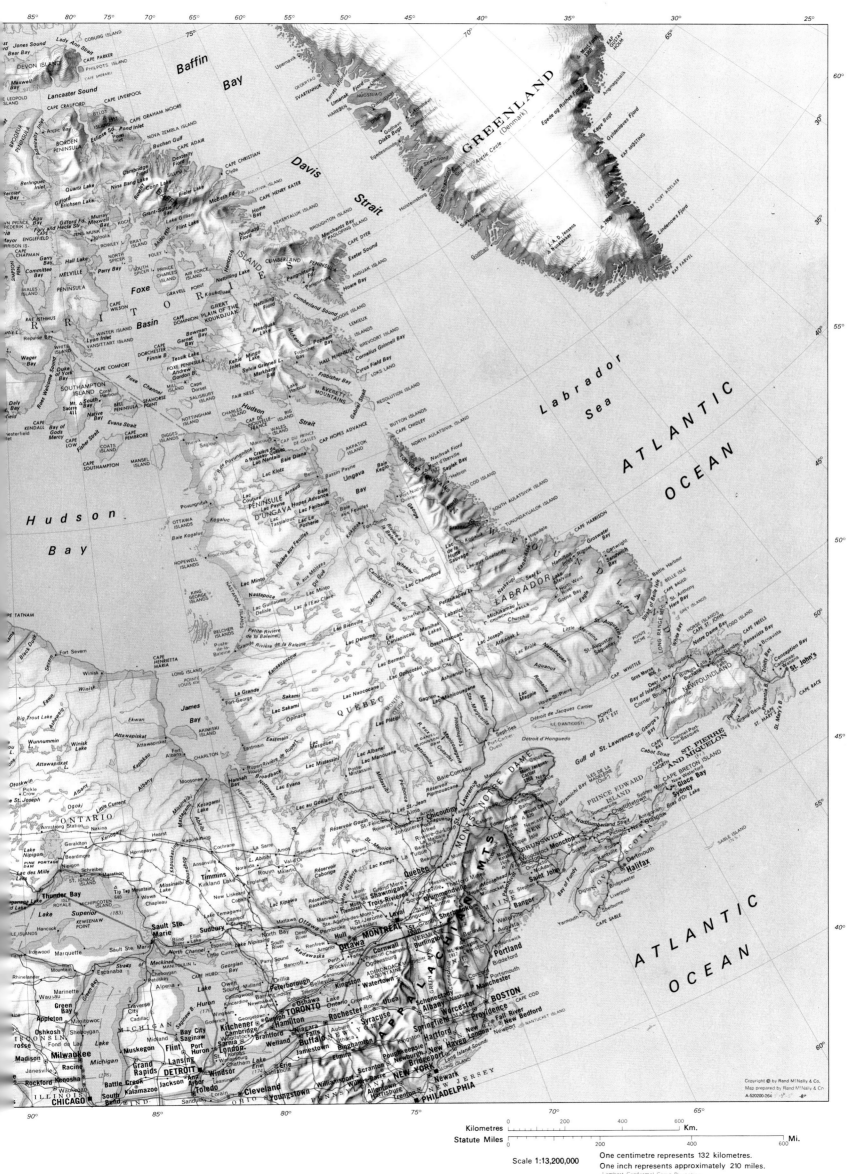

Copyright © by Rand McNally & Co.
Map prepared by Rand McNally & Co.
A-520200-264

Kilometres
0   200   400   600
Km.

Statute Miles
0   200   400   600
Mi.

Scale 1:13,200,000

One centimetre represents 132 kilometres.
One inch represents approximately 210 miles.

Lambert Conformal Conic Projection

161

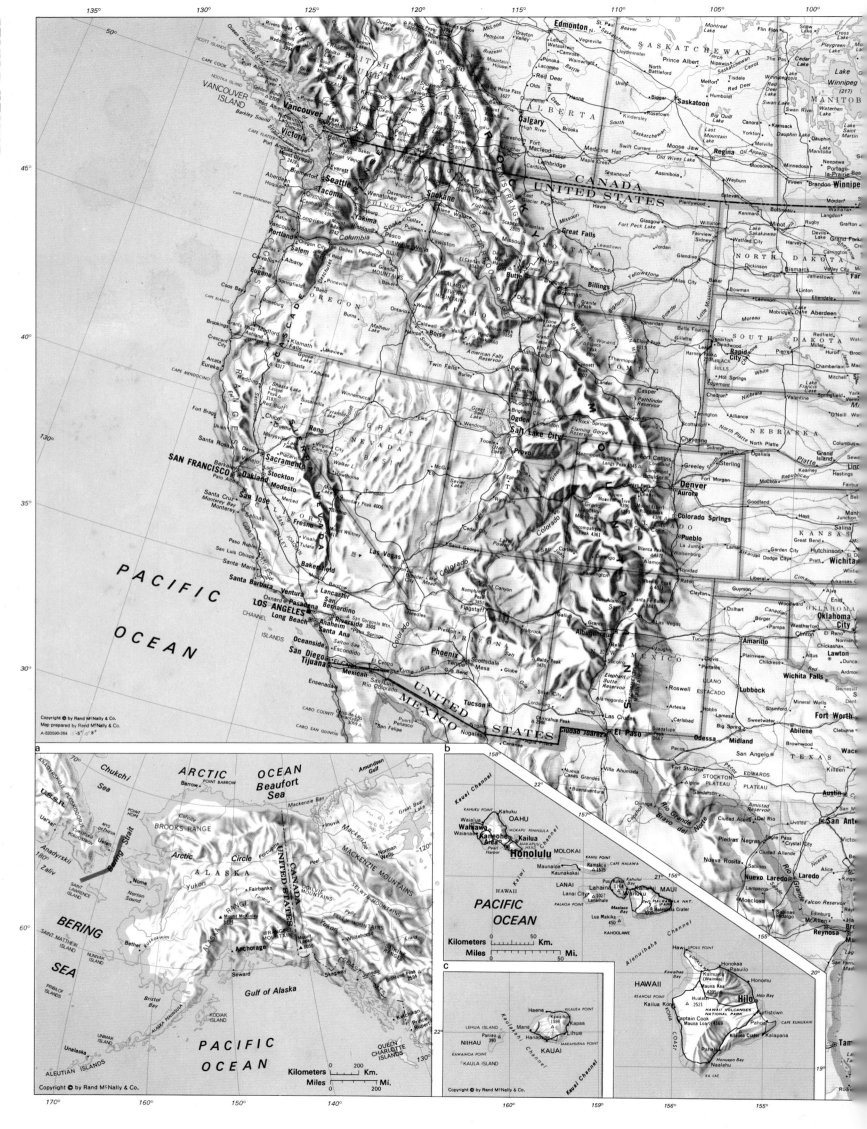

PACIFIC

OCEAN

Kilometres
0   200   400   600   Km.
Statute Miles
0   200   400   600   Mi.

Scale 1:13,200,000

One centimetre represents 132 kilometres.
One inch represents approximately 210 miles.
Albers Conical Equal-Area Projection

163

POLAR REGIONS

The Arctic and Antarctic each presents some of the harshest conditions found on earth. Other places have the intense winter cold, the lack of plant growth, the snow and ice for parts of the year. But nowhere else experiences these features so persistently. Add to them the eerie yet strangely beautiful long winter nights, with the sun always below the horizon, and contrasting period when the sun is always above.

Early polar travellers described these scenes most vividly. The Norwegian explorer and humanitarian, Fridtjof Nansen, in his book *Farthest North* (1898), described the long polar night over the Arctic ice sheet:

The sky is like an enormous cupola, blue at the zenith, shading down into green and then into lilac and violet at the edges. Over the ice fields there are cold violet-blue shadows, with lighter pink tints where a ridge here and there catches the last reflection of the vanished day .... Presently the aurora borealis shakes over the vault of heaven its veil of glittering silver, changing now to yellow, now to green, now to red .... And all the time

this utter stillness, impressive as the symphony of infinitude.

Then Captain Scott and members of his party recorded their experiences of the often savage Antarctic 'summer', at the other end of the earth. Thus wrote Admiral Edward Evans in *South with Scott*:

The blizzard on the second day pursued its course with unabated violence, the temperature increased however and we experienced driving sleet. The tent floor cloths had pools of water on them and water dripped on our faces as we lay in our sleeping bags. Outside the scene was miserable enough, the poor ponies cowering behind their snow walls the picture of misery.

Yet, apart from the seasonal similarities and the trying weather conditions, the Polar Regions are of very differing character. One comprises the extremities of the great land masses of the Northern Hemisphere, Eurasia and North America, and a deep ocean basin across which they face. The other comprises the extremities of the great oceans of the Southern Hemisphere and the bleak, frozen wastes, which they encircle.

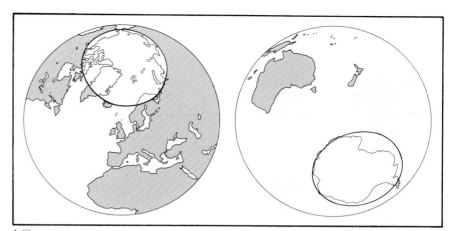

1 ▽

2 ◁

3 ▷

Opposite: Antarctic peninsula; 1 Weddell seal, Graham Land, Antarctic; 2 British Antarctic Survey relief ship landing field party in northern Marguerite Bay – research stations *have been set up to chart the wilderness; 3 Tromsö, Norway – the largest town north of the Arctic Circle; 4 Adélie penguins – most penguin species are found in Antarctica;*

4 ◁

The Arctic

This is an area of extreme cold surrounding the North Pole. Here, due to the fact that the earth's axis of rotation is not at right angles to an imaginary line joining the earth to the sun, latitude 66° 32′N marks the limits of the polar region within which the sun may be seen in the sky for 24 hours on at least one day in the year, the northern summer solstice, about 21 June. By contrast, at the northern winter solstice, about 22 December, the sun does not rise above the horizon at all. At the North Pole itself, the sun rises above the horizon at the spring equinox, about 21 March, and does not set again until the autumnal equinox, about 22 September. Thus, the area within the Arctic Circle, north of 66° 32′N is called the land of the midnight sun. However, within the Arctic Circle the sun, when seen, is always low in the sky.

At the heart of the region lies the huge Arctic Ocean which has an area of about 14 million km² (5.4 million sq ml). This is largely covered by an extensive ice sheet. Around the margins of the polar area, the northern extremities of a number of countries lie within the Arctic Circle: Norway, Sweden, Finland, the USSR, the USA (Alaska), Canada, Greenland and Iceland, as well as a large number of islands. Each of these countries, except Norway, whose coasts are washed by the warm North Atlantic Drift, has some of its coasts icebound for part, if not all the year.

Monthly average temperatures in the Arctic range from −40°C (−40°F) in the winter to as high as 15°C (59°F) in the summer. Surprisingly, in many places annual snowfall is low, being as little as 250 mm (10 in), equivalent to only 25 mm (1 in) of rainfall. Much of this becomes compacted into ice which, over the ages, has built up into the great ice sheet over the Arctic Ocean, and the ice caps and valley glaciers of Greenland, the other islands and parts of the mainlands.

At the North Pole the ice sheet is not exceptionally thick, so that an atomic submarine has been able to pass beneath it and then break through to the surface at the Pole itself. Just as the ice builds up in the coldest parts, so it must disperse at the margins, either by melting in situ, or by the breaking away of icebergs which float southward in the Atlantic and Pacific Oceans, there to melt slowly away. In contrast, the Greenland ice cap is as much as 3,000 m (10,000 ft) thick in places.

Where it is not permanently covered by ice, land in the Arctic has a tundra type of vegetation. Mosses, lichens, stunted grass and even dwarf trees cover the ground, as do bright flowers which bloom each spring. The area is also rich in wild life, including seals, walruses, foxes, wolves, reindeer, polar and grizzly bears, as well as a great variety of birds and fishes. These provide a livelihood for such peoples as the Lapps, Chukchees, Samoyeds and the Eskimos who herd, hunt, trap and trade.

The Arctic is also rich in mineral resources. Within the Soviet Arctic, coal, oil, uranium, nickel, copper and tin are all being developed. Norway and Sweden both have rich iron ore deposits. Silver, lead and cryolite are all found and mined in Greenland, while a great variety of resources in North America, especially oil in Alaska and north-west Canada are being exploited. These have attracted developers from the warmer parts of the respective countries who have established new towns.

The exploration of the Arctic has attracted less attention and romance than that of the Antarctic. In the late nineteenth and early decades of the twentieth centuries, attempts were made to explore on foot, to cross the Greenland ice cap, to lodge a ship in the ice and then see where it would be carried and to overfly the pole in a simple aircraft. In these ventures names like Nansen, Amundsen, Peary, Byrd and Watkins stand out.

Many and varied are the methods of transport in and over the Arctic. Walking with the aid of snow shoes and skis, sledging with dog teams and paddling through open water in kayaks are still practised by the native peoples. Mechanized transport on a local scale now includes light aircraft, helicopters and snowmobiles. For large-scale developments, the coastal ice may be broken through by icebreakers so that large ships may reach the northern coasts of Siberia, Alaska and Canada. More strangely, the Arctic silence is frequently broken by the distant roar of high-flying jet aircraft, for which the shortest route between many European, North American and Pacific centres lies across these cold lands.

Many world maps distort the spatial relationships of places surrounding the Arctic. Thus, the shortest distance between Archangel'sk and Fairbanks is not along the 65th parallel; it is along a line almost passing over the North Pole. Great Circle positions and distances, so important in strategic and political studies, are only shown on gnomonic map projections, see below.

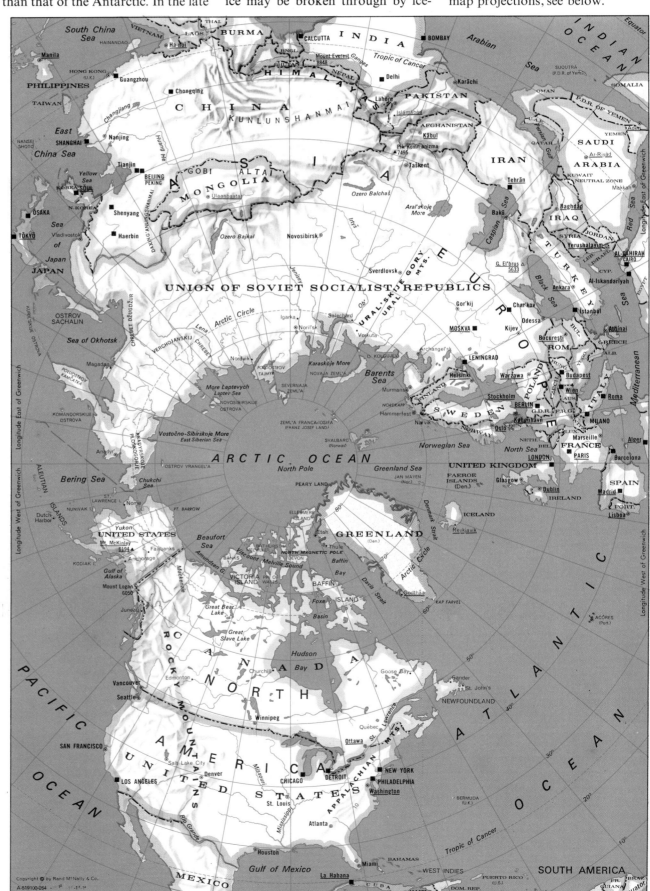

Antarctica

This is predominantly an ice-covered land which rises to considerable heights. Were all the ice to be removed, a very rugged landscape would be revealed; relieved of the weight of ice, the land would rise and the highest peaks would probably match those of the Himalayas.

Latitude 66° 32′S limits the geographical area within which, at the southern summer solstice, about 22 December, the sun may be seen in the sky for 24 hours. At the southern winter solstice, about 21 June, the sun does not rise above the horizon at all. At the South Pole, high up in the centre of the ice-covered land mass, the sun is above the horizon continuously from about 22 September till about 21 March, though it is usually low in the sky.

The Antarctic land mass is almost as big as the Arctic Ocean, covering some 13.2 million km² (5.1 million sq ml). Thus, it is larger than either Europe or Australia. In places the land extends north of the Antarctic Circle, as in the peninsula of Graham Land around 65°W and along the coast of Wilkes Land, between 90°E and 140°E. In other places, such as the head of the Ross Sea, the land margin is as near to the Pole as 85°S latitude.

The whole land is covered with ice and snow, except where high mountains project through the frozen surface. The highest point in the Vinson Massif is 5,140 m (16,864 ft) above sea level. Sea ice surrounds the continent, often way beyond the Antarctic Circle.

The climate of Antarctica is far more severe than even that of the Arctic. From the centre of this mass representing about 90 percent of the world's permanent ice and snow, bitter winds blow outwards. Winter average temperatures, as far as they are known, drop as low as −60°C (−76°F), and even in summer only rise to −20°C (−3°F) in the interior of the continent. Only at the land margins do summer monthly average temperatures rise above freezing.

The two largest seas, the Weddell and Ross, are covered by ice sheets fed from the land by great glaciers. From their margins, as well as the rest of the continent, the sea ice breaks away in icebergs to float northward into the Pacific, Atlantic and Indian Oceans. But these seas, being farther from other continents than their Arctic equivalents, never presented the same iceberg hazards to mariners as did the waters of the North Atlantic.

The Antarctic is almost completely without vegetation, and wild life is very limited. A few tiny invertebrates live on the margins of the land. There are two permanent residents, skuas and the emperor penguins. In addition, the Adelie penguin breeds on the land but lives mainly in the surrounding seas.

This continent has obviously never been appealing for permanent settlement, though its exploration has attracted much attention. When Captain Cook crossed the Antarctic Circle in 1773, he did not sight land. Then, in 1830, John Biscoe, one of the first English explorers to be backed by the newly established Royal Geographical Society, first sighted this continent.

Early in this century, three intrepid explorers were drawn to this virtually unknown continent. Of three expeditions which set out to reach the Pole, Shackleton's just failed but returned safely, and Amundsen's just beat Scott's to return triumphantly. Though successful in its objective, Scott's attempt resulted in the death of all five members of his polar party on their return journey, in an adventure which ranks among the greatest human dramas recalled to this day.

In 1957, International Geophysical Year, twelve nations conducted scientific studies in the continent. About 60 bases were built on the mainland and nearby islands. Studies of the ice, the underlying rocks, the ocean currents and the weather were made. In 1957/58, an ambitious expedition to cross the continent from one side to the other using modern tracked vehicles was successfully led by Sir Vivian Fuchs and Sir Edmund Hillary. At that time a number of countries including the UK, France, Australia and Norway had laid claim to territories in the Antarctic. However, following the International Geophysical Year, in 1959, a 30-year treaty was signed between all nations interested in polar research. All territorial claims have been suspended and the whole area is now free for scientific research, excluding nuclear experiments.

The mineral reserves of the continent are not really known. Coal was brought back by the explorers over 60 years ago, showing that far warmer climates were once enjoyed. Other minerals suspected include copper, nickel and, almost certainly, crude oil. Exploitation of these is, as yet, economically impossible. Except for the scientists and their supply links, by ship and transport aircraft which land on the ice, Antarctica remains a silent continent.

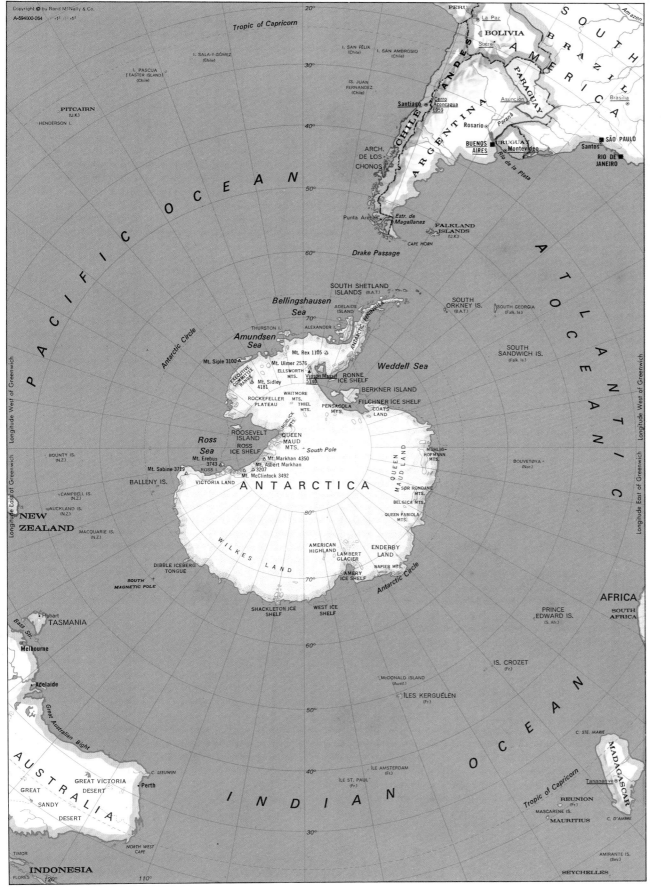

WORLD TO VIEW

The main value of thematic maps is to clarify the immensely varied patterns and distributions of world phenomena. Using appropriate symbols to show one class of geographical information at a time, maps can highlight such topics as the locations of mineral deposits, the distributions of farm animals, etc.

The simplest thematic maps are those which show where particular phenomena are found, with no quantification. For example, the Languages map below uses a series of colours to show where particular languages dominate. It does not show what proportions of the population or how many people speak that language. In the following pages the map of predominant economies also has no mathematical base. It shows

Opposite: Tibetan priests

areas of the world where particular types of economic activity dominate, though it does not show the extent to which other activities, though less important, are also found.

Other types of thematic maps may use a precisely calculated measure. On the Literacy map below, for instance, a percentage scale has been adopted to show the proportions of the population throughout the world who are literate. The average literacy rate for each whole country has been calculated and then plotted according to the selected scale and colour scheme. Only for those areas which are essentially uninhabited has the map been left uncoloured.

Two other maps on the following pages also have a mathematical base, but in neither are whole countries regarded as the essential units of area. Population densities can be calculated for individual parts of each

country, and then a general picture of world distributions plotted on a selected scale. Using a carefully graded colour scheme, with deepest colours for the greatest densities and vice versa, a clear impression of the greatest population pressure points can be given. Finally, using a combination of mathematical measures, a map such as that of climatic regions can be constructed.

Considering the two maps below: the areas of the world with the highest literacy rates are those with the most advanced economies, mainly in the temperate regions. State run services, including education, only come fully into their own with economic development. Thus, on the literacy map, much of Europe, the USSR, North America, Australia, New Zealand and Argentina appear as the countries with over 90 percent of their populations able to read. At

the other end of the scale, it is the countries of the Third World, particularly in Africa, southern and South-east Asia that have less than a third of their peoples thus qualified.

In recent historic times, languages have been carried around the globe by migrations, thus changing the original language distributions. Today some of the original native tongues have been displaced. Thus the Americas, at one time dominated by Indian languages, are now mainly using Germanic and Romance tongues – English and some French in the North, mainly Spanish and Portuguese in the Middle and South. English has also taken over from the native aboriginal and Polynesian languages in Australia and New Zealand. Likewise, in South Africa, the Bantu and other native tongues are still used, but the introduced languages are English and Afrikaans.

LANGUAGES

Bogdan Zaborski

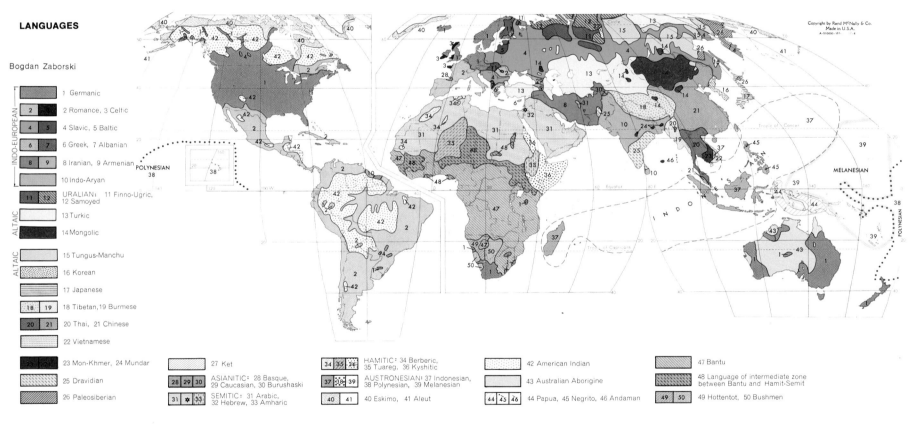

INDO-EUROPEAN
- 1 Germanic
- 2 Romance, 3 Celtic
- 4 Slavic, 5 Baltic
- 6 Greek, 7 Albanian
- 8 Iranian, 9 Armenian
- 10 Indo-Aryan

URALIAN: 11 Finno-Ugric, 12 Samoyed

ALTAIC
- 13 Turkic
- 14 Mongolic
- 15 Tungus-Manchu
- 16 Korean
- 17 Japanese
- 18 Tibetan, 19 Burmese
- 20 Thai, 21 Chinese
- 22 Vietnamese
- 23 Mon-Khmer, 24 Mundar
- 25 Dravidian
- 26 Paleosiberian

- 27 Ket
- ASIANITIC: 28 Basque, 29 Caucasian, 30 Burushaski
- SEMITIC: 31 Arabic, 32 Hebrew, 33 Amharic
- HAMITIC: 34 Berberic, 35 Tuareg, 36 Kyshitic
- AUSTRONESIAN: 37 Indonesian, 38 Polynesian, 39 Melanesian
- 40 Eskimo, 41 Aleut

- 42 American Indian
- 43 Australian Aborigine
- 44 Papua, 45 Negrito, 46 Andaman

- 47 Bantu
- 48 Language of intermediate zone between Bantu and Hamit-Semit
- 49 Hottentot, 50 Bushmen

LITERACY

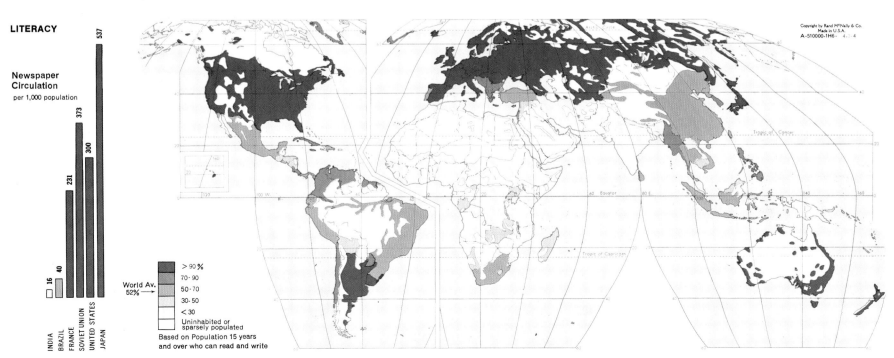

Newspaper Circulation
per 1,000 population

INDIA 16
BRAZIL 40
FRANCE 231
SOVIET UNION 300
UNITED STATES 373
JAPAN 537

World Av. 52%

- > 90 %
- 70 - 90
- 50 - 70
- 30 - 50
- < 30
- Uninhabited or sparsely populated

Based on Population 15 years and over who can read and write

Predominant Economies

Man is neither the master nor the plaything of his environment. His activities are not determined by it, but he is not entirely free to do what he likes where he likes. A modern world map of the patterns of man's economic activities shows every stage, from the simplest forms of making a living from the natural environment, to the most advanced economies of industrial societies. These locations and occupations show a considerable response to the environment, climate and landscape.

Earliest man lived by hunting wild animals and gathering the fruits of the earth. Today such simple activities are still found in some equatorial and tropical areas, both within the dense forest regions and in the dry areas. Many more of the world's dry areas are today used for extensive animal herding, the nomadic herds wandering from one place to another in search of fresh pasture.

Subtropical and temperate regions of the world have been most suited to the development of more intensive forms of farming, whether for growing crops or raising animals. Large-scale ranging of animals, cattle and sheep, dominates the economies of Soviet Central Asia, south-eastern South America, some western parts of North America and much of Australia. Elsewhere in North America and Europe as well as on the margins of the southern continents, the most prosperous crop farming and intensive animal farming has been developed.

The establishment of commercial farming in many parts of the world involved clearing the forests. Today forestry is concentrated in those parts which are often less inviting for other activities. Thus, on the northern margins of the developed lands of the Northern Hemisphere, softwood lumbering is a major activity. Hardwoods are felled quite widely in the world's warmer areas.

It is not in the vast farmed areas that man produces his greatest wealth. Extracting the world's mineral resources, producing the enormous array of manufactured goods, and providing the great range of commercial services for today's advanced societies, together form the greatest generators of wealth. Mineral resources may be very unevenly distributed throughout the world but the raw materials are easily transported. The great centres of manufacturing industry and commerce are located in the temperate climate areas most attractive to industrially-minded man. These are mainly in the Northern Hemisphere, particularly in Western and Central Europe, North America, the Soviet Union and Japan. Developments in China, India, Australia, South Africa and South America, though of importance in their own areas are not as significant in the world scene.

1 △

Apart from South Africa, Japan, Australia, New Zealand and the Argentine, the most advanced countries are in Europe and North America. The Soviet Union has made exceptional progress since World War II and must now rank with the USA as a world political and economic force. 1 The new trading centre in the Chilanzar district of Tashkent is the largest of its kind in central Asia; 2 Such commercial buildings are common in the United States where most development has been upwards, as shown in the modern buildings of Atlanta, Georgia; 3 There is very little comparable development in the Third World countries and much of Asia where subsistence farming predominates

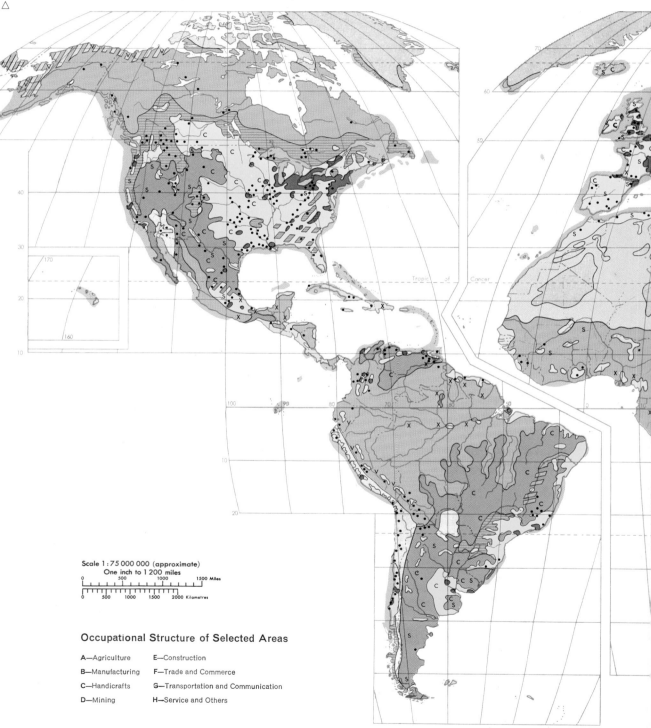

Scale 1 : 75 000 000 (approximate)
One inch to 1 200 miles

Occupational Structure of Selected Areas

A—Agriculture   E—Construction
B—Manufacturing   F—Trade and Commerce
C—Handicrafts   G—Transportation and Communication
D—Mining   H—Service and Others

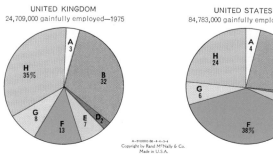

UNITED KINGDOM
24,709,000 gainfully employed—1975

A 3 · B 32 · D 2 · E 7 · F 13 · G 8 · H 35%

A—510000 06-4-4-3-4
Copyright by Rand M°Nally & Co.
Made in U.S.A.

UNITED STATES
84,783,000 gainfully employed—1975

A 4 · B 23 · D 1 · E 4 · F 38% · G 6 · H 24

CANADA
9,364,000 gainfully employed—1975

A 6 · B 20 · D 2 · E 6 · F 23 · G 8 · H 35%

76,41

2 △

3 △

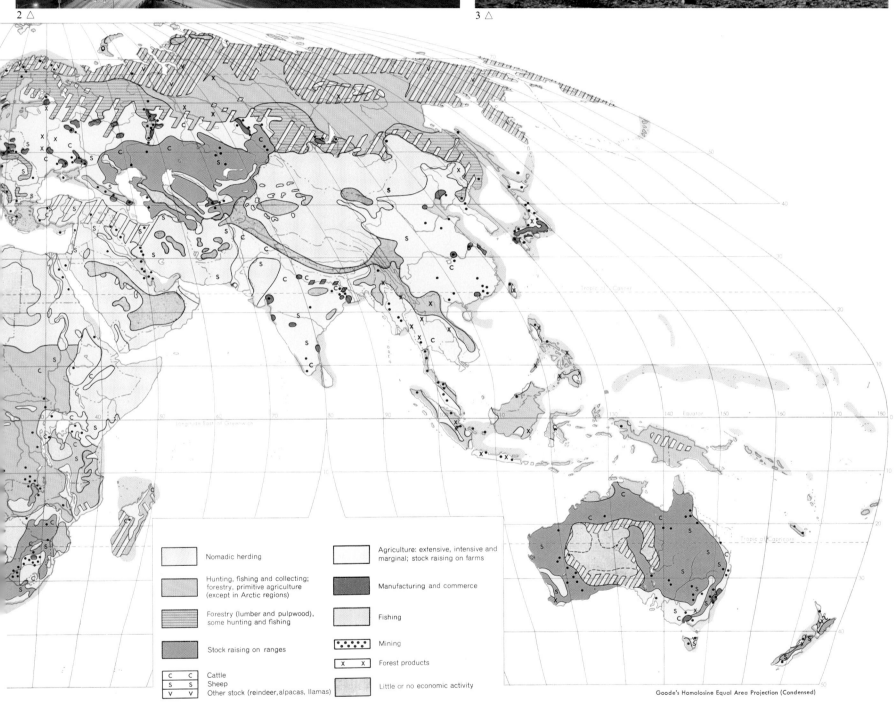

Nomadic herding

Hunting, fishing and collecting; forestry, primitive agriculture (except in Arctic regions)

Forestry (lumber and pulpwood), some hunting and fishing

Stock raising on ranges

C	C	Cattle
S	S	Sheep
V	V	Other stock (reindeer, alpacas, llamas)

Agriculture: extensive, intensive and marginal; stock raising on farms

Manufacturing and commerce

Fishing

| • • • | Mining |
| X | X | Forest products |

Little or no economic activity

Goode's Homolosine Equal Area Projection (Condensed)

ROPE
ployed—1975

B
31%

D
1

SOVIET UNION
117,094,000 gainfully employed—1975

A
22

H
25

G
10

F
6

E
9

D
2

B
26%

BRAZIL
29,545,400 gainfully employed—1970

H
25

G 4

F
9

E 3

D
1

B
14

A
44%

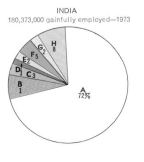

INDIA
180,373,000 gainfully employed—1973

H
8

G 2

F 5

E 2

D

C 3

B
1

A
72%

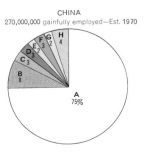

CHINA
270,000,000 gainfully employed—Est. 1970

H
4

G 3

F 2

E 2

D 1

C 3

B
8

A
75%

Population Density

Today the term 'population explosion' prompts varied reactions from the general public, from alarm to apathy. Total world population is growing at an ever increasing rate, yet individual areas have very different growth rates. World population grows at approximately 1.8 percent per annum. Some countries, however, presently have negative growth, while others exceed 4 percent per annum. Most of the high growth rates are in the Third World countries, some of which already have the highest total populations. Most countries of the developed world have growth rates well below the global average. Their total populations at present constitute less than a quarter of the world total.

Each country's average population density has been included in the country reference tables throughout the book. In many cases the distribution within a country is very uneven. Within Europe, where many of the countries have high average densities, local variations are great. In modern commercial and industrial cities densities can exceed 10,000 per km². In rural areas densities may be less than 10 per km². Such variations apply to UK, France and Germany.

Population densities in relation to a whole country may be very different from figures which relate total population to the area of land actually under cultivation. Australia has an average population density of 1.8 per km² (over 4 per sq ml) but with only six percent of the land area cultivated, there are nearly 30 people per square kilometre of cultivated land (76 per sq ml). Likewise Japan's average density of nearly 300 per km² (about 775 per sq ml) converts to a figure of nearly 2,000 per km² (over 5,000 per sq ml) in relation to cultivated land. Corresponding figures for the United Kingdom are 236 (630) and nearly 800 (nearly 2,000), and for the USA, 23 (58) and 104 (269).

A world map of population densities shows the great concentrations not only in the developed countries of Europe and parts of North America, but also in China, India and other developing countries of Southeast Asia. Within these two groups, it is interesting to consider the urban/rural balance. Countries seem to fall into three broad groups. Established industrial countries have the greater proportion of their populations in the towns – the United Kingdom 78 percent, Canada 76 percent, the USA 74 percent, France 70 percent. The developing countries have a much smaller proportion in the urban areas – China 29 percent, India 20 percent. Between these two extremes lie the mid-development countries which now have a near even split between urban and rural populations, the urban figures for them being – Japan 57 percent, Brazil 56 percent, and the USSR 56 percent.

1 △

Asia accounts for much of the world population explosion. 1 Intense overcrowding in cities such as Tokyo, Japan have led to a predominance of high-rise buildings and traffic chaos which the modern rail and expressways shown here do little to alleviate; 2 Hong Kong with its permanent boat dwellers, shanty town and influx of refugees from mainland China, reveals another heavily congested part of the continent; 3 In contrast, Canada, the world's second largest country, has only about one-tenth of the population of its neighbour, the USA, most of whom are concentrated in manufacturing towns near the US border. Small planes ferry people and supplies across vast uninhabited areas, especially in the far north.

Scale 1:75 000 000 (approximate)
One inch to 1 200 miles

Population Density
per square kilometre (per square mile)

of Total Area		of Cultivated Land
9 (24)	ARGENTINA	74 (192)
2 (5)	AUSTRALIA	30 (79)
13 (33)	BRAZIL	301 (780)
87 (229)	CHINA	650 (1684)
97 (252)	FRANCE	291 (728)
156 (653)	GERMANY	775 (2008)
150 (429)	INDIA & PAKISTAN	366 (949)
298 (777)	JAPAN	1989 (5152)
11 (40)	SOVIET UNION	183 (473)
229 (611)	UNITED KINGDOM	771 (1997)
23 (58)	UNITED STATES	104 (269)

2 △

3 △

Leningrad
Stockholm
Minsk
Moscow
Sverdlovsk
Chelyabinsk
Novosibirsk
Kuybyshev
Warsaw
Kiev
Volgograd
Bucharest
Istanbul
Baku
Tashkent
Harbin
Changchun
Sapporo
Athens
Tbilisi
Tehrān
Mukden
Pyongyang
Beirut
Baghdad
Tsientsin
Dairen
Taegu
Tokyo
Alexandria
Tel Aviv-Yafo
Sian
Tsingtao
Seoul
Pusan
Hiroshima
Fukuoka
Yokohama
Osaka
Cairo
Lahore
Chengtu
Nanking
Shanghai
Karāchi
Delhi
Kanpur
Chungking
Wuhan
Ahmedabad
Calcutta
Kunming
Taipei
Bombay
Poona
Hyderabad
Canton
Victoria
Madras
Bangalore
Rangoon
Bangkok
Manila
Colombo
Ho Chi Minh City
Singapore
Jakarta
Surabaya
Bandung
Sydney
Melbourne

Tropic of Cancer
Longitude East of Greenwich
Equator
Tropic of Capricorn
Arctic Circle

Goode's Homolosine Equal Area Projection (Condensed)

Per Sq. Km.	Per Sq. Mile
Uninhabited	Uninhabited
Under 1	Under 2
1-10	2-25
10-25	25-60
25-50	60-125
50-100	125-250
Over 100	Over 250

▫ Metropolitan areas over 2,000,000 population
○ Metropolitan areas 1,000,000 to 2,000,000 population

*Not all cities are named and some
are identified by initial letter only.*

Rural/Urban Population Ratios

Rural		Urban
17%	ARGENTINA	83%
14	AUSTRALIA	86
44	BRAZIL	56
24	CANADA	76
71	CHINA	29
30	FRANCE	70
80	INDIA	20
43	JAPAN	57
44	SOVIET UNION	56
65	TURKEY	35
22	UNITED KINGDOM	78
26	UNITED STATES	74

Climatic Regions

Each year, every place on the earth experiences a unique sequence of weather. Over a period of time a composite picture of the weather for each area can be worked out by taking the average of the individual years' records; such is a description of the local climate. Similar climates are, of course, experienced in different places. Scientists have noted these similarities and drawn up classifications for world climates.

Variable factors over the earth's surface influence climates. Latitude affects the amount of heat received, due to the differences in the height of the sun in the sky and the length of time it is there. Altitude must also be considered. Whatever the latitude, the higher the place the lower the temperature. Climate is also affected by the relative position of the nearest ocean or sea, the predominant wind direction, ocean currents, and large physical features such as mountains.

The simplest climatic classification relied solely on temperatures, resulting in the very general three-fold division of the world into frigid, temperate and torrid zones. The boundaries of these zones coincided with the Arctic and Antarctic Circles and the Tropics of Cancer and Capricorn. However, those lines do not coincide with the positions of the isotherms, lines joining places which have the same average temperatures. So, more accurate classifications, relying on the actual positions of the isotherms, have been devised.

According to the American scientist, Glenn T Trewartha, the first critical average monthly temperature is the 18°C (64.4°F) isotherm, below which most tropical plants will not grow. The next critical temperature is the 10°C (50°F) isotherm; many subtropical plants grow in places which have eight months above this level; places with less than four months are of limited use for farming. The most extreme locations have no month with the average temperature above 10°C (50°F).

Following such reasoning, broad zones far more meaningful than 'frigid', 'temperate' and 'torrid' are defined. Subdivisions have been made to allow for other particularly significant climatic features. Is the distribution of rainfall throughout the year even or uneven? Is there a monsoon pattern? Etc.

In large parts of the world evaporation is greater than precipitation. This results in semi-arid or steppe climates. Where evaporation is twice precipitation, true desert climates are found. Each of these two climatic groups cuts across the other main ones, and thus may possess tropical, subtropical or temperate characteristics. Finally, upland areas have very distinctive climates, in that temperatures are lower than might be expected and the annual precipitation, is comparatively high.

1 △

The range of climates throughout the world has an overriding effect on the varied lifestyles within each continental area. Africa possesses the world's largest desert, the Sahara. Similar conditions prevail in other parts of the world, as in south-east California, USA, where the main vegetation is cacti such as this Ocotillo in the Anzo-Borrego Desert State Park; Many deserts are now being made fertile in parts by irrigation schemes. 2 Water is continually being harnessed, too, to provide hydro-electric power, as at the famous Victoria Falls, Zambia; 3 In the Himalayas of Asia, the world's most physically extreme part, stands the magnificent Mount Everest, the highest point of our world.

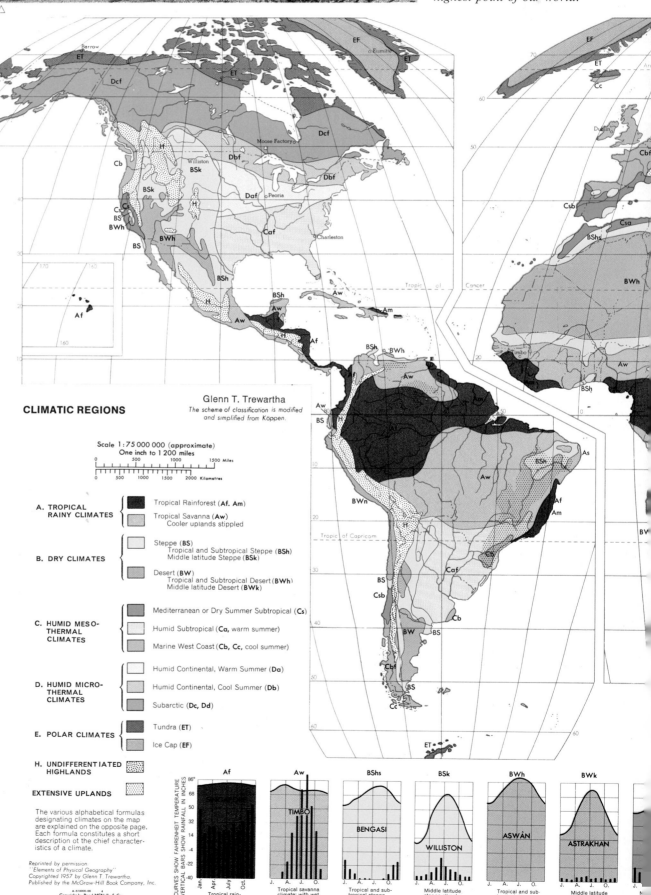

CLIMATIC REGIONS

Glenn T. Trewartha
The scheme of classification is modified and simplified from Köppen.

Scale 1:75 000 000 (approximate)
One inch to 1 200 miles

| A. TROPICAL RAINY CLIMATES | Tropical Rainforest (**Af. Am**) |
| | Tropical Savanna (**Aw**) Cooler uplands stippled |

| B. DRY CLIMATES | Steppe (**BS**) Tropical and Subtropical Steppe (**BSh**) Middle latitude Steppe (**BSk**) |
| | Desert (**BW**) Tropical and Subtropical Desert (**BWh**) Middle latitude Desert (**BWk**) |

C. HUMID MESO-THERMAL CLIMATES	Mediterranean or Dry Summer Subtropical (**Cs**)
	Humid Subtropical (**Ca**, warm summer)
	Marine West Coast (**Cb, Cc**, cool summer)

D. HUMID MICRO-THERMAL CLIMATES	Humid Continental, Warm Summer (**Da**)
	Humid Continental, Cool Summer (**Db**)
	Subarctic (**Dc, Dd**)

| E. POLAR CLIMATES | Tundra (**ET**) |
| | Ice Cap (**EF**) |

| H. UNDIFFERENTIATED HIGHLANDS | |

| EXTENSIVE UPLANDS | |

The various alphabetical formulas designating climates on the map are explained on the opposite page. Each formula constitutes a short description of the chief characteristics of a climate.

Reprinted by permission
''Elements of Physical Geography''
Copyrighted 1957 by Glenn T. Trewartha.
Published by the McGraw-Hill Book Company, Inc.
Copyright by Rand McNally & Co.
Made in U.S.A.

CURVES SHOW FAHRENHEIT TEMPERATURE
VERTICAL BARS SHOW RAINFALL IN INCHES

Af — Tropical rainforest climate

Aw TIMBO — Tropical savanna climate; with wet and dry seasons

BShs BENGASI — Tropical and subtropical steppe climate

BSk WILLISTON — Middle latitude steppe climate

BWh ASWAN — Tropical and subtropical desert climate

BWk ASTRAKHAN — Middle latitude desert climate

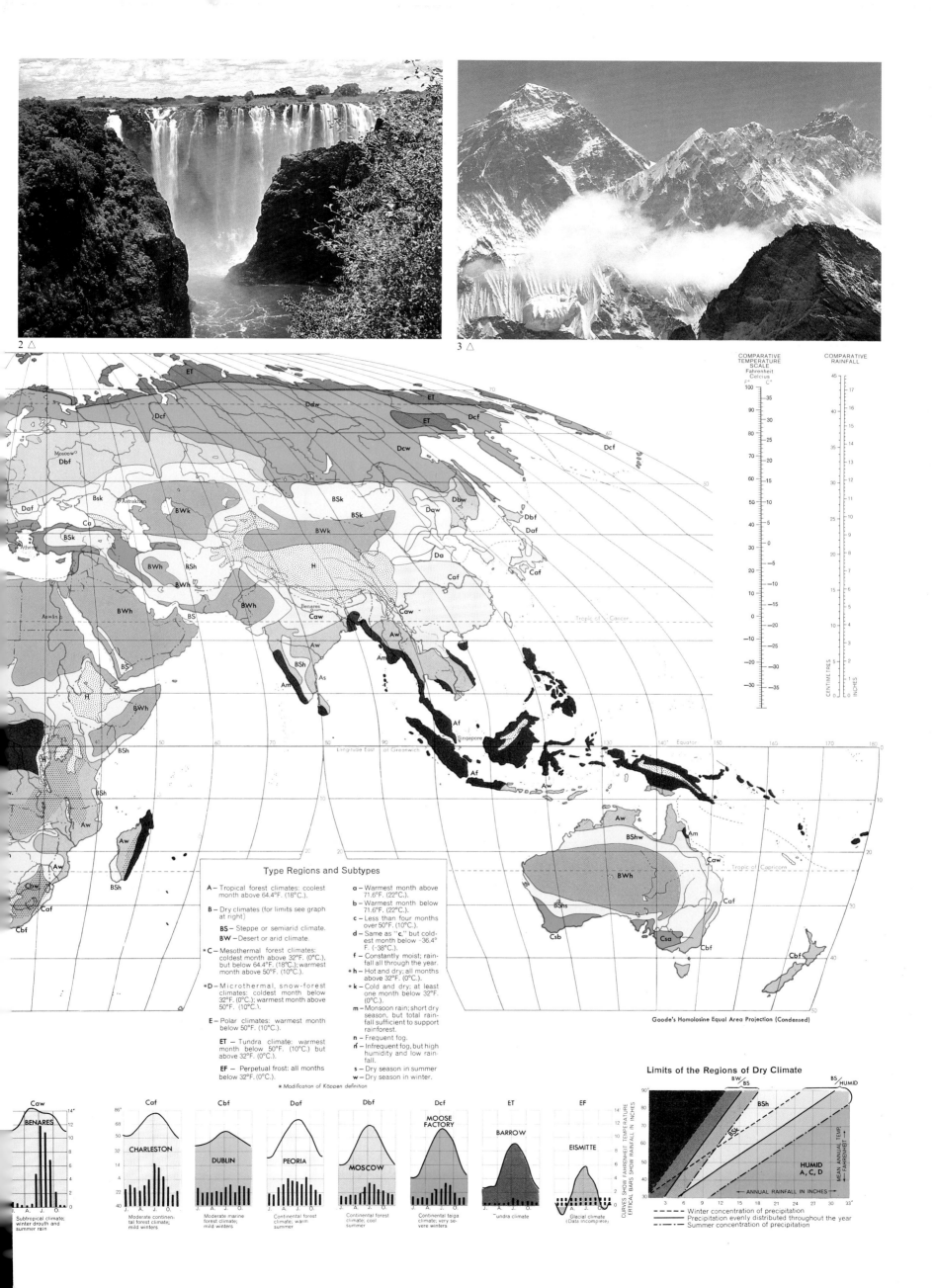

2 △

3 △

COMPARATIVE
TEMPERATURE
SCALE
Fahrenheit
Celcius

COMPARATIVE
RAINFALL

ET

Ddw

Dcf

ET

ET

Dcf

Dcw

Dcf

Moscow

Dbf

Daf

Bsk

Astrakhan

BWk

BSk

Daw

Dbw

Dbf

Ca

BWk

BSk

Da

Daf

Athens

BSk

Caf

H

Caf

BWh

BSh

BWh

BWh

Caw

Aswân

BWh

BS

Caw

Tropic of Cancer

Benares

Caw

BS

Aw

Am

BSh

Aw

Am

As

Am

Af

Singapore

Af

Longitude East   at Greenwich

Af

Equator

Aw

Af

Aw

Aw

Aw

BSh

BShw

Am

Cbw

BWh

Caw

Tropic of Capricorn

Caf

Cbf

Caf

BShs

Csa

Csb

Cbf

Goode's Homolosine Equal Area Projection (Condensed)

Type Regions and Subtypes

A – Tropical forest climates: coolest
month above 64.4°F. (18°C.).

B – Dry climates (for limits see graph
at right)

BS – Steppe or semiarid climate.

BW – Desert or arid climate.

*C – Mesothermal forest climates:
coldest month above 32°F. (0°C.),
but below 64.4°F. (18°C.); warmest
month above 50°F. (10°C.).

*D – Microthermal, snow-forest
climates: coldest month below
32°F. (0°C.); warmest month above
50°F. (10°C.).

E – Polar climates: warmest month
below 50°F. (10°C.).

ET – Tundra climate: warmest
month below 50°F. (10°C.) but
above 32°F. (0°C.).

EF – Perpetual frost: all months
below 32°F. (0°C.).

*Modification of Köppen definition

a – Warmest month above
71.6°F. (22°C.).
b – Warmest month below
71.6°F. (22°C.).
c – Less than four months
over 50°F. (10°C.).
d – Same as "c," but coldest month below –36.4°
F. (–38°C.).
f – Constantly moist; rainfall all through the year.
*h – Hot and dry; all months
above 32°F. (0°C.).
*k – Cold and dry; at least
one month below 32°F.
(0°C.).
m – Monsoon rain; short dry
season, but total rain-
fall sufficient to support
rainforest.
n – Frequent fog.
n' – Infrequent fog, but high
humidity and low rain-
fall.
s – Dry season in summer.
w – Dry season in winter.

Limits of the Regions of Dry Climate

BW/BS

BS/HUMID

BSh

BSk

HUMID
A, C, D

ANNUAL RAINFALL IN INCHES

CURVES SHOW FAHRENHEIT TEMPERATURE
VERTICAL BARS SHOW RAINFALL IN INCHES

MEAN ANNUAL TEMP.
FAHRENHEIT

Winter concentration of precipitation
Precipitation evenly distributed throughout the year
Summer concentration of precipitation

Caw

BENARES

Subtropical climate;
winter drouth and
summer rain

Caf

CHARLESTON

Moderate continen-
tal forest climate;
mild winters

Cbf

DUBLIN

Moderate marine
forest climate;
mild winters

Daf

PEORIA

Continental forest
climate; warm
summer

Dbf

MOSCOW

Continental forest
climate; cool
summer

Dcf

MOOSE
FACTORY

Continental taiga
climate; very se-
vere winters

ET

BARROW

Tundra climate

EF

EISMITTE

Glacial climate
(Data incomplete)

INDEX

The index includes in a single alphabetical list some 11,000 names appearing on the maps. Each name is followed by a page reference and by the location of the feature on the map. The map location is designated by latitude and longitude coordinates. If a page contains several maps, a lowercase letter identifies the inset map. The page reference for two-page maps is always to the left hand page.

Most map features are indexed to the largest-scale map on which they appear. Countries, mountain ranges, and other extensive features are generally indexed to the map that shows them in their entirety.

The features indexed are of three types: *point*, *areal*, and *linear*. For *point* features (for example, cities, mountain peaks, dams), latitude and longitude coordinates give the location of the point on the map. For *areal* features (countries, mountain ranges, etc.), the coordinates generally indicate the approximate centre of the feature. For *linear* features (rivers, canals, aqueducts), the coordinates locate a terminating point—for example, the mouth of a river, or the point at which a feature reaches the map margin.

NAME FORMS Names in the Index, as on the maps, are generally in the local language and insofar as possible are spelled according to official practice. Diacritical marks are included, except that those used to indicate tone, as in Vietnamese, are usually not shown. Most features that extend beyond the boundaries of one country have no single official name, and these are usually named in English. Many conventional English names and former names are cross referenced to the primary map name. All cross references are indicated by the symbol→. A name that appears in a shortened version on the map due to space limitations is given in full in the Index, with the portion that is omitted on the map enclosed in brackets, for example, Acapulco [de Juárez].

TRANSLITERATION For names in languages not written in the Roman alphabet, the locally official transliteration system has been used where one exists. Thus, names in the Soviet Union and Bulgaria have been transliterated according to the systems adopted by the academies of science of these countries. Similarly, the transliteration for mainland Chinese names follows the Pinyin system, which has been officially adopted in mainland China. For languages with no one locally accepted transliteration system, notably Arabic, transliteration in general follows closely a system adopted by the United States Board on Geographic Names.

ALPHABETIZATION Names are alphabetized in the order of the letters of the English alphabet. Spanish *ll* and *ch*, for example, are not treated as distinct letters. Furthermore, diacritical marks are disregarded in alphabetization—German or Scandinavian *ä* or *ö* are treated as *a* or *o*.

The names of physical features may appear inverted, since they are always alphabetized under the proper, not the generic, part of the name, thus: "Gibraltar, Strait of". Otherwise every entry, whether consisting of one word or more, is alphabetized as a single continuous entity. "Lakeland," for example, appears after "La Crosse" and before "La Salle." Names beginning with articles (Le Havre, Den Helder, Al-Qāhirah, As-Suways) are not inverted. Names beginning "Mc" are alphabetized as though spelled "Mac," and names beginning "St." and "Sainte" as though spelled "Saint."

In the case of identical names, towns are listed first, then political divisions, then physical features. Entries that are completely identical (including symbols, discussed below) are distinguished by abbreviations of their official country names and are sequenced alphabetically by country name. The many duplicate names in Canada, the United Kingdom, and the United States are further distinguished by abbreviations of the names of their primary subdivisions. (See list of abbreviations on pages 177 and 178).

ABBREVIATION AND CAPITALIZATION Abbreviation and styling have been standardized for all languages. A period is used after every abbreviation even when this may not be the local practice. The abbreviation "St." is used only for "Saint." "Sankt" and other forms of the term are spelled out.

All names are written with an initial capital letter except for a few Dutch names, such as 's-Gravenhage. Capitalization of noninitial words in a name generally follows local practice.

SYMBOL The symbols that appear in the Index graphically represent the broad categories of the features named, for example, ∧ for mountain (Everest, Mount ∧). Superior numbers following some symbols in the Index indicate finer distinctions, for example, $\wedge^1$ for volcano (Fuji-san $\wedge^1$). A complete list of the symbols and those with superior numbers is given on page 178.

LIST OF ABBREVIATIONS

	LOCAL NAME	ENGLISH
Afg.	Afghānestān	Afghanistan
Afr.	—	Africa
Ala., U.S.	Alabama	Alabama
Alaska, U.S.	Alaska	Alaska
Alg.	Algérie	Algeria
Alta., Can.	Alberta	Alberta
Am. Sam.	American Samoa	American Samoa
And.	Andorra	Andorra
Ang.	Angola	Angola
Anguilla	Anguilla	Anguilla
Ant.	—	Antarctica
Antig.	Antigua	Antigua
Arc. O.	—	Arctic Ocean
Arg.	Argentina	Argentina
Ariz., U.S.	Arizona	Arizona
Ark., U.S.	Arkansas	Arkansas
Ar. Sa.	Al-'Arabīyah as-Sa'ūdīyah	Saudi Arabia
As.	—	Asia
Atl. O.	—	Atlantic Ocean
Austl.	Australia	Australia
Ba.	Bahamas	Bahamas
Baḥr.	Al-Baḥrayn	Bahrain
Barb.	Barbados	Barbados
B.A.T.	British Antarctic Territory	British Antarctic Territory
B.C., Can.	British Columbia	British Columbia
Bdi.	Burundi	Burundi
Bel.	Belgique België	Belgium
Belize	Belize	Belize
Benin	Benin	Benin
Ber.	Bermuda	Bermuda
Ber. S.	—	Bering Sea
Bhārat	Bhārat	India
B.I.O.T.	British Indian Ocean Territory	British Indian Ocean Territory
Blg.	Bâlgarija	Bulgaria
Bngl.	Bangladesh	Bangladesh
Bol.	Bolivia	Bolivia
Bots.	Botswana	Botswana
Bra.	Brasil	Brazil
B.R.D.	Bundesrepublik Deutschland	Federal Republic of Germany
Bru.	Brunei	Brunei
Br. Vir. Is.	British Virgin Islands	British Virgin Islands
Calif., U.S.	California	California
Cam.	Cameroun	Cameroon
Can.	Canada	Canada
Can./End.	Canton and Enderbury	Canton and Enderbury
Carib. S.	—	Caribbean Sea
Cay. Is.	Cayman Islands	Cayman Islands
Centraf.	Empire centrafricain	Central African Empire
Česko.	Československo	Czechoslovakia
Chile	Chile	Chile
Christ. I.	Christmas Island	Christmas Island
C. Iv.	Côte d'Ivoire	Ivory Coast
C.M.I.K.	Chosŏn Minjujuŭi In'min Konghwaguk	North Korea
Cocos Is.	Cocos (Keeling) Islands	Cocos (Keeling) Islands
Col.	Colombia	Colombia
Colo., U.S.	Colorado	Colorado
Comores	Comores	Comoros
Congo	Congo	Congo
Conn., U.S.	Connecticut	Connecticut
Cook Is.	Cook Islands	Cook Islands
C.R.	Costa Rica	Costa Rica
Cuba	Cuba	Cuba
C.V.	Cabo Verde	Cape Verde
C.Z.	Canal Zone	Canal Zone
Dan.	Danmark	Denmark
D.C., U.S.	District of Columbia	District of Columbia
D.D.R.	Deutsche Demokratische Republik	German Democratic Republic
Del., U.S.	Delaware	Delaware
Den.	Danmark	Denmark
Djibouti	Djibouti	Djibouti
Dom.	Dominica	Dominica
D.Y.	Druk-Yul	Bhutan
Ec.	Ecuador	Ecuador
Eire	Eire	Ireland
Ellás	Ellás	Greece
El Sal.	El Salvador	El Salvador
Eng., U.K.	England	England
Esp.	España	Spain
Eur.	—	Europe
Falk. Is.	Falkland Islands	Falkland Islands (Islas Malvinas)
Fiji	Fiji	Fiji
Fla., U.S.	Florida	Florida
Før.	Føroyar	Faeroe Islands
Fr.	France	France
Ga., U.S.	Georgia	Georgia
Gabon	Gabon	Gabon
Gam.	Gambia	Gambia
Gaza	—	Gaza Strip
Ghana	Ghana	Ghana
Gib.	Gibraltar	Gibraltar
Gilb. Is.	Gilbert Islands	Gilbert Islands
Gren.	Grenada	Grenada
Grn.	Grønland	Greenland
Guad.	Guadeloupe	Guadeloupe
Guam.	Guam	Guam
Guat.	Guatemala	Guatemala
Guer.	Guernsey	Guernsey
Gui.-B.	Guinea-Bissau	Guinea-Bissau
Gui. Ecu.	Guinea Ecuatorial	Equatorial Guinea
Guinée	Guinée	Guinea
Guy.	Guyana	Guyana
Guy. fr.	Guyane française	French Guiana
Haï.	Haïti	Haiti
Haw., U.S.	Hawaii	Hawaii
H.K.	Hong Kong	Hong Kong
Hond.	Honduras	Honduras
H. Vol.	Haute-Volta	Upper Volta
Idaho, U.S.	Idaho	Idaho
I.I.A.	Ittiḥād al-Imārāt al-'Arabīyah	United Arab Emirates
Ill., U.S.	Illinois	Illinois
Ind., U.S.	Indiana	Indiana
Ind. O.	—	Indian Ocean
Indon.	Indonesia	Indonesia
I. of Man	Isle of Man	Isle of Man
Iowa, U.S.	Iowa	Iowa
Īrān	Īrān	Iran
'Irāq	Al-'Irāq	Iraq
Ísland	Ísland	Iceland
It.	Italia	Italy
Jam.	Jamaica	Jamaica
Jersey	Jersey	Jersey
Jugo.	Jugoslavija	Yugoslavia
Kam.	Kâmpŭchéa	Kampuchea
Kans., U.S.	Kansas	Kansas
Kenya	Kenya	Kenya
Kípros	Kípros Kıbrıs	Cyprus
Kuwayt	Al-Kuwayt	Kuwait
Ky., U.S.	Kentucky	Kentucky
La., U.S.	Louisiana	Louisiana
Lao	Lao	Laos
Leso.	Lesotho	Lesotho
Liber.	Liberia	Liberia
Lībiyā	Lībiyā	Libya
Liech.	Liechtenstein	Liechtenstein
Lubnān	Al-Lubnān	Lebanon
Lux.	Luxembourg	Luxembourg
Macau	Macau	Macau
Madag.	Madagasikara	Madagascar
Magreb	Al-Magreb	Morocco
Magy.	Magyarország	Hungary
Maine, U.S.	Maine	Maine
Malawi	Malawi	Malawi
Malay.	Malaysia	Malaysia
Mald.	Maldives	Maldives
Mali	Mali	Mali
Malta	Malta	Malta
Man., Can.	Manitoba	Manitoba
Mart.	Martinique	Martinique
Mass., U.S.	Massachusetts	Massachusetts
Maur.	Mauritanie	Mauritania
Maus.	Mauritius	Mauritius
Md., U.S.	Maryland	Maryland
Medit. S.	—	Mediterranean Sea
Méx.	México	Mexico
Mich., U.S.	Michigan	Michigan
Mid. Is.	Midway Islands	Midway Islands
Minn., U.S.	Minnesota	Minnesota
Miṣr	Miṣr	Egypt
Miss., U.S.	Mississippi	Mississippi
Mo., U.S.	Missouri	Missouri
Moç.	Moçambique	Mozambique
Monaco	Monaco	Monaco
Mong.	Mongol Ard Uls	Mongolia
Mont., U.S.	Montana	Montana
Monts.	Montserrat	Montserrat
Mya.	Myanma	Burma
N.A.	—	North America
Namibia	Namibia	Namibia
Nauru	Nauru	Nauru
N.B., Can.	New Brunswick	New Brunswick
N.C., U.S.	North Carolina	North Carolina
N. Cal.	Nouvelle-Calédonie	New Caledonia
N. Dak., U.S.	North Dakota	North Dakota
Nebr., U.S.	Nebraska	Nebraska
Ned.	Nederland	Netherlands
Ned. Ant.	Nederlandse Antillen	Netherlands Antilles
Nepāl	Nepāl	Nepal
Nev., U.S.	Nevada	Nevada
Newf., Can.	Newfoundland	Newfoundland
N.H., U.S.	New Hampshire	New Hampshire
N. Heb.	New Hebrides Nouvelles-Hébrides	New Hebrides
Nic.	Nicaragua	Nicaragua
Nig.	Nigeria	Nigeria
Niger	Niger	Niger
Nihon	Nihon	Japan
N. Ire., U.K.	Northern Ireland	Northern Ireland
Niue	Niue	Niue
N.J., U.S.	New Jersey	New Jersey
N. Mex., U.S.	New Mexico	New Mexico
Nor.	Norge	Norway
Norf. I.	Norfolk Island	Norfolk Island
N.S., Can.	Nova Scotia	Nova Scotia
N.W. Ter., Can.	Northwest Territories	Northwest Territories
N.Y., U.S.	New York	New York
N.Z.	New Zealand	New Zealand
Oc.	—	Oceania
Ohio, U.S.	Ohio	Ohio
Okla., U.S.	Oklahoma	Oklahoma
Ont., Can.	Ontario	Ontario
Oreg., U.S.	Oregon	Oregon
Öst.	Österreich	Austria
Pa., U.S.	Pennsylvania	Pennsylvania
Pac. O.	—	Pacific Ocean
Pāk.	Pākistān	Pakistan
Pan.	Panamá	Panama
Pap. N. Gui.	Papua New Guinea	Papua New Guinea
Para.	Paraguay	Paraguay
P.E.I., Can.	Prince Edward Island	Prince Edward Island
Perú	Perú	Peru
Pil.	Pilipinas	Philippines
Pit.	Pitcairn	Pitcairn
P.I.T.T.	Pacific Islands Trust Territory	Pacific Islands Trust Territory
Pol.	Polska	Poland
Poly. fr.	Polynésie française	French Polynesia
Port.	Portugal	Portugal
P.R.	Puerto Rico	Puerto Rico
P.S.N.Á.	Plazas de Soberanía en el Norte de África	Spanish North Africa
Qaṭar	Qaṭar	Qatar
Que., Can.	Québec	Quebec
Rep. Dom.	República Dominicana	Dominican Republic
Réu.	Réunion	Reunion
R.I., U.S.	Rhode Island	Rhode Island
Rom.	România	Romania
Rw.	Rwanda	Rwanda
S.A.	—	South America
S. Afr.	South Africa Suid-Afrika	South Africa
Sah. Occ.	Sahara Occidentale	Western Sahara
Sask., Can.	Saskatchewan	Saskatchewan
S.C., U.S.	South Carolina	South Carolina
S. Ch. S.	—	South China Sea
Schw.	Schweiz; Suisse; Svizzera	Switzerland
Scot., U.K.	Scotland	Scotland
S. Dak., U.S.	South Dakota	South Dakota
Sén.	Sénégal	Senegal
Sey.	Seychelles	Seychelles
Shq.	Shqipëri	Albania
Sing.	Singapore	Singapore
S.L.	Sierra Leone	Sierra Leone
S. Lan.	Sri Lanka	Sri Lanka
S. Mar.	San Marino	San Marino
Sol. Is.	Solomon Islands	Solomon Islands
Som.	Somaliya	Somalia
Sp.	España	Spain
S.S.R.	Sovetskaja Socialističeskaja Respublika	Soviet Socialist Republic
S.S.S.R.	Sojuz Sovetskich Socialističeskich Respublik	Union of Soviet Socialist Republics
St. Hel.	St. Helena	St. Helena
St. K.-N.	St. Kitts-Nevis	St. Kitts-Nevis
St. Luc.	St. Lucia	St. Lucia
S. Tom./P.	São Tomé e Príncipe	Sao Tome and Principe
St. P./M.	St.-Pierre-et-Miquelon	St. Pierre and Miquelon
St. Vin.	St. Vincent	St. Vincent
Sūd.	As-Sūdān	Sudan
Suomi	Suomi	Finland
Sur.	Suriname	Suriname
Sūriy.	As-Sūrīyah	Syria
Sval.	Svalbard og Jan Mayen	Svalbard and Jan Mayen
Sve.	Sverige	Sweden
Swaz.	Swaziland	Swaziland
T.a.a.f.	Terres australes et antarctiques françaises	French Southern and Antarctic Territories
Taehan	Taehan-Min'guk	South Korea
T'aiwan	T'aiwan	Taiwan
Tan.	Tanzania	Tanzania
Tchad	Tchad	Chad
T./C. Is.	Turks and Caicos Islands	Turks and Caicos Islands
Tenn., U.S.	Tennessee	Tennessee
Tex., U.S.	Texas	Texas
Thai.	Prathet Thai	Thailand
Togo	Togo	Togo
Tok. Is.	Tokelau Islands	Tokelau Islands
Tonga	Tonga	Tonga
Trin.	Trinidad and Tobago	Trinidad and Tobago
Tun.	Tunisie	Tunisia
Tür.	Türkiye	Turkey
Tuvalu	Tuvalu	Tuvalu
Ug.	Uganda	Uganda
U.K.	United Kingdom	United Kingdom
'Umān	'Umān	Oman
Ur.	Uruguay	Uruguay
Urd.	Al-Urdunn	Jordan
U.S.	United States	United States

Opposite: Antigua Bay, West Indies

Introduction to the Index

LIST OF ABBREVIATIONS CON'T.

	LOCAL NAME	ENGLISH
U.S.S.R.	Sojuz Sovetskich Socialističeskich Respublik	Union of Soviet Socialist Republics
Utah, U.S.	Utah	Utah
Va., U.S.	Virginia	Virginia
Vat.	Città del Vaticano	Vatican City
Ven.	Venezuela	Venezuela
Viet.	Viet-nam	Vietnam
Vir. Is., U.S.	Virgin Islands	Virgin Islands (U.S.)
Vt., U.S.	Vermont	Vermont
Wake I.	Wake Island	Wake Island
Wales, U.K.	Wales	Wales
Wal./F.	Wallis et Futuna	Wallis and Futuna
Wash., U.S.	Washington	Washington
Wis., U.S.	Wisconsin	Wisconsin
W. Sam.	Western Samoa	Western Samoa
W. Va., U.S.	West Virginia	West Virginia
Wyo., U.S.	Wyoming	Wyoming
Yai.	Yaitopya	Ethiopia
Yaman	Al-Yaman	Yemen
Yam. S.	Al-Yaman ash-Sha'bīyah	People's Democratic Republic of Yemen
Yis.	Yisra'el	Israel
Yukon, Can.	Yukon	Yukon
Zaïre	Zaïre	Zaire
Zam.	Zambia	Zambia
Zim. Rh.	Zimbabwe Rhodesia	Zimbabwe Rhodesia
Zhg.	Zhongguo	China

KEY TO SYMBOLS

- ⋀ Mountain
- ⋀¹ Volcano
- ⋀² Hill
- ⋀ Mountains
- ⋀¹ Plateau
- ⋀² Hills
-)(Pass
- ⋁ Valley, Canyon
- ≃ Plain
- ≃¹ Basin
- ≃² Delta
- ⊁ Cape
- ⊁¹ Peninsula
- ⊁² Spit, Sand Bar
- ○ Island
- ○¹ Atoll
- ○² Rock
- ○○ Islands
- ○○¹ Rocks
- ⫶ Other Topographic Features
- ⫶¹ Continent
- ⫶² Coast, Beach
- ⫶³ Isthmus
- ⫶⁴ Cliff
- ⫶⁵ Cave, Caves
- ⫶⁶ Crater
- ⫶⁷ Depression
- ⫶⁸ Dunes
- ⫶⁹ Lava Flow
- ≃ River
- ≃¹ River Channel
- ⌇ Canal
- ⌇¹ Aqueduct
- ⌇ Waterfall, Rapids
- ⋃ Strait
- C Bay, Gulf
- C¹ Estuary
- C² Fjord
- C³ Bight
- ⊜ Lake, Lakes
- ⊜¹ Reservoir
- ≋ Swamp
- ⌧ Ice Features, Glacier
- ⊤ Other Hydrographic Features
- ⊤¹ Ocean
- ⊤² Sea
- ⊤³ Anchorage
- ⊤⁴ Oasis, Well, Spring
- ✛ Submarine Features
- ✛¹ Depression
- ✛² Reef, Shoal
- ✛³ Mountain, Mountains
- ✛⁴ Slope, Shelf
- □ Political Unit
- □¹ Independent Nation
- □² Dependency
- □³ State, Canton, Republic
- □⁴ Province, Region, Oblast
- □⁵ Department, District, Prefecture
- □⁶ County
- □⁷ City, Municipality
- □⁸ Miscellaneous
- □⁹ Historical
- ʊ Cultural Institution
- ʊ¹ Religious Institution
- ʊ² Educational Institution
- ʊ³ Scientific, Industrial Facility
- ▪ Historical Site
- ♣ Recreational Site
- ⊠ Airport
- ■ Military Installation
- ▪ Miscellaneous
- ↗ Region
- ↗¹ Desert
- ↗² Forest, Moor
- ↗³ Reserve, Reservation
- ↗⁴ Transportation
- ↗⁵ Dam
- ↗⁶ Mine, Quarry
- ↗⁷ Neighborhood
- ↗⁸ Shopping Center

Index

Name	Page	Lat ° ′	Long ° ′
Arcachon	42	44.37 N	1.12 W
Archangel'sk	26	64.34 N	40.32 E
Arcos de la Frontera	50	36.45 N	5.48 W
Arda	54	41.39 N	26.29 E
Ardennes	36	50.10 N	5.45 E
Ardila	50	38.12 N	7.28 W
Arecibo	130	18.28 N	66.43 W
Arendal	28	58.27 N	8.48 E
Areq, Sebkha Bou	50	35.10 N	2.45 W
Arequipa	144	16.24 S	71.33 W
Arezzo	46	43.25 N	11.53 E
Argenta	46	44.37 N	11.50 E
Argentan	42	48.45 N	0.01 W
Argentera	46	44.10 N	7.18 E
Argentina	146	34.00 S	64.00 W
Argentino, Lago	146	50.13 S	72.25 W
Arghandāb	84	31.27 N	64.23 E
Argolikós Kólpos	54	37.33 N	22.45 E
Argonne	42	49.30 N	5.00 E
Árgos	54	37.39 N	22.44 E
Argostólion	54	38.10 N	20.30 E
Argun' (Eergu'nahe)	64	53.20 N	121.28 E
Århus	28	56.09 N	10.13 E
Ariano Irpino	46	41.09 N	15.05 E
Ariège	42	43.31 N	1.25 E
Arieș	54	46.26 N	23.59 E
Arima	130	10.38 N	61.17 W
Arizaro, Salar de	146	24.42 S	67.45 W
Arizgoiti	50	43.01 N	2.24 W
Arizona	162	34.00 N	112.00 W
Arkansas	162	34.50 N	93.40 W
Arkansas	162	33.48 N	91.04 W
Arkona, Kap	36	54.41 N	13.26 E
Arktičeskij, Mys	62	81.15 N	95.45 E
Arles	42	43.40 N	4.38 E
Arlington	162	38.52 N	77.05 W
Arlon	36	49.41 N	5.49 E
Armagh	32	54.21 N	6.39 W
Armavir	62	45.00 N	41.08 E
Armenia	144	4.31 N	75.41 W
Armentières	42	50.41 N	2.53 E
Armidale	116	30.31 S	151.39 E
Armstrong, Mount	160	63.12 N	133.16 W
Arnaud	160	59.59 N	69.46 W
Arnhem	36	51.59 N	5.55 E
Arnhem Land	116	13.10 S	134.30 E
Árnissa	54	40.48 N	21.50 E
Arno	46	43.41 N	10.17 E
Arnsberg	36	51.24 N	8.03 E
Arnstadt	36	50.50 N	10.57 E
Arona	46	45.46 N	8.34 E
Arorangi	114	21.13 S	159.49 W
Arosa, Ría de	50	42.28 N	8.57 W
Ar-Rab' al-Khālī	84	20.00 N	51.00 E
Arran, Island of	32	55.35 N	5.15 W
Arras	42	50.17 N	2.47 E
Arrats	42	44.06 N	0.52 E
Ar-Riyāḍ (Riyadh)	84	24.38 N	46.43 E
Arros	42	43.40 N	0.02 W
Arroux	42	46.29 N	3.58 E
Árta	54	39.09 N	20.59 E
Artemisa	130	22.49 N	82.46 W
Artigas	146	30.24 S	56.28 W
Aru, Kepulauan	82	6.00 S	134.30 E
Arua	102	3.01 N	30.55 E
Aruba	130	12.30 N	69.58 W
Arun	32	50.48 N	0.33 W
Arusha	104	3.22 S	36.41 E
Aruwimi	104	1.13 N	23.36 E
Arvika	28	59.39 N	12.36 E
Arzamas	26	55.23 N	43.50 E
Arzew	50	35.51 N	0.19 W
Arzew, Golfe d'	50	35.50 N	0.10 W
Arzew, Salines d'	50	35.40 N	0.15 W
Arzignano	46	45.31 N	11.20 E
Aš	36	50.10 N	12.10 E
Asahikawa	80	43.46 N	142.22 E
Asansol	84	23.41 N	86.58 E
Aschabad	62	37.57 N	58.23 E
Aschaffenburg	36	49.59 N	9.09 E
Aschersleben	36	51.45 N	11.27 E
Ascoli Piceno	46	42.51 N	13.34 E
Asenovgrad	54	42.01 N	24.52 E
Ashburton	118	43.55 S	171.45 E
Ashburton, Austl.	116	21.40 S	114.56 E
Ashburton, N.Z.	118	44.04 S	171.48 E
Asheville	162	35.34 N	82.33 W
Ashford	32	51.26 N	0.27 W
Ashikaga	80	36.20 N	139.27 E
Ashland	162	38.28 N	82.38 W
Ash-Shāriqah	84	25.22 N	55.23 E
Ash-Sharqīyah, Aṣ-Ṣaḥrā' (Eastern Desert)	102	28.00 N	32.00 E
Ashtabula	162	41.52 N	80.48 W
Asia Minor	84	39.00 N	32.00 E
Asilah	50	35.32 N	6.00 W
Asinara, Golfo dell'	46	41.00 N	8.30 E
Asinara, Isola	46	41.05 N	8.18 E
'Asīr	84	19.00 N	42.00 E
Asmera	102	15.20 N	38.53 E
Åsnen	28	56.38 N	14.42 E
Aso	46	43.06 N	13.51 E
Aspe	50	38.21 N	0.46 W
Aspromonte	46	38.10 N	15.55 E
Assad, Buḥayrat al-	20	36.00 N	38.00 E
Aṣ-Ṣaḥrā' al-Lībīyah (Libyan Desert)	102	24.00 N	25.00 E
Asse	36	50.55 N	4.12 E
Assen	36	52.59 N	6.34 E
Assiniboine, Mount	160	50.52 N	115.39 W
Assisi	46	43.04 N	12.37 E
As-Sulaymānīyah	84	35.33 N	45.26 E
As-Suwaydā'	84	32.42 N	36.34 E
As-Suways (Suez)	102	29.58 N	32.33 E
Asti	46	44.54 N	8.12 E
Astorga	50	42.27 N	6.03 W
Astrachan'	62	46.21 N	48.03 E
Asturias	50	43.20 N	6.00 W
Asuisui, Cape	113	13.47 S	172.29 W
Asunción	146	25.16 S	57.40 W
Aswān	102	24.05 N	32.53 E
Asyūṭ	102	27.11 N	31.11 E
Atacama, Desierto de	146	24.30 S	69.15 W
Atacama, Salar de	146	23.30 S	68.15 W
Atar	100	20.31 N	13.03 W
'Aṭbarah	102	17.42 N	33.59 E
'Aṭbarah (Atbara)	102	17.40 N	33.56 E
Athabasca	160	58.40 N	110.50 W
Athabasca, Lake	160	59.07 N	110.00 W
Athens	162	33.57 N	83.23 W
Atherton	116	17.16 S	145.29 E
Athínai (Athens)	54	37.58 N	23.43 E
Áthos	54	40.09 N	24.19 E
Ath-Thālith, Ash-Shallāl	102	19.49 N	30.19 E
Atlanta	162	33.45 N	84.23 W
Atlantic City	162	39.22 N	74.26 W
Atlas Mountains	100	33.00 N	2.00 W
Atlas Saharien	100	33.25 N	1.20 E
Atlas Tellien	100	36.00 N	3.00 E
Atrak (Atrek)	84	37.28 N	53.57 E
Ätran	28	56.53 N	12.30 E
Atrato	144	8.17 N	76.58 W
Atrek (Atrak)	84	37.28 N	53.57 E
Aṭ-Ṭā'if	84	21.16 N	40.24 E
Attawapiskat	160	52.57 N	82.18 W
Attikí	54	38.00 N	23.30 E
Attow, Ben	32	57.14 N	5.17 W
Atuel	146	36.17 S	66.50 W
Auasberge	104	22.45 S	17.22 E
Aubagne	42	43.17 N	5.34 E
Aubrac	42	44.40 N	3.00 E
Auburn	162	42.56 N	76.34 W
Aubusson	42	45.57 N	2.11 E
Auch	42	43.39 N	0.35 E
Auckland	118	36.52 S	174.46 E
Aude	42	43.13 N	3.14 E
Audincourt	42	47.29 N	6.50 E
Aue	36	50.35 N	12.42 E
Auerbach	36	50.41 N	12.54 E
Augsburg	36	48.23 N	10.53 E
Augusta, It.	46	37.13 N	15.13 E
Augusta, Ga., U.S.	162	33.29 N	81.57 W
Augusta, Maine, U.S.	162	44.19 N	69.47 W
Augusta, Golfo di	46	37.10 N	15.20 E
Augustów	36	53.51 N	22.59 E
Augustowski, Kanał	36	53.54 N	23.26 E
Auki	114	8.46 S	160.42 E
Aulne	42	48.17 N	4.16 W
Auob	104	26.25 S	20.35 E
Aurich	36	53.28 N	7.29 E
Aurillac	42	44.56 N	2.26 E
Aurora, Colo., U.S.	162	39.44 N	104.52 W
Aurora, Ill., U.S.	162	42.46 N	88.19 W
Ausangate, Nevado	144	13.48 S	71.14 W
Austin, Minn., U.S.	162	43.40 N	92.59 W
Austin, Tex., U.S.	162	30.16 N	97.45 W
Australia	116	25.00 S	135.00 E
Austria (Österreich)	36	47.20 N	13.20 E
Austvågøya	26	68.20 N	14.36 E
Autoua	112	16.21 S	167.45 E
Autun	42	46.57 N	4.18 E
Auvézère	42	45.12 N	0.51 E
Auxerre	42	47.48 N	3.34 E
Auyán-Tepuí	144	5.55 N	62.32 W
Avaloirs, Les	42	48.28 N	0.07 W
Avana	114	21.14 S	159.43 W
Avarua	114	21.12 S	159.46 W
Avatiu	114	21.12 S	159.47 W
Avatiu Harbour	114	21.11 S	159.47 W
Ave	50	41.20 N	8.45 W
Aveiro	50	40.38 N	8.39 W
Avellaneda	146	34.39 S	58.23 W
Avellino	46	40.54 N	14.47 E
Aven Armand	42	44.15 N	3.22 E
Aversa	46	40.58 N	14.12 E
Aves, Islas de	144	12.00 N	67.30 W
Avesta	28	60.09 N	16.12 E
Aveyron	42	44.05 N	1.16 E
Avezzano	46	42.02 N	13.25 E
Avignon	42	43.57 N	4.49 E
Ávila	50	40.39 N	4.42 W
Avilés	50	43.33 N	5.55 W
Avola	46	36.54 N	15.09 E
Avon	32	51.30 N	2.40 W
Avon	32	50.43 N	1.46 W
Avranches	42	48.41 N	1.22 W
Awash	102	11.45 N	41.05 E
Awe, Loch	32	56.15 N	5.15 W
Axiós (Vardar)	54	40.31 N	22.43 E
Ayacucho	144	13.07 S	74.13 W
Ayamonte	50	37.13 N	7.24 W
Aydın	54	37.51 N	27.51 E
Aydın Dağları	54	38.00 N	28.00 E
Ayers Rock	116	25.23 S	131.05 E
Áyion Óros	54	40.15 N	24.15 E
Áyios Nikólaos	54	35.11 N	25.42 E
Aylesbury	32	51.18 N	0.29 E
'Ayoûn el 'Atroûs	100	16.40 N	9.37 W
Ayr	32	55.28 N	4.38 W
Ayre, Point of	32	54.26 N	4.22 W
Ayrolle, Étang de l'	42	43.05 N	3.03 E
Ayvalık	54	39.18 N	26.41 E
Azaouak, Vallée de l'	100	15.30 N	3.18 E
Azovskoje More	62	46.00 N	36.00 E
Azuaga	50	38.16 N	5.41 W
Azuer	50	39.08 N	3.36 W
Azul	146	36.47 S	59.51 W
Azul, Cordillera	144	9.00 S	75.35 W
Azur, Côte d'	42	43.30 N	7.00 E
Aẓ-Ẓahrān (Dhahran)	84	26.18 N	50.08 E
Az-Zaqāzīq	102	30.35 N	31.31 E
Az-Zarqā'	84	32.05 N	36.06 E
Azzel Matti, Sebkha	100	25.55 N	0.56 E
B			
Ba	82	13.02 N	109.03 E
Baarn	36	52.13 N	5.16 E
Babaeski	54	41.26 N	27.06 E
Babelthuap	82	7.30 N	134.36 E
Babine Lake	160	54.45 N	126.00 W
Babuyan Islands	82	19.10 N	121.40 E
Bacabal	144	4.14 S	44.47 W
Bacău	54	46.34 N	26.55 E
Bačka	54	45.50 N	19.30 E
Bačka Palanka	54	45.15 N	19.24 E
Bačka Topola	54	45.49 N	19.38 E
Backnang	36	48.56 N	9.25 E
Bac-lieu (Vinh-loi)	82	9.17 N	105.44 E
Bacolod	82	10.40 N	122.57 E
Badajoz	50	38.53 N	6.58 W
Badalona	50	41.27 N	2.15 E
Bad Doberan	36	54.06 N	11.53 E
Bad Dürkheim	36	49.28 N	8.10 E
Bad Ems	36	50.20 N	7.43 E
Baden, Öst.	36	48.00 N	16.14 E
Baden, Schw.	42	47.29 N	8.18 E
Baden-Baden	36	48.46 N	8.14 E
Bad Freienwalde	36	52.47 N	14.01 E
Bad Harzburg	36	51.53 N	10.33 E
Bad Hersfeld	36	50.52 N	9.42 E
Bad Homburg [vor der Höhe]	36	50.13 N	8.37 E
Bad Honnef	36	50.39 N	7.13 E
Bad Ischl	36	47.43 N	13.37 E
Bad Kissingen	36	50.12 N	10.04 E
Bad Kreuznach	36	49.52 N	7.51 E
Badlands	162	46.45 N	103.30 W
Bad Langensalza	36	51.06 N	10.38 E
Bad Mergentheim	36	49.30 N	9.46 E
Bad Nauheim	36	50.22 N	8.44 E
Bad Oeynhausen	36	52.12 N	8.48 E
Bad Oldesloe	36	53.48 N	10.22 E
Bad Pyrmont	36	51.59 N	9.15 E
Bad Reichenhall	36	47.43 N	12.52 E
Bad Salzuflen	36	52.05 N	8.44 E
Bad Salzungen	36	50.48 N	10.13 E
Bad Schwartau	36	53.55 N	10.40 E
Bad Segeberg	36	53.56 N	10.17 E
Bad Tölz	36	47.46 N	11.34 E
Baena	50	37.37 N	4.19 W
Bafa Gölü	54	37.30 N	27.25 E
Bafatá	100	12.10 N	14.40 W
Baffin Bay	160	73.00 N	66.00 W
Baffin Island	160	68.00 N	70.00 W
Bafing	100	13.49 N	10.50 W
Baghdād	84	33.21 N	44.25 E
Bagheria	46	38.05 N	13.30 E
Bagnara Cálabra	46	38.18 N	15.49 E
Bagnères-de-Bigorre	42	43.04 N	0.09 E
Bagnols-sur-Cèze	42	44.10 N	4.37 E
Baguio	82	16.25 N	120.36 E
Bagzane, Monts	100	17.43 N	8.45 E
Bahamas	130	24.15 N	76.00 W
Bahāwalpur	84	29.24 N	71.41 E
Bahía, Islas de la	130	16.20 N	86.30 W
Bahía Blanca	146	38.43 S	62.17 W
Bahrain	84	26.00 N	50.30 E
Baia-Mare	54	47.40 N	23.35 E
Baidoa	102	3.04 N	43.48 E
Baie-Comeau	160	49.13 N	68.10 W
Bailén	50	38.06 N	3.46 W
Băilești	54	44.02 N	23.21 E
Baïse	42	44.07 N	0.17 E
Baja	36	46.11 N	18.57 E
Baja California	130	28.00 N	113.30 W
Bajdarackaja Guba	62	69.00 N	67.30 E
Bajkal, Ozero (Lake Baykal)	64	53.00 N	107.40 E
Baker, Mount	162	48.47 N	121.49 W
Baker Lake	160	64.15 N	96.00 W
Baker Lake	160	64.10 N	95.30 W
Bakersfield	162	35.23 N	119.01 W
Bakony	36	46.55 N	17.40 E
Bakoye	100	13.49 N	10.50 W
Baku	62	40.23 N	49.51 E
Balabac Strait	82	7.35 N	117.00 E
Balakovo	62	52.02 N	47.47 E
Balambangan, Pulau	82	7.15 N	116.55 E
Balassagyarmat	36	48.05 N	19.18 E
Balaton	36	46.50 N	17.45 E
Balboa Heights	130	8.57 N	79.33 W
Balchaš, Ozero	62	46.00 N	74.00 E
Baldy Peak	162	33.55 N	109.35 W
Baleares	50	39.30 N	3.00 E
Baleares, Islas (Balearic Islands)	50	39.30 N	3.00 E
Balen	36	51.10 N	5.09 E
Balfate	130	15.48 N	86.25 W
Bali	82	8.20 S	115.00 E
Balıkesir	54	39.39 N	27.53 E
Balikpapan	82	1.17 S	116.50 E
Balingen	36	48.16 N	8.51 E
Balintang Channel	82	19.49 N	121.40 E
Ballarat	116	37.34 S	143.52 E
Ballymena	32	54.52 N	6.17 W
Balsas	130	17.55 N	102.10 W
Baltic Sea	26	57.00 N	19.00 E
Baltijsk	26	54.39 N	19.55 E
Baltijskaja Kosa	36	54.25 N	19.35 E
Baltimore	162	39.17 N	76.37 W
Baluchistan	84	28.00 N	63.00 E
Bamako	100	12.39 N	8.00 W
Bambari	102	5.45 N	20.40 E
Bambatana	114	7.02 S	156.48 E
Bamberg	36	49.53 N	10.53 E
Bamenda	100	5.56 N	10.10 E
Bamingui	102	8.33 N	19.05 E
Banana	104	6.01 S	12.24 E
Banās, Ra's	102	23.54 N	35.48 E
Banat	54	45.20 N	20.40 E
Banbury	32	52.04 N	1.20 W
Banda, Laut (Banda Sea)	82	5.00 S	128.00 E
Bandama	100	5.10 N	5.00 W
Bandama Blanc	100	6.54 N	5.31 W
Bandama Rouge	100	6.54 N	5.31 W
Bandar Seri Begawan	82	4.56 N	114.55 E
Bandeira, Pico da	144	20.26 S	41.47 W
Bandırma	54	40.20 N	27.58 E
Bandundu	104	3.18 S	17.20 E
Bandung	82	6.54 S	107.36 E
Banes	130	20.58 N	75.43 W
Bangalore	84	12.58 N	77.36 E
Bangbu	80	32.58 N	117.24 E
Banggi, Pulau	82	7.17 N	117.12 E
Banghāzī	102	32.07 N	20.04 E
Bangka	82	2.15 S	106.00 E
Bangladesh	84	24.00 N	90.00 E
Bangor, N. Ire., U.K.	32	54.40 N	5.40 W
Bangor, Wales, U.K.	32	53.13 N	4.08 W
Bangor, Maine, U.S.	162	44.49 N	68.47 W
Bangui	102	4.22 N	18.35 E
Bangweulu, Lake	104	11.05 S	29.45 E
Bani	130	18.17 N	70.20 W
Bani	100	14.30 N	4.12 W
Banī Mazār	102	28.30 N	30.48 E
Banī Suwayf	102	29.05 N	31.05 E
Banja Luka	46	44.46 N	17.11 E
Banjarmasin	82	3.20 S	114.35 E
Banjul	100	13.28 N	16.39 W
Banks Island, B.C., Can.	160	53.25 N	130.10 W
Banks Island, N.W. Ter., Can.	160	73.15 N	121.30 W
Banks Islands	112	13.50 S	167.30 E
Bann	32	55.10 N	6.46 W
Bannu	84	32.59 N	70.36 E
Banská Bystrica	36	48.44 N	19.07 E
Banská Štiavnica	36	48.28 N	18.56 E
Baoding	80	38.52 N	115.29 E
Baoji	80	34.22 N	107.14 E
Baotou	80	40.40 N	109.59 E
Barabinskaja Step'	64	55.00 N	79.00 E
Baracoa	130	20.21 N	74.30 W
Baram	82	4.36 N	113.59 E
Barania Góra	36	49.37 N	19.00 E
Baranoviči	62	53.08 N	26.02 E
Baratang Island	84	12.13 N	92.45 E
Barat Daya, Kepulauan	82	7.25 S	128.00 E
Barbacena	144	21.14 S	43.46 W
Barbados	130	13.10 N	59.32 W
Barbas, Cabo	100	22.18 N	16.41 W
Barbastro	50	42.02 N	0.08 E
Barbate de Franco	50	36.12 N	5.55 W
Barbuda	130	17.38 N	61.48 W
Barcellona Pozzo di Gotto	46	38.09 N	15.13 E
Barcelona, Esp.	50	41.23 N	2.11 E
Barcelona, Ven.	144	10.08 N	64.42 W
Bardejov	36	49.18 N	21.16 E
Bárdenas Reales	50	42.10 N	1.25 W
Bardsey Island	32	52.45 N	4.45 W
Bareilly	84	28.20 N	79.25 E
Barents Sea (Barenc'ovo More)	26	69.00 N	40.00 E
Barfleur, Pointe de	42	49.42 N	1.16 W
Bari	46	41.07 N	16.52 E
Barīm	84	12.40 N	43.25 E
Barinas	144	8.38 N	70.12 W
Barisāl	84	22.42 N	90.22 E
Barito	82	3.32 S	114.29 E
Barka	102	18.13 N	37.35 E
Barkley Sound	160	48.53 N	125.20 W
Bar-le-Duc	42	48.47 N	5.10 E
Barletta	46	41.19 N	16.17 E
Barnaul	64	53.22 N	83.45 E
Barnsley	32	53.34 N	1.28 W
Barnstaple	32	51.05 N	4.04 W
Baro	102	8.26 N	33.13 E
Baroda	84	25.30 N	76.40 E
Barotseland	104	16.00 S	24.00 E
Barqah (Cyrenaica)	102	31.00 N	22.30 E
Barquisimeto	144	10.04 N	69.19 W
Barra, Ponta da	104	23.47 S	35.32 E
Barra Falsa, Ponta da	104	22.55 S	35.37 E
Barrafranca	46	37.23 N	14.13 E
Barra Mansa	144	22.32 S	44.11 W
Barrancabermeja	144	7.03 N	73.52 W
Barranquilla	144	10.59 N	74.48 W
Barre des Écrins	42	44.55 N	6.22 E
Barreiro	50	38.40 N	9.04 W
Barretos	144	20.33 S	48.33 W
Barrow-in-Furness	32	54.07 N	3.14 W
Barry	32	51.24 N	3.18 W
Barth	36	54.22 N	12.43 E
Bartoszyce	36	54.16 N	20.49 E
Barwon	116	30.00 S	148.05 E
Barycz	36	51.42 N	16.15 E
Basatongwulashan	80	33.05 N	91.30 E
Bascuñán, Cabo	146	28.51 S	71.30 W
Basel (Bâle)	42	47.33 N	7.35 E
Basento	46	40.21 N	16.50 E
Bașeu	54	47.44 N	27.15 E
Bashi Channel	82	22.00 N	121.00 E
Basilan	82	6.42 N	121.58 E
Basildon	32	51.35 N	0.25 E
Basingstoke	32	51.15 N	1.05 W
Bassano del Grappa	46	45.46 N	11.44 E
Bassas da India	104	21.25 S	39.42 E
Bassein	82	16.47 N	94.44 E
Basse-Terre, Guad.	130	16.00 N	61.44 W
Basseterre, St. K.-N.	130	17.18 N	62.43 W
Bass Strait	116	39.20 S	145.30 E
Bastia	42	42.42 N	9.27 E
Bata	100	1.51 N	9.45 E
Batabanó, Golfo de	130	22.15 N	82.30 W
Batajsk	62	47.10 N	39.44 E
Batak, Jazovir	54	41.59 N	24.11 E
Batangas	82	13.45 N	121.03 E
Batanghari	82	1.16 S	104.05 E
Bătdâmbâng	82	13.06 N	103.12 E
Bates, Mount	113	29.01 S	167.56 E
Bath	32	51.23 N	2.22 W
Bathgate	32	55.55 N	3.39 W
Bathurst	116	33.25 S	149.35 E
Bathurst Inlet	160	66.50 N	108.01 W
Bathurst Island, Austl.	116	11.37 S	130.27 E
Bathurst Island, N.W. Ter., Can.	160	76.00 N	100.30 W
Batna	100	35.34 N	6.11 E
Baton Rouge	162	30.23 N	91.11 W
Battle	160	52.42 N	108.15 W
Battle Creek	162	42.19 N	85.11 W
Batu	102	6.55 N	39.46 E
Batumi	62	41.38 N	41.38 E
Batu Pahat	82	1.51 N	102.56 E
Bauchi	100	10.19 N	9.50 E
Bauru	144	22.19 S	49.04 W
Bautzen	36	51.11 N	14.26 E
Bayamo	130	20.23 N	76.39 W
Bay City	162	43.36 N	83.53 W
Bayeux	42	49.16 N	0.42 W
Bayındır	54	38.13 N	27.40 E
Bayonne	42	43.29 N	1.29 W
Bayreuth	36	49.57 N	11.35 E
Bayrūt	84	33.53 N	35.30 E
Baza	50	37.29 N	2.46 W
Bazaruto, Ilha do	104	21.40 S	35.28 E
Beachy Head	32	50.44 N	0.16 E
Béarn	42	43.20 N	0.45 W
Beata, Isla	162	17.35 N	71.31 W
Beaucaire	42	43.48 N	4.38 E
Beauce	42	48.22 N	1.50 E
Beaufort Sea	160	73.00 N	140.00 W
Beaufort West	104	32.18 S	22.36 E
Beaujolais, Monts du	42	46.00 N	4.30 E
Beaumont	162	30.05 N	94.06 W
Beaune	42	47.02 N	4.50 E
Beauvais	42	49.26 N	2.05 E
Beaver	160	59.43 N	124.16 W
Bečej	54	45.37 N	20.03 E
Béchar	100	31.37 N	2.13 W
Beckley	162	37.46 N	81.13 W
Beckum	36	51.45 N	8.02 E
Bedford	32	52.08 N	0.29 W
Bedfordshire	32	52.05 N	0.30 W
Be'er Sheva'	84	31.15 N	34.47 E
Bega (Begej)	54	45.13 N	20.19 E
Begej (Bega)	54	45.13 N	20.19 E
Beian	80	48.15 N	126.30 E
Beihai	80	21.29 N	109.05 E
Beijing (Peking)	80	39.55 N	116.25 E
Beira	104	19.49 S	34.52 E
Beira Baixa	50	39.45 N	7.30 W
Beira Litoral	50	40.15 N	8.25 W
Beja, Port.	50	38.01 N	7.52 W
Béja, Tun.	100	36.44 N	9.11 E
Bejaïa	100	36.45 N	5.05 E
Bejaïa, Golfe de	50	36.45 N	5.25 E
Béjar	50	40.23 N	5.46 W
Békés	36	46.46 N	21.08 E
Békéscsaba	36	46.41 N	21.06 E
Bela Crkva	54	44.54 N	21.26 E
Belaja	62	56.00 N	54.32 E
Belaja Cerkov'	62	49.49 N	30.07 E
Belcher Islands	160	56.20 N	79.30 W
Bel'cy	62	47.46 N	27.56 E
Beled Weyne	102	4.47 N	45.12 E
Belém	144	1.27 S	48.29 W
Belfast	32	54.35 N	5.55 W
Belfast Lough	32	54.40 N	5.50 W
Belfort	42	47.38 N	6.52 E
Belgaum	84	15.52 N	74.31 E
Belgium	36	50.50 N	4.00 E
Belgorod	62	50.36 N	36.35 E
Beli Drim	54	42.06 N	20.25 E
Belize	130	17.30 N	88.12 W
Belize	130	17.15 N	88.45 W
Bell	160	49.48 N	77.38 W
Belledonne, Chaîne de	42	45.18 N	6.08 E
Belle-Île	42	47.20 N	3.10 W
Belle Isle	160	51.55 N	55.20 W
Bellingham	162	48.49 N	122.29 W
Bellingshausen Sea	167	71.00 S	85.00 W
Bellinzona	42	46.11 N	9.02 E
Bello	144	6.20 N	75.33 W
Belluno	46	46.09 N	12.13 E
Belmopan	130	17.15 N	88.46 W
Belo Horizonte	144	19.55 S	43.56 W
Beloit	162	42.31 N	89.02 W
Beloje, Ozero	62	60.11 N	37.37 E
Beloje More (White Sea)	62	65.30 N	38.00 E
Belomorsko-Baltijskij Kanal	26	62.48 N	34.48 E
Belovo	64	54.25 N	86.18 E
Belper	32	53.01 N	1.29 W
Belucha, Gora	64	49.48 N	86.40 E
Benavente	50	42.00 N	5.41 W
Bendigo	116	36.46 S	144.17 E
Bendorf	36	50.25 N	7.34 E
Benevento	46	41.08 N	14.45 E
Bengal, Bay of	84	15.00 N	90.00 E
Benguela	104	12.35 S	13.25 E
Benguérua, Ilha	104	21.58 S	35.28 E
Beni	144	10.23 S	65.24 W
Benicarló	50	40.25 N	0.26 E
Beni-Mellal	100	32.22 N	6.29 W
Benin	100	9.30 N	2.15 E
Benin, Bight of	100	5.30 N	3.00 E
Benin City	100	6.19 N	5.41 E
Beni Saf	50	35.19 N	1.23 W
Benmore, Lake	118	44.25 S	170.15 E
Benoni	104	26.19 S	28.27 E
Bénoué (Benue)	100	7.48 N	6.46 E
Bensheim	36	49.41 N	8.37 E
Benton Harbor	162	42.06 N	86.27 W
Benue (Bénoué)	100	7.48 N	6.46 E
Benxi	80	41.18 N	123.45 E
Beograd (Belgrade)	54	44.50 N	20.30 E
Beppu	80	33.17 N	131.30 E
Berat	54	40.42 N	19.57 E
Berbera	102	10.25 N	45.02 E
Berbérati	102	4.16 N	15.47 E
Berbice	144	6.17 N	57.32 W
Berd'ansk	62	46.45 N	36.49 E
Berens	160	52.21 N	97.02 W
Beretăul (Berettyó)	54	46.59 N	21.07 E
Berettyó (Beretăul)	54	46.59 N	21.07 E
Berettyóújfalu	36	47.14 N	21.32 E
Berezniki	62	59.24 N	56.46 E
Bergama	54	39.07 N	27.11 E
Bergamo	46	45.41 N	9.43 E
Bergen	28	60.23 N	5.20 E
Bergen [auf Rügen]	36	54.25 N	13.26 E
Bergen op Zoom	36	51.30 N	4.17 E
Bergerac	42	44.51 N	0.29 E
Bergisch	36	51.09 N	7.15 E
Bergisch Gladbach	36	50.59 N	7.07 E
Bergslagen	28	59.55 N	15.00 E
Bering Sea	162a	59.00 N	174.00 W
Bering Strait	162a	65.30 N	169.00 W
Berkane	50	34.59 N	2.20 W
Berkeley	162	37.57 N	122.18 W
Berkner Island	167	79.30 S	49.30 W
Berkshire	32	51.30 N	1.20 W
Berlenga	50	39.25 N	9.30 W
Berlin (West), B.R.D.	36	52.31 N	13.24 E
Berlin (Ost), D.D.R.	36	52.30 N	13.25 E
Berlin, N.H., U.S.	162	44.29 N	71.10 W
Bermejo, Arg.	146	31.52 S	67.22 W
Bermejo, S.A.	146	26.51 S	58.23 W
Bermen, Lac	160	53.35 N	68.55 W
Bermeo	50	43.26 N	2.43 W
Bermuda	130	32.20 N	64.45 W
Bern (Berne)	42	46.57 N	7.26 E
Bernalda	46	40.24 N	16.41 E
Bernau bei Berlin	36	52.40 N	13.35 E
Bernay	42	49.06 N	0.36 E
Bernburg	36	51.48 N	11.44 E
Berner Alpen	42	46.30 N	7.30 E
Bernina, Piz	42	46.21 N	9.51 E
Beroun	36	49.58 N	14.04 E
Berounka	36	50.00 N	14.24 E
Berre, Étang de	42	43.27 N	5.08 E
Berwick-upon-Tweed	32	55.46 N	2.00 W
Besançon	42	47.15 N	6.02 E
Beskid Mountains	36	49.40 N	20.00 E
Betanzos, Ría de	50	43.23 N	8.15 W
Bethlehem	104	28.15 S	28.15 E
Béthune	42	50.32 N	2.38 E
Beticos, Sistemas	50	37.00 N	4.00 W
Betpak-Dala	62	46.00 N	70.00 E
Betsiboka	104	16.03 S	46.36 E
Bette	102	22.00 N	19.12 E
Betzdorf	36	50.47 N	7.53 E
Beverley	32	53.52 N	0.26 W
Beverwijk	36	52.28 N	4.40 E
Bexhill	32	50.50 N	0.29 E
Beykoz	54	41.08 N	29.05 E
Béziers	42	43.21 N	3.15 E
Bhāgalpur	84	25.15 N	86.58 E
Bhaunagar	84	21.47 N	72.09 E
Bhopāl	84	23.15 N	77.25 E
Bhutan	84	27.30 N	90.30 E
Bia, Phou	82	18.59 N	103.09 E
Biafra, Bight of	100	4.00 N	8.00 E
Biała	36	50.03 N	20.55 E
Biała Podlaska	36	52.02 N	23.06 E
Białogard	36	54.01 N	16.00 E
Białystok	36	53.09 N	23.09 E
Biarritz	42	43.29 N	1.34 W
Biberach an der Riss	36	48.06 N	9.47 E
Bicaz	54	46.54 N	26.05 E
Bida	100	9.05 N	6.01 E
Biddeford	162	43.30 N	70.26 W
Bideford	32	51.01 N	4.13 W
Bié	104	12.22 S	16.56 E
Biebrza	36	53.37 N	22.56 E
Biel (Bienne)	42	47.10 N	7.12 E
Bielawa	36	50.41 N	16.38 E
Bielefeld	36	52.01 N	8.31 E
Bielersee	42	47.05 N	7.10 E
Biella	46	45.34 N	8.03 E
Bielsko-Biała	36	49.49 N	19.02 E
Bielsk Podlaski	36	52.47 N	23.12 E
Bien-hoa	82	10.57 N	106.49 E
Bietigheim	36	48.58 N	9.07 E
Biga	54	40.13 N	27.14 E
Bihać	46	44.49 N	15.52 E
Bijagós, Arquipélago dos	100	11.25 N	16.20 W
Bijeljina	54	44.45 N	19.13 E
Bijsk	64	52.34 N	85.15 E
Bīkaner	84	28.01 N	73.18 E
Bilāspur	84	22.05 N	82.08 E
Bilbao	50	43.15 N	2.58 W
Bilecik	54	40.09 N	29.59 E
Bili	102	4.50 N	22.29 E
Bílina	36	50.35 N	13.45 E
Billings	162	45.47 N	118.27 W
Bilo Gora	46	46.06 N	16.46 E
Biloxi	162	30.24 N	88.53 W
Bilugyun Island	82	16.24 N	97.32 E
Binche	36	50.24 N	4.10 E
Binga, Monte	104	19.45 S	33.04 E
Bingen	36	48.07 N	9.16 E
Binghamton	162	42.08 N	75.54 W
Binzert (Bizerte)	100	37.17 N	9.52 E
Bío-Bío	146	36.49 S	73.10 W
Birch	160	58.30 N	112.15 W
Birch Mountains	160	57.30 N	112.30 W
Bird Island	146	54.00 S	38.05 W
Birkenhead	32	53.24 N	3.02 W
Bîrlad	54	46.14 N	27.40 E
Bîrlad	54	45.36 N	27.31 E
Birmingham, Eng., U.K.	32	52.30 N	1.50 W
Birmingham, Ala., U.S.	162	33.31 N	86.49 W
Bîrzava	54	45.16 N	20.49 E
Birżebbuġa	46	35.49 N	14.32 E
Biscarosse, Étang de	42	44.20 N	1.10 E
Biscay, Bay of	42	44.00 N	4.00 W
Bisceglie	46	41.14 N	16.31 E
Bischofswerda	36	51.07 N	14.10 E
Bishop Auckland	32	54.40 N	1.40 W
Bishop's Stortford	32	51.53 N	0.09 E
Biskra	100	34.51 N	5.44 E
Bismarck	162	46.48 N	100.47 W
Bismarck Archipelago	116a	5.00 S	150.00 E
Bismarck Range	116a	5.30 S	144.45 E
Bissau	100	11.51 N	15.35 W
Bistcho Lake	160	59.40 N	118.40 W
Bistrița	54	47.08 N	24.30 E
Bitola	54	41.01 N	21.20 E
Bitonto	46	41.06 N	16.42 E
Bitterfeld	36	51.37 N	12.20 E
Biwa-ko	80	35.15 N	136.05 E
Bizerte, Lac de	46	37.12 N	9.52 E
Bjala Slatina	54	43.28 N	23.56 E
Bjelovar	46	45.54 N	16.51 E
Black (Da)	82	21.15 N	105.20 E
Blackburn	32	53.45 N	2.29 W
Black Hills	162	44.00 N	104.00 W
Blackpool	32	53.50 N	3.03 W
Black Range	130	33.20 N	107.50 W
Black Rock	146	53.39 S	41.48 W
Black Rock Desert	162	41.10 N	119.00 W
Black Sea	20	43.00 N	35.00 E
Blackstone	160	65.51 N	137.12 W
Black Volta (Volta Noire)	100	8.41 N	1.33 W
Blagoevgrad	54	42.01 N	23.06 E
Blagoveščensk	64	50.17 N	127.32 E
Blanc, Cap, Afr.	100	20.46 N	17.03 W
Blanc, Cap, Tun.	46	37.20 N	9.51 E
Blanc, Mont (Monte Bianco)	42	45.50 N	6.52 E
Blanca, Bahía	146	38.55 S	62.10 W
Blanca, Cordillera	144	9.10 S	77.35 W
Blanca Peak	162	37.35 N	105.29 W
Blankenburg	36	51.48 N	10.58 E
Blansko	36	49.22 N	16.39 E
Blantyre	104	15.47 S	35.00 E
Blenheim	118	41.31 S	173.57 E
Bletchley	32	52.00 N	0.46 W
Bleus, Monts, Afr.	102	1.30 N	30.30 E
Bleus, Monts, Zaïre	104	4.31 S	21.02 E
Blida	100	36.28 N	2.50 E
Bloemfontein	104	29.12 S	26.07 E
Blois	42	47.35 N	1.20 E
Bloody Foreland	32	55.09 N	8.17 W
Bloomington, Ill., U.S.	162	40.29 N	89.00 W
Bloomington, Ind., U.S.	162	39.10 N	86.32 W
Blouberg	104	23.01 S	28.59 E
Bludenz	36	47.09 N	9.49 E
Bluefields	130	12.00 N	83.45 W
Blue Mountain Peak	130	18.03 N	76.35 W
Blue Mountains	160	44.35 N	118.25 W
Blue Nile (Ābay)	102	15.38 N	32.31 E

Blue—Chih

Name	Page	Lat° ′	Long° ′
Blue Ridge	162	37.00 N	82.00 W
Blyth	32	55.07 N	1.30 W
Bo	100	7.56 N	11.21 W
Boaco	130	12.28 N	85.40 W
Boa Vista	100	16.05 N	22.50 W
Böblingen	36	48.41 N	9.01 E
Bobo Dioulasso	100	11.12 N	4.18 W
Bóbr	36	52.04 N	15.04 E
Bobrujsk	62	53.09 N	29.14 E
Boby, Pic	104	22.12 S	46.55 E
Bocas del Toro	130	9.20 N	82.15 W
Bochnia	36	49.58 N	20.26 E
Bocholt	36	51.50 N	6.36 E
Bochum	36	51.28 N	7.13 E
Bodele	102	16.30 N	16.30 E
Boden	26	65.50 N	21.42 E
Bodensee	42	47.35 N	9.25 E
Bodmin	32	50.29 N	4.43 W
Bodmin Moor	32	50.33 N	4.33 W
Bodø	26	67.17 N	14.23 E
Bodrog	54	48.07 N	21.25 E
Boeo, Capo	46	37.48 N	12.26 E
Bogale	82	16.17 N	95.24 E
Bognor Regis	32	50.47 N	0.41 W
Bogor	82	6.35 S	106.47 E
Bogotá	144	4.36 N	74.05 W
Bohemian Forest	36	49.15 N	12.45 E
Bois du Roi	42	47.00 N	4.02 E
Boise	162	43.37 N	116.13 W
Boizenburg	36	53.22 N	10.43 E
Bojador, Cabo	100	26.08 N	14.30 W
Bojeador, Cape	82	18.30 N	120.34 E
Boknafjorden	28	59.10 N	5.35 E
Bolama	100	11.35 N	15.28 W
Bolbec	42	49.34 N	0.29 E
Bolesławiec	36	51.16 N	15.34 E
Bolívar	144	4.21 N	76.10 W
Bolívar, Cerro	144	7.28 N	63.25 W
Bolívar, Pico	144	8.30 N	71.02 W
Bolivia	144	17.00 S	65.00 W
Bollnäs	28	61.21 N	16.25 E
Bollullos par del Condado	50	37.20 N	6.32 W
Bolmen	28	56.55 N	13.40 E
Bologna	46	44.29 N	11.20 E
Bolsena, Lago di	46	42.36 N	11.56 E
Bol'šoj Kavkaz (Caucasus)	62	42.30 N	45.00 E
Bolton	32	53.35 N	2.26 W
Bolzano (Bozen)	46	46.31 N	11.22 E
Boma	104	5.51 S	13.03 E
Bombay	84	18.58 N	72.50 E
Bomberai, Jazirah	82	3.00 S	133.00 E
Bomokandi	102	3.39 N	26.08 E
Bomu (Mbomou)	102	4.08 N	22.26 E
Bon, Cap	100	37.05 N	11.03 E
Bonaire	130	12.10 N	68.15 W
Bonavista Bay	160	48.45 N	53.20 W
Bondeno	46	44.53 N	11.25 E
Bone, Teluk	82	4.00 S	120.40 E
Bonifacio, Strait of	46	41.20 N	9.15 E
Bonifati, Capo	46	39.35 N	15.52 E
Bonn	36	50.44 N	7.05 E
Bonnet Plume	160	65.55 N	134.58 W
Bonthe	100	7.32 N	12.30 W
Boom	36	51.05 N	4.22 E
Boothia, Gulf of	160	71.00 N	91.00 W
Boquete	130	8.47 N	82.26 W
Bor, Jugo.	54	44.05 N	22.07 E
Bor, S.S.S.R.	26	56.22 N	44.05 E
Borah Peak	162	44.08 N	113.48 W
Borås	28	57.43 N	12.55 E
Borcea	54	44.40 N	27.53 E
Bordeaux	42	44.50 N	0.34 W
Bordighera	46	43.46 N	7.39 E
Bordj Bou Arreridj	50	36.04 N	4.46 E
Bordj Menaïel	50	36.44 N	3.43 E
Borgå (Porvoo)	28	60.24 N	25.40 E
Borghorst	36	52.07 N	7.23 E
Borgomanero	46	45.42 N	8.28 E
Borgosesia	46	45.43 N	8.16 E
Borisov	62	54.15 N	28.30 E
Borken	36	51.51 N	6.51 E
Borkum	36	53.35 N	6.41 E
Borlänge	28	60.29 N	15.25 E
Borna	36	51.19 N	13.11 E
Borneo (Kalimantan)	82	0.30 N	114.00 E
Bornholm	28	55.10 N	15.00 E
Bornova	54	38.27 N	27.14 E
Boro	102	8.52 N	26.11 E
Boroviči	26	58.24 N	33.55 E
Borșa	54	47.39 N	24.40 E
Bosanski Novi	46	45.03 N	16.23 E
Boshan	80	36.29 N	117.50 E
Bositenghu	80	42.00 N	87.00 E
Bosna	54	45.04 N	18.29 E
Bossangoa	102	6.29 N	17.27 E
Bosso, Dallol	100	12.25 N	2.50 E
Boston, Eng., U.K.	32	52.59 N	0.01 W
Boston, Mass., U.S.	162	42.21 N	71.04 W
Boston Mountains	162	35.50 N	93.20 W
Bosut	54	44.57 N	19.22 E
Boteti	104	20.08 S	23.23 E
Botev	54	42.43 N	24.55 E
Bothnia, Gulf of	28	63.00 N	20.00 E
Botoșani	54	47.45 N	26.40 E
Botrange	36	50.30 N	6.08 E
Botswana	104	22.00 S	24.00 E
Botte Donato	46	39.17 N	16.26 E
Bottenhavet (Selkämeri)	28	62.00 N	20.00 E
Bottrop	36	51.31 N	6.55 E
Botucatu	144	22.52 S	48.26 W
Bouaké	100	7.41 N	5.02 W
Bouar	102	5.57 N	15.36 E
Bougainville	114	6.00 S	155.00 E
Bougainville Strait	114	6.40 S	156.10 E
Bougar'oûn, Cap	50	37.06 N	6.28 E
Bouïra	50	36.23 N	3.54 E
Boulder	162	40.01 N	105.17 W
Boulogne-Billancourt	42	48.50 N	2.15 E
Boulogne-sur-Mer	42	50.43 N	1.37 E
Boundary Peak	162	37.51 N	118.21 W
Boundary Ranges	162a	59.00 N	134.00 W
Bourail	112	21.34 S	165.30 E
Bourg-en-Bresse	42	46.12 N	5.13 E
Bourges	42	47.05 N	2.24 E
Bourgoin	42	45.35 N	5.17 E
Bournemouth	32	50.43 N	1.54 W
Bou Saâda	100	35.12 N	4.11 E
Bøvågen	26	60.40 N	4.58 E
Bøverdal	26	61.43 N	8.21 E
Bow	160	49.56 N	111.42 W
Bowling Green	162	37.00 N	86.27 W
Boyer, Cap	112	21.37 S	168.06 E
Boz Burun	54	40.24 N	26.54 E
Boz Dağ	54	37.18 N	29.12 E
Bozeman	162	45.41 N	111.02 W
Bra	46	44.42 N	7.51 E
Brač, Otok	46	43.20 N	16.40 E
Bracciano, Lago di	46	42.07 N	12.14 E
Brad	54	46.08 N	22.47 E
Bradano	46	40.23 N	16.51 E
Bradenton	162	27.29 N	82.34 W
Bradford	32	53.48 N	1.45 W
Braga	50	41.33 N	8.26 W
Bragança	50	41.49 N	6.45 W
Brāhmani	84	20.45 N	87.00 E
Brahmaputra (Yaluzangbujiang)	84	24.02 N	90.55 E
Braich y Pwll	32	52.48 N	4.36 W
Brăila	54	45.16 N	27.58 E
Brăilei, Balta	54	45.00 N	28.00 E
Braine-l'Alleud	36	50.41 N	4.22 E
Braintree	32	51.53 N	0.32 E
Brake	36	53.19 N	8.28 E
Bran, Pasul	54	45.26 N	25.17 E
Brandberg	104	21.10 S	14.33 E
Brandenburg	36	52.24 N	12.32 E
Brandon	160	49.50 N	99.57 W
Brandýs nad Labem	36	50.10 N	14.41 E
Braniewo	36	54.24 N	19.50 E
Br'ansk	62	53.15 N	34.22 E
Brantford	160	43.08 N	80.16 W
Bras d'Or Lake	160	45.52 N	60.50 W
Brasília	144	15.47 S	47.55 W
Brașov	54	45.39 N	25.37 E
Brateș, Lacul	54	45.30 N	28.05 E
Bratislava	36	48.09 N	17.07 E
Bratsk	64	56.05 N	101.48 E
Braunau [am Inn]	36	48.15 N	13.02 E
Braunschweig	36	52.16 N	10.31 E
Brava, Costa	50	41.45 N	3.04 E
Bravo del Norte (Rio Grande)	162	25.55 N	97.09 W
Bray	32	53.12 N	6.06 W
Brazeau	160	52.55 N	115.15 W
Brazil	144	10.00 S	55.00 W
Brazos	162	28.53 N	95.23 W
Brazzaville	104	4.16 S	15.17 E
Brčko	54	44.53 N	18.48 E
Brda	36	53.07 N	18.08 E
Břeclav	36	48.46 N	16.53 E
Breda	36	51.35 N	4.46 E
Breë	104	34.24 S	20.50 E
Bregalnica	54	41.43 N	22.09 E
Bregenz	36	47.30 N	9.46 E
Bremen	36	53.04 N	8.49 E
Bremerhaven	36	53.33 N	8.34 E
Bremerton	162	47.34 N	122.38 W
Brenne	42	46.45 N	1.10 E
Brenner Pass	36	47.00 N	11.30 E
Brenta	46	45.11 N	12.18 E
Brentwood	32	51.38 N	0.18 E
Brescia	46	45.33 N	13.15 E
Bressanone	46	46.43 N	11.39 E
Bresse	42	46.30 N	5.15 E
Brest, Fr.	42	48.24 N	4.29 W
Brest, S.S.S.R.	62	52.06 N	23.42 E
Breton, Pertuis	42	46.25 N	1.20 W
Brezno	36	48.50 N	19.39 E
Briançon	42	44.54 N	6.39 E
Bridgend	32	51.31 N	3.35 W
Bridgeport	162	41.11 N	73.11 W
Bridgetown	130	13.06 N	59.37 W
Bridgwater	32	51.08 N	3.00 W
Bridgwater Bay	32	51.16 N	3.12 W
Bridlington	32	54.05 N	0.12 W
Bridlington Bay	32	54.04 N	0.08 W
Brienzer See	42	46.43 N	7.57 E
Brighton	32	50.50 N	0.08 W
Brilon	36	51.24 N	8.34 E
Brindisi	46	40.38 N	17.56 E
Brisbane	116	27.28 S	153.02 E
Bristol, Eng., U.K.	32	51.27 N	2.35 W
Bristol, Tenn., U.S.	162	36.36 N	82.11 W
Bristol Channel	32	51.20 N	4.00 W
British Antarctic Territory	167	60.00 S	45.00 W
British Columbia	160	54.00 N	125.00 W
British Mountains	162a	69.00 N	140.20 W
Brive-la-Gaillarde	42	45.10 N	1.32 E
Brixham	32	50.24 N	3.30 W
Brno	36	49.12 N	16.37 E
Brodnica	36	53.16 N	19.23 E
Broken Hill	116	31.57 S	141.27 E
Bromsgrove	32	52.20 N	2.03 W
Bronlund Peak	160	57.26 N	126.38 W
Bronte	46	37.48 N	14.50 E
Brooks Range	162a	68.00 N	154.00 W
Brownsville	162	25.54 N	97.30 W
Bruay-en-Artois	42	50.29 N	2.33 E
Bruchsal	36	49.07 N	8.35 E
Bruck an der Mur	36	47.25 N	15.16 E
Brugge	36	51.13 N	3.14 E
Brunei	82	4.30 N	114.40 E
Brunsbüttel	36	53.54 N	9.07 E
Brunswick	162	31.10 N	81.29 W
Bruntál	36	49.59 N	17.28 E
Bruxelles (Brussel)	36	50.50 N	4.20 E
Bryan	162	30.40 N	96.22 W
Brzeg	36	50.52 N	17.27 E
Brzesko	36	49.59 N	20.36 E
Bubaque	100	11.17 N	15.50 W
Būbiyān	84	29.47 N	48.10 E
Bucaramanga	144	7.08 N	73.09 W
Buchanan	100	5.57 N	10.02 W
Buchara	62	39.48 N	64.25 E
Bückeburg	36	52.16 N	9.02 E
Buckhaven	32	56.11 N	3.03 W
Buckinghamshire	32	51.45 N	0.48 W
București	54	44.26 N	26.06 E
Budapest	36	47.30 N	19.05 E
Bude Bay	32	50.50 N	4.37 W
Buenaventura	144	3.53 N	77.04 W
Buendia, Embalse de	50	40.25 N	2.43 W
Buenos Aires	146	34.36 S	58.27 W
Buffalo	162	42.54 N	78.53 W
Bug	20	52.31 N	21.05 E
Buga	144	3.54 N	76.17 W
Bugul'ma	26	54.33 N	52.48 E
Buhuși	54	46.43 N	26.41 E
Bujalance	50	37.54 N	4.22 W
Bujumbura	104	3.23 S	29.22 E
Buka Island	114	5.15 S	154.35 E
Buka Passage	114	5.25 S	154.41 E
Bukavu	104	2.30 S	28.52 E
Bükk	36	48.05 N	20.30 E
Bukovica	46	44.10 N	15.40 E
Bulawayo	104	20.09 S	28.36 E
Buldan	54	38.03 N	28.51 E
Bulgaria	54	43.00 N	25.00 E
Bunbury	116	33.19 S	115.38 E
Bundaberg	116	24.52 S	152.21 E
Bungo-suidō	80	33.00 N	132.13 E
Bunia	104	1.34 N	30.15 E
Burao	102	9.30 N	45.30 E
Buraydah	84	26.20 N	43.59 E
Burgas	54	42.30 N	27.28 E
Burgaski zaliv	54	42.30 N	27.33 E
Burg [bei Magdeburg]	36	52.16 N	11.51 E
Burgdorf, B.R.D.	36	52.27 N	10.00 E
Burgdorf, Schw.	42	47.04 N	7.37 E
Burghausen	36	48.09 N	12.49 E
Burgos	50	42.21 N	3.42 W
Burgos	50	42.20 N	3.40 W
Burgstädt	36	50.55 N	12.49 E
Burgsteinfurt	36	52.08 N	7.20 E
Burhaniye	54	39.30 N	26.58 E
Burhānpur	84	21.19 N	76.14 E
Burjasot	50	39.31 N	0.25 W
Burlington, Iowa, U.S.	162	40.49 N	91.14 W
Burlington, Vt., U.S.	162	44.29 N	73.13 W
Burma	82	22.00 N	98.00 E
Burnie	116	41.04 S	145.54 E
Burnley	32	53.48 N	2.14 W
Burntwood	160	56.08 N	96.30 W
Burriana	50	39.53 N	0.05 W
Bursa	54	40.11 N	29.04 E
Būr Sa'īd (Port Said)	102	31.16 N	32.18 E
Būr Sūdān (Port Sudan)	102	19.37 N	37.14 E
Burton-upon-Trent	32	52.49 N	1.36 W
Burundi	104	3.15 S	30.00 E
Bury	32	53.36 N	2.17 W
Bury Saint Edmunds	32	52.15 N	0.43 E
Busambra, Rocca	46	37.51 N	13.24 E
Bushimaie	104	6.02 S	23.45 E
Bushman Land	104	29.15 S	20.00 E
Busko Zdrój	36	50.28 N	20.44 E
Bussum	36	52.16 N	5.10 E
Busto Arsizio	46	45.37 N	8.51 E
Buta	100	2.48 N	24.44 E
Butare	104	2.36 S	29.44 E
Bute Inlet	160	50.37 N	124.53 W
Butler	162	40.52 N	79.54 W
Butte	162	46.00 N	112.32 W
Butterworth	82	5.25 N	100.24 E
Butuan	82	8.57 N	125.33 E
Bützow	36	53.50 N	11.59 E
Buxtehude	36	53.28 N	9.41 E
Buxton	32	53.15 N	1.55 W
Büyük Ağrı Dağı (Mount Ararat)	20	39.42 N	44.18 E
Büyükmenderes	54	37.27 N	27.11 E
Buzău	54	45.09 N	26.49 E
Buzău	54	45.26 N	27.44 E
Búzi	104	19.50 S	34.43 E
Bydgoski, Kanał	36	53.08 N	17.36 E
Bydgoszcz	36	53.08 N	18.00 E
Byrranga, Gory	64	75.00 N	104.00 E
Bystrzyca	36	51.13 N	16.54 E
Bytom (Beuthen)	36	50.22 N	18.54 E
Bytów	36	54.11 N	17.30 E
Bzura	36	52.23 N	20.09 E
C			
Caballería, Cabo de	50	40.05 N	4.05 E
Cabanatuan	82	15.29 N	120.58 E
Cabeza del Buey	50	38.43 N	5.13 W
Cabimas	144	10.23 N	71.28 W
Cabonga, Réservoir	160	47.20 N	76.35 W
Cabot Strait	160	47.20 N	59.30 W
Cabra	50	37.28 N	4.27 W
Cabrera	50	39.09 N	2.56 E
Čačak	54	43.53 N	20.21 E
Caccia, Capo	46	40.34 N	8.09 E
Cáceres	50	39.29 N	6.22 W
Cachimbo, Serra do	144	8.30 S	55.50 W
Cachoeiro de Itapemirim	144	20.51 S	41.06 W
Čadca	36	49.26 N	18.48 E
Cader Idris	32	52.42 N	3.54 W
Cádiz	50	36.32 N	6.18 W
Cádiz, Bahía de	50	36.32 N	6.16 W
Cádiz, Golfo de	50	36.50 N	7.10 W
Caen	42	49.11 N	0.21 W
Caernarvon Bay	32	53.05 N	4.30 W
Caerphilly	32	51.35 N	3.14 W
Cagayan	82	18.22 N	121.37 E
Cagayan de Oro	82	8.29 N	124.39 E
Cagliari	46	39.20 N	9.00 E
Cagliari, Golfo di	46	39.05 N	9.10 E
Cagnes	42	43.40 N	7.09 E
Caguas	130	18.14 N	66.02 W
Caha Mountains	32	51.45 N	9.45 W
Cahors	42	44.27 N	1.26 E
Caia	50	38.50 N	7.05 W
Caiapó, Serra	144	17.00 S	52.00 W
Caibarién	130	22.31 N	79.28 W
Caicos Islands	130	21.56 N	71.58 W
Caimanera	130	19.59 N	75.09 W
Cairns	116	16.55 S	145.45 E
Cairo Montenotte	46	44.24 N	8.15 E
Cajamarca	144	7.10 S	78.31 W
Cajàzeiras	144	6.54 S	38.34 W
Čakovec	46	46.23 N	16.26 E
Calabar	100	4.57 N	8.19 E
Calabozo	144	8.56 N	67.26 W
Calahorra	50	42.18 N	1.58 W
Calais	42	50.57 N	1.50 E
Calais, Pas de (Strait of Dover)	32	51.00 N	1.30 E
Calama	146	22.28 S	68.56 W
Călărași	54	44.11 N	27.20 E
Calatayud	50	41.21 N	1.38 W
Calbe	36	51.54 N	11.46 E
Calcutta	84	22.34 N	88.20 E
Caldas da Rainha	50	39.24 N	9.08 W
Caldeirão, Serra do	50	37.42 N	8.21 W
Caldey Island	32	51.38 N	4.41 W
Calf of Man	32	54.03 N	4.48 W
Calgary	160	51.03 N	114.05 W
Cali	144	3.27 N	76.31 W
Calicut	84	11.15 N	75.46 E
California	162	37.30 N	119.30 W
California, Golfo de	130	28.00 N	112.00 W
Călimani, Munții	54	47.07 N	25.03 E
Callao	144	12.04 S	77.09 W
Callosa de Segura	50	38.08 N	0.52 W
Călmățui	54	44.50 N	27.50 E
Caltagirone	46	37.14 N	14.31 E
Caltanissetta	46	37.29 N	14.04 E
Calw	36	48.43 N	8.44 E
Cam	32	52.21 N	0.15 E
Camagüey	130	21.23 N	77.55 W
Camaiore	46	43.56 N	10.18 E
Camargue	42	43.34 N	4.34 E
Camas	50	37.24 N	6.02 W
Ca-mau, Mui	82	8.38 N	104.44 E
Camborne	32	50.12 N	5.19 W
Cambrai	42	50.10 N	3.14 E
Cambrian Mountains	32	52.35 N	3.35 W
Cambridge, Ont., Can.	160	43.22 N	80.19 W
Cambridge, Eng., U.K.	32	52.13 N	0.08 E
Cambridge, Mass., U.S.	162	42.22 N	71.06 W
Cambridge Bay	160	69.03 N	105.05 W
Cambridgeshire	32	52.20 N	0.05 E
Camden	162	39.57 N	75.07 W
Cameron Hills	160	59.48 N	118.00 W
Cameroon	100	6.00 N	12.00 E
Cameroun, Mont	100	4.12 N	9.11 E
Campagna di Roma	46	41.50 N	12.35 E
Campeche	130	19.51 N	90.32 W
Campeche, Bahía de	130	20.00 N	94.00 W
Cam-pha	82	21.01 N	107.19 E
Campidano	46	39.30 N	8.50 E
Campina	50	37.45 N	4.45 W
Campina Grande	144	7.13 S	35.53 W
Campinas	144	22.54 S	47.05 W
Campobasso	46	41.34 N	14.39 E
Campo de Criptana	50	39.24 N	3.07 W
Campo Grande	144	20.27 S	54.37 W
Campos	144	21.45 S	41.18 W
Canada	160	60.00 N	95.00 W
Çanakkale	54	40.09 N	26.24 E
Çanakkale Boğazı (Dardanelles)	54	40.15 N	26.25 E
Canal Zone	130	9.10 N	79.48 W
Canarias, Islas (Canary Islands)	100	28.00 N	15.30 W
Canaveral, Cape	162	28.27 N	80.32 W
Canavese	46	45.20 N	7.40 E
Canberra	116	35.17 S	149.08 E
Cangkuang, Tanjung	82	6.51 S	105.15 E
Caniapiscau	160	57.40 N	69.30 W
Canicattì	46	37.21 N	13.51 E
Cannes	42	43.33 N	7.01 E
Cannock	32	52.42 N	2.09 W
Canosa [di Puglia]	46	41.13 N	16.04 E
Cantábrica, Cordillera	50	43.00 N	5.00 W
Cantal	42	45.10 N	2.40 E
Canterbury	32	51.17 N	1.05 E
Canterbury Bight	118	44.15 S	171.38 E
Canterbury Plains	118	44.00 S	171.45 E
Can-tho	82	10.02 N	105.47 E
Canton	162	40.48 N	81.22 W
Canton and Enderbury	10	2.50 S	171.43 W
Cantù	46	45.44 N	9.08 E
Čapajevsk	26	52.58 N	49.41 E
Capanaparo	144	7.01 N	67.07 W
Cape Breton Island	160	46.00 N	60.30 W
Cape Coast	100	5.05 N	1.15 W
Cape Town (Kaapstad)	104	33.55 S	18.22 E
Cape Verde	100	16.00 N	24.00 W
Cape York Peninsula	116	14.00 S	142.30 E
Cap-Haïtien	130	19.45 N	72.12 W
Capraia, Isola di	46	43.02 N	9.49 E
Capri, Isola di	46	40.33 N	14.13 E
Capua	46	41.06 N	14.12 E
Caracal	54	44.07 N	24.21 E
Caracas	144	10.30 N	66.56 W
Caransebeș	54	45.25 N	22.13 E
Caratasca, Laguna de	130	15.23 N	83.55 W
Caratinga	144	19.47 S	42.08 W
Caravaca	50	38.06 N	1.51 W
Caravaggio	46	45.30 N	9.38 E
Carbon, Cap	50	36.47 N	5.06 E
Carbonara, Capo	46	39.06 N	9.31 E
Carbonia	46	39.11 N	8.32 E
Carcagente	50	39.08 N	0.27 W
Carcans, Étang de	42	45.08 N	1.08 W
Carcassonne	42	43.13 N	2.21 E
Cárdenas	130	23.02 N	81.12 W
Cardiff	32	51.29 N	3.13 W
Cardigan Bay	32	52.30 N	4.20 W
Čardžou	62	39.06 N	63.34 E
Carei	54	47.42 N	22.28 E
Cares	50	43.19 N	4.36 W
Caribbean Sea	130	15.00 N	73.00 W
Cariboo Mountains	160	53.00 N	121.00 W
Caribou	160	59.20 N	94.44 W
Caribou Mountains	160	59.12 N	115.40 W
Carini	46	38.08 N	13.11 E
Carleton, Mount	160	47.23 N	66.53 W
Carlisle	32	54.54 N	2.25 W
Carmacks	160	62.05 N	136.18 W
Carmagnola	46	44.51 N	7.43 E
Carmarthen	32	51.52 N	4.19 W
Carmel Head	32	53.24 N	4.34 W
Carmona	50	37.28 N	5.38 W
Carnatic	84	12.30 N	78.15 E
Carniche, Alpi	46	46.40 N	13.00 E
Caroline Islands	82	8.00 N	140.00 E
Carpathian Mountains	20	48.00 N	24.00 E
Carpații Meridionali	54	45.30 N	24.15 E
Carpentaria, Gulf of	116	14.00 S	139.00 E
Carpentras	42	44.03 N	5.03 E
Carpi	46	44.47 N	10.53 E
Carranza, Cabo	146	35.36 S	72.38 W
Carrara	46	44.05 N	10.06 E
Carrauntoohill	32	52.00 N	9.45 W
Carreta, Punta	144	14.13 S	76.18 W
Carrickfergus	32	54.43 N	5.49 W
Carrión	50	41.53 N	4.32 W
Carson City	162	39.10 N	119.46 W
Carson Sink	162	39.45 N	118.30 W
Cartagena, Col.	144	10.25 N	75.32 W
Cartagena, Esp.	50	37.36 N	0.59 W
Cartago, Col.	144	4.45 N	75.55 W
Cartago, C.R.	130	9.52 N	83.55 W
Caruaru	144	8.17 S	35.58 W
Carúpano	144	10.40 N	63.14 W
Carvin	42	50.29 N	2.58 E
Carvoeiro, Cabo	50	39.21 N	9.24 W
Casablanca (Dar-el-Beida)	100	33.39 N	7.35 W
Casale Monferrato	46	45.08 N	8.27 E
Casarano	46	40.00 N	18.10 E
Cascade Bay	113	29.01 S	167.58 E
Cascade Range	162	49.00 N	120.00 W
Cascais	50	38.42 N	9.25 W
Cascina	46	43.41 N	10.33 E
Caserta	46	41.04 N	14.20 E
Casiquiare, Brazo	144	2.01 N	67.07 W
Čáslav	36	49.54 N	15.23 E
Casper	162	42.51 N	106.19 W
Caspian Sea	62	42.00 N	50.30 E
Cassai (Kasai)	104	3.06 S	16.57 E
Cassano allo Ionio	46	39.47 N	16.20 E
Cassiar Mountains	160	59.00 N	129.00 W
Cassino	46	41.30 N	13.49 E
Castelfranco Veneto	46	45.40 N	11.55 E
Castellamare del Golfo	46	38.01 N	12.53 E
Castellammare, Golfo di	46	38.10 N	12.55 E
Castellammare [di Stabia]	46	40.42 N	14.29 E
Castellaneta	46	40.37 N	16.57 E
Castellón	50	40.10 N	0.10 W
Castellón de la Plana	50	39.59 N	0.02 W
Castelo Branco	50	39.49 N	7.30 W
Castelsarrasin	42	44.02 N	1.06 E
Castelvetrano	46	37.41 N	12.47 E
Castilla	144	5.12 S	80.38 W
Castilla, Playa de	50	37.00 N	6.33 W
Castilla la Nueva	50	40.00 N	3.45 W
Castillo, Pampa del	146	45.58 S	68.24 W
Castle Mountain	160	64.35 N	135.55 W
Castletown	32	54.04 N	4.40 W
Castres	42	43.36 N	2.15 E
Castries	130	14.01 N	61.00 W
Castro del Río	50	37.41 N	4.28 W
Castuera	50	38.43 N	5.33 W
Cataluña	50	42.00 N	2.00 E
Catamarca	146	28.28 S	65.47 W
Catanduva	144	21.08 S	48.58 W
Catania	46	37.30 N	15.06 E
Catania, Golfo di	46	37.25 N	15.15 E
Catanzaro	46	38.54 N	16.36 E
Catarroja	50	39.24 N	0.24 W
Catbalogan	82	11.46 N	124.53 E
Cat Island	130	24.27 N	75.30 W
Catoche, Cabo	130	21.35 N	87.05 W
Cattolica	46	43.58 N	12.44 E
Čaunskaja Guba	64	69.20 N	170.00 E
Caura	144	7.38 N	64.53 W
Caux, Pays de	42	49.40 N	0.40 E
Cava [de'Tirreni]	46	40.42 N	14.42 E
Cavaillon	42	43.50 N	5.02 E
Caviana, Ilha	144	0.10 N	50.10 W
Cavite	82	14.29 N	120.55 E
Caxias	144	4.50 S	43.21 W
Cayambe	144	0.02 N	77.59 W
Cayenne	144	4.56 N	52.20 W
Cayman Brac	130	19.43 N	79.49 W
Cayman Islands	130	19.30 N	80.40 W
Cazaux, Étang de	42	44.30 N	1.10 W
Cazorla, Sierra de	50	37.55 N	2.55 W
Čeboksary	26	56.09 N	47.15 E
Cebu	82	10.18 N	123.54 E
Cecina	46	43.19 N	10.31 E
Cedar Lake	160	53.10 N	100.00 W
Cedar Rapids	162	41.59 N	91.40 W
Cedrino	46	40.23 N	9.44 E
Cedros, Isla	130	28.12 N	115.15 W
Cefalù	46	38.02 N	14.01 E
Cegléd	36	47.10 N	19.48 E
Ceglie Messapico	46	40.39 N	17.31 E
Cehegín	50	38.06 N	1.48 W
Čel'abinsk	62	55.10 N	61.24 E
Celaya	130	20.31 N	100.49 W
Celebes Sea	82	3.00 N	122.00 E
Celinograd	62	51.10 N	71.30 E
Celje	46	46.14 N	15.16 E
Celle	36	52.37 N	10.05 E
Čemerno	46	43.11 N	18.37 E
Čemerno	54	43.14 N	18.37 E
Cenderawasih, Teluk	82	2.30 S	135.20 E
Ceno	46	44.41 N	10.05 E
Cento	46	44.43 N	11.17 E
Central, Cordillera, Bol.	144	18.30 S	64.55 W
Central, Cordillera, Col.	144	5.00 N	75.00 W
Central, Massif	42	45.00 N	3.10 E
Central, Planalto	144	18.00 S	47.00 W
Central, Sistema	50	40.30 N	5.00 W
Central African Empire	102	7.00 N	21.00 E
Central Makrān Range	84	26.40 N	64.30 E
Centre, Canal du	42	46.27 N	4.07 E
Cère	42	44.55 N	1.53 E
Čeremchovo	64	53.09 N	103.05 E
Čerepovec	26	59.08 N	37.54 E
Cerignola	46	41.16 N	15.54 E
Čerkassy	62	49.26 N	32.04 E
Čern'achovsk	26	54.38 N	21.49 E
Černá hora	36	48.58 N	13.48 E
Cernavodă	54	44.21 N	28.01 E
Cernei, Munții	54	45.02 N	22.31 E
Černigov	62	51.30 N	31.18 E
Černi vrâh	54	42.34 N	23.17 E
Černovcy	54	48.18 N	25.56 E
Cerro de Pasco	144	10.41 S	76.16 W
Čerskogo, Chrebet	64	52.00 N	114.00 E
Cervati, Monte	46	40.17 N	15.29 E
Červen Brjag	54	43.16 N	24.06 E
Cervia	46	44.15 N	12.22 E
Cesena	46	44.08 N	12.15 E
Česká Lípa	36	50.42 N	14.32 E
Česká Třebová	36	49.54 N	16.27 E
České Budějovice	36	48.59 N	14.28 E
Český Těšín	36	49.45 N	18.37 E
Češskaja Guba	62	67.30 N	46.30 E
Cessnock	116	32.50 S	151.21 E
Cestos	100	5.40 N	9.10 W
Cetinje	54	42.23 N	18.55 E
Ceuta	100	35.53 N	5.19 W
Chabarovsk	64	48.27 N	135.06 E
Chablais	42	46.18 N	6.39 E
Chachani, Nevado	144	16.12 S	71.33 W
Chad	102	15.00 N	19.00 E
Chad, Lake (Lac Tchad)	102	13.20 N	14.00 E
Chadileuvú	146	37.46 S	66.00 W
Chafarinas, Islas	50	35.11 N	2.26 W
Chaidamupendi	80	37.00 N	95.00 E
Chaîne des Mongos	102	8.40 N	22.25 E
Chalbi Desert	102	3.00 N	37.20 E
Châlons-sur-Marne	42	48.57 N	4.22 E
Chalon-sur-Saône	42	46.47 N	4.51 E
Chalosse	42	43.45 N	0.30 W
Chambal	84	26.30 N	79.15 E
Chambéry	42	45.34 N	5.56 E
Chambi, Djebel	100	35.11 N	8.42 E
Chamonix-Mont-Blanc	42	45.55 N	6.52 E
Champaign	162	40.07 N	88.14 W
Champaquí, Cerro	146	31.59 S	64.56 W
Champlain, Lake	162	44.45 N	73.15 W
Chang, Ko	82	12.05 N	102.20 E
Changajn Nuruu	80	47.30 N	100.00 E
Changane	104	24.43 S	33.32 E
Changchun	80	43.53 N	125.19 E
Changhua	80	24.05 N	120.32 E
Changjiang (Yangtze)	80	31.48 N	121.10 E
Changsha	80	28.11 N	113.01 E
Changzhi	80	36.11 N	113.08 E
Changzhou	80	31.47 N	119.57 E
Chanka, Ozero (Xingkathu)	80	45.00 N	132.24 E
Channel Islands, Eur.	32	49.20 N	2.20 W
Channel Islands, Calif., U.S.	162	34.00 N	120.00 W
Chantilly	42	49.12 N	2.28 E
Chaoan	80	23.41 N	116.38 E
Chao Phraya	82	13.32 N	100.36 E
Chapala, Lago de	130	20.15 N	103.00 W
Charente	42	45.57 N	1.05 W
Chari	102	12.58 N	14.31 E
Char'kov	62	50.00 N	36.15 E
Charleroi	36	50.25 N	4.26 E
Charleston, S.C., U.S.	162	32.48 N	79.57 W
Charleston, W. Va., U.S.	162	38.21 N	81.38 W
Charleville-Mézières	42	49.46 N	4.43 E
Charlotte	162	35.14 N	80.50 W
Charlotte Amalie	130	18.21 N	64.56 W
Charlottesville	162	38.02 N	78.29 W
Charlottetown	160	46.14 N	63.08 W
Chartres	42	48.27 N	1.30 E
Char Us Nuur	80	48.00 N	92.10 E
Chatangskij Zaliv	62	73.30 N	109.00 E
Châteaubriant	42	47.43 N	1.23 W
Châteaudun	42	48.05 N	1.20 E
Châteauroux	42	46.49 N	1.42 E
Château-Thierry	42	49.03 N	3.24 E
Châtellerault	42	46.49 N	0.33 E
Chatham	32	51.23 N	0.32 E
Chattanooga	162	35.03 N	85.19 W
Chauk	82	20.54 N	94.50 E
Chaumont	42	48.07 N	5.08 E
Chauny	42	49.37 N	3.13 E
Chaves	50	41.44 N	7.28 W
Cheb	36	50.01 N	12.25 E
Chech, Erg	100	25.00 N	2.15 W
Chechaouene	50	35.10 N	5.16 W
Cheduba Island	82	18.48 N	93.38 E
Cheju	80	33.31 N	126.32 E
Cheju-do	80	33.20 N	126.30 E
Chelghoum el Aïd	50	36.10 N	6.10 E
Chélia, Djebel	100	35.19 N	6.42 E
Chelif, Oued	50	36.01 N	0.07 E
Chełm	36	51.10 N	23.28 E
Chełmno	36	53.22 N	18.26 E
Chelmsford	32	51.44 N	0.28 E
Chełmża	36	53.12 N	18.37 E
Cheltenham	32	51.54 N	2.04 W
Chengde	80	40.58 N	117.53 E
Chengdu	80	30.39 N	104.04 E
Cher	42	47.21 N	0.29 E
Cherbourg	42	49.39 N	1.39 W
Cherchell	50	36.36 N	2.12 E
Chergui, Chott ech	100	34.21 N	0.30 E
Cherson	62	46.38 N	32.35 E
Chesapeake	162	36.43 N	76.15 W
Chesapeake Bay	162	38.40 N	76.25 W
Cheshire	32	53.23 N	2.30 W
Chester	32	53.12 N	2.54 W
Chesterfield	32	53.15 N	1.25 W
Chesterfield, Île	104	16.20 S	43.58 E
Chew Bahir (Lake Stefanie)	102	4.40 N	36.50 E
Cheyenne	162	41.08 N	104.49 W
Cheyenne	162	44.40 N	101.15 W
Chi	82	15.11 N	104.43 E
Chiai	80	23.29 N	120.27 E
Chiang Mai	82	18.47 N	98.59 E
Chianti, Monti del	46	43.32 N	11.25 E
Chiari	46	45.32 N	9.56 E
Chiavari	46	44.19 N	9.19 E
Chiba	80	35.36 N	140.07 E
Chicago	162	41.53 N	87.38 W
Chicapa	104	6.26 S	20.47 E
Chichester	32	50.50 N	0.48 W
Chiclana de la Frontera	50	36.25 N	6.08 W
Chiclayo	144	6.46 S	79.51 W
Chico	162	39.44 N	121.50 W
Chico, Arg.	146	43.48 S	66.25 W
Chico, Arg.	146	49.56 S	68.32 W
Chicoutimi	160	48.26 N	71.04 W
Chidley, Cape	160	60.23 N	64.26 W
Chiemsee	36	47.54 N	12.29 E
Chieri	46	45.01 N	7.49 E
Chieti	46	42.21 N	14.10 E
Chihuahua	130	28.38 N	106.05 W

Chil—East

Name	Page	Lat ° ′	Long ° ′
Chile □[1]	146	30.00 S	71.00 W
Chilia, Brațul [1]	54	45.18 N	29.40 E
Chililabombwe (Bancroft)	104	12.18 S	27.43 E
Chilka Lake	84	19.45 N	85.25 E
Chilkat Pass	162a	59.43 N	136.35 W
Chillán	146	36.36 S	72.07 W
Chiloé, Isla de	146	42.30 S	73.55 W
Chilpancingo	130	17.33 N	99.30 W
Chilung	80	25.08 N	121.44 E
Chilwa, Lake	104	15.12 S	35.50 E
Chimborazo [1]	144	1.28 S	78.48 W
Chimbote	144	9.05 S	78.36 W
China □[1]	80	35.00 N	105.00 E
Chinandega	130	12.37 N	87.09 W
Chincha, Islas de	144	13.38 S	76.25 W
Chincha Alta	144	13.27 S	76.08 W
Chinchorro, Banco [4]	130	18.35 N	87.22 W
Chinde	104	18.37 S	36.24 E
Chindwin	82	21.26 N	95.15 E
Chingola	104	12.32 S	27.52 E
Chinhae	80	35.09 N	128.40 E
Chin Hills [2]	82	22.30 N	93.30 E
Chinju	80	35.11 N	128.05 E
Chinko	102	4.50 N	23.53 E
Chioggia	46	45.13 N	12.17 E
Chippenham	32	51.28 N	2.07 W
Chippewa	162	44.25 N	92.10 W
Chiquimula	130	14.48 N	89.33 W
Chirgis Nuur	80	49.12 N	93.24 E
Chiricahua Peak	162	31.52 N	109.20 W
Chiriquí, Golfo de	130	8.00 N	82.20 W
Chiriquí, Volcán de [1]	130	8.48 N	82.33 W
Chirripó, Cerro	130	9.29 N	83.30 W
Chisone	46	44.49 N	7.25 E
Chitré	130	7.58 N	80.26 W
Chittagong	84	22.20 N	91.50 E
Chiumbe	104	7.00 S	21.12 E
Chiuta, Lake	104	14.55 S	35.50 E
Chivasso	46	45.11 N	7.53 E
Chmel'nickij	62	49.25 N	27.00 E
Chochis, Cerro	144	18.04 S	60.03 W
Chodzież	36	52.59 N	16.56 E
Choiseul	114	7.05 S	157.00 E
Chojnice	36	53.42 N	17.34 E
Chojnów	36	51.17 N	15.56 E
Cholet	42	47.04 N	0.53 W
Choluteca	130	13.18 N	87.12 W
Chomutov	36	50.28 N	13.26 E
Ch'ŏnan	80	36.48 N	127.09 E
Chon Buri	82	13.22 N	100.59 E
Ch'ŏngjin	80	41.47 N	129.50 E
Ch'ŏngju	80	36.39 N	127.31 E
Chongqing	80	29.39 N	106.34 E
Chŏnju	80	35.49 N	127.08 E
Chonos, Archipiélago de los	146	45.00 S	74.00 W
Chop'or	62	49.36 N	42.19 E
Choszczno	36	53.10 N	15.26 E
Chovd	80	48.06 N	92.11 E
Chövsgöl Nuur	80	51.00 N	100.30 E
Christchurch, N.Z.	118	43.32 S	172.38 E
Christchurch, Eng., U.K.	32	50.44 N	1.45 W
Christina	160	56.40 N	111.03 W
Christmas Island □[2]	82	10.30 S	105.40 E
Chrudim	36	49.57 N	15.48 E
Chrzanów	36	50.09 N	19.24 E
Chukchi Sea [2]	64	69.00 N	171.00 W
Chulucanas	144	5.06 S	80.10 W
Ch'unch'ŏn	80	37.52 N	127.43 E
Ch'ungju	80	36.58 N	127.58 E
Chuquicamata	146	22.19 S	68.56 W
Chur	42	46.51 N	9.32 E
Churchill, Can.	160	58.47 N	94.12 W
Churchill, Newf., Can.	160	53.30 N	60.10 W
Churchill, Cape	160	58.46 N	93.12 W
Churchill Falls	160	53.35 N	64.27 W
Ciechanów	36	52.53 N	20.38 E
Ciego de Avila	130	21.51 N	78.46 W
Ciénaga	144	11.01 N	74.15 W
Cienfuegos	130	22.09 N	80.27 W
Cieszyn	36	49.45 N	18.38 E
Cieza	50	38.14 N	1.25 W
Cigüela	50	39.08 N	3.44 W
Cijara, Embalse de [1]	50	39.18 N	4.52 W
Cilento [1]	46	40.15 N	15.10 E
Cimarron	162	36.10 N	96.17 W
Čimkent	62	42.18 N	69.36 E
Cîmpina	54	45.08 N	25.44 E
Cîmpulung	54	45.16 N	25.03 E
Cîmpulung Moldovenesc	54	47.31 N	25.34 E
Cina, Tanjung	82	5.56 S	104.45 E
Cincar	46	43.54 N	17.04 E
Cincinnati	162	39.06 N	84.31 W
Çine	54	37.36 N	28.04 E
Ciociaria [1]	46	41.45 N	13.15 E
Cipolletti	146	38.56 S	67.59 W
Čirčik	62	41.29 N	69.35 E
Cirebon	82	6.44 S	108.34 E
Ciremay, Gunung	82	6.54 S	108.24 E
Cirencester	32	51.44 N	1.59 W
Ciriè	46	45.14 N	7.36 E
Čirpan	54	42.12 N	25.20 E
Čistopol'	26	55.21 N	50.37 E
Čita	64	52.03 N	113.30 E
Citlaltépetl, Volcán [1]	130	19.01 N	97.16 W
Città di Castello	46	43.27 N	12.14 E
Cittanova	46	38.21 N	16.05 E
Ciudad Bolívar	144	8.08 N	63.33 W
Ciudad del Carmen	130	18.38 N	91.50 W
Ciudad de México (Mexico City)	130	19.24 N	99.09 W
Ciudad de Valles	130	21.59 N	99.01 W
Ciudadela	50	40.02 N	3.50 E
Ciudad Guayana	144	8.22 N	62.40 W
Ciudad Guzmán	130	19.41 N	103.29 W
Ciudad Juárez	130	31.44 N	106.29 W
Ciudad Mante	130	22.44 N	98.57 W
Ciudad Obregón	130	27.29 N	109.56 W
Ciudad Ojeda	144	10.12 N	71.19 W
Ciudad Real	50	38.59 N	3.56 W
Ciudad Rodrigo	50	40.36 N	6.32 W
Ciudad Victoria	130	23.44 N	99.08 W
Civitanova Marche	46	43.18 N	13.44 E
Civitavecchia	46	42.06 N	11.48 E
Clacton-on-Sea	32	51.48 N	1.09 E
Clain	42	46.47 N	0.32 E
Claire, Lake	160	58.30 N	112.00 W
Clarence Island	167	61.09 S	54.06 W
Clarksburg	162	39.17 N	80.21 W
Clausthal-Zellerfeld	36	51.48 N	10.20 E
Clearwater	162	27.58 N	82.48 W
Cleethorpes	32	53.34 N	0.02 W
Clerke Rocks [1]	146	55.01 S	34.41 W
Clermont-Ferrand	42	45.47 N	3.05 E
Cleveland	162	41.30 N	81.41 W
Clinton	162	41.51 N	90.12 W
Clipperton [1]	130	10.17 N	109.13 W
Clonmel	32	52.21 N	7.42 W
Cloppenburg	36	52.50 N	8.02 E
Cloud Peak	162	44.25 N	107.10 W
Cluj	54	46.47 N	23.36 E
Clwyd □[6]	32	53.05 N	3.20 W
Clyde, Firth of [1]	32	55.42 N	5.00 W
Côa	50	41.05 N	7.06 W
Coast Mountains	160	55.00 N	129.00 W
Coast Ranges	162	41.00 N	123.30 W
Coatbridge	32	55.52 N	4.01 W
Coatzacoalcos	130	18.09 N	94.25 W
Cobán	130	15.29 N	90.19 W
Coburg	36	50.15 N	10.58 E
Cochabamba	144	17.24 S	66.09 W
Cochin	84	9.58 N	76.15 E
Cochrane, Lago (Lago Puyerredón)	146	47.20 S	72.00 W
Coco, Isla del	130	5.32 N	87.04 W
Cocoa	162	28.21 N	80.44 W
Coco Islands	82	14.05 N	93.18 E
Cod, Cape	162	41.42 N	70.15 W
Codogno	46	45.09 N	9.42 E
Codru-Moma, Munții	54	46.30 N	22.20 E
Coen	116	13.56 S	143.12 E
Coiba, Isla de	130	7.27 N	81.45 W
Coimbatore	84	11.00 N	76.57 E
Coimbra	50	40.12 N	8.25 W
Coín	50	36.40 N	4.45 W
Čojbalsan	80	48.34 N	114.50 E
Colatina	144	19.32 S	40.37 W
Colchester	32	51.54 N	0.54 E
Coleraine	32	55.08 N	6.40 W
Colhué Huapi, Lago	146	45.30 S	68.48 W
Colima	130	19.14 N	103.43 W
Coll	32	56.38 N	6.34 W
Colmar	42	48.05 N	7.22 E
Colnett, Cabo	130	30.58 N	116.19 W
Colombia □[1]	144	4.00 N	72.00 W
Colombo	84	6.56 N	79.51 E
Colón, Cuba	130	22.43 N	80.54 W
Colón, Pan.	130	9.22 N	79.54 W
Colonna, Capo	46	39.02 N	17.11 E
Coloradas, Lomas [2]	146	43.24 S	67.24 W
Colorado □[3]	162	39.30 N	105.30 W
Colorado, Arg.	146	39.50 S	62.08 W
Colorado, N.A.	162	31.54 N	114.57 W
Colorado, Tex., U.S.	162	28.36 N	95.58 W
Colorado Springs	162	38.50 N	104.49 W
Columbia, Mo., U.S.	162	38.57 N	92.20 W
Columbia, S.C., U.S.	162	34.00 N	81.03 W
Columbia	160	46.15 N	124.05 W
Columbia, Mount	160	52.09 N	117.25 W
Columbus, Ga., U.S.	162	32.29 N	84.59 W
Columbus, Ohio, U.S.	162	39.57 N	83.00 W
Colwyn Bay	32	53.18 N	3.43 W
Comacchio	46	44.42 N	12.11 E
Comayagua	130	14.25 N	87.37 W
Comilla	84	23.27 N	91.12 E
Comino, Capo	46	40.31 N	9.50 E
Comiso	46	36.56 N	14.37 E
Comitán	130	16.15 N	92.08 W
Comminges [1]	42	43.15 N	0.45 E
Como	46	45.47 N	9.05 E
Como, Lago di	46	46.00 N	9.20 E
Comodoro Rivadavia	146	45.52 S	67.30 W
Comorin, Cape	84	8.06 N	77.33 E
Comoros □[1]	104	12.10 S	44.10 E
Compiègne	42	49.25 N	2.50 E
Conakry	100	9.31 N	13.43 W
Concarneau	42	47.52 N	3.55 W
Concepción, Chile	146	36.50 S	73.03 W
Concepción, Para.	146	23.25 S	57.17 W
Concepción, Laguna	144	17.29 S	61.25 W
Concepción del Uruguay	146	32.29 S	58.14 W
Conception Bay	104	23.53 S	14.28 E
Conchos	130	29.35 N	104.25 W
Concord	162	43.12 N	71.32 W
Concordia	146	31.24 S	58.02 W
Conegliano	46	45.53 N	12.18 E
Confuso	146	25.09 S	57.34 W
Congleton	32	53.10 N	2.13 W
Congo □[1]	104	1.00 S	15.00 E
Congo (Zaire) (Zaïre)	104	6.04 S	12.24 E
Connaught □[9]	32	53.45 N	9.00 W
Connecticut □[3]	162	41.45 N	72.45 W
Conselheiro Lafaiete	144	20.40 S	43.48 W
Consett	32	54.51 N	1.49 W
Con Son	82	8.43 N	106.36 E
Constanța	54	44.11 N	28.39 E
Constantina	50	37.52 N	5.37 W
Constantine	100	36.22 N	6.37 E
Consuegra	50	39.28 N	3.36 W
Conversano	46	40.58 N	17.08 E
Conway	32	53.17 N	3.50 W
Cook, Cape	160	50.08 N	127.55 W
Cook, Mount	118	43.36 S	170.10 E
Cook Islands □[2]	10	20.00 S	158.00 W
Cook Strait	118	41.15 S	174.30 E
Cooktown	116	15.28 S	145.15 E
Copertino	46	40.16 N	18.03 E
Copiapó	146	27.22 S	70.20 W
Copparo	46	44.54 N	11.49 E
Coquimbo	146	29.58 S	71.21 W
Corabia	54	43.46 N	24.30 E
Coral Sea [2]	116	15.00 S	155.00 E
Corato	46	41.09 N	16.25 E
Corbeil-Essonnes	42	48.36 N	2.29 E
Corbières	42	42.55 N	2.38 E
Corby	32	52.29 N	0.40 W
Corcovado, Golfo	146	43.30 S	73.30 W
Corcovado, Volcán [1]	146	43.12 S	72.48 W
Córdoba, Arg.	146	31.24 S	64.11 W
Córdoba, Esp.	50	37.53 N	4.46 W
Córdoba, Méx.	130	18.53 N	96.56 W
Coria del Río	50	37.16 N	6.03 W
Corigliano Calabro	46	39.36 N	16.31 E
Corixa Grande	144	17.31 S	57.52 W
Cork	32	51.54 N	8.28 W
Cork □[6]	32	52.00 N	8.30 W
Corleone	46	37.49 N	13.18 E
Çorlu	54	41.09 N	27.48 E
Corner Brook	160	48.57 N	57.57 W
Corn Islands	130	12.15 N	83.00 W
Corno Grande	46	42.28 N	13.34 E
Cornwall	160	45.02 N	74.44 W
Cornwall □[6]	32	50.30 N	4.40 W
Coro	144	11.25 N	69.41 W
Coromandel Coast [2]	84	13.30 N	80.30 E
Coromandel Peninsula [1]	118	36.50 S	175.35 E
Coromandel Range	118	37.00 S	175.40 E
Coronation Island	167	60.37 S	45.30 W
Coronel	146	37.01 S	73.08 W
Coropuna, Nevado	144	15.31 S	72.42 W
Corozal	130	18.24 N	88.24 W
Corpus Christi	162	27.48 N	97.24 W
Correggio	46	44.46 N	10.47 E
Correnti, Isola delle	46	36.38 N	15.05 E
Corrib, Lough	32	53.05 N	9.10 W
Corrientes	146	27.28 S	58.50 W
Corrientes, Cabo, Col.	144	5.30 N	77.34 W
Corrientes, Cabo, Cuba	130	21.45 N	84.31 W
Corrientes, Cabo, Méx.	130	20.25 N	105.42 W
Corse (Corsica)	42	42.40 N	9.05 E
Corse, Cap	42	43.00 N	9.25 E
Cort Adelaer, Kap	160	62.00 N	42.00 W
Cortina d'Ampezzo	46	46.32 N	12.08 E
Cortona	46	43.16 N	11.59 E
Corubal	100	11.57 N	15.06 W
Çorum	54	39.14 N	28.27 E
Corumbá	144	19.01 S	57.39 W
Corvallis	162	44.34 N	123.16 W
Cosenza	46	39.17 N	16.15 E
Cosmoledo Group	104	9.43 S	47.35 E
Cosne-sur-Loire	42	47.24 N	2.55 E
Costa Rica □[1]	130	10.00 N	84.00 W
Costiera, Catena	46	39.20 N	16.05 E
Coswig	36	51.53 N	12.26 E
Cotabato	82	7.13 N	124.15 E
Cotentin [1]	42	49.30 N	1.30 W
Cotmeana	54	44.24 N	24.45 E
Cotonou	100	6.21 N	2.26 E
Cotopaxi [1]	144	0.40 S	78.26 W
Cotswold Hills [2]	32	51.45 N	2.10 W
Cottbus	36	51.45 N	14.19 E
Cottiennes, Alpes (Alpi Cozie)	46	44.45 N	7.00 E
Coubre, Pointe de la	42	45.41 N	1.13 W
Coulommiers	42	48.49 N	3.05 E
Council Bluffs	162	41.16 N	95.52 W
Courantyne (Corantijn)	144	5.55 N	57.05 W
Courcelles	36	50.28 N	4.22 E
Coventry	32	52.25 N	1.30 W
Covilhã	50	40.17 N	7.30 W
Covington	162	39.05 N	84.30 W
Cowdenbeath	32	56.07 N	3.21 W
Cowes	32	50.45 N	1.18 W
Cozumel, Isla de	130	20.25 N	86.55 W
Cradock	104	32.08 S	25.36 E
Crailsheim	36	49.08 N	10.04 E
Craiova	54	44.19 N	23.48 E
Cranbrook	160	49.31 N	115.46 W
Crasna (Kraszna)	54	48.09 N	22.20 E
Cratéus	144	5.10 S	40.40 W
Crato	144	7.14 S	39.23 W
Crawley	32	51.07 N	0.12 W
Cree	160	59.00 N	105.47 W
Cree Lake	160	57.30 N	106.30 W
Creil	42	49.16 N	2.29 E
Crema	46	45.22 N	9.41 E
Cremona	46	45.07 N	10.02 E
Cres, Otok	46	44.50 N	14.25 E
Crescent Group	82	16.31 N	111.38 E
Creuse	42	47.00 N	0.34 E
Crevillente	50	38.15 N	0.48 W
Crewe	32	53.05 N	2.27 W
Crimmitschau	36	50.49 N	12.23 E
Cristóbal Colón, Pico	144	10.50 N	73.41 W
Crișu Alb	54	46.42 N	21.17 E
Crișu Negru	54	46.42 N	21.16 E
Crișu Repede (Sebes Körös)	54	46.55 N	20.59 E
Crooked Island	130	22.45 N	74.13 W
Cross Fell	32	54.42 N	2.29 W
Crotone	46	39.05 N	17.07 E
Cruz, Cabo	130	19.51 N	77.44 W
Cruz del Eje	146	30.44 S	64.48 W
Cserhát	36	47.55 N	19.30 E
Csongrád	36	46.43 N	20.09 E
Cuando (Kwando)	104	18.27 S	23.32 E
Cuango (Kwango)	104	3.14 S	17.23 E
Cuanza	104	9.19 S	13.08 E
Cuba □[1]	130	21.30 N	80.00 W
Cubango (Okavango)	104	18.50 S	22.25 E
Cúcuta	144	7.54 N	72.31 W
Čudskoje Ozero	62	58.40 N	27.25 E
Cuenca, Ec.	144	2.53 S	78.59 W
Cuenca, Esp.	50	40.04 N	2.08 W
Cuernavaca	130	18.55 N	99.15 W
Cugir	54	45.50 N	23.22 E
Cuiabá	144	15.35 S	56.05 W
Cuilo (Kwilu)	104	3.22 S	17.22 E
Cuíto	104	18.01 S	20.48 E
Cuitzeo, Lago de	130	19.55 N	101.05 W
Culebra, Sierra de la	50	41.54 N	6.20 W
Culiacán	130	24.48 N	107.24 W
Cullera	50	39.10 N	0.15 W
Cumaná	144	10.28 N	64.10 W
Cumbal, Volcán de [1]	144	0.57 N	77.52 W
Cumberland	162	39.39 N	78.46 W
Cumberland	162	37.09 N	88.25 W
Cumberland Plateau [1]	162	36.00 N	85.00 W
Cumberland Sound	160	65.10 N	65.30 W
Cumbria □[6]	32	54.30 N	3.00 W
Čumerna	54	42.47 N	25.58 E
Cunene	104	17.20 S	11.50 E
Cuneo	46	44.23 N	7.32 E
Curaçao	130	12.11 N	69.00 W
Curepipe	104	20.19 S	57.31 E
Curicó	146	34.59 S	71.14 W
Curtea-de-Argeș	54	45.08 N	24.41 E
Curvelo	144	18.45 S	44.25 W
Cutro	46	39.02 N	16.59 E
Cuttack	84	20.26 N	85.53 E
Cuxhaven	36	53.52 N	8.42 E
Cuyuni	144	6.23 N	58.41 W
Cuzco	144	13.31 S	71.59 W
Cyangugu	104	2.29 S	28.54 E
Cyprus □[1]	20	35.00 N	33.00 E
Czechoslovakia □[1]	36	49.30 N	17.00 E
Czechowice-Dziedzice	36	49.54 N	19.00 E
Częstochowa	36	50.49 N	19.06 E
D			
Dacca	84	23.43 N	90.25 E
Dachau	36	48.15 N	11.27 E
Dagupan	82	16.03 N	120.20 E
Dahlak Archipelago	102	15.45 N	40.30 E
Dahlak Kebir Island	102	15.38 N	40.11 E
Dahra	50	36.25 N	1.00 E
Daḥy, Nafūd ad- [8]	84	22.20 N	45.35 E
Daimiel	50	39.04 N	3.37 W
Dajianshan	80	26.42 N	103.34 E
Dakar	100	14.40 N	17.26 W
Dakhla	100	23.43 N	15.57 W
Đakovica	54	42.23 N	20.25 E
Dalälven	28	60.38 N	17.27 E
Dallas	162	32.47 N	96.48 W
Daloa	100	6.53 N	6.27 W
Daly Waters	116	16.15 S	133.22 E
Damanhūr	102	31.02 N	30.28 E
Damāvand, Qolleh-ye	84	35.56 N	52.08 E
Danakil Plain	102	12.25 N	40.30 E
Da-nang	82	16.04 N	108.13 E
Danger Point	104	34.40 S	19.17 E
Danube	20	45.20 N	29.40 E
Danville, Ill., U.S.	162	40.08 N	87.37 W
Danville, Va., U.S.	162	36.35 N	79.24 W
Danzig, Gulf of	36	54.40 N	19.15 E
Dão	50	40.20 N	8.11 W
Darabani	54	48.11 N	26.35 E
Darchan	80	49.28 N	105.56 E
Dar-es-Salaam	104	6.48 S	39.17 E
Darling	116	34.07 S	141.55 E
Darling Range	116	32.00 S	116.30 E
Darlington	32	54.31 N	1.34 W
Darłowo	36	54.26 N	16.23 E
Darmstadt	36	49.53 N	8.40 E
Darnah	102	32.46 N	22.39 E
Darnétal	42	49.27 N	1.09 E
Darsser Ort	36	54.29 N	12.31 E
Dartmoor [3]	32	50.35 N	4.00 W
Dartmouth	160	44.40 N	63.34 W
Darwin	116	12.28 S	130.50 E
Darwin, Monte	146	54.45 S	69.29 W
Dasht	84	25.10 N	61.40 E
Datong	80	40.08 N	113.13 E
Datu, Tandjung	82	0.00 N	109.39 E
Datu Piang	82	7.01 N	124.30 E
Daugava (Zapadnaja Dvina)	62	57.04 N	24.03 E
Daugavpils	26	55.53 N	26.32 E
Daule	144	2.10 S	79.52 W
Davao	82	7.04 N	125.36 E
Davao Gulf	82	6.40 N	125.55 E
Davenport	162	41.32 N	90.41 W
David	130	8.26 N	82.26 W
Davis Mountains	162	30.35 N	104.00 W
Davis Strait	160	67.00 N	57.00 W
Davos	42	46.48 N	9.50 E
Dawa (Daua)	102	4.11 N	42.06 E
Dawlish	32	50.35 N	3.28 W
Dawna Range	82	16.50 N	98.15 E
Dawson	160	64.04 N	139.25 W
Dawson Range	160	62.40 N	139.00 W
Dax	42	43.43 N	1.03 W
Dayr az-Zawr	84	35.20 N	40.09 E
Dayrūṭ	102	27.33 N	30.49 E
Dayton	162	39.45 N	84.15 W
Daytona Beach	162	29.12 N	81.00 W
De Aar	104	30.39 S	24.00 E
Dead Sea	84	31.30 N	35.30 E
Deal	32	51.14 N	1.24 E
Dean Channel	160	52.33 N	127.13 W
Dearg, Beinn	32	57.48 N	4.57 W
Dease	160	59.54 N	128.30 W
Death Valley	162	36.30 N	117.00 W
Dębica	36	50.04 N	21.24 E
Dęblin	36	51.35 N	21.50 E
Debrecen	36	47.32 N	21.38 E
Debre Markos	102	10.20 N	37.45 E
Decatur, Ala., U.S.	162	34.36 N	86.59 W
Decatur, Ill., U.S.	162	39.51 N	89.32 W
Decazeville	42	44.34 N	2.15 E
Deccan [1]	84	17.00 N	78.00 E
Deception Island	167	62.57 S	60.38 W
Děčín	36	50.48 N	14.13 E
Decize	42	46.50 N	3.27 E
Dee	32	51.20 N	4.00 W
Deflotte, Cap	112	21.10 S	167.25 E
Deggendorf	36	48.51 N	12.59 E
Dehiwala-Mount Lavinia	84	6.51 N	79.52 E
Dehra Dūn	84	30.20 N	78.02 E
Deinze	36	50.59 N	3.32 E
Dej	54	47.09 N	23.52 E
Delaware □[3]	162	39.10 N	75.30 W
Delaware Bay	162	39.05 N	75.15 W
Delémont	42	47.22 N	7.21 E
Delft	36	52.00 N	4.21 E
Delfzijl	36	53.19 N	6.46 E
Delgado, Cabo	104	10.40 S	40.35 E
Delhi	84	28.37 N	77.12 E
Delicias	130	28.13 N	105.28 W
Delitzsch	36	51.31 N	12.20 E
Dellys	50	36.55 N	3.55 E
Delmenhorst	36	53.03 N	8.38 E
Demirci	54	39.03 N	28.40 E
Demir Kapija	54	41.24 N	22.15 E
Demmin	36	53.54 N	13.02 E
Dempo, Gunung	82	4.02 S	103.09 E
Denain	42	50.20 N	3.23 E
Dendermonde	36	51.02 N	4.07 E
Denham, Mount	130	18.13 N	77.32 W
Den Helder	36	52.54 N	4.45 E
Denizli	54	37.46 N	29.06 E
Denmark □[1]	28	56.00 N	10.00 E
Denmark Strait	26a	67.00 N	25.00 W
Denpasar	82	8.39 S	115.13 E
D'Entrecasteaux, Point	116	34.50 S	116.00 E
D'Entrecasteaux Islands	116a	9.30 S	150.40 E
Denver	162	39.43 N	105.01 W
Dera Ghāzi Khān	84	30.03 N	70.38 E
Dera Ismāīl Khān	84	31.50 N	70.54 E
Derby	32	52.55 N	1.29 W
Derbyshire □[6]	32	53.00 N	1.33 W
Derg, Lough	32	53.00 N	8.20 W
Derventa	54	44.58 N	17.55 E
Derwent	32	53.45 N	0.57 W
Desaguadero, Arg.	146	34.13 S	66.47 W
Desaguadero, Bol.	144	18.24 S	67.05 W
Deschambault Lake	160	54.40 N	103.35 W
Deschutes	162	45.38 N	120.54 W
Dese	102	11.05 N	39.41 E
Deseado	146	47.45 S	65.54 W
Desengaño, Punta	146	49.15 S	67.37 W
Desenzano del Garda	46	45.28 N	10.32 E
Des Moines	162	41.35 N	93.37 W
Desna	62	50.33 N	30.32 E
Dessau	36	51.50 N	12.14 E
Detmold	36	51.56 N	8.52 E
Detroit	162	42.20 N	83.03 W
Deutsche Bucht	36	54.30 N	7.30 E
Deva	54	45.53 N	22.55 E
Dévaványa	36	47.02 N	20.58 E
Deventer	36	52.15 N	6.10 E
Devès, Monts du	42	45.00 N	3.45 E
Devils Paw	162a	58.44 N	133.50 W
Devoll	54	40.49 N	19.51 E
Devon □[6]	32	50.45 N	3.50 W
Devon Island	160	75.00 N	87.00 W
Devonport	116	41.11 S	146.21 E
Dewsbury	32	53.42 N	1.37 W
Dezfūl	84	32.23 N	48.24 E
Dežneva, Mys	64	66.06 N	169.45 W
Dhamār	84	14.46 N	44.23 E
Dhaulāgiri	84	28.42 N	83.30 E
Dhodhekánisos (Dodecanese)	54	36.30 N	27.00 E
Diaka [1]	100	15.13 N	4.14 W
Diamantina	144	18.15 S	43.36 W
Dibble Iceberg Tongue	167	65.40 S	135.10 E
Diégo-Suarez	104	12.16 S	49.17 E
Diepholz	36	52.35 N	8.21 E
Dieppe	42	49.56 N	1.05 E
Digne	42	44.06 N	6.14 E
Digoin	42	46.29 N	3.59 E
Digul	82	7.07 S	138.42 E
Dijon	42	47.19 N	5.01 E
Dikhil	102	11.06 N	42.22 E
Dili	82	8.33 S	125.35 E
Dimashq (Damascus)	84	33.30 N	36.18 E
Dimasse, Rass	46	35.37 N	11.03 E
Dîmbovița	54	44.14 N	26.27 E
Dimitrovgrad, Blg.	54	42.03 N	25.36 E
Dimitrovgrad, S.S.S.R.	26	54.14 N	49.39 E
Dimlang	100	8.24 N	11.47 E
Dinan	42	48.27 N	2.02 W
Dinant	36	50.16 N	4.55 E
Dinara	46	43.50 N	16.35 E
Dinard	42	48.38 N	2.04 W
Dingalan Bay	82	15.18 N	121.25 E
Dingolfing	36	48.38 N	12.31 E
Dinkelsbühl	36	49.04 N	10.19 E
Diourbel	100	14.40 N	16.15 W
Dire Dawa	102	9.37 N	41.52 E
Disappointment, Cape, Falk. Is.	146	54.53 S	36.07 W
Disappointment, Cape, Wash., U.S.	162	46.18 N	124.03 W
Disko	160	69.50 N	53.30 W
Disko Bugt	160	69.15 N	52.00 W
District of Columbia □[5]	162	38.54 N	77.01 W
Disūq	102	31.08 N	30.39 E
Dithmarschen [1]	36	54.05 N	9.00 E
Divinópolis	144	20.09 S	44.54 W
Divisor, Serra do [1]	144	8.20 S	73.30 W
Dixon Entrance	162a	54.25 N	132.30 W
Diyarbakır	20	37.55 N	40.14 E
Dja	100	2.02 N	15.12 E
Djedi, Oued	100	34.28 N	6.05 E
Djemmal	46	35.37 N	10.46 E
Djénné	100	13.54 N	4.33 W
Djerba, Île de	100	33.48 N	10.54 E
Djerem	100	5.20 N	13.24 E
Djerid, Chott	100	33.42 N	8.26 E
Djibouti	102	11.36 N	43.09 E
Djibouti □[1]	102	11.30 N	43.00 E
Djidjelli	50	36.48 N	5.46 E
Djursholm	28	59.24 N	18.05 E
Dmitrija Lapteva, Proliv	64	73.00 N	142.00 E
Dnepr	62	46.30 N	32.18 E
Dneprodzeržinsk	62	48.30 N	34.37 E
Dnepropetrovsk	62	48.27 N	34.59 E
Dnestr	62	46.18 N	30.17 E
Döbeln	36	51.07 N	13.07 E
Doberai, Jazirah [1]	82	1.30 S	132.30 E
Doboj	54	44.44 N	18.06 E
Dobrudžansko plato [1]	54	43.32 N	27.50 E
Dodge City	162	37.45 N	100.01 W
Dodman Point	32	50.13 N	4.48 W
Dodoma	104	6.11 S	35.45 E
Doetinchem	36	51.58 N	6.17 E
Doiran, Lake	54	41.13 N	22.44 E
Dole	42	47.06 N	5.30 E
Dolisie	104	4.12 S	12.41 E
Dolomiti	46	46.25 N	11.50 E
Dombes [1]	42	46.00 N	5.03 E
Dombóvár	36	46.23 N	18.08 E
Domeyko, Cordillera	146	24.30 S	69.00 W
Dominica □[1]	130	15.30 N	61.20 W
Dominican Republic □[1]	130	19.00 N	70.40 W
Domodossola	46	46.07 N	8.17 E
Domuyo, Volcán [1]	146	36.38 S	70.26 W
Don	62	47.04 N	39.18 E
Donaueschingen	36	47.57 N	8.29 E
Don Benito	50	38.57 N	5.52 W
Doncaster	32	53.32 N	1.07 W
Dondra Head	84	5.55 N	80.35 E
Doneck	62	48.00 N	37.48 E
Donegal Bay	32	54.30 N	8.30 W
Donga	100	8.19 N	9.58 E
Donghaidao	80	21.02 N	110.25 E
Dong-nai	82	10.45 N	106.46 E
Dongshaqundao (Pratas Islands)	80	20.42 N	116.43 E
Dongtinghu	80	29.20 N	112.54 E
Donjek	160	62.35 N	140.00 W
Dorchester	32	50.43 N	2.26 W
Dordogne	42	45.02 N	0.35 W
Dordrecht	36	51.49 N	4.40 E
Dore, Monts	42	45.30 N	2.45 E
Dornbirn	36	47.25 N	9.44 E
Dorohoi	54	47.57 N	26.24 E
Dorset □[6]	32	50.47 N	2.20 W
Dortmund	36	51.31 N	7.28 E
Dos Hermanas	50	37.17 N	5.55 W
Dothan	162	31.13 N	85.24 W
Douai	42	50.22 N	3.04 E
Douala	100	4.03 N	9.42 E
Douarnenez	42	48.06 N	4.20 W
Doubs	42	47.10 N	6.25 E
Doubtful Sound	118	45.17 S	166.51 E
Douglas	32	54.09 N	4.28 W
Douglas Channel	160	53.30 N	129.12 W
Dourdou	42	44.00 N	2.41 E
Douro (Duero)	50	41.08 N	8.40 W
Douze	42	43.54 N	0.30 W
Dover, Eng., U.K.	32	51.08 N	1.19 E
Dover, Del., U.S.	162	39.10 N	75.32 W
Dover, N.H., U.S.	162	43.12 N	70.56 W
Dover, Strait of (Pas de Calais)	32	51.00 N	1.30 E
Dra, Hamada du [2]	100	29.00 N	6.45 W
Drâa, Oued	100	28.43 N	11.09 W
Drachten	36	53.06 N	6.05 E
Dračie Jaskyně [5]	36	49.05 N	19.35 E
Drăgășani	54	44.40 N	24.16 E
Dragonera, Isla	50	39.35 N	2.19 E
Draguignan	42	43.32 N	6.28 E
Drakensberg	104	27.00 S	30.00 E
Dráma	54	41.09 N	24.08 E
Drammen	28	59.44 N	10.15 E
Dranov, Ostrovul	54	44.52 N	29.15 E
Drau (Drava) (Dráva)	46	45.33 N	18.55 E
Drava (Drau) (Dráva)	46	45.33 N	18.55 E
Dravinja	46	46.22 N	15.57 E
Drawa	36	52.52 N	15.59 E
Dresden	36	51.03 N	13.44 E
Dreux	42	48.44 N	1.22 E
Drin	54	41.17 N	20.02 E
Drina	54	44.53 N	19.21 E
Drinit, Pellg i	54	41.45 N	19.28 E
Drobeta-Turnu-Severin	54	44.38 N	22.39 E
Drogheda	32	53.43 N	6.21 W
Dronne	42	45.02 N	0.09 W
Drummondville	160	45.53 N	72.29 W
Drwęca	36	53.00 N	18.42 E
Duarte, Pico	130	19.02 N	70.59 W
Dubawnt Lake	160	63.08 N	101.30 W
Dubayy	84	25.18 N	55.18 E
Dubbo	116	32.15 S	148.36 E
Dublin (Baile Átha Cliath)	32	53.20 N	6.15 W
Dublin □[6]	32	53.20 N	6.15 W
Dubrovnik	54	42.38 N	18.07 E
Dubuque	162	42.30 N	90.41 W
Dudelange	36	49.28 N	6.05 E
Dudley	32	52.30 N	2.05 W
Dudweiler	36	49.17 N	7.02 E
Duero (Douro)	50	41.08 N	8.40 W
Dufourspitze	42	45.55 N	7.52 E
Dugi Otok	46	44.00 N	15.04 E
Du Gué	160	57.21 N	70.45 W
Duin Dui	112	15.24 S	167.46 E
Duisburg	36	51.25 N	6.46 E
Duitama	144	5.50 N	73.02 W
Dülmen	36	51.51 N	7.16 E
Duluth	162	46.47 N	92.06 W
Dumaguete	82	9.18 N	123.18 E
Dumbarton	32	55.57 N	4.35 W
Dumbier	36	48.57 N	19.37 E
Dumfries	32	55.04 N	3.37 W
Dumyāṭ	102	31.25 N	31.48 E
Dunajec	36	50.15 N	20.44 E
Dunărea Veche	54	45.17 N	28.02 E
Dunaújváros	36	46.58 N	18.57 E
Duna-völgyi-főcsatorna	36	46.12 N	18.56 E
Dundalk	32	54.01 N	6.25 W
Dundee	32	56.28 N	3.00 W
Dundrum Bay	32	54.13 N	5.45 W
Dunedin	118	45.52 S	170.30 E
Dunfermline	32	56.04 N	3.29 W
Dungeness	32	50.55 N	0.58 E
Dunkerque	42	51.03 N	2.22 E
Dún Laoghaire	32	53.17 N	6.08 W
Dunstable	32	51.53 N	0.32 W
Durango, Esp.	50	43.10 N	2.37 W
Durango, Méx.	130	24.02 N	104.40 W
Durazno	146	33.22 S	56.31 W
Durban	104	29.55 S	30.56 E
Düren	36	50.48 N	6.28 E
Durham, Eng., U.K.	32	54.47 N	1.34 W
Durham, N.C., U.S.	162	35.59 N	78.54 W
Durham □[6]	32	54.45 N	1.45 W
Durmitor	54	43.08 N	19.01 E
Durrës	54	41.19 N	19.26 E
Dušanbe	62	38.35 N	68.48 E
Düsseldorf	36	51.12 N	6.47 E
Dvůr Králové [nad Labem]	36	50.26 N	15.48 E
Dyfed □[6]	32	52.00 N	4.30 W
Dyje (Thaya)	36	48.37 N	16.56 E
Džambul	62	42.54 N	71.22 E
Dzaoudzi	104	12.47 S	45.17 E
Dzavchan	80	48.54 N	93.23 E
Dzeržinsk	26	56.15 N	43.24 E
Dzierżoniów (Reichenbach)	36	50.44 N	16.39 E
E			
Eastbourne	32	50.46 N	0.17 E
East China Sea [2]	80	30.00 N	126.00 E
East Dereham	32	52.41 N	0.56 E
Eastern Ghāts	84	16.00 N	79.00 E
East Falkland	146	51.55 S	59.00 W
East Grinstead	32	51.08 N	0.01 W
East Kilbride	32	55.46 N	4.10 W
Eastleigh	32	50.58 N	1.22 W
East London (Oos-Londen)	104	33.00 S	27.55 E

Name	Page	Lat ° ′	Long ° ′
Eastmain ≃	160	52.15 N	78.35 W
East Retford	32	53.19 N	0.56 W
East Saint Louis	162	38.38 N	90.09 W
Eau Claire	162	44.49 N	91.31 W
Ebbw Vale	32	51.47 N	3.12 W
Eberbach	36	49.28 N	8.59 E
Eberswalde	36	52.50 N	13.49 E
Ebingen	36	48.13 N	9.01 E
Ebola ≃	102	3.20 N	20.57 E
Eboli	46	40.37 N	15.04 E
Ebro ≃	50	40.43 N	0.54 E
Ebro, Delta del ⊻[2]	50	40.43 N	0.54 E
Ebro, Embalse del ◎[1]	50	43.00 N	3.58 W
Écija	50	37.32 N	5.05 W
Eckernförde	36	54.28 N	9.50 E
Eckerö I	28	60.14 N	19.35 E
Ecuador □[1]	144	2.00 S	77.30 W
Eddystone Rocks II[1]	32	50.12 N	4.15 W
Ede, Ned.	36	52.03 N	5.40 E
Ede, Nig.	100	7.44 N	4.27 E
Eden ≃	32	54.57 N	3.01 W
Eder ≃	36	51.13 N	9.27 E
Édhessa	54	40.48 N	22.03 E
Edinburgh	32	55.57 N	3.13 W
Edirne	54	41.40 N	26.34 E
Edmonton	160	53.33 N	113.28 W
Edremit	54	39.35 N	27.01 E
Edremit Körfezi C	54	39.30 N	26.45 E
Edrengijn Nuruu ⛰	80	44.15 N	97.45 E
Edward, Lake ◎	104	0.25 S	29.30 E
Edwards Plateau ⛰[1]	162	31.20 N	101.00 W
Eeklo	36	51.11 N	3.34 E
Eergu'nahe (Argun') ≃	64	53.20 N	121.28 E
Egadi, Isole II	46	37.56 N	12.16 E
Egedesminde	160	68.42 N	52.45 W
Eger	36	47.54 N	20.23 E
Egypt □[1]	102	27.00 N	30.00 E
Éibar	50	43.11 N	2.28 W
Eichstätt	36	48.54 N	11.12 E
Eifel ⛰	36	50.15 N	6.45 E
Eilenburg	36	51.27 N	12.37 E
Einbeck	36	51.49 N	9.52 E
Eindhoven	36	51.26 N	5.28 E
Einsiedeln	42	47.08 N	8.45 E
Eisenach	36	50.59 N	10.19 E
Eisenberg	36	50.58 N	11.53 E
Eisenerz	36	47.33 N	14.53 E
Eisenerzer Alpen ⛰	36	47.28 N	14.45 E
Eisenhüttenstadt	36	52.10 N	14.39 E
Eisenstadt	36	47.51 N	16.32 E
Eisleben	36	51.31 N	11.32 E
Eislingen	36	48.42 N	9.42 E
Eitorf	36	50.46 N	7.26 E
Ejea de los Caballeros	50	42.08 N	1.08 W
Ekeren	36	51.17 N	4.25 E
El Aaiún	100	27.09 N	13.12 W
Elan ≃	54	46.07 N	28.04 E
El Arahal	50	37.16 N	5.33 W
El Asnam	100	36.10 N	1.20 E
Elâzığ	20	38.41 N	39.14 E
Elba, Isola d' I	46	42.46 N	10.17 E
El Banco	144	9.00 N	73.58 W
Elbasan	54	41.06 N	20.05 E
Elbe (Labe) ≃	36	53.50 N	9.00 E
Elbe-Havel-Kanal ☲	36	52.24 N	12.23 E
Elbert, Mount ▲	162	39.07 N	106.27 W
Elbeuf	42	49.17 N	1.00 E
Elbląg (Elbing)	36	54.10 N	19.25 E
Elbląski, Kanał ☲	36	53.43 N	19.53 E
El'brus, Gora ▲	62	43.21 N	42.26 E
El Cajon	162	32.48 N	116.58 W
Elche	50	38.15 N	0.42 W
Elda	50	38.29 N	0.47 W
El Djouf ◆[2]	100	20.30 N	8.00 W
Eldoret	104	0.31 N	35.17 E
Elektrostal'	62	55.47 N	38.28 E
Elephant Island I	167	61.10 S	55.14 W
Eleuthera I	130	25.10 N	76.14 W
Elevsís	54	38.02 N	23.32 E
El Ferrol del Caudillo	50	43.29 N	8.14 W
Elgin, Scot., U.K.	32	57.39 N	3.20 W
Elgin, Ill., U.S.	162	42.02 N	88.17 W
El Goléa	100	30.30 N	2.50 E
Elgon, Mount ▲	104	1.08 N	34.33 E
El Hank •[4]	100	24.30 N	7.00 W
Elhovo	54	42.10 N	26.34 E
Elila ≃	104	2.45 S	25.53 E
Elizabeth	116	34.43 S	138.40 E
El-Jadida	100	33.16 N	8.30 W
Ełk	36	53.50 N	22.22 E
Ełk ≃	36	53.31 N	22.47 E
El Kairouan	100	35.41 N	10.07 E
El Kala	46	36.50 N	8.30 E
El Kef	100	36.11 N	8.43 E
Elkhart	162	41.41 N	85.58 W
Ellice ≃	160	68.02 N	103.26 W
Ellwangen	36	48.57 N	10.07 E
El Mahdia	46	35.30 N	11.04 E
Elmira	162	42.06 N	76.49 W
El Moknine	100	35.38 N	10.54 E
El Mreyyé ◆[1]	100	19.30 N	7.00 W
Elmshorn	36	53.45 N	9.39 E
El Nevado, Cerro ▲	144	3.59 N	74.04 W
Elobey, Islas II	104	0.59 N	9.30 E
El Oued	100	33.20 N	6.58 E
El Paso	162	31.45 N	106.29 W
El Puerto de Santa María	50	36.36 N	6.13 W
Elsa	160	63.55 N	135.28 W
El Salvador □[1]	130	13.50 N	88.55 W
Elsterwerda	36	51.28 N	13.31 E
El Tigre	144	8.55 N	64.15 W
Elvas	50	38.53 N	7.10 W
Emden	36	53.22 N	7.12 E
Emmen	36	52.47 N	7.00 E
Emmendingen	36	48.07 N	7.50 E
Emmerich	36	51.50 N	6.15 E
Empalme	130	27.58 N	110.51 W
Emperor Range ⛰	114	5.45 S	154.55 E
Empoli	46	43.43 N	10.57 E
Ems ≃	36	53.30 N	7.00 E
Emsdetten	36	52.10 N	7.31 E
En (Inn) ≃	42	48.35 N	13.28 E
Encarnación	146	27.20 S	55.54 W
Encounter Bay C	116	35.35 S	138.44 E
Enderby Land ◆[1]	167	67.30 S	53.00 E
Engel's	62	51.30 N	46.07 E
England □[8]	32	52.30 N	1.30 W
English ≃	160	50.12 N	95.00 W
English Channel (La Manche) Ʉ	32	50.20 N	1.00 W
Enid	162	36.19 N	97.48 W
Enkhuizen	36	52.42 N	5.17 E
Enköping	28	59.38 N	17.04 E
Enna	46	37.34 N	14.17 E
Ennedi ⛰[1]	102	17.15 N	22.00 E
Enns	36	48.13 N	14.29 E
Enns ≃	36	48.14 N	14.32 E
Enschede	36	52.12 N	6.53 E
Ensenada	130	31.52 N	116.37 W
Entebbe	104	0.04 N	32.28 E
Entenbühl ▲	36	49.46 N	12.24 E
Entinas, Punta ➤	50	36.41 N	2.46 W
Enugu	100	6.27 N	7.27 E
Envalira, Port d')(	50	42.35 N	1.45 E
Enza ≃	46	44.54 N	10.31 E
Eo ≃	50	43.28 N	7.03 W
Eolie, Isole II	46	38.30 N	15.00 E
Épernay	42	49.03 N	3.57 E
Épinal	42	48.11 N	6.27 E
Epping	32	51.43 N	0.07 E
Epsom	32	51.20 N	0.16 W
Equatorial Guinea □[1]	100	2.00 N	9.00 E
Erba	46	45.48 N	9.15 E
Erciyeş Dağı ▲	20	38.32 N	35.28 E
Érd	36	47.23 N	18.56 E
Erdek	54	40.24 N	27.48 E
Erding	36	48.18 N	11.54 E
Erebus, Mount ▲	167	77.32 S	167.09 E
Erft ≃	36	51.11 N	6.44 E
Erfurt	36	50.58 N	11.01 E
Ergene ≃	54	41.01 N	26.22 E
Erges (Erjas) ≃	50	39.40 N	7.01 E
Erice	46	38.02 N	12.36 E
Erie	162	42.08 N	80.04 W
Erie, Lake ◎	162	42.15 N	81.00 W
Erímanthos ▲	54	37.59 N	21.51 E
Erjas (Erges) ≃	50	39.40 N	7.01 W
Erkelenz	36	51.05 N	9.19 E
Erlangen	36	49.36 N	11.01 E
Ermelo	104	26.34 S	29.58 E
Ermoúpolis	54	37.26 N	24.56 E
Erne, Lower Lough ◎	32	54.10 N	7.30 W
Erne, Upper Lough ◎	32	54.20 N	7.30 W
Eromanga I	112	18.45 S	169.05 E
Erzgebirge (Krušné hory) ⛰	36	50.30 N	13.10 E
Erzincan	20	39.44 N	39.29 E
Erzurum	20	39.55 N	41.17 E
Esbjerg	28	55.28 N	8.27 E
Esca ≃	50	42.37 N	1.03 W
Escarpada Point ➤	82	18.31 N	122.13 E
Escaut (Schelde) ≃	36	51.22 N	4.15 E
Esch-sur-Alzette	36	49.30 N	5.59 E
Eschwege	36	51.11 N	10.04 E
Eschweiler	36	50.49 N	6.16 E
Escondido	162	33.07 N	117.05 W
Escuintla	130	14.18 N	90.47 W
Escurial, Serra do ▲	144	10.04 S	41.05 W
Eşfahān	84	32.40 N	51.38 E
Eskilstuna	28	59.22 N	16.30 E
Eskişehir	20	39.46 N	30.32 E
Esmeraldas	144	0.59 N	79.42 W
Esmeraldas ≃	144	0.58 N	79.38 W
Espinhaço, Serra do ⛰	144	17.30 S	43.30 W
Espinho	50	41.00 N	8.39 W
Espíritu Santo I	112	15.50 S	166.50 E
Espoo (Esbo)	28	60.13 N	24.40 E
Esquel	146	42.54 S	71.19 W
Essaouira	100	31.30 N	9.47 W
Essen	36	51.28 N	7.01 E
Essequibo ≃	144	6.59 N	58.23 W
Esslingen	36	48.45 N	9.16 E
Est, Cap ➤	104	15.16 S	50.29 E
Est, Pointe de l' ➤	160	49.08 N	61.41 W
Estados, Isla de los I	146	54.47 S	64.15 W
Estats, Pique d' ▲	50	42.40 N	1.24 E
Este	46	45.14 N	11.39 E
Estelí	130	13.05 N	86.23 W
Estepona	50	36.26 N	5.08 W
Estrela ▲	50	40.19 N	7.37 W
Estrela, Serra da ⛰	50	40.20 N	7.38 W
Estremadura □[9]	50	39.15 N	9.10 W
Esztergom	36	47.48 N	18.45 E
Étampes	42	48.26 N	2.09 E
Étaples	42	50.31 N	1.39 E
Ethiopia □[1]	102	9.00 N	39.00 E
Etna, Monte ▲[1]	46	37.46 N	15.00 E
Etoshapan ⊻	104	18.45 S	16.15 E
Ettlingen	36	48.56 N	8.24 E
Eu	42	50.03 N	1.25 E
Eugene	162	44.02 N	123.05 W
Eugenia, Punta ➤	130	27.50 N	115.05 W
Eume ≃	50	43.25 N	8.08 W
Eupen	36	50.38 N	6.02 E
Euphrates (Al-Furāt) (Firat) ≃	84	31.00 N	47.25 E
Eureka	162	40.47 N	124.09 W
Europa, Picos de ⛰	50	43.12 N	4.48 W
Europa Point ➤	50	36.10 N	5.22 W
Euskirchen	36	50.39 N	6.47 E
Eutin	36	54.08 N	10.37 E
Eutsuk Lake ◎	160	53.20 N	126.44 W
Evanston	162	42.03 N	87.42 W
Evansville	162	37.58 N	87.35 W
Everest, Mount (Zhumulangmafeng) ▲	84	27.59 N	86.56 E
Everett	162	47.59 N	122.31 W
Evergem	36	51.07 N	3.42 E
Evesham	32	52.06 N	1.56 W
Évora	50	38.34 N	7.54 W
Évreux	42	49.01 N	1.09 E
Évros (Marica) (Meriç) ≃	54	40.52 N	26.12 E
Évvoia I	54	38.34 N	23.50 E
Exe ≃	32	50.37 N	3.25 W
Executive Committee Range ⛰	167	76.50 S	126.00 W
Exeter	32	50.43 N	3.31 W
Exmouth	32	50.37 N	3.25 W
Extremadura □[9]	50	39.00 N	6.00 W
Exuma Sound Ʉ	130	24.15 N	76.00 W
Eyasi, Lake ◎	104	3.40 S	35.05 E
Eyre North, Lake ◎	116	28.40 S	137.10 E
Eyre South, Lake ◎	116	29.30 S	137.20 E
Ezine	54	39.47 N	26.20 E

F

Name	Page	Lat ° ′	Long ° ′
Fabriano	46	43.20 N	12.54 E
Faddeja, Zaliv C	62	76.40 N	107.20 E
Faenza	46	44.17 N	11.53 E
Faeroe Islands □[2]	20	62.00 N	7.00 W
Fafen ≃	102	6.07 N	44.20 E
Făgăraş	54	45.51 N	24.58 E
Făgăraş, Munţii ⛰	54	45.35 N	25.00 E
Fagersta	28	60.00 N	15.47 E
Faguibine, Lac ◎	100	16.45 N	3.54 W
Fairbanks	162a	64.51 N	147.43 W
Fair Head ➤	32	55.13 N	6.09 W
Fair Isle I	32	59.30 N	1.40 W
Fairweather, Mount ▲	160	58.54 N	137.32 W
Falcon, Cap ➤	50	35.46 N	0.48 W
Falconara Marittima	46	43.37 N	13.24 E
Falémé ≃	100	14.46 N	12.14 W
Falkenberg	28	56.54 N	12.28 E
Falkensee	36	52.33 N	13.04 E
Falkenstein	36	50.29 N	12.22 E
Falkirk	32	56.00 N	3.48 W
Falkland Islands □[2]	146	51.45 S	59.00 W
Falkland Sound Ʉ	146	51.45 S	59.25 W
Falköping	28	58.10 N	13.31 E
Fall River	162	41.43 N	71.08 W
Falmouth	32	50.08 N	5.04 W
False Divi Point ➤	84	15.45 N	80.50 E
Falster I	28	54.48 N	11.58 E
Fălticeni	54	47.28 N	26.18 E
Falun	28	60.36 N	15.38 E
Famatina, Nevado de ⛰	146	29.00 S	67.51 W
Fano	46	43.50 N	13.01 E
Fan-si-pan ▲	82	22.15 N	103.46 E
Faraān, Jazā'ir II	84	16.48 N	41.54 E
Farafangana	104	22.49 S	47.50 E
Farah ≃	84	31.29 N	61.24 E
Farcăul ▲	54	47.56 N	24.27 E
Fareham	32	50.51 N	1.10 W
Farewell, Cape ➤	118	40.30 S	172.41 E
Farewell Spit ➤[2]	118	40.31 S	172.52 E
Fargo	162	46.52 N	96.48 W
Farilhões II	50	39.28 N	9.34 W
Farne Islands II	32	55.38 N	1.38 W
Faro	50	37.01 N	7.56 W
Faro ≃	100	9.21 N	12.55 E
Faro, Punta del ➤	46	38.17 N	15.39 E
Fårön I	28	57.56 N	19.08 E
Farquhar Group II	104	10.10 S	51.10 E
Fartak, Ra's ➤	84	15.38 N	52.15 E
Farvel, Kap ➤	160	59.45 N	44.00 W
Fasano	46	40.50 N	17.22 E
Favara	46	37.19 N	13.40 E
Favignana, Isola I	46	37.56 N	12.19 E
Faxaflói C	26a	64.25 N	23.00 W
Faxälven ≃	28	63.13 N	17.13 E
Fayetteville	162	35.03 N	78.54 W
Fazzān (Fezzan) ◆[1]	102	26.00 N	14.00 E
Fear, Cape ➤	162	33.50 N	77.58 W
Fécamp	42	49.45 N	0.22 E
Fedjadj, Chott el ☷	100	33.55 N	9.10 E
Fehérgyarmat	36	47.58 N	22.32 E
Fehmarn I	36	54.28 N	11.08 E
Fehmarn Belt Ʉ	36	54.35 N	11.15 E
Feia, Lagoa C	144	22.00 S	41.20 W
Feira de Santana	144	12.15 S	38.57 W
Feistritz ≃	36	47.01 N	16.08 E
Feldkirch	36	47.14 N	9.36 E
Felixstowe	32	51.58 N	1.20 E
Fellbach	36	48.48 N	9.15 E
Feltre	46	46.01 N	11.54 E
Femunden ◎	28	62.12 N	11.52 E
Fergana	62	40.23 N	71.46 E
Ferlo, Vallée du V	100	15.42 N	15.30 W
Fermo	46	43.09 N	13.43 E
Fernán-Núñez	50	37.40 N	4.43 W
Ferrara	46	44.50 N	11.35 E
Ferrat, Cap ➤	50	35.54 N	0.23 W
Ferrato, Capo ➤	46	39.18 N	9.38 E
Ferret, Cap ➤	42	44.37 N	1.15 W
Fès	100	34.05 N	4.57 W
Feteşti	54	44.23 N	27.50 E
Fethiye	54	36.37 N	29.07 E
Feyẕābād	84	35.01 N	58.46 E
Fianarantsoa	104	21.26 S	47.05 E
Fichtelberg ▲	36	50.26 N	12.57 E
Fichtelgebirge ⛰	36	50.26 N	12.57 E
Fidenza	46	44.52 N	10.03 E
Fier	54	40.43 N	19.34 E
Figueira da Foz	50	40.09 N	8.52 W
Figueras	50	42.16 N	2.58 E
Figuig	100	32.10 N	1.15 W
Fiji □[1]	111	18.00 S	175.00 E
Filchner Ice Shelf ⩍	167	79.00 S	40.00 W
Filicudi, Isola I	46	38.35 N	14.34 E
Fimi ≃	104	3.01 S	16.58 E
Finale Ligure	46	44.10 N	8.20 E
Finisterre, Cabo de ➤	50	42.53 N	9.16 W
Finland □[1]	26	64.00 N	26.00 E
Finland, Gulf of C	26	60.00 N	27.00 E
Finlay ≃	160	57.00 N	125.05 W
Finn ≃	32	54.50 N	7.29 W
Finspång	28	58.43 N	15.47 E
Finsterwalde	36	51.38 N	13.42 E
Fiora ≃	46	42.20 N	11.34 E
Firenze (Florence)	46	43.46 N	11.15 E
Firminy	42	45.23 N	4.18 E
Firth ≃	162a	69.32 N	139.22 W
Fischbacher Alpen ⛰	36	47.28 N	15.30 E
Fish ≃	104	28.07 S	17.45 E
Flagstaff	162	35.12 N	111.39 W
Flamborough Head ➤	32	54.07 N	0.04 W
Fläming ◆[1]	36	52.00 N	12.30 E
Flattery, Cape ➤	162	48.23 N	124.43 W
Fleetwood	32	53.56 N	3.01 W
Flensburg	36	54.47 N	9.26 E
Flint, Wales, U.K.	32	53.15 N	3.07 W
Flint, Mich., U.S.	162	43.01 N	83.41 W
Flint ≃	162	30.52 N	84.33 W
Florence	162	34.49 N	87.40 W
Florencia	144	1.36 N	75.36 W
Flores I	82	8.30 S	121.00 E
Floriano	144	6.47 S	43.01 W
Florida □[3]	162	28.00 N	82.00 W
Florida, Straits of Ʉ	130	25.00 N	79.45 W
Florida Keys II	162	24.45 N	81.00 W
Floridia	46	37.04 N	15.10 E
Flórina	54	40.47 N	21.24 E
Flumen ≃	50	41.43 N	0.09 W
Flumendosa ≃	46	39.26 N	9.38 E
Fluvia ≃	50	42.12 N	3.07 E
Foča	54	43.31 N	18.46 E
Focşani	54	45.41 N	27.11 E
Foggia	46	41.27 N	15.34 E
Fogo Island I	160	49.40 N	54.13 W
Fohnsdorf	36	47.13 N	14.41 E
Föhr I	36	54.43 N	8.30 E
Foia ▲	50	37.19 N	8.36 W
Foix ◆[1]	42	43.00 N	1.40 E
Foligno	46	42.57 N	12.42 E
Folkestone	32	51.05 N	1.11 E
Follonica, Golfo di C	46	42.54 N	10.43 E
Fond du Lac	162	43.47 N	88.27 W
Fondi	46	41.21 N	13.25 E
Fontainebleau	42	48.24 N	2.42 E
Fontenay-le-Comte	42	46.28 N	0.48 W
Forbach	42	49.11 N	6.54 E
Forchheim	36	49.43 N	11.04 E
Forel, Mont ▲	160	67.00 N	37.00 W
Forez, Monts du ⛰	42	45.35 N	3.48 E
Forggensee ◎	36	47.36 N	10.44 E
Forlì	46	44.13 N	12.03 E
Formby Point ➤	32	53.33 N	3.06 W
Formia	46	41.15 N	13.37 E
Formosa	146	26.11 S	58.11 W
Forst	36	51.44 N	14.39 E
Fortaleza	144	3.43 S	38.30 W
Fort Collins	162	40.35 N	105.05 W
Fort-Dauphin	104	25.02 S	47.00 E
Fort-de-France	130	14.36 N	61.05 W
Fort Dodge	162	42.30 N	94.10 W
Forth, Firth of C[1]	32	56.05 N	2.55 W
Fort Lauderdale	162	26.07 N	80.08 W
Fort McPherson	160	67.27 N	134.53 W
Fort Myers	162	26.37 N	81.54 W
Fort Pierce	162	27.27 N	80.20 W
Fort Portal	104	0.40 N	30.17 E
Fort Simpson	160	61.52 N	121.23 W
Fort Smith, N.W. Ter., Can.	160	60.00 N	111.53 W
Fort Smith, Ark., U.S.	162	35.23 N	94.25 W
Fort Victoria	104	20.05 S	30.50 E
Fort Wayne	162	41.04 N	85.09 W
Fort Worth	162	32.45 N	97.20 W
Foshan	80	23.03 N	113.09 E
Fossano	46	44.33 N	7.43 E
Foster, Mount ▲	162a	59.48 N	135.29 W
Fougères	42	48.21 N	1.12 W
Foulness Island I	32	51.36 N	0.55 E
Foumban	100	5.43 N	10.55 E
Foumbouni	104	11.50 S	43.30 E
Fourmies	42	50.00 N	4.03 E
Fouta Djallon ◆[1]	100	11.30 N	12.30 W
Foveaux Strait Ʉ	118	46.35 S	168.00 E
Foxe Basin C	160	68.25 N	77.00 W
Foxe Channel Ʉ	160	64.30 N	80.00 W
Foxen ◎	28	59.23 N	11.52 E
Foxe Peninsula ➤[1]	160	65.00 N	76.00 W
Foyle, Lough ◎	32	55.07 N	7.08 W
Fraïn, Chott el ◎	50	35.57 N	5.38 E
Franca	144	20.32 S	47.24 W
Francavilla Fontana	46	40.31 N	17.35 E
France □[1]	42	46.00 N	2.00 E
Frances Lake ◎	160	61.25 N	129.30 W
Francis Case, Lake ◎[1]	162	43.15 N	99.00 W
Francistown	104	21.11 S	27.32 E
Francofonte	46	37.13 N	14.53 E
Francs Peak ▲	162	43.58 N	109.20 W
Frankenberg	36	50.54 N	13.01 E
Frankfort	162	38.12 N	84.52 W
Frankfurt am Main	36	50.07 N	8.40 E
Frankfurt an der Oder	36	52.20 N	14.33 E
Fränkische Alb ⛰	36	49.00 N	11.30 E
Frascati	46	41.48 N	12.41 E
Fraser ≃	160	49.09 N	123.12 W
Fraserburgh	32	57.42 N	2.00 W
Frauenfeld	42	47.34 N	8.54 E
Fredericia	28	55.35 N	9.46 E
Fredericton	160	45.58 N	66.39 W
Frederikshavn	28	57.26 N	10.32 E
Fredrikstad	28	59.13 N	10.57 E
Freeport	130	26.30 N	78.45 W
Freetown	100	8.30 N	13.15 W
Fregenal de la Sierra	50	38.10 N	6.39 W
Freiberg	36	50.54 N	13.20 E
Freiburg [im Breisgau]	36	47.59 N	7.51 E
Freising	36	48.23 N	11.44 E
Freital	36	51.00 N	13.39 E
Fréjus	42	43.26 N	6.44 E
Fremantle	116	32.03 S	115.45 E
French Guiana □[2]	144	4.00 N	53.00 W
French Polynesia □[2]	10	15.00 S	140.00 W
Fresnillo	130	23.10 N	102.53 W
Fresno	162	36.45 N	119.45 W
Freudenstadt	36	48.28 N	8.25 E
Freycinet Peninsula ➤[1]	116	42.13 S	148.18 E
Fria, Cape ➤	104	18.30 S	12.01 E
Fribourg (Freiburg)	42	46.48 N	7.09 E
Friedberg	36	50.20 N	8.45 E
Friedrichshafen	36	47.39 N	9.28 E
Frio, Cabo ➤	144	22.53 S	42.00 W
Frisian Islands II	20	53.35 N	6.40 E
Friza, Proliv Ʉ	64	45.30 N	149.10 E
Frobisher Bay	160	63.44 N	68.28 W
Frome	32	51.14 N	2.20 W
Frome, Lake ◎	116	30.48 S	139.48 E
Frosinone	46	41.38 N	13.19 E
Frunze	62	42.54 N	74.36 E
Frýdek-Místek	36	49.41 N	18.22 E
Fucino, Conca del ⊻	46	42.01 N	13.31 E
Fuerte ≃	130	25.54 N	109.22 W
Fugløysund Ʉ	26	70.12 N	20.20 E
Fuji	80	35.09 N	138.39 E
Fuji-san ▲[1]	80	35.22 N	138.44 E
Fukui	80	36.04 N	136.13 E
Fukuoka	80	33.35 N	130.24 E
Fukushima	80	37.45 N	140.28 E
Fūlādī, Kūh-e ▲	84	34.38 N	67.32 E
Fulda	36	50.33 N	9.41 E
Fulda ≃	36	51.25 N	9.39 E
Funchal	100	32.38 N	16.54 W
Fundy, Bay of C	160	45.00 N	66.00 W
Furnas, Reprêsa de ◎[1]	144	20.45 S	46.00 W
Furneaux Group II	116	40.10 S	148.05 E
Fürstenfeldbruck	36	48.10 N	11.15 E
Fürstenwalde	36	52.21 N	14.04 E
Fürth	36	49.28 N	10.59 E
Fushun	80	41.52 N	123.53 E
Füssen	36	47.34 N	10.42 E
Fuxinshi	80	42.03 N	121.46 E
Fuzhou	80	26.06 N	119.17 E
Fyn I	28	55.20 N	10.30 E

G

Name	Page	Lat ° ′	Long ° ′
Gabas ≃	42	43.46 N	0.42 W
Gabès	100	33.53 N	10.07 E
Gabès, Golfe de C	100	34.00 N	10.25 E
Gabon □[1]	104	1.00 S	11.45 E
Gaborone	104	24.45 S	25.55 E
Gabrovo	54	42.52 N	25.19 E
Gadsden	162	34.02 N	86.02 W
Gaeta	46	41.12 N	13.35 E
Gaeta, Golfo di C	46	41.06 N	13.30 E
Gafsa	100	34.25 N	8.48 E
Gaggenau	36	48.48 N	8.19 E
Gagnoa	100	6.08 N	5.56 W
Gail ≃	36	46.36 N	13.53 E
Gainesville	162	29.40 N	82.20 W
Gainsborough	32	53.24 N	0.46 W
Gairdner, Lake ◎	116	31.35 S	136.00 E
Gal, Punta de ➤	50	39.10 N	1.05 E
Galán, Cerro ▲	146	25.55 S	66.52 W
Galana ≃	104	3.09 S	40.08 E
Galashiels	32	55.37 N	2.49 W
Galaţi	54	45.26 N	28.03 E
Galatina	46	40.10 N	18.10 E
Galera, Punta ➤	146	39.59 S	73.43 W
Galesburg	162	40.57 N	90.22 W
Galicia □[9]	50	43.00 N	8.00 W
Galka'yo	102	6.49 N	47.23 E
Gallarate	46	45.40 N	8.47 E
Galle	84	6.02 N	80.13 E
Gallinas, Punta ➤	144	12.28 N	71.40 W
Gallipoli	46	40.03 N	17.58 E
Gällivare	26	67.07 N	20.45 E
Gallo, Capo ➤	46	38.13 N	13.19 E
Gallura ◆[1]	46	41.05 N	9.15 E
Galveston	162	29.18 N	94.48 W
Galway	32	53.16 N	9.03 W
Gambia □[1]	100	13.30 N	15.30 W
Gambia (Gambie) ≃	100	13.28 N	16.34 W
Ganderkesee	36	53.02 N	8.32 E
Gandía	50	38.58 N	0.11 W
Gangdisishan ▲	80	31.29 N	80.45 E
Ganges (Ganga) (Padma) ≃	84	23.22 N	90.32 E
Gannett Peak ▲	162	43.11 N	109.39 W
Ganos Dağı ▲	54	40.47 N	27.16 E
Ganzhou	80	25.54 N	114.55 E
Gao	100	16.16 N	0.03 W
Gap	42	44.34 N	6.05 E
Garanhuns	144	8.54 S	36.29 W
García de Sola, Embalse de ◎[1]	50	39.15 N	5.05 W
Garda, Lago di ◎	46	45.40 N	10.41 E
Gardelegen	36	52.31 N	11.23 E
Gardone Val Trompia	46	45.41 N	10.11 E
Gardunha, Serra da ⛰	50	40.05 N	7.31 W
Gargano, Testa del ➤	46	41.49 N	16.12 E
Garmisch-Partenkirchen	36	47.29 N	11.05 E
Garonne ≃	42	45.02 N	0.36 W
Gartempe ≃	42	46.48 N	0.50 E
Gary	162	41.36 N	87.20 W
Gash (Al-Qash) ≃	102	16.48 N	35.51 E
Gastonia	162	35.16 N	81.11 W
Gatčina	26	59.34 N	30.08 E
Gateshead	32	54.58 N	1.37 W
Gatineau ≃	160	45.27 N	75.40 W
Gatooma	104	18.21 S	29.55 E
Gausta ▲	28	59.50 N	8.35 E
Gavá	50	41.18 N	2.01 E
Gave d'Aspe ≃	42	43.12 N	0.36 W
Gävle	28	60.40 N	17.10 E
Gaya	84	24.48 N	85.03 E
Gaziantep	20	37.05 N	37.22 E
Gdańsk (Danzig)	36	54.23 N	18.40 E
Gdynia	36	54.32 N	18.33 E
Gêba ≃	100	11.46 N	15.36 W
Gebze	54	40.48 N	29.25 E
Gediz ≃	54	38.35 N	26.48 E
Geel	36	51.10 N	5.00 E
Geelong	116	38.08 S	144.21 E
Geesthacht	36	53.26 N	10.22 E
Geislingen	36	48.37 N	9.51 E
Gejiu (Kokiu)	80	23.22 N	103.06 E
Gela	46	37.03 N	14.15 E
Gela, Golfo di C	46	37.00 N	14.10 E
Gelai ▲[1]	104	2.33 S	36.05 E
Geleen	36	50.58 N	5.52 E
Gelibolu	54	40.24 N	26.40 E
Gelibolu Yarımadası (Gallipoli Peninsula) ➤[1]	54	40.20 N	26.30 E
Gélise ≃	42	44.11 N	0.17 E
Gelsenkirchen	36	51.31 N	7.07 E
Gemlik	54	40.26 N	29.09 E
Genale ≃	102	5.43 N	40.53 E
General Carrera, Lago (Lago Buenos Aires) ◎	146	46.35 S	72.00 W
General Roca	146	39.02 S	67.35 W
Geneva, Lake ◎	42	46.25 N	6.30 E
Genève	42	46.12 N	6.09 E
Genil ≃	50	37.42 N	5.19 W
Genk	36	50.58 N	5.30 E
Gennargentu, Monti del ⛰	46	39.59 N	9.19 E
Genova (Genoa)	46	44.25 N	8.57 E
Genova, Golfo di C	46	44.10 N	8.55 E
Gent (Gand)	36	51.03 N	3.43 E
Genthin	36	52.24 N	12.09 E
Geographe Bay C	116	33.35 S	115.15 E
George ≃	160	58.49 N	66.10 W
George, Lake ◎	104	0.00 N	30.12 E
Georgetown, Cay. Is.	130	19.18 N	81.23 W
Georgetown, Gam.	100	13.30 N	14.47 W
Georgetown, Guy.	144	6.48 N	58.10 W
Georgia □[3]	162	32.50 N	83.15 W
Georgian Bay C	160	45.15 N	80.50 W
Gera	36	50.52 N	12.04 E
Gerlachovský štít ▲	36	49.12 N	20.08 E
German Democratic Republic (Deutsche Demokratische Republik) □[1]	36	52.00 N	12.30 E
Germany, Federal Republic of (Bundesrepublik Deutschland) □[1]	36	51.00 N	9.00 E
Germiston	104	26.15 S	28.05 E
Gerona	50	41.59 N	2.49 E
Gerrei ◆[1]	46	39.28 N	9.20 E
Gers ≃	42	44.09 N	0.39 E
Getafe	50	40.18 N	3.43 W
Gévora ≃	50	38.53 N	6.57 W
Geyser, Banc du ✧[2]	104	12.25 S	46.25 E
Ghana □[1]	100	8.00 N	2.00 W
Ghardaïa	100	32.31 N	3.37 E
Għawdex I	46	36.03 N	14.15 E
Ghazāl, Baḥr al- ≃	102	9.31 N	30.25 E
Ghazal, Baḥr el ≃	102	13.01 N	15.28 E
Ghazaouet	50	35.06 N	1.51 W
Ghaznī	84	33.33 N	68.26 E
Ghazzah	84	31.30 N	34.28 E
Gheorghe Gheorghiu-Dej	54	46.14 N	26.44 E
Gheorgheni	54	46.43 N	25.36 E
Gia-dinh	82	10.48 N	106.42 E
Gibraltar	50	36.09 N	5.21 W
Gibraltar □[2]	50	36.11 N	5.22 W
Gibraltar, Strait of (Estrecho de Gibraltar) Ʉ	50	35.57 N	5.36 W
Gibraltar Point ➤	32	53.05 N	0.19 E
Gien	42	47.42 N	2.38 E
Giessen	36	50.35 N	8.40 E
Gifhorn	36	52.29 N	10.33 E
Gifu	80	35.25 N	136.45 E
Giglio, Isola del I	46	42.21 N	10.54 E
Gijón	50	43.32 N	5.40 W
Gilbert Islands □[2]	10	4.00 S	175.00 E
Gilgit ≃	84	35.44 N	74.38 E
Gillingham	32	51.24 N	0.33 E
Gilo ≃	102	8.10 N	33.15 E
Giluwe, Mount ▲	116a	6.05 S	143.50 E
Gimone ≃	42	44.00 N	1.06 E
Ginosa	46	40.34 N	16.46 E
Gioia del Colle	46	40.48 N	16.56 E
Gioia Tauro	46	38.26 N	15.54 E
Girardot	144	4.18 N	74.48 W
Gironde C[1]	42	45.20 N	0.45 W
Girou ≃	42	43.46 N	1.23 E
Gisborne	118	38.40 S	178.01 E
Gisenyi	104	1.42 S	29.15 E
Gitega	104	3.26 S	29.56 E
Giugliano [in Campania]	46	40.56 N	14.12 E
Giulianova	46	42.45 N	13.57 E
Giurgiu	54	43.53 N	25.57 E
Givors	42	45.35 N	4.46 E
Gizo	114	8.06 S	156.51 E
Giżycko	36	54.03 N	21.47 E
Gjelma	102	36.28 N	7.26 E
Gjirokastër	54	40.05 N	20.10 E
Gjøvik	28	60.48 N	10.42 E
Gjuhëzës, Kep i ➤	54	40.25 N	19.18 E
Glace Bay	160	46.12 N	59.57 W
Gladbeck	36	51.34 N	6.59 E
Glåma ≃	28	59.12 N	10.57 E
Glarner Alpen ⛰	42	46.55 N	9.00 E
Glasgow	32	55.53 N	4.15 W
Glas Maol ▲	32	56.52 N	3.22 W
Glauchau	36	50.49 N	12.32 E
Glazov	26	58.09 N	52.40 E
Gleinalpe ⛰	36	47.15 N	15.03 E
Glens Falls	162	43.19 N	73.39 W
Glittertinden ▲	28	61.39 N	8.33 E
Gliwice (Gleiwitz)	36	50.17 N	18.40 E
Gliwicki, Kanał ☲	36	50.22 N	18.05 E
Głogów	36	51.40 N	16.05 E
Gloucester	32	51.53 N	2.14 W
Gloucestershire □[6]	32	51.47 N	2.15 W
Głowno	36	51.58 N	19.44 E
Głuchołazy	36	50.20 N	17.22 E
Glückstadt	36	53.47 N	9.25 E
Gmunden	36	47.55 N	13.48 E
Gniezno	36	52.31 N	17.37 E
Gnjilane	54	42.28 N	21.29 E
Gobabis	104	22.30 S	18.58 E
Gobi ◆[2]	80	43.00 N	105.00 E
Goce Delčev	54	41.34 N	23.44 E
Goch	36	51.41 N	6.10 E
Godāvari ≃	84	17.00 N	81.45 E
Gödöllő	36	47.36 N	19.22 E
Godoy Cruz	146	32.55 S	68.50 W
Gods ≃	160	56.22 N	92.51 W
Godthåb	160	64.11 N	51.44 W
Godwin Austen (K2) ▲	84	35.53 N	76.30 E
Goes	36	51.30 N	3.54 E
Goiana	144	7.33 S	34.59 W
Goiânia	144	16.40 S	49.16 W
Gökçeada I	54	40.10 N	25.50 E
Gölcük	54	40.44 N	29.48 E
Goleniów	36	53.36 N	14.50 E
Golfito	130	8.38 N	83.11 W
Goljama Kamčija ≃	54	43.03 N	27.29 E
Golo ≃	42	42.31 N	9.32 E
Gombe ≃	104	4.38 S	31.40 E
Gomel'	62	52.25 N	31.00 E
Gómez Palacio	130	25.34 N	103.30 W
Gonaïves	130	19.27 N	72.41 W
Gonder	102	12.40 N	37.30 E
Gondomar	50	41.09 N	8.32 W
Gönen	54	40.06 N	27.39 E
Gonggashan ▲	80	29.35 N	101.51 E
Gonggeershan ▲	80	38.37 N	75.20 E
Gongola ≃	100	9.30 N	12.04 E
Good Hope, Cape of ➤	104	34.24 S	18.30 E
Good Hope Mountain ▲	160	51.09 N	124.10 W
Goole	32	53.42 N	0.52 W
Göppingen	36	48.42 N	9.40 E
Gorakhpur	84	26.45 N	83.22 E
Gorda, Punta ➤	130	22.24 N	82.10 W
Gore	102	8.08 N	35.33 E
Gorinchem	36	51.50 N	5.00 E
Gorizia	46	45.57 N	13.38 E
Gor'kij (Gorky)	26	56.20 N	44.00 E
Gorlice	36	49.40 N	21.10 E
Görlitz	36	53.24 N	13.54 E
Gorlovka	62	48.18 N	38.03 E
Gorna Orjahovica	54	43.07 N	25.41 E
Goro	112	22.16 S	167.02 E
Gorontalo	82	0.33 N	123.03 E
Gorul, Muntele ▲	54	45.48 N	26.25 E
Gorzów Wielkopolski (Landsberg an der Warthe)	36	52.44 N	15.15 E
Goslar	36	51.54 N	10.25 E
Gostivar	54	41.47 N	20.54 E
Gostyń	36	51.53 N	17.00 E
Gostynin	36	52.26 N	19.29 E
Göta älv ≃	26	57.42 N	11.52 E
Göta kanal ☲	28	58.50 N	13.58 E
Göteborg (Gothenburg)	28	57.43 N	11.58 E
Gotha	36	50.57 N	10.41 E
Gotland I	28	57.30 N	18.33 E
Gotska Sandön I	28	58.23 N	19.16 E

Name	Page	Lat ° ′	Long ° ′
Göttingen	36	51.32 N	9.55 E
Gottwaldov	36	49.13 N	17.41 E
Gouda	36	52.01 N	4.43 E
Gouin, Réservoir ◎[1]	160	48.38 N	74.54 W
Goulburn	116	34.45 S	149.43 E
Goundam	100	16.25 N	3.40 W
Governador Valadares	144	18.51 S	41.56 W
Goya	146	29.08 S	59.16 W
Graaff-Reinet	104	32.14 S	24.32 E
Gračanica	54	44.42 N	18.19 E
Grado	46	45.40 N	13.23 E
Grafton	116	29.41 S	152.56 E
Graham Island I	160	53.40 N	132.30 W
Grahamstown	104	33.19 S	26.31 E
Grajewo	36	53.39 N	22.27 E
Grammichele	46	37.13 N	14.38 E
Grampian Mountains ⛰	32	56.45 N	4.00 W
Granada, Esp.	50	37.13 N	3.41 W
Granada, Nic.	130	11.56 N	85.57 W
Granby	160	45.24 N	72.44 W
Gran Canaria I	100	28.00 N	15.36 W
Gran Chaco ≚	146	23.00 S	60.00 W
Grand Bahama I	130	26.38 N	78.25 W
Grand Canal ≋	32	53.21 N	6.14 W
Grand Canyon ∨	162	36.10 N	112.45 W
Grand Cayman I	130	19.20 N	81.15 W
Grande ≈, Bol.	144	15.51 S	64.39 W
Grande ≈, Esp.	50	39.07 N	0.44 W
Grande, Bahía C[3]	146	50.45 S	68.45 W
Grande, Boca ≈[1]	144	8.38 N	60.30 W
Grande, Rio (Bravo del Norte) ≈	162	25.55 N	97.09 W
Grande Comore I	104	11.35 S	43.20 E
Grande do Gurupá, Ilha I	144	1.00 S	51.30 W
Grand Erg de Bilma ✦[2]	100	18.30 N	14.00 E
Grand Erg Occidental ✦[2]	100	30.30 N	0.30 E
Grand Erg Oriental ✦[2]	100	30.30 N	7.00 E
Grandes, Salinas ≚	146	29.37 S	64.56 W
Grand Forks	162	47.55 N	97.03 W
Grand Hers ≈	42	43.47 N	1.20 E
Grand Island	162	40.55 N	98.21 W
Grand Junction	162	39.05 N	108.33 W
Grand Lieu, Lac de ◎	42	47.06 N	1.40 W
Grand Rapids	162	42.58 N	85.40 W
Grand Teton ▲	162	43.44 N	110.48 W
Grand Turk	130	21.28 N	71.08 W
Granitola, Capo ➤	46	37.33 N	12.40 E
Granollers	50	41.37 N	2.18 E
Gran Paradiso ▲	46	45.32 N	7.16 E
Gran Sasso d'Italia ⛰	46	42.27 N	13.42 E
Grantham	32	52.55 N	0.39 W
Grant Range ⛰	162	38.25 N	115.30 W
Granville	42	48.50 N	1.36 W
Grass ≈	160	56.03 N	96.33 W
Grasse	42	43.40 N	6.55 E
Gravina in Puglia	46	40.49 N	16.25 E
Grays Peak ▲	162	39.37 N	105.45 W
Graz	36	47.05 N	15.27 E
Greaca, Lacul ◎	54	44.05 N	26.23 E
Great Abaco I	130	26.28 N	77.05 W
Great Artesian Basin ≚[1]	116	25.00 S	143.00 E
Great Astrolabe Reef ✢[2]	111	18.52 S	178.31 E
Great Australian Bight C[3]	116	35.00 S	130.00 E
Great Barrier Reef ✢[2]	116	18.00 S	145.50 E
Great Basin ≚[1]	162	40.00 N	117.00 W
Great Bear Lake ◎	160	66.00 N	120.00 W
Great Dividing Range ⛰	116	25.00 S	147.00 E
Greater Antilles II	130	20.00 N	74.00 W
Greater Sunda Islands II	82	2.00 S	110.00 E
Great Exuma I	130	23.32 N	75.50 W
Great Falls	162	47.30 N	111.17 W
Great Inagua I	130	21.05 N	73.18 W
Great Indian Desert (Thar Desert) ✦[2]	84	27.00 N	71.00 E
Great Karroo ⛰[1]	104	32.25 S	22.40 E
Great Malvern	32	52.07 N	2.19 W
Great Ruaha ≈	104	7.56 S	37.52 E
Great Salt Lake ◎	162	41.10 N	112.30 W
Great Sandy Desert ✦[2], Austl.	116	21.30 S	125.00 E
Great Sandy Desert ✦[2], Oreg., U.S.	162	43.35 N	120.15 W
Great Slave Lake ◎	160	61.30 N	114.00 W
Great Victoria Desert ✦[2]	116	28.30 S	127.45 E
Great Yarmouth	32	52.37 N	1.44 E
Gréboun, Mont ▲	100	20.00 N	8.35 E
Gredos, Sierra de ⛰	50	40.18 N	5.05 W
Greece (Ellás) □[1]	54	39.00 N	22.00 E
Greeley	162	40.25 N	104.42 W
Green Bay	162	44.30 N	88.01 W
Green Bay C	162	45.00 N	87.30 W
Greenland □[2]	160	70.00 N	40.00 W
Green Mountains ⛰	162	43.45 N	72.45 W
Greenock	32	55.57 N	4.45 W
Greensboro	162	36.04 N	79.47 W
Greenville, Miss., U.S.	162	33.25 N	91.05 W
Greenville, S.C., U.S.	162	34.51 N	82.23 W
Greifswald	36	54.05 N	13.23 E
Greifswalder Bodden C	36	54.15 N	13.35 E
Greiz	36	50.39 N	12.12 E
Grenada □[1]	130	12.07 N	61.40 W
Grenadine Islands II	130	12.40 N	61.15 W
Grenchen	42	47.11 N	7.24 E
Grenoble	42	45.10 N	5.43 E
Greven	36	52.05 N	7.36 E
Grevená	54	40.05 N	21.25 E
Grevenbroich	36	51.05 N	6.35 E
Grevesmühlen	36	53.51 N	11.10 E
Griesheim	36	49.50 N	8.34 E
Grijalva ≈	130	18.36 N	92.39 W
Grim, Cape ➤	116	40.41 S	144.41 E
Grimma	36	51.14 N	12.43 E
Grimmen	36	54.07 N	13.02 E
Grimsby	32	53.35 N	0.05 W
Grimselpass)(	42	46.34 N	8.21 E
Grintavec ▲	46	46.21 N	14.32 E
Grodno	62	53.41 N	23.50 E
Grodzisk Mazowiecki	36	52.07 N	20.37 E
Groix, Île de I	42	47.38 N	3.27 W
Grójec	36	51.52 N	20.52 E
Gronau	36	52.13 N	7.00 E
Groningen	36	53.13 N	6.33 E
Groot-Karasberge ⛰	104	27.20 S	18.40 E
Groot-Kei ≈	104	32.41 S	28.22 E
Groot-Swartberge ⛰	104	33.22 S	22.20 E
Groot-Vis ≈	104	33.30 S	27.08 E
Grootvloer ≚	104	30.00 S	20.40 E
Grossenhain	36	51.17 N	13.31 E
Grosser Arber ▲	36	49.07 N	13.07 E
Grosser Beerberg ▲	36	50.37 N	10.44 E
Grosser Feldberg ▲	36	50.14 N	8.26 E
Grosser Priel ▲	36	47.43 N	14.04 E
Grosseto	46	42.46 N	11.08 E
Grossglockner ▲	36	47.04 N	12.42 E
Grottaglie	46	40.32 N	17.26 E
Groznyj	62	43.20 N	45.42 E
Grudziądz	36	53.29 N	18.45 E
Gryfice	36	53.56 N	15.12 E
Guacanayabo, Golfo de C	130	20.28 N	77.30 W
Guadajira ≈	50	38.52 N	6.41 W
Guadajoz ≈	50	37.50 N	4.51 W
Guadalajara, Esp.	50	40.38 N	3.10 W
Guadalajara, Méx.	130	20.40 N	103.20 W
Guadalamar ≈	50	38.05 N	3.06 W
Guadalaviar ≈	50	40.21 N	1.08 W
Guadalcanal I	114	9.32 S	160.12 E
Guadalén ≈	50	38.05 N	3.32 W
Guadalentín ≈	50	37.59 N	1.04 W
Guadalmena ≈	50	38.19 N	2.56 W
Guadalope ≈	50	41.15 N	0.03 W
Guadalquivir ≈	50	36.47 N	6.22 W
Guadalupe, Sierra de ⛰	50	39.26 N	5.25 W
Guadalupe Peak ▲	162	31.50 N	104.52 W
Guadarrama, Puerto de)(	50	40.43 N	4.10 W
Guadazaón ≈	50	39.42 N	1.36 W
Guadeloupe □[2]	130	16.15 N	61.35 W
Guadiana ≈	50	37.14 N	7.22 W
Guadix	50	37.18 N	3.08 W
Gualdo Tadino	46	43.14 N	12.47 E
Gualeguaychú	146	33.01 S	58.31 W
Guam □[2]	82	13.28 N	144.47 E
Guampí, Sierra de ⛰	144	6.00 N	65.35 W
Guanajuato	130	21.01 N	101.15 W
Guane	130	22.12 N	84.05 W
Guangzhou (Canton)	80	23.06 N	113.16 E
Guantánamo	130	20.08 N	75.12 W
Guarda	50	40.32 N	7.16 W
Guardiato ≈	50	38.20 N	5.22 W
Guareña ≈	50	41.29 N	5.23 W
Guatemala	130	14.38 N	90.31 W
Guatemala □[1]	130	15.30 N	90.15 W
Guaviare ≈	144	4.03 N	67.44 W
Guayaquil	144	2.10 S	79.50 W
Guaymallén	146	32.54 S	68.47 W
Guaymas	130	27.56 N	110.54 W
Gubbio	46	43.21 N	12.35 E
Gubin	36	51.56 N	14.45 E
Gúdar, Sierra de ⛰	50	40.27 N	0.42 W
Gudenå ≈	28	56.29 N	10.13 E
Guebwiller	42	47.55 N	7.12 E
Guelma	100	36.28 N	7.26 E
Guelph	160	43.33 N	80.15 W
Güera	100	20.48 N	17.08 W
Guéret	42	46.10 N	1.52 E
Guernsey □[2]	20	49.28 N	2.35 W
Guernsey I	42	49.27 N	2.35 W
Guge ▲	102	6.10 N	37.26 E
Guildford	32	51.14 N	0.35 W
Guilin	80	25.11 N	110.09 E
Guimarães	50	41.27 N	8.18 W
Guinea □[1]	100	11.00 N	10.00 W
Guinea, Gulf ➤ C	100	2.00 N	2.30 E
Guinea-Bissau □[1]	100	12.00 N	15.00 W
Güines	130	22.50 N	82.02 W
Guingamp	42	48.33 N	3.11 W
Güira de Melena	130	22.48 N	82.30 W
Guiyang	80	26.35 N	106.43 E
Gujrānwāla	84	32.26 N	74.33 E
Gujrāt	84	32.34 N	74.05 E
Gulfport	162	30.22 N	89.06 W
Gulu	102	2.47 N	32.18 E
Gummersbach	36	51.02 N	7.34 E
Gunisao ≈	160	53.54 N	97.58 W
Guntūr	84	16.18 N	80.27 E
Günzburg	36	48.27 N	10.16 E
Gurara ≈	100	8.12 N	6.41 E
Gurghiului, Munții ⛰	54	46.41 N	25.12 E
Gurjev	62	47.07 N	51.56 E
Gurk ≈	36	46.36 N	14.31 E
Gurupi, Serra do ⛰[1]	144	5.00 S	47.30 W
Gurvan Sajchan Uul ⛰	80	43.50 N	103.30 E
Gusau	100	12.12 N	6.40 E
Gus'-Chrustal'nyj	26	55.37 N	40.40 E
Gusev	26	54.36 N	22.12 E
Guspini	46	39.32 N	8.38 E
Gustav Holm, Kap ➤	160	67.00 N	34.00 W
Güstrow	36	53.48 N	12.10 E
Gütersloh	36	51.54 N	8.23 E
Guyana □[1]	144	5.00 N	59.00 W
Gwda ≈	36	53.04 N	16.44 E
Gwelo	104	19.27 S	29.49 E
Gwent □[6]	32	51.43 N	2.57 W
Gwynedd □[6]	32	53.00 N	4.00 W
Gyldenløves Fjord C[2]	160	64.30 N	41.30 W
Gyöngyös	36	47.47 N	19.56 E
Győr	36	47.42 N	17.38 E
Gyula	36	46.39 N	21.17 E
H			
Haar	36	48.06 N	11.44 E
Haarlem	36	52.23 N	4.38 E
Habomai-shoto II	64	43.30 N	146.10 E
Hachinohe	80	40.30 N	141.29 E
Ḥadd, Ra's al- ➤	84	22.32 N	59.48 E
Haderslev	28	55.15 N	9.30 E
Ḥaḍramawt ✦[1]	84	15.00 N	50.00 E
Ḥaḍūr Shu'ayb ▲	102	15.18 N	43.59 E
Haeju	80	38.02 N	125.42 E
Haerbin	80	45.45 N	126.41 E
Hafnarfjörður	26a	64.03 N	21.56 W
Hafun, Ras ➤	102	10.27 N	51.26 E
Hagen	36	51.22 N	7.28 E
Hagenow	36	53.26 N	11.11 E
Hagerstown	162	39.39 N	77.43 W
Haggin, Mount ▲	162	46.05 N	113.05 W
Hague, Cap de la ➤	42	49.43 N	1.57 W
Haguenau	42	48.49 N	7.47 E
Haikou	80	20.06 N	110.21 E
Ḥā'il	84	27.33 N	41.42 E
Hailuoto I	28	65.02 N	24.42 E
Hainandao I	80	19.00 N	109.30 E
Haines Junction	160	60.45 N	137.30 W
Hai-phong	82	20.52 N	106.41 E
Haiti □[1]	130	19.00 N	72.25 W
Hajdúböszörmény	36	47.41 N	21.30 E
Hajdúnánás	36	47.51 N	21.26 E
Hajdúszoboszló	36	47.27 N	21.24 E
Hajnówka	36	52.45 N	23.36 E
Hakodate	80	41.45 N	140.43 E
Ḥalab (Aleppo)	84	36.12 N	37.10 E
Halberstadt	36	51.54 N	11.02 E
Halden	28	59.09 N	11.23 E
Haldensleben	36	52.18 N	11.26 E
Halifax, N.S., Can.	160	44.39 N	63.36 W
Halifax, Eng., U.K.	32	53.44 N	1.52 W
Halla-san ▲	80	33.22 N	126.32 E
Halle, Bel.	36	50.44 N	4.13 E
Halle, D.D.R.	36	51.29 N	11.58 E
Hallein	36	47.41 N	13.06 E
Halligen II	36	54.35 N	8.35 E
Hallstahammar	28	59.37 N	16.13 E
Halmahera I	82	1.00 N	128.00 E
Halmstad	28	56.39 N	12.50 E
Haltern	36	51.46 N	7.10 E
Haltiatunturi ▲	26	69.18 N	21.16 E
Hamadān	84	34.48 N	48.30 E
Ḥamāh	84	35.08 N	36.45 E
Hamamatsu	80	34.42 N	137.44 E
Hamar	28	60.48 N	11.06 E
Hamburg	36	53.33 N	9.59 E
Hämeenlinna	28	61.00 N	24.27 E
Hameln	36	52.06 N	9.21 E
Hamhŭng	80	39.54 N	127.32 E
Hamilton, Ber.	130	32.17 N	64.46 W
Hamilton, Ont., Can.	160	43.15 N	79.51 W
Hamilton, N.Z.	118	37.47 S	175.17 E
Hamilton, Scot., U.K.	32	55.47 N	4.03 W
Hamilton, Ohio, U.S.	162	39.26 N	84.30 W
Hamm	36	51.41 N	7.49 E
Hammamet	100	36.24 N	10.37 E
Hammamet, Golfe de C	46	36.05 N	10.40 E
Hammam Lif	46	36.44 N	10.20 E
Ḥammār, Hawr al- ◎	84	30.50 N	47.10 E
Hammerfest	26	70.40 N	23.42 E
Hampshire □[6]	32	51.05 N	1.15 W
Hampton	162	37.01 N	76.22 W
Hamra, Saguia el ∨	100	27.15 N	13.21 W
Hanang ▲	104	4.26 S	35.24 E
Hanau	36	50.08 N	8.55 E
Handan	80	36.37 N	114.29 E
Handen	28	59.10 N	18.08 E
Handlová	36	48.44 N	18.46 E
Hando	102	10.39 N	51.08 E
Hangzhou	80	30.15 N	120.10 E
Ḥanīsh, Jazā'ir II	84	13.45 N	42.45 E
Hannover	36	52.24 N	9.44 E
Ha-noi	82	21.02 N	105.51 E
Hanzhong	80	32.59 N	107.11 E
Hardangerfjorden C[2]	28	60.10 N	6.00 E
Harderwijk	36	52.21 N	5.36 E
Hareøen I	160	70.25 N	54.50 W
Harer	102	9.18 N	42.08 E
Hargeysa	102	9.30 N	44.03 E
Harīrūd (Tedžen) ≈	84	37.24 N	60.38 E
Harlingen, Ned.	36	53.10 N	5.24 E
Harlingen, Tex., U.S.	162	26.11 N	97.42 W
Harlow	32	51.47 N	0.08 E
Harmanli	54	41.56 N	25.54 E
Harney Peak ▲	162	44.00 N	103.30 W
Härnösand	28	62.38 N	17.56 E
Harper	100	4.25 N	7.43 W
Harrisburg	162	40.16 N	76.52 W
Harrison, Cape ➤	160	54.55 N	57.55 W
Harrogate	32	54.00 N	1.33 W
Harstad	26	68.46 N	16.30 E
Hart ≈	160	65.51 N	137.22 W
Hartford	162	41.46 N	72.41 W
Hartland Point ➤	32	51.02 N	4.31 W
Hartlepool	32	54.42 N	1.11 W
Harts ≈	104	28.24 S	24.17 E
Hārūt ≈	84	31.35 N	61.18 E
Harwich	32	51.57 N	1.17 E
Hase ≈	36	52.41 N	7.18 E
Ḥashā, Jabal al- ▲	84	13.43 N	44.31 E
Haskovo	54	41.56 N	25.33 E
Haslemere	32	51.06 N	0.43 W
Hasselt	36	50.56 N	5.20 E
Hassi el Ghella	50	35.28 N	1.03 W
Hässleholm	28	56.09 N	13.46 E
Hastings, N.Z.	118	39.38 S	176.51 E
Hastings, Eng., U.K.	32	50.51 N	0.36 E
Hathob, Oued el ∨	46	35.23 N	9.32 E
Hatteras, Cape ➤	162	35.13 N	75.32 W
Hattiesburg	162	31.19 N	89.16 W
Hatvan	36	47.40 N	19.41 E
Hat Yai	82	7.01 N	100.28 E
Haugesund	28	59.25 N	5.18 E
Haukivesi ◎	28	62.06 N	28.28 E
Haunstetten	36	48.18 N	10.54 E
Hauraki Gulf C	118	36.20 S	175.05 E
Haut Atlas ⛰	100	31.30 N	6.00 W
Hautes Fagnes ⛰	36	50.30 N	6.05 E
Hautmont	42	50.15 N	3.56 E
Havant	32	50.51 N	0.29 W
Havelland ✦[1]	36	52.25 N	12.45 E
Haverhill	32	50.51 N	0.59 W
Havířov	36	49.47 N	18.27 E
Havlíčkův Brod	36	49.36 N	15.35 E
Hawaii □[3]	162b	20.00 N	157.45 W
Hawaii I	162b	19.30 N	155.30 W
Hawick	32	55.25 N	2.47 W
Hawke Bay C	118	39.20 S	177.30 E
Hay, Mount ▲	162a	59.15 N	137.37 W
Hayange	42	49.20 N	6.03 E
Hayes ≈	160	57.03 N	92.09 W
Hayrabolu	54	41.12 N	27.06 E
Hay River	160	60.51 N	115.40 W
Hazebrouck	42	50.43 N	2.32 E
Hazleton	162	40.58 N	75.59 W
Hebrides II	32	57.00 N	6.30 W
Heerenveen	36	52.57 N	5.55 E
Heerlen	36	50.54 N	5.59 E
Ḥefa	84	32.49 N	35.00 E
Hefei	80	31.51 N	117.17 E
Hegang	80	47.24 N	130.17 E
Heide	36	54.12 N	9.06 E
Heidelberg	36	49.25 N	8.43 E
Heidenheim	36	49.01 N	10.44 E
Heilbronn	36	49.08 N	9.13 E
Heiligenstadt	36	51.23 N	10.09 E
Heilongjiang (Amur) ≈	64	52.56 N	141.10 E
Hekla ▲[1]	26a	64.00 N	19.39 W
Helagsfjället ▲	28	62.55 N	12.27 E
Helena	162	46.36 N	112.01 W
Helensburgh	32	56.01 N	4.44 W
Helgoland I	36	54.12 N	7.53 E
Helgoländer Bucht C	36	54.10 N	8.04 E
Hellín	50	38.31 N	1.41 W
Hell-Ville	104	13.25 S	48.16 E
Helmond	36	51.29 N	5.40 E
Helmstedt	36	52.13 N	11.00 E
Helsingborg	28	56.03 N	12.42 E
Helsingør (Elsinore)	28	56.02 N	12.37 E
Helsinki (Helsingfors)	28	60.10 N	24.58 E
Helska, Mierzeja ➤[2]	36	54.45 N	18.39 E
Helston	32	50.05 N	5.16 W
Hemel Hempstead	32	51.46 N	0.28 W
Hengelo	36	52.15 N	6.45 E
Hengyang	80	26.51 N	112.30 E
Hennebont	42	47.48 N	3.17 W
Hennef	36	50.46 N	7.16 E
Hennigsdorf	36	52.38 N	13.12 E
Henrietta Maria, Cape ➤	160	55.09 N	82.20 W
Henzada	82	17.38 N	95.28 E
Herāt	84	34.20 N	62.07 E
Hérault ≈	42	43.17 N	3.26 E
Hereford	32	52.04 N	2.43 W
Hereford and Worcester □[6]	32	52.10 N	2.30 W
Herford	36	52.06 N	8.40 E
Herisau	42	47.23 N	9.17 E
Hermosillo	130	29.04 N	110.58 W
Hernád (Hornád) ≈	36	47.56 N	21.08 E
Herne	36	51.32 N	7.13 E
Herne Bay	32	51.23 N	1.08 E
Herning	28	56.08 N	8.59 E
Herschel Island I	160	69.35 N	139.05 W
Herstal	36	50.40 N	5.38 E
Hertford	32	51.48 N	0.05 W
Hertfordshire □[6]	32	51.50 N	0.10 W
Hess ≈	160	63.34 N	133.57 W
Hettstedt	36	51.38 N	11.30 E
Heves	36	47.36 N	20.17 E
Heysham	32	54.02 N	2.54 W
Hidalgo del Parral	130	26.56 N	105.40 W
Hienghène	112	20.41 S	164.56 E
High Plains ≚	162	38.30 N	103.00 W
High Point	162	35.58 N	80.01 W
High Wycombe	32	51.38 N	0.46 W
Hiiumaa I	62	58.52 N	22.40 E
Ḥijāz, Jabal al- ⛰	84	19.45 N	41.55 E
Hilden	36	51.10 N	6.56 E
Hildesheim	36	52.09 N	9.57 E
Hillerød	28	55.56 N	12.19 E
Hilo	162b	19.43 N	155.05 W
Hilo Bay C	162b	19.44 N	155.05 W
Hilversum	36	52.14 N	5.10 E
Himalayas ⛰	84	28.00 N	84.00 E
Himeji	80	34.49 N	134.42 E
Ḥimṣ	84	34.44 N	36.43 E
Hindu Kush ⛰	84	36.00 N	71.30 E
Hingol ≈	84	25.23 N	65.28 E
Hinnøya I	26	68.30 N	16.00 E
Hinojosa del Duque	50	38.30 N	5.09 W
Hinterrhein ≈	42	46.49 N	9.25 E
Hirosaki	80	40.35 N	140.28 E
Hiroshima	80	34.24 N	132.27 E
Hirson	42	49.55 N	4.05 E
Hispaniola I	130	19.00 N	71.00 W
Hitachi	80	36.36 N	140.39 E
Hitra I	28	63.33 N	8.45 E
Hjälmaren ◎	28	59.15 N	15.45 E
Hjørring	28	57.28 N	9.59 E
Hlohovec	36	48.25 N	17.47 E
Hnilec ≈	36	48.53 N	21.01 E
Hobart	116	42.53 S	147.19 E
Hoboken	36	51.10 N	4.21 E
Hochalmspitze ▲	36	47.01 N	13.19 E
Hochkönig ▲	36	47.25 N	13.04 E
Hockenheim	36	49.19 N	8.33 E
Hódmezővásárhely	36	46.25 N	20.20 E
Hodna, Chott el ◎	100	35.25 N	4.45 E
Hodna, Monts du ⛰	50	35.50 N	4.50 E
Hodna, Plaine du ≚	50	35.38 N	4.30 E
Hodonín	36	48.51 N	17.08 E
Hof	36	50.18 N	11.55 E
Hofheim in Unterfranken	36	50.08 N	10.31 E
Hofors	28	60.33 N	16.17 E
Hog, Tanjong ➤	82	5.18 N	119.16 E
Hohe Acht ▲	36	50.23 N	7.00 E
Hohenlimburg	36	51.21 N	7.35 E
Hoher Dachstein ▲	36	47.28 N	13.35 E
Hökensås ⛰[2]	28	58.11 N	14.08 E
Hokkaidō I	80	44.00 N	143.00 E
Holbæk	28	55.43 N	11.43 E
Holguín	130	20.53 N	76.15 W
Hollam's Bird Island I	104	24.45 S	14.34 E
Holland	162	42.47 N	86.07 W
Hollywood	162	26.00 N	80.09 W
Holmsjön ◎	28	62.41 N	16.33 E
Holstebro	28	56.21 N	8.38 E
Holsteinsborg	160	66.55 N	53.40 W
Holyhead	32	53.19 N	4.38 W
Holy Island I, Eng., U.K.	32	55.41 N	1.48 W
Holy Island I, Wales, U.K.	32	53.18 N	4.37 W
Holzminden	36	51.50 N	9.27 E
Hombori Tondo ▲	100	15.16 N	1.40 W
Homburg	36	49.19 N	7.20 E
Hondsrug ⛰[2]	36	52.55 N	6.50 E
Honduras □[1]	130	15.00 N	86.30 W
Hønefoss	28	60.10 N	10.18 E
Honfleur	42	49.25 N	0.14 E
Hon-gai	82	20.57 N	107.05 E
Hong Kong □[2]	80	22.15 N	114.10 E
Honguedo, Détroit d' ∪	160	49.15 N	64.00 W
Honiara	114	9.26 S	159.57 E
Honolulu	162b	21.19 N	157.52 W
Honshū I	80	36.00 N	138.00 E
Hoogeveen	36	52.43 N	6.29 E
Hoorn	36	52.38 N	5.04 E
Hope, Ben ▲	32	58.24 N	4.36 W
Hopes Advance, Cap ➤	160	61.04 N	69.34 W
Horgen	42	47.15 N	8.36 E
Horn ➤	26a	66.28 N	22.28 W
Hornád (Hernád) ≈	36	47.56 N	21.08 E
Hornavan ◎	26	66.10 N	17.30 E
Hornomoravský úval ∨	36	49.25 N	17.20 E
Hornos, Cabo de (Cape Horn) ➤	146	55.59 S	67.16 W
Horsens	28	55.52 N	9.52 E
Horsham	32	51.04 N	0.21 W
Hørsholm	28	55.53 N	12.30 E
Horten	28	59.25 N	10.30 E
Horton ≈	160	70.00 N	126.53 W
Hoséré Batandji ▲	100	8.20 N	13.15 E
Hospitalet	50	41.22 N	2.08 E
Hoste, Isla I	146	55.15 S	69.00 W
Hot Springs National Park	162	34.30 N	93.03 W
Houston	162	29.46 N	95.22 W
Hove	32	50.49 N	0.10 W
Howe, Cape ➤	116	37.31 S	149.59 E
Howrah	84	22.35 N	88.20 E
Höxter	36	51.46 N	9.23 E
Hoyerswerda	36	51.26 N	14.14 E
Hradec Králové	36	50.12 N	15.50 E
Hranice	36	49.33 N	17.44 E
Hron ≈	36	47.49 N	18.45 E
Hronov	36	50.29 N	16.12 E
Hrubieszów	36	50.49 N	23.55 E
Hrubý Jeseník ⛰	36	50.00 N	17.20 E
Hsinchu	80	24.48 N	120.58 E
Hsinkao Shan ▲	80	23.28 N	120.57 E
Huacho	144	11.07 S	77.37 W
Huagaruancha, Cerro ▲	144	10.32 S	75.58 W
Huainan	80	32.40 N	117.00 E
Hualien	80	23.58 N	121.36 E
Huallaga ≈	144	5.10 S	75.32 W
Huambo	104	12.44 S	15.47 E
Huancayo	144	12.04 S	75.14 W
Huanghe ≈	80	37.32 N	118.19 E
Huangshi	80	30.13 N	115.05 E
Huánuco	144	9.55 S	76.14 W
Huaraz	144	9.32 S	77.32 W
Huascarán, Nevado ▲	144	9.07 S	77.37 W
Hubli	84	15.20 N	75.08 E
Huddersfield	32	53.39 N	1.47 W
Huddinge	28	59.14 N	17.59 E
Hudiksvall	28	61.44 N	17.07 E
Hudson Bay C	160	60.00 N	86.00 W
Hudson Strait ∪	160	62.30 N	72.00 W
Hue	82	16.28 N	107.36 E
Huehuetenango	130	15.20 N	91.28 W
Huelva	50	37.16 N	6.57 W
Huelva, Río de ≈	50	37.27 N	6.00 W
Huerva ≈	50	41.39 N	0.52 W
Huesca	50	42.08 N	0.25 W
Huhehaote	80	40.51 N	111.40 E
Huila, Nevado del ▲	144	3.00 N	76.00 W
Ḥukayyim, Bi'r al- ⊤[4]	102	31.36 N	23.29 E
Hull	160	45.26 N	75.43 W
Hulunchi ◎	80	49.01 N	117.32 E
Humbe, Serra do ⛰	104	12.13 S	15.25 E
Humber ≈	32	53.40 N	0.10 W
Humberside □[6]	32	53.50 N	0.30 W
Humboldt ≈	162	40.02 N	118.31 W
Humenné	36	48.56 N	21.55 E
Humphreys Peak ▲	162	35.20 N	111.40 W
Húnaflói C	26a	65.50 N	20.50 W
Hunedoara	54	45.45 N	22.54 E
Hungary (Magyarország) □[1]	36	47.00 N	20.00 E
Hŭngnam	80	39.50 N	127.38 E
Hunsberge ⛰	104	27.45 S	17.12 E
Hunsrück ⛰	36	49.50 N	6.40 E
Hunte ≈	36	52.30 N	8.19 E
Huntingdon	32	52.20 N	0.12 W
Huntington	162	38.25 N	82.26 W
Huntsville	162	34.44 N	86.35 W
Hunyani ≈	104	15.37 S	30.39 E
Huon Gulf C	116a	7.10 S	147.25 E
Huron, Lake ◎	162	44.30 N	82.15 W
Hürth	36	50.52 N	6.51 E
Huşi	54	46.40 N	28.04 E
Huskvarna	28	57.48 N	14.16 E
Husum	36	54.28 N	9.03 E
Hutchinson	162	38.05 N	97.56 W
Hüttental	36	50.54 N	8.02 E
Huy	36	50.31 N	5.14 E
Hvannadalshnúkur ▲	26a	64.01 N	16.41 W
Hvar, Otok I	46	43.09 N	16.45 E
Hvarski Kanal ∪	46	43.15 N	16.37 E
Hyderābād, Bhārat	84	17.23 N	78.29 E
Hyderābād, Pāk.	84	25.22 N	68.22 E
Hyères	42	43.07 N	6.07 E
Hyndman Peak ▲	162	43.50 N	114.10 W
Hyvinkää	28	60.38 N	24.52 E
I			
Ialomiţa ≈	54	44.42 N	27.51 E
Ialomiţei, Balta ≣	54	44.30 N	28.00 E
Iaşi	54	47.10 N	27.35 E
Ibadan	100	7.17 N	3.30 E
Ibagué	144	4.27 N	75.14 W
Ibar ≈	54	43.44 N	20.45 E
Ibarra	144	0.21 N	78.07 W
Ibb	84	14.01 N	44.10 E
Ibbenbüren	36	52.16 N	7.43 E
Ibérico, Sistema ⛰	50	41.00 N	2.30 W
Ibiza	50	38.54 N	1.26 E
Ibiza I	50	39.00 N	1.25 E
Ibo	104	12.20 S	40.35 E
Iboundji, Mont ▲	104	1.08 S	11.48 E
Ica	144	14.04 S	75.42 W
Iceland (Ísland) □[1]	26a	65.00 N	18.00 W
Ich Bogd Uul ⛰	80	44.55 N	100.20 E
Ichilo ≈	144	15.57 S	64.42 W
Ichkeul, Garaet ◎	46	37.10 N	9.40 E
Idaho □[3]	162	45.00 N	115.00 W
Idaho Falls	162	43.30 N	112.02 W
Idar-Oberstein	36	49.42 N	7.19 E
Iderijn ≈	80	49.16 N	100.41 E
Idfū	102	24.58 N	32.52 E
Ídhi Óros ▲	54	35.18 N	24.43 E
Ídhra I	54	37.20 N	23.32 E
Ieper	36	50.51 N	2.53 E
Iesi	46	43.31 N	13.14 E
Ife	100	7.30 N	4.30 E
Iforas, Adrar des ⛰	100	20.00 N	2.00 E
Iglesias	46	39.19 N	8.32 E
Iglesiente ✦[1]	46	39.20 N	8.40 E
İğneada Burnu ➤	54	41.54 N	28.03 E
Iguaçu ≈	146	25.36 S	54.36 W
Iguaçu, Saltos do (Iguassu Falls) ↳	146	25.41 S	54.26 W
Iguala	130	18.21 N	99.32 W
Igualada	50	41.35 N	1.38 E
Iguatu	144	6.22 S	39.18 W
Iguidi, Erg ●[8]	100	26.35 N	5.40 W
Iijoki ≈	28	65.20 N	25.17 E
Iivaara ▲[2]	28	65.47 N	29.40 E
Ijebu-Ode	100	6.50 N	3.56 E
Ijill, Kediet ▲	100	22.38 N	12.33 W
IJmuiden	36	52.27 N	4.36 E
IJsselmeer (Zuiderzee) ⊤[2]	36	52.45 N	5.25 E
Ikaría I	54	37.41 N	26.20 E
Ikerre	100	7.31 N	5.14 E
Ila	100	8.01 N	4.55 E
Ilan	80	24.45 N	121.44 E
Iława	36	53.37 N	19.33 E
Île-à-la-Crosse	160	55.27 N	107.53 W
Île-à-la-Crosse, Lac ◎	160	55.40 N	107.45 W
Île Desroches I	104	5.41 S	53.41 E
Ilesha	100	7.38 N	4.45 E
Ilhéus	144	14.49 S	39.02 W
Illampu, Nevado ▲	144	15.50 S	68.34 W
Iller ≈	36	48.23 N	9.58 E
Illimani, Nevado ▲	144	16.39 S	67.48 W
Illinois □[3]	162	40.00 N	89.00 W
Illinois ≈	162	38.58 N	90.27 W
Il'men', Ozero ◎	62	58.17 N	31.20 E
Ilmenau	36	50.41 N	10.55 E
Iloilo	82	10.42 N	122.34 E
Ilorin	100	8.30 N	4.32 E
Imandra, Ozero ◎	62	67.30 N	33.00 E
Imatra	28	61.10 N	28.46 E
Immenstadt	36	47.33 N	10.13 E
Imola	46	44.21 N	11.42 E
Imperia	46	43.53 N	8.03 E
Imperial de Aragón, Canal ≋	50	42.02 N	1.33 W
Inari ◎	26	69.00 N	28.00 E
Inca	50	39.43 N	2.54 E
Inch'ŏn	80	37.28 N	126.38 E
Indalsälven ≈	28	62.31 N	17.27 E
India □[1]	84	20.00 N	77.00 E
Indiana □[3]	162	40.00 N	86.15 W
Indianapolis	162	39.46 N	86.09 W
Indigirka ≈	64	70.48 N	148.54 E
Indispensable Strait ∪	114	9.00 S	160.30 E
Indonesia □[1]	82	5.00 S	120.00 E
Indore	84	22.43 N	75.50 E
Indrāvati ≈	84	18.43 N	80.17 E
Indre ≈	42	47.16 N	0.19 E
Indus ≈	84	24.20 N	67.47 E
İnegöl	54	40.05 N	29.31 E
Ingelheim	36	49.59 N	8.05 E
Ingolstadt	36	48.46 N	11.27 E
Inhaca, Ilha da I	104	26.03 S	32.57 E
Inhambane	104	23.51 S	35.29 E
Inharrime	104	24.29 S	35.01 E
Inírida ≈	144	3.55 N	67.52 W
Inishtrahull ✢[2]	32	55.26 N	7.14 W
Injasuti ▲	104	29.09 S	29.23 E
Inle Lake ◎	82	20.32 N	96.55 E
Inn (En) ≈	42	48.35 N	13.28 E
Innsbruck	36	47.16 N	11.24 E
Innviertel ✦[1]	42	48.10 N	13.15 E
Inowrocław	36	52.48 N	18.15 E
In Salah	100	27.12 N	2.28 E
Inta	26	66.02 N	60.08 E
Interlaken	42	46.41 N	7.51 E
Inthanon, Doi ▲	82	18.35 N	98.29 E
Inuvik	160	68.25 N	133.30 W
Invercargill	118	46.24 S	168.21 E
Inverness	32	57.27 N	4.15 W
Inyangani ▲	104	18.20 S	32.50 E
Ioánnina	54	39.40 N	20.50 E
Ionian Sea ⊤[2]	20	39.00 N	19.00 E
Iónioi Nísoi II	54	38.30 N	20.30 E
Íos I	54	36.42 N	25.24 E
Iowa □[3]	162	42.15 N	93.15 W
Iowa City	162	41.40 N	91.32 W
Ípeiros ✦[1]	54	39.40 N	20.50 E
Ipel'(Ipoly) ≈	36	47.49 N	18.52 E
Ipiales	144	0.50 N	77.37 W
Ipoh	82	4.35 N	101.05 E
Ipswich, Austl.	116	27.36 S	152.46 E
Ipswich, Eng., U.K.	32	52.04 N	1.10 E
Iquitos	144	3.46 S	73.15 W
Iráklion	54	35.20 N	25.09 E
Iran (Īrān) □[1]	84	32.00 N	53.00 E
Iran, Pegunungan ⛰	82	2.05 N	114.55 E
Irapuato	130	20.41 N	101.21 W
Iraq □[1]	84	33.00 N	44.00 E
Irazú, Volcán ▲[1]	130	9.58 N	83.53 W
Irbid	84	32.33 N	35.51 E
Irbīl	84	36.11 N	44.01 E
Ireland □[1]	32	53.00 N	8.00 W
Iri	80	35.56 N	126.57 E
Iringa	104	7.46 S	35.42 E
Irkutsk	64	52.16 N	104.20 E
Iroise C	42	48.15 N	4.55 W
Iron Gate ∨	54	44.41 N	22.31 E
Iron Gate Reservoir ◎[1]	54	44.30 N	22.00 E
Irrawaddy ≈	82	15.50 N	95.06 E
Irtyš ≈	62	61.04 N	68.52 E
Irún	50	43.21 N	1.47 W
Irvine	32	55.37 N	4.40 W
Isabella, Cordillera ⛰	130	13.45 N	85.15 W
Ísafjörður	26a	66.08 N	23.13 W
Isar ≈	36	48.49 N	12.58 E
Ischia	46	40.44 N	13.57 E
Ischia, Isola d' I	46	40.43 N	13.54 E
Ise	80	34.29 N	136.42 E
Iserlohn	36	51.22 N	7.41 E
Isernia	46	41.36 N	14.14 E
Iseyin	100	7.58 N	3.36 E
Ishikari ≈	80	43.15 N	141.23 E
Ishinomaki	80	38.25 N	141.18 E
Isiro	102	2.47 N	27.37 E
Iskâr, Jazovir ◎[1]	54	43.23 N	27.29 E
İskenderun	20	36.37 N	36.07 E
İskenderun Körfezi C	20	36.30 N	35.40 E
Islāmābād	84	33.42 N	73.10 E
Islands, Bay of C	160	49.10 N	58.15 W
Islay I	32	55.46 N	6.10 W
Isle ≈	42	44.55 N	0.15 W
Isle of Man □[2]	32	54.15 N	4.30 W
Isle of Wight □[6]	32	50.40 N	1.20 W
Ismaning	36	48.14 N	11.41 E
Isola della Scala	46	45.16 N	11.00 E
Isola di Capo Rizzuto	46	38.58 N	17.06 E
Isosyöte ▲[2]	28	65.37 N	27.35 E
Isparta	20	37.46 N	30.33 E
Israel □[1]	84	31.30 N	35.00 E

Name	Page	Lat ° ′	Long ° ′
Issoire	42	45.33 N	3.15 E
Issoudun	42	46.57 N	2.00 E
İstanbul	54	41.01 N	28.58 E
İstanbul Boğazı (Bosporus)	54	41.06 N	29.04 E
Istra	46	45.15 N	14.00 E
Istranca Dağları	54	41.50 N	27.30 E
Itabuna	144	14.48 S	39.16 W
Itagüí	144	6.10 N	75.36 W
Itajubá	144	22.26 S	45.27 W
Italy	46	42.50 N	12.50 E
Itapetininga	144	23.36 S	48.03 W
Ithaca	162	42.27 N	76.30 W
Itháki	54	38.24 N	20.42 E
Ituiutaba	144	18.58 S	49.28 W
Ituri	104	1.40 N	27.01 E
Itzehoe	36	53.55 N	9.31 E
Ivangrad	54	42.50 N	19.52 E
Ivano-Frankovsk	62	48.55 N	24.43 E
Ivanovo	26	57.00 N	40.59 E
Ivory Coast	100	8.00 N	5.00 W
Ivrea	46	45.28 N	7.52 E
Iwaki	80	37.03 N	140.55 E
Iwo	100	7.38 N	4.11 E
Iza	54	47.54 N	23.57 E
Izegem	36	50.55 N	3.12 E
Iževsk	26	56.51 N	53.14 E
Ižma	62	65.19 N	52.54 E
İzmir	54	38.25 N	27.09 E
İzmit (Kocaeli)	54	40.46 N	29.55 E
Iznajar, Embalse de	50	37.15 N	4.30 W
İznik Gölü	54	40.26 N	29.30 E
Izozog, Bañados de	144	18.48 S	62.10 W
Izu-shotō	80	32.00 N	140.00 E
J			
Jabalón	50	38.53 N	4.05 W
Jabalpur	84	23.10 N	79.57 E
Jablanica	54	43.07 N	21.57 E
Jablonec nad Nisou	36	50.44 N	15.10 E
Jablonovyj Chrebet (Yablonovy Range)	64	53.30 N	115.00 E
Jaboatão	144	8.07 S	35.01 W
Jacareí	144	23.19 S	45.58 W
Jackson, Mich., U.S.	162	42.15 N	84.24 W
Jackson, Miss., U.S.	162	32.18 N	90.12 W
Jacksonville, Fla., U.S.	162	30.20 N	81.40 W
Jacksonville, N.C., U.S.	162	34.45 N	77.26 W
Jacmel	130	18.14 N	72.32 W
Jacob	104	4.11 S	13.17 E
Jacobābād	84	28.17 N	68.26 E
Jacques-Cartier, Mont	160	48.59 N	65.57 W
Jadebusen	36	53.30 N	8.10 E
J.A.D. Jensens Nunatakker	160	62.45 N	48.00 W
Jaén	50	37.46 N	3.47 W
Jaffna	84	9.40 N	80.00 E
Jagst	36	49.14 N	9.11 E
Jaipur	84	26.56 N	75.50 E
Jajce	46	44.21 N	17.16 E
Jakarta	82	6.10 S	106.48 E
Jakobstad (Pietarsaari)	28	63.40 N	22.42 E
Jakupica	54	41.43 N	21.26 E
Jakutsk	64	62.13 N	129.49 E
Jalālābād	84	34.26 N	70.28 E
Jalapa Enríquez	130	19.32 N	96.55 W
Jalón	50	41.47 N	1.04 W
Jamaica	130	18.15 N	77.30 W
Jamal, Poluostrov	64	70.00 N	70.00 E
Jamantau, Gora	62	54.15 N	58.06 E
Jambes	36	50.28 N	4.52 E
Jambi	82	1.36 S	103.37 E
Jambol	54	42.29 N	26.30 E
Jambongan, Pulau	82	6.40 N	117.27 E
James Bay	160	53.30 N	80.30 W
Jamestown	162	42.06 N	79.14 W
Jammerbugten	28	57.20 N	9.30 E
Jammu and Kashmir	84	35.00 N	76.00 E
Jāmnagar	84	22.28 N	70.04 E
Jamshedpur	84	22.48 N	86.11 E
Jamuna	84	23.51 N	89.45 E
Janesville	162	42.41 N	89.01 W
Janskij Zaliv	64	71.50 N	136.00 E
Jantra	54	43.38 N	25.34 E
Japan	80	36.00 N	138.00 E
Japan, Sea of	80	40.00 N	135.00 E
Jarama	50	40.02 N	3.39 W
Jarocin	36	51.59 N	17.31 E
Jaroměř	36	50.21 N	15.55 E
Jaroslavl'	26	57.37 N	39.52 E
Jarosław	36	50.02 N	22.42 E
Järvenpää	28	60.28 N	25.06 E
Jasło	36	49.45 N	21.29 E
Jason Islands	146	51.05 S	61.00 W
Jászapáti	36	47.31 N	20.09 E
Jat, Uad el	100	26.45 N	13.03 W
Jataí	144	17.53 S	51.43 W
Játiva	50	38.59 N	0.31 W
Jaú	144	22.18 S	48.33 W
Javalambre	50	40.06 N	1.03 W
Javari (Yavarí)	144	4.21 S	70.02 W
Javor	54	44.05 N	18.55 E
Javorníky	36	49.20 N	18.20 E
Jawa (Java)	82	7.30 S	110.00 E
Jawa, Laut (Java Sea)	82	5.00 S	110.00 E
Jawor	36	51.03 N	16.11 E
Jaworzno	36	50.13 N	19.15 E
Jaya, Puncak	82	4.05 S	137.11 E
Jayapura (Sukarnapura)	82	2.32 S	140.42 E
Jędrzejów	36	50.39 N	20.18 E
Jefferson City	162	38.34 N	92.10 W
Jegorjevsk	26	55.23 N	39.02 E
Jekateriny, Proliv	64	53.53 N	140.25 E
Jelec	62	52.37 N	38.30 E
Jelenia Góra (Hirschberg)	36	50.55 N	15.46 E
Jelgava	26	56.39 N	23.42 E
Jelizavety, Mys	64	54.24 N	142.42 E
Jeloguj	64	63.13 N	87.45 E
Jember	82	8.10 S	113.42 E
Jena	36	50.56 N	11.35 E
Jenisej	62	71.50 N	82.40 E
Jenisejskij Kr'až	62	59.00 N	93.00 E
Jenisejskij Zaliv	62	72.30 N	80.00 E
Jequié	144	13.51 S	40.05 W
Jérémie	130	18.39 N	74.07 W
Jerevan	62	40.11 N	44.30 E
Jerez de la Frontera	50	36.41 N	6.08 W
Jerez de los Caballeros	50	38.19 N	6.46 W
Jergeni	62	47.00 N	44.00 E
Jersey	32	49.15 N	2.10 W
Jersey City	162	40.44 N	74.02 W
Jerte	50	39.58 N	6.17 W
Jesenice	46	46.27 N	14.04 E
Jevišovka	36	48.48 N	16.28 E
Jezerce	54	42.26 N	19.49 E
Jhang Maghiāna	84	31.16 N	72.19 E
Jhānsi	84	25.27 N	78.35 E
Jhelum	84	32.56 N	73.44 E
Jiamusi	80	46.50 N	130.21 E
Jiaozuo	80	35.15 N	113.18 E
Jičín	36	50.26 N	15.21 E
Jihlava	36	49.24 N	15.36 E
Jihlava	36	48.55 N	16.37 E
Jijia	54	46.54 N	28.05 E
Jilin	80	43.51 N	126.33 E
Jima	102	7.36 N	36.50 E
Jimbolia	54	45.47 N	20.43 E
Jinan (Tsinan)	80	36.40 N	116.57 E
Jindřichův Hradec	36	49.09 N	15.00 E
Jingdezhen	80	29.16 N	117.11 E
Jinja	104	0.26 N	33.12 E
Jinshajiang	80	28.50 N	104.36 E
Jinzhou	80	41.07 N	121.08 E
Jirjā	102	26.20 N	31.53 E
Jiu	54	43.47 N	23.48 E
Jixi	80	45.17 N	130.59 E
Jizera	36	50.10 N	14.43 E
João Pessoa	144	7.07 S	34.52 W
Jódar	50	37.50 N	3.21 W
Jodhpur	84	26.17 N	73.01 E
Joensuu	28	62.36 N	29.46 E
Johannesburg	104	26.15 S	28.00 E
Johanngeorgenstadt	36	50.26 N	12.43 E
Johnson City	162	36.19 N	82.21 W
Johnstown	162	40.20 N	78.55 W
Johor Baharu	82	1.28 N	103.45 E
Joliet	162	41.32 N	88.05 W
Jolo	82	6.03 N	121.00 E
Jönköping	28	57.47 N	14.11 E
Jonquière	160	48.24 N	71.15 W
Joplin	162	37.06 N	94.31 W
Jordan	84	31.00 N	36.00 E
Jos	100	9.55 N	8.53 E
Joškar-Ola	26	56.38 N	47.52 E
Juan Fernández, Islas	146	33.00 S	80.00 W
Juàzeiro	144	9.25 S	40.30 W
Juàzeiro do Norte	144	7.12 S	39.20 W
Jūbā	102	4.51 N	31.37 E
Juba	104	0.12 N	42.40 E
Juby, Cap	100	27.58 N	12.55 W
Júcar	50	39.09 N	0.14 W
Juchitán	130	16.26 N	95.01 W
Juddah (Jidda)	84	21.30 N	39.12 E
Judenburg	36	47.10 N	14.40 E
Juigalpa	130	12.05 N	85.24 W
Juist	36	53.40 N	7.00 E
Juiz de Fora	144	21.45 S	43.20 W
Juliaca	144	15.30 S	70.08 W
Julian Alps	46	46.00 N	14.00 E
Julianatop	144	3.41 N	56.32 W
Julianehåb	160	60.43 N	46.01 W
Jülich	36	50.55 N	6.21 E
Jullundur	84	31.20 N	75.35 E
Jumentos Cays	130	22.42 N	75.55 W
Jumet	36	50.26 N	4.25 E
Jumilla	50	38.29 N	1.17 W
Jundiaí	144	23.11 S	46.52 W
Juneau	162a	58.20 N	134.27 W
Jungfrau	42	46.32 N	7.58 E
Junín	146	34.35 S	60.57 W
Junín, Lago de	144	11.02 S	76.06 W
Jur	102	8.39 N	29.18 E
Jura	42	46.45 N	6.30 E
Jūrmala	26	56.58 N	23.42 E
Juruá	144	2.37 S	65.44 W
Jüterbog	36	51.59 N	13.04 E
Jutiapa	130	14.17 N	89.54 W
Juticalpa	130	14.42 N	86.15 W
Južno-Sachalinsk	64	46.58 N	142.42 E
Južnyj, Mys	64	57.45 N	156.45 E
Južnyj Bug	62	46.59 N	31.58 E
Jylland	28	56.00 N	9.15 E
Jyväskylä	28	62.14 N	25.44 E
K			
Kaap Plato	104	28.20 S	23.57 E
Kabale	104	1.15 S	29.59 E
Kab-hegy	36	46.58 N	17.30 E
Kabīr Kūh	84	33.25 N	46.45 E
Kabompo	104	14.10 S	23.11 E
Kābul	84	34.30 N	69.11 E
Kabwe (Broken Hill)	104	14.27 S	28.27 E
Kabylie	50	36.30 N	4.30 E
Kadan Kyun	82	12.30 N	98.22 E
Kadeï	102	3.31 N	16.05 E
Kadijevka	62	48.34 N	38.40 E
Kaduna	100	10.33 N	7.27 E
Kaduna	100	8.45 N	5.45 E
Kaédi	100	16.09 N	13.30 W
Kaesŏng	80	37.59 N	126.33 E
Kafirévs, Ákra	54	38.09 N	24.36 E
Kafu	104	1.08 N	31.05 E
Kafue	104	15.56 S	28.55 E
Kagera	104	0.57 S	31.47 E
Kagoshima	80	31.36 N	130.33 E
Kahayan	82	3.20 S	114.04 E
Kahler Asten	36	51.11 N	8.29 E
Kaieteur Fall	144	5.10 N	59.28 W
Kaifeng	80	34.51 N	114.21 E
Kailua	162b	21.24 N	157.44 W
Kailua Kona	162b	19.39 N	155.59 W
Kaïmakchalán	54	40.58 N	21.48 E
Kaiserslautern	36	49.26 N	7.46 E
Kajaani	28	64.14 N	27.41 E
Kalahari Desert	104	24.00 S	21.30 E
Kalámai	54	37.04 N	22.07 E
Kalamariá	54	40.35 N	22.58 E
Kalamazoo	162	42.17 N	85.32 W
Kalb, Ra's al-	84	14.02 N	48.40 E
Kalemi (Albertville)	104	5.56 S	29.12 E
Kalgoorlie	116	30.45 S	121.28 E
Kaliakra, nos	54	43.21 N	28.27 E
Kálimnos	54	36.57 N	26.59 E
Kalinin	26	56.52 N	35.55 E
Kaliningrad (Königsberg), S.S.S.R.	26	54.43 N	20.30 E
Kaliningrad, S.S.S.R.	62	55.55 N	37.49 E
Kalisz	36	51.46 N	18.06 E
Kalixälven	26	65.50 N	23.11 E
Kallavesi	28	62.50 N	27.45 E
Kallsjön	28	63.37 N	13.00 E
Kalmar	28	56.40 N	16.22 E
Kalmarsund	28	56.40 N	16.25 E
Kalničko Gorje	46	46.10 N	16.30 E
Kalocsa	36	46.32 N	18.59 E
Kalpeni Island	84	10.05 N	73.38 E
Kalsūbai	84	19.36 N	73.43 E
Kaluga	26	54.31 N	36.16 E
Kama	62	55.45 N	52.00 E
Kamaishi	80	39.16 N	141.53 E
Kamarān	84	15.21 N	42.34 E
Kamčatka, Poluostrov	64	56.00 N	160.00 E
Kamčatskij Zaliv	64	55.35 N	162.21 E
Kamčija	54	43.02 N	27.53 E
Kamensk-Ural'skij	62	56.28 N	61.54 E
Kamenz	36	51.16 N	14.06 E
Kamienna	36	51.06 N	21.47 E
Kamienna Góra	36	50.47 N	16.01 E
Kamina	104	8.44 S	25.00 E
Kamloops	160	50.40 N	120.20 W
Kampala	104	0.19 N	32.25 E
Kampen	36	52.33 N	5.54 E
Kampinoska, Puszcza	36	52.20 N	20.30 E
Kâmpóng Cham	82	12.00 N	105.27 E
Kâmpŭchéa	82	13.00 N	105.00 E
Kamskoje Vodochranilišče	62	58.52 N	56.15 E
Kamyšin	62	50.06 N	45.24 E
Kanaaupscow	160	53.39 N	77.09 W
Kananga (Luluabourg)	104	5.54 S	22.25 E
Kanazawa	80	36.34 N	136.39 E
Kandalakša	26	67.09 N	32.21 E
Kandik	162a	65.24 N	142.34 W
Kandy	84	7.18 N	80.38 E
Kaneohe	162b	21.25 N	157.48 W
Kanggye	80	40.58 N	126.34 E
Kangnŭng	80	37.45 N	128.54 E
Kanin, Poluostrov	62	68.00 N	45.00 E
Kanin Nos, Mys	62	68.39 N	43.16 E
Kanjiža	54	46.04 N	20.04 E
Kankakee	162	41.07 N	87.52 W
Kankan	100	10.23 N	9.18 W
Kanmaw Kyun	82	11.40 N	98.28 E
Kannapolis	162	35.30 N	80.37 W
Kano	100	12.00 N	8.30 E
Kānpur	84	28.28 N	80.21 E
Kansas	162	38.45 N	98.15 W
Kansas City, Kans., U.S.	162	39.07 N	94.39 W
Kansas City, Mo., U.S.	162	39.05 N	94.35 W
Kanye	104	24.59 S	25.19 E
Kaohsiung	80	22.38 N	120.17 E
Kaokoveld	104	21.00 S	14.20 E
Kaolack	100	14.09 N	16.04 W
Kapaonik	54	43.20 N	20.50 E
Kapfenberg	36	47.26 N	15.18 E
Kapos	36	46.44 N	18.30 E
Kaposvár	36	46.22 N	17.47 E
Kapuas	82	0.25 S	109.40 E
Kapuas Hulu, Pegunungan	82	1.25 N	113.15 E
Kapuskasing	160	49.49 N	82.00 W
Kapuvár	36	47.36 N	17.02 E
Kara-Bogaz-Gol, Zaliv	62	41.00 N	53.15 E
Karabük	20	41.12 N	32.37 E
Karacabey	54	40.13 N	28.21 E
Karāchi	84	24.52 N	67.03 E
Karaganda	62	49.50 N	73.10 E
Karaginskij Zaliv	64	58.50 N	164.00 E
Karagoš, Gora	64	51.44 N	89.24 E
Karakoram Range	84	35.30 N	77.00 E
Karakumskij Kanal	62	37.35 N	61.50 E
Karakumy	62	39.00 N	60.00 E
Karamürsel	54	40.42 N	29.36 E
Karatau, Chrebet	62	43.50 N	68.30 E
Karawanken	46	46.30 N	14.25 E
Karbalā'	84	32.36 N	44.02 E
Karcag	36	47.19 N	20.56 E
Kardhítsa	54	39.21 N	21.55 E
Kârdžali	54	41.39 N	25.22 E
Karhula	28	60.31 N	26.57 E
Kariba, Lake	104	17.00 S	28.00 E
Karimata, Selat (Karimata Strait)	82	2.05 S	108.40 E
Karl-Marx-Stadt (Chemnitz)	36	50.50 N	12.55 E
Karlovac	46	45.29 N	15.34 E
Karlovo	54	42.38 N	24.48 E
Karlovy Vary	36	50.11 N	12.52 E
Karlshamn	28	56.10 N	14.51 E
Karlskoga	28	59.20 N	14.31 E
Karlskrona	28	56.10 N	15.35 E
Karlsöarna	28	57.17 N	17.58 E
Karlsruhe	36	49.03 N	8.24 E
Karlstad	28	59.22 N	13.30 E
Karnāli	84	28.45 N	81.16 E
Karnobat	54	42.39 N	26.59 E
Kárpathos	54	35.40 N	27.10 E
Karpenísion	54	38.55 N	21.40 E
Karrats Isfjord	160	71.20 N	54.00 W
Kars	20	40.36 N	43.05 E
Karşıyaka	54	38.27 N	27.07 E
Karskoje More (Kara Sea)	62	76.00 N	80.00 E
Kartal	54	40.53 N	29.10 E
Kartuzy	36	54.20 N	13.12 E
Karviná	36	49.50 N	13.30 E
Kasai (Cassai)	104	3.06 S	16.57 E
Kashi (Kashgar)	80	39.29 N	75.59 E
Kásos	54	35.22 N	26.56 E
Kasr, Ra's	102	18.02 N	38.35 E
Kassalā	102	15.28 N	36.24 E
Kassel	36	51.19 N	9.29 E
Kastoría	54	40.31 N	21.15 E
Kasūr	84	31.07 N	74.27 E
Kaszuby	36	54.10 N	18.15 E
Katahdin, Mount	162	45.55 N	68.55 W
Katanga Plateau	104	10.30 S	25.30 E
Kateríni	54	40.16 N	22.30 E
Kates Needle	162a	57.03 N	132.03 W
Katherine	116	14.28 S	132.16 E
Kāthiāwār	84	21.58 N	70.30 E
Kātmāndu	84	27.43 N	85.19 E
Katowice	36	50.16 N	19.00 E
Katrīnah, Jabal	102	28.31 N	33.57 E
Katrineholm	28	59.00 N	16.12 E
Katsina	100	13.00 N	7.32 E
Katsina Ala	100	7.45 N	9.05 E
Kattegat	28	57.00 N	11.00 E
Katwijk aan Zee	36	52.13 N	4.24 E
Katzenbuckel	36	49.28 N	9.02 E
Kauai	162b	22.00 N	159.30 W
Kaufbeuren	36	47.53 N	10.37 E
Kau Kau Bay	114	9.42 S	160.40 E
Kaukauveld	104	20.00 S	20.30 E
Kaunas	26	54.54 N	23.54 E
Kavajë	54	41.11 N	19.33 E
Kavála	54	40.56 N	24.25 E
Kavieng	116a	2.35 S	150.50 E
Kavīr, Dasht-e	84	34.40 N	54.30 E
Kawasaki	80	35.32 N	139.43 E
Kawm Umbū	102	24.28 N	32.57 E
Kayes	100	14.27 N	11.26 W
Kayseri	20	38.43 N	35.30 E
Kazan'	26	55.49 N	49.08 E
Kazanlâk	54	42.38 N	25.21 E
Kazbek, Gora	62	42.42 N	44.31 E
Kazincbarcika	36	48.16 N	20.37 E
Kéa	54	37.34 N	24.22 E
Kebnekaise	26	67.53 N	18.33 E
Kecel	36	46.32 N	19.16 E
Kech	84	26.00 N	62.44 E
Kecskemét	36	46.54 N	19.42 E
Kediri	82	7.49 S	112.01 E
Kędzierzyn	36	50.20 N	18.12 E
Keele Peak	160	63.26 N	130.19 W
Keetmanshoop	104	26.36 S	18.08 E
Kefallinía	54	38.15 N	20.35 E
Keflavík	26a	64.02 N	22.36 W
Ke-ga, Mui	82	12.53 N	109.28 E
Keglo, Baie	160	59.10 N	65.50 W
Kehl	36	48.35 N	7.50 E
Kékes	36	47.55 N	20.02 E
Kelamayi	80	45.37 N	84.53 E
Kelang	82	3.02 N	101.27 E
Kelantan	82	6.11 N	102.15 E
Kelbia, Şebkra	46	35.51 N	10.16 E
Keleti-főcsatorna	36	48.01 N	21.20 E
Kelheim	36	48.55 N	11.52 E
Kelibia	46	36.51 N	11.06 E
Keluang	82	2.02 N	103.19 E
Kem'	26	64.57 N	34.36 E
Kemerovo	64	55.20 N	86.05 E
Kemi	28	65.49 N	24.32 E
Kemijärvi	26	66.40 N	27.25 E
Kemijoki	28	65.47 N	24.30 E
Kemmuna	46	36.00 N	14.20 E
Kempen	36	51.22 N	6.25 E
Kempten [allgäu]	36	47.43 N	10.19 E
Kemul, Kong	82	1.52 N	116.11 E
Kendal	32	54.20 N	2.45 W
Kenema	100	7.52 N	11.12 W
Kenitra	100	34.16 N	6.40 W
Kennebec	162	44.00 N	69.50 W
Kennedy, Mount	160	60.30 N	139.00 W
Kenogami	160	51.06 N	84.28 W
Kenosha	162	42.35 N	87.49 W
Kent	32	51.15 N	0.40 E
Kentucky	162	37.30 N	85.15 W
Kenya	104	1.00 N	38.00 E
Kenya, Mount	104	0.10 S	37.20 E
Kępno	36	51.17 N	17.59 E
Kerava	28	60.24 N	25.07 E
Kerč'	62	45.22 N	36.27 E
Kerinci, Gunung	82	1.42 S	101.16 E
Kerkenna, Îles	100	34.44 N	11.12 E
Kérkira (Corfu)	54	39.36 N	19.56 E
Kérkira	54	39.40 N	19.42 E
Kerkrade	36	50.52 N	6.04 E
Kerkrade [-Holz]	36	50.52 N	6.04 E
Kermān	84	30.17 N	57.05 E
Kermānshāh	84	34.19 N	47.04 E
Kerme Körfezi	54	36.50 N	28.00 E
Kerulen (Cherlen) (Kelulunhe)	80	48.48 N	117.00 E
Keşan	54	40.51 N	26.37 E
Keszthely	36	46.46 N	17.15 E
Ketchikan	162a	55.21 N	131.35 W
Kętrzyn (Rastenburg)	36	54.06 N	21.23 E
Kettering	32	52.24 N	0.44 W
Kevelaer	36	51.35 N	6.15 E
Keweenaw Point	162	47.30 N	87.50 W
Key West	162	24.33 N	81.48 W
Kežmarok	36	49.08 N	20.25 E
Khalkís	54	38.28 N	23.36 E
Khambhāt, Gulf of	84	21.00 N	72.30 E
Khānewāl	84	30.18 N	71.56 E
Khanh-hung	82	9.36 N	105.58 E
Khaniá	54	35.31 N	24.02 E
Khark, Jazīreh-ye	84	29.15 N	50.20 E
Khāsh	84	31.11 N	62.05 E
Khersan	84	31.33 N	50.22 E
Khíos	54	38.22 N	26.08 E
Khíos	54	38.22 N	26.00 E
Khon Kaen	82	16.26 N	102.50 E
Khorramshahr	84	30.25 N	48.11 E
Khouribga	100	32.54 N	6.57 W
Khulna	84	22.48 N	89.33 E
Khūryān Mūryān	84	17.30 N	56.00 E
Khyber Pass	84	34.05 N	71.10 E
Kičevo	54	41.31 N	20.57 E
Kiel	36	54.20 N	10.08 E
Kielce	36	50.52 N	20.37 E
Kieler Bucht	36	54.35 N	10.35 E
Kiffa	100	16.37 N	11.24 W
Kifisiá	54	38.04 N	23.48 E
Kigali	104	1.57 S	30.04 E
Kii-suidō	80	33.55 N	134.55 E
Kijev	62	50.26 N	30.31 E
Kijevskoje Vodochranilišče	62	51.00 N	30.25 E
Kikinda	54	45.50 N	20.28 E
Kikládhes	54	37.30 N	25.00 E
Kikwit	104	5.02 S	18.49 E
Kilimanjaro	104	3.04 S	37.22 E
Kilkenny	32	52.39 N	7.15 W
Kilkís	54	41.00 N	22.53 E
Killeen	162	31.08 N	97.44 W
Kilmarnock	32	55.36 N	4.30 W
Kilombero	104	8.31 S	37.22 E
Kiltān	84	11.29 N	73.00 E
Kim	100	5.28 N	11.07 E
Kimberley	104	28.43 S	24.46 E
Kimch'aek	80	40.41 N	129.12 E
Kimry	26	56.52 N	37.21 E
Kinabalu, Gunong	82	6.05 N	116.33 E
Kindia	100	10.04 N	12.51 W
Kindu-Port-Empain	104	2.57 S	25.56 E
Kinel'	26	53.14 N	50.39 E
Kinešma	26	57.26 N	42.09 E
King George Island	167	62.00 S	58.15 W
King's Lynn	32	52.45 N	0.24 E
Kingsport	162	36.32 N	82.33 W
Kingston, Jam.	130	18.00 N	76.48 W
Kingston, Norf. I.	113	29.03 S	167.58 E
Kingston, N.Y., U.S.	162	41.56 N	74.00 W
Kingston upon Hull	32	53.45 N	0.20 W
Kingstown	130	13.09 N	61.14 W
King William Island	160	69.00 N	97.30 W
King William's Town	104	32.51 S	27.22 E
Kinkony, Lac	104	16.08 S	45.50 E
Kinnairds Head	32	57.42 N	2.00 W
Kinshasa (Léopoldville)	104	4.18 S	15.18 E
Kintyre	32	55.32 N	5.35 W
Kinyeti	102	3.57 N	32.54 E
Kipengere Range	104	9.10 S	34.15 E
Kipushi	104	11.46 N	27.14 E
Kira Kira	114	10.27 S	161.55 E
Kirchheim	36	48.10 N	10.30 E
Kirgizskij Chrebet	62	42.30 N	74.00 E
Kırıkkale	20	39.50 N	33.31 E
Kırkağaç	54	39.06 N	27.40 E
Kirkcaldy	32	56.07 N	3.10 W
Kirkland Lake	160	48.09 N	80.02 W
Kırklareli	54	41.44 N	27.12 E
Kirkūk	84	35.28 N	44.28 E
Kirkwall	32	58.59 N	2.58 W
Kirov	26	58.38 N	49.42 E
Kirovabad	62	40.40 N	46.22 E
Kirovakan	62	40.48 N	44.30 E
Kirovograd	62	48.30 N	32.18 E
Kirovsk	26	67.37 N	33.35 E
Kīrthar Range	84	27.00 N	67.10 E
Kiruna	26	67.51 N	20.16 E
Kisangani (Stanleyville)	104	0.30 N	25.12 E
Kisel'ovsk	64	54.00 N	86.39 E
Kišin'ov	62	47.00 N	28.50 E
Kiskőrös	36	46.38 N	19.17 E
Kiskunfélegyháza	36	46.43 N	19.52 E
Kiskunhalas	36	46.26 N	19.30 E
Kisújszállás	36	47.13 N	20.46 E
Kisumu	104	0.06 S	34.45 E
Kisvárda	36	48.13 N	22.05 E
Kita	100	13.03 N	9.29 W
Kitakyūshū	80	33.53 N	130.50 E
Kitami	80	43.48 N	143.54 E
Kitchener	160	43.27 N	80.29 W
Kíthira	54	36.20 N	22.58 E
Kíthnos	54	37.25 N	24.28 E
Kitimat	160	54.03 N	128.33 W
Kitwe	104	12.49 S	28.13 E
Kitzbühel	36	47.27 N	12.23 E
Kitzingen	36	49.44 N	10.09 E
Kivu, Lac	104	2.00 S	29.10 E
Kızıl	20	41.44 N	35.58 E
Kjustendil	54	42.17 N	22.41 E
Kladno	36	50.08 N	14.05 E
Klagenfurt	36	46.38 N	14.18 E
Klaipėda (Memel)	26	55.43 N	21.07 E
Klamath	162	41.33 N	124.04 W
Klamath Falls	162	42.13 N	121.46 W
Klarälven (Trysilelva)	28	59.23 N	13.32 E
Klatovy	36	49.24 N	13.18 E
Klerksdorp	104	26.58 S	26.39 E
Klet'	36	48.52 N	14.17 E
Kleve	36	51.48 N	6.09 E
Klin	26	56.20 N	36.44 E
Klingenthal	36	50.21 N	12.28 E
Klínovec	36	50.24 N	12.58 E
Kłobuck	36	50.55 N	18.57 E
Kłodzko	36	50.27 N	16.39 E
Klondike	160	63.30 N	139.00 W
Klosterneuburg	36	48.18 N	16.20 E
Klosterwappen	36	47.46 N	15.48 E
Kluane Lake	160	61.15 N	138.40 W
Kluczbork	36	50.59 N	18.13 E
Knaresborough	32	54.00 N	1.27 W
Kneža	54	43.30 N	24.05 E
Knin	46	44.02 N	16.12 E
Knittelfeld	36	47.14 N	14.50 E
Knokke	36	51.21 N	3.17 E
Knox, Cape	160	54.11 N	133.04 W
Knoxville	162	35.58 N	83.56 W
Kobar Sink	102	14.00 N	40.30 E
Kōbe	80	34.41 N	135.10 E
København (Copenhagen)	28	55.40 N	12.35 E
Koblenz	36	50.21 N	7.35 E
Kočani	54	41.55 N	22.25 E
Kocher	36	49.14 N	9.12 E
Kōchi	80	33.33 N	133.33 E
Kodiak Island	162a	57.30 N	153.30 W
Köflach	36	47.04 N	15.05 E
Koforidua	100	6.03 N	0.17 W
Kōfu	80	35.39 N	138.35 E
Kogaluc	160	59.40 N	77.35 W
Kogaluc, Baie	160	59.20 N	77.50 W
Køge	28	55.27 N	12.11 E
Køge Bugt, Dan.	28	55.30 N	12.20 E
Køge Bugt, Grn.	160	65.00 N	40.30 W
Kohāt	84	33.35 N	71.26 E
Kohtla-Järve	26	59.24 N	27.15 E
Kokand	62	40.33 N	70.57 E
Kokemäenjoki	28	61.33 N	21.42 E
Kokkola (Gamlakarleby)	28	63.50 N	23.07 E
Kokomo	162	40.29 N	86.08 W
Kokopo	116a	4.20 S	152.15 E
Kokšaalatau, Chrebet	62	41.00 N	78.00 E
Kolárovo	36	47.52 N	18.02 E
Kolding	28	55.31 N	9.29 E
Kolea	50	36.38 N	2.46 E
Kolgujev, Ostrov	62	69.05 N	49.15 E
Kolhāpur	84	16.42 N	74.13 E
Kolín	36	50.01 N	15.13 E
Köln (Cologne)	36	50.56 N	6.59 E
Koło	36	52.12 N	18.38 E
Kołobrzeg	36	54.12 N	15.33 E
Kolomna	26	55.05 N	38.49 E
Kolovrat, Mount	114	9.10 S	161.05 E
Kolpino	26	59.45 N	30.36 E
Kol'skij Poluostrov (Kola Peninsula)	62	67.30 N	37.00 E
Kolubara	54	44.40 N	20.15 E
Kolwezi	104	10.43 S	25.28 E
Kolyma	64	69.30 N	161.00 E
Kom	54	43.10 N	23.03 E
Komadugu Gana	100	13.05 N	12.24 E
Komadugu Yobe	100	13.43 N	13.20 E
Komárno	36	47.45 N	18.09 E
Komárom	36	47.44 N	18.08 E
Komló	36	46.12 N	18.16 E
Kommunarsk	62	48.30 N	38.47 E
Kommunizma, Pik	62	38.57 N	72.01 E
Komoé	100	5.12 N	3.44 W
Komotiní	54	41.08 N	25.25 E
Komovi	54	42.40 N	19.40 E
Kompasberg	104	31.45 S	24.32 E
Komsomol'sk-na-Amure	64	50.35 N	137.02 E
Koné	112	21.04 S	164.52 E
Königssee	36	47.36 N	12.59 E
Konin	36	52.13 N	18.16 E
Könkämäälv	26	68.29 N	22.17 E
Konkouré	100	9.58 N	13.42 W
Końskie	36	51.12 N	20.26 E
Konstantinovka	26	56.41 N	50.53 E
Konstanz	36	47.40 N	9.10 E
Konya	20	37.52 N	32.31 E
Kópavogur	26a	64.06 N	21.50 W
Kopejsk	62	55.07 N	61.37 E
Koper	42	45.33 N	13.44 E
Köping	28	59.31 N	16.00 E
Koppány	36	46.35 N	18.26 E
Koprivnica	46	46.10 N	16.50 E
Korab	54	41.47 N	20.34 E
Koralpe	36	46.50 N	14.58 E
Korbach	36	51.16 N	8.52 E
Korçë	54	40.37 N	20.46 E
Korčula, Otok	46	42.57 N	16.50 E
Korčulanski Kanal	46	43.03 N	16.40 E
Korea, North	80	40.00 N	127.00 E
Korea, South	80	36.30 N	128.00 E
Korea Bay	80	39.00 N	124.00 E
Korea Strait	80	34.00 N	129.00 E
Korhogo	100	9.27 N	5.38 W
Korinthiakós Kólpos	54	38.19 N	22.04 E
Kórinthos (Corinth)	54	37.56 N	22.56 E
Korínthou, Dhiórix	54	37.57 N	22.56 E
Kőris-hegy	36	47.18 N	17.45 E
Kōriyama	80	37.24 N	140.23 E
Korneuburg	36	48.21 N	16.20 E
Korónia, Límni	54	40.41 N	23.05 E
Körös	36	46.43 N	20.12 E
Korso	28	60.21 N	25.06 E
Korsør	28	55.20 N	11.09 E
Kortrijk (Courtrai)	36	50.50 N	3.16 E
Kos	54	36.50 N	27.10 E
Kościan	36	52.06 N	16.38 E
Kościerzyna	36	54.08 N	18.00 E
Kosciusko, Mount	116	36.27 S	148.16 E
Košice	36	48.43 N	21.15 E
Kosovska Mitrovica	54	42.53 N	20.52 E
Kosteröarna	28	58.54 N	11.02 E
Kostroma	26	57.46 N	40.55 E
Kostrzyn	36	52.37 N	14.39 E
Koszalin (Köslin)	36	54.12 N	16.09 E
Kőszeg	36	47.23 N	16.33 E
Kota Baharu	82	6.08 N	102.15 E
Kota Kinabalu (Jesselton)	82	5.59 N	116.04 E
Kotel'nyj, Ostrov	64	75.45 N	138.44 E
Köthen	36	51.45 N	11.58 E
Kotka	28	60.28 N	26.55 E
Kotlas	26	61.16 N	46.35 E
Kotlenski prohod	54	42.53 N	26.27 E
Kotto	102	4.14 N	22.02 E
Koudougou	100	12.15 N	2.22 W
Koulikoro	100	12.53 N	7.33 W
Koumac	112	20.33 S	164.17 E
Koussi, Emi	102	19.50 N	18.30 E
Koutiala	100	12.23 N	5.28 W
Kouvola	28	60.52 N	26.42 E
Kovrov	26	56.22 N	41.18 E
Kowkcheh	84	37.10 N	69.23 E
Kowloon (Jiulong)	80	22.18 N	114.10 E
Kozáni	54	40.18 N	21.47 E
Koźle	36	50.20 N	18.08 E
Kra, Isthmus of	82	10.20 N	99.00 E
Kragujevac	54	44.01 N	20.55 E
Kraków	36	50.03 N	19.58 E
Kralendijk	130	12.10 N	68.17 W
Kraljevo	54	43.43 N	20.41 E
Kralupy nad Vltavou	36	50.11 N	14.18 E
Kramatorsk	62	48.43 N	37.32 E
Kranj	46	46.15 N	14.21 E
Kraśnik	36	50.56 N	22.13 E
Kraśnik Fabryczny	36	50.58 N	22.12 E
Krasnodar	62	45.02 N	39.00 E
Krasnojarsk	64	56.01 N	92.50 E
Krasnyj Luč	26	57.04 N	30.05 E
Krasnystaw	36	50.59 N	23.10 E
Kraszna (Crasna)	54	48.09 N	22.20 E
Krbava	46	44.40 N	15.35 E
Krefeld	36	51.20 N	6.34 E
Kremenčug	62	49.04 N	33.25 E
Krems an der Donau	36	48.25 N	15.36 E
Krishna	84	15.43 N	80.55 E
Kristiansand	28	58.10 N	8.00 E
Kristianstad	28	56.02 N	14.08 E
Kristiansund	28	63.07 N	7.45 E
Kristinehamn	28	59.20 N	14.07 E
Kríti	54	35.29 N	24.42 E
Kritikón Pélagos	54	35.46 N	23.54 E
Krivaja	54	44.27 N	18.09 E
Krivoj Rog	62	47.55 N	33.21 E
Krk, Otok	46	45.05 N	14.35 E
Krn	42	46.16 N	13.40 E
Krnov	36	50.05 N	17.41 E
Krokodil	104	24.12 S	26.52 E
Kroměříž	36	49.18 N	17.24 E
Kronach	36	50.14 N	11.20 E
Kronockij Zaliv	64	54.12 N	160.36 E
Kronštadt	26	59.59 N	29.45 E
Kroonstad	104	27.46 S	27.12 E
Kroppefjäll	28	58.40 N	12.13 E
Krosno	36	49.42 N	21.46 E
Krotoszyn	36	51.42 N	17.26 E
Krugersdorp	104	26.05 S	27.35 E
Krung Thep (Bangkok)	82	13.45 N	100.31 E
Kruševac	54	43.35 N	21.20 E
Krymskij Poluostrov	62	45.00 N	34.00 E
Krynica	36	49.25 N	20.56 E
Krzna	36	52.08 N	23.31 E
Ksar el Boukhari	50	35.51 N	2.52 E
Ksar-el-Kebir	100	35.01 N	5.54 W

Name	Page	Lat° '	Long° '
Ksar Hellal	46	35.39 N	10.54 E
Ksour Essaf	46	35.25 N	11.00 E
Kuala Lumpur	82	3.10 N	101.42 E
Kuala Terengganu	82	5.20 N	103.08 E
Kuantan	82	3.48 N	103.20 E
Kuban'	62	45.20 N	37.30 E
Kuching	82	1.33 N	110.20 E
Kudymkar	26	59.01 N	54.37 E
Kufstein	36	47.35 N	12.10 E
Kujawy	36	52.45 N	18.30 E
Kujbyšev	26	53.12 N	50.09 E
Kujū-san	80	33.05 N	131.15 E
Kula, Jugo.	54	45.36 N	19.32 E
Kula, Tür.	54	38.32 N	28.40 E
Kula Kangri	84	28.03 N	90.27 E
Kulmbach	36	50.06 N	11.27 E
Kuma	62	44.56 N	47.00 E
Kumamoto	80	32.48 N	130.43 E
Kumanovo	54	42.08 N	21.43 E
Kumasi	100	6.41 N	1.35 W
Kumla	28	59.08 N	15.08 E
Kummerower See	36	53.49 N	12.52 E
Kumo	100	10.03 N	11.13 E
Kungwe Mount	104	6.07 S	29.48 E
Kunhegyes	36	47.22 N	20.38 E
Kunlunshanmai	80	36.30 N	88.00 E
Kunming	80	25.05 N	102.40 E
Kunsan	80	35.58 N	126.41 E
Kuopio	28	62.54 N	27.41 E
Kupang	82	10.10 S	123.35 E
Kurashiki	80	34.35 N	133.46 E
Kure	80	34.14 N	132.34 E
Kurgan	62	55.26 N	65.18 E
Kuril'skije Ostrova (Kuril Islands)	64	46.10 N	152.00 E
Kursk	62	51.42 N	36.12 E
Kurume	80	33.19 N	130.31 E
Kuşadası Körfezi	54	37.50 N	27.08 E
Kusawa Lake	160	60.20 N	136.15 W
Kuş Gölü	54	40.10 N	27.57 E
Kushiro	80	42.58 N	144.23 E
Kustanaj	62	53.10 N	63.35 E
Kūstī	102	13.10 N	32.40 E
Kut, Ko	82	11.40 N	102.35 E
Kütahya	20	39.25 N	29.59 E
Kutaisi	62	42.15 N	42.40 E
Kutch, Gulf of	84	22.36 N	69.30 E
Kutina	36	45.29 N	16.46 E
Kutná Hora	36	49.57 N	15.16 E
Kutno	36	52.15 N	19.23 E
Kuusankoski	28	60.54 N	26.38 E
Kuwait	84	29.30 N	47.45 E
Kuzneck	26	53.07 N	46.36 E
Kuzneckij Alatau	62	54.45 N	88.00 E
Kvænangen	26	70.05 N	21.13 E
Kvarner	36	44.45 N	14.15 E
Kwando (Cuando)	104	18.27 S	23.32 E
Kwangju	80	35.09 N	126.54 E
Kwango (Cuango)	104	3.14 S	17.23 E
Kwenge	104	4.50 S	18.42 E
Kwidzyn	36	53.45 N	18.56 E
Kwilu (Cuilo)	104	3.22 S	17.22 E
Kwisa	36	51.35 N	15.25 E
Kymijoki	28	60.30 N	26.52 E
Kyoga, Lake	104	1.30 N	33.00 E
Kyŏngju	80	35.51 N	129.14 E
Kyōto	80	35.00 N	135.45 E
Kyūshū	80	33.00 N	131.00 E
Kyzylkum	62	42.00 N	64.00 E
Kzyl-Orda	62	44.48 N	65.28 E
L			
La Alcarria	50	40.30 N	2.45 W
La Baule	42	47.17 N	2.24 W
Labé	100	11.19 N	12.17 W
Labe (Elbe)	36	53.50 N	9.00 E
Laberge, Lake	160	61.11 N	135.12 W
La Blanquilla	144	11.51 N	64.37 W
Laborec	36	48.31 N	21.54 E
Labrador	160	54.00 N	62.00 W
Labrador Sea	160	57.00 N	53.00 W
Labuan, Pulau	82	5.21 N	115.13 E
Labuk	82	5.54 N	117.30 E
Lacanau, Étang de	42	44.58 N	1.07 E
La Carolina	50	38.15 N	3.37 W
Laccadive Islands	84	10.00 N	73.00 E
La Ceiba	130	15.47 N	86.50 W
Lac-giao	82	12.40 N	108.03 E
La Chaux-de-Fonds	42	47.06 N	6.50 E
La Chorrera	130	8.53 N	79.47 W
La Ciotat	42	43.10 N	5.36 E
La Coruña	50	43.22 N	8.23 W
La Crosse	162	43.49 N	91.15 W
Ladākh	84	34.45 N	76.30 E
La Dorada	144	5.27 N	74.40 W
Ladožskoje Ozero (Lake Ladoga)	62	61.00 N	31.30 E
Ladue	162a	63.09 N	140.25 W
Ladysmith	104	28.34 S	29.45 E
Lae	116a	6.45 S	147.00 E
La Encantada, Cerro de	130	31.00 N	115.24 W
Læsø	28	57.16 N	11.01 E
Lafayette, Ind., U.S.	162	40.25 N	86.53 W
Lafayette, La., U.S.	162	30.14 N	92.01 W
Lafia	100	8.30 N	8.30 E
La Flèche	42	47.42 N	0.05 W
Lafnitz	36	46.57 N	16.16 E
La Galite	100	37.32 N	8.56 E
Lagan	28	56.33 N	12.56 E
Lågen	28	61.08 N	10.25 E
Laghouat	100	33.50 N	2.59 E
Lagny	42	49.37 N	2.55 E
Lagos	100	6.27 N	3.24 E
La Goulette	46	36.49 N	10.18 E
La Grand'Combe	42	44.13 N	4.02 E
La Grande	160	53.50 N	79.00 W
La Gran Sabana	144	5.30 N	61.30 W
La Guaira	144	10.36 N	66.56 W
La Habana (Havana)	130	23.08 N	82.22 W
Lahaina	162b	20.52 N	156.41 W
Lahore	84	31.35 N	74.18 E
Lahr	36	48.20 N	7.52 E
Lahti	28	60.58 N	25.40 E
Lainioälven	26	67.22 N	23.39 E
Laizhouwan	80	37.36 N	119.30 E
La Jara	50	39.42 N	4.54 W
Lajosmizse	36	47.02 N	19.34 E
Lake Charles	162	30.13 N	93.12 W
Lakeland	162	28.03 N	81.57 W
Laksefjorden	26	70.58 N	27.00 E
La Libertad	130	16.47 N	90.07 W
La Linea	50	36.10 N	5.19 W
La Maddalena	46	41.13 N	9.24 E
La Mancha	50	39.05 N	3.00 W
La Manche (English Channel)	32	50.20 N	1.00 W
Lamap	112	16.26 S	167.43 E
Lambaréné	104	0.42 S	10.13 E
Lambasa	111	16.26 S	179.24 E
Lambay Island	32	53.29 N	6.01 W
Lambert Glacier	167	71.00 S	70.00 E
Lamenu	112	16.34 S	168.11 E
Lamia	54	38.54 N	22.26 E
Lampang	82	18.18 N	99.31 E
Lampedusa, Isola di	46	35.31 N	12.35 E
Lampertheim	36	49.35 N	8.28 E
Lanai	162b	20.50 N	156.55 W
Lancashire	32	53.45 N	2.40 W
Lancaster, Eng., U.K.	32	54.03 N	2.48 W
Lancaster, Ohio, U.S.	162	39.43 N	82.36 W
Lancaster, Pa., U.S.	162	40.02 N	76.19 W
Lancaster Sound	160	74.13 N	84.00 W
Lanciano	46	42.14 N	14.23 E
Łańcut	36	50.05 N	22.13 E
Landau	36	49.12 N	8.07 E
Landerneau	42	48.27 N	4.15 W
Landösjön	28	63.35 N	14.04 E
Landsberg [am Lech]	36	48.05 N	10.55 E
Land's End	32	50.03 N	5.44 W
Landshut	36	48.33 N	12.09 E
Landskrona	28	55.52 N	12.50 E
Langano, Lake	102	7.35 N	38.48 E
Langeberg	104	34.00 S	20.40 E
Langeland	28	55.00 N	10.50 E
Langenfeld	36	51.07 N	6.56 E
Langenhagen	36	52.27 N	9.44 E
Langenthal	42	47.13 N	7.47 E
Langeoog	36	53.46 N	7.32 E
Langjökull	26a	64.42 N	20.12 W
Langkawi, Pulau	82	6.22 N	99.50 E
Langnau	42	46.57 N	7.47 E
Langøya	26	68.44 N	14.50 E
Langres	42	47.52 N	5.20 W
Lang-son	82	21.50 N	106.44 E
Lannion	42	48.44 N	3.28 W
Lansing	162	42.43 N	84.34 W
Lanzhou	80	36.03 N	103.41 E
Laoag	82	18.12 N	120.36 E
Laon	42	49.34 N	3.40 E
La Orchila	144	11.48 N	66.09 W
La Oroya	144	11.32 S	75.54 W
Laos	82	18.00 N	105.00 E
Laou, Oued	50	35.29 N	5.04 W
La Palma	130	8.25 N	78.09 W
La Paz, Bol.	144	16.30 S	68.09 W
La Paz, Méx.	130	24.10 N	110.18 W
Lapland	26	68.00 N	25.00 E
La Plata	146	34.55 S	57.57 W
Lappeenranta	28	61.04 N	28.11 E
Laptevych, More (Laptev Sea)	64	76.00 N	126.00 E
L'Aquila	46	42.22 N	13.22 E
Larache	100	35.12 N	6.10 W
Laramie Mountains	162	42.00 N	105.40 W
Larche, Col de	42	44.25 N	6.53 E
Laredo	162	27.31 N	99.30 W
Largo, Cayo	130	21.38 N	81.28 W
La Rioja	146	29.26 S	66.51 W
La Rioja	50	42.20 N	0.22 W
Lárisa	54	39.38 N	22.25 E
Lārkāna	84	27.33 N	68.13 E
Larne	32	54.51 N	5.49 W
La Rochelle	42	46.10 N	1.10 W
La Roche-sur-Yon	42	46.40 N	1.26 W
La Roda	50	39.13 N	2.09 W
Larvik	28	59.04 N	10.00 E
Larzac, Causse du	42	44.00 N	3.15 E
Lasa (Lhasa)	80	29.40 N	91.09 E
La Sagra	50	37.57 N	2.34 W
Las Casitas, Cerro	130	23.32 N	109.59 W
Lascaux, Grotte de	42	45.01 N	1.08 E
Las Cruces	162	32.23 N	106.29 W
La Selle, Pic	130	18.22 N	71.59 W
La Serena	146	29.54 S	71.16 W
La Serena	50	38.45 N	5.30 W
La Seyne	42	43.06 N	5.53 E
La Sila	46	39.15 N	16.30 E
Las Marismas	50	37.00 N	6.15 W
Las Minas, Cerro	130	14.33 N	88.39 W
La Solana	50	38.56 N	3.14 W
Las Palmas de Gran Canaria	100	28.06	15.24 W
La Spezia	46	44.07 N	9.50 E
Las Piedras	146	34.44 S	56.13 W
Lassen Peak	162	40.29 N	121.31 W
Las Tablas	130	7.46 N	80.17 W
Lastovski Kanal	46	42.50 N	16.59 E
Las Vegas	162	36.11 N	115.08 W
Lata	113	14.14 S	169.29 W
La Teste-de-Buch	42	44.38 N	1.09 W
Latina	46	41.28 N	12.52 E
Latorica	36	48.28 N	21.50 E
La Tortuga, Isla	144	10.56 N	65.20 W
Lauchhammer	36	51.30 N	13.47 E
Lauf an der Pegnitz	36	49.30 N	11.17 E
Lau Group	111	18.20 S	178.30 W
Launceston	116	41.26 S	147.08 E
La Unión, El Sal.	130	13.20 N	87.51 W
La Unión, Esp.	50	37.37 N	0.52 W
Laurie Island	167	60.45 S	44.35 W
Lauritsala	28	61.04 N	28.16 E
Lausanne	42	46.31 N	6.38 E
Laut, Pulau	82	4.43 N	107.59 E
Lautoka	111	17.37 S	177.27 E
Lava, Nosy	104	14.33 S	47.36 E
Laval, Qué., Can.	160	45.33 N	73.44 W
Laval, Fr.	42	48.04 N	0.46 W
Lavant	36	46.38 N	14.57 E
Lavapié, Punta	146	37.09 S	73.35 W
La Vega	130	19.13 N	70.31 W
Lavello	46	41.03 N	15.48 E
La Vera	50	40.20 N	5.30 W
Lawers, Ben	32	56.33 N	4.15 W
Lawrence, Kans., U.S.	162	38.58 N	95.14 W
Lawrence, Mass., U.S.	162	42.42 N	71.09 W
Lawton	162	34.37 N	98.25 W
Lawz, Jabal al-	84	28.40 N	35.18 E
Leavenworth	162	39.19 N	94.55 W
Łeba	36	54.47 N	17.33 E
Lebanon	84	33.50 N	35.50 E
Lębork	36	54.33 N	17.44 E
Lebrija	50	36.55 N	6.04 W
Łebsko, Jezioro	36	54.44 N	17.24 E
Le Cateau	42	50.06 N	3.33 E
Lecce	46	40.23 N	18.11 E
Lecco	46	45.51 N	9.23 E
Lech	36	48.44 N	10.56 E
Lechtaler Alpen	36	47.15 N	10.30 E
Le Creusot	42	46.48 N	4.26 E
Łęczyca	36	52.04 N	19.13 E
Led'anaja, Gora	64	61.53 N	171.09 W
Leech Lake	162	47.09 N	94.23 W
Leeds	32	53.50 N	1.35 W
Leer	36	53.14 N	7.26 E
Leeuwarden	36	53.12 N	5.46 E
Leeward Islands	130	17.00 N	63.00 W
Legazpi	82	13.08 N	123.44 E
Legionowo	36	52.25 N	20.56 E
Legnago	46	45.11 N	11.18 E
Legnano	46	45.36 N	8.54 E
Legnica (Liegnitz)	36	51.13 N	16.09 E
Le Havre	42	49.30 N	0.08 E
Lehrte	36	52.22 N	9.59 E
Leicester	32	52.38 N	1.05 W
Leicestershire	32	52.40 N	1.10 W
Leiden	36	52.09 N	4.30 E
Leighton Buzzard	32	51.55 N	0.40 W
Leinster	32	53.05 N	7.00 W
Leipzig	36	51.19 N	12.20 E
Leitha (Lajta)	36	47.54 N	17.17 E
Leizhoubandao	80	21.15 N	110.09 E
Lekkous, Oued	50	34.58 N	5.52 W
Lelishan	80	33.26 N	81.42 E
Le Locle	42	47.03 N	6.45 E
Le Madonie	46	37.55 N	14.00 E
Le Maire, Estrecho de	146	54.50 S	65.00 W
Le Mans	42	48.00 N	0.12 E
Lemberg	36	48.09 N	8.45 E
Lemesós	84	34.40 N	33.02 E
Lemgo	36	52.02 N	8.54 E
Le Murge	46	40.52 N	16.42 E
Lena	64	72.25 N	126.40 E
Lenakel	112	19.32 S	169.16 E
Lenina, Pik	62	39.20 N	72.55 E
Leninabad	62	40.17 N	69.37 E
Leninakan	62	40.48 N	43.50 E
Leningrad	26	59.55 N	30.15 E
Leninogorsk	26	54.36 N	52.30 E
Leninsk-Kuzneckij	64	54.38 N	86.10 E
Lens	42	50.26 N	2.50 E
Lentini	46	37.17 N	15.00 E
Leoben	36	47.23 N	15.06 E
León, Esp.	50	42.36 N	5.34 W
León, Méx.	130	21.07 N	101.40 W
León, Nic.	130	12.26 N	86.53 W
León	50	42.00 N	6.00 W
León, Montes de	50	42.30 N	6.18 W
Leonberg	36	48.48 N	9.01 E
Leonforte	46	37.39 N	14.24 E
Lepe	50	37.15 N	7.12 W
Lepontine, Alpi	42	46.25 N	8.40 E
Le Port	104	20.55 S	55.18 E
Le Puy	42	45.02 N	3.53 E
Lerici	46	44.04 N	9.55 E
Lérida	50	41.37 N	0.37 E
Lerwick	32	60.09 N	1.09 W
Les Cayes	130	18.12 N	73.45 W
Leskovac	54	42.59 N	21.57 E
Lesotho	104	29.30 S	28.30 E
Les Sables-d'Olonne	42	46.30 N	1.47 W
Lesser Antilles	130	15.00 N	61.00 W
Lesser Slave Lake	160	55.25 N	115.30 W
Lésvos	54	39.10 N	26.20 E
Leszno	36	51.51 N	16.35 E
Letea, Ostrovul	54	45.20 N	29.20 E
Lethbridge	160	49.42 N	112.50 W
Letsók-aw Kyun	82	11.37 N	98.15 E
Leucate, Étang de	42	42.51 N	3.00 E
Leuna	36	51.19 N	12.01 E
Leuven	36	50.53 N	4.42 E
Levádhia	54	38.25 N	22.54 E
Leverkusen	36	51.03 N	6.59 E
Levice	36	48.13 N	18.37 E
Levítha	54	37.00 N	26.28 E
Lévka Óri	54	35.18 N	24.01 E
Levkás	54	38.50 N	20.41 E
Levkás	54	38.39 N	20.27 E
Levkosía	84	35.10 N	33.22 E
Levuka	111	17.41 S	178.50 E
Lewes	32	50.52 N	0.01 E
Lewis, Isle of	32	58.10 N	6.40 W
Lewiston, Idaho, U.S.	162	46.25 N	117.01 W
Lewiston, Maine, U.S.	162	44.06 N	70.13 W
Lexington	162	38.03 N	84.30 W
Leyre	42	44.39 N	1.01 W
Lhut	102	10.25 N	51.05 E
Liaodongbandao	80	40.00 N	122.20 E
Liaodongwan	80	40.30 N	121.30 E
Liaoyang	80	41.17 N	123.11 E
Liaoyuan	80	42.54 N	125.07 E
Liberec	36	50.46 N	15.03 E
Liberia	130	10.38 N	85.27 W
Liberia	100	6.30 N	9.30 W
Libourne	42	44.55 N	0.14 W
Libreville	104	0.23 N	9.27 E
Libya	102	27.00 N	17.00 E
Licata	46	37.05 N	13.56 E
Lichfield	32	52.42 N	1.48 W
Lichtenfels	36	50.09 N	11.04 E
Lidingö	28	59.22 N	18.08 E
Lidköping	28	58.30 N	13.10 E
Lidzbark	36	53.17 N	19.49 E
Lidzbark Warmiński	36	54.09 N	20.35 E
Liechtenstein	20	47.09 N	9.35 E
Liège	36	50.38 N	5.34 E
Lienz	36	46.50 N	12.47 E
Liepāja	26	56.31 N	21.01 E
Lier	36	51.08 N	4.34 E
Liestal	42	47.29 N	7.44 E
Liévin	42	50.25 N	2.46 E
Lifou, Île	112	20.53 S	167.13 E
Ligurian Sea	46	43.30 N	9.00 E
Lihue	162b	21.59 N	159.22 W
Likasi (Jadotville)	104	10.59 S	26.44 E
Likoma Island	104	12.05 S	34.45 E
Likouala	104	0.50 S	17.11 E
Lille	42	50.38 N	3.04 E
Lillestrøm	28	59.57 N	11.05 E
Lilongwe	104	13.59 S	33.44 E
Lim	54	43.45 N	19.13 E
Lima, Perú	144	12.03 S	77.03 W
Lima, Ohio, U.S.	162	40.46 N	84.06 W
Lima (Limia)	50	41.41 N	8.50 W
Limburg an der Lahn	36	50.23 N	8.04 E
Limeira	144	22.34 S	47.24 W
Limerick	32	52.40 N	8.38 W
Limfjorden	28	55.55 N	9.10 E
Limia (Lima)	50	41.41 N	8.50 W
Límnos	54	39.54 N	25.21 E
Limoges	42	45.50 N	1.16 E
Limón	130	10.00 N	83.02 W
Limousins, Plateau du	42	45.30 N	1.15 E
Limoux	42	43.04 N	2.14 E
Limpopo	104	25.15 S	33.30 E
Linares, Chile	146	35.51 S	71.36 W
Linares, Esp.	50	38.05 N	3.38 W
Lincoln, Eng., U.K.	32	53.14 N	0.33 W
Lincoln, Nebr., U.S.	162	40.48 N	96.42 W
Lincolnshire	32	52.55 N	0.22 W
Lindau	36	47.33 N	9.41 E
Lindenows Fjord	160	60.45 N	43.30 W
Linderödsåsen	28	55.53 N	13.56 E
Lindesnes	28	58.00 N	7.02 E
Lindi	104	10.00 S	39.43 E
Lindi	104	0.33 N	25.05 E
Lindlar	36	51.01 N	7.23 E
Lingayen Gulf	82	16.15 N	120.14 E
Lingen	36	52.31 N	7.19 E
Lingga, Kepulauan	82	0.05 S	104.35 E
Linh, Ngoc	82	15.04 N	107.59 E
Linköping	28	58.25 N	15.37 E
Linlithgow	32	55.59 N	3.37 W
Linnhe, Loch	32	56.37 N	5.25 W
Linosa, Isola di	46	35.52 N	12.52 E
Lins	144	21.40 S	49.45 W
Linz	36	48.18 N	14.18 E
Lion, Golfe du	42	43.00 N	4.00 E
Lipa	82	13.57 N	121.10 E
Lipari, Isola	46	38.30 N	14.57 E
Lipeck	62	52.37 N	39.35 E
Lipenská přehrada	42	48.43 N	14.04 E
Lipno	36	52.51 N	19.10 E
Lipova	54	46.05 N	21.40 E
Lippe	36	51.39 N	6.38 E
Lippstadt	36	51.40 N	8.19 E
Liptovský Mikuláš	36	49.06 N	19.37 E
Lisboa (Lisbon)	50	38.43 N	9.08 W
Lisburn	32	54.31 N	6.03 W
Lisburne, Cape	112	15.40 S	166.43 E
Liscia	46	41.11 N	9.19 E
Lisičansk	62	48.55 N	38.26 E
Lisieux	42	49.09 N	0.14 E
Lismore	116	28.48 S	153.17 E
Litoměřice	36	50.35 N	14.09 E
Little Cayman	130	19.41 N	80.03 W
Little Inagua	130	21.30 N	73.00 W
Little Karroo	104	33.45 S	21.30 E
Little Minch	32	57.35 N	6.45 W
Little Ouse	32	52.30 N	0.22 E
Little Rock	162	34.44 N	92.15 W
Little Scarcies	100	8.51 N	13.09 W
Little Smoky	160	55.42 N	117.38 W
Litvínov	36	50.37 N	13.36 E
Liuzhou	80	24.22 N	109.32 E
Livanjsko Polje	46	43.55 N	16.45 E
Liverpool	32	53.25 N	2.55 W
Livingston	130	15.50 N	88.45 W
Livingstone	104	17.50 S	25.53 E
Livingstone, Chutes de	104	4.50 S	14.30 E
Livingston Island	167	62.35 S	60.30 W
Livorno (Leghorn)	46	43.33 N	10.19 E
Lizard Point	32	49.56 N	5.13 W
Ljubljana	46	46.03 N	14.31 E
Ljungan	28	62.19 N	17.23 E
Ljungby	28	56.50 N	13.56 E
Ljusnan	28	61.12 N	17.08 E
Llandudno	32	53.19 N	3.49 W
Llanelli	32	51.42 N	4.10 W
Llanos	144	5.00 N	70.00 W
Llobregat	50	41.19 N	2.09 E
Lluchmayor	50	39.29 N	2.54 E
Llullaillaco, Volcán	146	24.43 S	68.33 W
Loa	146	21.26 S	70.04 W
Loanatit	112	19.22 S	169.14 E
Loange (Luangue)	104	4.17 S	20.02 E
Lobatse	104	25.11 S	25.40 E
Löbau	36	51.05 N	14.40 E
Lobaye	102	3.41 N	18.35 E
Lobito	104	12.20 S	13.34 E
Lobos de Afuera, Islas	144	6.57 S	80.42 W
Locarno	42	46.10 N	8.48 E
Lodi	46	45.19 N	9.30 E
Łódź	36	51.46 N	19.30 E
Loffa	100	6.36 N	11.08 W
Lofoten	26	68.30 N	15.00 E
Logan	162	41.44 N	111.50 W
Logan, Mount	160	60.34 N	140.24 W
Logone	102	12.06 N	15.02 E
Logroño	50	42.28 N	2.27 W
Logudoro	46	40.38 N	8.38 E
Lohjanjärvi	28	60.15 N	23.55 E
Lohne	36	52.42 N	8.12 E
Lohr	36	50.00 N	9.34 E
Loir	42	47.33 N	0.32 W
Loire	42	47.16 N	2.11 W
Loja, Ec.	144	4.00 S	79.13 W
Loja, Esp.	50	37.10 N	4.09 W
Lokeren	36	51.06 N	4.00 E
Lokoro	104	1.43 S	18.23 E
Lol	102	9.13 N	28.59 E
Lolland	28	54.46 N	11.30 E
Lolowai	112	15.18 S	168.00 E
Lom	54	43.49 N	23.14 E
Lom	100	5.20 N	13.24 E
Loma Mansa	100	9.13 N	11.07 W
Lomami	104	0.46 N	24.16 E
Lomé	100	6.08 N	1.13 E
Lommel	36	51.14 N	5.18 E
Lomond, Loch	32	56.08 N	4.38 W
Łomża	36	53.11 N	22.05 E
London, Ont., Can.	160	42.59 N	81.14 W
London, Eng., U.K.	32	51.30 N	0.10 W
London	32	51.30 N	0.10 W
Londonderry	32	55.00 N	7.19 W
Longa	104	10.15 S	13.30 E
Long Beach	162	33.46 N	118.11 W
Long Eaton	32	52.54 N	1.15 W
Long Island, Ba.	130	23.15 N	75.07 W
Long Island, N.Y., U.S.	162	40.50 N	73.00 W
Long Island Sound	162	41.05 N	72.58 W
Long Range Mountains	160	49.20 N	57.30 W
Longs Peak	162	40.15 N	105.37 W
Longview, Tex., U.S.	162	32.30 N	94.44 W
Longview, Wash., U.S.	162	46.08 N	122.57 W
Longwy	42	49.31 N	5.46 E
Long-xuyen	82	10.23 N	105.25 E
Lons-le-Saunier	42	46.40 N	5.33 E
Lookout, Cape	162	34.35 N	76.32 W
Loop Head	32	52.34 N	9.56 W
Lopez, Cap	104	0.37 S	8.43 E
Lora del Rio	50	37.39 N	5.32 W
Lorain	162	41.28 N	82.10 W
Lorca	50	37.40 N	1.42 W
Lorient	42	47.45 N	3.22 W
Lörrach	36	47.37 N	7.40 E
Los Angeles, Chile	146	37.28 S	72.21 W
Los Angeles, Calif., U.S.	162	34.03 N	118.15 W
Los Mochis	130	25.45 N	108.57 W
Los Palacios y Villafranca	50	37.10 N	5.56 W
Los Roques, Islas	144	11.50 N	66.45 W
Lot	42	44.18 N	0.20 E
Lota	146	37.05 S	73.10 W
Lotrului, Munții	54	45.30 N	23.52 E
Lotsane	104	22.41 S	28.11 E
Lotta	26	68.36 N	31.06 E
Louangphrabang	82	19.52 N	102.08 E
Louga	100	15.37 N	16.13 W
Louge	42	43.27 N	1.20 E
Loughborough	32	52.47 N	1.11 W
Louisiana	162	31.15 N	92.15 W
Louis Trichardt	104	23.01 S	29.43 E
Louisville	162	38.16 N	85.45 W
Louny	36	50.19 N	13.46 E
Lourdes	42	43.06 N	0.03 W
Louth	32	53.22 N	0.01 W
Louviers	42	49.13 N	1.10 E
Lovat'	62	58.14 N	31.28 E
Loveč	54	43.08 N	24.43 E
Lowell	162	42.39 N	71.18 W
Lower Hutt	118	41.13 S	174.55 E
Lower Red Lake	162	48.00 N	94.50 W
Lowestoft	32	52.29 N	1.45 E
Łowicz	36	52.07 N	19.56 E
Loyauté, Îles (Loyalty Islands)	112	21.00 S	167.00 E
Lozère, Mont	42	44.25 N	3.45 E
Loznica	54	44.32 N	19.13 E
Lua	102	2.46 N	18.26 E
Lualaba	104	0.26 N	25.20 E
Luanda	104	8.48 S	13.14 E
Luando	104	10.19 S	16.40 E
Luangue (Loange)	104	4.17 S	20.02 E
Luanguinga	104	15.11 S	22.56 E
Luangwa (Aruângua)	104	15.36 S	30.25 E
Luanshya	104	13.08 S	28.24 E
Luapula	104	9.26 S	28.33 E
Lubań	36	51.08 N	15.18 E
Lubango	104	14.55 S	13.30 E
Lübben	36	51.56 N	13.53 E
Lübbenau	36	51.52 N	13.57 E
Lubbock	162	33.35 N	101.51 W
Lübeck	36	53.52 N	10.40 E
Lübecker Bucht	36	54.00 N	10.55 E
Lubelska, Wyżyna	36	51.00 N	23.00 E
L'ubercy	62	55.41 N	37.53 E
Lubilash	104	6.02 S	23.45 E
Lubin	36	51.24 N	16.13 E
Lublin	36	51.15 N	22.35 E
Lubliniec	36	50.40 N	18.41 E
Lubsko	36	51.46 N	14.59 E
Lubudi	104	6.51 S	21.18 E
Lubudi	104	9.13 S	25.38 E
Lubumbashi (Élisabethville)	104	11.40 S	27.28 E
Lucania	46	40.30 N	16.00 E
Lucania, Mount	160	61.01 N	140.28 W
Lucca	46	43.50 N	10.29 E
Luce Bay	32	54.47 N	4.50 W
Lucena, Esp.	50	37.24 N	4.29 W
Lucena, Pil.	82	13.56 N	121.37 E
Lučenec	36	48.20 N	19.40 E
Lucera	46	41.30 N	15.20 E
Luck	62	50.44 N	25.20 E
Luckenwalde	36	52.05 N	13.10 E
Lucknow	84	26.50 N	80.52 E
Lucon	42	46.27 N	1.10 W
Lüda (Dairen)	80	38.53 N	121.35 E
Luda Kamčija	54	43.03 N	27.29 E
Lüdenscheid	36	51.13 N	7.38 E
Lüderitz	104	26.38 S	15.10 E
Ludhiāna	84	30.55 N	75.51 E
Ludvika	28	60.09 N	15.11 E
Ludwigsburg	36	48.53 N	9.11 E
Ludwigsfelde	36	52.17 N	13.16 E
Ludwigshafen	36	49.29 N	8.26 E
Ludwigslust	36	53.19 N	11.30 E
Luena	104	12.31 S	22.34 E
Lugano	42	46.01 N	8.58 E
Lugano, Lago di	46	46.00 N	9.00 E
Luganville	112	15.32 S	167.08 E
Lugenda	104	11.25 S	38.33 E
Lugo, Esp.	50	43.00 N	7.34 W
Lugo, It.	46	44.25 N	11.54 E
Lugoj	54	45.41 N	21.54 E
Luino	46	46.00 N	8.44 E
Lukanga Swamp	104	14.25 S	27.45 E
Łuków	36	51.56 N	22.23 E
Luleå	28	65.34 N	22.10 E
Luleälven	26	65.35 N	22.03 E
Lüleburgaz	54	41.24 N	27.21 E
Luma	113	14.14 S	169.32 W
Lund	28	55.42 N	13.11 E
Lundi	104	21.43 S	32.34 E
Lundy	32	51.10 N	4.40 W
Lune	32	54.02 N	2.50 W
Lüneburg	36	53.15 N	10.23 E
Lüneburger Heide	36	53.10 N	10.20 E
Lünen	36	51.36 N	7.32 E
Lunéville	42	48.36 N	6.30 E
Lunga	104	14.34 S	26.25 E
Lungué-Bungo	104	14.19 S	23.14 E
Lūni	84	24.40 N	71.15 E
Lunndörrsfjällen	28	63.00 N	13.00 E
Luobubo (Lop Nor)	80	40.20 N	90.15 E
Luoyang	80	34.41 N	112.28 E
Lupeni	54	45.22 N	23.13 E
Lurgan	32	54.28 N	6.20 W
Lúrio	104	13.35 S	40.32 E
Lusaka	104	15.25 S	28.17 E
Lusambo	104	4.58 S	23.27 E
Lushnje	54	40.56 N	19.42 E
Lüshun (Port Arthur)	80	38.47 N	121.13 E
Lūt, Dasht-e	84	33.00 N	57.00 E
Luton	32	51.53 N	0.25 W
Luwegu	104	8.31 S	37.23 E
Luxembourg	42	49.36 N	6.09 E
Luxembourg	20	49.45 N	6.05 E
Luy	42	43.39 N	1.08 W
Luzern	42	47.03 N	8.18 E
Luzhou	80	28.54 N	105.27 E
Luzon	82	16.00 N	121.00 E
Luzon Strait	82	20.30 N	121.00 E
L'vov	62	49.50 N	24.00 E
Lyallpur	84	31.25 N	73.05 E
Lyme Bay	32	50.38 N	3.00 W
Lynchburg	162	37.24 N	79.10 W
Lyon	42	45.45 N	4.51 E
Lyonnais, Monts du	42	45.40 N	4.30 E
Łysica	36	50.54 N	20.55 E
Lytham Saint Anne's	32	53.45 N	2.57 W
M			
Maas (Meuse)	36	51.49 N	5.01 E
Maastricht	36	50.52 N	5.43 E
Mababe Depression	104	18.50 S	24.15 E
Mabeul	46	36.27 N	10.46 E
McAllen	162	26.12 N	98.15 W
Macapá	144	0.02 N	51.03 W
Macau (Aomen)	80	22.14 N	113.35 E
Macau	80	22.10 N	113.33 E
Macclesfield	32	53.16 N	2.07 W
Macdui, Ben	32	57.04 N	3.40 W
Maceió	144	9.40 S	35.43 W
Macerata	46	43.18 N	13.27 E
MacFarlane	160	59.12 N	107.58 W
Machaćkala	62	42.58 N	47.30 E
Machala	144	3.16 S	79.58 W
Macias Nguema Biyogo	100	3.30 N	8.40 E
Macina	100	14.30 N	5.00 W
Mackay	116	21.09 S	149.11 E
Mackenzie	160	69.15 N	134.08 W
Mackinac, Straits of	162	45.49 N	84.42 W
McKinley, Mount	162a	63.30 N	151.00 W
McLeod	160	54.08 N	115.42 W
Macmillan	160	62.52 N	135.55 W
Macocha	36	49.23 N	16.45 E
Macomer	46	40.16 N	8.46 E
Mâcon, Fr.	42	46.18 N	4.50 E
Macon, Ga., U.S.	162	32.50 N	83.38 W
Mada	100	7.59 N	7.55 E
Madagascar	104	19.00 S	46.00 E
Madang	116a	5.15 S	145.50 E
Madawaska	160	45.27 N	76.21 W
Maddalena, Isola	46	41.13 N	9.24 E
Maddaloni	46	41.02 N	14.23 E
Madeira	100	32.44 N	17.00 W
Madeira	144	3.22 S	58.45 W
Mädelegabel	42	47.18 N	10.18 E
Madeleine, Îles de la	160	47.30 N	61.45 W
Madidi	144	12.32 S	66.52 W
Madīnat ash-Sha'b	84	12.50 N	44.56 E
Madison	162	43.05 N	89.22 W
Madiun	82	7.37 S	111.31 E
Madras	84	13.04 N	80.16 E
Madre, Laguna, Méx.	130	25.00 N	97.40 W
Madre, Laguna, Tex., U.S.	162	27.00 N	97.35 W
Madre, Sierra	82	16.20 N	122.00 E
Madre de Dios	144	10.59 S	66.08 W
Madre Occidental, Sierra	130	25.00 N	105.00 W
Madre Oriental, Sierra	130	22.00 N	99.30 W
Madrid	50	40.24 N	3.41 W
Madurai	84	9.56 N	78.08 E
Maebashi	80	36.23 N	139.04 E
Mae Klong	82	13.21 N	100.00 E
Maesteg	32	51.37 N	3.40 W
Maestra, Sierra	130	20.00 N	76.45 W
Mafeking	104	25.53 S	25.39 E
Mafia Island	104	7.50 S	39.50 E
Magadan	64	59.34 N	150.48 E
Magangué	144	9.14 N	74.45 W
Magdalena	144	11.06 N	74.51 W
Magdalena, Isla	146	44.40 S	73.10 W
Magdeburg	36	52.07 N	11.38 E
Magelang	82	7.28 S	110.13 E
Magenta	46	45.28 N	8.53 E
Magerøya	26	71.03 N	25.45 E
Maggiore, Lago	46	46.00 N	8.40 E
Magina	50	37.43 N	3.28 W
Magnitogorsk	62	53.27 N	59.04 E
Maguarinho, Cabo	144	0.18 S	48.22 W
Mahābhārat Range	84	27.40 N	84.30 E
Mahajamba, Baie de la	104	15.24 S	47.05 E
Mahakam	82	0.35 S	117.17 E
Mahalapye	104	23.05 S	26.51 E
Mahébourg	104	20.24 S	57.42 E
Mahé Island	104	4.40 S	55.28 E
Mahia Peninsula	118	39.10 S	177.53 E
Mahón	50	39.53 N	4.15 E
Maidenhead	32	51.32 N	0.44 W
Maidstone	32	51.17 N	0.32 E
Maiduguri	100	11.51 N	13.10 E
Main	36	50.00 N	8.18 E
Mai-Ndombe, Lac	104	2.00 S	18.20 E
Maine	162	45.15 N	69.15 W
Mainland	32	60.20 N	1.22 W
Mainz	36	50.01 N	8.16 E
Maipo, Volcán	146	34.10 S	69.50 W
Maipú	146	36.52 S	57.52 W
Maiquetía	144	10.36 N	66.57 W
Maitland	116	32.44 S	151.33 E
Maizuru	80	35.27 N	135.20 E
Majkop	62	44.35 N	40.07 E
Majunga	104	15.43 S	46.19 E
Makasar, Selat (Makassar Strait)	82	2.00 S	117.30 E
Makaza	54	41.16 N	25.26 E
Makejevka	62	48.02 N	37.58 E
Makeni	100	8.53 N	12.03 W
Makgadikgadi Pans	104	20.45 S	25.30 E
Makkah (Mecca)	84	21.27 N	39.49 E

Name	Page	Lat	Long
Makó	36	46.13 N	20.29 E
Makurdi	100	7.45 N	8.32 E
Malabar Coast ≗[2]	84	11.00 N	75.00 E
Malabo	100	3.45 N	8.47 E
Malacca, Strait of ᴜ	82	2.30 N	101.20 E
Malacky	36	48.27 N	17.00 E
Málaga	50	36.43 N	4.25 W
Malaita I	114	9.00 S	161.00 E
Malakāl	102	9.31 N	31.39 E
Mala Kapela ⋏	46	44.50 N	15.30 E
Malang	82	7.59 S	112.37 E
Malanje	104	9.32 S	16.20 E
Mała Panew ≏	36	50.44 N	17.52 E
Mälaren ⊜	28	59.30 N	17.12 E
Malatya	20	38.21 N	38.19 E
Malawi ⬜[1]	104	13.30 S	34.00 E
Malay Peninsula ≗[1]	82	6.00 N	101.00 E
Malaysia ⬜[1]	82	2.30 N	112.30 E
Malbork	36	54.02 N	19.01 E
Maldegem	36	51.13 N	3.27 E
Maldives ⬜[1]	10	3.15 N	73.00 E
Maléa, Ákra ⋗	54	36.26 N	23.12 E
Malé Karpaty ⋏	36	48.30 N	17.20 E
Maekula I	112	16.15 S	167.30 E
Malheur Lake ⊜	162	43.20 N	118.45 W
Mali ⬜[1]	100	17.00 N	4.00 W
Mali I	84	25.43 N	97.29 E
Malik, Wādī al- ∨	102	18.02 N	30.58 E
Malkara	54	40.53 N	26.54 E
Mallawī	102	27.44 N	30.50 E
Mallorca I	50	39.30 N	3.00 E
Malmberget	26	67.10 N	20.40 E
Malmö	28	55.36 N	13.00 E
Małopolska ≗[1]	36	50.10 N	21.30 E
Malo Strait ᴜ	112	15.50 S	167.10 E
Malpaso, Presa de ⊜[1]	130	17.10 N	93.40 W
Malpelo, Isla de I	144	3.59 N	81.35 W
Målselva ≏	26	69.14 N	18.30 E
Malta ⬜[1]	22	35.50 N	14.35 E
Malta I	46	35.53 N	14.27 E
Maluku, Laut (Molucca Sea) ⇥[2]	82	0.00 S	125.00 E
Malý Dunaj ≏	36	48.08 N	17.09 E
Malyj Kavkaz ⋏	62	41.00 N	44.35 E
Malyj Uzen' ≏	62	48.50 N	49.39 E
Mambéré ≏	102	3.31 N	16.03 E
Mamoré ≏	144	10.23 S	65.23 W
Mamou	100	10.23 N	12.05 W
Mamry, Jezioro ⊜	36	54.08 N	21.42 E
Man	100	7.24 N	7.33 W
Mana ≏	144	5.44 N	53.54 W
Manacor	50	39.34 N	3.12 E
Manado	82	1.29 N	124.51 E
Managua	130	12.09 N	86.17 W
Managua, Lago de ⊜	130	12.20 N	86.20 W
Manakara	104	22.08 S	48.01 E
Mananjary	104	21.13 S	48.20 E
Manās ≏	84	26.13 N	90.38 E
Manaus	144	3.08 S	60.01 W
Manchester, Eng., U.K.	32	53.30 N	2.15 W
Manchester, N.H., U.S.	162	42.59 N	71.28 W
Mand ≏	84	28.11 N	51.17 E
Mandala, Puncak ⋏	82	4.44 S	140.20 E
Mandalay	82	22.00 N	96.05 E
Mandara Mountains ⋏	100	10.45 N	13.40 E
Mandeb, Bāb el- ᴜ	102	12.40 N	43.20 E
Manduria	46	40.24 N	17.38 E
Manfalūṭ	102	27.19 N	30.58 E
Manfredonia	46	41.38 N	15.55 E
Manfredonia, Golfo di C	46	41.35 N	16.05 E
Mangalore	84	12.52 N	74.52 E
Mangkalihat, Tanjung ⋗	82	1.02 N	118.59 E
Mangoky ≏	104	23.27 S	45.13 E
Manhattan	162	39.11 N	96.35 W
Manicouagan ≏	160	49.11 N	68.13 W
Manila	82	14.35 N	121.00 E
Manisa	54	38.36 N	27.26 E
Manitoba ⬜[4]	160	54.00 N	97.00 W
Manitoba, Lake ⊜	160	51.00 N	98.45 W
Manitoulin Island I	162	45.45 N	82.30 W
Manitowoc	162	44.06 N	87.40 W
Manizales	144	5.05 N	75.32 W
Mankato	162	44.10 N	94.01 W
Mannheim	36	49.29 N	8.29 E
Manning Strait ᴜ	114	7.24 S	158.00 E
Mannu ≏	46	40.50 N	8.23 E
Manono	104	7.18 S	27.25 E
Manresa	50	41.44 N	1.50 E
Mansfield, Eng., U.K.	32	53.09 N	1.11 W
Mansfield, Ohio, U.S.	162	40.46 N	82.31 W
Manta	144	0.57 S	80.44 W
Mantes-la-Jolie	42	48.59 N	1.43 E
Mantova	46	45.09 N	10.48 E
Manua Islands II	113	14.13 S	169.35 W
Manukau	118	37.02 S	174.54 E
Manukau Harbour C	118	37.01 S	174.44 E
Manyara, Lake ⊜	104	3.35 S	35.50 E
Manyč ≏	62	47.15 N	40.00 E
Manzanares	50	39.00 N	3.22 W
Manzanares ≏	50	40.19 N	3.32 W
Manzanillo, Cuba	130	20.21 N	77.07 W
Manzanillo, Méx.	130	19.03 N	104.20 W
Manzini	104	26.30 S	31.25 E
Maouri, Dallol ∨	100	12.05 N	3.32 E
Maputo (Lourenço Marques)	104	25.58 S	32.35 E
Mara ≏	104	1.31 S	33.56 E
Maracá, Ilha de I	144	2.05 N	50.25 W
Maracaibo	144	10.40 N	71.37 W
Maracaibo, Lago de ⊜	144	9.50 N	71.30 W
Maracay	144	10.15 N	67.36 W
Maradi	100	13.29 N	7.06 E
Marahuaca, Cerro ⋏	144	3.34 N	65.27 W
Marajó, Baía de C	144	1.00 S	48.30 W
Marajó, Ilha de I	144	1.00 S	49.30 W
Marano [di Napoli]	46	40.54 N	14.11 E
Marañón ≏	144	4.30 S	73.27 W
Maraş	20	37.36 N	36.55 E
Marburg an der Lahn	36	50.49 N	8.46 E
Marcal ≏	36	47.41 N	17.32 E
March	32	52.33 N	0.06 E
March (Morava) ≏	36	48.10 N	16.59 E
Marchena	50	37.20 N	5.24 W
Mar Chiquita, Laguna ⊜	146	30.42 S	62.36 W
Mardān	84	34.12 N	72.02 E
Mar del Plata	146	38.00 S	57.33 W
Maré, Île I	112	21.30 S	168.00 E
Mare, Muntele ⋏	54	46.29 N	23.14 E
Mareeba	116	17.00 S	145.26 E
Maremma ≗[1]	46	42.30 N	11.30 E
Marettimo, Isola I	46	37.58 N	12.04 E
Margarita, Isla de I	144	11.00 N	64.00 W
Margate	32	51.24 N	1.24 E
Margeride, Monts de la ⋏	42	44.50 N	3.30 E
Margherita Peak ⋏	104	0.22 N	29.51 E
Margilan	62	40.29 N	71.44 E
Mārgow, Dasht-e ≗[2]	84	30.45 N	63.10 E
Mariana Islands II	82	16.00 N	145.30 E
Marianao	130	23.05 N	82.26 W
Mariánské Lázně	36	49.59 N	12.43 E
Mariato, Punta ⋗	130	7.13 N	80.53 W
Maribor	46	46.33 N	15.39 E
Marica (Évros) (Meriç) ≏	54	40.52 N	26.12 E
Marie-Galante I	130	15.56 N	61.16 W
Mariental	104	24.36 S	17.59 E
Mariestad	28	58.43 N	13.51 E
Marietta	162	33.57 N	84.33 W
Mariga ≏	100	9.40 N	5.55 E
Marignane	42	43.25 N	5.13 E
Marília	144	22.13 S	49.56 W
Marinette	162	45.06 N	87.38 W
Marino	46	41.46 N	12.39 E
Marion, Ind., U.S.	162	40.33 N	85.40 W
Marion, Ohio, U.S.	162	40.35 N	83.08 W
Marion, Lake ⊜[1]	162	33.30 N	80.25 W
Maritime Alps ⋏	42	44.15 N	7.10 E
Marka	102	1.47 N	44.52 E
Markerwaard ⇥[1]	36	52.33 N	5.15 E
Markham, Mount ⋏	167	82.51 S	161.21 E
Marktredwitz	36	50.00 N	12.06 E
Marmande	42	44.30 N	0.10 E
Marmara Denizi (Sea of Marmara) ⇥[2]	54	40.40 N	28.15 E
Marmolada ⋏	36	46.26 N	11.51 E
Marne ≏	42	48.49 N	2.24 E
Marne au Rhin, Canal de la ☰	42	48.35 N	7.47 E
Maromokotro ⋏	104	14.01 S	48.59 E
Maroni (Marowijne) ≏	144	5.45 N	53.58 W
Maros (Mureş) ≏	54	46.15 N	20.13 E
Marovoay	104	16.06 S	46.39 E
Marowijne (Maroni) ≏	144	5.45 N	53.58 W
Marquette	162	46.33 N	87.24 W
Marrah, Jabal ⋏	102	13.04 N	24.21 E
Marrakech	100	31.38 N	8.00 W
Marsala	46	37.48 N	12.26 E
Marseille	42	43.18 N	5.24 E
Marsfjället ⋏	26	65.05 N	15.28 E
Marsica ≗[1]	46	41.50 N	13.45 E
Märsta	28	59.37 N	17.51 E
Martaban, Gulf of C	84	16.30 N	97.00 E
Martigny	42	46.06 N	7.04 E
Martigues	42	43.24 N	5.03 E
Martin ≏	50	41.18 N	0.19 W
Martina Franca	46	40.42 N	17.21 E
Martinique ⬜[2]	130	14.40 N	61.00 W
Martinsville	162	36.41 N	79.52 W
Martos	50	37.43 N	3.58 W
Marum, Mount ⋏	112	16.15 S	168.07 E
Marungu ⋏	104	7.42 S	30.00 E
Maryborough	116	37.03 S	143.45 E
Maryland ⬜[3]	162	39.00 N	76.45 W
Maryport	32	54.43 N	3.30 W
Marysville	162	39.09 N	121.35 W
Marzūq, Idehan ⇥[1]	102	24.30 N	13.00 E
Masai Steppe ≗[1]	104	4.45 S	37.00 E
Masaka	104	0.20 S	31.44 E
Masan	80	35.11 N	128.32 E
Masaya	130	11.58 N	86.06 W
Mascara	100	35.45 N	0.01 E
Maseru	104	29.28 S	27.30 E
Mashābih I	84	25.37 N	36.29 E
Mashhad	84	36.18 N	59.36 E
Māshkel, Hāmūn-i- ⓶	84	28.15 N	63.00 E
Maṣīrah, Khalīj al- C	84	20.10 N	58.15 E
Masoala, Presqu'île ⋗[1]	104	15.40 S	50.12 E
Mason City	162	43.09 N	93.12 W
Massa	46	44.01 N	10.09 E
Massachusetts ⬜[3]	162	42.15 N	71.50 W
Massafra	46	40.35 N	17.07 E
Massa Marittima	46	43.03 N	10.53 E
Massarosa	46	43.52 N	10.20 E
Massive, Mount ⋏	162	39.12 N	106.28 W
Masterton	118	40.57 S	175.40 E
Mat ≏	54	41.39 N	19.34 E
Matabeleland ≗[1]	104	19.30 S	28.00 E
Matachel ≏	50	38.50 N	6.17 W
Matadi	104	5.49 S	13.27 E
Matagalpa	130	12.55 N	85.55 W
Matamoros	130	25.53 N	97.30 W
Matandu ≏	104	8.45 S	39.19 E
Matanzas	130	23.03 N	81.35 W
Mataró	50	41.32 N	2.27 E
Matatula, Cape ⋗	113	14.15 S	170.34 W
Matautu	113	13.57 S	171.56 W
Matavera	114	21.13 S	159.44 W
Matehuala	130	23.39 N	100.39 W
Matera	46	40.40 N	16.37 E
Mateur	46	37.03 N	9.40 E
Matlock	32	53.08 N	1.32 W
Mato, Cerro ⋏	144	7.15 N	65.14 W
Matočkin Šar, Proliv ᴜ	62	73.20 N	55.21 E
Mato Grosso, Planalto do ≗[1]	144	15.30 S	56.00 W
Matopo Hills ≗[2]	104	20.36 S	28.28 E
Matosinhos	50	41.11 N	8.42 W
Mátra ⋏	36	47.55 N	20.00 E
Maṭraḥ	84	23.38 N	58.34 E
Maṭrūḥ	102	31.21 N	27.14 E
Matsue	80	35.28 N	133.04 E
Matsumoto	80	36.14 N	137.58 E
Matsu Shan I	80	26.09 N	119.56 E
Matsuyama	80	33.50 N	132.45 E
Mattagami ≏	160	50.43 N	81.29 W
Matterhorn ⋏	42	45.59 N	7.43 E
Maturín	144	9.45 N	63.11 W
Maubeuge	42	50.17 N	3.58 E
Ma-ubin	82	16.44 N	95.39 E
Mauga Silisili ⋏	113	13.35 S	172.27 W
Maui I	162b	20.45 N	156.15 W
Mauna Kea ⋏	162b	19.50 N	155.28 W
Mauna Loa ⋏[1]	162b	19.29 N	155.36 W
Mauritania ⬜[1]	100	20.00 N	12.00 W
Mauritius ⬜[1]	104	20.17 S	57.33 E
Mayaguana I	130	22.23 N	72.57 W
Mayagüez	130	18.12 N	67.09 W
Mayen	36	50.19 N	7.13 E
Mayenne	42	48.18 N	0.37 W
Mayenne ≏	42	47.30 N	0.33 W
Maymyo	82	22.02 N	96.28 E
Mayo ≏	160	63.35 N	135.54 W
Mayon Volcano ⋏[1]	82	13.15 N	123.41 E
Mayotte ⬜[2]	104	12.50 S	45.10 E
Mayotte I	104	12.50 S	45.10 E
Mazamet	42	43.30 N	2.24 E
Mazara del Vallo	46	37.39 N	12.36 E
Mazār-e Sharīf	84	36.42 N	67.06 E
Mazaruni ≏	144	6.25 N	58.38 W
Mazatenango	130	14.32 N	91.30 W
Mazatlán	130	23.13 N	106.25 W
Mazoe ≏	104	16.32 S	33.25 E
Mazowsze ≗[1]	36	52.30 N	20.40 E
Mazury ≗[1]	36	53.45 N	21.00 E
Mba	111	17.33 S	177.41 E
Mbabane	104	26.18 S	31.06 E
Mbale	104	1.05 N	34.10 E
Mbandaka (Coquilhatville)	104	0.04 N	18.16 E
Mbanza-Ngungu	104	5.15 S	14.52 E
Mbari ≏	102	4.34 N	22.43 E
Mbeya	104	8.50 S	33.22 E
Mbomou (Bomu) ≏	102	4.08 N	22.26 E
Mbuji-Mayi (Bakwanga)	104	6.09 S	23.38 E
Meath ⬜[9]	32	53.40 N	7.00 W
Meaux	42	48.57 N	2.52 E
Mechelen	36	51.02 N	4.28 E
Mecklenburger Bucht C	36	54.20 N	11.40 E
Mecsek ⋏	36	46.15 N	18.05 E
Medan	82	3.35 N	98.40 E
Medanosa, Punta ⋗	146	48.06 S	65.55 W
Médéa	50	36.17 N	2.58 E
Medellín	144	6.15 N	75.35 W
Medford	162	42.19 N	122.52 W
Medgidia	54	44.15 N	28.16 E
Mediaş	54	46.10 N	24.21 E
Medicine Hat	160	50.03 N	110.40 W
Medina del Campo	50	41.18 N	4.55 W
Mediterranean Sea ⇥[2]	20	36.00 N	15.00 E
Medjerda, Monts de la ⋏	46	36.35 N	8.15 E
Médoc ≗[1]	42	45.20 N	1.00 W
Medvedica ≏	62	49.35 N	42.41 E
Medvežji Ostrova II	64	70.52 N	161.26 E
Medway ≏	32	51.27 N	0.44 E
Meerane	36	50.51 N	12.28 E
Meerut	84	29.00 N	77.43 E
Mégara	54	38.01 N	23.21 E
Meghna ≏	84	22.50 N	90.50 E
Meiktila	82	20.52 N	95.52 E
Meiningen	36	50.34 N	10.25 E
Meissen	36	51.10 N	13.28 E
Mekele	102	13.33 N	39.30 E
Mekerrhane, Sebkha ⓶	100	26.19 N	1.20 E
Meknès	100	33.53 N	5.37 W
Mekong ≏	82	10.33 N	105.24 E
Mékrou ≏	100	12.24 N	2.49 E
Melaka (Malacca)	82	2.12 N	102.15 E
Melbourne	116	37.49 S	144.58 E
Melegnano	46	45.21 N	9.19 E
Melfi	46	40.59 N	15.40 E
Melilla	100	35.19 N	2.58 W
Melitopol'	62	46.50 N	35.22 E
Mellègue, Oued ≏	46	36.32 N	8.51 E
Mělník	36	50.20 N	14.29 E
Melo	146	32.22 S	54.11 W
Melrhir, Chott ⓶	100	34.20 N	6.20 E
Melton Mowbray	32	52.46 N	0.53 W
Melun	42	48.32 N	2.40 E
Melville, Lake ⊜	160	53.45 N	59.30 W
Melville Hills ≗[2]	160	69.20 N	122.00 W
Melville Island I, Austl.	116	11.40 S	131.00 E
Melville Island I, N.W. Ter., Can.	160	75.15 N	110.00 W
Melville Peninsula ⋗[1]	160	68.00 N	84.00 W
Melvin, Lough ⊜	32	54.26 N	8.10 W
Melzo	46	45.30 N	9.25 E
Memmingen	36	47.59 N	10.11 E
Memphis	162	35.08 N	90.03 W
Mende	42	44.30 N	3.30 E
Menden	36	51.26 N	7.47 E
Mendip Hills ≗[2]	32	51.15 N	2.40 W
Mendocino, Cape ⋗	162	40.25 N	124.25 W
Mendoza	146	32.53 S	68.49 W
Menemen	54	38.36 N	27.04 E
Menfi	46	37.36 N	12.58 E
Menor, Mar C	50	37.43 N	0.48 W
Menorca I	50	40.00 N	4.00 E
Mentawai, Kepulauan II	82	2.00 S	99.30 E
Mentawai, Selat ᴜ	82	1.56 S	100.12 E
Menton	42	43.47 N	7.30 E
Menzel Bourguiba	46	37.10 N	9.48 E
Meppel	36	52.42 N	6.11 E
Meppen	36	52.41 N	7.17 E
Merano (Meran)	46	46.40 N	11.09 E
Mercedes, Arg.	146	33.40 S	65.28 W
Mercedes, Ur.	146	33.16 S	58.01 W
Merenkurkku (Norra Kvarken) ᴜ	28	63.36 N	21.43 E
Mergui	82	12.26 N	98.36 E
Mergui Archipelago II	82	12.00 N	98.00 E
Mérida, Esp.	50	38.55 N	6.20 W
Mérida, Méx.	130	20.58 N	89.37 W
Mérida, Ven.	144	8.36 N	71.08 W
Mérida, Cordillera de ⋏	144	8.40 N	71.00 W
Meridian	162	32.22 N	88.42 W
Mérignac	42	44.50 N	0.42 W
Mersea Island I	32	51.47 N	0.55 E
Merseburg	36	51.21 N	11.59 E
Mersin	20	36.48 N	34.38 E
Merthyr Tydfil	32	51.46 N	3.23 W
Meru ⋏	104	3.14 S	36.45 E
Merzig	36	49.27 N	6.36 E
Mesa	162	33.25 N	111.50 W
Mesagne	46	40.33 N	17.49 E
Meschede	36	51.20 N	8.17 E
Mesewa (Massaua)	102	15.38 N	39.28 E
Mesolóngion	54	38.21 N	21.17 E
Mesopotamia ≗[1]	84	34.00 N	44.00 E
Messalo ≏	104	11.40 S	40.26 E
Messina	46	38.11 N	15.33 E
Messina, Stretto di ᴜ	46	38.15 N	15.35 E
Messini	54	37.04 N	22.00 E
Mesta (Néstos) ≏	54	40.41 N	24.44 E
Mestre	46	45.29 N	12.15 E
Metallifere, Colline ⋏	46	43.15 N	11.00 E
Mettmann	36	51.15 N	6.58 E
Metz	42	49.08 N	6.10 E
Meurthe ≏	42	48.47 N	6.09 E
Meuse (Maas) ≏	42	51.49 N	5.01 E
Mexiana, Ilha I	144	0.02 S	49.35 W
Mexicali	130	32.40 N	115.29 W
Mexico ⬜[1]	130	23.00 N	102.00 W
Mexico, Gulf of C	130	25.00 N	90.00 W
Mezen' ≏	62	66.11 N	43.59 E
Mezőberény	36	46.50 N	21.02 E
Mezőkövesd	36	47.50 N	20.34 E
Mezőtúr	36	47.00 N	20.38 E
M'goun, Irhil ⋏	100	31.31 N	6.25 W
Miami	162	25.46 N	80.12 W
Miami Beach	162	25.47 N	80.08 W
Miass	62	54.59 N	60.06 E
Michalovce	36	48.45 N	21.55 E
Michigan ⬜[3]	162	44.00 N	85.00 W
Michigan, Lake ⊜	162	44.00 N	87.00 W
Michigan City	162	41.43 N	86.54 W
Michikamau Lake ⊜	160	54.00 N	64.00 W
Michipicoten Island I	160	47.45 N	85.45 W
Mičurinsk	62	52.54 N	40.30 E
Middelburg	36	51.30 N	3.37 E
Middle Andaman I	84	12.30 N	92.50 E
Middlesbrough	32	54.35 N	1.14 W
Middletown	162	39.29 N	84.24 W
Mid Glamorgan ⬜[6]	32	51.40 N	3.30 W
Midi, Canal du ☰	42	43.36 N	1.59 E
Midland, Mich., U.S.	162	43.37 N	84.14 W
Midland, Tex., U.S.	162	32.00 N	102.05 W
Midway Islands ⬜[2]	10	28.13 N	177.22 W
Międzyrzec Podlaski	36	52.00 N	22.47 E
Międzyrzecz	36	52.28 N	15.35 E
Mielec	36	50.18 N	21.25 E
Mieres	50	43.15 N	5.45 W
Miguel Alemán, Presa ⊜[1]	130	18.13 N	96.32 W
Mihajlovgrad	54	43.25 N	23.13 E
Mikkeli	28	61.41 N	27.15 E
Mikkwa ≏	160	58.25 N	114.43 W
Mikołów	36	50.11 N	18.53 E
Milagro	144	2.07 S	79.36 W
Milano (Milan)	46	45.28 N	9.12 E
Milâs	54	37.19 N	27.47 E
Milazzo	46	38.13 N	15.15 E
Miletto, Monte ⋏	46	41.27 N	14.22 E
Milford Haven	32	51.44 N	5.02 W
Millau	42	44.06 N	3.05 E
Mille Lacs Lake ⊜	162	46.15 N	93.40 W
Millevaches, Plateau de ⋏[1]	42	45.40 N	2.00 E
Milos I	54	36.41 N	24.15 E
Milwaukee	162	43.02 N	87.55 W
Minas	146	34.23 S	55.14 W
Minatitlán	130	17.59 N	94.31 W
Mindanao I	82	8.00 N	125.00 E
Mindanao Sea ⇥[2]	82	9.10 N	124.25 E
Mindelo	100	16.53 N	25.00 W
Minden	36	52.17 N	8.55 E
Mindoro I	82	12.50 N	121.05 E
Mindoro Strait ᴜ	82	12.20 N	120.40 E
Minervino Murge	46	41.05 N	16.05 E
Minho ⬜[9]	50	41.40 N	8.30 W
Minho (Miño) ≏	50	41.52 N	8.51 W
Minna	100	9.37 N	6.33 E
Minneapolis	162	44.59 N	93.13 W
Minnesota ⬜[3]	162	46.00 N	94.15 W
Minnesota ≏	162	44.54 N	93.10 W
Miño (Minho) ≏	50	41.52 N	8.51 W
Minot	162	48.14 N	101.18 W
Minsk	62	53.54 N	27.34 E
Mińsk Mazowiecki	36	52.11 N	21.34 E
Minto, Lac ⊜	160	51.00 N	73.37 W
Minturno	46	41.15 N	13.45 E
Mira	46	45.26 N	12.08 E
Mira ≏	50	37.43 N	8.47 W
Miramichi Bay C	160	47.08 N	65.08 W
Miranda de Ebro	50	42.41 N	2.57 W
Mirandola	46	44.53 N	11.04 E
Miravete, Puerto de)(	50	39.43 N	5.43 W
Miri	82	4.23 N	113.59 E
Mīrpur Khās	84	25.32 N	69.00 E
Misāḥah, Bi'r ⓶[4]	102	22.12 N	27.57 E
Mishmi Hills ≗[2]	84	29.00 N	96.00 E
Misilmeri	46	38.01 N	13.27 E
Miskitos, Cayos II	130	14.23 N	82.46 W
Miskolc	36	48.06 N	20.47 E
Mişrātah	102	32.23 N	15.06 E
Mississippi ⬜[3]	162	32.50 N	89.30 W
Mississippi ≏	162	29.00 N	89.15 W
Mississippi Delta ≗[2]	162	29.10 N	89.15 W
Missoula	162	46.52 N	114.01 W
Missouri ⬜[3]	162	38.30 N	93.30 W
Missouri ≏	162	38.50 N	90.08 W
Misterbianco	46	37.31 N	15.01 E
Misti, Volcán ⋏[1]	144	16.18 S	71.24 W
Mistretta	46	37.56 N	14.22 E
Mita, Punta de ⋗	130	20.47 N	105.33 W
Mitchell, Mount ⋏	162	35.46 N	82.16 W
Mitilíni	54	39.06 N	26.32 E
Mito	80	36.22 N	140.28 E
Mitsio, Nosy I	104	12.54 S	48.36 E
Mittellandkanal ☰	36	52.16 N	11.41 E
Mittweida	36	50.59 N	12.59 E
Mitumba, Monts ⋏	104	6.00 S	29.00 E
Miyakonojō	80	31.44 N	131.04 E
Miyazaki	80	31.54 N	131.26 E
Mizen Head ⋗	32	51.27 N	9.49 W
Mjölby	28	58.19 N	15.08 E
Mjøsa ⊜	28	60.40 N	11.00 E
Mladá Boleslav	36	50.23 N	14.59 E
Mława	36	53.06 N	20.23 E
Mljet, Otok I	46	42.45 N	17.30 E
Mljetski Kanal ᴜ	46	42.48 N	17.35 E
Moa ≏	100	6.59 N	11.36 W
Mobile	162	30.42 N	88.05 W
Moçambique	104	15.03 S	40.42 E
Moçâmedes	104	15.10 S	12.09 E
Mochudi	104	24.28 S	26.05 E
Möckeln ⊜	28	56.40 N	14.10 E
Môco, Serra ⋏	104	12.28 S	15.10 E
Močurica ≏	54	42.31 N	26.32 E
Modena	46	44.40 N	10.55 E
Modesto	162	37.39 N	121.00 W
Modica	46	36.51 N	14.47 E
Mödling	36	48.05 N	16.17 E
Modra Špilja ⊜[5]	46	43.00 N	16.02 E
Moe	116	38.10 S	146.15 E
Moers	36	51.27 N	6.37 E
Mogadishu	102	2.01 N	45.20 E
Mogi das Cruzes	144	23.31 S	46.11 W
Mogil'ov	62	53.54 N	30.21 E
Mogliano Veneto	46	45.33 N	12.14 E
Mohács	36	45.59 N	18.42 E
Mohammedia	100	33.44 N	7.24 W
Moheli I	104	12.15 S	43.45 E
Moinești	54	46.28 N	26.29 E
Mojave Desert ≗[2]	162	35.00 N	117.00 W
Mokp'o	80	34.48 N	126.22 E
Mokrisset	100	34.59 N	5.20 W
Mokša ≏	62	54.44 N	41.53 E
Mol	36	51.11 N	5.06 E
Mola di Bari	46	41.04 N	17.05 E
Moldova ≏	54	46.54 N	26.58 E
Moldoveanu ⋏	54	45.36 N	24.44 E
Molepolole	104	24.25 S	25.30 E
Moletta ≏	46	41.12 N	16.36 E
Molina de Segura	50	38.03 N	1.12 W
Moline	162	41.30 N	90.31 W
Molins de Rey	50	41.25 N	2.01 E
Mollendo	144	17.02 S	72.01 W
Mölln	36	53.37 N	10.41 E
Molokai I	162b	21.07 N	157.00 W
Molopo ≏	104	28.30 S	20.13 E
Mombasa	104	4.03 S	39.40 E
Momski Chrebet ⋏	64	66.00 N	146.00 E
Møn I	28	55.00 N	12.20 E
Mona, Isla I	130	18.05 N	67.54 W
Monaco ⬜[1]	42	43.42 N	7.23 E
Monaco	42	43.42 N	7.23 E
Monadhliath Mountains ⋏	32	57.15 N	4.10 W
Monastir	46	35.47 N	10.50 E
Moncalieri	46	45.00 N	7.41 E
Moncegorsk	62	67.54 N	32.58 E
Monclova	130	26.54 N	101.25 W
Mönchengladbach	36	51.12 N	6.28 E
Moncton	160	46.06 N	64.47 W
Mondovì	46	44.23 N	7.49 E
Mondragone	46	41.07 N	13.53 E
Monfalcone	46	45.49 N	13.32 E
Monforte de Lemos	50	42.31 N	7.30 W
Mongolia ⬜[1]	80	46.00 N	105.00 E
Mongol Altajn Nuruu ⋏	80	47.00 N	92.00 E
Mono ≏	100	6.17 N	1.51 E
Mono Lake ⊜	162	38.00 N	119.00 W
Monopoli	46	40.57 N	17.19 E
Monreale	46	38.05 N	13.17 E
Monroe	162	32.33 N	92.07 W
Monrovia	100	6.18 N	10.47 W
Mons	36	50.27 N	3.56 E
Montalto ⋏	46	38.10 N	15.55 E
Montana ⬜[3]	162	47.00 N	110.00 W
Montargis	42	48.00 N	2.45 E
Montauban	42	44.01 N	1.21 E
Montbéliard	42	47.31 N	6.48 E
Montbrison	42	45.36 N	4.03 E
Montceau [-les-Mines]	42	46.40 N	4.22 E
Mont-de-Marsan	42	43.53 N	0.30 W
Montecristi	130	19.52 N	71.39 W
Montecristo, Isola di I	46	42.20 N	10.19 E
Montego Bay	130	18.28 N	77.55 W
Montélimar	42	44.34 N	4.45 E
Monte Lindo ≏	146	23.56 S	57.12 W
Monterey	162	36.37 N	121.55 W
Monterey Bay C	162	36.45 N	121.55 W
Montería	144	8.46 N	75.53 W
Monterotondo	46	42.03 N	12.37 E
Monterrey	130	25.40 N	100.19 W
Monte Sant'Angelo	46	41.42 N	15.57 E
Monte Santu, Capo di ⋗	46	40.05 N	9.44 E
Montes Claros	144	16.43 S	43.52 W
Montevarchi	46	43.31 N	11.34 E
Montevideo	146	34.53 S	56.11 W
Montgomery	162	32.23 N	86.18 W
Monti	46	40.48 N	9.20 E
Montichiari	46	45.25 N	10.24 E
Montiel, Campo de ≗[1]	50	38.46 N	2.44 W
Montijo, Port.	50	38.42 N	8.58 W
Montijo, Esp.	50	38.55 N	6.37 W
Montilla	50	37.35 N	4.38 W
Montluçon	42	46.20 N	2.36 E
Montmorillon	42	46.26 N	0.52 E
Montpelier	162	44.15 N	72.34 W
Montpellier	42	43.36 N	3.53 E
Montréal	160	45.31 N	73.34 W
Montreal Lake ⊜	160	54.20 N	105.40 W
Montreux	42	46.26 N	6.55 E
Montrose	32	56.43 N	2.29 W
Montserrat ⬜[2]	130	16.45 N	62.12 W
Monywa	82	22.05 N	95.08 E
Monza	46	45.35 N	9.16 E
Moorhead	162	46.53 N	96.45 W
Moosburg	36	48.29 N	11.57 E
Moosehead Lake ⊜	162	45.40 N	69.40 W
Moose Jaw	160	50.23 N	105.32 W
Mopti	100	14.30 N	4.12 W
Mór	36	47.23 N	18.12 E
Mora	50	39.41 N	3.46 W
Morādābād	84	28.50 N	78.47 E
Mórahalom	36	46.13 N	19.54 E
Moraleda, Canal ᴜ	146	44.30 S	73.30 W
Morant Cays II	130	17.24 N	75.59 W
Moratalla	50	38.12 N	1.53 W
Moratuwa	84	6.46 N	79.53 E
Morava (March) ≏	36	48.10 N	16.59 E
Moray Firth C[1]	32	57.50 N	3.30 W
More, Ben ⋏	32	56.23 N	4.31 W
Moreau ≏	162	45.18 N	100.43 W
Morecambe	32	54.04 N	2.53 W
Morelia	130	19.42 N	101.07 W
Morena, Sierra ⋏	50	38.15 N	5.00 W
Morghāb (Murgab) ≏	84	38.18 N	61.12 E
Morioka	80	39.42 N	141.09 E
Morlaix	42	48.35 N	3.50 W
Morocco ⬜[1]	100	32.00 N	5.00 W
Morogoro	104	6.49 S	37.40 E
Moro Gulf C	82	6.51 N	123.00 E
Morón	130	22.06 N	78.38 W
Morondava	104	20.17 S	44.17 E
Morón de la Frontera	50	37.08 N	5.27 W
Moroni	104	11.41 S	43.16 E
Morpeth	32	55.10 N	1.41 W
Morro, Punta ⋗	146	27.07 S	70.57 W
Mortara	46	45.15 N	8.44 E
Morvan ≗[1]	42	47.05 N	4.00 E
Mosbach	36	49.21 N	9.08 E
Mosel (Moselle) ≏	42	50.22 N	7.36 E
Moshi	104	3.21 S	37.20 E
Moskenesøya I	26	67.59 N	13.00 E
Moskva (Moscow)	62	55.45 N	37.35 E
Mosonmagyaróvár	36	47.51 N	17.17 E
Mosquitos, Golfo de los C	130	9.00 N	81.15 W
Moss	28	59.26 N	10.42 E
Mosselbaai	104	34.11 S	22.08 E
Mossoró	144	5.11 S	37.20 W
Most	36	50.32 N	13.39 E
Mostaganem	100	35.51 N	0.07 E
Mostar	46	43.20 N	17.49 E
Møsting, Kap ⋗	160	64.00 N	41.00 W
Motala	28	58.33 N	15.03 E
Motherwell	32	55.48 N	4.00 W
Motril	50	36.45 N	3.31 W
Motru ≏	54	44.44 N	22.59 E
Motutapu I	114	21.14 S	159.43 W
Mou	114	21.05 S	165.26 E
Moulins	42	46.34 N	3.20 E
Moulmein	82	16.30 N	97.38 E
Moulouya, Oued ≏	100	35.05 N	2.25 W
Moundou	100	8.34 N	16.05 E
Mounier, Mont ⋏	42	44.09 N	6.58 E
Mountain Nile (Baḥr al-Jabal) ≏	102	9.30 N	30.30 E
Mount Gambier	116	37.50 S	140.46 E
Mount Isa	116	20.44 S	139.30 E
Mount Roskill	118	36.55 S	174.45 E
Mount's Bay C	32	50.03 N	5.25 W
Mount Wellington	118	36.54 S	174.51 E
Mourdi, Dépression du ≗[7]	102	18.10 N	23.00 E
Mourne Mountains ⋏	32	54.10 N	6.04 W
Moxos, Llanos de ≏	144	15.00 S	65.00 W
Moyen Atlas ⋏	100	33.30 N	5.00 W
Moyeuvre-Grande	42	49.15 N	6.02 E
Mozambique ⬜[1]	104	18.15 S	35.00 E
Mozambique Channel ᴜ	104	19.00 S	41.00 E
Možga	62	56.23 N	52.17 E
Mrągowo	36	53.52 N	21.19 E
Mrhila, Djebel ⋏	46	35.25 N	9.14 E
Msaken	46	35.44 N	10.35 E
M'Sila	100	35.46 N	4.31 E
Mtwara	104	10.16 S	40.11 E
Muar	82	2.02 N	102.34 E
Muchinga Mountains ⋏	104	12.00 S	31.45 E
Mudanjiang	80	44.35 N	129.36 E
Mufulira	104	12.33 S	28.14 E
Mugello ∨	46	43.55 N	11.30 E
Mugía	50	43.06 N	9.13 W
Mugodžáry ⋏[2]	62	49.00 N	58.40 E
Mühlacker	36	48.57 N	8.50 E
Mühldorf	36	48.15 N	12.32 E
Mühlhausen	36	51.12 N	10.27 E
Mühlviertel ≗[1]	36	48.25 N	14.13 E
Mukačevo	54	48.27 N	22.45 E
Mulde ≏	36	51.10 N	12.48 E
Mulhacén ⋏	50	37.03 N	3.19 W
Mulhouse	42	47.45 N	7.20 E
Mull, Island of I	32	56.27 N	6.00 W
Multán	84	30.11 N	71.29 E
Mun ≏	82	15.19 N	105.30 E
Muna, Pulau I	82	5.00 S	122.30 E
München (Munich)	36	48.08 N	11.34 E
Muncie	162	40.11 N	85.23 W
Munster ⬜[9]	32	52.30 N	8.15 W
Munster	36	52.59 N	10.05 E
Münster, B.R.D.	36	51.57 N	7.37 E
Münster, B.R.D.	36	52.59 N	8.00 E
Muqayshiṭ I	84	24.12 N	53.42 E
Mura (Mur) ≏	46	46.18 N	16.53 E
Muradiye	54	38.39 N	27.21 E
Murchison ≏	116	27.42 S	114.09 E
Murchison Falls ᴸ	102	2.17 N	31.41 E
Murcia	50	37.59 N	1.07 W
Murcia ⬜[9]	50	38.30 N	1.45 W
Murgab (Morghāb) ≏	84	38.18 N	61.12 E
Muri	114	21.14 S	159.43 W
Müritz ⊜	36	53.25 N	12.40 E
Murmansk	62	68.58 N	33.05 E
Muroran	80	42.18 N	140.58 E
Murrumbidgee ≏	116	34.43 S	143.12 E
Murter, Otok I	46	43.48 N	15.37 E
Murud, Gunong ⋏	82	3.52 N	115.30 E
Mürzzuschlag	36	47.36 N	15.41 E
Musala ⋏	54	42.11 N	23.34 E
Mus-Chaja, Gora ⋏	64	62.35 N	140.50 E
Mushin	100	6.32 N	3.22 E
Muskegon	162	43.14 N	86.16 W
Muskogee	162	35.45 N	95.22 W
Mussomeli	46	37.35 N	13.45 E
Mustafakemalpaşa	54	40.02 N	28.24 E
Mutsu-wan C	80	41.05 N	140.55 E
Mwanza	104	2.31 S	32.54 E
Mweru, Lake ⊜	104	9.00 S	28.45 E
Myanaung	82	18.17 N	95.19 E
Myingyan	82	21.28 N	95.23 E
Myitkyiná	82	25.23 N	97.24 E
Myjava	36	48.45 N	17.34 E
Mymensingh	84	24.45 N	90.24 E
Myślenice	36	49.51 N	19.56 E
Mysłowice	36	50.15 N	19.07 E
Mysore	84	12.18 N	76.39 E
My-tho	82	10.21 N	106.21 E
Mytišči	62	55.55 N	37.46 E
Mzuzu	104	11.27 S	33.55 E

Name	Page	Lat ° ′	Long ° ′
N			
Naab ≃	36	49.01 N	12.02 E
Naach, Jbel ▲	50	34.53 N	3.22 W
Nabeul	100	36.27 N	10.44 E
Nabī Shu'ayb, Jabal an- ▲	84	15.18 N	43.59 E
Nābulus	84	32.13 N	35.15 E
Náchod	36	50.25 N	16.10 E
Nachodka	64	42.48 N	132.52 E
Nacka	28	59.18 N	18.10 E
Nădlac	54	46.10 N	20.45 E
Nador	50	35.12 N	2.55 W
Næstved	28	55.14 N	11.46 E
Naga	82	13.37 N	123.11 E
Nagano	80	36.39 N	138.11 E
Nagaoka	80	37.27 N	138.51 E
Nagasaki	80	32.48 N	129.55 E
Nagoya	80	35.10 N	136.55 E
Nāgpur	84	21.08 N	79.04 E
Nagykanizsa	36	46.27 N	17.00 E
Nagykáta	36	47.25 N	19.45 E
Nagykőrös	36	47.02 N	19.43 E
Naha	80	26.13 N	127.40 E
Nahe ≃	36	49.58 N	7.57 E
Nairobi	104	1.17 S	36.49 E
Najin	80	42.15 N	130.18 E
Najramdal Uul ▲	80	49.10 N	87.52 W
Nakhon Pathom	82	13.49 N	100.03 E
Nakhon Ratchasima	82	14.58 N	102.07 E
Nakhon Sawan	82	15.41 N	100.07 E
Nakhon Si Thammarat	82	8.26 N	99.58 E
Nakło nad Notecią	36	53.08 N	17.35 E
Nakskov	28	54.50 N	11.09 E
Nakuru	104	0.17 S	36.04 E
Nal'čik	62	43.29 N	43.37 E
Namak, Daryācheh-ye ⊜	84	34.45 N	51.36 E
Namangan	62	41.00 N	71.40 E
Nam-dinh	82	20.25 N	106.10 E
Namib Desert •[2]	104	23.00 S	15.00 E
Namibia □[2]	104	22.00 S	17.00 E
Namp'o	80	38.45 N	125.23 E
Nampula	104	15.07 S	39.15 E
Namsen ≃	26	64.27 N	11.28 E
Namuchabawashan ▲	80	29.38 N	95.04 E
Namuhu ⊜	80	30.42 N	90.30 E
Namur	36	50.28 N	4.52 E
Namysłów	36	51.05 N	17.42 E
Nan ≃	82	15.42 N	100.09 E
Nanaimo	160	49.10 N	123.56 W
Nanchang	80	28.41 N	115.53 E
Nanchong	80	30.48 N	106.04 E
Nancy	42	48.41 N	6.12 E
Nanda Devi ▲	84	30.23 N	79.59 E
Nandi	111	17.48 S	177.25 E
Nandi Bay C	111	17.44 S	177.25 E
N'andoma	26	61.40 N	40.12 E
Nānga Parbat ▲	84	35.15 N	74.36 E
Nanjing	80	32.03 N	118.47 E
Nanling ⛰	80	25.00 N	112.00 E
Nanning	80	22.48 N	108.20 E
Nansa ≃	50	43.22 N	4.29 W
Nansei-shotō (Ryukyu Islands) II	80	26.30 N	128.00 E
Nantes	42	47.13 N	1.33 W
Nantong	80	32.02 N	120.53 E
Nantucket Island I	162	41.16 N	70.03 W
Nanuque	144	17.50 S	40.21 W
Nanyang	80	33.00 N	112.32 E
Nanyuki	104	0.01 N	37.04 E
Nao, Cabo de la >	50	38.44 N	0.14 E
Náousa	54	40.37 N	22.05 E
Napier	118	39.29 S	176.55 E
Napoli (Naples)	46	40.51 N	14.17 E
Napoli, Golfo di C	46	40.43 N	14.10 E
Nara	80	34.41 N	135.50 E
Nārāyanganj	84	23.37 N	90.30 E
Narbonne	42	43.11 N	3.00 E
Nardò	46	40.11 N	18.02 E
Narew ≃	36	52.26 N	20.42 E
Narinda, Baie de C	104	14.55 S	47.30 E
Narni	46	42.31 N	12.31 E
Naro	46	37.17 N	13.48 E
Narodnaja, Gora ▲	62	65.04 N	60.09 E
Narovorovo	112	15.13 S	168.09 E
Narva	26	59.23 N	28.12 E
Narvik	26	68.26 N	17.25 E
Nashua	162	42.46 N	71.27 W
Nashville	162	36.09 N	86.48 W
Näsijärvi ⊜	28	61.37 N	23.42 E
Nāsik	84	19.59 N	73.47 E
Nassau	130	25.05 N	77.21 W
Nasser, Lake ⊜[1]	100	22.40 N	32.00 E
Nässjö	28	57.39 N	14.41 E
Natal	144	5.47 S	35.13 W
Natewa Bay C	111	16.35 S	179.40 E
Natron, Lake ⊜	104	2.25 S	36.00 E
Nattastunturit ▲	26	68.12 N	27.20 E
Nauen	36	52.36 N	12.52 E
Naumburg	36	51.09 N	11.48 E
Nauru □[1]	10	0.32 S	166.55 E
Nausori	111	18.02 S	175.32 E
Navarra □[4]	50	42.40 N	1.30 W
Navia ≃	50	43.33 N	6.44 W
Navojoa	130	27.06 N	109.26 W
Návpaktos	54	38.23 N	21.50 E
Návplion	54	37.34 N	22.48 E
Nawābshāh	84	26.15 N	68.25 E
Náxos I	54	37.02 N	25.35 E
Naze	80	28.23 N	129.30 E
Nazilli	54	37.55 N	28.21 E
Ndjamena (Fort-Lamy)	102	12.07 N	15.03 E
Ndola	104	12.58 S	28.38 E
Ndreketi ≃	111	16.34 S	178.53 E
Neagh, Lough ⊜	32	54.38 N	6.24 W
Neajlov ≃	54	44.11 N	26.12 E
Neath	32	51.40 N	3.48 W
Nebraska □[3]	162	41.30 N	100.00 W
Nebrodi ⛰	46	37.55 N	14.35 E
Neckar ≃	36	49.31 N	8.26 E
Neckarsulm	36	49.12 N	9.13 E
Nédroma	50	35.01 N	1.45 W
Negombo	84	7.13 N	79.50 E
Negra, Cordillera ⛰	144	9.25 S	77.40 W
Negra, Punta >	144	6.06 S	81.09 W
Negro ≃, Arg.	146	41.02 S	62.47 W
Negro ≃, Bol.	144	14.11 S	63.07 W
Negro ≃, S.A.	144	3.08 S	59.55 W
Negros I	82	10.00 N	123.00 E
Neheim-Hüsten	36	51.27 N	7.57 E
Neiges, Piton des ▲	104	21.05 S	55.29 E
Neijiang	80	29.35 N	105.03 E
Neisse (Nysa Łużycka) (Nisa) ≃	36	52.04 N	14.46 E
Neiva	144	2.56 N	75.18 W
Nelson	118	41.17 S	173.17 E
Nelson ≃	160	57.04 N	92.30 W
Nelspruit	104	25.30 S	30.58 E
Néma	100	16.37 N	7.15 W
Neman (Nemunas) ≃	62	55.18 N	21.23 E
Nemuna, Bjeshkët e ⛰	54	42.27 N	19.47 E
Nemunas (Neman) ≃	62	55.18 N	21.23 E
Nemuro	80	43.20 N	145.35 E
Nepal (Nepāl) □[1]	84	28.00 N	84.00 E
Nera ≃	46	42.26 N	12.24 E
Nerastro, Sarīr •[2]	102	24.20 N	20.37 E
Neretva ≃	54	43.40 N	17.59 E
Nerva	50	37.42 N	6.32 W
Ness, Loch ⊜	32	57.15 N	4.30 W
Nesselrode, Mount ▲	162a	58.58 N	134.18 W
Netanya	84	32.20 N	34.51 E
Netherlands □[1]	36	52.15 N	5.30 E
Netherlands Antilles □[2]	130	12.15 N	69.00 W
Neto ≃	46	39.13 N	17.08 E
Nettilling Lake ⊜	160	66.30 N	70.40 W
Nettuno	46	41.27 N	12.39 E
Neubrandenburg	36	53.33 N	13.15 E
Neuburg an der Donau	36	48.44 N	11.11 E
Neuchâtel	42	46.59 N	6.56 E
Neuchâtel, Lac de ⊜	42	46.52 N	6.50 E
Neu-Isenburg	36	50.03 N	8.41 E
Neumarkt in der Oberpfalz	36	49.16 N	11.28 E
Neumünster	36	54.04 N	9.59 E
Neunkirchen	36	47.43 N	16.05 E
Neunkirchen/saar	36	49.20 N	7.10 E
Neuquén	146	38.57 S	68.04 W
Neuruppin	36	52.55 N	12.48 E
Neusiedler See ⊜	36	47.50 N	16.46 E
Neuss	36	51.12 N	6.41 E
Neustadt an der Weinstrasse	36	49.21 N	8.08 E
Neustadt in Holstein	36	54.06 N	10.48 E
Neustrelitz	36	53.21 N	13.04 E
Neutral Zone □[2]	84	29.10 N	45.30 E
Neu-Ulm	36	48.23 N	10.01 E
Neuwied	36	50.25 N	7.27 E
Nevada □[3]	162	39.00 N	117.00 W
Nevada, Sierra ⛰, Esp.	50	37.05 N	3.10 W
Nevada, Sierra ⛰, Calif., U.S.	162	38.00 N	119.15 W
Nevado, Cerro ▲	146	35.35 S	68.30 W
Nevers	42	47.00 N	3.09 E
Nevinnomyssk	62	44.38 N	41.56 E
Nevis I	130	17.10 N	62.34 W
Nevis, Ben ▲	32	56.48 N	5.01 W
New Amsterdam	144	6.15 N	57.31 W
Newark, N.J., U.S.	162	40.44 N	74.10 W
Newark, Ohio, U.S.	162	40.04 N	82.24 W
Newark-upon-Trent	32	53.05 N	0.49 W
New Bedford	162	41.38 N	70.56 W
New Britain I	116a	6.00 S	150.00 E
New Brunswick □[4]	160	46.30 N	66.15 W
Newburgh	162	41.30 N	74.01 W
Newbury	32	51.25 N	1.20 W
New Caledonia □[2]	112	21.30 S	165.30 E
Newcastle, Austl.	116	32.56 S	151.46 E
Newcastle, S. Afr.	104	27.49 S	29.55 E
New Castle, Pa., U.S.	162	41.00 N	80.20 W
Newcastle-under-Lyme	32	53.00 N	2.14 W
Newcastle upon Tyne	32	54.59 N	1.35 W
Newcastle Waters	116	17.24 S	133.24 E
New Delhi	84	28.36 N	77.15 E
Newfoundland □[4]	160	52.00 N	56.00 W
New Georgia I	114	8.15 S	157.30 E
New Georgia Group II	114	8.30 S	157.20 E
New Glasgow	160	45.35 N	62.39 W
New Hampshire □[3]	162	43.35 N	71.40 W
New Hanover I	116a	2.30 S	150.15 E
New Haven	162	41.18 N	72.56 W
New Hebrides □[2]	112	16.00 S	167.00 E
New Hebrides (Nouvelles-Hébrides) II	112	16.00 S	167.00 E
New Ireland I	116a	3.20 S	152.00 E
New Jersey □[3]	162	40.15 N	74.30 W
New London	162	41.21 N	72.07 W
Newmarket	32	52.15 N	0.25 E
New Mexico □[3]	162	34.30 N	106.00 W
New Orleans	162	29.58 N	90.07 W
New Plymouth	118	39.04 S	174.05 E
Newport, Eng., U.K.	32	50.42 N	1.18 W
Newport, Wales, U.K.	32	52.01 N	4.51 W
Newport, R.I., U.S.	162	41.13 N	71.18 W
Newport News	162	37.04 N	76.28 W
New Providence I	130	25.02 N	77.24 W
Newquay	32	50.25 N	5.05 W
Newry	32	54.11 N	6.20 W
Newton Abbot	32	50.32 N	3.36 W
Newtownabbey	32	54.42 N	5.54 W
Newtownards	32	54.36 N	5.41 W
New Westminster	160	49.12 N	122.55 W
New York	162	40.43 N	74.01 W
New York □[3]	162	43.00 N	75.00 W
New Zealand □[1]	118	41.00 S	174.00 E
Ngami, Lake ⊜	104	20.37 S	22.40 E
Ngatangiia	114	21.14 S	159.43 W
Ng'iro, Ewaso ≃	104	0.28 N	39.55 E
Ngoko ≃	104	1.40 N	16.03 E
Nguru	100	12.52 N	10.27 E
Nha-trang	82	12.15 N	109.11 E
Niagara Falls, Ont., Can.	160	43.06 N	79.04 W
Niagara Falls, N.Y., U.S.	162	43.06 N	79.02 W
Niamey	100	13.31 N	2.07 E
Nias, Pulau I	82	1.05 N	97.35 E
Nicaragua □[1]	130	13.00 N	85.00 W
Nicaragua, Lago de ⊜	130	11.30 N	85.30 W
Nicastro (Lamezia Terme)	46	38.59 N	16.20 E
Nice	42	43.42 N	7.15 E
Nicobar Islands II	82	8.00 N	93.30 E
Nicosia	46	37.45 N	14.24 E
Nida ≃	36	50.18 N	20.52 E
Nidd ≃	32	54.01 N	1.12 W
Nidzica	36	53.22 N	20.26 E
Niedere Tauern ⛰	36	47.18 N	14.00 E
Nienburg	36	52.38 N	9.13 E
Niger □[1]	100	16.00 N	8.00 E
Niger ≃	100	5.33 N	6.33 E
Nigeria □[1]	100	10.00 N	8.00 E
Nigrita	54	40.55 N	23.30 E
Niigata	80	37.55 N	139.03 E
Nijmegen	36	51.50 N	5.50 E
Nikolajev	62	46.58 N	32.00 E
Nikopol'	62	47.35 N	34.25 E
Nikšić	54	42.46 N	18.56 E
Nile (Nahr an-Nīl) ≃	102	30.10 N	31.06 E
Nimba, Mont ▲	100	7.37 N	8.25 W
Nimba Mountains ⛰	100	7.30 N	8.30 W
Nîmes	42	43.50 N	4.21 E
Nine Degree Channel ⊔	84	9.00 N	72.50 E
Ninety Mile Beach •[2]	116	38.13 S	147.23 E
Ningbo	80	29.52 N	121.31 E
Nioro du Sahel	100	15.15 N	9.35 W
Niort	42	46.19 N	0.27 W
Nipigon, Lake ⊜	160	49.50 N	88.30 W
Nipissing, Lake ⊜	160	46.17 N	80.00 W
Niš	54	43.19 N	21.54 E
Nišava ≃	54	43.22 N	21.46 E
Niscemi	46	37.08 N	14.24 E
Nisling ≃	160	62.27 N	139.30 W
Nissan ≃	28	56.40 N	12.51 E
Niterói	144	22.53 S	43.07 W
Nitra	36	48.20 N	18.05 E
Nitra ≃	36	47.46 N	18.10 E
Niue □[2]	10	19.02 S	169.52 W
Nive ≃	42	43.30 N	1.29 W
Nivelles	36	50.36 N	4.20 E
Nizke Beskydy ⛰	36	49.20 N	21.30 E
Nizke Tatry ⛰	36	48.54 N	19.40 E
Nižnekamsk	26	55.32 N	51.58 E
Nižnij Tagil	62	57.55 N	59.57 E
Njombe ≃	104	6.56 S	35.06 E
Nkongsamba	100	4.57 N	9.56 E
Nmai ≃	80	25.42 N	97.30 E
Nobeoka	80	32.35 N	131.40 E
Noce ≃	46	46.09 N	11.04 E
Nocera [Inferiore]	46	40.44 N	14.38 E
Nogales, Méx.	130	31.20 N	110.56 W
Nogales, Ariz., U.S.	162	31.20 N	110.56 W
Nogent-le-Rotrou	42	48.19 N	0.50 E
Noginsk	26	55.51 N	38.27 E
Noir, Causse ⛰[1]	42	44.10 N	3.15 E
Noirmoutier, Île de I	42	47.00 N	2.15 W
Nokia	28	61.28 N	23.30 E
Nola	46	40.55 N	14.33 E
Nong Khai	82	17.52 N	102.44 E
Noordoost Polder ◆[1]	36	52.42 N	5.45 E
Nora Islands II	102	16.02 N	39.58 E
Norden	36	53.36 N	7.12 E
Nordenham	36	53.29 N	8.28 E
Norderney I	36	53.42 N	7.10 E
Nordhausen	36	51.30 N	10.47 E
Nordhorn	36	52.27 N	7.05 E
Nordkapp >	26	71.11 N	25.48 E
Nördlingen	36	48.51 N	10.30 E
Nord-Ostsee-Kanal ⊔	36	53.53 N	9.08 E
Nordpfälzer Bergland ⛰	36	49.40 N	7.40 E
Nordre Strømfjord C[2]	160	67.50 N	52.00 W
Nordstrand I	36	54.30 N	8.53 E
Norfolk	162	36.40 N	76.14 W
Norfolk □[6]	32	52.35 N	1.00 E
Norfolk Island □[2]	113	29.02 S	167.57 E
Noril'sk	64	69.20 N	88.06 E
Normanton	116	17.40 S	141.05 E
Norra Storfjället ▲	26	65.52 N	15.18 E
Nørresundby	28	57.04 N	9.55 E
Norrköping	28	58.36 N	16.11 E
Norrtälje	28	59.46 N	18.42 E
Norte, Canal do ⊔	144	0.30 N	50.30 W
North, Cape >[2]	160	47.02 N	60.25 W
Northampton	32	52.14 N	0.54 W
Northamptonshire □[6]	32	52.20 N	0.50 W
North Andaman I	84	13.15 N	92.55 E
North Bay	160	46.19 N	79.28 W
North Carolina □[3]	162	35.30 N	80.00 W
North Channel ⊔, Ont., Can.	160	46.02 N	82.50 W
North Channel ⊔, U.K.	32	55.10 N	5.40 W
North Dakota □[3]	162	47.30 N	100.15 W
North Downs ⛰[1]	32	51.20 N	0.10 E
Northeim	36	51.42 N	10.00 E
Northern Indian Lake ⊜	160	57.20 N	97.20 W
Northern Ireland □[8]	32	54.40 N	6.45 W
North Foreland >	32	51.23 N	1.27 E
North Frisian Islands II	26	54.50 N	8.12 E
North Island I	118	39.00 S	176.00 E
North Platte ≃	162	41.15 N	100.45 W
North Saskatchewan ≃	160	53.15 N	105.06 W
North Sea ▾[2]	20	55.20 N	3.00 E
Northumberland □[6]	32	55.15 N	2.05 W
Northwest Territories □[4]	160	70.00 N	100.00 W
North Yorkshire □[6]	32	54.15 N	1.30 W
Norway □[1]	26	62.00 N	10.00 E
Norwegian Sea ▾[2]	26	70.00 N	2.00 E
Norwich	32	52.38 N	1.18 E
Nossi-Bé I	104	13.20 S	48.15 E
Nossob (Nossop) ≃	104	26.55 S	20.37 E
Noteć ≃	36	52.44 N	15.26 E
Notikewin ≃	160	57.15 N	117.05 W
Noto	46	36.53 N	15.05 E
Noto, Golfo di C	46	36.50 N	15.15 E
Noto-hantō >[1]	80	37.20 N	137.00 E
Notre Dame, Monts ⛰	160	48.10 N	68.00 W
Nottingham	32	52.58 N	1.10 W
Nottinghamshire □[6]	32	53.00 N	1.00 W
Nouadhibou	100	20.54 N	17.04 W
Nouakchott	100	18.06 N	15.57 W
Nouméa	112	22.16 S	166.27 E
Nouvelle-Calédonie I	112	21.30 S	165.30 E
Nova Friburgo	144	22.16 S	42.32 W
Novaja Zemľa II	62	74.00 N	57.00 E
Novara	46	45.28 N	8.38 E
Nova Scotia □[4]	160	45.00 N	63.00 W
Nova Zagora	54	42.29 N	26.01 E
Novelda	50	38.23 N	0.46 W
Nové Město nad Váhom	36	48.46 N	17.49 E
Nové Zámky	36	47.59 N	18.11 E
Novgorod	26	58.31 N	31.17 E
Novi Bečej	54	45.36 N	20.08 E
Novi Ligure	46	44.46 N	8.47 E
Novi Pazar, Blg.	54	43.21 N	27.12 E
Novi Pazar, Jugo.	54	43.08 N	20.31 E
Novi Sad	54	45.15 N	19.50 E
Novočerkassk	62	47.25 N	40.06 E
Novokujbyševsk	26	53.07 N	49.58 E
Novokuzneck	64	53.45 N	87.06 E
Novomoskovsk	62	54.05 N	38.13 E
Novorossijsk	62	44.45 N	37.45 E
Novošachtinsk	62	47.47 N	39.56 E
Novosibirsk	64	55.02 N	82.55 E
Novosibirskije Ostrova II	64	75.00 N	142.00 E
Nový Bohumín	36	49.56 N	18.20 E
Nový Jičín	36	49.36 N	18.00 E
Nowa Ruda	36	50.35 N	16.31 E
Nowa Sól (Neusalz)	36	51.48 N	15.44 E
Nowshāk ▲	84	36.26 N	71.50 E
Nowshera	84	34.01 N	71.59 E
Nowy Dwór Mazowiecki	36	52.26 N	20.43 E
Nowy Sącz	36	49.38 N	20.42 E
Nowy Targ	36	49.29 N	20.02 E
Noya ≃	50	41.28 N	1.56 E
Noyon	42	49.35 N	3.00 E
Nsawam	100	5.50 N	0.20 W
Ntem ≃	100	2.15 N	9.45 E
Nūbah, Jibāl an- ⛰	102	12.00 N	30.45 E
Nubian Desert •[2]	102	20.30 N	33.00 E
Nueces ≃	162	27.50 N	97.30 W
Nueva, Isla I	146	55.13 S	66.30 W
Nueva Gerona	130	21.53 N	82.48 W
Nueva Rosita	130	27.57 N	101.13 W
Nuevitas	130	21.33 N	77.16 W
Nuevo Laredo	130	27.30 N	99.31 W
Nuevo Mundo, Cerro ▲	144	21.55 S	66.53 W
Nûgssuaq >[1]	160	71.45 N	53.00 W
Nullarbor Plain ⌣	116	31.00 S	129.00 E
Numazu	80	35.06 N	138.52 E
Nuneaton	32	52.32 N	1.28 W
Nuoro	46	40.19 N	9.20 E
Nürnberg	36	49.27 N	11.04 E
Nurra ◆[1]	46	40.45 N	8.15 E
Nürtingen	36	48.38 N	9.20 E
Nusa Tenggara (Lesser Sunda Islands) II	82	9.00 S	120.00 E
Nushan ⛰	80	26.50 N	99.03 E
Nuweveldberge ⛰	104	32.13 S	21.40 E
Nyala	102	12.03 N	24.53 E
Nyanza	104	2.21 S	29.45 E
Nyasa, Lake ⊜	104	12.00 S	34.30 E
Nyborg	28	55.19 N	10.48 E
Nybro	28	56.45 N	15.54 E
Nyíregyháza	36	47.59 N	21.43 E
Nykøbing	28	54.46 N	11.53 E
Nyköping	28	58.45 N	17.00 E
Nymburk	36	50.11 N	15.03 E
Nynäshamn	28	58.54 N	17.57 E
Nyon	42	46.23 N	6.14 E
Nyong ≃	100	3.17 N	9.54 E
Nysa	36	50.29 N	17.20 E
Nysa Kłodzka ≃	36	50.49 N	17.50 E
Nzérékoré	100	7.45 N	8.49 W
Nzi ≃	100	5.57 N	4.50 W
O			
Oahu I	162b	21.30 N	158.00 W
Oakland	162	37.47 N	122.13 W
Oamaru	118	45.06 S	170.58 E
Oaxaca	130	17.00 N	96.30 W
Ob' ≃	62	66.45 N	69.30 E
Ober Ennstal V	36	47.28 N	14.10 E
Oberhausen	36	51.28 N	6.50 E
Oberursel	36	50.11 N	8.35 E
Obihiro	80	42.55 N	143.12 E
Obock	102	11.59 N	43.16 E
Obra ≃	36	52.36 N	15.28 E
Obščij Syrt ▲	62	52.00 N	51.30 E
Obskaja Guba C	62	69.00 N	73.00 E
Obuasi	100	6.14 N	1.39 W
Ocaña	144	8.15 N	73.20 W
Occidental, Cordillera ⛰, Col.	144	5.00 N	76.00 W
Occidental, Cordillera ⛰, Perú	144	14.00 S	74.00 W
Oceanside	162	33.12 N	117.23 W
Ochtrup	36	52.13 N	7.11 E
Ocotal	130	13.38 N	86.29 W
Ocotlán	130	20.21 N	102.46 W
Ocreza, Ribeira da ≃	50	39.32 N	7.50 W
Oda	100	5.55 N	0.59 W
Oda, Jabal ▲	102	20.21 N	36.39 E
Ödemiş	54	38.13 N	27.59 E
Odendaalsrus	104	27.48 S	26.45 E
Odense	28	55.24 N	10.23 E
Odenwald ⛰	36	49.40 N	9.00 E
Oder (Odra) ≃	36	53.32 N	14.38 E
Oderbruch ◆[1]	36	52.40 N	14.15 E
Odessa, S.S.S.R.	62	46.28 N	30.44 E
Odessa, Tex., U.S.	162	31.51 N	102.22 W
Odorheiu Secuiesc	54	46.18 N	25.18 E
Oelde	36	51.49 N	8.08 E
Oelsnitz	36	50.24 N	12.10 E
Ofanto ≃	46	41.22 N	16.13 E
Offenbach	36	50.08 N	8.47 E
Offenburg	36	48.28 N	7.57 E
Ogbomosho	100	8.08 N	4.15 E
Ogden	162	41.14 N	111.58 W
Ogden, Mount ▲	162a	58.26 N	133.23 W
Ogilvie Mountains ⛰	160	65.00 N	139.30 W
Ogliastra ◆[1]	46	40.00 N	9.30 E
Oglio ≃	46	45.02 N	10.39 E
Ogooué ≃	104	0.49 S	9.00 E
O'Higgins, Lago (Lago San Martín) ⊜	146	49.00 S	72.40 W
Ohio □[3]	162	40.15 N	82.45 W
Ohio ≃	162	36.59 N	89.08 W
Ohrid	54	41.07 N	20.47 E
Ohrid, Lake ⊜	54	41.02 N	20.43 E
Oise ≃	42	49.00 N	2.04 E
Ōita	80	33.14 N	131.36 E
Ojos del Salado, Cerro ▲	146	27.06 S	68.32 W
Oka ≃	62	56.20 N	43.59 E
Okanogan ≃	162	48.06 N	119.43 W
Okāra	84	30.49 N	73.27 E
Okavango (Cubango) ≃	104	18.50 S	22.25 E
Okavango Swamp ≋	104	18.45 S	22.45 E
Okayama	80	34.39 N	133.55 E
Okeechobee, Lake ⊜	162	26.55 N	80.45 W
Okhotsk, Sea of (Ochotskoje More) ▾[2]	64	53.00 N	150.00 E
Okinawa-jima I	80	26.30 N	128.00 E
Oklahoma □[3]	162	35.30 N	98.00 W
Oklahoma City	162	35.28 N	97.32 W
Oksskolten ▲	26	65.59 N	14.15 E
Olanchito	130	15.30 N	86.35 W
Öland I	28	56.45 N	16.38 E
Olavarría	146	36.54 S	60.17 W
Oława	36	50.57 N	17.17 E
Olbia	46	40.55 N	9.29 E
Old Crow	160	67.35 N	139.50 W
Old Crow ≃	162a	67.35 N	139.50 W
Oldenburg	36	53.08 N	8.13 E
Oldenburg [in Holstein]	36	54.17 N	10.52 E
Oldenzaal	36	52.19 N	6.56 E
Oldham	32	53.33 N	2.07 W
Old Wives Lake ⊜	160	50.06 N	106.00 W
Olen'okskij Zaliv C	64	73.20 N	121.00 E
Oléron, Île d' I	42	45.56 N	1.15 W
Oleśnica	36	51.13 N	17.23 E
Olhão	50	37.02 N	8.50 W
Olib, Otok I	46	44.22 N	14.48 E
Olimbos ▲ Ellás	54	40.05 N	22.21 E
Olimbos ▲ Kipros	84	34.56 N	32.52 E
Olinda	144	8.01 S	34.51 W
Oliva	50	38.55 N	0.07 W
Oliva de la Frontera	50	38.16 N	6.55 W
Olomouc	36	49.36 N	17.16 E
Olongapo	82	14.50 N	120.16 E
Oloron-Sainte-Marie	42	43.12 N	0.36 W
Olot	50	42.11 N	2.29 E
Olpe	36	51.02 N	7.52 E
Olsztyn (Allenstein)	36	53.48 N	20.29 E
Olt ≃	54	43.43 N	24.51 E
Olten	42	47.21 N	7.54 E
Olteniţa	54	44.05 N	26.39 E
Oluan Pi >	80	21.54 N	120.51 E
Ol'utorskij, Mys >	64	59.55 N	170.27 E
Olympia	162	47.03 N	122.53 W
Olympus, Mount ▲	162	47.48 N	123.43 W
Omagh	32	54.36 N	7.18 W
Omaha	162	41.16 N	95.57 W
Oman □[1]	84	22.00 N	58.00 E
Oman, Gulf of C	84	24.30 N	58.30 E
Omegna	46	45.53 N	8.24 E
Ometepe, Isla de I	130	11.30 N	85.35 W
Omineca ≃	160	56.05 N	124.30 W
Omo ≃	102	4.32 N	36.04 E
Omsk	64	55.00 N	73.24 E
Omul ▲	54	45.26 N	25.26 E
Omulew ≃	36	53.05 N	21.32 E
Ōmuta	80	33.02 N	130.27 E
Onda	50	39.58 N	0.15 W
Ondava ≃	36	48.27 N	21.48 E
Ondo	100	7.04 N	4.47 E
Onega ≃	26	63.58 N	37.55 E
Onežskoje Ozero ⊜	62	61.30 N	35.45 E
Onitsha	100	6.09 N	6.47 E
Onon ≃	80	51.42 N	115.50 E
Ontario □[4]	160	51.00 N	85.00 W
Ontario, Lake ⊜	162	43.45 N	78.00 W
Onteniente	50	38.49 N	0.37 W
Oostelijk Flevoland ◆[1]	36	52.30 N	5.45 E
Oostende (Ostende)	36	51.13 N	2.55 E
Oosterhout	36	51.38 N	4.51 E
Opava	36	49.56 N	17.54 E
Opladen	36	51.04 N	7.00 E
Opoczno	36	51.23 N	20.17 E
Opole (Oppeln)	36	50.41 N	17.55 E
Oradea	54	47.03 N	21.57 E
Oran	100	35.43 N	0.43 W
Oran, Sebkha d' ⊜	50	35.30 N	1.00 W
Orange, Austl.	116	33.17 S	149.06 E
Orange, Fr.	42	44.08 N	4.48 E
Orange (Oranje) ≃	104	28.41 S	16.28 E
Orange, Cabo >	144	4.24 N	51.33 W
Oranienburg	36	52.45 N	13.14 E
Oranje Gebergte ⛰	144	3.00 N	55.05 W
Oranjestad	130	12.33 N	70.06 W
Orăştie	54	45.50 N	23.12 E
Orb ≃	42	43.15 N	3.18 E
Orbetello	46	42.27 N	11.13 E
Orbieu ≃	42	43.14 N	2.54 E
Orce ≃	50	37.44 N	2.28 W
Orchon ≃	80	50.21 N	106.05 E
Ordžonikidze	62	43.03 N	44.40 E
Örebro	28	59.17 N	15.13 E
Orechovo-Zujevo	26	55.49 N	38.59 E
Oregon □[3]	162	44.00 N	121.00 W
Orenburg	62	51.54 N	55.06 E
Orense	50	42.20 N	7.51 W
Orestiás	54	41.30 N	26.31 E
Orford Ness >	32	52.05 N	1.34 E
Oriental, Cordillera ⛰, Col.	144	6.00 N	73.00 W
Oriental, Cordillera ⛰, Perú	144	13.00 S	72.00 W
Orihuela	50	38.05 N	0.57 W
Orillia	160	44.37 N	79.25 W
Orinoco ≃	144	8.37 N	62.15 W
Oristano	46	40.00 N	8.40 E
Orizaba	130	18.51 N	97.06 W
Orkney Islands □[4]	32	59.00 N	3.00 W
Orlando	162	28.32 N	81.23 W
Orléanais □[9]	42	47.50 N	2.00 E
Orléans	42	47.55 N	1.54 E
Orléans, Canal d' ⊔	42	47.54 N	1.55 E
Orlová	36	49.50 N	18.24 E
Ormoc	82	11.00 N	124.37 E
Örnsköldsvik	28	63.18 N	18.43 E
Or'ol	62	52.59 N	36.05 E
Orosei, Golfo di C	46	40.10 N	9.50 E
Orosháza	36	46.34 N	20.40 E
Oroszlány	36	47.30 N	18.19 E
Orša	26	54.30 N	30.24 E
Orsasjön ⊜	28	61.07 N	14.34 E
Orta Nova	46	41.19 N	15.42 E
Ortegal, Cabo >	50	43.45 N	7.53 W
Ortigueira, Ría de C[1]	50	43.42 N	7.51 W
Ortles ▲	46	46.31 N	10.33 E
Ortón ≃	144	10.50 S	66.04 W
Ortona	46	42.21 N	14.24 E
Oruro	144	17.59 S	67.09 W
Orvieto	46	42.43 N	12.07 E
Orzyc ≃	36	52.47 N	21.13 E
Oš	62	40.33 N	72.48 E
Osa, Peninsula de >[1]	130	8.34 N	83.31 W
Ōsaka	80	34.40 N	135.30 E
Osâm ≃	54	43.42 N	24.51 E
Oschatz	36	51.17 N	13.07 E
Oschersleben	36	52.01 N	11.13 E
Oshawa	160	43.54 N	78.51 W
Oshkosh	162	44.01 N	88.33 W
Oshogbo	100	7.47 N	4.34 E
Osijek	54	45.33 N	18.41 E
Osimo	46	43.29 N	13.29 E
Oskarshamn	28	57.16 N	16.26 E
Oslava ≃	36	49.05 N	16.22 E
Oslo	28	59.55 N	10.45 E
Oslofjorden C[2]	28	59.20 N	10.35 E
Osnabrück	36	52.16 N	8.02 E
Osorno	146	40.34 S	73.09 W
Oss	36	51.46 N	5.31 E
Ossa, Mount ▲	116	41.54 S	146.01 E
Osse ≃, Fr.	42	44.07 N	0.17 E
Osse ≃, Nig.	100	6.10 N	5.20 E
Osterholz-Scharmbeck	36	53.14 N	8.47 E
Osterode	36	51.44 N	10.11 E
Östersund	28	63.11 N	14.39 E
Ostrava	36	49.50 N	18.17 E
Ostredok ▲	36	48.55 N	19.04 E
Ostróda	36	53.43 N	19.59 E
Ostrołęka	36	53.06 N	21.34 E
Ostrov	36	50.17 N	12.57 E
Ostrov ◆[1]	36	47.55 N	17.35 E
Ostrowiec Świętokrzyski	36	50.57 N	21.23 E
Ostrów Mazowiecka	36	52.49 N	21.54 E
Ostrów Wielkopolski	36	51.39 N	17.49 E
Ostuni	46	40.44 N	17.35 E
Osum ≃	54	40.48 N	19.52 E
Ōsumi-shotō II	80	30.30 N	130.00 E
Osuna	50	37.14 N	5.07 W
Oswestry	32	52.52 N	3.04 W
Oświęcim	36	50.03 N	19.12 E
Otaru	80	43.13 N	141.00 E
Otava ≃	36	49.26 N	14.12 E
Oti ≃	100	8.40 N	0.13 E
Otjiwarongo	104	20.29 S	16.36 E
Otoskwin ≃	160	52.13 N	88.06 W
Otra ≃	28	58.09 N	8.00 E
Otradnyj	26	53.22 N	51.21 E
Otranto, Strait of ⊔[1]	54	40.00 N	19.00 E
Otrokovice	36	49.13 N	17.31 E
Ōtsu	80	35.00 N	135.52 E
Ottawa	160	45.25 N	75.42 W
Ottawa ≃	160	45.20 N	73.58 W
Ottumwa	162	41.01 N	92.25 W
Otwock	36	52.07 N	21.16 E
Ötztaler Alpen ⛰	46	46.45 N	10.55 E
Ou ≃, Afr.	102	9.18 N	18.14 E
Ou ≃, Lao	82	20.04 N	102.13 E
Ouagadougou	100	12.22 N	1.31 W
Ouahigouya	100	13.35 N	2.25 W
Ouaka ≃	102	4.59 N	19.56 E
Ouarane ◆[1]	100	21.00 N	10.30 W
Ouargla	100	31.59 N	5.25 E
Oubangui (Ubangi) ≃	100	1.15 N	17.50 E
Oudenaarde	36	50.51 N	3.36 E
Oudtshoorn	104	33.35 S	22.14 E
Ouémé ≃	100	6.29 N	2.32 E
Ouenza	46	35.57 N	8.04 E
Ouessant, Île d' I	42	48.28 N	5.05 W
Ouezzane	100	34.52 N	5.35 W
Ouidah	100	6.22 N	2.05 E
Oujda	100	34.41 N	1.45 W
Oulu	28	65.01 N	25.28 E
Oulujärvi ⊜	28	64.20 N	27.15 E
Oulujoki ≃	28	65.01 N	25.25 E
Oum er Rbia, Oued ≃	100	33.19 N	8.21 W
Ouro Prêto	144	20.23 S	43.30 W
Ourthe ≃	36	50.38 N	5.35 E
Ouse ≃	32	53.42 N	0.41 W
Oust ≃	42	47.39 N	2.06 W
Ovalle	146	30.36 S	71.12 W
Overflakkee I	36	51.45 N	4.10 E
Oviedo	50	43.22 N	5.50 W
Oviksfjällen ⛰	28	63.02 N	13.51 E
Owensboro	162	37.46 N	87.07 W
Owen Sound	160	44.34 N	80.56 W
Owen Stanley Range ⛰	116a	9.20 S	147.55 E
Owl ≃	160	57.51 N	92.44 W
Owo	100	7.15 N	5.37 E
Oxelösund	28	58.40 N	17.06 E
Oxford	32	51.46 N	1.15 W
Oxfordshire □[6]	32	51.50 N	1.15 W
Oxnard	162	34.12 N	119.11 W
Oyo	100	7.15 N	3.56 E
Oyonnax	42	46.15 N	5.40 E
Ozamiz	82	8.08 N	123.50 E
Ozark Plateau ⛰[1]	162	36.30 N	92.30 W
Ozarks, Lake of the ⊜[1]	162	38.10 N	92.50 W
Ózd	36	48.14 N	20.18 E
Ozieri	46	40.35 N	9.00 E
Ozorków	36	51.58 N	19.19 E
P			
Paarl	104	33.45 S	18.56 E
Pabianice	36	51.40 N	19.22 E
Pachino	46	36.42 N	15.06 E
Pachuca	130	20.07 N	98.44 W
Pacific Islands Trust Territory □[2]	82	10.00 N	143.00 E
Padang	82	0.57 S	100.21 E
Paderborn	36	51.43 N	8.45 E
Padirac, Gouffre de •[5]	42	44.44 N	1.27 E
Padova	46	45.25 N	11.53 E
Paducah	162	37.05 N	88.36 W
Pădurea Craiului, Munții ⛰	54	46.55 N	22.20 E
Paektu-san ▲	80	42.00 N	128.03 E
Pagalu I	104	1.25 S	5.36 E
Paget, Mount ▲	146	54.26 S	36.33 W
Pago Pago	113	14.16 S	170.42 W
Pago Pago Harbor C	113	14.17 S	170.40 W
Pahang ≃	82	3.32 N	103.28 E
Paignton	32	50.26 N	3.34 W
Päijänne ⊜	28	61.35 N	25.30 E
Painted Desert •[2]	162	36.00 N	111.20 W
Paisley	32	55.50 N	4.26 W

Name	Page	Lat °′	Long °′
Reykjanes ≻[1]	26a	63.49 N	22.43 W
Reykjavík	26a	64.09 N	21.51 W
Reynosa	130	26.07 N	98.18 W
Rezā'īyeh	84	37.33 N	45.04 E
Rezā'īyeh, Daryācheh-ye ⊜	84	37.40 N	45.30 E
Rezé	42	47.12 N	1.34 W
Rhaetian Alps ⋏	42	46.30 N	10.00 E
Rheda-Wiedenbrück	36	51.50 N	8.18 E
Rheine	36	52.17 N	7.26 E
Rheinfelden	36	47.33 N	7.47 E
Rheinhausen	36	51.24 N	6.44 E
Rheydt	36	51.10 N	6.25 E
Rhine (Rhein) (Rhin) ≃	36	51.52 N	6.02 E
Rhir, Cap ≻	100	30.38 N	9.55 W
Rho	46	45.32 N	9.02 E
Rhode Island □[3]	162	41.40 N	71.30 W
Rhodope Mountains ⋏	54	41.30 N	24.30 E
Rhondda	32	51.40 N	3.27 W
Rhône ≃	42	43.20 N	4.50 E
Rhône au Rhin, Canal du ≍	42	47.06 N	5.19 E
Rhue ≃	42	45.23 N	2.29 E
Rhyl	32	53.19 N	3.29 W
Riaza ≃	50	41.42 N	3.55 W
Ribagorza ◆[1]	50	42.15 N	0.30 E
Ribble ≃	32	53.44 N	2.50 W
Ribeirão Prêto	144	21.10 S	47.48 W
Ribera	46	37.30 N	13.16 E
Ribnitz-Damgarten	36	54.15 N	12.28 E
Riccione	46	43.59 N	12.39 E
Richard's Bay C	104	28.50 S	32.02 E
Richland	162	46.17 N	119.18 W
Richmond, Ind., U.S.	162	39.50 N	84.54 W
Richmond, Va., U.S.	162	37.30 N	77.28 W
Riesa	36	51.18 N	13.17 E
Riesi	46	37.17 N	14.05 E
Rieti	46	42.24 N	12.51 E
Rif ⋏	100	35.00 N	4.00 W
Rift Valley V	104	3.00 S	29.00 E
Rīga	26	56.57 N	24.06 E
Rīgestān ◆[1]	84	31.00 N	65.00 E
Rigi ∧	42	47.05 N	8.30 E
Riihimäki	28	60.45 N	24.46 E
Riječki Zaljev C	46	45.15 N	14.25 E
Rijeka	46	45.20 N	14.27 E
Rijssen	36	52.18 N	6.30 E
Rila ⋏	54	42.08 N	23.33 E
Rima ≃	100	13.04 N	5.10 E
Rimavská Sobota	36	48.23 N	20.02 E
Rimini	46	44.04 N	12.34 E
Rîmna ≃	54	45.39 N	27.19 E
Rîmnicu-Sărat	54	45.23 N	27.03 E
Rîmnicu-Vîlcea	54	45.06 N	24.22 E
Ringvassøya I	26	69.55 N	19.15 E
Rinjani, Gunung ∧	82	8.24 S	116.28 E
Riobamba	144	1.40 S	78.38 W
Rio Benito	100	1.35 N	9.37 E
Rio Branco	144	9.58 S	67.48 W
Rio Claro	144	22.24 S	47.33 W
Río Cuarto	146	33.08 S	64.21 W
Rio de Janeiro	144	22.54 S	43.14 W
Río Gallegos	146	51.38 S	69.13 W
Riom	42	45.54 N	3.07 E
Río Negro, Embalse del ⊜[1]	146	32.45 S	56.00 W
Rio Negro, Pantanal do ≡	144	19.00 S	56.00 W
Rionero in Vulture	46	40.56 N	15.41 E
Ripon	32	54.08 N	1.31 W
Riva	46	45.53 N	10.50 E
Rivas	130	11.26 N	85.50 W
Rive-de-Gier	42	45.32 N	4.37 E
Rivera	146	30.54 S	55.31 W
Riverside	162	33.59 N	117.22 W
Rivoli	46	45.04 N	7.31 E
Rižskij Zaliv C	20	57.30 N	23.35 E
Rizzuto, Capo ≻	46	38.54 N	17.06 E
Roanne	42	46.02 N	4.04 E
Roanoke	162	37.16 N	79.57 W
Roatán, Isla de I	130	16.23 N	86.30 W
Roberts Peak ∧	160	52.57 N	120.32 W
Robson, Mount ∧	160	53.07 N	119.09 W
Roca, Cabo da ≻	50	38.47 N	9.30 W
Rocas, Atol das I[1]	144	3.52 S	33.59 W
Rocciamelone ∧	46	45.12 N	7.05 E
Rochdale	32	53.38 N	2.09 W
Rochefort	42	45.57 N	0.58 W
Rochester, Minn., U.S.	162	44.02 N	92.29 W
Rochester, N.Y., U.S.	162	43.10 N	77.36 W
Rockall I	20	57.35 N	13.48 W
Rockefeller Plateau ⋏[1]	167	80.00 S	135.00 W
Rockford	162	42.17 N	89.06 W
Rockhampton	116	23.23 S	150.31 E
Rock Island	162	41.30 N	90.34 W
Rocky Mount	162	35.56 N	77.48 W
Rocky Mountains ⋏	162	48.00 N	116.00 W
Rodez	42	44.21 N	2.35 E
Ródhos (Rhodes)	54	36.26 N	28.13 E
Ródhos I	54	36.10 N	28.00 E
Rodnei, Munţii ⋏	54	47.35 N	24.40 E
Roermond	36	51.12 N	6.00 E
Roeselare	36	50.57 N	3.08 E
Rogagua, Lago ⊜	144	13.43 S	66.54 W
Rogen ⊜	28	62.19 N	12.23 E
Rogers, Mount ∧	162	36.39 N	81.33 W
Rogoaguado, Lago ⊜	144	12.52 S	65.43 W
Rokycany	36	49.45 N	13.36 E
Roma (Rome)	46	41.54 N	12.29 E
Roman	54	46.55 N	26.56 E
Romania (România) □[1]	54	46.00 N	25.30 E
Roman-Koš, Gora ∧	62	44.37 N	34.15 E
Romano, Cayo I	130	22.04 N	77.50 W
Romans[-sur-Isère]	42	45.03 N	5.03 E
Rome, Ga., U.S.	162	34.16 N	85.11 W
Rome, N.Y., U.S.	162	43.13 N	75.27 W
Romilly-sur-Seine	42	48.31 N	3.43 E
Romorantin-Lanthenay	42	47.22 N	1.45 E
Ronda	50	36.44 N	5.10 W
Ronda, Serranía de ⋏	50	36.44 N	5.03 W
Ron-ma, Mui ≻	82	18.07 N	106.22 E
Rønne	28	55.06 N	14.42 E
Ronneburg	36	50.51 N	12.10 E
Ronneby	28	56.12 N	15.18 E
Ronse	36	50.45 N	3.36 E
Roosevelt Island I	167	79.30 S	162.00 W
Roraima, Mount ∧	144	5.12 N	60.44 W
Rorschach	42	47.29 N	9.30 E
Rosario	146	32.57 S	60.40 W
Rosarito, Embalse de ⊜[1]	50	40.05 N	5.15 W
Rosarno	46	38.29 N	15.59 E
Rosas, Golfo de C	50	42.10 N	3.15 E
Roseau	130	15.18 N	61.24 W
Rosenheim	36	47.51 N	12.07 E
Rosica ≃	54	43.15 N	25.42 E
Rosignano Marittimo	46	43.24 N	10.28 E
Roşiori-de-Vede	54	44.07 N	25.00 E
Roskilde	28	55.39 N	12.05 E
Roslags-Näsby	28	59.26 N	18.04 E
Ross ≃	160	61.59 N	132.26 W
Ross, Point ≻	113	29.04 S	167.56 E
Rossano	46	39.35 N	16.39 E
Rossel, Cap ≻	112	20.23 S	166.36 E
Ross Ice Shelf ⊡	167	81.30 S	175.00 W
Rosslau	36	51.53 N	12.14 E
Rosso	100	16.30 N	15.49 W
Ross Sea ⊤[2]	167	76.00 S	175.00 W
Rostavatn ⊜	26	68.45 N	20.30 E
Rostock	36	54.05 N	12.07 E
Rostov-na-Donu	62	47.14 N	39.42 E
Roswell	162	33.24 N	104.32 W
Rota	50	36.37 N	6.21 W
Rotenburg	36	53.06 N	9.24 E
Rothaargebirge ⋏	36	51.05 N	8.15 E
Rothenburg ob der Tauber	36	49.23 N	10.10 E
Rotherham	32	53.26 N	1.20 W
Rotorua	118	38.09 S	176.15 E
Rotterdam	36	51.55 N	4.28 E
Rottweil	36	48.10 N	8.37 E
Roubaix	42	50.42 N	3.10 E
Roudnice	36	50.22 N	14.16 E
Rouen	42	49.26 N	1.05 E
Rouyn	160	48.15 N	79.01 W
Rovaniemi	26	66.34 N	25.48 E
Rovato	46	45.34 N	10.00 E
Rovereto	46	45.53 N	11.02 E
Rovigo	46	45.04 N	11.47 E
Rovno	62	50.37 N	26.15 E
Roxas (Capiz)	82	11.35 N	122.45 E
Royal Canal ≍	32	53.21 N	6.15 W
Royale, Isle I	162	48.00 N	89.00 W
Royal Leamington Spa	32	52.18 N	1.31 W
Royan	42	45.37 N	1.01 W
Rozewie, Przylądek ≻	36	54.51 N	18.21 E
Rožňava	36	48.40 N	20.32 E
Roztocze ∧	36	50.30 N	23.20 E
Ruahine Range ⋏	118	40.00 S	176.06 E
Rubcovsk	64	51.33 N	81.10 E
Ruby Mountains ⋏	162	40.25 N	115.35 W
Ruda Śląska	36	50.18 N	18.51 E
Rudnyj	62	52.57 N	63.07 E
Rudolf, Lake ⊜	102	3.30 N	36.00 E
Rudolstadt	36	50.43 N	11.20 E
Rufisque	100	14.43 N	17.17 W
Rugby	32	52.23 N	1.15 W
Rukatunturi ∧[2]	28	66.09 N	29.10 E
Rukwa, Lake ⊜	104	8.00 S	32.25 E
Ruma	54	45.00 N	19.49 E
Rum Cay I	130	23.40 N	74.53 W
Rumia	36	54.35 N	18.25 E
Runaway, Cape ≻	118	37.32 S	177.59 E
Rungwa ≃	104	7.36 S	31.50 E
Ruse	54	43.50 N	25.57 E
Rusken ⊜	28	57.17 N	14.20 E
Rüsselsheim	36	50.00 N	8.25 E
Rustavi	62	41.33 N	45.02 E
Rustenburg	104	25.37 S	27.08 E
Ruvuma (Rovuma) ≃	104	10.29 S	40.28 E
Ružomberok	36	49.36 N	19.18 E
Rwanda □[1]	104	2.30 S	30.00 E
Rybačij, Poluostrov ≻[1]	62	69.42 N	32.36 E
Rybinsk	62	58.03 N	38.52 E
Rybinskoje Vodochranilišče ⊜[1]	62	58.30 N	38.25 E
Rybnik	36	50.06 N	18.32 E
Ryde	32	50.44 N	1.10 W
Rzeszów	36	50.03 N	22.00 E
Ržev	62	56.16 N	34.20 E
S			
Saale ≃	36	51.57 N	11.55 E
Saalfeld	36	50.39 N	11.22 E
Saarbrücken	36	49.14 N	6.59 E
Saaremaa I	62	58.25 N	22.30 E
Saarlouis	36	49.21 N	6.45 E
Şab, Tônlé ⊜	82	13.00 N	104.00 E
Šabac	54	44.45 N	19.42 E
Sabadell	50	41.33 N	2.06 E
Sabhah	102	27.03 N	14.26 E
Sabi (Save) ≃	104	21.00 S	35.02 E
Sabina ◆[1]	46	42.15 N	12.42 E
Sabine ≃	162	30.00 N	93.45 W
Sable, Cape ≻, N.S., Can.	160	43.25 N	65.35 W
Sable, Cape ≻, Fla., U.S.	162	25.12 N	81.05 W
Sable Island I	160	43.55 N	59.50 W
Sabor ≃	50	41.10 N	7.07 W
Săcele	54	45.37 N	25.42 E
Sachalin, Ostrov (Sakhalin) I	64	51.00 N	143.00 E
Sachalinskij Zaliv C	64	53.45 N	141.30 E
Sachigo ≃	160	55.06 N	88.58 W
Šachty	62	47.42 N	40.13 E
Säckingen	36	47.33 N	7.56 E
Sacramento	162	38.35 N	121.30 W
Sacramento ≃	162	38.03 N	121.56 W
Sacramento Mountains ⋏	162	33.10 N	105.50 W
Sa'dah	84	16.52 N	43.37 E
Sado I	80	38.00 N	138.25 E
Safata Bay C	113	14.00 S	171.50 W
Säffle	28	59.08 N	12.56 E
Safi	100	32.20 N	9.17 W
Safīd Kūh, Selseleh-ye ⋏	84	34.30 N	63.30 E
Saga	80	33.15 N	130.18 E
Saginaw	162	43.25 N	83.58 W
Saginaw Bay C	162	43.50 N	83.40 W
Sagua la Grande	130	22.49 N	80.05 W
Sahara ◆[2]	100	26.00 N	13.00 E
Sahāranpur	84	29.57 N	77.48 E
Sahel, Oued ≃	50	36.45 N	5.04 E
Sāhīwāl	84	30.40 N	73.06 E
Saïda	100	34.50 N	0.09 E
Saidpur	84	25.47 N	88.54 E
Saimaa ⊜	28	61.15 N	28.15 E
Saint Albans	32	51.46 N	0.21 W
Saint Aldhelm's Head ≻	32	50.34 N	2.04 W
Saint-Amand-les-Eaux	42	50.26 N	3.26 E
Saint-Amand-Mont-Rond	42	46.44 N	2.30 E
Saint-André, Cap ≻	104	16.11 S	44.27 E
Saint Andrews	32	56.20 N	2.48 W
Saint Anne's	32	53.45 N	3.02 W
Saint Austell	32	50.20 N	4.48 W
Saint-Avold	42	49.06 N	6.42 E
Saint-Barthélemy I	130	17.54 N	62.50 W
Saint-Brieuc	42	48.31 N	2.47 W
Saint Catherine's Point ≻	32	50.34 N	1.15 W
Saint-Chamond	42	45.28 N	4.30 E
Saint Christopher I	130	17.20 N	62.45 W
Saint-Claude	42	46.23 N	5.52 E
Saint Cloud	162	45.33 N	94.10 W
Saint Croix I	130	17.45 N	64.45 W
Saint David's Head ≻	32	51.55 N	5.19 W
Saint-Denis, Fr.	42	48.56 N	2.22 E
Saint-Denis, Réu.	104	20.52 S	55.28 E
Saint-Dié	42	48.17 N	6.57 E
Saint-Dizier	42	48.38 N	4.57 E
Saint Elias, Mount ∧	160	60.18 N	140.55 W
Saint Elias Mountains ⋏	162a	60.30 N	139.30 W
Saint-Étienne	42	45.26 N	4.24 E
Saint Francis, Cape ≻	104	34.14 S	24.49 E
Saint George's	130	12.03 N	61.45 W
Saint George's Channel U	32	52.00 N	6.00 W
Saint-Germain	42	48.54 N	2.05 E
Saint Helena Bay C	104	32.43 S	18.05 E
Saint Helier	32	49.12 N	2.37 W
Saint Ignace Island I	160	48.48 N	87.55 W
Saint James, Cape ≻	160	51.56 N	131.01 W
Saint-Jean	160	45.19 N	73.16 W
Saint-Jean, Lac ⊜	160	48.35 N	72.05 W
Saint-Jean-d'Angély	42	45.57 N	0.31 W
Saint-Jean-de-Luz	42	43.23 N	1.40 W
Saint-Jérôme	160	45.47 N	74.00 W
Saint John	160	45.16 N	66.03 W
Saint John, Cape ≻	160	50.00 N	55.32 W
Saint Johns, Antig.	130	17.06 N	61.51 W
Saint John's, Newf., Can.	160	47.34 N	52.43 W
Saint Joseph	162	39.46 N	94.51 W
Saint Joseph, Lake ⊜	160	51.05 N	90.35 W
Saint-Junien	42	45.53 N	0.54 E
Saint Kilda I	32	57.49 N	8.36 W
Saint Lawrence ≃	160	49.30 N	67.00 W
Saint Lawrence, Gulf of C	160	48.00 N	62.00 W
Saint-Lô	42	49.07 N	1.05 W
Saint-Louis, Sén.	100	16.02 N	16.30 W
Saint Louis, Mo., U.S.	162	38.38 N	90.11 W
Saint Lucia □[1]	130	13.53 N	60.58 W
Saint Lucia, Lake ⊜	104	28.05 S	32.26 E
Saint-Malo	42	48.39 N	2.01 W
Saint-Malo, Golfe de C	42	48.45 N	2.00 W
Saint-Marc	130	19.07 N	72.42 W
Sainte-Marguerite ≃	160	50.09 N	66.36 W
Sainte-Marie, Cap ≻	104	25.36 S	45.08 E
Saint Mary's, Cape ≻	160	46.49 N	54.12 W
Saint-Mathieu, Pointe de ≻	42	48.20 N	4.46 W
Saint-Maur[-des-Fossés]	42	48.48 N	2.30 E
Saint-Nazaire	42	47.17 N	2.12 W
Saint Neots	32	52.14 N	0.17 W
Saint-Omer	42	50.45 N	2.15 E
Saint Paul	162	44.58 N	93.07 W
Saint Paul ≃	100	7.10 N	10.00 W
Saint Peter Port	32	49.27 N	2.32 W
Saint Petersburg	162	27.46 N	82.38 W
Saint-Pierre	104	21.19 S	55.29 E
Saint Pierre and Miquelon □[2]	160	46.55 N	56.10 W
Saint-Quentin	42	49.51 N	3.17 E
Saint-Raphaël	42	43.25 N	6.46 E
Saintes	42	45.45 N	0.52 W
Saint Thomas I	130	18.21 N	64.55 W
Saint Vincent □[2]	130	13.15 N	61.12 W
Saint-Vincent, Baie de C	112	22.00 S	166.05 E
Saint-Vincent, Cap ≻	104	21.57 S	43.16 E
Saipan I	82	15.12 N	145.45 E
Sajama, Nevado ∧	144	18.06 S	68.54 W
Sajó ≃	36	47.56 N	21.08 E
Sajószentpéter	36	48.13 N	20.44 E
Sak ≃	104	30.52 S	20.25 E
Sakakawea, Lake ⊜[1]	162	47.50 N	102.20 W
Sakania	104	12.45 S	28.34 E
Sakata	80	38.55 N	139.50 E
Sakau	112	16.49 S	168.24 E
Sal ≃	62	47.31 N	40.45 E
Salado ≃, Arg.	146	38.49 S	64.57 W
Salado ≃, Arg.	146	31.42 S	60.44 W
Salado ≃, Méx.	130	26.52 N	99.19 W
Salamanca, Esp.	50	40.58 N	5.39 W
Salamanca, Méx.	130	20.34 N	101.12 W
Salamis	54	37.59 N	23.28 E
Salat ≃	42	43.10 N	0.58 E
Salavat	62	53.21 N	55.55 E
Salé	100	34.04 N	6.50 W
Salem, Bhārat	84	11.39 N	78.10 E
Salem, Oreg., U.S.	162	44.57 N	123.01 W
Salentina, Penisola ≻[1]	46	40.25 N	18.00 E
Salerno	46	40.41 N	14.47 E
Salerno, Golfo di C	46	40.32 N	14.42 E
Salford	32	53.28 N	2.18 W
Salgótarján	36	48.07 N	19.48 E
Salihli	54	38.29 N	28.09 E
Salīmah, Wāḥat ⊤[4]	102	21.22 N	29.19 E
Salina	162	38.50 N	97.37 W
Salina, Isola I	46	38.34 N	14.51 E
Salina Cruz	130	16.10 N	95.12 W
Salinas	162	36.40 N	121.38 W
Salinas, Cabo de ≻	50	39.16 N	3.03 E
Salisbury, Rh.	104	17.50 S	31.03 E
Salisbury, Zim. Rh.	32	51.05 N	1.48 W
Salisbury Plain ≚	32	51.12 N	1.55 W
Salmon ≃	162	45.51 N	116.46 W
Salmon River Mountains ⋏	162	44.45 N	115.00 W
Salo	28	60.23 N	23.08 E
Salon-de-Provence	42	43.38 N	5.06 E
Salonta	54	46.48 N	21.40 E
Salop □[6]	32	52.40 N	2.40 W
Salor ≃	50	39.39 N	7.03 W
Saloum ≃	100	13.50 N	16.45 W
Salpausselkä ∧	28	61.00 N	26.30 E
Salso ≃	46	37.05 N	13.57 E
Salt ≃	162	33.23 N	112.18 W
Salta	146	24.47 S	65.25 W
Saltash	32	50.24 N	4.12 W
Saltcoats	32	55.38 N	4.47 W
Saltillo	130	25.25 N	101.00 W
Salt Lake City	162	40.46 N	111.53 W
Salto	146	31.23 S	57.58 W
Salto ≃	46	42.23 N	12.54 E
Salton Sea ⊜	162	33.19 N	115.50 W
Saluafata Harbour C	113	13.50 S	171.34 W
Saluzzo	46	44.39 N	7.29 E
Salvador	144	12.59 S	38.31 W
Salween (Nujiang) ≃	80	17.30 N	97.30 E
Salza ≃	36	47.40 N	14.43 E
Salzach ≃	36	48.12 N	12.56 E
Salzburg	36	47.48 N	13.02 E
Salzgitter	36	52.10 N	10.25 E
Salzkammergut ◆[1]	36	47.45 N	13.30 E
Salzwedel	36	52.51 N	11.09 E
Samālūṭ	102	28.18 N	30.42 E
Samar I	82	12.00 N	125.00 E
Samara ≃	62	53.10 N	50.04 E
Samarai	116a	10.37 S	150.40 E
Samarinda	82	0.30 S	117.09 E
Samarkand	62	39.40 N	66.48 E
Sambor	62	49.32 N	23.11 E
Sambre ≃	42	50.28 N	4.52 E
Samokov	54	42.20 N	23.33 E
Sámos I	54	37.48 N	26.44 E
Sam Rayburn Reservoir ⊜[1]	162	31.27 N	94.37 W
Samsun	20	41.17 N	36.20 E
Samui, Ko I	82	9.30 N	100.00 E
San	100	13.18 N	4.54 W
Şan'ā'	84	15.23 N	44.12 E
Sanaga ≃	100	3.35 N	9.38 E
San Agustín, Cape ≻	82	6.16 N	126.11 E
San Andrés, Isla de I	144	12.32 N	81.42 W
San Andrés Tuxtla	130	18.27 N	95.13 W
San Angelo	162	31.28 N	100.26 W
San Antonio, Chile	146	33.35 S	71.38 W
San Antonio, Tex., U.S.	162	29.28 N	98.31 W
San Antonio, Cabo ≻	130	21.52 N	84.57 W
San Baudilio de Llobregat	50	41.21 N	2.03 E
San Benedetto del Tronto	46	42.57 N	13.53 E
San Benito	130	16.55 N	89.54 W
San Bernardino	162	34.06 N	117.17 W
San Bernardo	146	33.36 S	70.43 W
San Blas, Cape ≻	162	29.40 N	85.22 W
San Carlos, Gui. Ecu.	100	3.27 N	8.33 E
San Carlos, Pil.	82	15.55 N	120.20 E
San Carlos de Bariloche	146	41.09 S	71.18 W
San Cataldo	46	37.29 N	14.04 E
Sánchez	130	19.14 N	69.36 W
San Clemente Island I	162	32.54 N	118.29 W
San Cristóbal	144	7.46 N	72.14 W
San Cristóbal I	114	10.36 S	161.45 E
San Cristóbal las Casas	130	16.45 N	92.38 W
Sancti-Spíritus	130	21.56 N	79.27 W
Sandakan	82	5.50 N	118.07 E
San Diego	162	32.43 N	117.09 W
San Diego, Cabo ≻	146	54.38 S	65.07 W
Sandnes	28	58.51 N	5.44 E
Sandomierz	36	50.41 N	21.45 E
San Donà di Piave	46	45.38 N	12.34 E
Sandown	32	50.39 N	1.09 W
Sandusky	162	41.27 N	82.42 W
Sandviken	28	60.37 N	16.46 E
Sandwich, Port C	112	16.27 S	167.46 E
Sandy Lake ⊜	160	53.00 N	93.07 W
Sandžak ◆[1]	54	43.10 N	19.30 E
San Felipe	144	10.20 N	68.44 W
San Feliu de Guíxols	50	41.47 N	3.02 E
San Fernando, Chile	146	34.35 S	71.00 W
San Fernando, Esp.	50	36.28 N	6.12 W
San Fernando, Pil.	82	16.37 N	120.19 E
San Fernando, Pil.	82	15.01 N	120.41 E
San Fernando, Trin.	130	10.17 N	61.28 W
San Fernando de Apure	144	7.54 N	67.28 W
San Francisco, Arg.	146	31.26 S	62.05 W
San Francisco, Calif., U.S.	162	37.48 N	122.24 W
San Francisco, Cabo de ≻	144	0.40 N	80.05 W
San Francisco de Macorís	130	19.18 N	70.15 W
Sangay, Volcán ∧[1]	144	2.00 S	78.20 W
Sangayán, Isla de I	144	13.51 S	76.28 W
Sangerhausen	36	51.28 N	11.17 E
Sangha ≃	104	1.13 S	16.49 E
Sangihe, Kepulauan II	82	3.00 N	125.30 E
San Giovanni in Fiore	46	39.16 N	16.42 E
San Giovanni in Persiceto	46	44.38 N	11.11 E
San Giovanni Rotondo	46	41.42 N	15.44 E
San Giovanni Valdarno	46	43.34 N	11.32 E
San Gorgonio Mountain ∧	162	34.06 N	116.50 W
San Gottardo, Passo del)(	42	46.33 N	8.34 E
San Isidro	146	34.27 S	58.30 W
San Joaquin Valley V	162	36.50 N	120.10 W
San Jorge, Golfo C	146	46.00 S	67.00 W
San Jorge, Golfo de C	50	40.53 N	1.00 E
San José, C.R.	130	9.56 N	84.05 W
San Jose, Calif., U.S.	162	37.20 N	121.53 W
San José de Mayo	146	34.20 S	56.42 W
San Juan, Arg.	146	31.32 S	68.31 W
San Juan, P.R.	130	18.28 N	66.07 W
San Juan, Rep. Dom.	130	18.48 N	71.14 W
San Juan del Norte	130	10.55 N	83.42 W
San Juan de los Morros	144	9.55 N	67.21 W
San Juan del Sur	130	11.15 N	85.52 W
San Juan Mountains ⋏	162	37.35 N	107.10 W
Sankt Gallen	42	47.25 N	9.23 E
Sankt Ingbert	36	49.17 N	7.06 E
Sankt Pölten	36	48.12 N	15.37 E
Sankt Veit an der Glan	36	46.46 N	14.21 E
San Lázaro, Cabo ≻	130	24.48 N	112.19 W
San Lorenzo, Isla I	144	12.05 S	77.15 W
Sanlúcar de Barrameda	50	36.47 N	6.21 W
San Lucas, Cabo ≻	130	22.52 N	109.53 W
San Luis, Arg.	146	33.18 S	66.21 W
San Luis, Guat.	130	16.14 N	89.27 W
San Luis, Lago de ⊜	144	13.45 S	64.00 W
San Luis Potosí	130	22.09 N	100.59 W
San Luis Río Colorado	130	32.29 N	114.48 W
San Marino	46	43.55 N	12.28 E
San Marino □[1]	20	43.56 N	12.25 E
San Martín ≃	144	13.08 S	63.43 W
San Matías, Golfo C	146	41.30 S	64.15 W
San Miguel	130	13.29 N	88.11 W
San Miguel ≃	144	13.52 S	63.56 W
San Miguel de Tucumán	146	26.49 S	65.13 W
San Miniato	46	43.41 N	10.51 E
Sannicandro Garganico	46	41.50 N	15.34 E
San Nicolás de los Arroyos	146	33.20 S	60.13 W
San Nicolas Island I	162	33.15 N	119.31 W
Sanok	36	49.34 N	22.13 E
San Pablo	82	14.04 N	121.19 E
San Pablo, Punta ≻	130	27.14 N	114.29 W
San Pedro, Punta ≻	146	25.30 S	70.38 W
San Pedro, Volcán ∧[1]	146	21.53 S	68.25 W
San Pedro de las Colonias	130	25.45 N	102.59 W
San Pedro de Macorís	130	18.27 N	69.18 W
San Pedro Mártir, Sierra ⋏	130	30.45 N	115.13 W
San Pedro Sula	130	15.27 N	88.02 W
San Pietro, Isola di I	46	39.08 N	8.18 E
San Quintín, Cabo ≻	130	30.21 N	116.00 W
San Rafael	146	34.36 S	68.20 W
San Remo	46	43.49 N	7.46 E
San Salvador	130	13.42 N	89.12 W
San Salvador (Watling Island) I	130	24.02 N	74.28 W
San Salvador de Jujuy	146	24.11 S	65.18 W
San Sebastián	50	43.19 N	1.59 W
Sansepolcro	46	43.34 N	12.08 E
San Severo	46	41.41 N	15.23 E
Sanshawan C	80	26.35 N	119.50 E
Santa Ana, El Sal.	130	13.59 N	89.34 W
Santa Ana, Calif., U.S.	162	33.43 N	117.54 W
Santa Bárbara, Méx.	130	26.48 N	105.49 W
Santa Barbara, Calif., U.S.	162	34.25 N	119.42 W
Santa Catalina Island I	162	33.23 N	118.26 W
Santa Clara	130	22.24 N	79.58 W
Santa Cruz, Bol.	144	17.48 S	63.10 W
Santa Cruz, Calif., U.S.	162	36.58 N	122.01 W
Santa Cruz del Sur	130	20.43 N	78.00 W
Santa Cruz Island I	162	34.01 N	119.45 W
Santa Fe, Arg.	146	31.38 S	60.42 W
Santa Fe, N. Mex., U.S.	162	35.42 N	106.57 W
Santa Fe Baldy ∧	162	35.50 N	105.46 W
Santa Inés, Isla I	146	53.45 S	72.45 W
Santa Isabel I	114	8.00 S	159.00 E
Santa Margherita Ligure	46	44.20 N	9.12 E
Santa Maria	162	34.57 N	120.26 W
Santa Maria, Cabo de ≻	104	13.25 S	12.32 E
Santa Maria Capua Vetere	46	41.05 N	14.15 E
Santa Maria di Leuca, Capo ≻	46	39.47 N	18.22 E
Santa Marta	144	11.15 N	74.13 W
Santander	50	43.28 N	3.48 W
Sant'Antioco, Isola di I	46	39.00 N	8.25 E
Santarém, Bra.	144	2.26 S	54.42 W
Santarém, Port.	50	39.14 N	8.41 W
Santa Rita	130	15.09 N	87.53 W
Santa Rosa, Arg.	146	32.20 S	65.12 W
Santa Rosa, Hond.	130	14.47 N	88.46 W
Santa Rosa, Calif., U.S.	162	38.26 N	122.43 W
Santa Rosa Island I	162	33.58 N	120.06 W
Santa Teresa, Embalse de ⊜[1]	50	40.40 N	5.30 W
Sant'Eufemia, Golfo di C	46	38.50 N	16.00 E
Santiago, Chile	146	33.27 S	70.40 W
Santiago, Pan.	130	8.06 N	80.59 W
Santiago, Rep. Dom.	130	19.27 N	70.42 W
Santiago de Compostela	50	42.53 N	8.33 W
Santiago de Cuba	130	20.01 N	75.49 W
Santiago del Estero	146	27.47 S	64.16 W
Säntis ∧	42	47.15 N	9.21 E
Santo Antão I	100	17.05 N	25.10 W
Santo Antônio	104	1.39 N	7.26 E
Santo Domingo	130	18.28 N	69.54 W
Santos	144	23.57 S	46.20 W
San Valentín, Monte ∧	146	46.36 S	73.20 W
San Vicente	130	13.38 N	88.48 W
San Vicente de Baracaldo	50	43.18 N	2.59 W
San Vito, Capo ≻	46	38.11 N	12.43 E
San Vito dei Normanni	46	40.39 N	17.42 E
São Carlos	144	22.01 S	47.54 W
São Francisco ≃	144	10.30 S	36.24 W
São João da Boa Vista	144	21.58 S	46.47 W
São João da Madeira	50	40.54 N	8.30 W
São João del Rei	144	21.09 S	44.16 W
São José do Rio Prêto	144	20.48 S	49.23 W
São José dos Campos	144	23.11 S	45.53 W
São Luís	144	2.31 S	44.16 W
Saône ≃	42	45.44 N	4.50 E
São Paulo	144	23.32 S	46.37 W
São Roque, Cabo de ≻	144	5.29 S	35.16 W
São Sebastião, Ponta ≻	104	22.07 S	35.30 E
São Tiago I	100	15.05 N	23.40 W
São Tomé	104	0.20 N	6.44 E
São Tomé I	104	0.12 N	6.39 E
São Tomé, Cabo de ≻	144	21.59 S	40.59 W
São Tomé, Pico de ∧	104	0.16 N	6.33 E
Sao Tome and Principe □[1]	104	1.00 N	7.00 E
São Vicente	144	23.58 S	46.23 W
São Vicente I	100	16.50 N	25.00 W
São Vicente, Cabo de ≻	50	37.01 N	9.00 W
Sapele	100	5.54 N	5.41 E
Sapitwa ∧	104	15.57 S	35.36 E
Sapporo	80	43.03 N	141.21 E
Sapt Kosi ≃	84	26.31 N	86.58 E
Sarajevo	54	43.52 N	18.25 E
Saransk	26	54.11 N	45.11 E
Sarapul	26	56.28 N	53.48 E
Sarasota	162	27.20 N	82.34 W
Saratov	62	51.34 N	46.02 E
Sarayköy	54	37.55 N	28.58 E
Sarcidano ◆[1]	46	39.55 N	9.05 E
Sarektjåkkå ∧	26	67.25 N	17.46 E
Sargodha	84	32.05 N	72.40 E
Sarh	102	9.09 N	18.23 E
Sariwŏn	80	38.31 N	125.44 E
Sark I	32	49.26 N	2.21 W
Sarmiento, Monte ∧	146	54.27 S	70.50 W
Sărnena ⋏	54	42.35 N	25.10 E
Sarnia	160	42.58 N	82.23 W
Sarno	46	40.49 N	14.37 E
Saronno	46	45.38 N	9.02 E
Saros Körfezi C	54	40.30 N	26.20 E
Sárospatak	36	48.19 N	21.34 E
Šar Planina ⋏	54	42.05 N	20.50 E
Sarpsborg	28	59.17 N	11.07 E
Sarrath, Oued V	46	35.59 N	8.23 E
Sarreguemines	42	49.06 N	7.03 E
Sarthe ≃	42	47.30 N	0.32 W
Sárvár	36	47.15 N	16.57 E
Sárvíz ≃	36	46.24 N	18.41 E
Sarzana	46	44.07 N	9.58 E
Sasebo	80	33.10 N	129.43 E
Saskatchewan □[4]	160	54.00 N	105.00 W
Saskatoon	160	52.07 N	106.38 W
Sassandra ≃	100	4.58 N	6.05 W
Sassari	46	40.44 N	8.33 E
Sassnitz	36	54.31 N	13.38 E
Sassuolo	46	44.33 N	10.47 E
Sata-misaki ≻	80	30.59 N	130.40 E
Sátoraljaújhely	36	48.24 N	21.39 E
Sātpura Range ⋏	84	22.00 N	78.00 E
Satsunan-shotō II	80	29.00 N	130.00 E
Satu Mare	54	47.48 N	22.53 E
Saudi Arabia □[1]	84	25.00 N	45.00 E
Sauerland ◆[1]	36	51.10 N	8.00 E
Sault Sainte Marie	160	46.31 N	84.20 W
Sault Ste. Marie	162	46.30 N	84.21 W
Saumur	42	47.16 N	0.05 W
Sauveterre, Causse ⋏[1]	42	44.20 N	3.10 E
Sauwald ◆[3]	36	48.28 N	13.40 E
Sava	46	40.24 N	17.34 E
Sava ≃	54	44.50 N	20.26 E
Savai'i I	113	13.35 S	172.25 W
Savannah	162	32.04 N	81.05 W
Savannakhét	82	16.33 N	104.45 E
Savanna-la-Mar	130	18.13 N	78.08 W
Save (Sabi) ≃, Afr.	104	21.00 S	35.02 E
Save ≃, Fr.	42	43.47 N	1.17 E
Saverne	42	48.44 N	7.22 E
Savigliano	46	44.38 N	7.40 E
Savona	46	44.17 N	8.30 E
Savusavu	111	16.16 S	179.21 E
Sawdā', Jabal as- ⋏[2]	102	28.40 N	15.30 E
Sawdā', Qurnat as- ∧	84	34.18 N	36.07 E
Sawel Mountain ∧	32	54.49 N	7.02 W
Sawhāj	102	26.33 N	31.42 E
Sawqarah, Dawḥat C	84	18.35 N	57.15 E
Sayan Mountains (Sajany) ⋏	62	52.45 N	96.00 E
Say'ūn	84	15.56 N	48.47 E
Sazanit I	54	40.30 N	19.16 E
Sázava ≃	36	49.53 N	14.24 E
Scafell Pikes ∧	32	54.27 N	3.12 W
Scapegoat Mountain ∧	162	47.19 N	112.50 W
Scarborough, Trin.	130	11.11 N	60.44 W
Scarborough, Eng., U.K.	32	54.17 N	0.24 W
Schaffhausen	42	47.42 N	8.38 E
Schelde (Escaut) ≃	36	51.22 N	4.15 E
Schenectady	162	42.47 N	73.53 W
Schiedam	36	51.55 N	4.24 E
Schiermonnikoog I	36	53.28 N	6.15 E
Schiltigheim	42	48.36 N	7.45 E
Schio	46	45.43 N	11.21 E
Schkeuditz	36	51.24 N	12.13 E
Schleswig	36	54.31 N	9.33 E
Schmalkalden	36	50.43 N	10.26 E
Schmölln	36	50.53 N	12.20 E
Schneeberg	36	50.36 N	12.38 E
Schönebeck	36	52.01 N	11.44 E
Schorndorf	36	48.48 N	9.31 E
Schouwen I	36	51.43 N	3.50 E
Schramberg	36	48.13 N	8.23 E
Schwabach	36	49.20 N	11.01 E
Schwäbische Alb ⋏	36	48.25 N	9.30 E
Schwäbisch Gmünd	36	48.48 N	9.47 E
Schwäbisch Hall	36	49.07 N	9.44 E
Schwandorf in Bayern	36	49.20 N	12.08 E
Schwarza ≃	36	47.43 N	16.13 E
Schwarze Elster ≃	36	51.49 N	12.51 E
Schwarzwald ⋏	36	48.00 N	8.15 E
Schwechat	36	48.08 N	16.29 E
Schwedt	36	53.03 N	14.17 E
Schweinfurt	36	50.03 N	10.14 E
Schwerin	36	53.38 N	11.25 E
Schweriner See ⊜	36	53.45 N	11.28 E
Schwetzingen	36	49.23 N	8.34 E
Schwyz	42	47.02 N	8.40 E
Sciacca	46	37.30 N	13.06 E
Scicli	46	36.47 N	14.43 E

Name	Page	Lat	Long
Scilly, Isles of ‖	32	49.55 N	6.20 W
Scordia	46	37.18 N	14.51 E
Scorno, Punta di ➤	46	41.07 N	8.19 E
Scotland □[8]	32	57.00 N	4.00 W
Scottsdale	162	33.30 N	111.56 W
Scranton	162	41.24 N	75.40 W
Scrivia ≃	46	45.03 N	8.54 E
Scunthorpe	32	53.36 N	0.38 W
Scutari, Lake ◎	54	42.12 N	19.18 E
Seaham	32	54.52 N	1.21 W
Seal ≃	160	59.04 N	94.48 W
Seattle	162	47.36 N	122.20 W
Seattle, Mount ∧	162a	60.06 N	139.11 W
Sebastián Vizcaíno, Bahía C	130	28.00 N	114.30 W
Sebeş	54	45.58 N	23.34 E
Sebnitz	36	50.58 N	14.16 E
Secchia ≃	46	45.04 N	11.00 E
Sèd ≃	36	47.00 N	18.31 E
Sədan	42	42.42 N	4.57 E
Sedova, Pik ∧	62	73.29 N	54.58 E
Sefton, Mount ∧	118	43.41 S	170.03 E
Segama ≃	82	5.27 N	118.48 E
Segeža	26	63.44 N	34.19 E
Ségou	100	13.27 N	6.16 W
Segovia	50	40.57 N	4.07 W
Segura ≃	50	38.06 N	0.38 W
Segura, Sierra de ✗	50	38.00 N	2.43 W
Sein, Île de ‖	42	48.02 N	4.51 W
Seinäjoki	28	62.47 N	22.50 E
Seine ≃, Ont., Can.	160	48.40 N	92.49 W
Seine ≃, Fr.	42	49.26 N	0.26 E
Seine, Baie de la ⊂	42	49.30 N	0.30 W
Sejm ≃	62	51.27 N	32.34 E
Sekondi-Takoradi	100	4.59 N	1.43 W
Selagskij, Mys ➤	64	70.06 N	170.26 E
Selatan, Tanjung ➤	82	4.10 S	114.38 E
Selb	36	50.10 N	12.08 E
Selby	32	53.48 N	1.04 W
Selçuk	54	37.56 N	27.22 E
Selenga (Selenge Mörön) ≃	64	52.16 N	106.16 E
Selenge Mörön (Selenga) ≃	62	52.16 N	106.16 E
Sélestat	42	48.16 N	7.27 E
Seliger, Ozero ◎	62	57.13 N	33.05 E
Selkirk Mountains ✗	160	51.00 N	117.40 W
Selvagens, Ilhas ‖	100	30.05 N	15.55 W
Selvas ✗[3]	144	5.00 S	68.00 W
Selwyn Mountains ✗	160	63.10 N	130.20 W
Seman ≃	54	40.56 N	19.24 E
Semara	100	26.44 N	14.41 W
Semarang	82	6.58 S	110.25 E
Semenic, Munţii ✗	54	45.05 N	22.05 E
Semeru, Gunung ∧	82	8.06 S	112.55 E
Semipalatinsk	64	50.28 N	80.13 E
Semliki ≃	104	1.14 S	30.28 E
Sendai	80	38.15 N	140.53 E
Senegal (Sénégal) □[1]	100	14.00 N	14.00 W
Senftenberg	36	51.31 N	14.00 E
Senica	36	48.41 N	17.22 E
Senigallia	46	43.43 N	13.13 E
Senlis	42	49.12 N	2.35 E
Sennestadt	36	51.59 N	8.37 E
Sens	42	48.12 N	3.17 E
Senta	54	45.56 N	20.04 E
Sepi	114	8.33 S	159.50 E
Sepik ≃	116a	3.51 S	144.34 E
Seraing	36	50.36 N	5.29 E
Seram (Ceram) ‖	82	3.00 S	129.00 E
Seram, Laut (Ceram Sea) ⊤[2]	82	2.30 S	128.00 E
Sered'	36	48.17 N	17.44 E
Seremban	82	2.43 N	101.56 E
Serengeti Plain ≃	104	2.50 S	35.00 E
Seria	82	4.39 N	114.23 E
Sérifos ‖	54	37.11 N	24.31 E
Serov	62	59.29 N	60.31 E
Serowe	104	22.25 S	26.44 E
Serpuchov	26	54.55 N	37.25 E
Sérrai	54	41.05 N	23.32 E
Serrat, Cap ➤	46	37.14 N	9.13 E
Servi Burnu ➤	54	41.40 N	28.06 E
Sesia ≃	46	45.05 N	8.37 E
Sessa Aurunca	46	41.14 N	13.56 E
Sestao	50	43.18 N	3.00 W
Sestri Levante	46	44.16 N	9.24 E
Sète	42	43.24 N	3.41 E
Sete Lagoas	144	19.27 S	44.14 W
Sétif	100	36.09 N	5.26 E
Settat	100	33.04 N	7.37 W
Setúbal	50	38.32 N	8.54 W
Seul, Lac ◎	160	50.20 N	92.30 W
Sevastopol'	62	44.36 N	33.32 E
Sevčenko	62	43.35 N	51.05 E
Severn ≃, Ont., Can.	160	56.02 N	87.36 W
Severn ≃, Eng., U.K.	32	51.35 N	2.40 W
Severnaja Dvina ≃	62	64.32 N	40.30 E
Severnaja Zeml'a ‖	64	79.30 N	98.00 E
Severnyje Uvaly ✗[2]	62	59.30 N	49.00 E
Severodvinsk	26	64.34 N	39.50 E
Severomorsk	26	69.05 N	33.24 E
Severskij Donec ≃	62	48.20 N	40.15 E
Sevier ≃	162	39.04 N	113.06 W
Sevier Lake ◎	162	38.55 N	113.09 W
Sevilla, Col.	144	4.16 N	75.57 W
Sevilla, Esp.	50	37.23 N	5.59 W
Sevlievo	54	43.01 N	25.06 E
Seward	162a	60.06 N	149.26 W
Seychelles □[1]	4	4.35 S	55.40 E
Sfax	100	34.44 N	10.46 E
Sfîntu-Gheorghe	54	45.52 N	25.47 E
Sfîntu Gheorghe, Braţul ≃[1]	54	44.53 N	29.36 E
Sfîntu Gheorghe, Ostrovul ‖	54	45.07 N	29.22 E
's-Gravenhage (The Hague)	36	52.06 N	4.18 E
Shabani	104	20.20 S	30.02 E
Shag ≃	118	45.29 S	170.49 E
Shag Rocks ‖[1]	146	53.33 S	42.02 W
Shahdād, Namakzār-e ⇄	84	30.30 N	58.30 E
Shaki	100	8.39 N	3.25 E
Shala, Lake ◎	102	7.35 N	38.30 E
Shām, Jabal ash- ∧	84	23.13 N	57.16 E
Shamo, Lake ◎	102	5.49 N	37.35 E
Shandongbandao ➤[1]	80	37.00 N	121.00 E
Shangani ≃	104	18.41 S	27.10 E
Shanghai	80	31.14 N	121.28 E
Shangqiu	80	34.27 N	115.42 E
Shannon ≃	32	52.36 N	9.41 W
Shantou (Swatow)	80	23.23 N	116.41 E
Shaoguan	80	24.50 N	113.37 E
Shaoxing	80	30.00 N	120.35 E
Shaoyang	80	27.06 N	111.25 E
Sharbaţāt, Ra's ash- ➤	84	17.52 N	56.22 E
Sharon	162	41.14 N	80.31 W
Shashi	80	30.19 N	112.14 E
Shasta, Mount ∧[1]	162	41.20 N	122.20 W
Shasta Lake ◎[1]	162	40.50 N	122.25 W
Shawinigan	160	46.33 N	72.45 W
Shaybārā ‖	84	25.27 N	36.48 E
Shaykh 'Uthmān	84	12.52 N	44.59 E
Shebele (Shebelle) ≃	102	0.50 N	43.10 E
Sheboygan	162	43.46 N	87.36 W
Sheffield	32	53.23 N	1.30 W
Shenyang (Mukden)	80	41.48 N	123.27 E
Sheppey, Isle of ‖	32	51.24 N	0.50 E
Sherbro Island ‖	100	7.45 N	12.55 W
Sherbrooke	160	45.24 N	71.54 W
Sherman	162	33.38 N	96.36 W
's-Hertogenbosch	36	51.41 N	5.19 E
Sheyenne ≃	162	47.05 N	96.50 W
Shibām	84	15.56 N	48.38 E
Shibīn al-Kawm	102	30.33 N	31.01 E
Shijiazhuang	80	38.03 N	114.28 E
Shikārpur	84	27.57 N	68.38 E
Shikoku ‖	80	33.45 N	133.30 E
Shimonoseki	80	33.57 N	130.57 E
Shinkolobwe ➤	104	11.02 S	26.35 E
Shiono-misaki ➤	80	33.26 N	135.45 E
Shire ≃	104	17.42 S	35.19 E
Shiretoko-misaki ➤	80	44.14 N	145.17 E
Shizuoka	80	34.58 N	138.23 E
Shkodër	54	42.05 N	19.30 E
Shkumbin ≃	54	41.01 N	19.26 E
Sholāpur	84	17.40 N	75.55 E
Shoshone Mountains ✗	162	39.25 N	117.15 W
Shreveport	162	32.30 N	93.45 W
Shrewsbury	32	52.43 N	2.45 W
Shuangyashan	80	46.37 N	131.22 E
Shwebo	82	22.34 N	95.42 E
Siālkot	84	32.30 N	74.31 E
Šiauliai	26	55.56 N	23.19 E
Šibenik	46	43.44 N	15.54 E
Siberut, Pulau ‖	82	1.20 S	98.55 E
Sibir' (Siberia) ✗[1]	62	65.00 N	110.00 E
Sibiu	54	45.48 N	24.09 E
Sibu	82	2.18 N	111.49 E
Sibuyan Sea ⊤[2]	82	12.50 N	122.40 E
Sichote-Alin' ✗	64	48.00 N	138.00 E
Sicilia (Sicily) ‖	46	37.30 N	14.00 E
Sicily, Strait of ⋃	46	37.20 N	11.20 E
Sidheros, Ákra ➤	54	35.19 N	26.19 E
Sidi bel Abbès	100	35.13 N	0.10 W
Sidi Ifni	100	29.24 N	10.12 W
Sidmouth	32	50.41 N	3.15 W
Sidney Lanier, Lake ◎[1]	162	34.15 N	83.57 W
Siedlce	36	52.11 N	22.16 E
Siegburg	36	50.47 N	7.12 E
Siegen	36	50.52 N	8.02 E
Siemianowice Śląskie	36	50.19 N	19.01 E
Siena	46	43.19 N	11.21 E
Sieradz	36	51.36 N	18.45 E
Sierpc	36	52.52 N	19.41 E
Sierra Leone □[1]	100	8.30 N	11.30 W
Sierre	42	46.18 N	7.32 E
Sífnos ‖	54	36.59 N	24.40 E
Sighetul Marmaţiei	54	47.56 N	23.54 E
Sighişoara	54	46.13 N	24.48 E
Siglufjördur	26a	66.10 N	18.56 W
Sigmaringen	36	48.05 N	9.13 E
Siguiri	100	11.25 N	9.10 W
Sikanni Chief ≃	160	57.47 N	122.15 W
Sikaram ∧	84	34.50 N	69.55 E
Sikasso	100	11.19 N	5.40 W
Sikéai	54	36.46 N	22.56 E
Siliana, Oued ≃	46	36.33 N	9.25 E
Silistra	54	44.07 N	27.16 E
Siljan ◎	28	60.50 N	14.45 E
Silkeborg	28	56.10 N	9.34 E
Sillon de Talbert ➤[1]	42	48.53 N	3.05 W
Silvretta ✗	36	46.50 N	10.05 E
Simav ≃	54	40.23 N	28.31 E
Simeria	54	45.51 N	23.01 E
Simeto ≃	46	37.24 N	15.06 E
Simferopol'	62	44.57 N	34.06 E
Sími ‖	54	36.35 N	27.52 E
Simplon Pass)(	42	46.15 N	8.02 E
Sīnā' (Sinai Peninsula), Shib Jazīrat ➤[1]	102	29.30 N	34.00 E
Sinaia	54	45.21 N	25.33 E
Sincelejo	144	9.18 N	75.24 W
Sindelfingen	36	48.42 N	9.00 E
Siné ⋁	100	14.10 N	16.28 W
Singapore	82	1.17 N	103.51 E
Singapore □[1]	82	1.22 N	103.48 E
Singatoka	111	18.08 S	177.30 E
Singen [hohentwiel]	36	47.46 N	8.50 E
Sinni ≃	46	40.09 N	16.42 E
Sînnicolau Mare	54	46.05 N	20.38 E
Sinnūris	102	29.25 N	30.52 E
Sinoe, Lacul ◎	54	44.38 N	28.53 E
Sint-Niklaas	36	51.10 N	4.08 E
Sint-Truiden	36	50.48 N	5.12 E
Sinŭiju	80	40.05 N	124.24 E
Sió ≃	36	46.23 N	18.55 E
Siófok	36	46.54 N	18.04 E
Sion	36	46.14 N	7.21 E
Sioule ≃	42	46.21 N	3.19 W
Sioux City	162	42.30 N	96.23 W
Sioux Falls	162	43.32 N	96.44 W
Siping	80	43.12 N	124.20 E
Siracusa	46	37.04 N	15.17 E
Sīrajganj	84	24.27 N	89.43 E
Sīrhān, Wādī as- ⋁	84	30.30 N	38.00 E
Sirino, Monte ∧	46	40.08 N	15.50 E
Sir James MacBrien, Mount ∧	160	62.07 N	127.41 W
Síros ‖	54	37.26 N	24.54 E
Sīrrī, Jazīreh-ye ‖	84	25.55 N	54.32 E
Sisak	46	45.29 N	16.23 E
Sīstān, Daryācheh-ye ◎	84	31.00 N	61.15 E
Sitka	162a	57.03 N	135.20 W
Sitnica ≃	54	42.41 N	21.01 E
Sittang ≃	82	17.10 N	96.58 E
Sittard	36	51.00 N	5.53 E
Sittwe (Akyab)	82	20.09 N	92.54 E
Sivas	84	39.45 N	37.02 E
Sjælland ‖	28	55.30 N	11.45 E
Sjeništa ∧	54	43.42 N	18.37 E
Sjujutlijka ≃	54	42.17 N	25.55 E
Skagen	28	57.44 N	10.36 E
Skagerrak ⋃	28	57.45 N	9.00 E
Skalka ◎	28	66.50 N	18.46 E
Skamlingsbanke ∧[2]	28	55.25 N	9.34 E
Skarżysko-Kamienna	36	51.08 N	20.53 E
Skawina	36	49.59 N	19.49 E
Skeena ≃	160	54.09 N	130.02 W
Skegness	32	53.10 N	0.21 E
Skellefteå	28	64.46 N	20.57 E
Skellefteälven ≃	28	64.42 N	21.06 E
Skiddaw ∧	32	54.38 N	3.08 W
Skien	28	59.12 N	9.36 E
Skierniewice	36	51.58 N	20.08 E
Skiftet ⋃	28	60.15 N	21.05 E
Skikda	100	36.55 N	6.58 E
Skive	28	56.34 N	9.02 E
Skopje	54	41.59 N	21.26 E
Skövde	28	58.24 N	13.50 E
Skye, Island of ‖	32	57.15 N	6.10 W
Skyring, Seno ⋃	146	52.35 S	72.00 W
Slagelse	28	55.24 N	11.22 E
Slamet, Gunung ∧	82	7.14 S	109.12 E
Slancy	26	59.06 N	28.04 E
Slanské Vrchy ✗	36	48.50 N	21.30 E
Slaný	36	50.14 N	14.06 E
Slatina	54	44.26 N	24.22 E
Slav'ansk	62	48.51 N	37.36 E
Slave ≃	160	61.18 N	113.39 W
Slavonija ≃	54	45.00 N	18.00 E
Slavonska Požega	46	45.20 N	17.41 E
Slavonski Brod	54	45.09 N	18.01 E
Sławno	36	54.22 N	16.40 E
Sliedrecht	36	51.49 N	4.45 E
Sligo	32	54.17 N	8.28 W
Sliven	54	42.40 N	26.19 E
Slobozia	54	44.34 N	27.23 E
Slovenské rudohorie ✗	36	48.45 N	20.00 E
Słupia ≃	36	54.35 N	16.50 E
Słupsk (Stolp)	36	54.28 N	17.02 E
Smederevo	54	44.40 N	20.56 E
Smethwick	32	52.30 N	1.58 W
Smith Island ‖	167	62.59 N	62.32 W
Smoky ≃	160	56.10 N	117.21 W
Smolensk	26	54.47 N	32.03 E
Smoljan	54	41.35 N	24.41 E
Smygehuk ➤	28	55.21 N	13.23 E
Smythe, Mount ∧	160	57.54 N	124.53 W
Snaefell ∧	32	54.16 N	4.27 W
Snake ≃, Yukon, Can.	160	65.58 N	134.10 W
Snake ≃, U.S.	162	46.12 N	119.02 W
Snasahögarna ∧	28	63.13 N	12.21 E
Sneek	36	53.02 N	5.40 E
Snežnik ∧	46	45.35 N	14.27 E
Śniardwy, Jezioro ◎	36	53.46 N	21.44 E
Snina	36	48.59 N	22.07 E
Snowdon ∧	32	53.04 N	4.05 W
Sobat ≃	102	9.22 N	31.33 E
Sobral	144	3.42 S	40.21 W
Sochaczew	36	52.14 N	20.14 E
Soči	62	43.35 N	39.45 E
Socuéllamos	50	39.17 N	2.48 W
Sodankylä	26	67.29 N	26.32 E
Söderhamn	28	61.18 N	17.03 E
Södertälje	28	59.12 N	17.37 E
Soest, B.R.D.	36	51.34 N	8.07 E
Soest, Ned.	36	52.09 N	5.18 E
Sofia ≃	104	15.27 S	47.23 E
Sofija (Sofia)	54	42.41 N	23.19 E
Sogamoso	144	5.43 N	72.56 W
Sognafjorden C[2]	28	61.06 N	5.10 E
Sohano	114	5.27 S	154.40 E
Soissons	42	49.22 N	3.20 E
Sôjosôn-man C	80	39.20 N	124.50 E
Sôkch'o	80	38.12 N	128.36 E
Söke	54	37.45 N	27.24 E
Sokodé	100	8.59 N	1.08 E
Sokol	26	59.28 N	40.10 E
Sokołka	36	53.25 N	23.31 E
Sokolov	36	50.09 N	12.40 E
Sokołów	36	50.14 N	22.07 E
Sokoto	100	13.04 N	5.16 E
Sokoto ≃	100	11.20 N	4.10 E
Sol, Costa del ⋆[2]	50	36.30 N	4.30 W
Sofa ≃	36	50.04 N	19.13 E
Solbad Hall in Tirol	36	47.17 N	11.31 E
Soledad	144	10.55 N	74.46 W
Solihull	32	52.25 N	1.45 W
Solikamsk	62	59.39 N	56.47 E
Solingen	36	51.10 N	7.05 E
Sollentuna	28	59.28 N	17.54 E
Solna	28	59.22 N	18.01 E
Solomon Islands □[1]	114	8.00 S	159.00 E
Solomon Sea ⊤[2]	116	8.00 S	155.00 E
Solothurn	42	47.13 N	7.32 E
Šolta, Otok ‖	46	43.23 N	16.15 E
Soltau	36	52.59 N	9.49 E
Solway Firth C[2]	32	54.50 N	3.35 W
Soma	54	39.10 N	27.33 E
Somalia □[1]	102	10.00 N	49.00 E
Sombor	54	45.46 N	19.07 E
Somerset □[6]	32	51.08 N	3.00 W
Someşu Cald ≃	54	46.44 N	23.22 E
Sommen ◎	28	58.01 N	15.15 E
Sömmerda	36	51.10 N	11.07 E
Somosomo Strait ⋃	111	16.47 S	179.58 E
Somport, Puerto de)(	50	42.48 N	0.31 W
Sønderborg	28	54.55 N	9.47 E
Søndershausen	36	51.22 N	10.52 E
Søndre Strømfjord C[2]	160	67.30 N	52.00 W
Sondrio	46	46.10 N	9.52 E
Songhuahu ◎[1]	80	43.20 N	127.07 E
Songhuajiang ≃	80	47.44 N	132.32 E
Songkhla	82	7.12 N	100.36 E
Songnim	80	38.44 N	125.38 E
Sonmiāni Bay C	84	25.15 N	66.30 E
Sonneberg	36	50.22 N	11.10 E
Sonora ≃	130	28.48 N	111.33 W
Sonsón	144	5.42 N	75.18 W
Sonsonate	130	13.43 N	89.44 W
Sonthofen	36	47.31 N	10.17 E
Sopot	36	54.28 N	18.34 E
Sopron	36	47.41 N	16.36 E
Sora	46	41.43 N	13.37 E
Sorel	160	46.02 N	73.07 W
Soria	50	41.46 N	2.28 W
Sorocaba	144	23.29 S	47.27 W
Sorol ‖[1]	82	8.08 N	140.23 E
Soroti	104	1.43 N	33.37 E
Sorraia ≃	50	38.56 N	8.53 W
Sorrento	46	40.37 N	14.22 E
Sorsatunturi ∧	26	67.24 N	29.38 E
Sortavala	26	61.42 N	30.41 E
Sösjöfjällen ✗	28	63.53 N	13.15 E
Sosnogorsk	26	63.37 N	53.51 E
Sosnowiec	36	50.18 N	19.08 E
Sotteville	42	49.25 N	1.06 E
Soûl (Seoul)	80	37.33 N	126.58 E
Souris ≃	160	49.39 N	99.34 W
Sousse	100	35.49 N	10.38 E
South Africa □[1]	104	30.00 S	26.00 E
Southampton	32	50.55 N	1.25 W
Southampton Island ‖	160	64.20 N	84.40 W
South Andaman ‖	84	11.45 N	92.45 E
South Bend	162	41.41 N	86.15 W
South Carolina □[3]	162	34.00 N	81.00 W
South Dakota □[3]	162	44.15 N	100.00 W
South Downs ✗[1]	32	50.55 N	0.25 W
South East Cape ➤	116	43.39 S	146.50 E
Southend-on-Sea	32	51.33 N	0.43 E
Southern Alps ✗	118	43.30 S	170.30 E
Southern Indian Lake ◎	160	57.10 N	98.40 W
South Foreland ➤	32	51.09 N	1.23 E
South Georgia ‖	146	54.15 S	36.45 W
South Glamorgan □[6]	32	51.30 N	3.20 W
South Island ‖, Kenya	102	2.38 N	36.36 E
South Island ‖, N.Z.	118	43.00 S	171.00 E
South Orkney Islands ‖	167	60.35 S	45.30 W
Southport, Austl.	116	27.58 S	153.25 E
Southport, Eng., U.K.	32	53.39 N	3.01 W
South Saskatchewan ≃	160	53.15 N	105.05 W
South Shetland Islands ‖	167	62.00 S	58.00 W
South Shields	32	55.00 N	1.25 W
Sovetsk (Tilsit)	26	55.05 N	21.53 E
Spa	36	50.30 N	5.52 E
Spain (España) □[1]	50	40.00 N	4.00 W
Spalding	32	52.47 N	0.10 W
Spanish North Africa □[2]	50	35.53 N	5.19 W
Spanish Town	130	17.59 N	76.57 W
Spartanburg	162	34.57 N	81.55 W
Spartel, Cap ➤	50	35.48 N	5.56 W
Spartivento, Capo ➤	46	37.55 N	16.04 E
Spátha, Ákra ➤	54	35.42 N	23.44 E
Spencer Gulf C	116	34.00 S	137.00 E
Sperkhiós ≃	54	38.52 N	22.34 E
Speyer	36	49.19 N	8.26 E
Spiekeroog ‖	36	53.46 N	7.42 E
Spišská Nová Ves	36	48.57 N	20.34 E
Spittal an der Drau	36	46.48 N	13.30 E
Split	46	43.31 N	16.27 E
Spokane	162	47.40 N	117.23 W
Spratly Island ‖	82	8.38 N	111.55 E
Spreča ≃	54	44.45 N	18.06 E
Spremberg	36	51.34 N	14.22 E
Springfield, Ill., U.S.	162	39.47 N	89.40 W
Springfield, Mass., U.S.	162	42.07 N	72.36 W
Springfield, Mo., U.S.	162	37.14 N	93.17 W
Springfield, Ohio, U.S.	162	39.55 N	83.49 W
Spring Mountains ✗	162	36.10 N	115.40 W
Spruce Knob ∧	162	38.42 N	79.32 W
Spulico, Capo ➤	46	39.58 N	16.39 E
Spurn Head ➤	32	53.34 N	0.07 E
Squaline, Golfo di C	46	38.50 N	16.50 E
Squinzano	46	40.26 N	18.02 E
Srbobran	54	45.33 N	19.48 E
Sredinnyj Chrebet ✗	64	56.00 N	158.00 E
Sredna Gora ✗	54	42.30 N	25.00 E
Srednesibirskoje Ploskogorje ✗[1]	62	65.00 N	105.00 E
Śrem	36	52.08 N	17.01 E
Sremska Mitrovica	54	44.58 N	19.37 E
Sri Lanka □[1]	84	7.00 N	81.00 E
Srīnagar	84	34.05 N	74.49 E
Środa Wielkopolski	36	52.14 N	17.17 E
Stade	36	53.36 N	9.28 E
Stadskanaal	36	53.00 N	6.55 E
Stadthagen	36	52.19 N	9.13 E
Stafford	32	52.48 N	2.07 W
Staffordshire □[6]	32	52.50 N	2.00 W
Staines	32	51.26 N	0.31 W
Stalin (Kuçovë)	54	40.48 N	19.54 E
Stamford	32	52.39 N	0.29 W
Standerton	104	26.58 S	29.07 E
Stanke Dimitrov	54	42.16 N	23.07 E
Stanley	146	51.42 S	57.51 W
Stanley Falls ⌣	104	0.15 N	25.30 E
Stann Creek	130	16.58 N	88.13 W
Stanovoj Chrebet ✗	64	56.20 N	126.00 E
Stanovoje Nagorje (Stanovoy Mountains) ✗	64	56.00 N	114.00 E
Starachowice	36	51.03 N	21.04 E
Staraja Russa	26	58.00 N	31.23 E
Stara Planina (Balkan Mountains) ✗	54	43.15 N	25.00 E
Stara Zagora	54	42.25 N	25.38 E
Stargard Szczeciński (Stargard in Pommern)	36	53.20 N	15.02 E
Star Harbour C	114	10.47 S	162.18 E
Stari Vlah ✗	54	43.35 N	20.15 E
Starnberg	36	48.00 N	11.20 E
Starnberger See ◎	36	47.55 N	11.18 E
Starogard Gdański	36	53.59 N	18.33 E
Start Point ➤	32	50.13 N	3.38 W
Stassfurt	36	51.51 N	11.34 E
Stavanger	28	58.58 N	5.45 E
Stavropol'	62	45.02 N	41.59 E
Steinkjer	28	64.01 N	11.30 E
Stellenbosch	104	33.58 S	18.50 E
Stelvio, Passo dello)(	46	46.32 N	10.27 E
Stendal	36	52.36 N	11.51 E
Steps Point ➤	113	14.22 S	170.45 W
Sterling	162	41.48 N	89.42 W
Sterlitamak	62	53.37 N	55.58 E
Šternberk	36	49.44 N	17.18 E
Steubenville	162	40.22 N	80.37 W
Stevenage	32	51.55 N	0.14 W
Stewart ≃	160	63.18 N	139.25 W
Stewart Island ‖	118	47.00 S	167.50 E
Şteyr	36	48.03 N	14.25 E
Štiavnické vrchy ✗	36	48.20 N	18.50 E
Stikine ≃	162a	56.40 N	132.30 W
Štilo, Punta ➤	46	38.28 N	16.36 E
Ştirinisoara, Munţii ✗	54	47.10 N	26.00 E
Stirling, Austl.	116	31.54 S	115.67 E
Stirling, Scot., U.K.	32	56.07 N	3.57 W
Stockerau	36	48.23 N	16.13 E
Stockholm	28	59.20 N	18.03 E
Stockport	32	53.25 N	2.10 W
Stockton	162	37.57 N	121.17 W
Stockton Plateau ✗[1]	162	30.30 N	102.30 W
Stoke-on-Trent	32	53.00 N	2.10 W
Stolberg	36	50.46 N	6.13 E
Stolica ∧	36	48.48 N	20.11 E
Storå ≃	28	56.19 N	8.19 E
Stora Alvaret ≃	28	56.27 N	16.30 E
Storavan ◎	28	65.40 N	18.15 E
Storm Bay C	116	43.10 S	147.32 E
Storsjön ◎	28	63.12 N	14.18 E
Storvättneshägna ∧	28	62.07 N	12.27 E
Storvindeln ◎	28	65.43 N	17.05 E
Stour ≃	32	50.43 N	1.46 W
Stradella	46	45.05 N	9.18 E
Strakonice	36	49.16 N	13.55 E
Stralsund	36	54.19 N	13.05 E
Strangford Lough C	32	54.28 N	5.36 W
Stranraer	32	54.55 N	5.02 W
Strasbourg	42	48.35 N	7.45 E
Stratford-upon-Avon	32	52.12 N	1.41 W
Strathy Point ➤	32	58.35 N	4.01 W
Straubing	36	48.53 N	12.34 E
Strausberg	36	52.35 N	13.53 E
Stresa	46	45.53 N	8.32 E
Strickland ≃	116a	6.00 S	142.15 E
Stroud	32	51.45 N	2.12 W
Struma (Strimón) ≃	54	40.47 N	23.51 E
Strumble Head ➤	32	52.02 N	5.04 W
Strumica	54	41.26 N	22.38 E
Strzegom	36	50.57 N	16.21 E
Strzelce Opolskie	36	50.31 N	18.19 E
Strzelin	36	50.47 N	17.03 E
Studen Kladenec, Jazovir ◎[1]	54	41.37 N	25.30 E
Stupino	26	54.53 N	38.05 E
Stuttgart	36	48.46 N	9.11 E
Suakin Archipelago ‖	102	18.42 N	38.30 E
Subotica	54	46.06 N	19.39 E
Suceava	54	47.39 N	26.16 E
Suceava ≃	54	47.33 N	26.18 E
Suchona ≃	62	60.46 N	46.24 E
Suchumi	62	43.01 N	41.02 E
Sucre	144	19.02 S	65.17 W
Sudan □[1]	102	15.00 N	30.00 E
Sudbury	160	46.30 N	81.00 W
Sude ≃	36	53.22 N	10.45 E
Sudety ✗	36	50.30 N	16.00 E
Sue ≃	102	7.41 N	28.03 E
Sueca	50	39.12 N	0.19 W
Suffolk □[6]	32	52.10 N	1.00 E
Suhl	36	50.36 N	10.41 E
Sukkertoppen	160	65.25 N	52.53 W
Sukkur	84	27.42 N	68.52 E
Sul, Canal do ⋃	144	0.10 S	49.30 W
Sulaimān Range ✗	84	30.30 N	70.10 E
Sulawesi (Celebes) ‖	82	2.00 S	121.00 E
Sulcis ⋆[1]	46	39.00 N	8.45 E
Sulechów	36	52.06 N	15.37 E
Sulitelma ∧	28	67.08 N	16.24 E
Sullana	144	4.53 S	80.41 W
Sulmona	46	42.03 N	13.55 E
Sulu Archipelago ‖	82	6.00 N	121.00 E
Sulu Sea ⊤[2]	82	8.00 N	120.00 E
Sulzbach	36	49.18 N	7.07 E
Sulzbach-Rosenberg	36	49.30 N	11.45 E
Šumadija ≃	54	44.10 N	20.50 E
Sumatera (Sumatra) ‖	82	0.05 S	102.00 E
Sumba ‖	82	10.00 S	120.00 E
Sumbawa ‖	82	8.40 S	118.00 E
Šumen	54	43.16 N	26.55 E
Šumgait	62	40.35 N	49.38 E
Šumperk	36	49.58 N	16.58 E
Sumter	162	33.55 N	80.20 W
Sunda, Selat ⋃	82	6.00 S	105.45 E
Sundarbans ≃	84	22.00 N	89.00 E
Sundbyberg	28	59.22 N	17.58 E
Sunderland	32	54.55 N	1.23 W
Sundsvall	28	62.23 N	17.18 E
Suoche (Yarkand)	80	38.25 N	77.16 E
Superior	162	46.44 N	92.06 W
Superior, Lake ◎	162	48.00 N	88.00 W
Supraśl ≃	36	53.12 N	22.57 E
Suqutrā ‖	84	8.30 N	54.00 E
Sūr	84	22.34 N	59.32 E
Sura ≃	62	56.06 N	46.00 E
Surabaya	82	7.15 S	112.45 E
Surakarta	82	7.35 S	110.50 E
Surat	84	21.12 N	72.50 E
Surat Thani	82	9.08 N	99.19 E
Surigao	82	9.45 N	125.30 E
Suriname □[1]	144	4.00 N	56.00 W
Surt	102	31.12 N	16.35 E
Surt, Khalīj C	102	31.30 N	18.00 E
Surud Ad ∧	102	10.41 N	47.18 E
Suspiro del Moro, Puerto)(	50	37.04 N	3.39 W
Sussex, East □[6]	32	50.55 N	0.15 E
Susten Pass)(	42	46.44 N	8.27 E
Susurluk	54	39.54 N	28.10 E
Sutton-in-Ashfield	32	53.08 N	1.15 W
Suva	111	18.08 S	178.25 E
Suva Planina ✗	54	43.10 N	22.10 E
Suwałki	36	54.07 N	22.56 E
Suways, Khalīj as- C	102	29.00 N	32.50 E
Suways, Qanāt as- ≃	102	29.55 N	32.33 E
Suwŏn	80	37.17 N	127.01 E
Suzhou	80	31.18 N	120.37 E
Svartenhuk ➤[1]	160	71.55 N	55.00 W
Sv'atoj Nos, Mys ➤	62	68.10 N	39.45 E
Svendborg	28	55.03 N	10.37 E
Sverdlovsk	62	56.51 N	60.36 E
Svilengrad	54	41.46 N	26.12 E
Svir' ≃	62	60.30 N	32.48 E
Svištov	54	43.37 N	25.20 E
Svitavy	36	49.45 N	16.27 E
Svratka ≃	36	49.11 N	16.38 E
Swakopmund	104	22.41 S	14.32 E
Swale ≃	32	54.06 N	1.20 W
Swan Island ‖	130	17.25 N	83.55 W
Swansea	32	51.38 N	3.57 W
Swarzędz	36	52.26 N	17.05 E
Swaziland □[1]	104	26.30 S	31.30 E
Sweden □[1]	26	62.00 N	15.00 E
Świdnica (Schweidnitz)	36	50.51 N	16.29 E
Świdnik	36	51.14 N	22.41 E
Świdwin	36	53.47 N	15.47 E
Świebodzice	36	50.52 N	16.19 E
Świebodzin	36	52.15 N	15.32 E
Świecie	36	53.25 N	18.28 E
Świętokrzyskie, Góry ✗	36	50.55 N	21.00 E
Swindon	32	51.34 N	1.47 W
Swinford	32	53.57 N	8.57 W
Świnoujście (Swinemünde)	36	53.53 N	14.14 E
Switzerland □[1]	20	47.00 N	8.00 E
Sydney, Austl.	116	33.52 S	151.13 E
Sydney, N.S., Can.	160	46.09 N	60.11 W
Sydney Bay C	113	29.04 S	167.57 E
Syktyvkar	26	61.40 N	50.46 E
Sylhet	84	24.54 N	91.52 E
Sylsjön ◎	28	62.56 N	12.11 E
Sylt ‖	36	54.54 N	8.20 E
Syracuse	162	43.03 N	76.09 W
Syrdarya (Syr-Darya) ≃	62	46.03 N	61.00 E
Syria □[1]	84	35.00 N	38.00 E
Syzran'	26	53.09 N	48.27 E
Szamos (Someş) ≃	54	48.07 N	22.20 E
Szamotuły	36	52.37 N	16.35 E
Szarvas	36	46.52 N	20.34 E
Szczecin (Stettin)	36	53.24 N	14.32 E
Szczecinek (Neustettin)	36	53.43 N	16.42 E
Szczytno	36	53.34 N	21.00 E
Szeged	36	46.15 N	20.09 E
Szeghalom	36	47.01 N	21.11 E
Székesfehérvár	36	47.12 N	18.25 E
Szekszárd	36	46.21 N	18.42 E
Szentendre	36	47.40 N	19.05 E
Szentes	36	46.39 N	20.16 E
Szolnok	36	47.10 N	20.12 E
Szombathely	36	47.14 N	16.38 E
Szprotawa	36	51.34 N	15.33 E
Szzarviz ≃	36	46.24 N	18.41 E

T

Name	Page	Lat	Long
Tabatinga, Serra da ✗[1]	144	10.25 S	44.00 W
Tabernes de Valldigna	50	39.04 N	0.16 W
Tábor	36	49.25 N	14.41 E
Tabora	104	5.01 S	32.48 E
Tabrīz	84	38.05 N	46.18 E
Tabwemasana, Mount ∧	112	15.20 S	166.44 E
Tacloban	82	11.15 N	125.00 E
Tacna	144	18.01 S	70.15 W
Tacoma	162	47.15 N	122.27 W
Tacuarembó	146	31.44 S	55.59 W
Tademaït, Plateau du ✗[1]	100	28.30 N	2.00 E
Tadjoura	102	11.47 N	42.54 E
Taegu	80	35.52 N	128.35 E
Taejŏn	80	36.20 N	127.26 E
Tafassasset, Oued ⋁	100	21.20 N	10.10 E
Taga	113	13.46 S	172.28 W
Taganrog	62	47.12 N	38.56 E
Tagus (Tejo) (Tajo) ≃	50	38.40 N	9.24 W
Tahan, Gunong ∧	82	4.38 N	102.14 E
Tahoe, Lake ◎	162	39.06 N	120.03 W
Tahoua	100	14.54 N	5.16 E
Taibaishan ∧	80	33.54 N	107.46 E
T'aichung	80	24.09 N	120.41 E
T'ainan	80	23.00 N	120.11 E
Tainaron, Ákra ➤	54	36.23 N	22.29 E
T'aipei	80	25.03 N	121.30 E
Taiping	82	4.51 N	100.44 E
Taisetsu-zan ∧	80	43.30 N	142.57 E
Taitao, Península de ➤[1]	146	46.30 S	74.25 W
T'aitung	80	22.44 N	121.09 E
Taiwan (T'aiwan) □[1]	80	24.00 N	121.00 E
Taiyuan	80	37.55 N	112.30 E
Taizhou	80	32.30 N	119.58 E
Ta'izz	84	13.34 N	44.04 E
Tajmyr, Poluostrov ➤[1]	64	76.00 N	104.00 E
Tajumulco, Volcán ∧[1]	130	15.02 N	91.55 W
Tajuña ≃	50	40.07 N	3.35 W
Takamatsu	80	34.20 N	134.03 E
Takaoka	80	36.45 N	137.01 E
Takapuna	118	36.45 S	174.47 E
Takasaki	80	36.20 N	139.01 E
Taku ≃	162a	58.26 N	133.59 W
Takuam, Mount ∧	114	6.27 S	155.36 E
Talara	144	4.34 S	81.17 W
Talasea	116a	5.20 S	150.05 E
Talaud, Kepulauan ‖	82	4.20 N	126.50 E
Talavera de la Reina	50	39.57 N	4.50 W
Talca	146	35.26 S	71.40 W
Talcahuano	146	36.43 S	73.07 W
Talimu ≃	80	41.05 N	86.40 E
Talimupendi (Takla Makan) ✗[2]	80	39.00 N	83.00 E
Tallahassee	162	30.25 N	84.16 W
Tallinn	26	59.25 N	24.45 E
Talo ∧	102	10.44 N	37.55 E
Talodi	102	10.38 N	30.23 E
Tamale	100	9.25 N	0.50 W
Tamanrasset	100	22.56 N	5.30 E
Tâmega ≃	50	41.05 N	8.21 W
Tamiahua, Laguna de C	130	21.35 N	97.35 W
Tampa	162	27.57 N	82.27 W
Tampa Bay C	162	27.45 N	82.35 W
Tampere	26	61.30 N	23.45 E
Tampico	130	22.13 N	97.51 W
Tamworth	116	31.05 S	150.55 E
Tana ≃	102	2.32 S	40.31 E
Tana, Lake ◎	104	12.00 N	37.20 E
Tandil	146	37.19 S	59.09 W
Tanew ≃	36	50.31 N	22.16 E

Name	Page	Lat	Long
Mocha → Al-Mukhā	84	13.19 N	43.15 E
Mogadiscio → Mogadisho	102	2.01 N	45.20 E
Mogilev → Mogil'ov	62	53.54 N	30.21 E
Molotov → Perm'	62	58.00 N	56.15 E
Molotovsk → Severodvinsk	26	64.34 N	39.50 E
Molucca Sea → Maluku, Laut ⊤²	82	0.00 S	125.00 E
Monastir → Bitola	54	41.01 N	21.20 E
Montgomery → Sāhiwāl	84	30.40 N	73.06 E
Moppo → Mokp'o	80	34.48 N	126.22 E
Moravská Ostrava → Ostrava	36	49.50 N	18.17 E
Moscow → Moskva,	26	55.45 N	37.35 E
Mosul → Al-Mawlsil	84	36.20 N	43.08 E
Mozambique → Moçambique	104	15.03 S	40.42 E
Mukalla → Al-Mukallā	84	14.32 N	49.08 E
Mukden → Shenyang	80	41.48 N	123.27 E
München-Gladbach → Mönchengladbach	36	51.12 N	6.28 E
Munich → München	36	48.08 N	11.34 E
Munkács → Mukačevo	54	48.27 N	22.45 E
Muscat → Masqaṭ	84	23.37 N	58.35 E
Muscat and Oman → Oman □¹	84	22.00 N	58.00 E
Mutanchiang → Mudanjiang	80	44.35 N	129.36 E
Mutankiang → Mudanjiang	80	44.35 N	129.36 E
Myeik → Mergui	82	12.26 N	98.36 E
Mytilene → Mitilíni	54	39.06 N	26.32 E
Mytischi → Mytišči	26	55.55 N	37.46 E

N

Name	Page	Lat	Long
Nagybánya → Baia-Mare	54	47.40 N	23.35 E
Nagyvárad → Oradea	54	47.03 N	21.57 E
Nalchik → Nal'čik	62	43.29 N	43.37 E
Namcha Barwa → Namuchabawashan ∧	80	29.38 N	95.04 E
Namslau → Namysłów	36	51.05 N	17.42 E
Nanching → Nanjing	80	32.03 N	118.47 E
Nanch'ung → Nanchong	80	30.48 N	106.04 E
Nanhai → Foshan	80	23.03 N	113.09 E
Nanking → Nanjing	80	32.03 N	118.47 E
Nanshan → Qilianshanmai ∧	80	39.06 N	98.40 E
Nantung → Nantong	80	32.02 N	120.53 E
Naples → Napoli	46	40.51 N	14.17 E
Nase → Naze	80	28.23 N	129.30 E
Nawa → Naha	80	26.13 N	127.40 E
Neichiang → Neijiang	80	29.35 N	105.03 E
Neidenburg → Nidzica	36	53.22 N	20.26 E
Neikiang → Neijiang	80	29.35 N	105.03 E
Neisse → Nysa	36	50.29 N	17.20 E
Neuenburg → Neuchâtel	42	46.59 N	6.56 E
Neurode → Nowa Ruda	36	50.35 N	16.31 E
Neusalz → Nowa Sól	36	51.48 N	15.44 E
Neusatz → Novi Sad	54	45.15 N	19.50 E
Neusohl → Banská Bystrica	36	48.44 N	19.07 E
Neustadt in Oberschlesien → Prudnik	36	50.19 N	17.34 E
Neustettin → Szczecinek	36	53.43 N	16.42 E
New Guinea, Territory of → Papua New Guinea □¹	116a	6.00 S	150.00 E
New Sarum → Salisbury	32	51.05 N	1.48 W
New Windsor → Windsor	32	51.29 N	0.38 W
Nicosia → Levkosía	84	35.10 N	33.22 E
Nictheroy → Niterói	144	22.53 S	43.07 W
Nijvel → Nivelles	36	50.36 N	4.20 E
Nikolayev → Nikolajev	62	46.58 N	32.00 E
Ningpo → Ningbo	80	29.52 N	121.31 E
Ningsia → Yinchuan	80	38.30 N	106.18 E
Nish → Niš	54	43.19 N	21.54 E
Nizhny Novgorod → Gor'kij	26	56.20 N	44.00 E
Noremberg → Nürnberg	36	49.27 N	11.04 E
North Cape → Nordkapp ⟩	26	71.11 N	25.48 E
Northern Dvina → Severnaja Dvina	62	64.32 N	40.30 E
North Korea → Korea, North □¹	80	40.00 N	127.00 E
North Vietnam → Vietnam □¹	82	16.00 N	108.00 E
Nova Lisboa → Huambo	104	12.44 S	15.47 E
Novocherkassk → Novočerkassk	62	47.25 N	40.06 E
Novokuznetsk → Novokuzneck	64	53.45 N	87.06 E
Novonikolayevsk → Novosibirsk	64	55.02 N	82.55 E
Novorossiysk → Novorossijsk	62	44.45 N	37.45 E
Novoshakhtinsk → Novošachtinsk	62	47.47 N	39.56 E
Nuremberg → Nürnberg	36	49.27 N	11.04 E

O

Name	Page	Lat	Long
Ödenburg → Sopron	36	47.41 N	16.36 E
Oels → Oleśnica	36	51.13 N	17.23 E
Ohlau → Oława	36	50.57 N	17.17 E
Olympus, Mount → Ólimbos ∧	54	40.05 N	22.21 E
Omdurman → Umm Durmān	102	15.38 N	32.30 E
Ōmuda → Ōmuta	80	33.02 N	130.27 E
Onega, Lake → Onežskoje Ozero ⊘	62	61.30 N	35.45 E
Oporto → Porto	50	41.11 N	8.36 W
Oppeln → Opole	36	50.41 N	17.55 E
Ordzhonikidze → Ordžonikidze	62	43.03 N	44.40 E
Orekhovo-Zuyevo → Orechovo-Zujevo	26	55.49 N	38.59 E
Orel → Or'ol	62	52.59 N	36.05 E
Orléansville → El Asnam	100	36.10 N	1.20 E
Ortelsburg → Szczytno	36	53.34 N	21.00 E
Osh → Oš	62	40.33 N	72.48 E
Osipenko → Berd'ansk	62	46.45 N	36.49 E
Ost-Berlin → Berlin (Ost)	36	52.30 N	13.25 E
Ostende → Oostende	36	51.13 N	2.55 E
Osterode → Ostróda	36	53.43 N	19.59 E
Otu → Ōtsu	80	35.00 N	135.52 E
Ouahran → Oran	100	35.43 N	0.43 W
Oudjda → Oujda	100	34.41 N	1.45 W

P

Name	Page	Lat	Long
Padua → Padova	46	45.25 N	11.53 E
Pakhoi → Beihai	80	21.29 N	109.05 E
Pakistan, East → Bangladesh □¹	84	24.00 N	90.00 E
Pampeluna → Pamplona	50	42.49 N	1.38 W
Pangfou → Bangbu	80	32.58 N	117.24 E
Paochi → Baoji	80	34.22 N	107.14 E
Paoki → Baoji	80	34.22 N	107.14 E
Paoting → Baoding	80	38.52 N	115.29 E
Paotow → Baotou	80	40.40 N	109.59 E
Pará → Belém	144	1.27 S	48.29 W
Parahyba → João Pessoa	144	7.07 S	34.52 W
Parnahyba → Parnaiba	144	2.54 S	41.47 W
Parral → Hidalgo del Parral	130	26.56 N	105.40 W
Patras → Pátrai	54	38.15 N	21.44 E
Paulis → Isiro	102	2.47 N	27.37 E
Pechora → Pečora ≃	62	68.13 N	54.15 E
Peian → Beian	80	48.15 N	126.30 E
Peiching → Beijing	80	39.55 N	116.25 E
Peihai → Beihai	80	21.29 N	109.05 E
Peking → Beijing	80	39.55 N	116.25 E
Peipsi Järv → Čudskoje Ozero ⊘	62	58.54 N	27.25 E
Peiskretscham → Pyskowice	36	50.24 N	18.38 E
Penang → Pinang	82	5.25 N	100.20 E
Pengpu → Bangbu	80	32.58 N	117.24 E
Penhsi → Benxi	80	41.18 N	123.45 E
Penki → Benxi	80	41.18 N	123.45 E
Perim → Barīm I	84	12.40 N	43.25 E
Pernambuco → Recife	144	8.03 S	34.54 W
Persia → Iran □¹	84	32.00 N	53.00 E
Pescadores → P'enghu Liehtao II	80	23.30 N	119.30 E
Petrograd → Leningrad	26	59.55 N	30.15 E
Petrovgrad → Zrenjanin	54	45.23 N	20.24 E
Petrozsény → Petroşani	54	45.25 N	23.22 E
Philippeville → Skikda	100	36.50 N	6.58 E
Philippopolis → Plovdiv	54	42.09 N	24.45 E
Phnom Penh → Phnum Pénh	82	11.33 N	104.55 E
Phra Nakhon → Krung Thep	82	13.45 N	100.31 E
Pietarsaari → Jakobstad	28	63.40 N	22.42 E
Pillau → Baltijsk	26	54.39 N	19.55 E
Pindus Mountains → Pindhos Óros ∧	54	39.49 N	21.14 E
Pinkiang → Haerbin	80	45.45 N	126.41 E
Piraeus → Piraiévs	54	37.57 N	23.38 E
Pless → Pszczyna	36	49.59 N	18.57 E
Ploesti → Ploieşti	54	44.56 N	26.02 E
Podgorica → Titograd	54	42.26 N	19.14 E
Pointe-des-galets → Le Port	104	20.55 S	55.18 E
Pola → Pula	46	44.52 N	13.50 E
Politz → Police	36	53.35 N	14.33 E
Polotsk → Polock	26	55.31 N	28.46 E
Ponthierville → Ubundi	104	0.21 S	25.29 E

Name	Page	Lat	Long
Poona → Pune	84	18.32 N	73.52 E
Port → Le Port	104	20.55 S	55.18 E
Port Arthur → Thunder Bay, Ont., Can.	160	48.23 N	89.15 W
Port Arthur → Lüshun, Zhg.	80	38.47 N	121.13 E
Port-Étienne → Nouadhibou	100	20.54 N	17.04 W
Port Láirghe → Waterford	32	52.15 N	7.06 W
Port-Lyautey → Kenitra	100	34.16 N	6.40 W
Port Said → Būr Sa'īd	102	31.16 N	32.18 E
Port Stanley → Stanley	146	51.42 S	57.51 W
Port Sudan → Būr Sūdān	102	19.37 N	37.14 E
Portuguese Guinea → Guinea-Bissau □¹	100	12.00 N	15.00 W
Port Victoria → Victoria	104	4.38 S	55.27 E
Porvoo → Borgå	28	60.24 N	25.40 E
Poshan → Boshan	80	36.29 N	117.50 E
Pozsony → Bratislava	36	48.09 N	17.07 E
Prague → Praha	36	50.05 N	14.26 E
Pratas Islands → Dongshaqundao II	80	20.42 N	116.43 E
Pripjat → Prip'at' ≃	62	51.21 N	30.09 E
Prokopyevsk → Prokopjevsk	64	53.53 N	86.45 E
Proskurov → Chmel'nickij	62	49.25 N	27.00 E
Puerto Limón → Limón	130	10.00 N	83.02 W
Puerto Ordaz → Ciudad Guayana	144	8.22 N	62.40 W
Pulj → Pula	46	44.52 N	13.50 E
Pursat → Poŭthĭsăt	82	12.32 N	103.55 E
Pushkin → Puškin	26	59.43 N	30.25 E
Pyatigorsk → P'atigorsk	62	44.03 N	43.04 E
Pyrgos → Pírgos	54	37.41 N	21.28 E

Q

Name	Page	Lat	Long
Qena → Qinā	102	26.10 N	32.43 E
Qingyuan → Baoding	80	38.52 N	115.29 E
Quelpart Island → Cheju-do I	80	33.20 N	126.30 E
Queluz → Conselheiro Lafaiete	144	20.40 S	43.48 W

R

Name	Page	Lat	Long
Ragusa → Dubrovnik	54	42.38 N	18.07 E
Rampur Boalia → Rājshāhi	84	24.22 N	88.36 E
Rashin → Najin	80	42.15 N	130.18 E
Rastenburg → Kętrzyn	36	54.06 N	21.23 E
Ratisbon → Regensburg	36	49.01 N	12.06 E
Renaix → Ronse	36	50.45 N	3.36 E
Rheims → Reims	42	49.15 N	4.02 E
Rhodes → Ródhos	54	36.26 N	28.13 E
Rhodes → Ródhos I	54	36.10 N	28.00 E
Rieka → Rijeka	46	45.20 N	14.27 E
Riga, Gulf of → Rižskij Zaliv C	20	57.30 N	23.35 E
Rijssel → Lille	36	50.38 N	3.04 E
Riyadh → Ar-Riyāḍ	80	24.38 N	46.43 E
Rome → Roma	46	41.54 N	12.29 E
Roulers → Roeselare	36	50.57 N	3.08 E
Royal Tunbridge Wells → Tunbridge Wells	32	51.08 N	0.16 E
Rubtsovsk → Rubcovsk	64	51.33 N	81.10 E
Rügenwalde → Darłowo	36	54.26 N	16.23 E
Ruschuk → Ruse	54	43.50 N	25.57 E
Ryazan' → R'azan'	26	54.38 N	39.44 E
Ryojun → Lüshun	80	38.47 N	121.13 E
Ryukyu Islands → Nansei-shotō II	80	26.30 N	128.00 E

S

Name	Page	Lat	Long
Saarlautern → Saarlouis	36	49.21 N	6.45 E
Sagan → Żagań	36	51.37 N	15.19 E
Sai-gon → Thanh-pho Ho Chi Minh	82	10.45 N	106.40 E
Ste. → Saint		0.00	0.00
St. → Saint, Sankt, Sint		0.00	0.00
Sainte → Saint		0.00	0.00
Saint-Gall → Sankt Gallen	42	47.25 N	9.23 E
Saint Johns → Saint-Jean	160	45.19 N	73.16 W
Saint-Niklaas → Sint-Nicolaas	36	51.10 N	4.08 E
Saint Petersburg → Leningrad	26	59.55 N	30.15 E
Saint Thomas → Charlotte Amalie	130	18.21 N	64.56 W
Saishu-to → Cheju-do I	80	33.20 N	126.30 E
Sakhalin → Sachalin, Ostrov I	64	51.00 N	143.00 E
Salonika → Thessaloníki	54	40.38 N	22.56 E
Salvador, El → El Salvador □¹	130	13.50 N	88.55 W
Samara → Kujbyšev	26	53.12 N	50.09 E

Name	Page	Lat	Long
San Buenaventura → Ventura	162	34.17 N	119.18 W
San Felipe de Puerto Plata → Puerto Plata	130	19.48 N	70.41 W
Santa Isabel → Malabo	100	3.45 N	8.47 E
Santiago → Santiago de Compostela	50	42.53 N	8.33 W
Santorini → Thíra I	54	36.24 N	25.29 E
Santo Tomé de Guayana → Ciudad Guayana	144	8.22 N	62.40 W
São Salvador → Salvador	144	12.59 S	38.31 W
Saragossa → Zaragoza	50	41.38 N	0.53 W
Sarajevo → Sarajevo	54	43.52 N	18.25 E
Sarrebruck → Saarbrücken	36	49.14 N	6.59 E
Schivelbein → Świdwin	36	53.47 N	15.47 E
Schneidemühl → Piła	36	53.10 N	16.44 E
Schönlanke → Trzcianka	36	53.03 N	16.28 E
Schweidnitz → Świdnica	36	50.51 N	16.29 E
Schwiebus → Świebodzin	36	52.15 N	15.32 E
Scutari → Shkodër, Shq.	54	42.05 N	19.30 E
Scutari → Üsküdar, Tür.	54	41.01 N	29.01 E
Sebenico → Šibenik	46	43.44 N	15.54 E
Segesvar → Sighişoara	54	46.13 N	24.48 E
Seishin → Ch'ŏngjin	80	41.47 N	129.50 E
Senne II → Sennestadt	36	51.59 N	8.37 E
Senqu → Orange ≃	104	28.41 S	16.28 E
Sensburg → Mrągowo	36	53.52 N	21.19 E
Seoul → Sŏul	80	37.33 N	126.58 E
Serayevo → Sarajevo	54	43.52 N	18.25 E
Serpukhov → Serpuchov	26	54.55 N	37.25 E
Seville → Sevilla	50	37.23 N	5.59 W
Shakhty → Šachty	62	47.42 N	40.13 E
Shangch'iu → Shangqiu	80	34.27 N	115.42 E
Shantung Peninsula → Shandongbandao ⟩¹	80	37.00 N	121.00 E
Shaohing → Shaoxing	80	30.00 N	120.35 E
Shaohsing → Shaoxing	80	30.00 N	120.35 E
Shaokuan → Shaoguan	80	24.50 N	113.37 E
Shawinigan Falls → Shawinigan	160	46.33 N	72.45 W
Shcherbakov → Rybinsk	26	58.03 N	38.52 E
Shihchiachuang → Shijiazhuang	80	38.03 N	114.28 E
Shihkiachwang → Shijiazhuang	80	38.03 N	114.28 E
Shingishū → Sinŭiju	80	40.05 N	124.24 E
Shufu → Kashi	80	39.29 N	75.59 E
Shwangliao → Liaoyuan	80	42.54 N	125.07 E
Siam → Thailand □¹	82	15.00 N	100.00 E
Siam, Gulf of → Thailand, Gulf of C	82	10.00 N	101.00 E
Sian → Xi'an	80	34.15 N	108.52 E
Siangtan → Xiangtan	80	27.51 N	112.54 E
Siberia → Sibir' ⋗¹	62	65.00 N	110.00 E
Sicily → Sicilia I	46	37.30 N	14.00 E
Sidra, Gulf of → Surt, Khalīj C	102	31.30 N	18.00 E
Sienna. → Siena	46	43.19 N	11.21 E
Siking → Xi'an	80	34.15 N	108.52 E
Simbirsk → Uljanovsk	26	54.20 N	48.24 E
Simonoseki → Shimonoseki	80	33.57 N	130.57 E
Sinai Peninsula → Sīnā', Shibh Jazīrat ⟩¹	102	29.30 N	34.00 E
Singora → Songkhla	82	7.12 N	100.36 E
Sinhai → Xinhailian	80	34.39 N	119.16 E
Sinsiang → Xinxiang	80	35.20 N	113.51 E
Siros → Ermoúpolis	54	37.26 N	24.56 E
Sizuoka → Shizuoka	80	34.58 N	138.23 E
Slavonia → Slavonija ⋗¹	54	45.00 N	18.00 E
Smara → Semara	100	26.44 N	11.41 W
Smyrna → İzmir	54	38.25 N	27.09 E
Soch'e → Suoche	80	38.25 N	77.16 E
Sochi → Soči	62	43.35 N	39.45 E
Socotra → Suquṭrā I	84	12.30 N	54.00 E
Soerabaja → Surabaya	82	7.15 S	112.45 E
Sofia → Sofija	54	42.41 N	23.19 E
Sogcho → Sŏkch'o	80	38.12 N	128.36 E
Sogne Fjord → Sognafjorden C²	28	61.06 N	5.10 E
Sohåg → Sawhāj	102	26.33 N	31.42 E
Soleure → Solothurn	42	47.13 N	7.32 E
Solimões → Amazon ≃	144	0.05 S	50.00 W
Solo → Surakarta	82	7.35 S	110.50 E
Somali Republic → Somalia □¹	102	10.00 N	49.00 E
Sommerfeld → Lubsko	36	51.46 N	14.59 E
Sŏngjin → Kimch'aek	80	40.41 N	129.12 E

Name	Page	Lat	Long
Soo → Sault Sainte Marie	162	46.30 N	84.21 W
Soochow → Suzhou	80	31.18 N	120.37 E
Sorau → Żary	36	51.38 N	15.09 E
Southern Yemen → Yemen, People's Democratic Republic of □¹	84	15.00 N	48.00 E
South Korea → Korea, South □¹	80	36.30 N	128.00 E
South Norfolk → Chesapeake	162	36.43 N	76.15 W
South Vietnam → Vietnam □¹	82	16.00 N	108.00 E
Soviet Union → Union of Soviet Socialist Republics □¹	62	60.00 N	80.00 E
Spalato → Split	46	43.31 N	16.27 E
Spanish Sahara → Western Sahara □²	100	24.30 N	13.00 W
Sparta → Spárti	54	37.05 N	22.27 E
Spezia → La Spezia	46	44.07 N	9.50 E
Spires → Speyer	36	49.19 N	8.26 E
Sprottau → Szprotawa	36	51.34 N	15.33 E
Ssup'ing → Siping	80	43.12 N	124.20 E
Stalin → Varna, Blg.	54	43.13 N	27.55 E
Stalin → Braşov, Rom.	54	45.39 N	25.37 E
Stalinabad → Dušanbe	62	38.35 N	68.48 E
Staling → Doneck	62	48.00 N	37.48 E
Stalinogorsk → Novomoskovsk	62	54.05 N	38.13 W
Stalinogród → Katowice	36	50.16 N	19.00 E
Stalinsk → Novokuzneck	64	53.45 N	87.06 E
Stanislav → Ivano-Frankovsk	62	48.55 N	24.43 E
Stanisławów → Ivano-Frankovsk	62	48.55 N	24.43 E
Stanleyville → Kisangani	104	0.30 N	25.12 E
Stanovoy Mountains → Stanovoje Nagorje ∧	64	56.00 N	114.00 E
Stavropol → Toljatti	26	53.31 N	49.26 E
Steinamanger → Szombathely	36	47.14 N	16.38 E
Stolp → Słupsk	36	54.28 N	17.01 E
Stolpmünde → Ustka	36	54.35 N	16.50 E
Strehlen → Strzelin	36	50.47 N	17.03 E
Striegau → Strzegom	36	50.57 N	16.21 E
Stuhlweissenburg → Székesfehérvár	36	47.12 N	18.25 E
Suchou → Suzhou	80	31.18 N	120.37 E
Süchow → Xuzhou	80	34.16 N	117.11 E
Suez → As-Suways	102	29.58 N	32.33 E
Suez, Gulf of → Suways, Khalīj as- C	102	29.00 N	32.50 E
Suez Canal → Suways, Qanāt as- ≖	102	29.55 N	32.33 E
Sufu → Kashi	80	39.29 N	75.59 E
Suifu → Yibin	80	28.47 N	104.38 E
Sukhumi → Suchumi	62	43.01 N	41.02 E
Sütschou → Xuzhou	80	34.16 N	117.11 E
Swatow → Shantou	80	23.23 N	116.41 E
Swinemünde → Świnoujście	36	53.53 N	14.14 E
Syracuse → Siracusa	46	37.04 N	15.17 E
Syr-Darya → Syrdarja ≃	62	46.03 N	61.00 E
Szabadka → Subotica	54	46.06 N	19.39 E
Szatmárnémeti → Satu Mare	54	47.48 N	22.53 E
Szeping → Siping	80	43.12 N	124.20 E

T

Name	Page	Lat	Long
Tagdempt → Tiaret	100	35.28 N	1.21 E
Taiden → Taejŏn	80	36.20 N	127.26 E
Taif → Aṭ-Ṭā'if	84	21.16 N	40.24 E
Taihoku → T'aipei	80	25.03 N	121.30 E
T'aihsien → Taizhou	80	32.30 N	119.58 E
Taikyu → Taegu	80	35.52 N	128.35 E
Taira → Iwaki	80	37.03 N	140.55 E
Takao → Kaohsiung	80	22.38 N	120.17 E
Takla Makan → Taklimupendi ⋗²	80	39.00 N	83.00 E
Takoradi → Sekondi-Takoradi	100	4.59 N	1.43 W
Takow → Kaohsiung	80	22.38 N	120.17 E
Talien → Lüda	80	38.53 N	121.35 E
Tammerfors → Tampere	28	61.30 N	23.45 E
Tananarive → Antananarivo	104	18.55 S	47.31 E
Tangier → Tanger	100	35.48 N	5.45 W
T'an'san' → Tien Shan ∧	80	42.00 N	80.00 E
Targu-Mures → Tîrgu Mureş	54	46.33 N	24.33 E
Tarim → Talimuhe ≃	80	41.05 N	86.40 E
Tarnopol → Ternopol'	62	49.34 N	25.36 E
Tashkent → Taškent	62	41.20 N	69.18 E
Tatar Strait → Tatarskij Proliv ⋃	64	50.00 N	141.15 E
Tat'ung → Datong	80	40.08 N	113.13 E

ठ